WITHDRAWN

Harmonious Tensions

Johann Christoph Friedrich Schiller. From a painting by Ludovike Simanowitz.

Harmonious Tensions

The Writings
of Friedrich Schiller

Steven D. Martinson

DELAWARE

Newark: University of Delaware Press
London: Associated University Presses

Associated University Presses
440 Forsgate Drive
Cranbury, NJ 08512

Associated University Presses
16 Barter Street
London WC1A 2AH, England

Associated University Presses
P.O. Box 338, Port Credit
Mississauga, Ontario
Canada L5G 4L8

The paper used in this publication meets the requirements
of the American National Standard for Permanence of Paper
for Printed Library Materials Z39.48-1984.

Library of Congress Cataloging-in-Publication Data

Martinson, Steven D., 1949–
    Harmonious tensions : the writings of Friedrich Schiller / Steven
D. Martinson.
        p. cm.
    Includes bibliographical references and index.
    ISBN 0-87413-568-0 (alk. paper)
    1. Schiller, Friedrich, 1759–1805—Criticism and interpretation.
I. Title.
PT2492.M36   1996
831′.6—dc20   95-47381
                                                                                    CIP

For my children Elisa, Eric, and Lori
in memory of Marbach a.N. 1990/91
"Alles Vergängliche
Ist nur ein Gleichnis"
(Goethe, Faust II)

Contents

Preface

JOHANN Christoph Friedrich Schiller was not only one of the most talented German poets. He was also a philosopher, physiologist, and historian, as well as a reviewer, editor, and writer of letters. Schiller became a regimental doctor in Stuttgart, theater critic in Mannheim, professor of philosophy in Jena, and co-director of the Court Theater in Weimar. Since the pioneering book by Benno von Wiese in 1959,[1] the diverse nature of Friedrich Schiller's activities as a writer has received little attention in scholarship. While there are many splendid interpretations of specific works,[2] there are but few monographs that explore Schiller's oeuvre considered as a whole.[3] An important exception is Lesley Sharpe's *Friedrich Schiller: Drama, Thought and Politics,* the first full-length study in English of the writer and his works in over forty years.[4]

For the first time, the present study seeks to investigate the thematics, form, and function of the writings of Friedrich Schiller (1759–1805) in the light of the writer's multidisciplinary activities. One of the most basic aspects of Schiller's oeuvre is the integration of literature, physiology, philosophy, history, and music. The employment of various approaches is informed by Schiller's idea that while art is primarily concerned with intuitive comprehensions (*Anschauungen*), science strives to generate ever clearer and more reliable concepts (*Begriffe*). A closer study of Schiller's texts discloses that the writer operated as if these two understandings of knowledge were mutually cooperative. For Schiller, both sources of knowledge generate a powerful vehicle for the exploration, understanding, and criticism of multifarious objects of study.

One reason why Benno von Wiese's book on Schiller (*Friedrich Schiller*) has remained so challenging owes to the author's appreciation of the multidisciplinary nature of the writer's work. However, von Wiese treated Schiller's activities as storyteller, philosopher, and historian in individual chapters, thus creating the impression that all of these various activities, except the writer's work as philosopher and poet, function relatively independently of one another. This dividing line cannot be maintained even on the basis of one of von Wiese's own assumptions. "Schiller was . . . a philosopher, poet and historian *in one person*" [emphasis mine].[5] In Schiller's case, the act of writing was a moment in which not one but several or more activities cooperated simultaneously.

Johann Wolfgang Goethe, Alexander von Humboldt, and Friedrich Schil-

9

ler—all of these and many more prolific German writers of the late eighteenth and early nineteenth centuries—believed firmly in the interconnectedness and reciprocal cooperation of all facets of knowledge. In their important anthology of Schiller's medical works, *Friedrich Schiller: Medicine, Psychology and Literature,* Kenneth Dewhurst and Nigel Reeves reminded us that the eighteenth century did not yet know of the strict divisions between the disciplines characterizing our universities and fields of research today.[6] The current resistance to cross-disciplinary investigation on the part of many scholars of literature may have to do with the fact that interdisciplinary studies problematize the traditional understanding of literature as beautiful art.[7] On a practical level, non-traditional research means the expansion of knowledge across intellectual, departmental, institutional and political lines.[8]

In exploring what he termed the attack on literature, Rene Wellek underscored the fact that the eighteenth century was already working with a much more expansive concept of literature than we are today.[9] On this point, we need only recall the numerous books Gotthold Ephraim Lessing, Johann Gottfried Herder and other writers of the late eighteenth century reviewed in the area of "literature" in periodicals like *Letters Concerning the Most Recent Literature* [*Briefe, die neueste Literatur betreffend* (1759f.)] and *Concerning Recent German Literature* [*Über die neuere deutsche Literatur* (1766–67)] to comprehend just how narrow the term had become by the mid-twentieth century with the advent of the New Criticism.

In his report on the state of Schiller research, Helmut Koopmann spoke of the need for integral interpretations of Schiller's work, "which could treat the variety of his works and his changing positions from a convincing comprehensive understanding."[10] In the present study, I will attempt to trace lines of continuity that unify Schiller's work, while remaining sensitive to the differences in the historical development of that body of writings. Whereas German scholars generally herald Schiller as one of their great classical writers, British scholars and professors of English in North America tend to see only the romantic in Schiller. The present study enters this debate from the perspective of the writer's multidisciplinary activities in an attempt to narrow the gap between German and Anglo-Saxon scholarship.

Finally, I hope to refuel the dynamics of Schiller's diverse writings by opening them up to reassessment in the arena of contemporary critical thinking. In the epilogue, I endeavor to map the reception of Schiller's writings among German philosophers in the late twentieth century, while adding some critical commentary of my own.

Acknowledgments

THIS study on the nature of Friedrich Schiller's writings was supported by the Alexander von Humboldt-Foundation in Bonn, Federal Republic of Germany, in the form of a generous research fellowship (1990–91). The fabulous holdings of the German Archive for Literature (Deutsches Literaturarchiv), in Schiller's hometown of Marbach am Neckar near Stuttgart, greatly enhanced my understanding of the life and work of this gifted writer. I am indebted to my mentors Dorothea Kuhn (Marbach/Weimar), Ulrich Ott (Marbach), and Dieter Kimpel (Frankfurt am Main) for the many engaging conversations concerning both eighteenth-century German literature and contemporary German culture. Undoubtedly, the profound act of German reunification in 1990 leaves its imprint on this study. Conversations with Hans-Georg Gadamer (Heidelberg) and Jürgen Habermas (Frankfurt) formed two of the high points of my experiences during that fourteen-month stay in the new-old Germany. I very much appreciate the support, encouragement, and critical commentary I received from each of these individuals.

I am likewise indebted to many other colleagues for stimulating exchanges on a variety of subjects. To Lesley Sharpe (Exeter, England) I extend my thanks for the delightful conversations on Schiller and current German events while in Marbach. Heartfelt thanks to Claus and Ingeborg Beyer for taking my family under their wing, especially during the time of the Gulf War. My work was augmented by two trips to Weimar and the Goethe-Schiller Archive. Hans-Dietrich and Vera Dahnke (Weimar) were most gracious in opening their home to me and my wife Elizabeth. I will always remember our conversations about the difficult transition from the German Democratic Republic to the Federal Republic of Germany. Despite our ideological differences, perhaps our friendly exchanges confirm the existence of a province of the human. I also wish to thank Leonid Zhmud of St. Petersburg, Russia, for the lively discussion of the possible intellectual affinities between Schiller and Pythagoras on the grounds of the Ludwigsburg Castle. Our exchange of ideas would not have occurred, nor would portions of it have been incorporated into the present study without the commitment of the Alexander von Humboldt-Foundation to cross-cultural dialogue.

Here, at home, my colleague Louis F. Helbig took a keen interest in my work. His critical discernment helped bring the study to a timely conclusion. The highly competent secretarial assistance and advice I received from Birgit Haerle, a native of Swabia, and Anuradha Ruhil were greatly appreciated.

I am also grateful to the former Dean of the Faculty of Humanities, Annette Kolodny, and the Dean of the new College of Humanities, Charles Tatum, for supporting the final stages of the book with research supplements. John McCarthy's (Vanderbilt University) critical reading of portions of the text was, as always, insightful and exacting. Finally, I wish to thank Karl S. Guthke (Harvard) and Wulf Koepke (Texas A & M) for their constructive criticisms of the original manuscript. Any errors in judgment are mine alone.

Two of my four published articles on the work of Friedrich Schiller mark the inception of this study. "Friedrich Schiller's *Der Verbrecher aus verlorener Ehre,* or the Triumph of the Moral Will" appeared in *Sprachkunst. Beiträge zur Literaturwissenschaft* 18 (1987): 1–9, a publication of the Austrian Academy of Sciences. "Filling in the Gaps: 'The Problem of World-Order' in Friedrich Schiller's Essay on Universal History" was published in *Eighteenth-Century Studies* 22 (1988): 24–46. The first part of chapter three is a revised version of the former article, whereas a slightly revised version of the latter article constitutes the first half of chapter four. I refer to two other articles, one on Schiller's relationship to the Jacobin thinker Johann Benjamin Erhard and the other on the concept of imagination in Schiller's book reviews, in the course of the study. A fifth article on Schiller is forthcoming in the *Festschrift* for Wolfgang Wittkowski.

All illustrations are from *Marbacher Schillerbuch* (Stuttgart/Berlin: J. G. Cotta, 1905).

Introduction: Portraits of Schiller's Life and Intellectual Development: The Writings of Wilhelm von Humboldt and Caroline von Wolzogen

Humboldt's Portrait

THE account of Schiller's intellectual development by Wilhelm von Humboldt, one of the writer's closest friends, has left an indelible mark on scholarship. In his essay *Concerning Schiller and the Course of His Intellectual Development* [*Über Schiller und den Gang seiner Geistesentwicklung*], the brother of Alexander von Humboldt extolled the genius of the man Friedrich Schiller. In his writing, Humboldt returned repeatedly to his friend's sense of liberation from the confines of physical reality whenever his intellectual powers were enlivened.

As captivating as Humboldt's account of Schiller is, the writer did not come to terms with Schiller's consciousness of the, at times, agonizing struggle between body and mind. For Schiller's unique characteristic ("besondere Eigentümlichkeit"), his genius, according to Humboldt, manifested itself "on the basis of an intellectuality . . . , which wished to unite everything into a whole by tying things together."[1] The subjunctive form of the German verb employed here—*möchte*—suggests that a deeper reality underlies Humboldt's characterization.

For one thing, the author makes no mention of Schiller's work as a physiologist or of the mind-body problem in general. Rather, Humboldt concentrated on the intellectual-artistic merits of his friend's activities. Humboldt contends that, of poetry, Schiller demanded a deeper penetration of thought, forming everything in his purview into an intellectual unity. This was accomplished, he argues, by applying a more rigid form of art to the raw material of reality. Treating each of his poetic works in this way, Schiller expanded the individuality of the material, unarbitrarily and of itself, to the wholeness of an idea. Thus, "The [writer's] advantages rest on these properties, which Schiller holds to be characteristic."[2] In the final analysis, there can be no doubt that Wilhelm von Humboldt was most interested in preserving his friend's advantages ("Vorzüge") and not his apparent weaknesses.

Peering beneath the beautiful facade, Humboldt's characterization

13

strongly indicates that Schiller's work embraces a larger and more interesting project than the mere subsumption of reality under the wholeness of a
central idea. Humboldt took his friend's search for wholeness at face value
and appreciated the beauty of the enterprise. Yet, the very choice of words
he employs to portray Schiller's ambitions betrays the fact that a different
energy is at work. While there is no question that Schiller constantly struggled with the demands and limitations of his body, the writer Wilhelm von
Humboldt embellished Schiller's frequent bouts with illness, not wishing, I
surmise, to make his friend appear weak. After all, he was a genius, and
a German genius at that. "The continuous self-activation of the mind
never left him, and gave in only to the strongest cases of corporeal ill-
temperedness. This [self-activity] appeared to be [a form of] recuperation,
not strenuousness."[3]

Influenced as he was by the new school of romanticism and rising tide
of idealism, Humboldt submitted that thought ("der Gedanke") must then
comprise the very substance of Schiller's life ("das Element seines
Lebens"). I am not convinced that Schiller viewed everything from the
privileged position of rationality since, according to his own writings, intro-
spection, observation, and experience presuppose the tension-filled interdependence of the physical and mental components of the human being.
Having been schooled in the Enlightenment, Schiller was well aware of both
the potentialities and the limitations of human activities.

The limits of Humboldt's characterization are most pronounced when he
idolizes Schiller as a great German. Referring to Schiller's "Germanness"
("Deutschheit") and to the German nation, Humboldt expressed what was
most deeply Teutonic: "The more profound and truer direction in the German lies in his greater inwardness, which holds him closer to the truth of
Nature, in the tendency to concern oneself with ideas and the sensations
related to them as well as in everything that is tied to this."[4] The service
into which Humboldt enlisted his friend was so important to him that he
used Schiller as an example to distinguish the Germans from most other
peoples, including the ancient Greeks. In short, Humboldt transformed the
historical person Friedrich Schiller into a mythical representative of a superior German intellect.

But here we must be careful to differentiate between concepts of genius
in the eighteenth and early nineteenth centuries. In Schiller's own education,
it was not so much the genius cult of the Storm-and-Stress movement, as it
was the work of philosophical doctors and Schiller's instructor in philosophy, Jakob Friedrich Abel, that left an indelible mark on the writer's work.
It is a curious fact that the writings of eighteenth-century philosophical
doctors, work on the nature of genius almost always emphasized harmony.[5]
In his electrifying speech on genius ("Rede über das Genie") before members of the Carlsschule in 1776, J. F. Abel advocated that the harmonious
relationship between all powers of the soul, together, constitutes genius, and

that the great mind ("der große Geist") is "at the same time a work of Nature and education."[6] For Abel, "Correctness of concepts is often a sign of genius," and "Harmony and genius are always together."[7] The concept of genius Schiller appropriated and developed thus differs markedly from Wilhelm von Humboldt's romantic notion of the same.

The portrait of Schiller that Humboldt builds up in the course of his essay is diametrically opposed to Schiller's clear awareness of the limits of his own theorizing. By sidestepping this key aspect of Schiller's writings, as well as the writer's medical dissertations, Humboldt overemphasized Schiller's seemingly utopian gestures. The goal, toward which Schiller's writings seem to be directed, is the mutual cooperation of all of the human being's capacities—not the detachment of the rational from the physical-material but, rather, the greatest degree of cooperative interaction between mind and body. Furthermore, Schiller's friend overlooked the fact that even the attainment of the ideals to which the writer refers on occasion is, perhaps, best characterized by harmonious tension. These aspects of Schiller's writings disclose a deeper-lying problematic over which Humboldt's narrative casts a dark, albeit enchanting shadow.

Von Wolzogen's Portrait

Benno von Wiese once suggested that the elder of the two von Wolzogen sisters, Caroline, was "the stronger, more intellectual personality";[8] at the same time, however, she was also "more dissonant, more abrupt and demanding than her sister."[9] Not only in the light of these personality traits, but also as compared to Wilhelm von Humboldt's writing, the sobriety of Baroness von Wolzogen's judgment in her two-volume biography of Friedrich Schiller, *Schillers Leben* of 1830, is especially striking.

Schiller's sister-in-law Caroline von Wolzogen (1763–1847), born von Lengefeld, was a perceptive individual. Already near the beginning of her biography she recorded that Schiller's revised medical dissertation of 1780 "does not seem to have been so well known as it deserved to be."[10] As we know, it is only recently that Schiller scholarship has taken serious note of the importance of the medical dissertations for an understanding of the author and his work.

On a personal level, von Wolzogen respected Schiller's behavior toward women. "For him, love was always something serious—a divinity—the youth who marries Psyche, not the foolish, flattering lad."[11] Of Schiller's demeanor in general, the female writer remarks: "High seriousness and graceful, witty ease of an open, unspoiled mind were always present [lively] in Schiller's company."[12] At the same time, however, she cannot refrain from romanticizing the nature of her conversations with him: " . . . people journeyed in conversations with him as between the unchanging stars of heaven and earth's flowers."[13] As a person, Schiller seems to have been a

most charming gentleman, and his social behavior appears to be consistent
with the ideals of the Carlsschule in Stuttgart. For one of Duke Carl Eugen's
major missions was to prepare students like Schiller for diplomatic service.

Concerning politics, von Wolzogen perceived that Schiller privileged the
individual human being over the State. The biographer excerpted the following from a letter by Schiller to Caroline von Beulwitz of November 27, 1788:
"The greatest state is a work of the human being; the human being is a work
of unattainable, great Nature . . . The state is only the product [effect] of
the power of the human being, only a work of thought; but the human being
is the source of power itself and the creator of thought."[14] In his person, she
writes, Schiller combined "the power of development [formation]" ("Bildun-
gskraft") with diligence.[15] Happiness ("Glückseligkeit"), for him, lay in the
"power of his mind" ("Kraft seines Geistes").[16] One evening, in late 1789,
after having assumed his responsibilities as professor of philosophy in Jena,
Schiller conveyed the following to her: " . . . if I should remain happy, then
I must attain to the feeling of my powers."[17] By his own admission, the
combined exercise of his talents reached fruition in the creative production
of works of art.[18] On this point, there is close agreement between von Wolzogen and Humboldt concerning the native talents of their mutual friend.

True self-love, von Wolzogen submits, which combines a love and respect
for others, permeates Schiller's writings. "It is not egotism, not even pride;
it is a yearning to regard oneself highly that is inseparable from love."[19]
Genuine self-love was something from which the individual human being
could draw strength, especially when experiencing physical pain. Unlike
Wilhelm von Humboldt, then, Caroline von Wolzogen did not downplay the
agony and suffering of the body that the man Friedrich Schiller experienced
repeatedly throughout his short life. She notes, candidly, that "attacks of
severe chest pains [cramps] were not absent, and intruded, disturbingly, into
his happy spiritual life."[20] At times, pain overpowered the mind. Repeatedly,
von Wolzogen notes the anguish Schiller experienced because of a lung
ailment and the negative effect this had on his disposition. Still, Schiller
embraced this, too, as part of the greater power of Nature. "We must give
ourselves over to the all-prevailing spirit of Nature," he said, "and be active
as long as we are able."[21] This amounts to significantly more than Stoic
perseverance in the face of peril. According to von Wolzogen, Schiller did
not perceive the suffering attending corporeal restrictions as an encroach-
ment on freedom but, rather, as an inherent part of Nature itself. In general,
Schiller's writings exhibit a constant, unresolved, yet ever fruitful tension
between the limitations of the body and the freedom of the mind.

Caroline's biography is also a beautiful testimony to the loving friendship
between Schiller and the early romantic writer Novalis (Friedrich von Hardenberg). After Schiller's traumatic, physical attack in Erfurt (while attending
a concert), in 1791, from which the man never fully recovered, Novalis,
more than anyone else, attended to his friend's needs.[22] Von Wolzogen char-

acterized their relationship in the following terms: "The pure lute of his heart, his religious feeling, his longing for the eternal remain precious to all those who feel alike."[23] Suffering marked Schiller's final days. "This is certainly the most rending pain for a human heart to see the beautiful harmony of the mind destroyed and the tender bond, which on earth ties one to one's loved one, torn; to see those eyes from which soul-filled love radiates directed at us with a glassy, confused look."[24] The highly moving style of writing is a credit to the female writer as well as a tribute to the man she admired and, perhaps, from afar, even loved. But the most remarkable quality of the phrases is how much they complement the main metaphors and motifs of so many of Schiller's writings. As we shall see, one of the central themes of Schiller's work is the relation between harmony and rupture in Nature.

Caroline von Wolzogen's portrait of her brother-in-law in the closing pages of the second volume of her biography commands attention. For she submits that Schiller was neither the servant of his time nor its guide. Perhaps it was this, more than his assumed genius, that earned him the respect of his compatriots.[25] Unquestionably, Caroline von Wolzogen had something radically different than world conquest in mind when she wrote: "so Schiller stood alone in the world, listening only to the sound of great Nature within him, which sound the voice of the nation echoed back."[26]

Nevertheless, like Humboldt, von Wolzogen tended to glorify the writer. Enlisting the powerful Homeric and romantic topos of life as a sea, the writer painted a captivating picture of Friedrich Schiller. "That person is happy, who, like Schiller, rests firmly in the idea of truth and beauty and who, through one's inner self, is able to save oneself time and again from the smashing storm, in order to land on the green, flowery shore of pure humanity."[27] According to von Wolzogen, truth and love comprised the religion of Schiller's heart.[28] To be sure, Caroline von Wolzogen's biography is an expression of love. "This is the way the spiritual image of my friend stands before my soul," she wrote upon concluding her work.[29] Given the relatively late appearance of her biography, it is clear that von Wolzogen's love for her friend continued long after the writer's death.

In sum, where Wilhelm von Humboldt idealized his friend and propagated a myth of German genius, Caroline von Wolzogen tended to romanticize the man she admired. In the final analysis, the female writer's account exhibits greater sobriety of judgment than the male writer. It also supplies us with a fuller account of Schiller's activities. Unlike Wilhelm von Humboldt, Caroline von Wolzogen comes to terms with the struggle between mind and body in Schiller's person and opens up the possibility that, for him, illness was not only the cause of pain but, at the same time, an opportunity for healing and a source of critical-creative thinking. Though the form and content of Humboldt's and von Wolzogen's writings are different, both accounts are still united in their love for the main object of study: Friedrich Schiller. The very fact that, at times, Humboldt idealized and von Wolzogen romanticized Schiller calls up the question of the great variations in writing, even firsthand accounts of a given author. Because we cannot know the man personally, perhaps it is best to concentrate on the writer's true legacy: his writings. By studying more closely the thematics, form, and function of that body of writings, we might also gain a keener sense of what the man Friedrich Schiller stood for and thus be able to situate him in history. Finally, I submit that the recurrent themes, multidisciplinary texture, and general import of Schiller's writings can activate and inform critical-creative thinking today.

Harmonious Tensions

1

"Harmonious Tension" and the Field of Tension Between Anthropology and Metaphysics: The Medical Dissertations

THE term "harmonious tension" ("harmonische Spannung") was coined by the Jewish-German writer Moses Mendelssohn, the friend of the enlightened philosopher Gotthold Ephraim Lessing and the grandfather of the composer Felix Mendelssohn-Bartholdy. While scholarship is aware of Lessing's indebtedness to Mendelssohn's essay *Letters Concerning the Sensations* [*Briefe über die Empfindungen*] (1755) for the development of ideas on the nature of tragedy in the *Hamburg Dramaturgy* [*Hamburgische Drama-turgie*] (1776–67), it has not yet appreciated the impact which the concept and image of harmonious tension had on Friedrich Schiller. Along with Adam Ferguson's work on moral philosophy and Adam Smith's theory of sensation, Moses Mendelssohn's *Letters Concerning the Sensations* had a profound effect on the thought of the younger and later writer. This is confirmed not only by the fact that, when Schiller died, a copy of Mendelssohn's essay was lying on his desk,[1] but also by a close examination of the language of Schiller's writings.

In the Tenth Letter by Theocles (Palemon) to Euphranor in Mendelssohn's *Letters Concerning the Sensations,* the author refers to "the tangled knot" ("den verwirrten Knoten") of "sensuous delight" ("sinnliche Lust"), noting that such delights often exert a more powerful influence on both the body and the soul than "rational pleasures" ("die verständlichen Vergnügungen").[2] What do body and soul have in common that enables them to both be sources of pleasure? Mendelssohn's answer calls up the idea of the mixed nature of body and mind.

> Analysts of the human body have taught that the sinewy vessels are so delicately intertwined in a thousand labyrinthine passageways, that in the entire structure of the body everything is tied to everything else. The degrees of tension are distributed harmoniously from nerve to nerve, and never does a change occur in one part which does not, to a certain extent, have an influence on the whole. Those who appreciate art call this harmonious tension tone.[3]

21

And:

> Should, then, one member or part of the human body be gently stimulated; then
> the effect of it is transferred to the most distant limbs. All vessels are set in a
> healthy tension, in harmonious tone, which relays the activity of the human body
> and fosters its continuation.[4]

Clearly, harmony does not mean the cessation of activity. On the contrary.
The healthy body and, by extension, mind are characterized by harmonious
tension. Knowledge of the nervous system in particular, and of physiology
in general, suggests that a different concept of harmony than the standard
one offered by writers such as Alexander Baumgarten and Georg Friedrich Meier was exerting its influence on so-called classical writers like
Friedrich Schiller.

In his *Large, Complete Universal-Lexicon* [*Großes vollständiges
Universal-Lexikon*], Johann Heinrich Zedler noted "that the creation of
sound is to be explained by quivering motion alone."[5] In the case of stringed
instruments, the length of the sounding string ("die Länge der klingenden
Seyte") is determined by its tightening force ("die anspannende Kraft").[6]
We may conclude that all sounds, including the most beautiful, melodic, and
harmonious ones, are not only produced, but also sustained by tension.

One of the most fruitful and most frequently employed metaphors animat-
ing Schiller's writings is the finely tuned stringed instrument. This metaphor
appears early, already in Schiller's earliest public speech, his medical dissertations, and his first poems, titled *Anthology for the Year 1782* [*Anthologie
auf das Jahr 1782*].

As part of the celebration of the Countess Franziska von Hohenheim's
birthday on January 10, 1779, the nineteen-year-old medical student at Duke
Carl Eugen's Military Academy in Stuttgart delivered a speech titled
"Speech Concerning the Question: Is All-too-much Goodness, Amiability,
and Great Generosity in the Narrow Sense Attributed to Virtue?" ["Rede
über die Frage: Gehört allzuviel Güte, Leutseeligkeit und grosse Freygebig-
keit im engsten Verstande zur Tugend?"] In this essay, Schiller exhibits his
love of happiness ("Liebe zur Glükseeligkeit") and enthusiasm for endless,
magnificent Nature ("unendliche, große Natur").[7] Here, he conceived of
Nature as being masterfully knitted together ("so meisterhafft zusam-
mengefüget") through divine wisdom. This, in turn, animates God's eternal
clockwork ("Ewiges Uhrwerk") (NA 20: 8). Through wisdom, God's thousand vibrating strings sound melodiously ("Durch sie [Gottes Weisheit]
klingen melodisch zusammen deine tausend zitternde Saiten!") (NA 20: 8).

The eternal, unchanging laws ("ewige unwandelbare Gesetze") (NA 20:
4) not only establish order but also melody, or harmony ("Wohlklang")
(NA 20: 4). Taken literally, a "Wohl-Klang" is a sound that is not simply
pleasurable but also therapeutic, for it makes us feel good ("wohl"), that is,

well. In the text of his speech, young Schiller defines virtue ("Tugend") numerous times as the harmonious bond of love and wisdom ("das harmonische Band von Liebe und Weisheit") (NA 20: 4,5,6,7,8). In and through the exercise of virtue, the human being associates oneself with God and thus shares God's divinity.

It is important to note that the plural form of the German word for bond (*Band*) is related, semantically, to the word *Fesseln* (chains or fetters). Through virtue, then, one is chained to God and, by extension, to Creation, which is Nature. We have seen that, already in this early essay, the writer had associated the musical metaphor of the stringed instrument with the source of all Creation.

Schiller's first attempt to write a dissertation was titled *Philosophy of Physiology* [*Philosophie der Physiologie*] (1779). The work recaptures some of the arguments presented by Moses Mendelssohn in the *Letters Concerning the Sensations*. The writer states that a pleasurable experience is a sign of both beauty and melodic harmony, whereas displeasure is evoked by ugliness and discordant tones.[8] For the philosophical physiologist, however, the analogy between music and physiology is much stronger than in Mendelssohn's work. The clavier plays an essential role in Schiller's description of the nature of human physiology. The reference to that "system of chains" ("Kettensystem"; NA 20: 23) which is human anatomy is complemented by allusions to both music and optical science.

The writer advances what he calls an analogical proof ("einen analogischen Beweis"). With respect to the science of acoustics, he states: "If I put two pianos beside one another and play a key on one of them, producing a note, the same string on the other piano, and that alone, will sound without my touching it. The same note will play, though admittedly more softly" (D/R, p. 160; NA 20: 24).[9] For the former, Schiller substitutes the world, that is, the sensuous organs or "nerve spirit" ("Nervengeist") and, for the latter, the brain ("Denkorgan"). "There are as many strings in the external world as there are objects, and as many fibres in the organ of thought as there are strings in the external world. And both reality and the organ of thought, and the strings in the one and the fibres in the other correspond as precisely as the two pianos when their strings sound and resound" (D/R, p. 161; NA 20: 24).[10]

The question here is to what extent experience improves or harms one's own material condition as a corporeal human being. Upon studying the early dissertations, it becomes clear that the writer sought to cultivate the experience of melodic, harmonious sounds, especially the sounds of music, initially for therapeutic reasons.

In his third and final dissertation of 1780 *Study of the Connection Between the Animal and Intellectual Natures of the Human Being* [*Versuch über den Zusammenhang der tierischen Natur des Menschen mit seiner geistigen*][11], the young medical student compared the relationship between body and mind to "two . . . finely-tuned stringed instruments . . . , which are placed next to each other" ("zweien gleichgestimmten Saiteninstrumenten . . . , die nebeneinander gestellt sind") (NA 20: 63). "When a string on one is plucked and produces a certain note, the equivalent string on the other instrument will sound of its own accord and reproduce the same note, only somewhat weaker. Thus, keeping this metaphor, the joyful string in the body wakes the joyful string in the soul, and the sad note of the one wakes the sad note in the other" (D/R, p. 275; NA 20: 63–64).[12] Perfect health of mind and of body presupposes a state of harmonious tension. In order for there to be a harmonizing effect, however, the instrument must first be played.

A closer analysis of the language of Schiller's writing reveals that the metaphor of the stringed instrument assumes symbolic significance as a sign of Nature's operations. When discussing the indispensability of sensation, for instance, the writer builds up an image of the soul in a state of physical pain, exclaiming: "that was the initial stimulus, the first ray of light in the night of dormant faculties, a golden resonant note from Nature's lute" (D/R, p. 264; NA 20: 50).[13] Throughout this study, I will explore the function of the metaphor and symbol of the stringed instrument as a model of Nature and as a sign for the harmonious tensions operative in Schiller's writings.[14]

The young medical student was convinced that the body first alerted the mind to the phenomena of Nature, an act that "made the world interesting and significant, because it had rendered them [natural phenomena] indispensable to the mind" (D/R, p. 268; NA 20: 54).[15] He argues that the formation of ideas owes a great deal to the data provided by the natural world and the cooperation of sensation and experience. At this moment in his intellectual development Schiller already had begun to appreciate the compatibility of the study of physiology and aesthetics as complementary sources of knowledge about human nature in particular and Nature in general. Though the former is based in science, i.e., distinct concepts, and the latter in art, i.e., representations, there is really no indication in the writings of the young Friedrich Schiller that the two cultures of knowledge were in any way irreconcilable.

The vast secondary literature on Friedrich Schiller contains countless references to the dualistic, antithetical, dichotomous, and even contradictory nature of the author's work. Time and again, however, scholarship has characterized Friedrich Schiller either as a classical or a romantic writer and his literature as exhibiting harmony. But is the simultaneous emphasis on the dualistic, yet harmonious nature of Schiller's writings as contradictory as the split in the scholarship on Schiller suggests? Perhaps, the seemingly irresolvable tension in the secondary literature is a product of the very nature of the author's writings. In my reading, the concept of harmonious tension best characterizes the form and function of Schiller's works. Here it is helpful to recall Andreas Streicher's observation that his friend Schiller was impressed that Albrecht von Haller could be both a scientist ("Naturf-

The Solitude near Stuttgart. From a painting by Viktor Heideloff.

orscher") and a great poet ("ein grosser Dichter").[16] Rather than characterize Schiller's oeuvre in terms of the binary opposition between two distinct
and sharply opposed entities (indeed, the words dualism and antithesis leave
no room for the simultaneous, interrelated operation of manifold phenomena), I seek to appreciate the tensions that inhere in and throughout Schiller's multifarious writings. The full power of expression here, I believe, can
be comprehended both conceptually and imagistically, i.e., metaphorically/
symbolically [see, for instance, the work of Reinhart Koselleck and Hans
Blumenberg]. A central example of the tense fusion of concept and image
is captured by the symbol of the stringed instrument in Schiller's writings.
The richness of the symbol and metaphors relating to the stringed instrument is confirmed by the fact that it is also politically charged. In short, it
has a basis in reality.

Schiller's passionate love of music is evidenced by the personal testimony
of his friend, Andreas Streicher (himself a concert pianist and composer),
and recent scholarship.[17] A close reading of his works discloses the creative
recurrence of references to the stringed instrument, especially to the lute
and the piano.[18] Calling up several forgotten facts will help to illuminate this
important dimension of Schiller's writings, while, at the same time, grounding our discussion in the writer's experiences.

Duke Carl Eugen, for example, played the harp, the guitar, and the cembalo and even performed in several recitals with his own orchestra at the

Ludwigsburg castle. Schiller's wife, Charlotte von Lengefeld, played guitar—the one exhibited in the house where Schiller was born (*Geburtshaus*), in Marbach am Neckar. It is very likely that Schiller was inspired to write poetry while listening to music performed by Charlotte as well as by Andreas Streicher and others.[19] In fact, Goethe was irritated by what he called Schiller's tic of speaking to himself while listening to music.[20] Furthermore, Schiller's mother, Elizabeth Kodweiß, played the lute. I have not been able to determine with certainty whether or not Schiller himself could play an instrument. Following conversations with several Schiller experts, I believe it to be highly unlikely.[21] The most important fact is that the metaphor and symbol of the stringed instrument were employed and developed not only in the writer's poetry, but also in the medical dissertations, the dramas, and the historical and philosophical writings. This unifying element proves to be of crucial importance for an appreciation and understanding of the confluence of Schiller's multidisciplinary activities in his writings.

Harmony

In their *German Dictionary* [*Deutsches Wörterbuch*] the Grimm brothers understood that the term "Harmonie" was firmly rooted in the German language. The concept was also developed in the field of music earlier in the eighteenth century, as in Johann George Sulzer's influential *General Theory of the Beautiful Arts* [*Allgemeine Theorie der Schönen Künste*] (1774). We know that this work was used as a textbook at the Hohe Carlsschule in Stuttgart. Already very early in his career, Schiller drew several connections between music and poetry. The Grimm brothers record that the word harmony had appeared "since the second half of the previous [18th] century, . . . at which time especially Schiller enjoyed using it."[22] The large majority of lines from drama and poetry, which the Grimms cite, are from Schiller's writings. Excerpts from the early poem "Laura at the Piano" ("Laura am Klavier") and the early drama *The Robbers* [*Die Räuber*] are especially interesting in the light of our topic:

> seelenvolle harmonien wimmeln,
> ein wollüstig ungestüm,
> aus den saiten

> [soulful harmonies are teeming,
> a sensual turmoil
> out of strings]

> wie zwo flammen sich ergreifen, wie
> harfentöne in einander spielen
> zu der himmelvollen harmonie

[like two flames seizing one another,
like the sounds of harps' playing in
each other; to heaven-filled harmony][23]

According to both J. G. Sulzer and the Grimm brothers, harmony originates "from [a] mixture or uniting of several sounds" ("aus [einer] Vermischung oder Vereinigung mehrerer Töne").[24] It proceeds "from the tie of
individual simultaneously striking sounds to a melodious whole" ("aus der
verbindung von einzelnen gleichzeitig angeschlagenen tönen zu einem wohl-
klingenden ganzen").[25] But do these lines from Schiller's early writings just
cited not suggest something else? As unrefined as "Laura at the Piano" may
seem, it is precisely these kinds of word combinations that call up the presence of tension, as well as the idea that tension is not completely suspended
or negated (*aufgehoben*) in harmony itself.

In her detailed study *The Analogue of Harmony,* Margaret Ives isolated
more than twelve uses of the term in Schiller's theoretical works. But even
with the naming of semantically related metaphors from the field of music,
Ives understands the word in the traditional sense as balance, symmetry,
and proportion, that is, as correspondences or a mathematical grid. Such a
characterization fails to convey the dynamics of tension. The central question is what configured harmony for the writer Friedrich Schiller. What is
the relationship, for instance, between rupture and harmony in Schiller's
writings? Dewhurst and Reeves maintain that already at the time of the
writing of the third dissertation the writer championed "the ideal of harmony
that later informed the whole of Weimar Classicism, an ideal which can thus
be seen to have roots in the psycho-physical theories of Enlightenment
medicine" (D/R, pp. 290–91). As I am suggesting here, however, Schiller's
development of the motif and symbol of the stringed instrument, which are
deeply embedded in world literature, presupposes not only harmony but
the problem of tension. I am also advocating that the "melodious whole"
("wohlklingendes ganze"), which the Grimms and other philologists of the
nineteenth century called harmony, calls up the question of harmonious
tension.[26]

It is not coincidental that the entries for the terms "Spannung" (tension)
and "spannen" (to taughten) in the *German Dictionary* should contain several quotations from Schiller's works. The newly developed science of physiology in the eighteenth century had a strong influence on the writing of
these entries. "Spannung," for instance, is defined as the "condition of individual parts of the human body; the tension of nerves" ("zustand einzelner
theile des menschlichen Körpers; spannung der nerven").[27] Here, too, we
find quite a few secondary meanings that create analogies between the harmony of the universe and music. The close association between science and
music implies a fusion of the modern, the Copernican, and the ancient,
Pythagorean conceptions of the world: "a correspondence of the movement

of planets and of their distance from the sun with the registers and intervals, or distances between notes in music" ("eine übereinstimmung der bewegung der planeten und ihrer weite von der sonne mit den stimmen und intervallis oder den notenweiten in der musik").[28]

Contemplating the production of a sound on a stringed instrument, it is clear that all strings must not only be taut, but properly tightened in order to create melodic music. In the case of stringed instruments in particular, beautiful sounds are created *only* with the aid of tension. In the production of beautiful music, tension and harmony are necessarily interrelated. The very creation of a beautiful note is an active and tense moment. Harmony is not a mere state of rest. Schiller's writings suggest that activity is necessary not only for the achievement but also for the maintenance of harmony, beauty, completion, and perfection. Already the first dissertation *Philosophy of Physiology* contains statements about human physiology that are analogous to stringed instrumentation. The nerve spirit ("Nervengeist"), for example, is described as an entity whose strings ("Saiten") constantly vibrate ("zittern").[29] This transmutative force ("Mittelkraft") is said to reverberate throughout the body including the brain. The brain is referred to, interchangeably, as "the general sensorium" ("das allgemeine Sensorium"), "the organ of thought" ("das Denkorgan"), and "the instrument of the intellect" ("das Instrument des Verstandes") (D/R, p. 157; NA 20: 20).

When strings are strung too tightly, the danger exists that they will tear or break. Schiller's writings contain numerous references to critical moments such as these. Some of the most frequently employed words are "reißen," "zerreißen," and "entreißen," which signify tearing, shredding, or ripping things apart. In Schiller's writings, these linguistic signs refer to a fundamental problem inhering in life, namely to rupture ("Riß" and "Zerrissenheit"). The writer's concern with rupture is first intimated in the first medical dissertation, the *Philosophy of Physiology,* where he refers to the potential danger of rupture in Nature. Perceiving that "Geist" (spirit/mind) and the object ("Gegenstand") are both present and that an additional force exists, the young scholar submits: "Its disappearance has created a rift between world and mind. Its presence illuminates, animates everything about it—I shall call it the transmutative force ("Mittelkraft")" (D/R, p. 152; NA 20: 13).[30] This transmutative force is said to reside in the nerve. "If I damage the nerve, the link between world and soul is destroyed" (D/R, p. 154; NA 20: 16).[31] The question is whether this nerve is "an elastic string" ("eine elastische Saite") or some other substance. Though he does not know of what the nerve actually consists, the student of science goes on to offer a few insights into the phenomena of the nerves. The most important point here is that the writer describes parts of human anatomy in terms of strings which, once torn or severed, lead to the destruction of the body and, if the body, then also the mind.

Rupture

The word "Riß" (rupture) can be traced back to the Latin *ruptura*, which denotes the separation of something that has been fashioned together. In his *Large, Complete Universal-Lexicon* J. H. Zedler approached a definition from an exclusively theological perspective. He understands "rupture" as the consequence of God's judgment and the division between God and His people, that is, as "punishment and plague because of sins committed and a great defeat of transgressors."[32] The secondary meaning is analogous to a fissure in a wall which must be plugged "so that the enemy does not penetrate the city."[33] Only with the advent of natural science did the word acquire greater meaning. Immanuel Kant, for instance, used the word "Riß" to denote the rift ("Kluft") between the internal and external worlds (phenomenal reality and noumenal reality). Goethe appropriated the semantically related term *hiatus* to differentiate between the animate and inanimate worlds (organic and inorganic matter). The problem with which Schiller grappled in his many writings, then, was not only his own. It also characterized the nature of late eighteenth-century German culture.

In his earliest poems, the writer wrestled with the problem of death. Within his poetic writings, rupture is the term for the rift between life and death. The problem of rupture, then, is of both anthropological and metaphysical interest.[34] Schiller's early dramatic practice as well exhibits the division between the internal, moral sphere of the main protagonists and the external world, as evidenced, for instance, by Karl and Franz Moor in *The Robbers* (see chapter 3). Insofar as rupture signifies the split between the private and the public, it will have political consequences. Thus, the employment of the word rupture ("Riß"-"Zerrissenheit") in Schiller's writings marks a crisis. Appearing much later than Zedler's universal lexicon, Grimms' *German Dictionary* lists numerous meanings for the term *Riß*. One meaning associated with the term reads: "in common usage [dialect] having to do with a sudden excitation of the nerves, fright, anger, etc."[35] Thus the word "rupture" signals a critical condition, especially in the area of human health.

At the very center of his book *Critique and Crisis* [*Kritik und Krise*] Reinhart Koselleck (Bielefeld) discussed Friedrich Schiller's role in the indirect appropriation of political power by the learned middle class and his contribution to the program of the European Enlightenment. In a lengthy footnote to that section of his influential work, the German theoretical historian traced the common origin of the words "criticism" and "crisis" back to the ancient Greek. In ancient times, "crisis" referred to the administration of justice and the practice of law. The primary meaning of "crisis" at the time of the ancient Greeks was "discrimination and dispute but also decision, in the sense of a final judgment or appeal, [or of judgment in general]."[36] A question arises here concerning the extent to which Schiller's concept of the tribunal and of judgment, as well as his use of metaphors connoting apocalypse, stem from his knowledge of "crisis." It is an interesting fact that Friedrich Schiller was first a student of religion, then of law, and, finally, of medicine. Koselleck's determination that, in Latin, the crisis of illness and medical judgment are complementary concepts that restricted the concept of crisis to the medical field,[37] is especially interesting in the light of Schiller's lifelong battle with illness and his own medical studies. But, to what extent did Schiller employ the term?

The term "crisis" was employed very often in medical discussions at Duke Carl Eugen's academy, which Schiller attended from 1773 to 1780. For example, on one page of Schiller's second dissertation in Latin, concerning the nature of fevers—a work rarely cited in scholarship—the word "Krisis" (crisis) is used no fewer than three times. In this writing, young Schiller ascertained that "it is not the small blockages in the pulmonary vessels that destroy the human machine but Nature in its hundreds and thousands of attempts to burst through these blockages" (D/R, pp. 205–6).[38] "The disease and its gravity result from Nature's active attempt to combat the morbific matter" (D/R, p. 206).[39] No less surprising is Schiller's conclusion, which draws on a quotation from Shakespeare's *Hamlet*.

> Let us, therefore, beware of making over-extravagant statements about the significance of the terms ebullition and crisis and of divorcing our doctrines from the nature of the diseases! I was certainly lost in various labyrinths of error before I was persuaded that the natural order is not as we have arranged it in our textbooks.
>
> > There are more things in Heaven and Earth
> > Than are dreamt of in our [*sic*] philosophy
> > [science] (D/R, p. 206).[40]

The dissertation was rejected.

The most remarkable idea here is that, in the case of fevers, Nature combats itself. Instead of maintaining order, it produces disorder, yes even the destruction of the body. Schiller's writing thus suggests that creation and destruction are inextricably related. If successful, the momentary crisis, to which the medical student referred, will help restore order. We recall that in his universal lexicon, J. H. Zedler focused exclusively on the healing power of Nature when defining the word *crisis*.[41] According to Schiller's dissertation, Nature itself can create crisis situations. We know that, in his own life, Schiller was often at the crossroads of sickness and healing. Thus, personal experience and the scientific observation of Nature together had a significant effect on the formation of Schiller's concept of harmony in particular.

The tension-filled relationship between physical and/or political enchainment and mental or spiritual freedom surfaces time and again in Schiller's writings. It is quite transparent, for instance, in Karl Moor's and Christian Wolf's struggles to come to terms with the social order as well as in the dramatic conflict between Mary Stuart and Queen Elizabeth. Already as a student of medicine, the writer came to appreciate struggle and conflict as inherent aspects of Nature. The first paragraph of the third and final dissertation *Concerning the Connection Between the Animal and Spiritual/ Intellectual Natures of the Human Being* outlines the basic problem.

> A good many philosophers have asserted that the body is, as it were, the prison-house of the spirit [mind], chaining it only too firmly to the earth and hindering its so-called flight to perfection. On the other hand, many a philosopher has been more or less convinced that knowledge and virtue are not only the end but the means to happiness and that man's every excellence resides in the improvement of his body[42] (D/R, p. 256; NA 20: 40).

In the third, revised dissertation of 1780 the writer attempted to come to terms with the debate among ancients (e.g., Pythagoras, Epicurus [materialism] and Plato [idealism]) and moderns (e.g., Haller and Schiller's own instructors) concerning the actual relationship between body and mind. Though Schiller wished to determine that "middle line of truth" ("die Mittellinie der Wahrheit"; NA 20: 40), the attempt to maintain a balance between the two positions actually creates a tense situation, for this middle ground is located at the dividing line between two competing perspectives.[43]

Having surveyed the then current debate between materialism and idealism, the writer submits that "the more common error, however, has been to over-emphasize the strength of the human spirit and to neglect the body in claiming the independence of the mind" (D/R, p. 257; NA 20: 40–41).[44] Schiller states unequivocally that his main concern in the dissertation is to chart the influence of the body on the mind. At the same time, he sought to dissociate himself from the extremes of the Epicurean worldview.

Kenneth Dewhurst and Nigel Reeves have underscored the influence of Moses Mendelssohn's idea of the harmonious fusion of body and soul (voiced through Theocles) in *Letters Concerning the Sensations* (D/R, pp. 121–22) on the young Schiller. It is no less clear that Schiller was impressed with the empirically based philosophies of Jakob Friedrich Abel, the attempt by Gottfried Wilhelm Leibniz to synthesize British empiricism and French rationalism,[45] and the emphasis on the value of feeling and obscure perception, the correspondence between external reality and mental perception (D/R, p. 121), as well as the metaphysics of harmony in Moses Mendelssohn's *Letters*. The young writer's thesis concerning the interaction between mind and body and the indispensability of the network of senses and sensations in the "animal" component of the human being in particular may be understood as an attempt to explore the then prevalent anthropological theories concerning the nature of the human being while, at the same

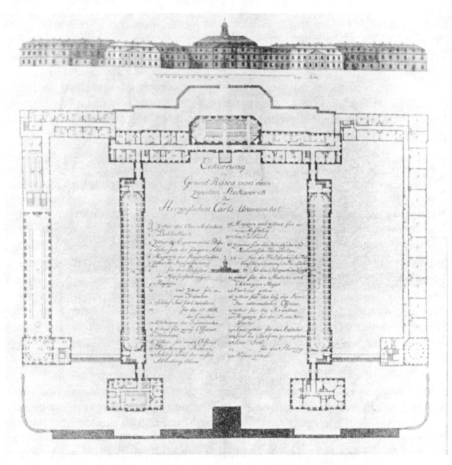

Floor plan of the main floor of the Carl's School, by M. Balleis, 1779.

time, developing a coherent theory of the universe. The tension produced by this mission reverberates throughout Schiller's writings as a whole. Indeed, the tension itself points up both the strength and limitations of the writer's enterprise.

Schiller wrote his third dissertation partially in order to express his dissatisfaction with traditional defenses of the dominance of the body over the mind. At the same time, however, he acknowledged the potentially strong influence of corporeal matter over the mind. An important chapter in this debate is his criticism of the theses propounded by Julien Offroy de La Mettrie (1709–51) in *The Human Being: A Machine* [*L'Homme machine*]. The virtual absence of direct references to this work in the medical dissertation is conspicuous, particularly suspicious since we know that one of Schiller's favorite instructors (J. F. Abel) ascribed to the empiricist underpinnings of de La Mettrie's work (D/R, pp. 116–17). Let us, then, compare and contrast de La Mettrie's work and Schiller's dissertation while expanding on several key aspects of Schiller's writings.

Schiller and de La Mettrie

In *L'Homme machine,* de La Mettrie conceived of the human body as a machine. He characterized his conception more vividly by employing the Cartesian metaphor of clockwork.[46] The idea that the human machine functions like a clock constitutes the basis of de La Mettrie's materialist view of the human being. It is quite clear already from the opening remarks of his essay that the Frenchman was no friend of metaphysics. Experience and observation alone, he stated, cut through and illuminate the "labyrinth of the human being."[47] De La Mettrie's categorical rejection of metaphysics is diametrically opposed to the several statements in Schiller's medical dissertations that testify to a divine Creation.

With the writing of the *Philosophy of Physiology* young Schiller considered the question of the determination or destiny of the human being ("Bestimmung des Menschen"). He conceived of the universe as "the creation of an infinite intelligence and designed in accordance with an excellent plan" ("das Werk eines unendlichen Verstandes . . . entworffen nach einem treflichen Plane"; D/R, p. 150; NA 20: 10). As we have seen, at the very beginning of this project, the writer had introduced the metaphor of the stringed instrument to represent the way in which Nature functions. All forces of omnipotent divine power "act both alone and together with others like notes from a thousand-stringed instrument sounding a single melody" (D/R, p. 150).[48] The human mind should function in this way when exploring "the grand design of the whole" ("den grosen Plan des Ganzen"; NA 20: 10). By emulating the sublime grandeur of the Creator, the human being will remain on the right path to "Gottgleichheit" [equality with God], which is our true destiny. Recognizing, however, that the mind of the human being is not as powerful as the mind of God, the writer concedes that, though it will continue to develop eternally, the human mind will "never attain its ideal" ("es [sein Ideal] niemals erreichen"; NA 20: 10). It would seem that, already from the start of his career, Friedrich Schiller was consciously aware of the limits of his own theorizing.

Another important example of the attempt to reconcile the claims of materialists and metaphysicians appears in the third, revised dissertation. In this work, young Schiller advanced the "irrefutable truth" that both philosophy and, especially, religion are capable of strengthening and uplifting the spirits of those who are seriously ill. Both philosophy (or, more specifically, a courageous mind) and religion can overcome the influence of animal sensations by storming the senses, thus tearing ("reißen") the soul away from all agreement or coherence with matter (NA 20: 66). In this way, rupture performs a therapeutic function. But crisis is first necessary. At this point, the accepted dissertation dovetails with the second one on the nature of fevers. Not only "the thought of God," but also "the harmony of one's past life, and the prescience of eternal future bliss" can cast a bright light over every thought, whereas the soul of a fool and an unbeliever "is thrust into [read: surrounded by] the night of all those dark sensations emanating from the bodily mechanism" (D/R, p. 278; NA 20: 67).[49]

Here, too, the act of writing helps form Schiller's concept of harmony. Reflecting on the unusual cheerfulness that the mortally ill sometimes experience, the writer reintroduces the concept of tone, submitting that "The soul enjoys an illusory sense of well-being because it is rid of a chronic feeling of pain" (D/R, p. 278; NA 20: 67).[50] But the soul is free of pain "not because the tone of its instruments has been restored, but because it no longer experiences their discord. Sympathy [between body and soul] ceases, as soon as the connection is severed" (D/R, p. 278; NA 20: 67).[51]

In his *Letters Concerning the Sensations,* Moses Mendelssohn had noted the necessity of maintaining harmonious tone and had drawn a connection to harmony in music. Dewhurst and Reeves have observed: "Music, it is suggested by Mendelssohn, has the power to harmonise, to bring out and to fulfill the diverse sides of the human being" (D/R, p. 122). For young Schiller, a courageous mind and religion possessed the power to reinstate harmony, no matter how momentarily.

A central question, then, is how to tap and further develop the human being's capacity to shape reality. One way, as suggested by the medical dissertations, is by drawing upon the harmony in Nature and cultivating it in human nature. But if rupture also inheres in Nature, then this will be a formidable, if not impossible task for the human being. Here, I believe, is one of the profound reasons for the writer's frequent employment of the metaphor of the stringed instrument and one source of his confidence in the power of culture, as articulated in the later writing *Concerning the Aesthetic Education of the Human Being in a Series of Letters* [*Über die ästhetische Erziehung des Menschen in einer Reihe von Briefen*] (1793–95).

To return to de La Mettrie's essay *The Human Being: A Machine* [*L'homme machine*], the French philosopher understands bodily reactions to be only responses to physical stimuli. Though he speaks of the harmony created by the law of cause and effect, his analysis deals exclusively with causality. Still, there is a moment in his writing when he employs the metaphor of the stringed instrument. "As a violin string or a harpsichord key vibrates and gives forth sound, so the cerebral fibres, struck by waves of sound, are stimulated to render or repeat the words that strike them."[52] Unlike Schiller's writings, de La Mettrie's reference to the stringed instrument does not suggest the possibility of harmoniously tense interaction between mind and body, let alone harmonious tone. The analogy is employed simply to underscore the effect of physical stimuli on the mind. The process he describes is purely mechanical. Body and mind are not mutually cooperative. Matter determines mind. It was precisely such narrowly conceived materialistic anthropology against which Schiller, together with several of his German instructors, was arguing.

Another significant difference between Schiller and de La Mettrie surfaces when the French anthropologist reduces the moral law to mere feeling. Morality is not a positive expression of love and concern. It is construed only negatively. Morality, for de La Mettrie, teaches us not to do something because we do not wish to have someone else do that thing to us. Though he does not exclude the possibility of a higher being, which he still deems plausible, de La Mettrie assumes neither revelation nor the existence of a divine lawgiver, from which and through whom the human being might receive direction.

De La Mettrie subscribes to the ideas of a chain of being and a unity of purposes in the universe. However, this chain is purely material, and as such is infrangible. He asks: "Why then would it be absurd to think that there are physical causes by reason of which everything has been made, and to which the whole chain of this vast universe is so necessarily bound and held that nothing which happens, could have failed to happen . . . ?"[53] He therefore concedes that the soul is "but an empty word, of which no one has any idea . . ."[54] Though he devotes some space to a discussion of the soul, de La Mettrie does not attribute any spiritual or metaphysical significance to it. It is "but a principle of motion or a material and sensible part of the brain."[55] Nonetheless, the soul influences all other major motivating forces of the human machine.[56]

In de La Mettrie's account, the human machine is depicted in such a way that the human being appears almost lifeless. De La Mettrie's purely descriptive account of the human machine is diametrically opposed to Schiller's lively articulation of a dynamic, perpetually active and interactive universe, wherein the human being is "Nature's greatest masterpiece" ("das gröste Meisterstück der Natur"; D/R, p. 269; NA 20: 55–56).

In his medical dissertations, Schiller refers periodically to the human machine and, on occasion, employs the metaphors of the machine and clockwork. The difference between the German writer and de La Mettrie on this point, however, lies in the fact that Schiller's medical dissertations disclose the tension between the traditional mechanistic philosophy of Nature and the new natural, scientific conception of the universe as an organism. Unlike the Frenchman, who constructed reality from a narrowly scientific perspective, the writer Friedrich Schiller conjoined scientific concepts with intuitive comprehensions (*Anschauungen*), which he then enlivened with the aid of imagination.[57]

Whereas de La Mettrie's approach is analytical, Schiller's is both critical *and* creative. Schiller's critical-creative approach to reality helps account for the tension between anthropology and metaphysics in his writings. The tension between anthropology and metaphysics also discloses a crisis in

German culture of the late eighteenth century. For, by the late eighteenth century, the physicotheological view of the world, which purported to have reconciled the dictates of traditional religion, specifically Christianity, with the findings of the New Science,[58] was in the process of collapsing. The new science of anthropology had begun to undermine the traditional religious explanations of the meaning and destiny of the human being in the world. In this context, it is important to recall Wolfgang Riedel's observation (*Die Anthropologie des jungen Schiller*) that Schiller's medical writings were indebted to eighteenth-century philosophical doctors.[59]

Taking the middle position, the writer focused on the fundamental connection between the competing forces of the sensuous system of the body and the intellectual-spiritual network of the mind. Schiller's interactionist theory of the relationship between mind and body presupposes reciprocal cooperation.[60] Whatever harmony may be achieved via this approach, it necessarily embodies a tension-filled field of activity. As the writer stated in the second paragraph of his dissertation, the sensuous nature of the human being first activates the mind.[61] This statement is particularly important; primarily because it underscores Schiller's appreciation of the natural components of human existence. Not only was Schiller's idea of the body first stimulating the mind influenced by Abel, Consbruch, and eighteenth-century philosophical doctors,[62] it was already a strong current of thought in Moses Mendelssohn's *Letters Concerning the Sensations.* Referring to the harmonious tension of the nerves and physiological activity in general, Mendelssohn added: "All of these effects spring from a marvelous mechanical drive before the thinking component of the human being is brought into play."[63]

But in what, according to Schiller's writings, does the perfection of the human species consist? "Man's [the human being's] perfection consists in the exercise of his [one's] powers through observing the design of the world; and as the extent to his [one's] powers and the end towards which they are working have to correspond with the most harmonious precision, perfection must consist in the greatest possible activity of these powers and their mutual subordination one to another" (D/R, p. 258; NA 20: 41).[64] Even in his medical dissertations, Schiller's anthropology does not exclude metaphysical considerations, for the writer retained the idea of a world plan ("Weltplan").[65] Indeed, a closer analysis of this section of the *Philosophy of Physiology* discloses one of the most characteristic elements of Schiller's manner of argumentation. For the writer's repeated qualifications of his statements serve to scan the limits of his own theorizing.

> But the activity of the human soul is tied to the activity of matter. . . . Changes in the corporeal world must be modified and, as it were, refined by a special group of intermediary organic forces, the *senses,* before they can produce a perception in me; and then further organic forces, the instruments of voluntary movements, must come between the soul and the world in order to transmit the change in the

former to the latter. Finally, even the operations of thinking and feeling must correspond to certain movements of the inner sensorium. All this together constitutes the organism of psychic activities. (D/R, p. 258; NA 20: 41–42).[66]

Again, the writer qualifies his argument.

But matter is the victim of eternal change and wears itself away as it works. In the course of movement an element is broken down, driven off and lost. (D/R, p. 258; NA 20: 42).[67]

Qualifications such as these permeate Schiller's writings from early on. The point here is that though matter sets the mind into motion, it cannot keep pace with mental activity.

The interaction between mind and body entails a process of reciprocal delimitation and dependence. While the body holds the mind within its bounds, the mind regulates the activities of the body, safeguarding it against possible destruction. To be sure, Ernst Platner, in his *Anthropology for Doctors and Philosophers* [*Anthropologie für Ärzte und Weltweisen*] (1772) had maintained that the "community of the soul and the body" ("Gemeinschaft der Seele und des Körpers") forms a relationship of "mutual dependence" ("gegenseitige Abhängigkeit").[68] For Schiller, however, the interactive nature of the relationship between body and mind forms an equilibrium, the suspension or overtaxing of which can have destructive consequences. This is true not only of human physiology but of all areas of human activity.

In sum, harmonious tension characterizes the nature of even the most perfect relationship between mind and body. The influence of his instructor, Jakob Abel, is also apparent in this context, where Schiller asserts: "This is that wonderful and remarkable sympathy that welds man's [the human being's] heterogeneous principles into a *single* being—man [the human being] is not soul and body but the most intimate blend of both these substances" (D/R, p. 276; NA 20: 64).[69] In his *Anthropology for Doctors and Philosophers,* Ernst Platner had defined the relationship in similar terms. "The human being is neither body nor soul alone; he/she is the harmony of both."[70] The key difference, however, between Platner's and Schiller's definitions turns on the nature of the agreement between mind and body. Rather than employ the term "Harmonie," the young Schiller advocated that the human being is the innermost *mixture,* or blend ("die innigste Vermischung") of body and mind. This mixture, I am arguing, presupposes harmonious tension.

In his *General Theory of the Beautiful Arts* Johann George Sulzer defined the word "Harmonie" as follows: "Since, then, the pleasantness of a sound originates, without question, from this harmonious blending or unity of several tones, why should one not follow this sign of Nature and make the song multivocal as Nature has made every single tone?"[71] It is easy to overlook the fact that music, harmony *and* Nature are not only associated with each other in idea, but actually connected to each other. Their existence depends on the proper blending or mixing of other elements. Since, for the eighteenth-century writer, music can stand as a model of harmonious nature, its absence suggests discord or rupture.

The conception of music as a model of harmonious nature surfaces time and again in Friedrich Schiller's multifarious writings. A closer study of Schiller's method of argumentation suggests that, as long as the human being is a physiological being, the tension between mind and body cannot cease. We may conclude, then, that the more harmonious the tension between mind and body, the healthier the human being. This is characteristic not only of Schiller's poetic, dramatic, and prose works, but also of his writings on history and philosophy. Though, at times, denied, Schiller's writings were clearly informed by the direct encounter with and observation of Nature, a term which also includes human nature.

Taking a closer look at the form of Schiller's published dissertation, it is significant that dramatic practice and theory should be intertwined with the scientific philosophical narrative. Attempting to prove his thesis that spiritual pain can lead to paralysis of the nerves (paragraph 15), the writer quotes a passage from his own drama *The Robbers,* which appears here under a different title and bears the name of a fictitious author. Where examples from the draft of a dramatic text are used as proofs to support a theoretical text dealing with medicine, the dramatic text is also enriched by the exploration of the central problem of physiology, the relationship between mind and body. The intertextual nature of Schiller's medical dissertation serves, perhaps, as the first tangible sign of the interdisciplinary character of Schiller's writings.

It is not surprising that the members of Schiller's dissertation committee should have criticized the candidate's seemingly unscientific approach to the study of physiology. The appendixes to the first part of Heinrich Wagner's two-volume history of Duke Carl's School in Stuttgart contain the written evaluations of Schiller's dissertations.[72] In these evaluations by Schiller's committee members, Johann Friedrich Consbruch, Christian Konrad Klein, and Christian Gottlieb Reuß, the student's style and manner of argumentation are critically scrutinized. In the committee's joint report, the writer was chastized for allowing himself to "be carried away too much by his imagination. Hence the poetic turns of phrase that so frequently disturb the calm flow of the philosophical style" (D/R, p. 286).[73] I would argue, however, that the committee's critical remarks concerning all three dissertations disclose the critical-creative quality of the writer's work.[74] In Schiller's many, diverse writings, the artistic and the scientific are inextricably bound. It is now clear that Schiller's medical writings disclose the harmonious tension between a purely conceptual and wholly imaginative manner of observation.[75] Sensuous experience and rational deliberation, that is, creativity and criticism inform the nature, form and function of Schiller's multifarious writings.

The first of four examples from the dissertation, to which the committee objected, was "the reverberating harmony of Nature's great lute."[76] The metaphor of the lute had appeared contemporaneously in two poems included in the *Anthology for the Year 1782*: "The Majesty of Creation: A Fantasy" ["Die Herrlichkeit der Schöpfung: Eine Phantasie"] and "Love's Triumph" ["Der Triumf der Liebe"]. The latter poem contains two beautiful, romantic-like lines that are important for an understanding of Schiller's work: "Liebe, Liebe lispelt nur / Auf der Laute der Natur" (Literally: Love, love lisps only / On the lute of Nature) (ll. 160–61; NA 1: 80). The metaphor of the stringed instrument and the analogy to broken strings would form a recurrent pattern in Schiller's writings.

Of the criticism leveled against Schiller by his committee members, Johann Friedrich Abel's comments seem quite ironic. His criticism of the writer's dissertation—"rash, lacking in proof, or only postulated by one class of philosopher" (D/R, p. 287)—[77]comes as somewhat of a surprise since Abel, in his own lectures, used many examples from poetry to support his philosophical insights. In fact, it was Abel who first introduced Schiller to Shakespeare.

The decisive point, however, is that the writing of the early medical dissertations reflects the convergence of science and art. In the all-encompassing province of knowledge, the convergence of science and art became a vital source of inspiration for the writer's formation of concepts and metaphors.

The employment of various forms of the German substantives *Anspannung* ["strain," or "tension"], *Abspannung* ["relaxation"], *Entspannung* or "Nachlaß" ["untightening," or "reduction of tension"], and *Überspannung* ["overexertion"] in Schiller's medical dissertations also demonstrates the centrality of harmonious tension in his writings. Time and again in his early work, the writer emphasized the necessity of restoring harmonious tone ("den harmonischen Ton"; NA 20: 74). Sleep, for example, is indispensable because it helps restore the healthy balance ("jenes heilsame Gleichgewicht"; NA 20: 74) that ensures survival ("die Fortdauer unsers Daseins"; NA 20: 74). For it unravels all the knotted ideas and sensations ("krampfichte Ideen und Empfindungen"; NA 20: 74) caused by the overly strenuous activities ("überspannte Tätigkeiten"; NA 20: 74) of the day. Through this type of relaxation, the writer submits, the harmony of the psychic processes ("die Harmonie der Seelenwirkungen" [NA 20: 74]) is restored.

Exploring the question of tension more closely, we find that Schiller developed a basic law of mixed natures ("Fundamentalgesetz der gemischten Naturen"): "the activities of the body correspond to the activities of the mind, i.e., any over-exertion of the mind will always result in an over-exertion of certain bodily functions, just as the equilibrium of the former or the harmonious activity of our spiritual faculties is associated with the most perfect balance of the latter. Further, mental sluggishness makes bodily movements sluggish, while mental inactivity causes them to cease altogether" (D/R, p. 270; NA 20: 57).[78] The equilibrium and balance to which the writer refers do not suggest a state of rest. On the contrary, they are animated by the activity that inheres in harmony.

The metaphor of the stringed instrument plays an essential role in Schiller's elaboration of the mind-body problem. The author criticizes the wide majority of people for allowing "the brain's strings" ["die Saiten des Denkorgans"] to doze ("erschlaffen") even when slightly taxed. The greater tension underlying and informing Schiller's early writings is expressed through the employment of juxtaposed metaphors and other tropes such as the yoke of despotism ("Joch des Despotismus"), chains and fetters of various kinds versus the metaphors of wings and the motif of flight. Together, they form a dynamic field of tension. Many of Schiller's writings recommmend themselves anew precisely because of the juxtaposition of the imprisonment of the body and the freedom of the mind. In short, the world constitutes a precarious balance, wherein crisis is immanent. The tapestry of the world is in constant threat of rupture. Schiller's writings seem to suggest that this danger can only be overcome by cultivating the original, active, yet tense harmony between all things. Indeed, the general movement of Schiller's writings from the medical dissertations to *William Tell* [Wilhelm Tell] testifies, time and again, to the rootedness of the human species in Nature.

For the writer of the medical dissertations, illness is the consequence of imbalance, that is, of the absence of the proper limitation of the forces of the soul. Thus, disturbances or breaks in the free flow of feelings and ideas, in either direction, work against the maintenance of good health. The medical student then posits a circle ("Zirkel") of reciprocal influence between the mind's sensations ("geistige Empfindungen") and the movements of the nerves ("Bewegungen der Nerven"; NA 20: 72–73). In sum, the harmonious tone of the healthy human being stems from the harmonious tension between mind and body.

Julius's Theosophy

"Julius's Theosophy" is the oldest section of the *Philosophical Letters* [*Philosophische Briefe*]. It was published in 1786 in Schiller's periodical *Thalia*. The original manuscript most likely dates back to the time of *The Robbers* and the *Anthology for the Year 1782*. Several scholars have focused on the young writer's theoretical reflections on the nature of love in this work.[79] At this point, I wish to explore the contents of this theoretical essay from the perspective of the field of tension between metaphysics and anthropology in Schiller's writings.[80]

Gerhard Kaiser has suggested that the utopia of happiness in Schiller's theosophy does not lie in the delimiting harmony of the I and the Thou but, rather, in the expectation "that reciprocal perfection leads rational creatures to likeness with God."[81] Part of the unifying theme of Schiller's work—death—is, in Kaiser's estimation, the determination of the divinity of the human being ("Bestimmung des Menschen zur Göttlichkeit").[82] This posture is complicated by the absence of any specific reference to original sin and by the writer's Baroque-like depictions of death. Isolating some basic differences between Schiller and past traditions, Kaiser alerts the reader to the problem of rupture: "for he [Schiller] sees death in a manner which was prepared in the Baroque—not actually Christian as the recompense of sin but as the great rift of the world, in which its entire dubious nature becomes clear, as the limit and measure of the human being."[83] In short, Schiller's work constitutes a break with the Christian tradition concerning original sin. In my view, this is a result of the writer's physiological anthropology.

In "Julius's Theosophy," the writer underscores the problem of rupture in Nature. Because Schiller's works reflect neither the assumed secular optimism of the Enlightenment nor the religious optimism of the Baroque, the question concerning the likeness of the human being to God becomes quite problematic. As Kaiser asks: "How can the human being be like God when death is still the final reality?"[84] Gerhard Kaiser quotes the words Schiller had assigned to Julius in the *Philosophical Letters:* "—wretched contradiction of Nature—this free upward soaring mind is made (woven) into the rigid, unalterable clockwork of a mortal body, mixed with its petty needs, yoked to its small fate—this God is relegated to a world of worms" (NA 20: 112).[85] The metaphors of the yoke and chains underscore the idea and sense of entrapment in physical nature, from which, apparently, only death is a means of liberation. Julius's words express the crisis caused by the debilitating limitation of the mortal body, of which the writer himself was painfully aware.

Julius extrapolates: "all people strive for the condition of the greatest free expression of their powers, all possess the common drive to expand their activity, to draw everything to themselves, to collect things within them, to adopt what they recognize to be good, splendid and charming" (NA 20: 117).[86] These and other statements comprising the text underscore the human being's freedom to express and develop oneself, albeit within the confines of the body. Julius's exclamation—"Reason is a torch in a prison" ("Die Vernunft ist eine Fackel im Kerker") (NA 20: 117)—strikes the heart of the truth concerning the relationship between the mind and the body in Schiller's writings. It is a major anthropocentric moment in the metaphysics of "Julius's Theosophy."

Because Julius conceives of perfection as a perpetual process, he can assert that the human being can obtain the values of the beautiful, the true, and the good, albeit only in instants of time. "In that moment in which we imagine them [the beautiful, the true, and the good], we are the owners of a virtue, creators of a deed, discoverers of a truth, bearers of a happiness. We ourselves become the experienced object" (NA 20: 117).[87] Schiller's language suggests that these values can be made one's own through intellectual effort, through the development of a moral state of mind. For, "Whatever state we perceive, we ourselves enter into it" (NA 20: 117).[88] This statement presages the writing not only of later theoretical works such as *Concerning the Aesthetic Education of the Human Being in a Series of Letters* but also of later dramatic texts such as *Mary Stuart [Maria Stuart (1800)]*. It establishes a thematic link, diachronically, between Schiller's earliest and later work, as it does synchronically, between the theoretical, dramatic, historical, poetic, and scientific writings.

According to Julius, one of the major tasks of being human is to cultivate the consciousness of one's own ennoblement ("das Bewußtsein eigener Veredlung") (NA 20: 119). The individual human being, then, if at all interested in the improvement of the species, will actively cultivate the full range of potentiality contained within his or her own nature. Here, the early essay introduces an essential part of the later program of education in *Concerning the Aesthetic Education of the Human Being in a Series of Letters,* where the writer's language waxes biblical: "Whatever beauty, whatever splendor, whatever enjoyment I summon outside me, I summon within me; whichever I neglect, destroy, I deny myself." (NA 20: 119).[89] In short, the improvement of society begins with oneself, and, if society is improved, then so is history.

The writer's employment of the word "Veredlung" (ennoblement) bears both moral and political significance. One of Schiller's major accomplishments is having transformed the concept of nobility into a task for every individual. Conceiving of the mission of the Enlightenment as individual responsibility in the spirit of moral freedom, Schiller redefined the term "edel" (noble). No longer was a sense of nobility reserved for aristocratic members of society; it could be appropriated by every individual, irrespective of social standing. By emphasizing the development of noble, that is, moral character and, in this way, transcending the traditional political denotation of the term, Schiller, through the dissemination of his writings, challenged the practice of arbitrary rule. No longer one's political standing but one's actions became the ultimate criterion for assessing the value of the individual.

In retrospect, the key to developing oneself, and thereby advancing the goals of the Enlightenment, lies in the continuous process of cultivating the harmonious tension between all aspects of life. By drawing on the tension between the body and the soul (or mind), then, the individual human being cultivates ever closer harmony with Nature. I will argue later that this idea reaches fruition in the writing of *William Tell.*

When discussing the nature of love, young Schiller's argument shifts directions. Everything, we are told, emanates and is subsumed under the concept of God, the Creator. But something more than the traditional idea of the

Christian God is at work here. For divinity inclines toward the greatest unity in diversity. The entire Creation, we are told, "flows into his personality" (NA 20: 121).[90] At this point in the argument, Julius indicts the pseudo-enlightenment of his time. "I fear that the philosophy of our times contradicts this teaching."[91] It has been spun ("gesponnen") by "a wretched egoism" ("einem dürftigen Egoismus"; NA 20: 121). Julius's argument that the age has made its own limitation the standard by which it judges the Creator constitutes a criticism of the anthropology of his day. Instead of egoism, the young writer advocates "the reality of an unselfish love" ("die Wirklichkeit einer uneigennützigen Liebe") (NA 20: 121). With this admonition, however, the writer has, in effect, reinstated the Christian tradition. For the source of this doctrine of love is Jesus Christ—"Be perfect, as your Father in Heaven is perfect, says the founder of our faith" (NA 20: 125).[92] Perhaps it is from this perspective that we should appreciate the frequently cited statement: "Love, then, . . . is the ladder upon which we clamber above to godlike nature" (NA 20: 124).[93]

Schiller describes the essence of love with reference to the metaphor of the stringed instrument, and thereby illuminates the nature of harmony. "Love does not occur among monotonous souls but, rather, among harmonious ones" (NA 20: 121).[94] The idea of being created in God's own image, as the writer suggests, presupposes that the human being resembles the Creator without being equal to God. To this extent, the human being shares in the divinity of the Godhead. "All manifestations of perfection in the universe are united in God" (NA 20: 123).[95] In the final analysis, however, the human being cannot be perfect, for perfection resides only in the Godhead.[96] Rather, the true value and worth of the human being is determined in striving towards perfection, which itself is an endless process of becoming.

In retrospect, the young writer underscored the mutually exclusive relationship between love and egoism in his essay "Julius's Theosophy." Whereas the goal of the former is unity, the latter generates only loneliness ("Einsamkeit"). The writer's language is politically charged. "Love is the co-ruling citizen of a blossoming free state; egoism a despot in a ravaged creation" (NA 20: 123).[97] In view of young Schiller's frustrations caused by the tyrannical conditions at the Duke Carl Eugen's Military Academy in Stuttgart, the philosophies of love and ennoblement of character advanced in this essay seem grounded in the writer's personal history. They were also to become an essential part of his concept of culture, which was to be worked out in the course of writing the letters *Concerning the Aesthetic Education of the Human Being*.

While stressing the importance of love, Schiller scanned the limits of self-love. "A mind that loves only itself is an atom swimming in immeasurably empty space" (NA 20: 122).[98] The simile clearly betrays the influence of the New Science on Schiller's language. In particular, the essay reflects the influence of astronomy and physics, as well as optical science when, for

Schiller's mother, Elisabeth Kodweiß.

instance, the writer refers to the existing structure of Nature as an "optical lense," or "prism" (NA 20: 124). No matter how uneasily at times the disciplines of natural science and philosophy are united, on the metaphorical and thematic planes of Schiller's language they achieve harmony.

In his second speech "Virtue in Light of Its Consequences" ["Die Tugend in ihren Folgen betrachtet"] delivered on January 10, 1780, to commemorate the birthday of the Imperial Countess Franziska von Hohenheim, the student of medicine and of life addressed the crisis of a world without love. Referring to the physics of love, he submitted: "Should love die within Creation—how soon—how soon would the ties between things be ruptured, how soon the immeasurable realm of spirits grow wild in anarchic pandemonium, just as the entire foundation of the corporeal world would collapse and all the wheels of Nature come to a final standstill should the law of attraction be suspended" (NA 20: 32).[99] In addition to the numerous allusions to various fields of inquiry, this passage discloses one of the major themes of Schiller's writings. It is the first time that the writer mentions the idea of cancellation or suspension (*Aufhebung*). Love is the true gravitational center of the universe.[100] If destroyed, the physical and metaphysical center of one's life implodes. Once this occurs, then the fabric of society is torn, and, if the fabric of society, then also the fabric of history.

At both the beginning and end of the essay "Julius's Theosophy," the writer addresses the nature of concept formation ("Begriffsbildung"). Wolfgang Riedel has noted Schiller's positive reception of the concept of Nature as a book or God's writing generated by the physicotheology of the early eighteenth century. The writer advanced the idea that all of the various expressions of the thinking mind can be encoded symbolically. "Everything in me and outside me is only a hieroglyph of a force that is similar to me. The laws of Nature are the chiffres which the thinking being fits together in order to make them understandable to the thinking being—the alphabet by way of which all minds negotiate with the most perfect mind (spirit) and with itself" (NA 20: 116).[101] The world is understood as a grand text in need of interpretation. One of the functions of Schiller's writings, then, is to decode the message inscribed on all manifestations of God's Creation. For the young Schiller, this entailed comprehending the physical constitution of the world, the binary nature of the human being, and one's relationship to both God and society.

In Paragraph Twenty-Five of the third and final medical dissertation, Schiller subscribed to the law of the association of ideas ("Ideenverbindung"; NA 20: 72). The association of ideas functions like the principle of analogy. In his edition of Albrecht Haller's *First Lines of Physiology* [*Grundriß der Physiologie*] (1746), Lester S. King noted, that while the process of analogy is fallible, since it applies to unobservable objects, early scientists availed themselves of this method in order to expand the intellectual horizon when no other means were available to them.[102] Johann Georg Zimmermann, one

of the leading philosophical doctors of the eighteenth century, also appreciated the value of induction and analogy. In his *Concerning Experience in
Medicine* [*Von der Erfahrung in der Arzneykunst*] (1763), Zimmermann
noted that analogy is useful, especially when the doctor is unsure of the
cause of illness. "Analogy connects a number of particular, yet different
appearances together as well as other ones through certain general statements."[103] Zimmermann is careful to note, however, that the physician is to
keep in mind the highest degree of probability. Since this work seems to
have influenced Schiller's thinking (according to Riedel), it is telling that
Zimmermann should have cited Moses Mendelssohn at this point. According to Zimmermann and Mendelssohn, the various levels of probability
can provide a ladder to certainty.[104] In Schiller's writings, we find a structural affinity between the association of ideas, the analogical method, and
the employment of metaphor, all of which expanded those areas of exploration limited by scientific and philosophical inquiry. The essay "Julius's Theosophy," as well as the first and third medical dissertations, are rich in their
application of these approaches to the decoding of the signs of Nature.

An essential part of the twenty-fifth paragraph of the third dissertation
concerning the association of ideas is the idea that "every feeling, no matter
of what kind, immediately affects another feeling of the same kind and thus
enlarges itself" (D/R, p. 282; NA 20: 72).[105] Furthermore, "every mental
feeling is associated with a similar animal sensation, or in other words: every
sensation produces a greater or lesser movement of the nerves, depending
on its extent and its degree of strength. Thus, as mental feelings increase,
the movements in the nervous system must also grow more intense" (D/R,
p. 282; NA 20: 72).[106] The writer describes this relationship in terms of an
ebb and flow of spiritual intellectual sensations and movements within the
system of nerves. The description discloses an appreciation of the tense
relationship that exists in and between all things. In retrospect, we recall
that Moses Mendelssohn had termed the active cooperation of the nerves
"harmonious tension" ("harmonische Spannung"). It is now apparent that
Schiller expanded this term, seeing in the harmonious tension of the body
also a prime mover of ideas.

In the section "Idee" of "Julius's Theosophy," the writer offers a unique
description of the states of human condition ("Zustand"). Whereas, in the
medical dissertation, he had associated impulses of the mind with certain
drives of the body, Schiller now establishes a structural affinity between the
physical state of the human being and conditions in the natural, physical
world. At the beginning of this early essay, Julius is given to declare: "Every
condition of the human soul has some parabola or another in physical Creation by which it is marked" (NA 20: 116).[107] He goes on to advocate "that
even the future destiny of the human mind is proclaimed in advance in the
dark oracle of physical Creation" (NA 20: 116).[108] All artists, poets, and
abstract thinkers, the writer maintains, have created from the vast store-

house of Nature. Appreciating natural physical bodies, however, the writer's eye is clearly focused on the world of real objects. In short, Schiller's use of language establishes an intimate connection between the physical and metaphysical realms of human existence.

In this early essay, the writer seems to have replaced the four elements of ancient Greek cosmology—earth, air, fire, and water—with the modern elements of "Ich" (the I), "Natur" (Nature), "Gott" (God), and "Zukunft" (the future). When brought into conjunction with specific disciplines, these designations mark the fields of philosophy, natural science, theology, and history, respectively. Schiller's writing thus denotes the confluence of these fields of inquiry, and art. "I confer with the infinite through the instrument of Nature, through world history—I read the soul of the artist in his/her Apollo" (NA 20: 116).[109] A good writer must also be a good reader. As a good reader and writer Friedrich Schiller was well versed in diverse fields of knowledge. The fact that he investigated their interrelation is confirmed by the harmonious tensions inhering in his own writings. One of the primary purposes of the present investigation is to illuminate this dynamic aspect of Schiller's oeuvre.

Near the end of "Julius's Theosophy," Schiller addresses the problem of concept formation directly. Even the purest concepts cannot reflect the true nature of things, for they are simply their determined and coexisting signs. Neither God, the soul, nor the world are really what we think they are. By inhabiting this world, the writer argues, we follow the pattern of thinking endemic to our world. "Our ideas of these things are only the endemic forms wherein the planet which we inhabit hands them down to us—our minds belong to this planet, hence also the idioms of the concepts in which they are preserved" (NA 20: 127).[110] The physical environment cannot restrict the free play of the human soul, which is constant: "the power of the soul is characteristic, necessary, and always true to itself" (NA 20: 127).[111] Though unaffected by the material world, the soul can express itself through that world: "the capriciousness of materials, upon which it [the soul] expresses itself, changes nothing about the eternal laws, according to which it expresses itself . . . as long as the sign remains completely true to the signed."[112]

The theory of palingenesis informs Schiller's remarks. Already in 1770, one of Charles Bonnet's (1720–93) major works appeared in German translation as the *Analytischer Versuch über die Seelenkräfte* [*Analytic Investigation of the Powers of the Soul*]. This work was received very positively by Albrecht von Haller in his study *On the Powers of the Soul* [*Ueber die Seelenkräfte*]. Wolfgang Riedel notes that Schiller was well aware of Bonnet's work.[113] Indeed, the first medical dissertation includes discussions of both Bonnet and Haller. The writer was struck especially by the preface to Bonnet's work. Though Schiller is critical of Bonnet elsewhere, this attraction is understandable given the Swiss writer's emphasis on the mixed nature of the human being. According to Bonnet, all natural life, from the smallest parts of the plant world to intelligent beings in distant parts of the universe follows a pattern or chain of gradation, in which there are no gaps.[114] Throughout the many worlds of planets, Bonnet argued, there is a harmonious pattern of development. Unlike Bonnet's work, however, Schiller's writings testify to the harmonious tensions informing all aspects of life.

Karl S. Guthke has seen that, in the sixteenth century, the ancient belief in plurality first received scientific credibility. Galileo's confirmation of Copernicus's theory of the universe did not mean that humankind was no longer at the center of the universe, as both Goethe and Nietzsche mistakenly believed. "The real shock of heliocentrism was not that it moved man out of the center, but that it gave scientific support to the idea of a plurality of worlds. It did so through the analogy of earth to the other planets: they all circle around the sun, they all are composed of the same matter."[115] In short, the scientific revolution changed the status of the concept of plurality. Thus the nagging idea that, perhaps, the human race inhabiting the Earth might be inferior or less capable than other races on other planets was keenly felt already at the time of the Enlightenment.

To what extent Friedrich Schiller embraced Bonnet's idea of the migration of the soul from planet to planet after death is not completely clear. In the essay "Julius's Theosophy," the writer testifies to the power of the soul ("Kraft der Seele"). We learn, however, that this power is not completely separable from the material world; indeed, it interacts with it. In sum, Schiller's attraction to some of the theories of Charles Bonnet is attributable to both the Swiss writer's belief in the mixed nature of the human being (anthropology) and his doctrine of the indestructability of the human soul (metaphysics), the latter idea of which drew Schiller to Moses Mendelssohn's *Phaedon*.[116] Thus, between the claims of the medical dissertations and the essay "Julius's Theosophy," there lies a dynamic field of tension.

Schiller's acceptance of Albrecht von Haller's definition of the human being as a "wretched in-between of angel and animal" ("unseliges Mittelding von Engel und Vieh") in the final, revised dissertation may have been a political strategy to appease the members of his dissertation committee.[117] In any event, the definition (which stems from St. Augustine) underscores the idea that the essence of the human being lies, or is caught *between* the divine and the terrestrial spheres.

A Tentative Conclusion

Schiller's medical dissertations and the essay "Julius's Theosophy" should be read together. Indeed, anthropology and metaphysics form a tension-filled relationship that reverberates throughout Schiller's writings.

From both biographical and autobiographical sources we are well-informed about the physical pain Friedrich Schiller experienced throughout his life. It is important to appreciate the fact that the man also attempted to compensate for the rupture in his own nature through constant mental activity. Though Schiller's letter of August 31, 1794, to Goethe has often been cited by scholars as one of the two letters that christened their undying friendship, Schiller's contribution to the exchange of letters has not been fully appreciated. For the writer's earliest letters to Goethe actually disclose an uneasy tension generated by the competition between the material-sensuous and intellectual-spiritual natures of the human being: "and so I hover like a hybrid entity *between* the concept and intuition, *between* the rule and sensation, *between* the technical intellect and genius" (NA 27: 32)[118] [emphasis mine]. The tense, yet dynamic state of being common to the most diverse entities of life may well have been the source of the greatest creative-critical activity for the writer Friedrich Schiller.

In the same letter to Goethe, Schiller qualified the hope that he would be able to master the discrepancy between imagination and abstractions and between cold understanding and poetry. Again, he refers to physical suffering: "unfortunately, however, after I have gotten to know and use my moral powers sickness threatens to bury my physical strength. I will hardly have time to complete a great and sweeping revolution of the mind, but I will do what I can and, when the structure finally collapses, perhaps I will have indeed rescued what is worthy of survival from the flame" (NA 27: 32).[119] With the aid of his mental powers Schiller attempted not so much to overcome physical suffering as to shape it. One thing is clear, however. The agonizing tension between the physical and the mental could not be canceled or suspended (*aufgehoben*).

Gradually, it seems, Schiller began to realize that tension is indispensable for the attainment of a sense of harmony with oneself, as well as with Nature, society, and history. In addition to the academic interest in the new science of physiology, perhaps it was from this perspective that Schiller was drawn to the problem of the relation between mind and body, in consideration of which he developed his theory of interaction. At the same time, this may well have been the major source of inspiration for the formation of the metaphors of the chains and the yoke as well as of the motif of flight, all of which can be traced back to the modern conception of the universe as a tautly strung stringed instrument.

Finally, the influence of the natural sciences on Schiller's writings has received very little attention. However, the impress of the natural sciences on Schiller's thinking is evident in his language. The widely disseminated notion that Schiller and Goethe differed in this respect can no longer be supported. At the Carlsschule, for example, the study of natural science (and not simply philosophy per se) formed what Dorothea Kuhn has termed a "cornerstone of instruction" ("Grundpfeiler des Unterrichts").[120] Indeed, young Schiller even won academic awards for excellence in both botany and surgery. Furthermore, on the basis of available biographical documents, it

Schiller's father, Johann Caspar Schiller, as a lieutenant.

is reasonable to assume that young Fritz was proud of his father's position as superintendent of the beautiful English and French gardens at the original Nursery (Pflanzschule) at the Solitude (1763–67), the home of Duke Carl Eugen's Military Academy. Young Fritz arrived there in 1773. The Academy became the headquarters of the writer's formal education in law, diplomacy, and medicine.

Dewhurst and Reeves note that the main development in the newly formed medical school, in 1775, was the introduction of physiology, osteology, and natural history into the curriculum and they underscore the point that the course of study in Stuttgart was no more theoretical than at any other German university of that time. Indeed, by the end of the eighteenth century, it was one of the very best medical faculties in the German states. In point of fact, the pupils were supplied with plenty of anatomical specimens, both dead and alive (D/R, p. 34). Schiller's own close examinations of and detailed reports on the ailing Joseph Grammont, for instance, indicate that the young writer was well-schooled in empirically based studies of nature. Dewhurst and Reeves observed that Schiller clearly appreciated "the interaction between mind and body in relation to Grammont's illness" (D/R, p. 182).

Friedrich Schiller's keen interest in his father's work is confirmed by the fact that he later edited Johann Caspar's *The Cultivation of Trees in General* [*Von der Baumzucht im Großen*] (1793) with Michaelis in Neustrelitz.[121] Michaelis was the publisher of Friedrich Schiller's *Poetic Annuals* [*Musenalmanach*]. This raises an intriguing question that must await a separate study. To what extent was Friedrich Schiller influenced by developments in natural science *before* his friendship with Goethe? I end the first chapter of our study with a quotation from Johann Caspar Schiller. "The human being certainly will not always become what the conditions dictate, otherwise he or she would be completely a machine."[122]

2

The Early Poetic Writings

In 1776, the year in which Schiller's first poem appeared, H. Steiner and associates in Winterthur, Switzerland, published *Dr. [Johann Heinrich] Sulzer's Shortened History of INSECTS According to the Linaean System [of Classification]* [*Dr. Sulzers Abgekürzte Geschichte der INSECTEN Nach dem Linaeischen System*]. This large, colorful volume was dedicated to prominent members of the Naturforschende Gesellschaft (Natural-Scientific Society) in Zürich. In this work, Sulzer classified seven species of insects. His system of classification was based on the different types of winged, half-winged, and non-winged insects.

In the essay "Julius's Theosophy" ["Die Theosophie des Julius"], Schiller noted his own interest in Linaeus's taxonomy. Other earlier writings address the fascinating relationship between the earthbound and heavenbound condition of the human being. In the third medical dissertation, concerning the evolution of humankind, the writer concludes: "Once again, then: the human being had to be [an] animal before he knew that he was mind; he had to crawl in the dirt before he dared take the Newtonian flight through the universe" (NA 20: 56).[1] As Dorothea Kuhn has pointed out, students attending the Military Academy in Stuttgart were given access to Duke Carl Eugen's natural history collection ("Naturalienkabinett"), parts of which consisted of "minerals, petrifications, prehistoric bones of mammals from Canstatt, birds, snakes, crodociles, sea creatures and, above all, insects."[2] There is no question that young Schiller was familiar with the collection. It is unlikely to be coincidence, then, that the writer's language is animated by the tension between earthbound existence and extraterrestrial flight, and a probable source of this tension is such natural science of his day.

The foreword ("Vorbericht") to Sulzer's work complements the idea of the Great Chain of Being. According to Sulzer, "the astonishing diversity" ("die erstaunliche Mannigfaltigkeit") of the world of insects helps document the conception of the universe as a multifold chain.[3] This chain consists of "a series of rings, which ascends from feelingless stone to the seraph, . . . from the lifeless little sun particle to the highest organization [of natural forms]."[4] All of these creations, the writer states, are "impregnated with the power of the essence-rich Word [of God]."[5] In Sulzer's theocentric view

52

of the universe the spiritual and material worlds are intricately intertwined: "What plasticity of matter! What fullness of Creation! Nowhere any leap, any gap—everything is constant, everything is filled and intermeshed—infinite in its simple, as well as composite parts, and, yet, [comprising] only a single unit—one harmonious, enormous body!"[6] The scientific writer's taxonomy of the complex diversity of the insect world calls up the sublime dimensions of the universe. Though he understood the cosmos to constitute a harmonious whole, the entomologist tended to foreground the great diversity and sublime enormity of Nature. Wolfgang Düsing describes Schiller as prioritizing the idea of a unified image of the world. However, the scholar's language discloses a deeper lying tension within Nature. Düsing states: "In ever greater intensity ["Anspannung"] the imagination seeks to capture the universe in a single image."[7] In this chapter, I will examine Schiller's early poetic writings in their complexity and uniqueness as documents that attest to the tensions inhering in all of Nature.

Schiller's "Fantasy to Laura" ["Phantasie an Laura"] turns as much to the purely physical, physiological world as it does to the metaphysical. Laura's kisses evoke an immediate, almost violent physiological reaction. What is it, the poet asks, that "Commands my heart to ever quicker impulses, / Wildly, feverishly takes my blood away"? [Meinem Herzen raschern Schwung gebietet, / Fiebrisch will mein Blut von hinnen reißt?] (ll. 27–28; NA 1: 47). For, "Out of their confines all senses swell / Blood overflows its banks, / Body desires to rush into body, / Souls burn in united flame" [Aus den Schranken schwellen alle Sennen [sic], / Seine Ufer überwallt das Blut, / Körper will in Körper über stürzen, / Lodern Seelen in vereinter Glut" (strophe 8; NA 1: 47)]. Though the potential threat of destruction was one aspect of both Friedrich Gottlieb Klopstock's and the young Goethe's poetry (e.g., "Frühlingsfeyer" and "Seefahrt"), analogies to human physiology in those writers' poetic works are conspicuously absent. In the poetic works of all three prominent, eighteenth-century German writers, catastrophe is averted. The ninth strophe of Schiller's poem is representative.

> Gleich allmächtig wie dort in der todten
> Schöpfung ewgen Federtrieb,
> Herrscht im arachneischen Gewebe
> Der empfindenden Natur die Lieb'.

> [Equally omnipotent as in the dead
> creation of the eternal spring mechanism,
> Love rules in the arachnean web
> of sensitive Nature.]

Though the metaphysics of love in this poem has been underscored in scholarship, the analogy to the arachnean web of sensitive nature in Schiller's writings has yet to be fully appreciated.

Scorpions, spiders, and mites are included in the class of anthropods. The various classes of arachnia are characterized not simply by four pairs of walking legs and antennae but also by their lack of wings. In short, they are utterly earthbound. The writer focuses on the web-like texture of sensitive nature. The universe, it would seem, is a labyrinth of multifarious, often knotted associations and interrelations. Schiller's early poetic writings contain several related metaphors of spinning, within which the knot forms one of the crisis points. The metaphor of the web in Schiller's early writings complements the conception of the universe as a whirlpool.

In short, there is an intimate connection between human physiology and entomology in Schiller's poetic writings. In "[Ode] to the Fates" ["An die Parzen"], for instance, both the seventh and eighth strophes link the "nerve threads of our life" ("Nervenfaden unsers Lebens"; NA 1: 73) with a "spider's web" ("Spinnewebe"; l. 28). In the eleventh strophe of the same poem, the writer relates a web's strings to human emotion. "Often in sensual, sweet hours / The thread was almost too finely [woven] for me, / More often so at the horrible abyss of melancholy / It had to be too tightly spun" [Oft in wollüstig süser Stunde / War mir der Faden fast zu fein, / Noch öfter an der Schwermut Schauerschlunde / Mußt' er zu fest gesponnen seyn] (strophe 11; NA 1: 74). Keeping in mind the concept of harmonious tension explored by Moses Mendelssohn in the *Letters Concerning the Sensations,* the image of too fine a thread—one that might be severed—and a thread too tautly wound—one that might rupture—captures the psychological conditions of sweet, but trivial passion or debilitating melancholy. Undulating in the infinite expanses of the universe, the thread of life ("Faden") ties the multifarious aspects of existence together. The final strophe of the poem reads:

> Laß ins Unendliche den Faden wallen,
>   Er wallet durch ein Paradis,
> Dann, Göttinn, laß die böse Scheere fallen!
>   O laß sie fallen, Lachesis!

> [Let the thread flow into the Infinite,
> It undulates through a paradise,
> Then, goddess, let the evil scissors fall!
> O let them fall, Lachesis!]

(Strophe 15; NA 1: 74)

Danger looms since the disposer of lots (Lachesis) is able to unravel the knot and cut the cord of life. The sinister scissors ("Todenschere"; l. 51) represent death. However, since Clotho and Lachesis are implored to let the scissors fall, the final decision is really in favor of life. At the same time, the writer also acknowledges life's precarious nature.

In the poem "To the Sun" ["An die Sonne"], the sun appears as the "daughter of Heaven" ("Tochter des Himmels"). Casting its radiance, it animates all of Nature. "Alle Fluren baden in deines Angesichts Abglanz /

Sich; und es wirbelt der Chor / Des Gevögels aus der vergoldeten Grüne der Wälder / Freudenlieder hinauf; Alle Wesen taumeln wie am Busen der Wonne: / Seelig die ganze Natur!" ["All fields and meadows bathe in the reflection of your countenance / And the chorus whirls / The joyful songs of the birds heavenwards from the forests' gilded green / All creatures sway as at bliss' bosom: / All of Nature is blessed!"] (NA 1: 51; ll. 21–26). Nature flows from the sun's "divine love" (l. 27b). Similar to the work of Barthold Brockes and Friedrich Klopstock, Schiller's "To the Sun" praises the "Father of the Saints" ("Vater der Heiligen"): "O forgive me that I fall on my face / And worship your work!" [O vergieb mir, daß ich auf mein Angesicht falle / Und anbete dein Werk!] (ll. 29–30; NA 1: 51). The act of worshipping God in Nature (Brockes) and expressing the wonders of Nature as an inspired poet (Klopstock) inform the poetry of the young Schiller.

But there are significant differences between Schiller and his forerunners. For, in this poem, the sun hovers ("schwebet") both above the domain of kings (political society) and the boundless waters of Creation (Nature). One of the most significant differences consists in the fact that as Schiller's vision of life on earth widens, his fascination with death intensifies. For, beneath the sun, all other thrones decay and the Earth appears as but a mound of dead bodies ("Grabeshügel"). In the end, however, the sun endures, smiling in the face of the murderess known as Time. To be sure, the sun stands at the center of the cosmological drama of Schiller's poetry.[8] However, scholarship has not accounted for the writer's awareness of the threat of extinction to the center of the solar system in eighteenth-century scientific circles. The Copernican Turn thus brought with it not only a new philosophical focus. It also evoked a fear of extinction—even at the time of the Enlightenment. For, unlike earlier German poetry, several of Schiller's early poetic writings convey the idea that the sun will one day burn out. Characterized as the "Magnificent Example of the Lofty" (l. 41a), the stars will be reproached one day by Eternity, "And you [sun] will yourself fade away" (l. 44). It is interesting to discover that this issue was being discussed in scientific circles at the very time Schiller was composing his first poetic writings.

The monthly issues of the *Schwäbisches Magazin von gelehrten Sachen* [*Swabian Magazine Of Learned Matters*] (1775–80) each contained a special section devoted to recent developments in scholarly circles. In the Sixth Piece for 1776, a short announcement appeared informing the reading public of a feud between an astronomer and a philosopher in Uppsala concerning whether or not the sun would eventually die out. The astronomer maintained that, within a million years, it would do so. The philosopher embraced the idea that, as one of God's creations, the sun would last forever. Apparently, arguments became so heated, and even insulting, that the local ruler felt inclined to silence the debate.[9] Not only did Schiller's first published poem "Evening" appear contemporaneously with this announcement, it appeared in the same journal.

By way of contrast, we note that, in Albrecht von Haller's "Unfinished Ode on Eternity," the sun is viewed as lasting forever. "O GOD, you alone are the source of everything / You, sun, are the measure of immeasurable time / You stay standing constant in power and light / You never went out and will never set / A single moment in you / is sheer eternity."[10] Though he felt, at times, like a small, insignificant worm in comparison to the infinite universe, Haller, the poet and scientist, maintained his trust in the spirit, but he also emphasized the reciprocal relationship between mind and body. "And with the body the mind grew. / It then tested its unpracticed power / Like insects when agitated by the warmth / Half worms they are desiring flight."[11] The connection between astronomy, physiology, and entomology in the language of Haller's poetry is not surprising given the fact that the Swiss writer and professor in Göttingen was recognized widely as the leading physiologist in Europe.

Near the end of the century, Friedrich Klopstock would stress the complementation between the two heavenly bodies of the sun and the earth in the poem "The Sun and the Earth" ["Die Sonne und die Erde"] (1796). In this poetic dialogue, the Earth is given a voice: "Let the path / that was laid out for us, float with joyfulness! / that of life / Let us enjoy and be glad in [it]."[12] In Schiller's poetic writings, however, the extinction of the sun serves not only as a metaphor for the Apocalypse or for the darkness of battle (as "In a Battle. By an Officer" ["In einer Bataille. Von einem Offizier"] for instance), which means death. We have seen that it also has a basis in the scientific discussions of the writer's own time.

Wolfgang Düsing has maintained that Schiller conceived of the cosmos as an organism, not as a machine.[13] A close analysis of each of Schiller's early poetic writings, especially when viewed in the light of the medical dissertations and dramas, actually discloses an unresolved tension between the mechanistic worldview of the seventeenth and early eighteenth centuries and the explanation of the universe as organic in nature. In part, this tension demonstrates the impact of the emerging sciences of physiology, biology, and botany in the mid to late eighteenth century. The metaphors in Schiller's language that refer to physiology and astronomy, for instance, suggest a more fundamental connection between the operations of the human circulatory system and planetary motion.[14] The following lines from the erotic poem "The Venus Wagon" ["Der Venuswagen"] provide a vivid example: "Pious anger favors fervid inclinations, / Gives the blood free sway and movement" ["Fromme Wut begünstigt heiße Triebe, / Gibt dem Blute freien Schwung und Lauf"] (ll. 185–86; NA 1: 20). The structural affinity between these two spheres of activity, as marked by poetic metaphor, shares the same source: Nature.

A closer look at Schiller's "Laura" poems reveals essential aspects of the writer's work. Though "Laura at the Piano" ["Laura am Klavier"] may seem to complement the "Fantasy to Laura" ["Phantasie an Laura"], it actually challenges the latter. Taken together, however, they form a dynamic field of tension. Whereas, in "Fantasy," the poet focuses on the corporeal world and develops the motif of flight, in "Laura at the Piano," the metaphor of the stringed instrument and the spiritual world predominates.[15] When Laura plays the stringed instrument, the poetic "I" loses its senses and turns into lifeless stone. The writer's choice of words here is especially significant since "entgeistert" and "entkörpert" can be taken literally to mean that the poet has been "de-spiritualized" and "de-bodied" (NA 1: 53; ll. 2 and 3, respectively). As long as Laura [the human being] continues to play, she commands life. References to the nervous system also abound. "Powerfully as from thousand webs of nerves / Souls demand Philadelphia [brotherly love]" [Mächtig wie von tausend Nervgeweben / Seelen fordert Philadelphia;] (ll. 5–6; NA 1: 53). Souls united in love resemble thousands of nerve tissues. All those who listen to the body are compelled by the sounds of Philadelphia's music. The human body is receptive to the music of the heavenly spheres. One of the most intimate connections between anthropology and metaphysics in Schiller's works is thereby disclosed.

We have noted how impassioned Schiller would become whenever he listened to either cheerful or tragic music, especially to music produced by stringed instruments.[16] "Laura at the Piano" is a moving testimony to the power of music to stir the writer's soul. The language of the poem suggests that music permeates and enlivens all facets of the universe. Perhaps we could subtitle the poem "the birth of the universe out of the spirit of music." The third strophe in particular underscores the forging of creation out of chaos.

> Seelenvolle Harmonieen wimmeln,
>   Ein wollüstig Ungestüm,
> Aus den Saiten, wie aus ihren Himmeln
>   Neugebohrne Serafim;
> Wie, des Chaos Riesenarm entronnen,
> Aufgejagt vom Schöpfungssturm die Sonnen
>   Funkend fuhren aus der Finsternuß,
>   Strömt der goldne Saitenguß.

> [Soulful harmonies are teeming,
>   A sensual turmoil,
> Out of the strings, from their heavens
>   New-born seraphim;
> As from the giant arm of chaos escaping
>   Roused by the storm of Creation the suns
> Sparking, driven from the darkness
> the golden affusion of strings flows forth.]

(Strophe 3; NA 1: 53)

The numerous similes and action verbs contained here create an impression of the dynamic energy of life. While silver-bright floods of water ("Fluten") trickle softly ("lieblich"), their splendor can be as majestic "As thunder's organ sound" ("Wie des Donners Orgelton"; ll. 23–26).

Because the accomplished pianist in Schiller's poem seems to commune with the higher spirits, the poet asks if Laura's communication through the medium of the stringed instrument could itself be the language of Elysium (strophe 5). With the melodic, "soulful harmonies" of music, the poetic I is afforded an, albeit momentary, glimpse behind the veil separating the world of appearance from the innermost mysteries of the universe. As in a whirl-wind ("Wirbel"), the poet is caught up into the heavenly heights. Though a new dawn emerges above the grave, the moment also marks a violent new beginning. For "The seats of the suns of new spirits / Beckon through the crevices of ruptured skies" [Neuer Geister Sonnensize / Winken durch zer-rißner Himmel Rize"] (ll. 46–47; NA 1: 54). In the German, "Ri[t]ze" (crev-ices) rhymes with "Insektenwi[t]ze" (insect intelligence) (l. 49).

It has been suggested that the metaphor of the cosmic wheel and the image of the universe as a clock contributed to the formation of the metaphor of the circle in Schiller's poetry.[17] Whatever the sequence of developments, there is an intimate connection. A prime example is found in the poem "The Secret of Reminiscence" ("Das Geheimniss der Reminiszenz"). In this text, two lovers tear the veil masking Nature, exposing the hidden wheels that drive the labyrinth of Creation (NA 1: 104f.). But, the poetic writer asks if, at some time in the past, their spirits had been intertwined ("verflochten"): "Were we in the ray of extinguished suns / In those days of long-buried delights / Already dissolved [meshed] into one?" [Waren wir im Stral *er-loschner Sonnen* / In den Tagen lang begrabner Wonnen / Schon in *Eins* zerronnen?] (ll. 23–25; NA 1: 104). Next to "Liebe" (love), "Tod" (death), and "Grab" (grave), the word "Wirbel" (whirlpool) is one of the most fre-quently employed words in Schiller's early poetic writings. "Glieder" (limbs or links), "Schwung" (momentum or leap), and "Wollust" (sensuality or ec-stasy) are also used extensively.

In "The Magnificence of Creation" ["Die Herrlichkeit der Schöpfung"], subtitled "A Fantasy" ["Eine Phantasie"], Schiller developed the motif of flying. As on wings of Nature, the poet again takes flight ("im Flug"). When referring to the celestial sphere, music begins to play the central role. The final lines of the poem read: "And what melodies / Surge up here? what inexpressible sound / Pounds my enchanted ear? . . . the great song of praise / Sounds on Nature's lute! . . . In harmonies, / Lost like a sweet death, / My spirit [praises] the Lord of All!" [Und welche Melodien / Dringen herauf? welch unaussprechlicher Klang / Schlägt mein entzüktes Ohr? . . . Der grose Lobgesang / Tönt auf der Laute der Natur! . . . In Harmonien, / Wie einen süsen Tod verlohren, preißt / Den herrn des Alls mein Geist!] (ll. 46b-51; NA 1: 56). We recall that it was precisely the incorporation of the metaphor of Nature's lute into the final medical dissertation to which the members of Schiller's committee had objected. Because of their interest in only one aspect of the candidate's work, namely the scientific, they were unable to appreciate the vital function of this central metaphor. Hence, the members of Schiller's dissertation committee overlooked the multidisciplinary texture of the candidate's writings.

The metaphor of the stringed instrument recurs in the poem "Love's Triumph" ["Der Triumf der Liebe"]. Schiller's early writings exhibit great sensitivity to mood and music. Invoking the name of Laura, the writer summons the theme of love. This motif is brought into conjunction with the metaphors of flight and musical instruments. "The silvery stream murmurs love, / Love teaches it to surge more softly; / It breathes soul into the lament / Of elegiac nightingales, / Inimitable feeling / In the strings the play of delight, / When they sound *Laura!* / Love, only love lisps / On Nature's lute" [Liebe rauscht der Silberbach, / Liebe lehrt ihn sanfter wallen; / Seele haucht sie in das Ach / Klagenreicher Nachtigallen, / Unnachahmliches Gefühl / In der Saiten Wonnespiel / Wenn sie *Laura!* hallen. / Liebe Liebe lispelt nur / Auf der Laute der Natur" (ll. 154–61; NA 1: 79–80). Hovering in the celestial sphere, the poetic I observes, below, shimmering imperial cities ("Königsstädte"). The political setting, however, quickly shifts to Nature, as the writer notes "the most beautiful mixture of blossoming fields, / Golden seeds and greening forests" (ll. 27–28). Even within the fullness of Nature, however, there lie "a long army of cliffs" and "gruesome rock wastelands" (ll. 33–34). Nature is not simply beautiful and majestic. It is also fearsome.

The occasional poem "Sensations of Gratitude" ["Empfindungen der Dankbarkeit"] records the artist's praise of the beautiful harmony exuded by one of Duke Carl Eugen's favorite companions, the Duchess Franziska von Hohenheim. When comparing her to their tyrannical, sensual monarch, the pupils at the Carlsschule must have seen in the Duchess the embodiment of virtue. In this poem, "Only cheerful thanks soar heavenward" [Nur froher Dank steigt himmelwärts] (l. 18; NA 1: 11). The political order is secure, but only as long as the Duchess's "sweet name flies high on the wings of glory" [holder Nahme fliegt hoch auf des Ruhmes Flügeln] (l. 33). The divine strains of the angel's harp are now internalized and secularized. "Elysian feelings move / The strings of the heart to song" [Elisische Gefühle drängen / Des Herzens Saiten zu Gesängen] (ll. 1–2 of 2. "Von der Ecole des Demoiselles"; NA 1: 12). In this world, nothing is silent. Though "every mouth" declares its allegiance to "virtue," it is the "mother" Franziska, not God, who instills virtue in her admirers. Hence, the strings of the human heart are themselves divine. The question, then, is how the strings should be played, or whether or not they are played at all.

The poetic I of Schiller's early poetic writings observes the operations of Nature. It is often a visual experience ("ich seh" [I see]). But Schiller was far more than a passive observer of Nature. Rather like a seer, the inspired writer apprehends the shaping forces of Nature. Most of all, his poetic writings continually highlight the creative struggle in which all Nature is forever engaged. A close analysis of the early poetry discloses that the writer's experience of life was also auditory in nature. In short, Schiller's poetry conveys sensitive knowledge of the world. As in the medical dissertations, sensuousness ("Sinnlichkeit") performs a vital function in the poet's quest for enlightenment.

In his earliest published poem "Evening" ["Der Abend"] (1776),[18] the writer focused on the soul of the poet, incorporated the motifs of wings and flight, and employed various metaphors suggesting melodic sounds and song. These are interlaced with analogies to science. The first eight lines of the second strophe crystallize the poet's earliest literary interests and theosophical viewpoints. "The poet's spirit now swells to divine melodies, / Let them flow, O Lord, from higher feeling, / Let enthusiasm swing the bold wings, / To you, to you, the goal of soaring flight. / I, lifted up heavenwards above the spheres, / Carried by marvelous feeling, / Praising the evening and the evening's creator / Penetrated by paradisial feeling" [Jezt schwillt des Dichters Geist zu göttlichen Gesängen, / Laß strömen sie, o HErr, aus höherm Gefühl, / Laß die Begeisterung die kühnen Flügel schwingen, / Zu dir, zu dir, des hohen Fluges Ziel. / Mich über Sphären, himmelan, gehoben, / Getragen sein vom herrlichen Gefühl, / Den Abend und des Abends Schöpfer loben, / Durchströmt vom paradisischen Gefühl] (ll. 9–16; NA 1: 3).

Though many of the poems in the Anthology for the Year 1782 and the half-dozen earlier poems not included in the volume emulate the exclamatory pathos of Baroque poetry, they constitute far more than "rhetorical poesy."[19] For when understood in the light of the philosophies of nature and science in his day, Schiller's poetic writings, like his writings on medicine, also disclose a tension between the claims of mechanistic philosophy and the conception of the universe as a living organism. The writer's early poetry contains innumerable references and allusions to a dynamic cosmos.[20] Indeed, this body of writings marks an encounter with reality in all its objective-material and subjective-spiritual manifestations. Though becoming and striving are major themes of this body of literature, Schiller's writings also emphasize the precarious relationship between creation and destruction, harmony and chaos.

Though scholarship has pointed time and again to young Schiller's preoccupation with death,[21] the tension between the modern, scientific view of the universe (anthropology) and the central tenets of Christian thought (religion) also animates the writer's work. The poem "Evening," for instance, calls up a close affiliation between science and religion.

Gott thuts, wenn in den weiten Himmeln
Planeten und Kometen wimmeln,

Wenn Sonnen sich um Axen drehn,
Und an der Erd vorüberwehn.

[God is at work when in the spacious skies
Planets and comets teem,
When suns turn on their axes
Drifting past the earth.]

(ll. 72–75; NA 1: 5)

The Earth is but one planet in a vast sea of worlds. The universe is teeming with life. Everything is dynamic, melodic, and joyful.

Ha, wie es schwärmt und lebt von tausend Leben
Die alle dich, Unendlicher, erheben,
Zerflossen in melodischem Gesang,
Wie tönt des Jubels himmlischer Gesang!
Wie tönt der Freude hoch erhabner Klang!
Und ich allein bin stumm—nein, tön es aus, o Harfe,
Schall Lob des HErrn in seines Staubes Harfe.

[Ha, how it stirs and lives from a thousand lives,
Which all raise you up, Eternal One,
United in melodious song,
How the heavenly song of joy resounds!
How the noble, sublime chord of joy resounds!
And I alone am mute—No! fade away, oh harp,
Ring the praise of the Lord in his harp of dust.]

(ll. 60–65; NA 1: 4)

Musical allusions abound in Schiller's early poetic writings. In short, God's Creation resembles a finely tuned instrument. There is harmony, but the state of harmony is one of harmonious tension.

Though the sixteen-year-old writer drew inspiration from God in "Evening," the poet is not depicted as being divinely inspired. The Platonic element characterizing some Storm-and-Stress poetry is not evident here.[22] Though the word "Gefühl" (feeling) is repeated three times, it is preceded by the adjectives "höher" (higher), "herrlich" (magnificent), and "paradiesisch" (paradisiacal). These modifiers point to something grander and nobler: not the unleashing of passion, but the refinement of emotion.

Clearly, the young writer experimented with some of the most pervasive traditions in German poetry. In the light of German literary history, "Evening" contains elements of the Baroque (including the work of Second Silesian School poets), early eighteenth-century physicotheology, and idyllic poetry. Combining, as it does, various elements of German poetry, Schiller's "Evening" constitutes an experiment in writing. Though Benno von Wiese detected the influence of Klopstock, Bürger, Schubart, Ewald von Kleist, and Albrecht von Haller in the shaping of Schiller's early poetic writings,[23] he was not attentive enough to the writer's scientific awareness. Indeed, von Wiese's own language reveals that there is something more fundamental at play in Schiller's poetry. "Schiller's metaphorism serves the (sensuous) symbolization of the abstract and its dialectical tensions. The taut existence of the human being between Elysium and death must always become more and more contradictory."[24] The tautness of existence and the dialectics of tension von Wiese perceives in Schiller's work, however, challenge his own view of the classical writer whose work, he says, exhibits both harmony and balance.

The vacillation between hope and despair, a sense of fulfillment and annihilation becomes especially transparent when juxtaposing the poems "Hymn to the Infinite" ["Hymne an den Unendlichen"] and "The Spaciousness of the World" ["Die Größe der Welt"]. In the first poem, the soul of the writer is caught up into the ocean of the air "between Heaven and Earth." Reeling from the dizzying heights, he thinks immediately of the Eternal One. Amazed by the sublimity of Nature ("Ungeheure Natur!"), the writer likens it to a mirror of the infinite. The potential threat of the thunderstorm in this poem is no more ominous, however, than the one described by Friedrich Gottlieb Klopstock in his famous poem "Spring Celebration" ("Frühlingsfeyer"). Unlike in Klopstock's ode, however, the storm in Schiller's poem, itself a manifestation of sublime Nature, is associated with music: "Listen! it plays like an organ" ("Horch! er orgelt") (NA 1: 101; l. 13). The Lord appears in the natural phenomenon of a lightening bolt. The last line of the poem affirms the human being's trust in God, itself a sign of the writer's respect for Nature.

Wolfgang Düsing has suggested that Schiller followed both Haller and Klopstock in depicting spatial and temporal infinity.[25] For him, this means the suspension of time ("die Aufhebung der Zeit") and the desire to transcend limits: "the attempt to break the chains of finitude."[26] However, by privileging the "classical," Schiller's interest in the suspension of time, Düsing overlooked the writer's candid recognition of the limits of human existence. Schiller's early poetic writings do not encourage escaping the chains of the finite world. The revised medical dissertation, for instance, with its acknowledgment of the limits of both the body *and* the mind, demonstrates that the writer knew that the human being cannot escape limitation. The more challenging question is how one comes to terms with the reality of limitation, not how one can transcend it.

In "The Spaciousness of the World," the focus shifts from the You (namely, Jehova) to the I. Whereas, in the hymn, flight was only implied, here the motif is consciously developed: "Through the suspended world, I fly the flight of the wind" ("Durch die schwebende Welt flieg ich des Windes Flug"; l. 2). A sense of dynamic movement has been created through the juxtaposition of the German verbs for "blowing" ("wehen") and "standing" ("stehen") (NA 1: 102). As in the poetry of the North German poet Barthold Brockes, visual observation of Nature plays a central role in the poet's experience. But, for Schiller, seeing is not so much believing, as it is understanding.

The simple past form of the verb "sehen" (to see) is employed three times in the second strophe. It complements the verbs "auferstehen" (to arise), "gehn" (to go), and "spielen" (to play). Traversing the outer reaches of the universe, the I encounters a pilgrim who asks what the I is looking for in the infinite expanses of space. The poetic I is depicted as that "bold sailor" ("kühne Seglerin") imagination ("Phantasie") who has set sail, albeit in vain ("du segelst umsonst"). The depiction suggests that, without reason, imagination is incapable of comprehending the infinite expanses of the universe. At times, such as at this moment in Schiller's development as a writer, the early poetic writings anticipate the content of the later theoretical essays. The idea of the reciprocal cooperation of reason and imagination had already begun to inform the nature of Schiller's book reviews, for instance.[27] As we will have occasion to observe later, the idea of the reciprocity of understanding and imagination also informed Schiller's later theory of the sublime.

"The Spaciousness of the World" shows that, while one may well wish to investigate other worlds, imagined or real, it is also crucial that one has a solid footing in the world. Taking this poem and "Hymn to the Infinite" together, the tension between anthropological and metaphysical considerations constitutes an essential part of the writer's enterprise. In addition to the formal experimentation with traditional and modern forms of poetry, we have seen that in his early poetic writings Schiller was shaping and reshaping certain understandings that were to form thematic links and harmonious tensions between the early and later writings. This line of continuity and the thematic unity of Schiller's collected works have not yet been fully appreciated.[28] At the same time, we will endeavor to determine various changes in Schiller's development as a writer.

In his earliest poetry, the young writer combined the science of modern physiology with a poetics of mythology. Promethean energy is expressed through the lines of "The Venus Wagon": "Oh, there the gods learn what it means to be human, / And lower themselves almost to the level of animals" ["O da lernen Götter—menschlich fühlen, / Laßen sich fast sehr herab zum—Vieh"] (ll. 65–66; NA 1: 17). Schiller's theory of the animal and intellectual natures of human beings developed in the third, revised dissertation has left its imprint. The twentieth strophe warns of the threat of a new barbarism to compassionate hearts.

> Pains of Hell gnaw through the nerves
> Turning them [the gods] into wild tigers.

[Durch die Nerfen bohren Höllenschmerzen
Kehren sie [die Götter] zu wilden Tigern um.]

(ll. 79–80; NA 1: 17)

"The Venus Wagon" contains comparably more references to strings and sounds than any of the other early poems, but they are also more violent. With the threat of rupture, crisis seems imminent.

"The Venus Wagon" is also unique in that it is the first poem in which the writer introduced the metaphor of ripping, or tearing, and of torn strings. The verb *reißen* (tearing) indicates an extreme state of tension. Its introduction here is coupled with moral criticism. For virtue, the poet writes, dies in the laps of Athenian courtesans. The spirit ("Geist") flies away, "Like the silver tone of torn strings" ("Wie aus rißnen Saiten Silberton"; l. 132).[29] "Venus's finger breaks the spirit's strength, / Plays godlessly . . ." ("Venus' Finger bricht des Geistes Stärke, / Spielet gottlos . . . "; l. 133). *Gottlos spielen* (to play godlessly) may well mean that Venus's fingers play with the body, i.e., sexually, rather than with the mind (spiritually-intellectually)— hence, the moral invective: "Melodious sound never flows from dead ruins" ("Wohlklang fließt aus toten Trümmern nie"; l. 140). Schiller's interest in physiology and poetry converge at this point. Deadened nerves denote lust and lasciviousness (ll. 145–46). Most significant, perhaps, the very absence of allusions to agitated nerves means the destruction of the cooperative interaction of body and mind. Hence, the science of physiology and moral criticism cooperate in Schiller's writings.

"Elegy on the Death of Captain Wiltmaister" ("Trauer-Ode auf den Todt des Hauptmanns Wiltmaister"), another example of the writer's occasional poetry, serves to introduce the *Anthology for the Year 1782*. The tone is serious and urgent. The trochaic lines contain several analogies to the body. "Grimly does death affect our limbs!" ("Grimmig wirgt der Todt durch unsre Glieder!"; NA 1: 31; l. 1) The wing metaphor plays an essential role. In this context, however, the metaphor augments the motif of tearing ("reißen"): "When, tearing, it [death] breaks our limbs apart" ("Wann er [der Tod] reißend durch die Glieder bricht"; l. 45). The broken strings of the body, together with the broken wings of the mind, spell certain death. Nonetheless, faith prevails and hope is maintained. For, in the end, joy will one day reign again above ("droben"), that is, beyond the rift between life and death.

Schiller's repeated acknowledgment of the fact of rupture challenges the traditional conception of the universe as a chain of being. This candid recognition places the writer at the crossroads of ancient and modern times, a theory of which was to be worked out later in the essay *Concerning Naive and Sentimental Poetry* [*Über naive und sentimentalische Dichtung*] (1795).

Wolfgang Riedel has described Schiller's analogies to physics and metaphysics as "building blocks for a history of metaphor."[30] He discerns that the writer's acceptance of the inclination toward selfless sympathy ("Sympathie") grounded in the network of human drives provides a key to a deeper understanding of the metaphysics of the essay "Julius's Theosophy." Like "the great connecting band" ("das große Band des Zusammenhangs"), to which Schiller refers in the essay "Virtue in Light of Its Consequences" (NA 20: 32), love exerts as much power in the spiritual-moral realm as does gravitation in the physical-material world.[31] In "Julius's Theosophy," love, perceived as the attraction of spirits/minds ("Anziehung der Geister") is analogous to the attraction of elements ("Anziehung der Elemente"; NA 20: 124).[32] Love is defined as "the omnipotent magnet in the spiritual world" ("der allmächtige Magnet in der Geisterwelt"; NA 20: 119).

In retrospect, the metaphors in Schiller's language illuminate the deeper physiological and psychological dynamics of the human being, serving as signs of the taut relationship between body and mind. This artistic depiction has little to do with poetic metaphors as rhetorical decoration or ornamentation.[33] Rather, it forms an analogy. We are told that God first constructed the "world of bodies" and the "realm of the spirits" according to a single principle. In the poem "The Triumph of Love," for example, love not only makes heaven more divine, it forms a bond between heaven and earth. Schiller's emphasis on love also establishes a closer affinity between himself and Goethe. For love is part of the answer to Faust's question as to what holds the world together in its innermost parts ("Was die Welt im Innersten zusammenhält" [*Faust I;* ll. 382–83). The kind of love described here is not Christ's love for humankind but, simply, the love of one human being for another. The writer's anthropological interest is suggested by the statement that human beings can be like God since, through love, they are blissful ("selig"), that is, virtuous. We can, therefore, identify a thematic link between the poem "The Triumph of Love" and the theoretical essay "Julius's Theosophy."

"In young Schiller's worldview, love, like gravity, has the status of a God-given natural law, the suspension of which could collapse the order of the Creation."[34] The potential crisis caused by the absence of love is unmistakable. For disintegration and loss of connectedness would be the end result of a world driven merely by egoism and self-preservation. A passage from Schiller's essay "Julius's Theosophy" supports this general understanding. "A mind that loves only itself is an atom swimming in immeasurably empty space" (NA 20: 122).[35] Without love, then, society itself will collapse, as, without gravity, the heavenly bodies would be dispersed, aimlessly, throughout the universe. In short, gravity in the physical world and love in the metaphysical realm are indispensable to the maintenance of the universe and society. If these essential elements are in any way jeopardized, there is crisis, and if crisis, then also perhaps rupture.

The possibility of this kind of crisis situation becomes all the more apparent in the light of Karl S. Guthke's recent investigation of the nervous reactions of major thinkers in the Western intellectual tradition to the Copernican and Galilean Turns. In *The Last Frontier* (1990) [*Der Mythos der Neuzeit* (1983)], Guthke submitted that the pressing question concerning the uniqueness of the individual human being and one's relative importance vis-à-vis the "higher" forms of life on other planets has been at the center of scientific discussions since the time of the Copernican Turn.[36] One of the most important results of his study is that the gap between the two cultures of humanistic learning and scientific investigation practically vanishes. Taken together, both avenues of inquiry form "a single coherent vision" ("eine[] übergreifende[] Gesamtanschauung").[37]

In his chapter on the Enlightenment, Guthke sees in the opening line of Schiller's "Ode to Joy" ("An die Freude") (1785)—"Seid umschlungen, Millionen!" [Be embraced, you millions!]—-one type of reaction to the Copernican-Galilean Turn and the representation of the plurality of inhabited planets. He describes this as "a sense of relief at not being alone; but this reaction may suddenly turn into its opposite, a terror of being lost precisely in such an infinitely populated universe."[38] The visionary Giordano Filippo Bruno (1548–1600) was one of the first to question Aristotle's division of the cosmos into four elements, while underscoring the multiplicity and equality of the suns and planets.

In Schiller's Laura poem "Blissful Moments" ["Die seeligen Augenblike"], the writer describes the sensation of love in terms of space travel. "Whirled away by death's delight, / We land on another sun, / Laura!" (ll. 46–47; NA 1: 65). But it is immediately dismissed as a mere dream (l. 48). Instead, loss of memory (anamnesis) and death prevail. "But, oh! Waves give chase into the ocean of death / Waves—Above this rapture beat / Already the whirlpool of forgetfulness" (ll. 52–54). Perhaps there is some spiritual affinity here to the work of the romantic Friedrich von Hardenberg ("Novalis"), as Guthke suggests. Novalis's sixteenth *Blütenstaub* fragment, for instance, reads: "We dream of journeys through the universe. But is not the universe within us?"[39] For Schiller, however, subject and object are not identical. The real tie between Schiller and Novalis may well be the subject of death. From Caroline von Wolzogen and others we know how close the personal relationship between the two writers was. Still, Schiller's interest in death should not be confused with the romantic mysticism of death.[40]

Most important, Karl Guthke's study poses a serious challenge to the longstanding account of the Great Chain of Being described by Arthur O. Lovejoy.[41] According to Lovejoy, all living beings, from the simplest to the most complex (the human being) form a ladder of gradation. This ladder holds strictly to the geocentric worldview and its theological and teleological structure. As we have seen, this view also informed *Dr. Sulzer's Shortened History of Insects*. Referring to Bruno, Guthke highlights the competing tradition of the ubiquity of life in a post-Copernican universe and the innumerable systems of planets. With the emergence of the New Science, the neo-Platonic idea of the golden chain linking all forms of being collapses. In the final analysis, then, Lovejoy's work masked the discontinuity between the neo-Platonic and modern scientific conception of plurality.[42] To my understanding, this was the philosopher's way of filling in the gaps in the natural order of things. As we shall see, the later Schiller was well aware of the implications of this orientation. According to Guthke, the originality of the modern post-Copernican conception consists in the idea "that the many life-forms in nature were no longer arranged in a vertical hierarchy—like rungs on a ladder—within the geocentric system of spheres; instead they were spread out in all directions within the heliocentric model of the universe."[43] Guthke understands that the idea of vertical continuity and the concept of the plurality of worlds are two different conceptions that cannot be subsumed under the concept of a chain of being. Our own analysis of Schiller's early poetic writings has disclosed that, though the writer employed metaphors suggesting the connecting links between things, Schiller was also acutely aware of the problems of rupture and world order.

In the first two lines of the "Fantasy to Laura" ["Phantasie an Laura"], the image of the universe as a whirlpool is informed by the study of physiology. "Laura, mine! Name me the whirlpool, / Which pulls one body mightily to another" [Meine Laura! Nenne mir den Wirbel, / Der an Körper Körper mächtig reißt] (NA 1: 46). The frequent use of the verb *reißen,* especially in association with *Wirbel,* strengthens the idea of collision, thereby heightening the possibility of destruction. The next two lines are restorative. *Geist* (mind/spirit) is both the stabilizing agent and the source of knowledge. The connection between astronomy and physiology is thereby reestablished. The first strophe, wherein two bodies and minds are conjoined, is followed immediately by a reference to the "hovering planets" ("die schwebenden Planeten") which "flee in perpetual circles around the sun" ("Ewgen Ringgangs um die Sonne fliehn"; ll. 5–6; NA 1: 46). The fourth strophe builds up an image of a universe whose harmony is first established by love.

> Little sun particles join with others
>> In intimate harmony,
> Love drives spheres into each other
>> World-systems endure only through her [love].

> [Sonnenstäubchen paart mit Sonnenstäubchen
>> Sich in trauter Harmonie,
> Sphären in einander lenkt die Liebe,
>> Weltsysteme dauern nur durch sie.]

(Strophe 4; NA 1: 46)

In *Ideas on the Philosophy of the History of Humankind* (*Ideen zur Philosophie der Geschichte der Menschheit*) [1784], which Schiller later studied, Johann Gottfried Herder asserted that the task of the human being was to construct order out of the apparent chaos created by post-Copernican cosmologists.[44] But Herder's efforts tended to veil the problem of disorder. Young Schiller, I am arguing, was well aware of the implications. We recall that, in his *Philosophy of Physiology,* he wrote of the potential crisis that could result from "rupture between the world and the spirit" ("Riß zwischen Welt und Geist"). Though the idea was not worked out explicitly, Schiller's early writings suggest the possibility of rupture inherent in Nature itself, as witnessed especially by the second dissertation on the nature of fevers and the poem "The Venus Wagon."

It is a curious fact that, despite the writer's acute awareness of mortality, there is no allusion in Schiller's poetic writings to the Baroque and early Enlightenment view of the transitoriness or fragility of the body. By way of contrast, I cite Carl Friedrich Drollinger's poem "To Professor Haller, on the death of his first dear wife" ("An den Herrn Professor Haller, Uber das Absterben seiner ersten Frau Eheliebsten").[45]

> You know the structure of the body;
> Its weak construction can not last.
> You know that, what one sees in it,
> A personification of the greatest masterpieces,
> Yet ever so fragile as beautiful.[46]

To be sure, Drollinger accentuates the imperishable nature of the soul, as does young Schiller. However, the very absence of the idea of the transitoriness of the body in Schiller's poetic writings is a distinguishing factor.

For Albrecht Haller, as Karl Richter has observed, "the human being is body, as body matter and, like all matter, originating from nothing, transitory and subject to necessity."[47] At the same time, however, the human being is also mind: "originates, as mind, from one of God's thoughts, immaterial, free and immortal."[48] The scholar's language suggests a deeper tension. "He [the human being] is half animal, half angel. . . . What one's own fragmentation conveys to him establishes at the same time his unique position in Creation. A large part of the tensions are traced back to the dualistic nature of the human being, as brought out in Haller's poems. All tensions, especially here, prove not to be the unresolved remainder of an unsuccessful striving for harmony. They are the consequence of a clear definition of the dual nature of the human being."[49] Richter concludes: "Nature is sentimental wherever it penetrates Haller's poetry."[50] In Schiller's work, however, I perceive not so much the dualism, that is, the binary tug-of-war between two competing entities, as I do the tension between various spheres of influence. This is depicted especially well in Schiller's writings by metaphors of the web and spinning.

The elder Gerhard Storz came to appreciate the tensions at work in Schiller's writings. He now maintains that personal experience ("Erlebnis") and philosophy were conjoined in Schiller's work from the earliest poems.[51] The jeu d'esprit of Schiller's poetry stems "from the powerful tension between piety and revolt, between human inspiration and despondent anguish."[52] It is clear, however, that Storz still privileges the poet Friedrich Schiller, overlooking other writings such as the medical dissertations. As highly refined as Storz's aesthetic sensibility for the dramatic texture of this body of poetry may be, he excludes the simultaneous operation of other fields of interest informing Schiller's act of writing. Rather than foreground the work of the poet or Schiller's "poetic vision" ("dichterische Schau") over the student of science, I believe it is more accurate to trace the crosscurrents of these activities in each of Schiller's writings, irrespective of genre. Let us now take a closer look at the relation between science and metaphysics in Schiller's early poetic writings.

Fritz Wagner has traced the genesis of the idolization of Sir Isaac Newton in the eighteenth century. "Newton is presented as the archetype of European, yes even of human history."[53] Wagner's study complements Hans Blumenberg's account of the Copernican Turn. Concerning the history of Copernicus's reception, Blumenberg submitted: "Copernicus is much less a figure of the history of *science* in modern times than, much more, of the history of *consciousness*. An emanation proceeds from the figure of Copernicus, which is recognizable at the beginning of the seventeenth century, and whose connection with the sober reality of the Frauenburg canon and his work can no longer by determined *historically*."[54] According to Hans Blumenberg, the founder of metaphorology,[55] the metaphorization of Copernicus accounts for the tremendous impact of his ideas. Where Blumenberg traces the reactions *against* Copernicus, Wagner scanned the history of Newton-reception among the scientists' admirers. Both studies illuminate the power as well as the limitations of the reception of important thinkers in the history of writing.[56] Blumenberg's study calls attention to the problem of the transposition of history into metaphor. It seems to me, however, that Blumenberg's thought-provoking work presents an even stronger case for the necessity of more rigorous historical research. Nevertheless, I agree that "the realism of metaphor in the formation of historical life is a factor of primary significance,"[57] one example of which is the work of Friedrich Schiller.

Both Karl Richter's and Wolfgang Düsing's studies on the influence of natural science on the literature of the early Enlightenment and on Schiller's poetry, respectively, are indebted to Blumenberg's work. They may be viewed as companion pieces to the extent that Richter assesses the impact of the Copernican Turn in eighteenth-century poetry in general (from Brockes to Klopstock), whereas Düsing analyzes the metaphorical references to the cosmos in Schiller's poetry in the light of the intellectual development mapped by Richter. According to Richter's account, the poetic metaphors of the early eighteeenth century complement natural science through their generation of a compressed image of Nature. With the aid of metaphors, writers could express the self-affirmation of the human being in an expanded but increasingly material ("versachlicht") world.

A closer look at Schiller's early poetic writings reveals that Newton had come to represent the *crisis* of a world without love. As we have seen, gravity and love—the magnets of the physical and metaphysical worlds— are required for the maintenance of physical, social, and personal order. The fifth strophe of the "Fantasy to Laura" ["Phantasie an Laura"], for instance, reads: "Cast it [love] from the clockwork of natures— / Disintegrating, the universe springs apart, / Your worlds thunder into chaos, / Newton, decry their colossal fall!" [Tilge sie (die Liebe) vom Uhrwerk der Naturen— / Trümmernd auseinander springt das All, / In das Chaos donnern eure Welten, / Weint, Newtone, ihren Riesenfall!] (NA 1: 46). Without love, humankind will destroy Creation. The same kind of crisis may threaten the human body. "Drive the goddess [of love] out of the Order of Spirits, / They will grow stiff as dead bodies / Without love, spring cannot return, / Without love, no creature will praise God!" [Tilg die Göttin aus der Geister Orden, / Sie erstarren in der Körper Tod, / Ohne Liebe kehrt kein Frühling wieder, / Ohne Liebe preißt kein Wesen Gott!] (ll. 21–22; NA 1: 46). Clearly, the young writer did not simply accept the history of consciousness of the famous English scientist. For Schiller, since love sustains the universe, it also sustains the law of gravity. As in the relationship between body and mind, there is also interaction between the physical and the metaphysical. As I suggested in chapter one, in Schiller's work, the fields of anthropology and metaphysics form a taut relationship.

Love rescues the writer and his Laura from ruin. "Look Laura, cheerfulness embraces / The excessiveness of wild pains, / Warming on the breast of love's hope / Stiff despair" [Siehe Laura, Frölichkeit umarmet / Wilder Schmerzen Ueberschwung, / An der Hoffnung Liebesbrust erwarmet / Starrende Verzweifelung] (strophe 10; NA 1: 47). "Fantasy to Laura" is one of Schiller's first poems that employs the metaphor of wings. On the wings of love ("Mit Liebe Flügel"), the writer adds, future and past are united eternally (strophe 15). The metaphysics of love, explored in theory in the early essay "Julius's Theosophy," forms one of the essential components of Schiller's most important early poetic writings.

The writer's treatment of the Judeo-Christian tradition in his early poetry is significant. A poem like the "Elegy on the Death of a Young Man" ["Elegie auf den Tod eines Jünglings" (Johann Christian Weckherlin)] provides some insight into the possible religious convictions of the young man. "Slumber peacefully until we meet again! / Until, on this hill full of corpses / The omnipotent trumpet sounds, / And following opened [aufgerißnen] bolts of death / God's stormy gale sets [vibrates] these corpses into motion— / Until, impregnated with Jehova's breath, / Graves will circle—Upon his mighty threat / In melting planets' smoke / The graves regurgitate their prey." [Schlummre ruhig bis auf Wiedersehn! / Bis auf diesen leichenvollen Hügeln / Die allmächtige Posaune klingt, / Und nach aufgerißnen Todesriegeln / Gottes Sturmwind diese Leichen in Bewegung schwingt / Bis befruchtet von Jehovas Hauche / Gräber kreisen—auf sein mächtig Dräun / In zerschmelzender Planeten Rauche / Ihren Raub die Grüfte wiederkäun] (ll. 76–84; NA 1: 59). Essential tenets of the Christian religion are evident here, especially the doctrines of the Final Judgment and the resurrection of the dead. Consistent with the image of the whirlpool of the universe, God returns in a windstorm, breathing new life into the dead. An image complementing the view of the sun as a transitory heavenly body is only one sign of this, namely the image of the melting suns. Despite the threat of some sort of apocalypse, however, both immaterial spirit and love are said to withstand any destruction of the physical universe.

> Earth may return to earth,
>   The spirit still flies away from the decaying house!
> Its ashes may be strewn by the stormy gale,
>   Its love still lasts forever!

> [Erde mag zurük in die Erde stäuben,
>   Fliegt der Geist doch aus dem morschen Hauß!
> Seine Asche mag der Sturmwind treiben,
>   Seine Liebe dauert ewig aus!]

(ll. 105–108; NA 1: 60)

As we recall, the oscillation between hope and despair and fulfillment and emptiness, especially between knowledge of the presence of God in the universe and knowledge of the void, surfaced when we juxtaposed the "Hymn to the Infinite" and "The Spaciousness of the World." The first poem was indebted to Klopstock's hymns, whereas the second resembles Haller's elegiac poetic voice. In the poetic hymn, the I and the You [= Nature] form an intimate relationship and the text concludes with all creatures ("we" / "wir") acknowledging the Lord. In the latter poem, a pilgrim wanders from one solar system to another, setting sail, aimlessly, in the infinite expanses of the universe. Klopstock's ode "The Worlds" ["Die Welten"], written as early as 1759, also incorporated the topos of the pilot on the ocean of the universe. In that poem, worlds run aground and the ship is lost. This poetic temperament is rare in Klopstock's poetry, whereas Schiller's early poems, more like Haller's, focus on the precarious nature of life in recognition of the infinite depths of the universe. For Schiller, crisis could be averted, not simply by praising God, but by exploring the labyrinth of human nature and, on the basis of that experience, discovering the path to one's true self.

In retrospect, German scholars have viewed Schiller's early poetry from the perspective of the classical, that is, later writer. As Wolfgang Düsing maintains, "From the standpoint of Classicism, Schiller lacks intuitiveness ("Anschaulichkeit") and idealized objectivity with this negative, depiction of an absolute being that negates every image."[58] It is clear that the scholar overlooked the multifarious, multidisciplinary aspects of Schiller's early poetry as expressions of a younger and, in some respects, different writer. Even though he prejudices his view of the writer by adopting the perspective of classicism, Düsing does establish a tie between the early poetry and the essay "Julius's Theosophy." Like Gerhard Storz and others, however, he completely overlooks the medical dissertations. In short, Düsing was unable to appreciate the fact that Schiller's later theories were informed by his early poetic and philosophical-scientific writings. Rather than constitute a search for an ideal state of being, which, traditionally, has served as one of the hallmarks of German classicism, Schiller's early poetic writings signal the confrontation with reality in all its variety.

Following his flight from Stuttgart, the refuge in Bauerbach, and his engagement as theater critic in Mannheim, Friedrich Schiller moved to Dresden, in 1785. Here, he developed a lasting friendship with the musician Christian Gottfried Körner. The famous poem "Ode to Joy" ["An die Freude"] was written at this time (1785), though it did not appear in print until early 1786 in *Thalia*. As in the earlier poetry, "Ode to Joy" exhibits the tension between the mechanistic worldview and the emerging appreciation of an organically evolving universe. Strophe Seven, for instance, reads: "Joy is the strong spring / in eternal Nature. / Joy, Joy drives the wheels / in the grand world-clock. / It draws flowers from their seeds, / Suns from the firmament, / It rolls the spheres in the [heavenly] spaces, / which [even] the seer's scope cannot know" [Freude heißt die starke Feder / in der ewigen Natur. / Freude, Freude treibt die Räder / in der großen Weltenuhr. / Blumen lockt sie aus den Keimen, / Sonnen aus dem Firmament, / Sphären rollt sie in den Räumen, / Die des Sehers Rohr nicht kennt!] (NA 1: 170). Whereas the first lines refer to the mechanistic philosophy of the seventeenth century, the lines that follow immediately thereafter signal the advancement of the New Science and the eighteenth-century view of organic nature.

Joy permeates and enlivens the celestial spheres, the outermost reaches of which the astronomer's telescope cannot purvey. Beyond the observable phenomena of Nature and the limits of scientific analysis lie other physical worlds which may be inhabited. Karl Guthke's insight that the Copernican and Galilean Turns fostered the idea of life on other planets applies with equal force to Schiller's writings. For the gentle wing ("sanfter Flügel"; l. 8) of joy embraces not only millions of people but millions of planets: "Seid umschlungen, Millionen!" In Schiller's poem, joy is also depicted as the daughter of Elysium. It stands as a sign for the state of happy coexistence informing all Creation. Like love, joy overcomes the threat of death. Though standing amid a chorus of angels, joy radiates "Through the crevice of opened coffins" ("Durch den Riß gesprengter Särge"; l. 55). Experiencing this happy state of being oneself, the poet expressed confidence in controlling the effects of the body. For, in a happy state, one possesses "Bold courage in intense suffering" ("Festen Mut in schwerem Leiden"; l. 85). As we shall see, this insight into a happy state of being foreshadows the later theory of the sublime and the drama *Mary Stuart*. The experience of exultation is also of political relevance. For joy provides "Rescue from tyrannts' chains" ("Rettung von Tyrannenketten"; l. 97).

On a biographical level, Schiller's move to Saxony and, eventually, to Thuringia provided a means of rescue from the hands of Duke Carl Eugen which instilled in him the hope of a happier (spiritual) existence. Yet, the "Ode to Joy" is certainly not representative of all of Schiller's poetry. For Schiller's writings are as multifarious as the multidisciplinary activities in which he was engaged.

Toward a Conclusion

Concerning the reception of Schiller's poetic writings in the early nineteenth century, the anonymous author of the book *Klopstock und Schiller, Oder: Kritische Versuche über einige lyrische Gedichte des Letztern, in poetischer und moralischer Hinsicht* (Ellwangen/Gmünd: Ritter, 1821) [*Klopstock and Schiller, Or: Critical Investigations of Several Lyrical Poems by the Latter, from a Poetic and Moral Perspective*] assailed the apparent contradiction in Schiller's word choices in "Laura at the Piano" ["Laura am Klavier"] and the apparent illogic of some of the lines: "entgeistern, entkörpern, wer kann das?"[59] The critic asks: "Im *Wirbel* sich *drehen* und doch *hingeschmiedet* stehn, kann das seyn?"[60] The critic's most serious reservation actually provides evidence of the tension at play in Schiller's poetry. With respect to the line "Seelenvolle Harmonien wimmeln," the author insists: "Harmony alone can never be called soulful. Melody is the soul; harmony only the body and lining of the same. Harmony can be learned, not melody; Nature must produce *it*. The more it teems with harmony, the more soulless it becomes. It is nothing more than a buzzing and humming, crossing, hurrying, [and] entangling of sounds, which one's ear cannot apprehend, distinguish, [or] enjoy. The word 'swarming' already expresses it."[61] The critic fails to appreciate the fact that Schiller's writings underscore the harmonious tension of the universe. In the light of our reading, "soul-filled harmonies" do "swarm," like bees. Melody and harmony, and the dynamic tension they presuppose, combine to challenge the ancient Pythagorean worldview.

The anonymous critic continues, however: "Strings, breakable steel strings, Heavens! Sounds, reborn seraphim! The ground of resonance, perhaps chaos! Like the storm of Creation, the wild beating and rumbling on the keys next to the reset pedal!—Are these not images born of the gigantic arms of a spirit of chaos?"[62] The rationalistic moralist has completely overlooked the fact that the harmonious sounds emanating from the tautly strung instrument do create a sense of harmony with the world. Unlike the Pythagorean worldview, however, Schiller has not sidestepped the problem of chaos. He has confronted it.

In this body of poetic writings, the concert-like rhythm of the universe is maintained; but it is always tension-filled because the cosmos possesses the potential for both harmony and rupture. This idea brings us to the crossroads between Schiller and pre-Socratic thought. For, unlike in the Pythagorean worldview, the modern writer was acutely aware of the crisis of rupture. By comparison, the Pythagorean concept of the harmony of the spheres reflects no awareness of either the necessity of taut strings for the production of melodic sounds or the danger of broken strings. Schiller's work thus challenges the ancient symbol of the universe as a beautifully sounding lyre. Employing the metaphor in this way, the writer Friedrich Schiller effectively reinscribed ancient tradition.

3

The Thematic Unities of
Criminal Out of Infamy and the Early
Dramatic Texts

I. *Criminal Out of Infamy* [*Der Verbrecher aus verlorener Ehre*]

THE problem of crime is as acute in the prose work *Criminal Out of Infamy* (1786)[1] as it is in Schiller's entire dramatic oeuvre. In particular, the story discloses the labyrinths of human nature and social behavior. Because of the earnestness of his search for identity, it is difficult to condemn the hero completely. In his quest, the main hero Christian Wolf gains knowledge of self and acts as a free and responsible moral being. The narrative affirms the power of the moral will. The postmortem examination of Christian's vice discloses not only the conditions under which his lascivious behavior had grown. It also necessitates a confrontation with his true self. Experiencing a number of trying situations, the hero comes to a recognition of self and restores his honor as a man of moral integrity. Let us take a closer look at how this stage of development is attained in the course of the narrative before moving to three of Schiller's early dramas.

Station 1: Christian Wolf and Franz Moor

Christian Wolf was born ugly. "Nature had neglected his body."[2] Women are repulsed by his unsightly appearance (as Amalia is by Franz!), and he becomes the laughingstock of his friends. Earlier interpretations of the story have overemphasized the fact that society has cast him out.[3] Already from birth, Christian has been cheated by nature. On account of this imbalance, the Sonnenwirt (Sun Host), like his literary ancestor Franz Moor, desires compensation for the inequities of life. "He wanted to obtain by importunity what was refused him" (NA 16: 10).[4] In order to gain favor in the eyes of a young girl, Christian resorts to stealing. Hannchen's jealous lover Robert, however, has Christian indicted for poaching, an action which turns Robert into an enemy for life.

A heavy feeling of privation conjoined with a sense of hurt pride. Misery and jealousy together overpower his sensitivity. Hunger drives him into the wide world. Revenge and passion hold him in their power (NA 16: 11).[5]

A prisoner of his sensuous nature, Christian commits one crime after another. Each time his enemy prevails and the punishment grows increasingly severe. Finally, in poor health, he is completely consumed by his desire for revenge ("Hunger nach Rache").

In the early stages of the narrative the physiological and psychological affinities between Christian Wolf and Franz Moor are so remarkable that they can hardly be superficial. We know that, while in the course of writing *The Robbers* [*Die Räuber*] (1781), Schiller had learned of the case of the infamous Swabian thief Friedrich Schwan from one of his favorite professors at the Hohe Carlsschule. By and large, Franz Moor's machinations in the drama are motivated by his inability to come to terms with his unsightly appearance, as well as with the fact that he was born second. Now he desires compensation through the exercise of a will to power. The violence of tearing things apart and severing relations becomes the major form of retribution or compensation.

> *Franz.* I will crush everything that stands
> in the way of my becoming master. And master
> I must be, to force my way to goals that I
> shall never gain through kindness.[6]

Though he thinks of himself as a freely acting agent, Franz is actually controlled by sensuous desire, that is by those animal sensations ("tierische Empfindungen") which Schiller had analyzed in his revised dissertation *Concerning the Connection Between the Animal and Intellectual Natures of the Human Being*. Although the young doctor desired the reciprocal cooperation of body and mind—the healthy human being is moderate and well-balanced—he candidly acknowledges the fact that an imbalance in one or the other leads to some kind of physical derangement ("Zerrüttung"). "In a word: the state of greatest mental anguish is also that of the greatest physical sickness" (D/R, p. 272; NA 20: 59).[7] This is an apt characterization of father Moor's behavior. As a result of the mental anguish he experiences upon losing his favorite son, Moor's physical constitution has become weak and sickly. He appears pale ("blaß") from the very beginning of the play to his death, which is the result of mental exhaustion.

Schiller's interactionist theory of the relation between body and mind is also the key to an appreciation of the kinship between Franz Moor and Christian Wolf. Scoffing at the idea that the dissonance between body and mind produces psychological imbalance in act II, scene 1, Franz Moor becomes the victim of the very yoke of mechanical laws ("Joch des Mechanismus") which he had hoped to overcome.[8] Resentful and utterly unwilling to be anything less than the master of all things, Franz is unable to gain freedom from material necessitation. Ultimately, his anti-religious philosophy of despair drives him to self-annihilation. In the second edition of *The Robbers* (1782), the writer establishes the connection between emotional obsession and fatalistic masochism through the character of Pastor Moser. The employment of the metaphor of the arachnidic world and the employment of the verb *zerreißen* (to tear apart) expose the torn fabric of human nature. "These spiders' webs of systems can be torn to pieces with the single word: you must die!" (L 145; NA 3: 122).[9] Contemporaneous with the writing of the drama, Schiller arrived at a similar conclusion in the revised dissertation.

One can, therefore, state with certainty that exaggerated physical activity hastens death as much as the greatest disharmony or the most severe illness (D/R, p. 283; NA 20: 74).[10]

Schiller's Christian Wolf is both guilty and innocent of his crimes. For society shares the blame for his tragedy. This is underscored not only by Robert's actions, but also by the young lad. Upon returning home, Christian is recognized immediately. Rather than experience a homecoming, he is met with contempt. The young lad returns Christian's act of kindness with a hateful glance and throws the Groschen he had handed him back in Christian's face. This reflex action actually indicts society as a whole. The writer's social criticism is especially pronounced at this point in the narrative. For the boy's act is a practical example of society's insensitivity to the needs of one of their own. One inhumane act leads to another. Spying Johanne, whose heinous illness ("schändliche Krankheit") is the result of her state of moral depravity (yet another tie to the medical dissertation), Christian derives some sinister pleasure in calling her a whore in public. At this moment, it is clear that Wolf has lost all moral scruples and even begins to take sadistic pleasure in the misfortunes of others. His joy in the misfortune of others (*Schadenfreude*) is of the most devious kind. He refuses to maintain even the semblance of an honorable man and gives himself over wholly to a life of corruption. "I wanted to do something malevolent . . . I wanted to earn my fate" (NA 16: 14).[11] At this juncture, there is a significant transition in Wolf's psychological portrayal away from the self-pitying Franz Moor to the self-punishing Karl Moor.

Station 2: The Inner Narrative and Christian's Likeness to Karl Moor

At the very center of the story, we are led on a journey into the interior of Christian Wolf's character. Already turned within himself and fleeing into the forest ("waldeinwärts"), the social outcast suddenly detects the gruff commanding voice of a hoary wild man carrying a bludgeon. This bizarre apparition has not been taken seriously by scholars. The man resembles a villainous character. He is referred to in the text both as a villain ("Böse-wicht") and a robber ("Räuber") whose figure takes on superhuman proportions ("ging ins Riesenmäßige"). With this unexpected occurrence (*unerhörte Begebenheit*), the reader is transported beyond the creative representation of the history of Wolf/Schwan to the true story ("wahre Geschichte"), which is not history but the encounter with the I, that is, with Christian Wolf's true self.[12] The issue of the relation between history and story which the narrator addresses at the very beginning of the novella is of secondary importance to the more urgent problem of self-actualization. In the light of this theme, Schiller's story is indebted to the Enlightenment philosophy of self-development (*Bildung*) and the experimental psychology (*Erfahrungsseelenkunde*) of his time.[13]

Immediately preceding the inner narrative, the central figure concedes that the quicker he had tried to flee the scene of Robert's murder, the more critical his crisis of conscience ("Gewissensangst") had become. His experiences testify to emotional shipwreck. "I was now given a choice between a life full of restless fear of death and a violent suicide ["Entleibung"], and I had to choose. I did not have the heart to leave the world through suicide and was horrified by the prospect of remaining in it" (NA 16: 17).[14] This type of border situation is also depicted in the characterization of Karl Moor. For the dramatic hero had wrestled with the idea of suicide as a possible remedy for the debilitating despair he had experienced because of his brother's machinations. Yet, Karl was able to overcome the idea of self-extinction. But is there any connection here to the main character of Schiller's prose work?

Tormented by frightening mental images, Christian is forced to come to terms with himself while in the very act of trying to run from himself. Driven by the "Führer" through a wood, which becomes more and more labyrinthine ("abschüssiger, unwegsamer und wilder") with each step, Christian awakens out of a state of delirium only to find himself standing on the edge of an abyss, "at the steep precipice of a cliff, which peered into a deep crevasse" (NA 16: 20).[15] This reference to Nature is a sign for the abyss of life. Here, he stands completely alone ("allein vor dem Abgrund").

The imagery accompanying this unheard-of occurrence may remind us of the sublime landscapes by eighteenth- and early nineteenth-century painters such as Caspar Wolf and David Friedrich. Only here, the sinister and potentially destructive character of the sublime completely undermines the cultivation of inspiration and superior might ("Übermacht") which the writer was to associate with the sublime moment in his later theoretical works (e.g., "Concerning the Sublime" [*Über das Erhabene*]). Christian is given to say: "I looked into the chasm which was to receive me; it reminded me darkly of the abyss of Hell, from where there is no longer any salvation" (NA 16: 21).[16] A ladder appears out of nowhere and Christian climbs down into the abyss deafened by the shrill scornful laughter of Hell ("Hohn-gelächter der Hölle"): "What does a murderer have to risk?" (NA 16: 21).[17] In the very depths of his own soul, Wolf has no choice ("keine Wahl") but to come to terms with the reality of his criminal self.[18] Almost a decade later, in the essay *Concerning Naive and Sentimental Poetry,* Schiller would write: Abandoned by the ladder that carried you, no other choice is left but to seize the law with free consciousness and will, or to fall without hope into a bottomless pit" (NA 20: 428).[19]

Christian Wolf becomes the leader ("Anführer") of a band of thieves, and like Karl Moor, becomes disenchanted with the troops under his command: "Envy, suspicion and jealousy raged inside of this condemned gang" (NA 16: 23).[20] At this moment, his peace is disturbed by the fear of death ("ewige Todesangst"). Pangs of conscience return together with the desire for repentance: "his naturally good understanding ["Verstand"] finally triumphed over his sad deception" (NA 16: 24).[21] Only now does he come to terms with himself. "He now sensed how deeply he had fallen. . . . With tears, he wished that he could retrieve the past; he now knew with certainty that he would repeat it much differently. . . . At the highest point of his corruption, he was closer to the good than he perhaps had been before his first erring step" (NA 16: 24–25).[22] Drawing upon his potential for good, Christian now wishes to turn himself over to the authorities voluntarily ("freiwillig"), just as Karl Moor had turned himself over willingly into the hands of justice. He desires atonement for the past through a philanthropic act. His wish is similar to Karl Moor's, who had desired to compensate for his criminal acts against society. His letter to the prince evidences that he is a changed man.

My execution will be an example for the world but no restitution for my actions. I hate vice, and passionately long for uprightness and virtue (NA 16: 25).[23]

Another mark of the writer's social criticism is the suggestion that Christian's moral conversion is too advanced for the times. Knowing that he desires the impossible, Christian receives no response to any of the three attempts to gain mercy. Who would believe that he could possibly experience a genuine moral conversion after having committed such a reprehensible act? To be sure, it truly would have been something unheard of ("etwas Unerhörtes") had he received a pardon. Consistent with his newly won sense of honor, and having overcome his fear of death, Christian desires to die a brave soldier.

Leaving the robber band behind, Christian happens upon a small country town. While seated on a stolen horse, he is captured by the townspeople and brought before the magistrate. Seeing in the judge an honorable man, one who is worthy of trust and respect,[24] Christian confides in him and, through an exercise of free moral will ("aus freier Wahl"), reveals his true identity. His sincere confession, however, can mean only certain death. The final words of the narrative—"I am the Sun Host" ("Ich bin der Sonnen-wirt"; NA 16: 29)—evidence the fact that Christian Wolf has accepted the person he has become. For had he not revealed his identity, he may well have been able to escape. Like Karl Moor, Christian Wolf comes to terms with his own personal history.

II. *The Robbers*

There is a very close affinity between Schiller's medical dissertations and his early dramatic practice. Grimm's observation of Karl Moor, who has just received the shocking news that his father will not forgive him, is a striking example of the interrelation between spiritual or mental strain and physical illness: "He's as pale as a corpse" ("Er ist bleich wie die Leiche") (L 42; NA 3: 25). The German words for "pale" ("bleich") and "corpse" ("Leiche") rhyme. As he had done in his medical dissertation, the writer of *The Robbers* again pointed out the negative consequences of extreme behavior and alluded to the potential in the human being to exercise moral-divine will. "And does not the bodily pain which accompanies every excess bear the fingerprint of the divine will?" (L 31; NA 3: 17).[25]

On the basis of Franz Moor's, Christian Wolf's, and even Karl Moor's patterns of behavior, the reader observes that spiritual or psychological imbalance leads to animal-like ("viehisches") behavior. Physiognomy, one part of the theory of affects explored in the third dissertation, plays a key role in contrasting the dramatis personae.[26] Act II begins with a monologue, wherein we gain greater insight into Franz's psychological makeup. There is an important reference here to the iron yoke of mechanical laws ("das eiserne Joch des Mechanismus" [NA 3: 38]). The character's exclamatory question is of significance: "Is my high-flying spirit to be bound to the snail's pace of material necessity?" (L 56; NA 3: 38).[27] The writer has assigned words from the medical dissertation to the dramatic antagonist: "Doctors and philosophers have taught me how finely the motions of the mind are attuned to those of the machine that houses it. Convulsive attacks are accompanied by dissonant vibrations in the machine; passions disturb the vital force; the overburdened spirit weighs down its vehicle" (L 56; NA 3: 38).[28] The statement describes the nature of Franz's diabolical cunning. It accords well with the writer's own condemnation of Franz Moor as the frightfully distorted picture of materalism ("Schreck—und Zerrbild des Material-ismus") or anti-type ("Antityp"), and Julius's hostile brother ("feindlicher Bruder des Julius").[29] Here, we are able to appreciate not only the interrelationship of Schiller's theory and practice, but also the affinity between Franz's statements and one of the central metaphors of his collected writings: the stringed instrument.[30]

In general, the blossoming of the mind or spirit (*Geist*) is a source of strength for human beings. In *The Robbers,* Spiegelberg serves as a good example. He exclaims, "Great thoughts are taking shape in my soul! . . . Curse me for sleeping! . . . for letting my energies lie fettered, my prospects barred and thwarted; I am awake, I feel what I am—what I must and shall be!" (L 40; NA 3: 24).[31] Though only momentarily, the mind seems to free itself from the chains of the body and the physical environment of which one is a part.

It is important to note, however, that the liberation of the mind is sparked by the senses. Karl Moor's behavior, for example, is portrayed as a reaction to (imagined) injustice: "My spirit thirsts for deeds, my lungs for freedom— murderers, robbers!" (L 49; NA 3: 32).[32] When venting his animosity toward his father for (apparently) having rejected him, Karl rails: "Why was this spirit not formed into a tiger, that fastens its savage jaws in human flesh? Is this a father's devotion? Is this love for love? Would that I were a bear, and could raise the bears of the north against this race of murderers" (L 48; NA 3: 31).[33] Animal imagery is incorporated very frequently in Schiller's earliest published drama. References to various types of animals abound: "tiger," "bear," "crocodile," "lion," and "lamb," "leopard," and even spiders. All of these references function to underscore the perpetual influence of the animal nature of the human being and, at times, the extremes and entanglements of human emotion.

Franz Moor represents the breakdown of the interaction between the animal and intellectual-spiritual natures, which is represented by the following metaphor: "my wit is the bite of scorpions" ("aber mein Witz ist Skorpionstich") (L 29; NA 3: 14). The connection the writer draws between emotions and animals is especially evident in Franz's case, for whom "anger" is a "wolf," "care" a "worm," and "grief" a "viper." Franz works his plan as a spider spins its web. His actions are on a plane with the insects which crawl along and are chained to the earth. References to tearing and ripping apart ("zerreißen" and "reißen") also abound. One of the most dramatic examples is father Moor's fear that his son Karl has been torn apart like Joseph's robe in the biblical account: "'an evil beast hath devoured him; Joseph is without doubt rent in pieces'" (L 70; NA 3: 52).[34]

Concerning the robbers, Roller states that without Karl Moor they are "body without soul" ("Leib ohne Seele"), for "the beast must have its head" ("das Thier muß auch seinen Kopf haben") (L 47; NA 3: 30). Though Karl Moor is described as someone in whom the harmonious tension between body and mind is embodied, in reality, his actions throughout most of the play do not exhibit the cooperative interaction between mind and body. By the end of the drama, however, Karl seems to have recaptured the harmonious tension between them, and completely on his own.

But what is the relation between this dimension of the play and the central metaphor of the stringed instrument? Franz Moor makes a mockery of the analogy. Trying to force Amalia into marrying him, Franz alleges that his relationship with his brother was harmonious: "our souls were always as

one" ("unsere Seelen stimmten so zusammen") (L 54; NA 3: 36). Amalia
rejects this interpretation out of hand. Still, Franz insists: "Oh, they were
as one, in such sweet harmony, I always thought that we should have been
twins!" (L 54; NA 3: 36).[35] Franz manipulates the metaphor of the stringed
instrument in an attempt to gain purely personal satisfaction. Employed
in this manner, the relationship between Franz and Amalia is effectively
destroyed. Rupture, not unity, is the result.

In *The Robbers* the writer adds several other direct references to the
metaphor of the strings and the problem of rupture. While playing the piano
(Act II), Amalia sings "Hector, wilt thou bid farewell for ever" in the presence of father Moor, who is moved by it. The story of the parting of An-
dromachas and Hector is transformed into music in order to underscore the
tragic love relationship between Amalia and Karl. It is a song that Amalia
and Karl used to sing quite often together—to the sound of the lute
("Laute") (NA 3: 45). Amalia sings of undying love and how they shall both
meet again in Elysium (NA 3: 45). Thinking that Karl has died, she dreams
of their being reunited "There, there beyond the stars" ("Droben, droben
über den Sonnen") (L 68; NA 3: 50). Amalia grows envious of the ailing
father, for dying, she imagines, means "to fly to his [Karl's] arms" ("Flug in
seine Arme") (L 69; NA 3: 51).

Interlude

Comparing the modern and ancient stories of Hector and Andromaches,
Schiller's allusion to the departure scene in Homer's *Iliad* (Book VI) is
without humor. Whereas Homer's account is sad, yet touching and the hero
and heroine share tears of joy, Schiller's song evokes only tragic pathos.
Furthermore, both the lover and the innocent child are missing from the
modern version of the ancient story. Amalia's song, however, is a testimony
of undying love, for "Lethe shall not drown thy Hector's love" ("Hektors
Liebe stirbt im Lethe nicht") (L 64; NA 3: 46). Unlike yearning ("mein
Sehnen") and thinking ("mein Denken"), love is imperishable.

The writer begins Act III by having Amalia play a lute in a garden. This
time, she is singing a different song. The third strophe evokes a sense of
love, passion, and harmony: "And his kiss—o taste of paradise! / As two
burning flames will grasp and cling, / As two harps will join their melodies /
And their heavenly harmonies will sing" (L 93; NA 3: 74).[36] Still, the song
ends tragically as reality supplants desire. "He is gone! . . . / and life is now
but pain, / All joy expiring in a dying gasp" (L 93; NA 3: 74).[37]

Amalia in the Garden

The central strophe of Amalia's poetic song contains the three lines which
the Grimm brothers were to include in their *German Dictionary* in the entry

"Harmonie." This strophe refers to the harmonious tension of their love relationship, which, though evident in the consummation of their love, is now a thing of the past. Upon closer examination, it becomes clear that the poem cannot really be characterized as a love song in the traditional sense. Rather, there exists a crisis, to which the past forms of the verbs refer. Indeed, it is as if love had died; hence, the collapse of the social order. The crisis in this case has led not to healing but to oblivion. We find no evidence of a yearning for love in the present, in the future, or even beyond death. All possible enjoyment of life expires in a dying gasp. These words convey a clear recognition of the passing of love and the unbridgeable gap between Amalia and her lover.

It has already been pointed out that this song resembles the heart-rending arias of the heroines of Italian opera, which, in Schiller's day, were very popular, and that there are direct echoes ("wörtliche Anklänge") of the same in Schiller's own operatic writing *Semele*.[38] But Amalia is no "love-sick heroine"[39] like the heroines of Niccolo Jommelli's operas, which Duke Carl Eugen regarded so highly and often had performed.[40] With the purely formal analysis of this song set to music, scholarship has not inquired further into the content of the melodious sounds of the language ("Wohllaut der Sprache") or the directness of expression ("Unmittelbarkeit des Aus-drucks").[41] Closer study reveals that this beautiful song is not a love song, but rather a song of death ("Totenlied"),[42] as Amalia herself understands it. It is a curious fact that, at the premiere performance of the work in Mann-heim, the song was sung to the accompaniment of stringed instruments, in this instance to the violin and the cembalo.

A key to the interpretation of the lyrical song "Amalia in the Garden" is found in the original stage directions. It reads: "AMALIA in her garden, playing upon the lute" (L 93; NA 3: 73).[43] We recall the critical remarks by the members of Schiller's dissertation committee concerning the "reverber-ating golden sound on the lute of Nature" ("tönende[n] Goldklang auf der Laute der Natur") which, in the medical writing, serves as a model of Na-ture. Amalia's song is sung "in the garden," that is, at a location where concord between the human being and Nature should reign. To be sure, the strings of Nature still sound, but the song is robbed of its content, namely of love. Rather than unity, the rupture between mind ("Geist") and world ("Welt") is now fully exposed.

It has not been observed that thematic unity exists between Amalia's lamentation in the garden (3.1) and Karl's insights in the important scene at the Danube (3.2). Karl thinks back on the Elysian-like moments ("Ely-siumsszenen") of his childhood at a beautiful scenic location where peace and harmony should reign and recognizes that these Elysian scenes will "never return" ("nimmer zurückkehren"). Neither Amalia's song of death nor Karl's confession is sentimental or melodramatic. For in both scenes there is a clear break with the past, a split that is not simply acknowledged, but accepted. This clear recognition of the past and the incurable split between the lovers provide evidence of an historian at work even in the writing of poetry. For Schiller, this comes early, well before the publication of *Concerning Naive and Sentimental Poetry* [*Über naive und sentimentalische Dichtung*] in 1795. The loss of love in the world, as depicted in *The Robbers*, may well constitute a sharp criticism of the predominant social order of late eighteenth-century Germany. In 1784, in the announcement in the *Rheinische Thalia*, where Schiller wrote of how the play had cost him both family and fatherland, he also recorded that the bonds to Duke Carl Eugen, who "until then was my father" ("der 'bis dahin mein Vater war'") "are rent apart" ("sind zerrissen") (NA 2/2: 51).

Amalia is again in the garden in act 4, scene 4. This time, she pleads that God not tear ("entreissen") Karl away from her (NA 3: 101). Despite the obstacles impeding their path, Amalia holds fast to the hope that love unites. The metaphors the writer introduces here complement others we have come to appreciate, for we read that "oceans and mountains and horizons [stand] between the lovers" (L 123; NA 3: 102).[44] Having returned home, Karl responds that lovers' words animate the experience of love. Wondering if there is not a better world, wherein those who lament may find joy and lovers may be reunited, Karl responds: "Yes, a world where all veils are rent, and love sees itself again, in terror—Eternity is its name" (L 123; NA 3: 102).[45]

In the Löffler edition (1782), Karl joined Amalia in singing "Do you, Hector, wish to tear yourself from me . . .?" Both lovers are playing the lute (NA 3: 103). But after singing only two lines, wherein "Kriegestanze" (the dance of war) is made to rhyme with "Todeslanze" (the lance of death) Karl throws the lute aside and flees. The revised edition for the Mannheim stage production omitted this important scene, no doubt trying to downplay the operatic quality of Schiller's work.

Interlude

Rudolf Zumsteeg, one of Schiller's closest associates, composed the music for the premiere performance of *The Robbers*, which took place on January 13, 1782, in Mannheim.[46] His *Songs from the Play The Robbers* [*Gesänge aus dem Schauspiel Die Räuber*] appeared the same year in Mannheim with the Schwan publishing house.[47] Ludwig Finscher has identified some essential differences between Schiller's own early operetta *Semele* and the music of Duke Carl Eugen's chief director Niccoli Jommelli.[48] According to Finscher, Schiller's "Wortmusik" (music of words) went beyond the formal tradition of the time. He describes Schiller's operetta as "a musical drama" ("ein musikalisches Drama") or "word-opera" ("Wort-Oper").[49] Carl Dahlhaus, in his attempt to extract an aesthetics of music from Schiller's writings, ascertains that tension ("die Spannung") characterizes the nature of the classical and romantic instrumental music of that day.[50]

The Robbers Continued

Act III, scene 2, begins with a song in which the robbers form the chorus and three individual characters sing a solo. The scene consists of an exchange among the robbers who are encamped somewhere along the Danube in a nearby forest, that is, in Nature. As beautiful and magnificent as the sunset which they observe may be, the moment is representative not simply of the loss of the innocence of youth, but also of decline and death. The apocalyptic atmosphere of the scene (wherein Spiegelberg murders Razmann) draws out both the metaphysical dimensions and moral implications of the dramatic writing.

In the stillness of the evening, Karl Moor sings the song of Brutus and Caesar. Once again, he is playing the lute. Finishing the song, Karl sets the lute aside and contemplates suicide. It is a particularly moving moment, one that is lost to the Mannheim performance. In the revised version, it is not Karl Schiller has play music but Karl's cohorts. Exhausted, Karl seeks the recuperative power of music, i.e., art. "Play, I say!—I must hear music so my slumbering mind ("Genius") can awaken again" (NA 3: 210).[51] As will become apparent later, there is an affinity between Karl Moor and Wallenstein concerning the healing power of music. Thematically, there is also a connection on this score between *The Robbers* and the later theoretical work *Concerning the Aesthetic Education of the Human Being*.

In general, the Mannheim stage version works against the interplay of harmony and rupture in Schiller's writings. This is all the more interesting when we consider the writer's development of the symbol of the stringed instrument. Contemplating suicide, the protagonist of the Löffler version of the play speaks of "labyrinths of confusion—no way out—no star to guide" (L 130; NA 3: 109).[52] Despairing, Karl poses a challenging question: "But why this burning hunger for happiness? Why this ideal of unattained perfection?" (L 130; NA 3: 109).[53] Is an unachievable ideal not merely an idea? The question the writer raises through his protagonist suggests discord between the inanimate, material world and the life of reason. "There is such divine harmony in the world of inanimate nature, why such discord ["Mißklang"] in the world of reason?" (L 131; NA 3: 109).[54] As in Schiller's early poetic writings, the metaphor of the chains accentuates the interrelated nature of time and eternity. At this moment, Karl raises the pistol to his head and declares: "Time and eternity—linked together by a single moment!" (L 131; NA 3: 109).[55]

Though the human being is free to choose between life and death, Schiller's hero is forced to reflect more deeply on the meaning of suicide. He imagines a grey key that locks the door to the prison of life ("das Gefängnis des Lebens"), while, in front of him, he perceives the unbarring of "the dwelling of eternal night" ("die Behausung der ewigen Nacht") (L 131; NA 3: 109). As in the early poem "Greatness of the World" ("Die Größe der

Welt") Karl is overwhelmed by the thought of infinity: "Strange, undiscovered country!" ("Fremdes, nie umgesegeltes Land!") (L 131; NA 3: 109). Rather ironically, perhaps, Karl's thought of suicide is a moment of awakening. "Be what thou wilt, nameless *Beyond*—if but my own self to me is true" [the translation is curiously Shakespearean] (L 131; NA 3: 110).[56] This is the context of Karl's frequently cited pronouncement: "I am my heaven and my hell" ("*Ich* bin mein Himmel und meine Hölle") (L 131; NA 3: 110). Clearly, this is a moment of enlightenment—not one of defiance. Much like Christian Wolf in the early novella, Karl Moor accepts all that life affords. "And am I to die out of fear of a life of suffering? Am I to grant misery this victory over me?—No! I will endure it! [*Throwing the pistol away*]" (L 132; NA 3: 110).[57]

The monologue which we have cited here at length is especially important because of its allusions to spinning, weaving, and the threadlike nature of the universe. An awareness of tension is also apparent in Karl's words. Referring to the infinite depths of eternity, Schiller's protagonist exclaims: "See, [hu]mankind grows weak before such visions, the tensile force of finitude is relaxed, and fancy, wilful ape of our senses, spins strange shadows to deceive our credulous mind" (L 131; NA 3: 109).[58] The hero insists that, if the infinite expanses of death should be but "lonely night and everlasting desolation," he would "people the silent emptiness with my imagination, and should have all eternity to pick apart the tangled threads of universal misery" (L 131; NA 3: 110).[59] Indeed, Karl attains self-realization when he accepts his own ties to the strings that hold the universe together. Instead of severing the bond between the general and the individual, Schiller's protagonist decides in favor of life and, as a result of accepting all that life holds for the individual, comes to terms with his true self. Indeed, Karl achieves true self-awareness by accepting his own history. As we have seen, the hero of the prose work *Criminal Out of Infamy* undergoes a similar process of self-enlightenment.

Reassessing the Character of Franz von Moor

Karl's brother Franz tends in the opposite direction. His anti-developmental character is mirrored by a philosophy of despair that offers no genuine self-determination. The words the writer assigns to Pastor Moser complement the metaphorical texture of Schiller's early poetic language: "These spiders' webs of systems can be torn to pieces with the single word: you die!" (L 145; NA 3: 122).[60] Franz Moor has turned his own study of medicine and that of the philosophical doctors of the eighteenth century into a negative, self-serving philosophy. "I have always read that our being is but a motion of the blood, and when the last drop of blood has ebbed, with it go mind and spirit too. They suffer all the infirmities of our body, will not they also cease when it is destroyed? go up in vapour as it rots?

Let a drop of water find its way into our brain, and your life makes a sudden pause, and that pause is like the end of being, and its continuation is death. . . . Our sensibility is the vibration of certain cords—and a broken instrument will sound no more" (L 145; NA 3: 121).[61] The writer has made very effective use of his anthropology and, in particular, the metaphor of the stringed instrument in his depiction of dramatic personae.

In his thought-provoking article on body language and enlightenment, Gerhard Sautermeister explored some of the ramifications of the 1982 performance of Schiller's *Robbers* at the Teatro Eliseo in Rome for scholarly interpretation. On the basis of this work, Sautermeister sees that body language and enlightenment "form a multifaceted relationship of tension."[62] He notes that Schiller's theater is composed of an "interdisciplinary dialogue."[63] In studying Franz von Moor's characterization, Sautermeister observes that "the injustice of Nature is tailor-made for him [literally: written on his body]."[64] But this reading of the antagonist, informed as it is by Norbert Elias's critique of civilization, can only engender compassion for Franz, an effect that runs counter to the portrayals in the original text editions. The association Sautermeister draws between Franz's physiognomy and music— "This primal sound [of the suffering animal ("Kreatur")] takes on the form of a gesture in his hobbleing"[65]—has nothing to do with the central problem of harmony. In contradistinction to Sautermeister and the Italian staging of the piece, Schiller's text does not present Karl Moor as a hero of the underprivileged or handicapped. His actions are inglorious, destructive to society, and (a point missed by Sautermeister) self-destructive. In short, Sautermeister has bypassed the writer's moral concerns.

Franz employs the model of the universe as a mechanism in order to manipulate others such as his father. John Neubauer has seen that Franz does not consider the mechanistic worldview valid for himself because he introduces the rhetorical question: "But must my plans submit to the iron yoke of mechanical laws?"[66] Though he thinks he is a freely acting agent, Franz is actually controlled by sensuous desire, that is, by animal sensations.[67] As a slave of sensuous drives, Franz becomes, ironically, the prisoner of his own machinations. His second rhetorical question, not cited by Neubauer, reads: "Is my high-flying spirit to be bound to the snail's pace of material necessity?" (L 56; NA 3: 38).[68] The affirmative answer to the question helps clarify Franz's actions. The analogy to the world of crawling creatures is not coincidental. In his announcement to the public ("Der Verfasser an das Publikum"), Schiller portrayed Franz negatively as "a hypocritical, insidious sniper" ("ein heuchlerischer heimtückischer Schleicher").[69] At the same time, he referred to him as "broken apart in his own expressions" ("gesprengt in seinen eigenen Minen"). It should be noted that the word "gesprengt" also has a specific, medical connotation. For it may refer to vessels that rupture or burst.[70]

Franz Moor tries to compensate for his own will to power. Cold-blooded and ruthlessly calculating, this power-hungry individual ("Why am I not the only one?" he asks) adheres only to the dictates of the body. In this state, however, he is incapable of gaining freedom from material necessity. In short, Franz is a deceived deceiver.[71] Thinking he is in control of his life, when in fact he is not, his inability to accept the conditions of his own existence precludes the possibility of knowing himself. His act of self-extinction seems to be consistent with the incapacity to determine himself. In the final analysis, Franz von Moor is a prototypical example of the law of mechanics ("das Gesetz des Mechanismus") and blind necessity ("blinde Notwendigkeit"), as defined in the writer's third medical dissertation (NA 20: 43f.).

As we have seen, the metaphor of the stringed instrument in Franz's vocabulary represents rupture of the senses. Indeed, the very absence of love means rupture.[72] According to Franz, once the body has ceased to function, nothing exists. As an anti-doctor, one who militates against healing, Franz can only reject Pastor Moser's words. For Franz, there is no "inner tribunal" ("innerer Tribunal") (NA 3: 122). His self-serving philosophy of life thus leads him to deny the existence of God. "There is no God!" ("Es ist kein Gott!"), he exclaims (NA 3: 121). The animal instincts in Franz are foregrounded when he attacks Pastor Moser and threatens to tear out his tongue (NA 3: 123). Between Franz and Moser there can be no genuine dialogue, because each of them generates a mutually exclusive perspective and forcefully defends his position. The gulf not only between Franz and Karl but also between Franz and Amalia and Franz and Moser, indeed between every other character in the drama is unbridgeable.

The tension between metaphysics and anthropology reaches a crisis point in this early drama. The rupture between mind and body leads Franz to commit suicide, at which point in the text the word *reißen* (to tear) is employed. Now insane, Franz *"tears the golden cord from his hat and strangles himself"* (L 150; NA 3: 126).[73] Schweizer then asks, "Where has he crept to, the vermin?" (L 150; NA 3: 126).[74] The situation is described with the aid of a simile suggesting animal behavior. Schwarz: "laid out like a dead cat" (L 150; NA 3: 127).[75] In the English translation by F. J. Lamport this statement is made to rhyme, and quite fittingly, with the thrice repeated simile: "He is as dead as a rat" ["Er ist maustodt"] (L 150; NA 3: 127). It is now graphically clear that the writer's word choices highlight the fact that Franz represents the extremes of animal behavior in human beings. He is also characterized as crawling near the ground. In the end, there can be no harmonious tension between body and mind for Franz. Nor does he desire any such harmony.

My point is that the absence of harmony between Karl and Franz Moor testifies not only to the social conflict between two competing brothers; it illuminates the rupture within their own natures. As the drama progresses, it seems that Franz represents more and more the world ("Welt"), whereas

Karl takes on the characteristics of mind or spirit ("Geist"). We recall that, in the *Philosophy of Physiology,* the writer had suggested that the absence of a transmutative force ("Mittelkraft") leads to "rupture between world and mind/spirit" ("Riß zwischen Welt und Geist"), whereas its presence animates and enlivens everything around it (NA 20: 13). As will soon become apparent, the character constellation in *The Robbers* anticipates the split between Mary Stuart and Queen Elizabeth in *Mary Stuart* (1800).

Reassessing Karl von Moor

Karl Moor perceives the supreme being to be a God of wrath. Lacking the self-love of Schiller's essay "Julius's Theosophy," he cannot forgive himself. Perhaps because of the self-incriminating knowledge of his own actions, Karl rebukes the Pietist belief in conversion. "Can so great a sinner still mend his ways? So great a sinner cannot mend his ways, that I should have known long ago" (L 157; NA 3: 133).[76] The thrust of this statement and other central declarations complements the original title of the drama, *The Prodigal Son* [*Der Verlorene Sohn*].[77] Even Amalia renounces love, desiring death at the hands of her former lover. Karl's description of his fate near the end of the play draws upon the analogy to the abyss: "here I stand at the limit ("Rand") of a life of horror, and see now with weeping and gnashing of teeth, that *two men such as I would destroy the whole moral order of creation*" (L 159; NA 3: 135).[78] Like Christian Wolf later, Karl stands at the precipice between life and death. Unlike Christian, however, Karl believes that world order demands a sacrifice. The nemesis which scholars attribute to the dramatic events, however, actually extends from the natures of the individual heroes themselves, i.e., from Nature.[79] The human being, as represented in part by Karl Moor, is endowed with the natural propensity to do good. Schiller's language is especially interesting here because the hero is concerned about how he can heal ("heilen") "the order which I have violated" ("die mißhandelte Ordnung") (L 160; NA 3: 135). One way of doing this is to restore the harmonious tension within one's own bifold nature. In Karl's case, critical discernment and rational self-reflection, based on bitter experience, create the catalyst for Karl's moral (self-) conversion. Restoring harmony and healing to the damaged social order is now uppermost on his mind. Having come to terms with his own personal history, Karl's final actions demonstrate the attainment of sublime, moral character.[80] In this way, Schiller anticipates the later characterization of Mary Stuart.

Karl's thought of suicide is amplified by allusions to music and harmony. Karl scolds his cohorts and asks: "do you suppose the harmony of creation will be restored by such blasphemous discord?" ("meinet ihr die Harmonie der Welt werde durch diesen gottlosen Mißlaut gewinnen?"). Answering the question negatively, the dramatic hero decides in favor of earthly existence.[81]

Like Odoardo Galotti in Lessing's *Emilia Galotti,* Karl Moor turns himself over to the legal authorities for trial. Thinking Karl has lost his mind, the robbers wish to enchain him, but Karl Moor's decision to accept the legal order and his own history constitutes a rational-moral act which his cohorts are unable to comprehend. Reaching this decision, Karl is able to break the chains of rebellion, which means that he is no longer a slave to his animal instincts. Moral actions, Karl insists, can cleanse the soul. Standing alone, and with a cheerful spirit, the Robber Moor of the Mannheim stage edition recognizes that he is still a good citizen. For he has observed the law. Like the Löffler text, the stage play ends with a philanthropic gesture.

In retrospect, I cannot agree (with Schiller and his friends like Petersen, in the account by J. F. Abel) that the Mannheim stage text rid the published text of its errors and mistakes. It seems to me that the Löffler text is the more intellectually stimulating of the two editions, especially in the light of the continuity and crisis of Schiller's writings we are tracing.

In his announcement to the public, Schiller wrote that his characterization of Karl von Moor constitutes "the portrait of a lost great soul."[82] Though "torn . . . from one vice to another," and driven to despair, Karl was still "sublime and honorable, great and majestic in misfortune, and bettered through misfortune."[83] Recognizing the error of his ways, Schiller's dramatic hero also accepts the truth of his own past history without, however, the hope of salvation in the social order of which he is still a part. The moral fortitude he exhibits in accepting his situation, then, is not at all idealistic but, rather, wholly realistic.[84]

Concerning the nature of Karl's conversion, Schiller himself stated "that the invisible hand of providence also can use the villain as a tool for its own purposes and judgments and, astonishingly, disentangle the most intricate knot of fate."[85] On the metaphorical level of Schiller's language, there is a close affinity between knots and strings. Most important, perhaps, we note the writer's conscious awareness of the knot-like texture of "fate," i.e., life in the universe, and his confidence that, through the exercise of free moral will, the knot of human existence can be disentangled.

III. *Intrigue and Love* [*Kabale und Liebe*]

Schiller's *Intrigue and Love* opens up on the living room of the musician Miller who is in the act of putting his violoncello aside. Rather than accept Major von Walter as his daughter's husband, money or no money, he would rather destroy his stringed instrument. "I'll go around begging with my violin and give a concert for something warm. . . . I'll smash my cello and stick manure in the soundingboard before I'll eat from the money my own child has earned with her soul and her salvation."[86] Luise herself feels that "Heaven and Ferdinand are tugging [reißen: tearing at] my bleeding soul" (P 9; NA 5: 11–12).[87] The reference to torn strings represents the experience of rupture associated with the arbitrary nature of the politics of absolutism. When viewed in the light of social history, the dramatic crisis is heightened by the fact that Miller and his wife refuse to allow the prince to take their daughter as his mistress. This results in the clash of two systems of morality.

Following her renunciation of Ferdinand in act 3, scene 3, Luise and Ferdinand meet for the first time on the stage. The stage directions concerning Luise read: "*She sinks down pale and faint on a chair*" (NA 5: 13).[88] Ferdinand's first words refer to the fact that Luise is pale, as was Father Moor in *The Robbers*. Luise attributes the gradual destruction of their love to an outside force. Rupture is imminent: "They will separate us!" ("Man trennt uns!") (P 12; NA 5: 14). Ferdinand, however, insists that the power of love will overcome all obstacles. His desperate question draws on one of the main metaphors of Schiller's language. "Who can dissolve the bond of two hearts, or rip apart the tones of a chord?" (P 12; NA 5: 14).[89] Because he is a nobleman ("Edelmann"), the son of an autocratic ruler, Ferdinand believes that he possesses the power to change the situation. Society, however, proves to be far more complex.

The chasm, on the political level, between courtly and lower middle-class society and the rupture, on the metaphysical level, between worldly society and the harmony of Nature preclude the possibility of a successful love relationship. Given the limits of eighteenth-century German society, as depicted in this drama, Luise's renunciation of Ferdinand proves to be a realistic act. At the same time, the non-actualization of love in political society is being criticized. Schiller was to reintroduce this theme later in the dramatic writing *Wallenstein*.

Another reason why the relationship is doomed to fail has a great deal to do with Ferdinand's egocentric pursuits. Ferdinand's "idealism," though it has been interpreted as a cry for love within a seemingly loveless society, is not informed by any vision of a better and more egalitarian social order. On the contrary. Ferdinand's actions are grounded in self-interest. Though I am convinced from the text that Luise loves Ferdinand, Ferdinand's "ideal of happiness" suggests that, in the final analysis, Luise is but an object of desire, one which Ferdinand wishes to possess. The possessive adjective "my," for instance, is employed repeatedly. His words recall similar statements of Werther to Lotte in the novel *The Sufferings of Young Werther* [*Die Leiden des jungen Werthers*] (1774). Ferdinand says:

> My ideal of good fortune withdraws more contentedly within myself. All my desires lie buried within my *heart* (P 19; NA 5: 21).[90]

Already in "Julius's Theosophy," Friedrich Schiller had differentiated sharply between love and egoism. "Egoism and love divide humanity into two highly dissimilar sexes whose borders never flow into one another."[91] The writer elaborates: "Egoism establishes its center in itself; love plants it outside itself in the axis of the eternal whole. Love is directed toward unity; egoism is loneliness. Love is the cooperative ruling citizen of a blossoming free State; egoism a despot in a ravaged Creation."[92] The political connotations are unmistakeable. Yet, the lament is directed not only against the arbitrary governance of that time, but also against the misuses and abuses of love by human beings in general. This becomes all the more clear when we consider that Ferdinand transfers the egotism of the despot to his love relationship. As I have suggested, Luise becomes the mere object of Ferdinand's unfulfilled desire.[93] The fact that he intentionally kills his loved one without achieving moral insight also reflects his egotism. Because of his purely self-interested action, Ferdinand von Walter is neither a heroic revolutionary freedom-fighter nor a "Kraftkerl" of the Storm and Stress. The problematics Schiller explores in his early writings run much deeper than the traditional idealist/realist dichotomy allows.

In Luise's presence, in act 2, scene 5, Ferdinand will insist: "You are *mine,* though heaven and hell come between us!" (P 36; NA 5: 39).[94] This is a decisive moment in the play. *Both* of Luise's parents criticize Ferdinand's exploits, and their language is rich in animal imagery. Frau Miller asks: "What has this lamb done that you should murder her?" (P 37; NA 5: 40).[95] With even greater resolve, and feeling that he is a man, Ferdinand exclaims: "But I shall penetrate his [his father's] cabals . . . I shall rend asunder all these iron chains of prejudice . . . freely, as a man, I shall choose, so that these insect-souls will grow dizzy looking aloft at the giant-handiwork of my love" (P 37–38; NA 5: 40).[96] In the end, it is *Ferdinand's* love ("my love") that takes precedence over everything else, including the woman who loves him. Defying his father, he exclaims:

> But to the ultimate only *love* can go . . . Here, Luise! Your hand in mine! (*He seizes it violently.*) As surely as God will not desert me in my final breath! . . . The moment that parts these two hands will also rip asunder the thread between *me* and *creation.*[97]
>
> (P 38; NA 5: 41)

The motif of severing the thread between Creation and the individual human being is yet another occurrence of the pervasive theme of rupture. Hence, it is not simply rhetoric that gives this passage its dramatic force, but also the content of Ferdinand's exclamation in the light of the writer's development of key metaphors.

Ferdinand's insistence on unconditional love fails to convince this reader of the efficacy of his actions. Indeed, his assumed love for Luise seems completely spurious in the light of his final actions: murdering the object of his love and extinguishing his own life. This is not heroism; it is behavior borne of frustration. The desires and emotional tantrums of the body overwhelm the rational mind. Indeed, there is some affinity here to Schiller's characterization of Franz von Moor. Ferdinand's frustration leads to acts of violence both against others and himself. Perhaps Pastor Moser's words are applicable to Ferdinand von Walter as well. "These spiders' webs of systems can be torn to pieces with the single word: you must die!" (L 145; NA 3: 122; fn. 60). Granted, Ferdinand von Walter does not resemble Franz von Moor in the matter of love. However, in the light of Schiller's medical dissertations, which establish the limits of both sensuous and rational behavior, there is indeed an unmistakable parallel between these two central dramatis personae. To be sure, Ferdinand's character does not represent the kind of self-love described in "Julius's Theosophy." It is therefore ironic that he should chastize his father with the words: "If you love yourself, no show of force!" (P 41; NA 5: 44),[98] for these words apply with even greater force to himself. By way of comparison, Schiller's "Ode to Joy" is diametrically opposed to the characterization of Ferdinand in the drama. As Christoph Bruckmann has suggested, joy is the feeling that can overcome the egoism of the individual human being.[99]

Act 2 opens on Lady Milford dreaming in front of a piano. She is dressed in a charming negligee. Consequently, the recipient's attention is directed to both the mind and the body. Milford fantasizes about marrying Ferdinand and then fleeing to the remotest desert of the world (P 24). Once and for all, she wishes to break the chains that bind her to the Duke: "Yes! of undoing it forever! of breaking that shameful chain forever!" (P 25; NA 5: 27–28).[100] Lady Milford's earlier history has not been taken seriously enough in the scholarly research. In 2.3, she divulges her personal history to Ferdinand. Upon the beheading of her father and the death of her mother, she fled with an attendant to Germany at the age of fourteen, with a chest of jewels. Speaking with ever increasing emotion ("Rührung"), she relays how she had arrived in Hamburg ill, alone, and without a name, "a foreign orphan" (P 31). Deprived of a formal education, Lady Milford was forced to fall back on her wealth. In the light of Schiller's writings, it is not surprising that one of her few possessions should be a piano ("Flügel"). Her bitter criticism of the political state of affairs—"The debauchery of the great of this world is the insatiable hyena that seeks victims with its ravening hunger" (P 32; NA 5: 34)[101]—is especially effective given the fact that the Duke had sworn his love to her, stolen her innocence, and then exercised his (political) claim to her.

The moral indictment of the politics of Schiller's day could not be plainer. Given the similarity in the dramatic action between *Intrigue and Love* and Lessing's *Emilia Galotti,* it cannot be coincidental that Lady Milford's first name should be Emilie. Furthermore, her descendants were of Norfolk blood, i.e., Mary Stuart's line. As we have seen, Schiller's Lady Emilie Milford imagines her marriage to Ferdinand to be a means to escape her stifling existence as the Duke's concubine. The metaphor of the broken bond underscores the Duke's moral depravity. He is described as an insatiable wild animal who ravages the land: "separating bride and bridegroom . . . even rending asunder the divine bond of marriages" (P 32; NA 5: 34).[102] Another frequently employed metaphor highlights the tension in Emilie's life: "I took a stand between lamb and tiger" (P 32; NA 5: 34).[103] In Walter's homeland, she first sensed a gentle hand. To Ferdinand, she bares her soul: "Walter I have blasted prisons open . . . torn up death sentences, and shortened many a hideous eternity in the galleys" (P 32; NA 5: 35).[104] Lady Milford is afflicted by "incurable wounds" ("unheilbare Wunden"). Longing for something good, which is denied her, and sick from anguish and abuse, Lady Milford proves to be a highly sympathetic character.

Ferdinand also bares his soul to Emilie, telling her of his love for a middle-class girl, Luise Millerin, the daughter of a musician. He captures her complete attention when narrating a story containing parallels to Lady Milford's own experiences. We discover that Luise is not a virgin. Ferdinand: "I *first* rent the golden peace of her innocence . . . lulled her heart with presumptuous hopes and treacherously exposed it to wild passion" (P 34; NA 5: 36).[105] Ferdinand's confession devastates Emilie. However she may act from this point on, the Lady knows that her hopes of marrying Ferdinand are dashed.

Concerning the political dimension of the play, the President is acutely aware of the problems created by his son's love for a young, lower middle-class woman. Like the prince in Lessing's *Emilia Galotti,* the President's aide attempts to turn the situation to his political advantage. To Wurm he exclaims, "You're taking [driving] me up to the edge of a ghastly abyss there" (P 44; NA 5: 48).[106] Wurm outlines his plan of action, spinning, as he says, a net of political intrigue: "Around the Major we shall spin a net of cunning" (P 45; NA 5: 49).[107] Somewhat in awe of his servant, the President exclaims: "The web is satanically fine" (P 46; NA 5: 50).[108] Personally familiar with middle-class mentality, Wurm plans to manipulate Luise's conscience. Self-interest plays a dominant role since Wurm would like to have Luise for himself. Overly confident, the President's aide believes that he will be able to pacify Luise's parents in the end. Schiller applies the metaphor of the stringed instrument to the parents' emotional responses. "Father and mother pitch their strings a trifle lower, and once they are thoroughly toned down . . . , they will wind up by acknowleding it as mercy when I give the daughter her reputation by the offer of my hand" (P 46; NA 5: 50).[109]

The metaphorical references to the insect world, especially to the spider's web, as well as the name of the President's aide, "Worm," form an analogy between the politics of Schiller's day and the animal nature of the human being. Hence, physiology and politics are intricately related not only in the poetic writings (see chapter 2) but also in Schiller's dramatic practice through the skillful incorporation of selected tropes. It is important to note that the metaphor of the stringed instrument is beginning to become a (if not the) central symbol of life in Schiller's writings.

Knowing who she is, namely a middle-class girl with an educated conscience, Luise is unable to flee her homeland with Ferdinand. Luise is fully aware that she is "renouncing an alliance that would rend asunder the seams of the bourgeois world and bring the universal and everlasting order down in ruins" (P 53; NA 5: 57).[110] Rather than direct her frustration outwardly against society, the middle-class young woman becomes a willing victim. Like Lessing's Emilia Galotti, she is victimized by her social environment. At the same time, like Goethe's Margareta in *Faust I*, Schiller's Luise incriminates herself: "*I* am the criminal . . . my heart has been given to wanton, foolish desires . . . my unhappiness is my *punishment*" (P 53; NA 5: 57).[111] It is a critical moment, "a parting [*trennende*] hour" (P 53; NA 5: 58), one that is underscored by the following stage directions.

(Ferdinand, in his distraction and fury, has seized a violin and tried to play on it.—Now he rips the strings apart, smashes the instrument on the floor, and bursts forth in loud laughter.)[112]

(P 53; NA 5: 57–58)

The moment is divisive not only because the political situation of the day disallows the lovers to marry (as Luise knows full well and, for better or for worse, accepts, no matter how reluctantly), but also because of Ferdinand's pure subjectivity. For he reduces the complexity of the public and private situations to a binary opposition: "Cold duty against fiery love!" (P 54; NA 5: 58).[113]

To return for a moment to this important stage direction, it is clear that Ferdinand destroys the central symbol of harmony in Schiller's writing. By act 3, scene 4, the recipient knows that the rupture in interpersonal relationships, especially the lovers' relationship, can only end in tragedy. The criticism of the ruling form of government is also clear. For love cannot perform its function of bonding society if it is locked in the human heart, i.e., not allowed to express itself outwardly. And where love is absent, worlds collide and the social order soon collapses. This, I believe, is one of the central messages of Schiller's *Intrigue and Love,* one that is tied thematically to the early essays and speeches.

In the end, the work encourages change through (albeit indirect) criticism by exposing both the limits which society imposes on the expression of love and the extremes of personal desire and selfish satisfaction in love. Early in his career, the writer Friedrich Schiller tied aesthetics to ethics. It appears, then, that in the work of the young Schiller, social engagement rather than aesthetic autonomy was the primary function of dramatic art. The fact that he conceived of the theater as a tribunal in his early theoretical writings undergirds this point. In short, Schiller's works are a prime example of the social efficacy of writing.

Luise's act of renunciation constitutes a sharp social criticism. With righteous indignation, she exlaims: "You are entrenched, you great ones . . .

entrenched against the truth behind your own vices" (P 57; NA 5: 62).[114] In Luise's eyes, Wurm, a representative of those in power, is simply a barbarian, one who blasphemes God and transgresses His order. However, in addition to its political relevance, the writing suggests that something more fundamental is at play. "This is tyrannical, O Heaven! Punish humans humanly if they offend Thee, but why crush me between two horrors? why dangle me back and forth between death and infamy? Why set this bloodsucking devil on my neck?" (P 59; NA 5: 63–64).[115] This reference to a state of being caught between the earthly and heavenly realms complements the tension in Schiller's many writings between anthropology and metaphysics. The interpenetration of politics and physiology is also denoted on the metaphorical level in Luise's language: "Oh you know all too well that our hearts are bound by our natural impulses as fast as by chains" (P 59; NA 5: 64).[116] The exploits of the shrewd psychologist, or mad doctor enchain Luise. Her language also establishes a connection between courtly intrigue (politics) and Hell (theology), the latter of which underscores the metaphysical dimension of the dramatic writing. "I yield to outwitting hell" ("Ich weiche der überlistenden Hölle") (P 59; NA 5: 64).

Ferdinand's behavior becomes more and more animal-like, the more he feels trapped. His criticism of his own social class contains several references to the animal world. He threatens the Chamberlain with the words: "I'll lead you around with me like some rare marmot or other. You shall dance like a tame monkey to the howling of the damned, fetch and carry, sit up and beg" (P 64; NA 5: 69).[117] Enraged, Ferdinand seizes the nobleman, shouting: "on my blossom . . . the vermin shall not crawl or . . . I will squash you to a pulp like this, and this, and again like this" (P 64; NA 5: 69).[118] "Creatures," "tarantulas," and "vermin" are just three of the metaphors based on the arachnean world that are employed to characterize the entanglements and intrigues of the political life of the court. Viewed in the light of Schiller's anthropology, the highest social class is thereby relegated to one of the lowest classes of animal life. It is not surprising, then, that in act 4, scene 5, both father and son are depicted as being entangled in the web of their own intrigues. President von Walter's earlier statement to Wurm—"The web is satanically fine"—is thus an apt characterization of the nature of courtly life. In the writer's language, the conjoining of the earthly and metaphysical realms forms a powerful criticism of the political structure of society.

The problem of harmony in a world out of balance with itself is captured by an oxymoron. Lady Milford says: "I tremble like a criminal at seeing this fortunate girl who feels so terribly in harmony with my heart" (P 67; NA 5: 72–73).[119] Lady Milford can understand the situation of her rival since both she and Luise were seduced as young women. A musical metaphor common to Schiller's early theoretical, poetic, and now dramatic writings is employed to represent this fact. "The first consecrating silvery tones on the untouched keyboard!" ("Auf dem unberührten Klavier der erste ein-weihende Silberton!") (P 69; NA 5: 74). We note that the central metaphor of the stringed instrument in Schiller's writings can also denote sexual activity. But, in this scene, it is rupture, not harmony that characterizes the relationship between Milford and Miller, and, ironically, it is not the lady of higher standing but Miller's common daughter who wins the battle of the words in act 4, scene 7. Interpreters of this dramatic writing have not appreciated the fact that the politically weaker individual triumphs in verbal warfare over the more powerful political individual. The dramatic climax in the relationship between the two major women characters in *Intrigue and Love* anticipates act 3, scene 4, of *Mary Stuart*, which was written some sixteen years later.

Though less frequently than in *The Robbers*, metaphors relating to the world of insects are also introduced, as we have seen, in Schiller's second major dramatic writing. On one level, they underscore the problem of conscience. Luise asks: "Who would go so far as to dream that Lady Milford kept an eternal scorpion for her conscience . . .?" (P 71; NA 5: 76).[120] *"Calmly and nobly,"* Luise shows compassion for Lady Milford's plight. In fact, even her own feelings seem to mirror Emilie's: "I had rent asunder ("zerrissen") my eternal claim to this world's joys" (P 71–72; NA 5: 77).[121] The problem of rupture in the emotional life of the human being is disclosed by the numerous distinctions between the microcosmic and infinite dimensions of the universe. The writer assigns Luise an important analogy: "Why, the insect in a drop of water feels as blissful as if it were in a heavenly kingdom, as happy and as joyous, until someone tells it about an ocean where navies and whales sport!" (P 72; NA 5: 77).[122]

Still desiring Ferdinand, Lady Milford threatens to tear the lovers apart. The references she uses were also employed in *The Robbers* and *The Criminal Out of Infamy:* "Cliffs and chasms I mean to throw between you; through the midst of your heaven I mean to pass like a Fury; my name shall frighten your kisses apart as a specter does criminals" (P 73; NA 5: 78).[123] Luise's depiction of their situation is apt: *"you* have demolished the heaven of two people in love, torn two hearts asunder that *God* had bound together" (P 73; NA 5: 79).[124] "Lady! To the ear of the Omniscient the final spasm of the trodden worm also cries" (P 74; NA 5: 79).[125]

Alone, and numbed by Luise's words, Lady Milford bemoans her fate: "Still, O Heaven! still my ear is rent by those dreadful words that condemn me: *Take him!"* (P 74; NA 5: 79).[126] Following intense emotional struggle, the Lady also decides to renounce Ferdinand. *"Put to shame* Emilia Milford may be. . . . but *disgraced* never! I *too* have strength to renounce" (P 74; NA 5: 80).[127] Similar to Karl Moor and Christian Wolf, Lady Milford achieves moral dignity through enlightened self-determination. Rupture seems indispensable since she gains insight by severing her relation with both the Duke and the President's son. Hence, rupture can also have a beneficial effect on the process of enlightened self-awareness. In Lady Milford's case, it constitutes a moral act:

> burst are all bonds between me and the Duke, this wild love is wrenched out of my heart!—Into thy arms I throw myself, Virtue! . . . Grand, like a setting sun, shall I sink today from the pinnacle of my loftiness; let my splendor die with my love, and let nothing but my *heart* accompany me into this proud exile.[128]
>
> (P 75; NA 5: 80)

Since the Lady also represents higher social strata, rupture can also represent a virtuous political act. Her letter to him confirms that her act is political: "I abhor demonstrations of favor that drip with the tears of subjects" (P 76–77; NA 5: 82).[129] On this level of the play, the writer's use of metaphor (the severing of strings or threads) represents a revolutionary act.

Lady Milford's act may also be understood as the defiance of a British princess over and against the Germans—"your *German people*" ("Ihr *Deutsches Volk*") (P 77; NA 5: 82). The letter is signed Joan Norfolk, Lady Emilie Milford. In a final act of philanthropy, reminiscent of Karl Moor's, the Lady opens her privy purse and distributes its contents to her servants. Political protest ends in positive, practical action, an act of humanity.

Luise is likewise strong. At the beginning of act 5, scene 1, she speaks to her father about the hard battle she has fought. "The battle has been decided. Father! People are wont to call our sex tender and frail. Do not believe that any more" (P 79; NA 5: 84).[130] The analogy the writer employs here relates again to the arachnean world. "Before a spider we shrink, but the black monster *Corruption* we clasp in our arms in sport" (P 79; NA 5: 84–85).[131] The metaphor of fetters is employed quite often at this point in the drama. It illustrates Luise's resolve and freedom of action in spite of her political enchainment. Concerning oaths that bind, Luise declares: "Oaths, father, may be binding upon the living; in death even the iron bond of the sacraments dissolves" (P 79; NA 5: 85).[132] Her letter to Ferdinand, which Miller reads aloud, includes an analogy to rupture: "A knavish trick without parallel has rent asunder the bond of our hearts, but a terrible vow held my tongue bound . . . I know of *another* place where no vow is binding any more" (P 79; NA 5: 85).[133] Miller notes how pale ("blaß") or sickly Luise has become and pleads that she not commit suicide. In one last desperate appeal, he reaches for a knife and asks his daughter to run it through her father's heart. Aghast at having to decide between Ferdinand and her father, Luise exclaims: "A criminal whichever way I turn!" ("Verbrecherin, wohin ich mich neige!") (P 82; NA 5: 88). Still, she decides in favor of her father. It is a dramatic reversal of the situation in Lessing's *Emilia Galotti*.

Toying with the idea that his daughter got into exile, Miller sees: "Our Lord God's bread grows everywhere, and He will provide ears for my fiddle too" (P 83; NA 5: 89).[134] Miller wishes to set her story of sorrow and grief to music—the music of the lute ("Laute"). He describes it as a song of a daughter, "who broke her heart to honor her father" ("die, ihren Vater zu ehren, ihr Herz zerriß") (P 83; NA 5: 89). The analogy between music and physiology is again in evidence. When Ferdinand enters, he finds that Luise is as pale as a ghost ("leichenblaß"). She is described as being pale as death ("Bleich wie der Tod!") and having the face of a corpse ("Leichengesicht") (NA 5: 90–91). Consistent with the interactionist theory of the early medical dissertations, Luise's mental and spiritual anguish is expressed in her physical constitution.

Some of Schiller's more frequently employed metaphors and motifs proliferate in the final act of *Intrigue and Love*. Even Ferdinand remarks: "My head is burning so feverishly" ("Mein Kopf brennt so fieberisch") (P 86; NA 5: 92). Ferdinand complains to Miller that his own father has deceived him: "You betrayed me and sold me scorpions" ("Er betrog mich, und verkaufte mir Skorpionen") (P 87; NA 5: 93). He laments that God plays so capriciously with human beings: "By slender, imperceptible cords often hang fearful weights" (P 87; NA 5: 93).[135] Recalling a time when he had wanted Miller to instruct him in the playing of the flute, Ferdinand characterizes his fate in terms of music: "Wretched flute playing, I should never have had the notion" (P 87; NA 5: 93).[136] In the fourth scene of the final act, Ferdinand chastizes himself for robbing Miller of his daughter. He describes the father as a man who has only his instrument and his child. In the course of the monologue, Ferdinand thinks that perhaps he should crush Luise before his father wounds her: "crush the adder before she stings her father too" (P 88; NA 5: 94).[137]

Act 5, scene 7, which has been omitted from some contemporary performances of the play in Germany, proves to be of special importance for an understanding of Schiller's writings. It forms the final climax in Ferdinand's and Luise's relationship. The scene begins with an invitation. Luise asks if Herr von Walter would like to accompany her at the fortepiano. After a period of silence, Ferdinand responds bitterly and sarcastically: "We will make a jollification out of this irksome duet, and with the aid of certain gallantries avenge ourselves on the caprices of love" (P 93; NA 5: 99).[138]

Many of the major metaphors and motifs employed throughout Schiller's early works also introduce the tragic denouement of *Intrigue and Love*. Verging on insanity, Ferdinand shouts: "Come in your monstrous terribleness, serpent, jump up on me, snake! . . . parade your hideous windings before me, rear your coils to the sky . . . as horrible as ever the pit beheld you. . . . Only no more angel . . . only no more angel now! . . . it is too late . . . I must crush you underfoot like an adder, or else despair . . . have pity!" (P 95; NA 5: 101).[139] The rhetorical exclamations in *Intrigue and Love* relate thematically to innumerable other references to Nature in Schiller's early works. Analogies to the animal and insect worlds abound. Very often, they capture the knotted, labyrinthine nature of the universe. The topic of political intrigue and the question of the entangled nature of physiology and sensation, i.e., human nature, are thereby also brought into closer alignment.

Ferdinand's destruction of the love relationship drives home the problem of the rupture in world order. This development is marked by the fact that singing or playing musical instruments has ceased. A duet is no longer possible. Indeed, harmonious Nature can no longer sound, for its strings have been ruptured. Yet, for all his ridicule of the harmony of love, Ferdinand perceives Luise's beauty, a beauty that radiates even in the face of death. "This fair work of the Heavenly Sculptor" ("Dieses schöne Werk des himmlischen Bildners") (P 95; NA 5: 101). Again, he notes: "And that sweet, melodious voice . . . how can so much harmony come out of torn strings? (*tarrying to glut his eyes on the sight of her*) Everything so beautiful . . . so full of proportion . . . so divinely perfect!" (P 95; NA 5: 101).[140] The words Schiller assigns to Ferdinand thematize the problem of harmony and rupture while drawing upon the conception of the universe as a grand stringed instrument. The musical allusions are also related to the writer's interest in physiology. When divulging the truth about the poisoned lemonade, for instance, Ferdinand determines: "Their delicate nerves stand firm against crimes that gnaw away the roots of humanity, and a miserable gram of arsenic overthrows them" (P 97; NA 5: 103).[141] Like Franz von Moor, Ferdinand von Walter appears to be a mad doctor.

In the final scene, Ferdinand's exchange of words with his father discloses the labyrinthine nature of the public and private spheres of society. "Sly and admirable, I confess, the trick was, to rend the bond of our hearts asunder by jealousy. . . . A master made the calculation, only it is a pity that angry *love* was not so responsive to the wire as your wooden puppet" (P 99; NA 5: 105).[142] The political scheme to tear the lovers apart has backfired. Instead, the strings devised to control the responses and actions of those under authority are severed by the power of angry love, i.e., the expression of personal emotions. Schiller's *Intrigue and Love* implicates Immanuel Kant's call for the separation of the public and private domains. We note that Kant's essay "In Answer to the Question: What Is Enlightenment?" ["Beantwortung der Frage: Was ist Aufklärung?"] appeared in the same year as Schiller's dramatic writing, namely in 1784.

Walter Pape recapped the reception of *Intrigue and Love* among Schiller's contemporaries: "others still criticize the 'long, pompous declamations', speak of 'bombast and platitudes', find 'the intonations too high and dissonant' and feel worn out by 'the eternal tension of language and the rich variety of sentences.'"[143] In his exacting study, Pape notes: "All of these [linguistic devices] are transgressions against the rules of rhetoric."[144] In response to some of Pape's sources, I would add that young Schiller's dramatic language certainly does not meet the requirements of the harmonious tone which Eschenburg and Lessing expected in the writing of tragedy. Ramler, for instance, in his reference to Winckelmann, insisted that "noble

simplicity" ("edle Einfalt") should dominate the tone of all dramatis personae.[145] The romantic Heinrich Wackenroder, however, praised Schiller's
drama. In a letter to Ludwig Tieck, he expressed the following sentiment:
"And the ending! There cannot be any greater tension [tensing] of passions!"
(NA 5: 231). August Wilhelm Schlegel, however, could not feel moved precisely because of the "overly tense tone of sentimentalism" ("überspannten
Ton der Empfindsamkeit") (NA 5: 231). In our own time, however, modern
critics and scholars still admire the pathos of Schiller's language ("pathetische Sprache"),[146] and, even recently, on German stages, *Intrigue and
Love* has been one of Schiller's most frequently performed plays.[147]

Interlude: Schiller in Bauerbach

While in exile in the Thuringian Forest, Friedrich Schiller wrote a number
of letters wherein the problem of rupture resurfaces. He wrote: "our intellectual powers must be played by minds ("Geister") like the strings of an
instrument" (NA 23: 67).[148] Besides complaining about the weather and his
health, he worried about the consequences of his actions, namely of having
forsaken his homeland of Swabia/Württemberg, "that it perhaps leaves a
tear ("Riß") in my whole future life (fate)" (NA 23: 73).[149] Though excited
about the Dom Karlos project at the time, Schiller was already thinking
about the story of Mary Stuart. His letters from this period convey a sense
of isolation and some signs of depression. He composed a missive to Rein-
wald, the main librarian in Meiningen (from whom Schiller requested more
and more snuff) and the future husband of Schiller's sister Caroline. This
letter captured the essence of his physical and emotional conditions with
the following words: "Loneliness, dissatisfaction over my fate, dashed
hopes, and perhaps also my changed lifestyle have, if I may say so, distorted
the sound ("Klang") of my disposition, and set out of tune the otherwise
pure instrument of my feeling" (NA 23: 76).[150] It is a telling fact that the
writer rarely refers to the strength ("Stärke") or weakness ("Schwäche") of
his body but, rather, to the quality of its tone ("Ton").

In retrospect, in *The Robbers* we had witnessed the tragic consequences
of the destruction of the paternal order, whereas in *Intrigue and Love,* the
attempt to maintain the paternal order bore tragic consequences. In his
early writings, Schiller directed his attention to the question of the nature of
human existence and the relationship of the human being to Nature without,
however, neglecting politics.

IV. *Don Carlos*

Though he began writing *Don Carlos* in the quiet village of Bauerbach, it
took Schiller three years to complete the work. The setting for the first act
of the verse drama is the beautiful Imperial garden in Aranjuez. The play

Christian Körner. From a painting by Anton Graff.

begins with Domingo's pronouncement that the lovely days in Aranjuez have now come to an end.[151] The Arcadian surroundings of Aranjuez are in flux. History soon begins to intervene. The sustained influence of Schiller's anthropology and his increased interest in working with historical material (history) coalesce in the act of writing the several versions of *Don Carlos*.

When Marquis Posa enters the stage, Carlos embraces his dear friend, and announces that their embrace heals his ailing soul (W 109; ll. 140c–41b; NA 6: 15).[152] Posa, however, cannot understand why his friend should be so concerned about his seemingly sick heart. In fact, he detects something odd about his friend: "The red that seems to burn / On your pale cheeks appears unnatural and / Your lips do tremble as if you were ill" (W 110; ll. 140c–41b; NA 6: 15).[153] Carlos's physical frailty contrasts sharply with the popular image of that "lion-hearted youth to whom / An oppressed people of heroic stock / Send me [Posa]" (W 110; ll. 161–62; NA 6: 16).[154] With Carlos's assistance, Posa hopes to save Flanders. However, his friend quickly dismisses the idea that he should be the one to usher in a new golden age. Rather than accept the intellectual challenge, Carlos bewails his state of loneliness. "Oh, let me weep, yes, weep / Hot, scalding tears and clutch you to my heart, / My only friend; for I have no one here, / And there is no one in this whole, wide world" (W 111; ll. 206b–209; NA 6: 17).[155] It seems that Don Carlos's self-centeredness short-circuits any genuine interest in others outside himself. In the early stages of the play, Carlos is depicted as a sentimentalist (*Schwärmer*) who lacks any specific program of action, political or otherwise.

Part of his childish behavior can be explained by the fact that Carlos is, more or less, fatherless. "I do not even know what 'father' means— / I am a king's son— . . ." (W 111; ll. 220–21a; NA 6: 18).[156] He sees his office as prince and heir to the throne of Spain as a purely political and hereditary commission. To the extent that he longs for genuine human contact within courtly society, Carlos's behavior seems quite understandable. From our knowledge of the daydreams about his childhood and the experiences he and Posa had while growing up like brothers ("brüderlich"), there can be no doubt that Carlos is ailing. The numerous allusions to human physiology and sickness in the text confirm this fact. Consistent with the First Law of the third medical dissertation and the ailment afflicting father Moor in *The Robbers,* Carlos's mental anguish manifests itself physically. Physiology and politics are again interrelated. As heir to the throne of Spain, what affects Carlos's body also affects the State.

Time and again, in the early running of the drama, political discussions are referred back to the private, human sphere. Cherishing his friend the Marquis, Carlos refers to their "soul's music played on fragile strings / Strung just alike at [the] dawning of our lives" (W 111; ll. 226–27; NA 6: 18).[157] Their spiritual kinship stems from all-creating Nature ("die schaffende Natur"; l. 224b; NA 6: 18).[158] Carlos's and Posa's childhood days were also

marked by imbalance. In short, the differences in temperament and physiology between Carlos and Posa were implanted from the beginning by Nature.
This is also true of the relationship between King Philipp and his son, as
Carlos asks, "Why did it [Nature] pick these two remote extremes / Of all
the human race—take him and me / To bind together in this holy bond?"
(W 115; ll. 339b–c, 341c–43; NA 6: 22).[159] The German adjective employed
to characterize the rupture between them is incurable ("unheilbar"). We
have seen this concept of Nature evolving in Schiller's writings already from
the beginning of the writer's career, in both *The Robbers* and *Criminal Out
of Infamy*.

Whereas Posa is embarassed by what he calls Carlos's "childish stories"
("kindischen/Geschichten") (W 112; ll. 253c–54a; NA 6: 19), Carlos cherishes them as a record of his own personal history. He feels that Posa could
tear his heart apart, but never separate them ("zerreißen konntest du mein
Herz, doch nie / von dir entfernen"; ll. 256–57b; NA 6: 19). The characterizations of Don Carlos and the Marquis Posa first set the stage for the later
battle between Mary Stuart and Queen Elizabeth in *Mary Stuart*. Indeed,
already in Bauerbach, while working on *Don Carlos,* Schiller first enter-
tained the idea of writing a drama about the Scottish queen.

In the discussion with Posa in act 1, scene 2, Carlos reminds Posa of the
oath they had pledged in their youth. At this point, we discover why Carlos
is so anxious to have a trusted friend in whom he can confide. Speaking of
a "fearful secret" ("entsetzliches/Geheimniß"; l. 300b; NA 6: 20) burning
within his breast, Carlos divulges the truth. He is in love with his stepmother
("meine Mutter"; NA 6: 21), the Queen. To his own mind, not only world
customs and Roman law, but also all Nature's order ("die Ordnung der
Natur") condemn his passion for her (NA 6: 21). Carlos's inner turmoil is
compounded by the fact that, though he feels he violates his father's right
("fühl's"), he loves the Queen anyway. In short, emotional desire overrides
the knowledge of what is right. His sensuous nature overpowers the faculty
of reason. "I love without all hope and sinfully" ("Ich liebe ohne Hoffnung—
lasterhaft") (W 113; l. 316; NA 6: 21). The gnawing sense of having violated
the social-moral (*sittlich*) code carries him to that abyss of the fear of death
("Todesangst") which, like Christian Wolf of *Criminal Out of Infamy,* instills
in him a sense of the precarious nature of life and its attendant dangers.
Despite this knowledge, Carlos exclaims: "I see that—oh, no matter, I still
love" (W 113; l. 317; NA 6: 21). Perhaps the fact that the Queen is characterized as being imprisoned in custom ("von Etikette ringsum eingeschlossen";
l. 323; NA 6: 21) heightens Carlos's desire to spend a moment alone with
her. To this end, and not out of political interest then, Carlos tries to enlist
the support of his friend. The fact that a private desire insists on its practical
realization, even in the public sphere, heightens the dramatic tension. The
same problem in late eighteenth-century German culture was evident not

only in Schiller's *Intrigue and Love* but also in young Goethe's sensational novel *The Sorrows of Young Werther.*

Carlos relays to Posa how nightmarish dreams have been haunting him "Like furies from the pit" ("Wie Furien des Abgrunds") (W 115; l. 386; NA 6: 24). Like Christian Wolf of Schiller's novella, Don Carlos experiences a moment of personal crisis. "My better self despairs, / And struggles with a host of monstrous plans; / Through labyrinthine subtleties my mind / In its most wretched contemplation moves / Until, when at the very edge of the / Declivity, it stops" (W 115; ll. 387b–91; NA 6: 24).[160] Posa suggests that, if Carlos and the Queen meet, they should meet in Aranjuez, where the tranquility of the geographical setting and the unrestrained customs of the land are most favorable for such a private encounter. In addition to the allusions to space, there is an increasing number of references to organic development. The articulation of feelings and experiences is responsible for much of the dramatic action.

As in *Criminal Out of Infamy,* the writer fully exploits the semantics of the word *Geschichte* ("history/story"). Already in act 1, scene 1, Carlos conveys to Domingo how he has always heard people say ("sagen hören") "That sundry spies and bearers of bad tales / Have carried out more evil in this world / Than poison or a dagger ever could" (W 107; ll. 72c–75; NA 6: 12).[161] For him, this cannot be true. Certainly, it was not true of the writer Friedrich Schiller, for whom writing, an essential aspect of culture, was the chief means of changing consciousness and furthering the claims of humanity. Unlike Don Carlos, however, for Schiller reason tempers the play of imagination.

The Queen also loves stories. Before her encounter with Carlos, Marquis Posa had already assumed the role of storyteller. In the beautiful, yet tragic story of powerful Fernando and divine Mathilde, in act 1, scene 4, the theme of union in love is reintroduced. "Now, neither nature nor the world before / Had fashioned fairer creatures for each other, / Ne'er was a choice so happy or so praised" (W 123; ll. 637–39; NA 6: 37).[162] In the story, Fernando was unaware of his uncle's claims on Mathilde. By narrating the events of a story, which comment on the events in the drama, Posa attempts to associate Don Carlos's desire and Fernando's fate. In the character of Marquis Posa, we have an excellent example of art (storytelling) as mere rhetoric and the manipulation of art for political purposes. Let me elaborate.

The very next scene (1.5) finds Carlos and the Queen alone. Unabashedly, Carlos claims the Queen for his rightful companion. "Once you were mine— mine in the world's eyes, / Promised to me by two great thrones and granted / By Heaven itself and Nature to be mine, / And it was Philipp, Philipp took you from me" (W 126; ll. 757–760; NA 6: 43).[163] The Queen is shocked by Carlos's lack of decorum. Challenging his father's claim to Elisabeth: ("Does he possess a heart to treasure you?" [W 127; ll. 764c–65; NA 6: 43]).[164] It

becomes clear that the dictates of Carlos's passionate heart outweigh all
other considerations.

Like Ferdinand von Walter in *Intrigue and Love,* Carlos loves uncondi-
tionally and selfishly: "My own heart, / That feels so ardently" ("Mein Herz /
das feurig fühlt") (W 127; ll. 804c–5b; NA 6: 45). Like Ferdinand, Carlos
wishes to possess the object of his love. In this way, both characters resemble the central hero of Goethe's narrative *The Sorrows of Young Werther.*
The difference, however, lies in the characterizations of Queen Elisabeth
and Luise Miller. For, whereas Luise had loved Ferdinand, the Queen resembles far more Goethe's Lotte in her observance of social propriety and her
acceptance of duty as Philipp's wife. Unlike the earlier drama and Goethe's
novel, however, the thematization of the Oedipus complex (Don Carlos loves
his "mother") is contrived. Since the Queen is only Carlos's stepmother,
the psychological power of the ancient problem is less commanding.[165] Like
Goethe's Werther, Schiller's Carlos wishes to possess the object of his obsession. Unlike Werther, however, Carlos contemplates the possible consequences of his action. "Hell / Lies in this feeling, but it would be Hell / If I
possessed you" (W 129; ll. 858c–60b; NA 6: 47).[166] Because he cannot balance emotion and reason, Carlos experiences physical ailment.

> Oh, alas, I cannot
> Conceive of this, my nerves begin to break.[167]
>
> (W 129; ll. 860b–61; NA 6: 47)

The pernicious influence of overly active senses articulated in the medical
dissertations is also registered in the dramatic poem *Don Carlos,* as it was
in *The Robbers* and *Criminal Out of Infamy.* The writer's position is reflected in the dramatic action when the twenty-three-year-old Carlos throws
himself at the Queen's feet. Carlos's behavior collides with the concept of
love in the early essay "Julius's Theosophy." There, the proper and universal
function of love, like gravity, is to draw things together and help maintain
the equilibrium between things. Here, however, Carlos is driven solely by
passion. In 1.6, Lerma senses the problem:

> The hot blood of Carlos one may fear,
> But not his heart.[168]
>
> (W 133; ll. 1018–19; NA 6: 55)

The scholarly debate concerning the question whether the human dilemma or the political debates are of primary significance in this work is
tempered by the fact that both aspects are equally at play. The character of
King Philipp is a good test case. Discovering that his wife is alone—itself a
suspicious situation, given the nature of courtly culture—Philipp notes that
though he be the richest man in the world, others before him had possessed,

and others following him will own the Empire's treasures. He recognizes that he is but one person in a long chain of rulers. For him, his Achilles' heel is his wife Elizabeth. "This is the point where I am a mere mortal" (W 133; l. 989; NA 6: 54).[169] The personal, human drama could not be clearer at this point. At the same time, however, Philipp is thinking about how to crush the rebellion in the Netherlands. "Now it is time. Most awful warnings must / Be given that the erring be converted" (W 134; ll. 1026–27; NA 6: 55).[170] Carlos serves as still another example. After all that we have witnessed, Carlos decides to intervene on Flanders's behalf, requesting that he, and not Alba, become the governor of the territories. Personal and political considerations are clearly intermeshed in Schiller's work—a simultaneous operation of the multiple dimensions of Schiller's writings.

The encounter between Philipp and Carlos in act 2, scene 2, is highly moving (*rührend*). At first, no matter how much his son appeals to his father's heart—"[I] want / To pull upon his heart with such great strength / That that rock-hard encasement built by doubt / Will fall away" (W 140; ll. 1258–59; NA 6: 67)[171]—Philipp is skeptical of Carlos's ability to rule responsibly. However, the father's heart is moved by the unpleasant thought that, like himself, his son must one day ascend the throne, where he will sit totally alone. The writer reactivates the human drama. With liveliness and warmth, Carlos again appeals to his father's heart. Anaphorically, Carlos impresses upon his father the feeling of delight and satisfaction in knowing:

> Our joys put color in another's cheeks,
> Our fears cause other hearts to palpitate,
> Our sorrows bring the tears to other eyes![172]
> (W 141; ll. 1287–89; NA 6: 68)

The possessive adjective "our," which receives the first full stress in these blank verse lines, together with the word "foreign" ("fremd"), forms a powerful rhetorical device that counteracts the idea of loneliness. Although sympathetic, the King senses that his son only harms himself by entertaining such thoughts. The choice of words recalls the First Law of Schiller's third medical dissertation.

> So [too] fiercely does the blood rush through
> your veins
> That you would only harm things.[173]
> (W 142; ll. 1335–36; NA 6: 70)

Carlos's insistence that he command the army is, in Philipp's view, the fanciful idea of a "dreamer" (l. 1367). "This task requires a real man" (W 143; ll. 1367c–68; NA 6: 71).[174] His arguments being of no avail, Carlos pleads that his father allow him to leave Madrid and thereby grant him the "healing" that a change of climate can afford. Philipp's response is not what his son anticipates, however.

> Such a sickness
> As you, my son, do suffer from requires
> That you be under constant care of doctors.
> You stay in Spain.[175]
>
> (W 144; ll. 1427c–30a; NA 6: 74).

In retrospect, a substantial part of Don Carlos's characterization is consistent with the writer's philosophy of physiology. For Don Carlos represents the potentially negative effects of an imbalance between the rational and sensuous natures of the human being. There is a moral. Out of touch with political reality and preoccupied with his own subjectivity, Carlos is easily outmaneuvered and ultimately defeated by the realm of politics, as the final scene of the play makes abundantly clear. A similar predicament will confront the central figure of *Wallenstein*. *Don Carlos* also foreshadows the program of political aesthetics developed in the series of letters *Concerning the Aesthetic Education of the Human Being*. For in that later work, the writer underscored the importance of personal development, i.e., the necessity of refining one's character in the interest of reshaping political society. Like Schiller's Queen Elizabeth in *Mary Stuart*, King Philipp is guided largely by the dictates of his office. For him, as for Queen Elizabeth later, politics outstrips moral considerations.[176] There is also a deeper affinity between Don Carlos and Max Piccolomini than recognized heretofore.[177] For both of Schiller's characters are essentially fatherless.[178] Because, for them, there is no truly paternal social order, they are left searching for alternatives to the status quo.[179] The problems of guidance and self-direction (i.e., Enlightenment) thus become acute.

In his early dramas *The Robbers, Intrigue and Love,* and *Don Carlos,* Schiller employed the epic element of letter writing in order to heighten the recipient's interest in the dramatic action. Like Karl Moor, who does not check to see if the letter he has received was actually written by his father, Don Carlos simply assumes that the letter he has is from the Queen. In actuality, it is from one of the Queen's ladies, Princess Eboli. Part of the dramatic action of this piece, then, illuminates problems stemming from the lack of critical discernment.

It is rather surprising that the scene between Eboli and Carlos has received no sustained investigation in the extensive secondary literature on *Don Carlos*. In act 2, scene 7, while Princess Eboli awaits Don Carlos in her chamber playing the lute and singing, she is interrupted by the page who, in error, tells of Carlos's love for her and the nature of his response to her letter. Wishing to surprise her lover, Eboli picks up the lute again and continues playing. Drawn to the sound of the lute, Carlos is shocked to find the princess and not the Queen. Trying to explain his appearance, Carlos recounts, in scene 8, the moments leading up to the present. It is an intriguing story.

> I heard
> That someone played upon a lute—was it
> A lute?
> *(He looks around uncertainly.)*
> Yes, I am right, for there it is—
> A lute—well, God in Heaven knows—I love
> A lute insanely, and as always am
> All ears. I think of nothing else. I rushed
> Into the room that I might look into
> The lovely eyes of the performer who
> Enchanted me and moved me so intensely.[180]
>
> (W 157; ll. 1831c-39; NA 6: 97).

Though Don Carlos may appear to be a hopeless aesthete, it is helpful to recall Friedrich Schiller's own love of stringed instruments, especially the lute and the piano. The memory of the sounds of lute music that drew Schiller to his mother's playing may well have helped shape his depiction of Don Carlos. Like the Fernando of Posa's story, who acted "on the wings of love" ("Auf der Liebe Flügeln"), Don Carlos flies on the wings of imagination. The metaphors of the flight of love and the flight of fancy disclose the imbalance in Don Carlos between mind and body. To this extent, Schiller's Carlos foreshadows Goethe's Euphorion, who, while on the wings of romantic imagination, soars into the stratosphere only to lose control, perishing at the feet of his parents Faust and Helena. Once again, Schiller's text has opened up a window on his times.

Though Carlos wishes to depart, Eboli beckons him to stay. Leading him to the sofa, she entices him not with sexuality but with the musical strains of her lute. "That song [aria], Prince Carlos, I most certainly / Will want to play again; your punishment / Will be to listen to me" (W 158; ll. 1874–76b; NA 6: 98).[181] Though admitting that her melody is "divinely beautiful," Carlos is still able to distinguish between the beauty of the song and the reality of the situation. "Such lovely words [the most beautiful text] from such a lovely mouth; / But certainly less true than they are fair" (W 158; ll. 1884–85; NA 6: 99).[182] From Carlos's perspective, through music Eboli offers him the healing he seeks. Appealing to his sensuous nature, the princess tries to manipulate a suffering Carlos. How curious that she should appeal to his need for relaxation (*Nachlaß* or *Abspannung*)!

> *(She seizes this moment to draw him to her
> on the sofa.)*
> Now you must rest, dear Carlos, for your blood

Is in an uproar —just sit here by me—
Away with these black fever fantasies![183]
(W 160; ll. 1933–35; NA 6: 101)

She tries to coerce him by suggesting that he is in need of healing (l. 1940c) and understanding, but also by reminding him of past indiscretions. In short, Eboli tries to fashion Carlos into an equal partner in love. Her crafty politics of love is still combined with more personal, human concern. For, as in the story of Mathilde and Fernando, a Duke who has befriended the King is now seeking the Princess's hand in marriage, even though she does not welcome his advances. In this convergence of epic narrative and dramatic action we observe an intertextual link between Princess Eboli's ambitions and Lady Milford's search for a lover in *Intrigue and Love*.

Carlos reacts quickly and positively to the suggestion that the princess should become a political sacrificial lamb. He perceives her to be a beautiful woman. Eboli purports that she wishes to give herself only once, but eternally to the man she loves. The writer employs analogies both to the sphere of music and the realm of organic nature to underscore this point. "My love will only make one person happy, / But this one it will make into a god. / Two souls' enchanting harmony—one kiss— / The pleasure of two lovers' hours together—And beauty's lofty and celestial magic / Are the related colors of *one* beam, / Are just the petals of *one* flower" (W 164–65; ll. 2088c–97; NA 6: 108).[184] Because he finds himself in the same kind of situation, his heart can go out to her. "I love and am not loved" ("Ich liebe und bin—nicht geliebt")(W 165; l. 2109; NA 6: 108). But the dramatic tension is fueled by yet another misunderstanding.

Carlos responds with tenderness and an embrace: "O sweet and tender maiden! / O creature most adorable!—I stand / All ears—all eyes—enchanted—full of wonder" (W 165; ll. 2114b–17a; NA 6: 109).[185] His highly emotive language leads the Princess to believe that he really does love her. For his part, however, Carlos sees in her only a comrade in arms and continues to dream about the Queen. Thinking he has discovered innocence and pure, unadulterated nature, Carlos says of Eboli: "at this court / You are the worthiest, the only one / Who understands my soul" (W 166; ll. 2148b–50b; NA 6: 110).[186] The Princess is correct to observe that Carlos is simply playing a game with her. At the same time, however, she also plays her game with him. For the virtue she appears to possess in Carlos's presence is, as Posa sees later, only the "selfishness of love" ("Eigennutz der Liebe").

In the dialogue between Alba and Domingo in act 2, we return to the political affairs of the court. Domingo entertains the chilling idea of Don Carlos as King of Spain and openly questions his ability to reign. Perceiving that Carlos is proud of his freedom and unaccustomed to compulsion ("Zwang"), the father confessor's exclamation recalls the problem of mind and body: "Tis' frightening, / This spirit in this body" ("Schrecklich ist / in diesem Körper dieser Geist") (W 173; ll. 2461c–62b; NA 6: 125). Don Carlos does not exhibit the healthy interaction between mind and body required (also) of a regent.

In act 3, scene 7, Alba narrates the story of the brave knight of Malta (NA 6: 171f.), Marquis Posa, who at the age of 18 disappeared from school in Alcala ("Alkala's hoher Schule" [l. 3396b–c]) and performed several selfless, heroic deeds. Before meeting the King, Posa vows to use the opportunity of a personal audience to tell the truth and "act in this belief" ("In diesem Glauben will ich handeln") (W 207; l. 3498b–c; NA 6: 177). The conversation between Posa and the King, in act 3, scene 10, is the structural center of the drama. Here, Schiller has Posa level a sharp criticism against the monarchial system of government: "I do love / Humanity, but in a monarchy / I dare love no one but myself" (W 210; ll. 3577c–79; NA 6: 181).[187] Underscoring the values of brotherly love, human dignity, and democratic ideals, Posa knows that "The age / Has not matured enough for my ideal. / I am a citizen of times to come" (W 211; ll. 3670c–72; NA 6: 185).[188] Political and humanistic concerns are thus fused in Schiller's *Don Carlos.*

That a human being should become like God is, for him, "Unhappy twist of Nature!" ("Unselige / Verdrehung der Natur") (ll. 3744c–45b). The reason given is insightful: "When you cast / Mankind [humankind] away to music of your lyre, / Who then could share your harmony?" (W 212; ll. 3745b–47b; NA 6: 187).[189] Employing the central metaphor of the stringed instrument, Posa succeeds in moving the King's soul "(By God, / He strikes me to the soul!)" (W 212; ll.3747c–48b; NA 6: 187).[190] As in *Intrigue and Love,* the symbol of the stringed instrument in *Don Carlos* becomes a form of political criticism. A monarchial system, wherein one human being stands, as a god, above all other human beings, appears to be an unnatural development. Indeed, Posa bewails the fact that, over the centuries, millions have been trampled by one man's private interest (l. 3753). Analogies to the arachnean world draw out the problem of autocratic and arbitrary governance.

Posa's vision "That only men [human beings]—not creatures of a higher / Variety—create world history!" (W 213; ll. 3789–90b; NA 6: 189)[191] anticipates the major theme of Schiller's inaugural lecture of 1789 ("What is, and to What End do we Study Universal History?"). The Marquis draws upon his knowledge of history in the hope of persuading the King to change his policies. For he has found the peoples of Flanders and Brabant to be strong, great, and good, and even divine. Once again, an analogy to breaking ties highlights the writer's (indirect) criticism of his times as well as his vision of the future. Unafraid, Posa now calls for exemplary, moral leadership.

> Give us what
> You took from us again, and you will be,
> Among a million other kings, the King.[192]
> (W 215; ll. 3852c–55b; NA 6: 191)

Encouraging Philipp to be a model for future generations, the Marquis exclaims, "Give us the right / To think with freedom" ("Geben Sie / Gedankenfreiheit") (W 215; ll. 3861c–62b; NA 6: 191), at which point he throws himself at the feet of the monarch. But his words receive the same cold response Carlos had received: "Strange and wondrous dreamer!" ("Sonderbarer Schwärmer!") (W 215; l. 3862b–c; NA 6: 192).

With respect to the political dynamics of the play, it is vitally important to bear in mind Posa's desperate attempt to convince the King of the merits of a natural social order which respects the rights of individual human beings.[193] But the voice of democracy—which was expressed already several years before the French Revolution in the German states—means too much of a sacrifice for King Philipp. For it would entail submitting himself to the will of the people and forsaking the power he enjoys in the absolutistic state. Though Phillip is struck by Posa's honesty and morality, and because of his unwillingness to divorce himself from his own self-interest, he is deaf to Posa's call to embrace the principle of humanity. Consistent with his character, Posa acts according to the *als-ob* (as if) of Kant's moral imperative, that is, from an ethically responsible political perspective.

Upon having Carlos arrested, Posa acknowledges the inconsistency of his actions. Self-observation leads him to the insight: "Who is the man [person] who will presume to take / The heavy rates of chance upon himself, / Although he does not claim to be omniscient?" (W 258; ll. 5002–4; NA 6: 266).[194] Not coincidentally, the writer added an analogy to the playing of strings.

> And does the lovely harmony that sleeps
> Within the lyre belong to one who buys
> It and who guards it with deaf ears? He has
> Bought up the right to smash it into pieces,
> But not the art to summon silvery tones
> And melt away into the song's delight.
> For truth is in existence for the wise
> And beauty for a feeling heart. The two
> Belong to one another. And this faith
> Cannot be shattered for me by some biased
> Belief.[195]
>
> (W 262; ll. 5158–5167; NA 6: 272).

Later, in act 5, Posa perceives that the web of politics and the frustration he experiences because of its entanglements have turned him into an animal. There is no way out of this dilemma, and that is one of the play's tragic elements.

> There's nothing—nothing—no way out—no help—
> Not in the whole extent of Nature! And

> Despair makes me a beast, a fury. I
> Then place my dagger on a woman's breast—
> But then a ray of light gleams in my soul.[196]
>
> (W 276; ll. 5487–91; NA 6: 295)

The Marquis is shot by mistake and dies in the arms of his friend.

Like Ferdinand von Walter in *Intrigue and Love,* Carlos draws his sword against his father. He blames the King for the deplorable political situation while referring to severed ties. "All human bonds are torn asunder. You / Yourself have rent them, Sire, in all your lands" (W 280; ll. 5585–86; NA 6: 301).[197] In his account of the events leading to this moment, Carlos accuses his father of his friend's death. The symbol of the stringed instrument underscores the problem of rupture. "This delicate stringed instrument was crushed / By your iron hand. For all that you could do / Was murder him" (W 281; ll. 5646–48a; NA 6: 303).[198] In Schiller's writings, metaphors also serve as means of social criticism. As the bonds of love and friendship had been cut by Posa's death, so Carlos renounces the kinship with his father. "I will renounce all that / Which might await me in this world. And you / May look at strangers searching for a son— / There lies my kingdom (W 282; ll. 5684b–84b; NA 6: 304).[199] The rupture between father and son results from the imbalance both within individuals and society. This point is driven home by the news that all of Madrid is armed and that a rebellion is about to occur. In Lerma's view, Philipp must now fear his own son. From the perspective of the status quo, Carlos's arrest would seem to be necessary.

In 5.8 we learn that Alba has intercepted the correspondence Posa had intended for Carlos via a courier, a Carthusian monk. The missive contains the plan to help the Netherlandic people free themselves from Spanish rule. The metaphor of chains ("Ketten") indicates the nature of the political dominance of Spain over the Netherlands. Alba can admire the design of the treasonous plan: "The / Design is fiendish, but in truth—divine!" ("ist teuflisch, aber wahrlich—göttlich") (W 289; l. 5850; NA 6: 315). The oxymoron complements the tragic denouement. In his characterization of the King, the writer once again heightens the tension between the political and moral dimensions of the play. "He [Carlos] had a friend, a friend who suffered death / For him—for him! With me he would have shared / My kingdom!" (W 290; ll. 5889–91b; NA 6: 318).[200] Philipp cannot comprehend devotion to a more fundamental good than the State. Envigorated by youthful power ("Jünglingskraft"), Philipp summons the Grand Inquisitor. Ironically, perhaps, as the stage directions inform us, the Inquisitor is ninety years old and blind! By characterizing the Inquisitor in this way, Schiller might have been suggesting the imminent close of that chapter in human history. The thesis that the Grand Inquisitor triumphs in the end and that Posa's ideas are thereby rendered hopeless ("chancenlos") cannot be accepted uncritically.[201] The victory seems to be momentary. In any event, Schiller's act of writing constitutes both a political statement and a moral indictment. At the same time, it has been noted that both Posa and Carlos describe the state of the future with metaphors that refer to organic Nature. Gerhard Kluge says: "This complex of images makes it clear that this State and the direction of its citizens, which will be world-citizens and not subjects, will originate in the Freedom of a natural-organic process of the cultivation and humanization of human beings and not through the realm of violence of a revolution or through guidance from above."[202] In the light of our discussion of *William Tell* in chapter nine, the implicit interest in activating all of one's powers of the soul and bringing them into alignment with the forces of Nature is an important first step toward what I will call natural justice.

Nearing a conclusion in our reading of *Don Carlos,* the metaphor of the rope represents the political power of the Church. "The tether / He dangled on was long but would not break" (W 295; ll. 6046b–47; NA 6: 327).[203] The Inquisitor admonishes the King for killing Posa since the Church itself had wanted to punish him. The historical antagonism between the Empire and the Church is thus clearly drawn. But because Phillip is willing to sacrifice his son, the Inquisitor puts aside their disagreement. King Philipp may receive the approval of the Church, but he does so by transgressing Nature. One act of inhumanity leads to another, all with the sanction of the Catholic Church. Reexposing this chapter in history, the writer launches a devastating criticism of absolutistic, autocratic, and arbitrary political power in whatever form it may appear.

Shortly before being taken prisoner, Don Carlos announces to the Queen his intention of leaving Spain for good and cutting the family ties to his father. The poetic language suggests that the act of severing relationships has been sanctioned by Nature itself. "The voice of Nature / Has totally departed from my breast" ("Ausgestorben ist / In meinem Busen die Natur") (W 302; ll. 6250c–51b; NA 6: 337). Carlos now hopes to save his suppressed people from the hand of a tyrant. But it may be too late, for the Queen detects the ringing of a bell: "I hear nought but the frightful bell that tolls / To mark our separation" (W 302; ll. 6270–71; NA 6: 338).[204] At that moment, the King appears, Carlos beholds the Grand Inquisitor, and the drama comes to an abrupt and shocking conclusion.

Preliminary Conclusions

Unlike Immanuel Kant, who did not ascribe value to nature and experience, Friedrich Schiller believed that experience plays an indispensable, indeed vital, role in the cultivation of true moral character.[205] In fact, it is the very depths of experience that first put Karl and Christian in touch with the moral principle. The turning point of *Criminal Out of Infamy* is the existential dilemma of the Sun Host in coming to terms with his criminal behavior and his higher potential as a human being. He first encounters the

Self in the "abyss of the Hell" of his own soul, which is the true unheard-of occurrence in the narrative.[206] In the end, even when shunned by the prince, Christian decides in favor of what he knows to be right and, as a result, can no longer despair. As Schiller wrote while working out his later theory of tragedy, "All other things have to; the human being is the creature that wills" ("Alle andere Dinge müssen; der Mensch ist das Wesen, welches will").[207] And what the human being wills is the good, often in the very face of evil and misfortune. In the final analysis, the moral will triumphs over the compulsion toward evil.[208] However, this triumph of the moral will can occur only when reason and sense are re-conjoined, that is, when the harmonious tension within human nature is recreated.

The human being may be an in-between of animal and angel, as Schiller propounded in the medical dissertation. Vice and virtue may be inextricably meshed "in one cradle" ("in einer Wiege"). And, yet, an important component of the "unchangeable structure of the human soul" ("unveränderliche Struktur der menschlichen Seele") is that the true human being (*Mensch*) wills the good, i.e., desires to cultivate the divine (*Engel*) over the animal (*Vieh*) within him. *Criminal Out of Infamy,* then, testifies to Schiller's unshakable belief in the power of the free will of the human being to decide in favor of the divine (*das Göttliche*). In Schiller's writings, indivisible nature is restored on a higher level, which, in view of the incompleteness of historical reality, still remains a task for the future. Herein, I believe, lies an important aspect of Schiller's relevance for our time.[209]

This expression of the existential-moral autonomy of the will to freedom is a sublime act.[210] For only in the sublime state does the mind act as if it operates only in accordance with its own laws. Hence, already before his intense study of the work of Immanuel Kant, Schiller's writings linked the principle of self-determination with the concept of moral autonomy. However, Schiller's literary practice demonstrates that the formation ("Bildung") of one's moral character is achieved only by experiencing the trial and tribulation of history which is tension, struggle, and strife. Later, in the essay *Something Concerning the First Human Society According to the Proscriptions of Mosaic Law* [*Etwas über die erste Menschengesellschaft nach dem Leitfaden der mosaischen Urkunde*], Schiller would emphasize the necessity of conflict and struggle with Nature in the transition of humankind to freedom and humanity: "only in this struggle could he [the human being] educate his reason and morality" (NA 17: 401).[211] The "depiction of moral independence in suffering" (die "Darstellung der moralischen Selbständigkeit im Leiden") (*Concerning the Sublime;* NA 20: 195) is already the intersecting point of Schiller's early narrative and dramatic practice. In both *The Robbers* and *Criminal Out of Infamy* we witness a decisive change of heart, a revolutionary act of moral character, which Kant was to propound in his essay *Religion within the Bounds of Reason* [*Die Religion innerhalb der Grenzen der bloßen Vernunft*] (1793) and which Schiller himself was to advocate in the series of letters *Concerning the Aesthetic Education of the Human Being* (1793–95). By having both Karl Moor and Christian Wolf turn themselves in to the authorities after a dramatic change of heart, Schiller also established a substantive link between the moral and legal spheres of influence. In doing so, he anticipated the work of Immanuel Kant. Therefore, Schiller's intensive study of the greatest German philosopher of the eighteenth century does not mark a break with the past and the beginning of a new, classical phase in the writer's literary career. Rather, it forms a happy point of culmination of what Schiller had already worked out, both in his early dramatic practice and in his earliest theoretical works.

As is clear from the foregoing, Schiller's medical dissertations, namely his physiology, together with his studies of science and Nature in general, helped shape the character of his literary practice. On the metaphorical level of Schiller's language and from the various biographies of the writer's life, we observe the impact of music, especially opera, on the quality of Schiller's writing.[212] In retrospect, already in the early phase of his career, Friedrich Schiller had brought all his multidisciplinary activities fruitfully to bear on the act of writing.

4

The Writing and Dramatization of History: The Essay on Universal History and *Wallenstein*

In his monumental work on the philosophy of the European Enlightenment, Ernst Cassirer noted that the "eighteenth century conception of history is less a finished form with clear outlines than a force exerting its influence in all directions."[1] Friedrich Schiller's essay "What Is and to What End Do We Study Universal History?" ["Was heißt und zu welchem Ende studiert man Universalgeschichte?"] (1789)[2] is a superb example of the complex, open-ended nature of conceptions of history in the eighteenth century. Unlike the work of many of his contemporaries, such as Bossuet, Kant, Herder, and members of the Göttingen circle of historians, Friedrich Schiller's writings demonstrate that world order is a real problem, one that would extend well beyond the limits of his own work. My initial task is to illuminate the writer's awareness of this problem, to determine how he treated it, and to survey the limits of his approach to it. My reflections are guided by the author's self-conscious awareness of the implications and limitations of his own exposition.[3] In this work, we can appreciate a marked increase in the number of qualifications to theses and positions advanced by the writer as his interest in history intensified.

I. *Critical Perspectives*

In his report on the state of Schiller research in the 1970s, Helmut Koopmann expressed surprise over the relative dearth of scholarship on Schiller's shorter historical writings.[4] This lacuna in research is unfortunate because these writings are instructive not only in locating the writer's position vis-à-vis the German Enlightenment, but also in disclosing the possible significance of Schiller's thought for our own times.

Schiller and History

A. In 1959, the year of the bicentennial celebration of Schiller's birth, Benno von Wiese characterized Schiller's inaugural lecture and other shorter essays as genuine "contributions to a philosophy of world-history,"[5] thereby liberating the author from the accounts of Johannes Janssen[6] and other nineteenth-century writings that decried the writer's apparent subjectivism and seeming disregard for "how it really was" ("wie es eigentlich gewesen [ist]" [Leopold von Ranke]). From the positivist point of view, Schiller's orientation with history was simply poetic, not historical. It was a form of art rather than a science. In 1970, the director of the Goethe Archives in Weimar, Karl-Heinz Hahn, contributed significantly to the demolition of the positivist claim that Schiller had provided only "constructions in place of historical depictions" by accentuating the writer's concern for factual authenticity ("sachliche Korrektheit").[7]

The issue is more complex, however, since we have come to appreciate the fact that the great historical writings of the late nineteenth century are also poetic in their foundations.[8] Nonetheless, there is still some truth to the positivist claim regarding Schiller, since, in the eighteenth century, history was viewed as a human science.[9] Schiller's models were the great historical essays of Herodotus, Thucydides, and Gibbon. No doubt in the light of this fact, some contemporary scholars have asserted that Schiller was most interested in elucidating the "inner truth" of poetry and history. Schiller's "historiographical idealism" consists in the *preservation of historical truth with the concomitant observance of poetic truth.*"[10]

I do not doubt that much of what Schiller had to say about history is analogous to his insights into the appropriation of history in his work as a poet. At the same time, however, we should appreciate the fact that it was both Schiller's aesthetic sensibility and his knowledge of the skillful employment of rhetoric that also informed the shorter writings on history.[11]

Schiller, the Idealist

B. A more serious problem in Schiller research is the widespread view of the writer as an idealist. This notion was advanced again by Klaus Berghahn in his provocative collection of essays, *Schiller: Ansichten eines Idealisten* (Frankfurt a.M.: Suhrkamp, 1986).

Charting the history of the image of Schiller as an idealist, Theodor Schieder's appraisal of the writer, in 1960, serves as an insightful yet problematic example of the complexity of this issue. For Schieder, a professional historian and erstwhile editor of the *Historische Zeitschrift,* Schiller's view of the progressive ennoblement and socialization of humankind underlies what he terms the writer's "dogmatic concept of universal history."[12] In responding to Schieder's assessment, however, we should be careful to note that Schiller, like Lessing before him, sought to acquire rather than to possess knowledge. Schiller's approach to truth casts serious doubt on the historian's claim that the writer advanced a dogmatic concept of universal history. Schiller's writings disclose the operation of a critical-creative mind, one that strove actively to expand the horizons of knowledge. At the same time, they demonstrate that the writer was clearly aware of the limits of speculation, especially idealistic contemplation. Our discussion of Schiller's relationship to Fichte in the ensuing chapter will help undergird this point. But let us return to the eminent German historian.

The significance of Schieder's viewpoint lies in his having acknowledged Schiller's "deep insight" that the realm of freedom as conceived in idea can never be realized in fact.[13] But Schieder makes of Schiller *his* contemporary, one who had ascertained that the final secret of history lay in its very "intransparency, the ostensible incompatibility of the course of events with any and all laws of reason."[14] While I agree that the writer was clearly aware of the disparity between the real and the ideal, he chose to retain the hope in the moral-social improvement of the human species. Furthermore, Schieder overlooks the *regulative* function of Schiller's ideas of humanity, the practical effect of which is to propel humanity beyond the moment.

For a moment, Schieder forgets his own insights into the dynamics of the writer's thought when characterizing Schiller as "an idealistic writer of history."[15] This view is not consistent with Schiller's candid recognition that the idea of humanity cannot be realized in fact, that is, in history, since the idea itself is always beyond history as given. We will observe this in the writer's dramatization of history, *Wallenstein* (1799). Insights like Schieder's suggest, then, that Schiller was more of an optimistic realist or realistic idealist than an idealist per se.[16] But, as my own working terminology suggests, attempts to characterize Schiller and his work in terms of any binary paradigm such as idealist-realist, clearly break down at this point. The relativization of the binary opposition means that the question of idealism in particular is a far more complex issue than recognized heretofore. The traditional view of Schiller as one of the founding fathers of German Idealism whose thought culminates in Hegel (encoded especially in philosophical studies of the writer)[17] is not informed by a rigorous analysis of the majority of Schiller's writings considered as a whole.

I have contended that even recent research on Schiller (Berghahn's book) is carrying this view forward without critical analysis of the term "idealist."[18] Hinrich Seeba, for instance (though his emphasis does lie elsewhere), describes the writer as an "idealistic portrayer of historical and poetic truth."[19] And the former East German scholar Eike Middell stresses "the idealistic philosophical-historical conception . . . behind his richly documented depiction,"[20] thereby challenging Hahn's view of the empirical ground of Schiller's historical thought. Clearly, this direction has been informed by Hegel's generally positive acceptance of Schiller's dialectical spirit. A good example of this orientation is Middell's literary biography of Schiller (1982), wherein Schiller's historical writings are viewed as precursory to and, by implication, of less significance than *Concerning the Aesthetic Education of the Human Being in a Series of Letters* and Hegel's later ruminations on the philosophy of history. By offering a rigorous appraisal of Schiller's reflections on universal history, I will suggest just how limited traditional views of the writer have been.

Schiller and Universal History

C. Benno von Wiese hesitated to embrace Schiller's reflections on the nature, function, and goal of universal history. For he entertains doubts (lingering from the positivists, perhaps) concerning the objective, i.e., empirical ground of the writer's views on this subject. Still, von Wiese defends the idea of the realization of humanity in the course of time.

Karl-Heinz Hahn's (former director of the Goethe/Schiller Archives in Weimar, now deceased) determination of the "material base" of Schiller's text in the seemingly objective and historical condition of that time and place, while prefiguring more recent developments in literary theory such as the "New Historicism,"[21] has the residual effect of shortcircuiting the possible meanings suggested both by Schiller's text and the critical reader's interpretation of the text. For, in Hahn's hands, the text is simply a historical document. Frozen in time and space, it can "say" no more than the author's times would allow. Such an approach to cultural artifacts restricts rather than opens up the possibilities of a text like Schiller's essay. Friedrich Schiller's approach to universal history accords well with the work of Hans-Georg Gadamer and Wolfhart Pannenberg, who, in the words of David Couzens Hoy, agree "that interpreters' understanding of the past is conditioned by their understanding of the present, including their expectations about the future."[22] Unlike Gadamer, however, Pannenberg argues that a text gains its fullest actualization in the understanding of the reader "in the horizon of universal history."[23] Though Pannenberg does not refer to Schiller's essay on universal history, there is, still, an intimate connection between the two writers.[24] One of my major tasks here is to determine and critically assess the nature of Schiller's hermeneutical reflection on the basis of the text itself.

II. Concerning the "Bread-Scholar" and the Philosophical Mind

The first part of Schiller's essay turns on the sharp distinction between the "bread-scholar" ("Brotgelehrter") and the philosophical mind ("philosophischer Kopf"). Whereas the former works only for monetary gain and considers toil to be arduous and tiring, the latter is motivated by a love of truth. This individual maintains a "cheerful disposition" ("frohen Muth") because one's inquiries are fueled by the quest for knowledge for its own sake. The "bread scholar" lacks the philosopher's grasp of the whole because of the narrow focus on the particulars of one's work (NA 17: 360f.). Whereas this type of scholar suffers from a kind of intellectual paralysis (he or she hovers "in perpetual intellectual standstill" ["in ewigem Geistesstill-stand"]), the philosophical mind strives continually to generate ever greater and finer thoughts. Herein lie the borders of Schiller's paradigm.

I see in this radical distinction an ironic form of self-criticism. We know that Schiller wrote the lengthier historical writings mainly in order to supplement his meager income. His great *History of the Thirty Years War* [*Geschichte des Dreissigjährigen Kriegs* (1790), for instance, appeared in the *Historical Diary for Women* [*Historischer Calender für Damen*], for which he received modest compensation. But, while projects such as these were understood as *Brotstudien* (studies written in order to earn money), none of them was merely that. For in the introductions to these works, as well as in the occasional generalizations found in the main body of each writing on history, there is evidence of a philosophical mind at work. This part of the writer's thinking, however, was not only interested in truth, but in performing the *labor* of the love of knowledge, for which Schiller still hoped to be compensated. Our writer may have been a gifted theorist, but he was also a practical man of affairs.

Schiller did not give free rein to the philosophical mind. Because this type of thinker loves truth more than one's own system of thought he or she is critically aware of the movement of one's own thinking. While actively pursuing truth, the philosopher must remain conscious of one's own limitations and potential to err. We could say, then, that the philosophical mind traces its own activity while endeavoring to expand the horizons of knowledge.

In the light of salaried professorships today, we can appreciate just how fluid the line is between the types of scholars the writer tries to play off against each other. It seems to me, however, that, if we accept both functions as legitimate methods of inquiry, we can better appreciate both the critical (analytical) and synthetic (unifying) powers of reason. Schiller's summarial statement reads as follows: "Where the 'bread'-scholar separates, the philosophical mind unites."[25] The point is that the human mind is capable of both operations at once and that Schiller's writings testify to this. It is likewise apparent that the distinction discloses the critical-creative nature of Schiller's own thinking.

A similar distinction between types of scholars was introduced, in 1980, by Geoffrey Hartman in *Criticism in the Wilderness* (New Haven: Yale University Press). Hartman differentiates, intially, between the "philosopher-critic" and the "scholar-critic." While Hartman's paradigm originates in the debate over New Criticism and what J. Hillis Miller proclaimed to be "the triumph of theory" in literary studies,[26] the critic does strive, in the end, for a synthesis of Anglo-American criticism ("scholarship") and Continental European hermeneutics ("philosophy").[27] I do not think it is necessary to accept the development of literary criticism as a distinct genre in order to appreciate Hartman's quest for mediation between these two influential traditions.

Whether or not Hartman is aware of the fact, his distinction can be traced back to Friedrich Schiller's essay on universal history. To conjoin Schiller's and Hartman's terms, it is the "Brotgelehrter" ("scholar-critic") who depends for his or her livelihood on the text, offering a painstaking analysis of that specific object, whereas the "philosophischer Kopf" ("philosopher-critic"), or "dialectician," exhibits "genuine dissemination," "a desire for perpetuation by spiritual means."[28] The point I wish to make here is that both directions of inquiry stand in a tense relationship of "reciprocal cooperation" ["gegenseitige Wechselwirkung"], to borrow a key phrase from Schiller's later theories of art.

III. The Transmission of History and Tradition

Contemporary theory has helped us appreciate the central role language plays in determining reality. One of the major precepts of this discussion was formulated by Hans-Georg Gadamer in his essay "Man [The Human Being] and Language" (1966). "We can only think in a language," he stated, "and just this residing of our thinking in a language is the profound enigma that language presents to thought."[29] Like some of his contemporaries, such as Johann Gottfried Herder in his *Essay Concerning the Origin of Language* [*Abhandlung über den Ursprung der Sprache*] (1772), Schiller knew that the nature of language informs our experience of reality. At the very heart of his essay on universal history, Schiller advanced the following thesis:

The source of all history is tradition, and the organ of tradition is language.[30]

This pronouncement complements one of the founding ideas of linguistic science. For, as his friend Wilhelm von Humboldt was to state later, "Language is the formative organ of thought."[31] Schiller knew then, as we realize now, that language drags along with it the very tradition that helps shape the present. But rather than naively accept what tradition dictates, the writer explored the problem of the codification of tradition in his own language.

This is the unstated reason why, in his reflections on universal history, the writer maintained that the philosophical historian selects those aspects of the past which facilitate an awareness of the present. In the first part of the essay on universal history, Schiller professed that the major task of the universal historian is to select from the total sum of human events those occurrences that have contributed in an essential way to the shaping of the present world. But Schiller was equally attendant to the future direction of history. In short, his account of history reflects the inseparability of past, present, and future. In contradistinction to Karl-Heinz Hahn, I submit that Schiller was aware of the fact that language mediates our understanding of reality. This being the case, the critical or enlightened writer must account for the transmission of tradition in his or her own language.

Whatever the force of tradition, then, even in the language we speak, there is still room for critical reflection. Critiquing Gadamer's work, we may agree that "the connection of understanding to tradition does not preclude criticism."[32] The exercise of critical, self-reflective intelligence first makes possible the objectification of experience. A by-product of self-reflection is that it seeks to account for what is *excluded* by the transmission of tradition.

Several years before the publication of two of Schiller's shorter historical essays, Immanuel Kant, in *Presumed Beginning of Human History* [*Mutmaßlicher Anfang der Menschengeschichte*], argued that, in the absence of documentation, conjecture (*Mutmaßungen*) plays an indispensable role in the recording of history.[33] The topic sentence of Kant's essay reflects the need to fill in the blanks in the historical record. "It is certainly permissible," he maintained, "to intersperse conjectures in the *continuing course* of history in order to fill in the *gaps* in reports: because what goes before as a distant cause and what follows as an effect can supply a fairly reliable direction in the discovery of the intermediate causes in order to make the transition comprehensible."[34] Filling in the gaps by way of "conjecture" is justified since the relation between what first occurred and what has happened subsequently can be inferred logically, that is, through the auspices of reason. Kant was well aware of the fact that a history or report composed solely of *Mutmaßungen* would be a wholly unreliable source of information, one which would not be much better than the draft of a novel. Therefore, it is necessary to distinguish between "conjecture," or inference based on data and mere contrivance, or fabrication ("eine bloße Erdichtung"). Whereas inference is based on a law of probability, contrivance assumes the status of mere fiction. Most important, however, Kant constructed a temporal line of development operating in analogy to Nature and the law of cause and effect. In short, since the historian cannot know everything that has occurred and must base conclusions on the available evidence, inference has a necessary and vital role to play in the construction of the historical record.

Kant's explanation leaves room for the judicious play of imagination in historical writing. For he defines inference as a movement involving imagination informed by reason.[35] In our own day, Russell Nye has argued for the use of imagination in historical writing, and therewith narrows the gap between history and literature. "Good historical writing," he asserted, "is under constant tension, with the imagination always pushing outward against the restraining discipline of historical plausibility."[36] But, whereas Kant had accepted inference based on the rational exercise of imagination, Nye appreciates more the very "contest between what the imagination wants to say and the rules of fact and temporality that restrict it."[37] In both history and literature, imagination is selective and interpretive. Where selection "brings order and meaning to the past, the other brings them to an experience beyond reality."[38] While transcending the limits of Kant's argument, Nye helps illuminate the nature of historical thought as propounded by the writer. For Schiller was more sensitive to the act of selection than Kant. In his prolegomenon to a universal history, indebted, as it was, to Kant's *Idea for a General History in Cosmopolitan Intent* [*Idee zu einer allgemeinen Geschichte in weltbürgerlicher Absicht*] (1784),[39] Schiller, to adopt Nye's terminology, sought to bring the order and meaning accorded to the past to an experience beyond reality as known.

IV. Filling in the Gaps

According to the writer Friedrich Schiller, the philosophical historian must fill in the gaps created by the incompleteness of the historical record in order to maintain a coherent account of history. But the writer is to do this without systematizing, for that would restrict rather than encourage historical development. What commends Schiller's reflections on the nature and goal of universal history is his candid recognition of the *disjunction* between actual, historical events ("die wirkliche Folge der Begebenheiten") and the rational, synthetic process of ordering, or structuring history. Hans-Georg Gadamer asserted that the hermeneutical process encompasses "the self-understanding of the interpreter as well as what is interpreted."[40] By scanning the limits of his own argument, Schiller exercised hermeneutical reflection. It is primarily this self-reflective movement, rather than the content of the work as such, that recommends Schiller's essay on universal history.

Schiller candidly admits that there are many gaps ("viele Lücken") and empty stretches ("leere Strecken") in history owing to the complete lack or near absence of historical documentation.[41] "There is, therefore, a noticeably visible incongruity between the course of the world and the course of world-history."[42] In the absence of such traces, it is necessary to invent certain artificial connecting links ("künstliche Bindungsglieder"), and this requires the activity of imagination. In other words, the retention of the idea of the orderly progression of history hinges on the invention of linkages.[43] Given this fact, it is not so much the causal relation between events as it is the creation of the linkages themselves that produces a semblance of historical order. Although Schiller claimed that the philosophical understanding was the agency lending coherence ("Zusammenhang") to world history, it is actually the linkages themselves that make historical development "coherent." For, "in as much as it [the philosophical understanding] chains these fragments together by way of artificial connecting links, it elevates the aggregate to a system, to a rationally interconnecting whole."[44]

Preservation of the idea of connectedness presupposes not only a temporal line but also a belief in the fundamental unity of all things. In the eighteenth century, the idea of an orderly, meaningful, coherent, and homogenous universe as informed by the conception of the great chain of being is still retained in Schiller's language.[45] One of the most frequently used verbs in the essay on universal history is "ineinandergreifen" (to mesh, or interlock). "A long chain of occurrences is drawn from the present moment to the beginning of the human race which meshes like cause and effect."[46] One of the central passages reads as follows:

> The more often, then, and with ever greater success, it [the philosophical mind] renews the attempt to tie the past to the present, the more it is inclined to connect as *means* and *intention* what it sees meshing as *cause* and *effect*.[47]

Yet, the conscious recognition that history contains many gaps and blank spaces challenges this idea. This is the reason why the idea of world order had become a problem for Schiller rather than a given. A major contribution of Schiller's essay on universal history, then, is its problematization of the intellectual tradition of the great chain of being: the limitation imposed on our knowledge of history by artificial connecting links calls into question the predominant idea of world order. This being the case, we may conclude that Schiller was critical of that tradition which language drags along with it into the present.

But what kept Schiller from rejecting the idea of an ordered and purposeful universe? After all, reason itself cannot *prove* the existence of an ordered universe.

Schiller's intensive study of human history, evidenced by the major historical writings on the fight for freedom in the Netherlands, the agonizing political tensions and devastation of the Thirty Years War, and the numerous uprisings in France, revealed that opposition, not unity, was one of the major characteristics of history. According to Schiller, the original break from Nature marking the beginning of the history of humankind was a violent moment. In his essay, *Something Concerning the First Human Society According to the Introduction of the Mosaic Testament* [*Etwas über die erste Menschengesellschaft nach Leitfaden der mosaischen Urkunde* (1789/90)], Schiller maintained that as soon as reason had welled up in the human being, Nature "threw" that person out of the cradle of purity and quiet repose into the "Kampf" [battle] of history. The "fall" from his own instinct, although introducing moral evil ("das moralische Übel"), was actually a necessary first step in making moral good ("das moralische Gute") possible. Harkening to the call of reason, the original human being "threw himself into the wild game of life, thus making his way along the dangerous path of moral freedom."[48] Such was the violent nature of the human being's propulsion into self-activity ("Selbsttätigkeit") and self-consciousness.

My point is that Schiller's own observations of the world and of Nature in its relation to history dictated anything but an ordered and purposeful universe. How, then, in the absence of proof, could Schiller retain the idea of world order? First, he simply assumed that the authentification ("Beglaubigung") of universal history "lies in the uniformity and unchangeable unity

of the laws of nature and of human intelligence."[49] Since human reason seeks
to unify the diverse and seemingly disparate phenomena of Nature and
history, the force of its own movement in the direction of unity is itself an
argument for an ordered and purposeful universe. Knowing, however, that
the evidence provided by history itself testified not to order but to strife,
struggle, and even disorder, Schiller was forced to admit that the idea of
world order was indeed a problem rather than an established fact.

By what means was the universal historian to relate the most essential
aspects of the historical past to the present and, ultimately, to the future?
Schiller began by adopting the analogical method of his day. "The method
of concluding by way of analogy is, as everywhere, also a powerful aid in
history. But it must be justified by a serious purpose and exercised with as
much caution as discernment."[50] But Schiller does not elaborate on why the
analogical method of his day had to be exercised with care. In our own day,
Paul Ricoeur has suggested that "reasoning by analogy is an illusion and
has no verifiable status in the empirical acquisition of human experience."[51]
It seems to me, however, that not only the transmission of tradition, as
Ricoeur understands it, but, analogy itself can "simulate the ordered succession of things," thus lending themselves "to a kind of causal explanation."[52]
Still, the very difference between the revolutionary development of Nature
and the seemingly "revolutionary" course of human history, of which Schiller was clearly aware, led the writer to circumscribe the limits to the then
current use of analogy as a method of historical explanation.

Unlike the "bread-scholar," the philosophical mind, Schiller asserts, cannot rest for long with the mere material of world history (i.e., with the facts
or particulars of history, so far as they are known) without feeling a drive
well up within him "which seeks harmony ["Übereinstimmung"] and strives
to assimilate everything around him to his own rational nature," thus giving
way to the compulsion "to elevate every appearance he encounters to the
highest effect, which he recognizes, to the *Idea*."[53] Herein we find the most
intimate connection between the universal historian in particular and the
philosophical mind in general. For the universal historian draws out of oneself ("aus sich selbst heraus") the underlying harmony of the world of appearances "and transplants them outside oneself into the order of things,
i.e., he introduces a rational purpose into the course of the world and a
teleological principle into world-history."[54]

Schiller's comparison of the tapestry of history (the appearances) and the
great "stage" ("Schauplatz") of the universe implies a distinction between
the surface reality of world history and the deep structure of the world order.
But Schiller's hermeneutical reflection ponders its own pre-understandings
("Vorverständnisse," to use Gadamer's term). For he openly admits that
while thousands of facts confirm the universal-historical orientation to the
course of history, many others actually refute it! But as long as important
connecting links are missing ("fehlen"), and ultimate destiny does not reveal

itself, the observer will declare the matter undecided. Hence, "that opinion will reign which offers the understanding the most satisfaction and the heart the greatest happiness."[55] Rather than give free rein to historical relativeness, Schiller opts to retain the simulation and semblance of the ordered succession of events. His argument discloses an appreciation of the limits of his own retention of the idea of a unified field of history from the past over the present into the future. Furthermore, he retained the idea of the purposiveness or finality of nature ("Zweckmäßigkeit"). Yet the act of faith informing these ideas does not really resolve what the writer himself calls "the problem of world-order." Perhaps this is the reason why Schiller was compelled to introduce this phrase only at the end of his essay.

V. A Critique

In the chapter, "Vom Nutzen und Nachteil der Historie für das Leben" in his *Untimely Observations* [*Unzeitgemäße Betrachtungen*] (1873–76), Friedrich Nietzsche launched a scathing attack on the positivists' view of history as science. Criticizing the purported "'objective' glance" ("'objektive[r]' Blick") of the scientific historian, Nietzsche cited a passage from Schiller's essay on universal history, on the basis of which he asserted that the writer was "completely clear about the obvious subjectivity of this claim" concerning the objectivity of historical thought. It is characteristic of Nietzsche's work that he did not name the author himself. In any case, the passage he cites is a central one in Schiller's essay. It reads: "One appearance after another begins to escape from blind chance and lawless freedom and to gain the ranks of a harmonious whole (which, to be sure, is present only in his mind ["Vorstellung"]) like a fitting link."[56] While it is true that Schiller acknowledged the subjective ground of historical thought, he himself was engaged in an objectifying process of critical self-reflection.

What attracted Nietzsche to Schiller in this instance, I think, were Schiller's efforts "to tie the past to the present." For, as Nietzsche was to assert: "*Only by virtue of the highest power of the present should you interpret the past.*"[57] Most important, the interjection in Schiller's statement above, which no doubt captured Nietzsche's full attention, discloses perhaps the true meaning of the statement. For it is now apparent that the overpowering of blind chance, or arbitrariness, depends on a consciously contrived idea of a coherent whole in the work of the philosophical historian. Upon closer analysis, we have seen that Schiller's essay on universal history actually exposes the *in*sufficiency of historical thought. At the same time, however, it generates a theory of universal history that, directed as it is toward the future, transcends, but cannot ultimately resolve, past and present historical problems.[58]

On a critical note, Schiller's essay tends to thwart our cognitive activity by "reducing" the problem of gaps to a more fundamental idea of a homogenous whole. For it is just as rational to assume the heterogeneity of reality as it is the homogeneity of the universe. In Schiller's experience, human history evidences the opposite of the fundamental unity of all things. This turn in Schiller's argument obviates the problem of absence created by the existence of the gaps, blanks, and lapses in history. Since, in the eighteenth century, history was perceived as developing analogously to Nature such a problem clearly impacts on the question of the nature of the universe. For Schiller, there still is a God; so problems transcending the limits of human thought were to find their ultimate resolution in the absolute knowledge of the Godhead. Not so, of course, for the post-Nietzschean thought of a Jacques Derrida, for whom, it might be said, absence has become *the* fundamental problem of philosophy. The decisive point here, however, is that, even in the face of the gaps in history, Schiller, by conscious election sought to preserve what Derrida later endeavored to disassemble, namely the idea of a centered structure.[59]

But there is an even deeper-lying source to Schiller's retention of the ideas of a contiguous line of historical development and the coherency of universal history. The fact of gaps, the absence of traces, historical blanks, or time-lapses is a fascinating yet perplexing problem because it forces us to come to terms with the fundamental problems of incompleteness, imperfection, and finite knowledge. While driving history forward in the quest for a better tomorrow, the regulative function of the idea of humanity actually serves to compensate for the unsettling possibility of a diffuse or heterogenous universe devoid of any ground or efficient cause. Yet, even this consequence of his idea did not escape Schiller's hermeneutical self-awareness. We recall that he urged the philosophical historian to exercise caution when applying the analogical method. Now, with respect to filling in the gaps, he notes that when applying this method, one runs the risk of forgetting "that this sequence of appearances, which took on so much regularity and purpose in his mind ["Vorstellung"], in reality denies these characteristics; it becomes hard for him to place under the blind mastery of necessity that which, in the borrowed light of understanding, had begun to take on such a cheerful form."[60]

At this point in the essay, Schiller offers a candid description of the conscious contrivance of order out of the sense of harmony dictated by his own reason. While serving as a vehicle of social progress, the study of universal history is also of therapeutic value. The following passage is decisive:

By training the human being to see oneself within the entire context of history and, on the basis of his conclusion, to rush ahead into the distant future: it [universal history] also conceals the limits of birth and death which encompass the life of the human being in such a narrow and oppressive manner; it expands its short existence into an infinite space creating an optical illusion, thus leading the individual, without noticing, into the species. [61]

By fabricating an "optical illusion," the universal historian confers a sense of immortality to that short being-in-the-world of the individual.[62] And how is this to be accomplished? By portraying the individual human being as an important link in the interconnected chain of historical being. Herein lies the utility of Schiller's program of universal history.

> A noble desire for the rich legacy of truth, morality, and freedom must enflame us, which we took over from the past world and which, in a richly augmented manner, we must again return to the future world, and make a contribution out of *our* means, and anchor our fleeting existence in the intransitory chain which is winding its way through all human generations.[63]

Finally, knowledge first becomes true knowledge for Schiller when the theoretical proves to be of practical value. The study of world-history is "as much an attractive as a useful enterprise."[64] But what is the purpose of the study of universal history?

As Schiller stated near the outset of his essay, our common mission ("Bestimmung") is "to develop ourselves as human beings." The ultimate end of history is not the Kantian state but the actualization of the idea of humanity (*Humanität*). This is an early anticipation of his idea, explored in *Concerning the Aesthetic Education of the Human Being,* that the moral *Bildung* of the human being is a necessary first step in the founding of the new Ethical State. Yet, while he was busy expounding the goal of universal history, the writer admitted that the barbarian vestiges ("barbarische Überreste") of past ages were still present in his own time. He perceived that there had been advances in civilization, but he conceded that the moral ennoblement ("Veredlung") of the human being would remain a task for the future, a never-ending assignment. But the problem of the recurrent manifestation of barbarism in modern times must, perforce, work against the utopian view of a morally liberated humanity. Perhaps, Schiller's candid recognition of the barbaric tendency of society signals an intuitive knowledge of the apparent irresolvability of this problem as well. The depiction of history in *Don Carlos* suggested this, as would *Wallenstein.*

In sum, the reiteration of the idea of the fundamental unity of all things generates a sense of constancy and permanence amid the disruption and sometimes radical changes of history. Embedded in Schiller's language is the idea of transitory being, one of the vestiges of the Baroque tradition, as well as the notion of the great chain of being, which informed the thought of the German Enlightenment from G. W. Leibniz on. In this essay, the writer endeavored to offset the facts of historical disruption and spiritual turbulence with a theory of universal history. For, by directing our attention to the unifying features of humankind and to the future, universal history generates some sense of security and permanence in life, thereby transcending the uncertainties and flux found in the isolated, empirical study of history and human experience. It is not surprising that, in this context, the writer of literature should have afforded the imagination greater liberty.

It follows then that the writing of history, like understanding in general, is not just a reconstructive act but a productive one. The movement of Schiller's thought as suggested by his writings objectifies; that is, "it lifts a thing [in this case, the argument itself] out of its context and makes it stand alone as an object before a consciousness."[65] As Wolfhart Pannenberg suggested, subjectivity is transcended when this type of objectifying language is coupled with a universal history.[66] In stressing the appropriation of the most essential aspects of the past in the present and then seeking to propel the present into the future by way of the dynamic yet regulative idea of a universal humanity, Friedrich Schiller developed a powerful, self-objectifying theory of historical transformation.

VI. At the Crossroads of Physiology and History: Schiller's *Wallenstein*

The numerous philosophical ruminations that Schiller interjected in *The History of the Thirty Years War* [*Die Geschichte des Dreißigjährigen Krieges*] (1790f.) draw the reader's attention to the intricacies of his work. In the second book, the writer expressed his sense of awe concerning the complex nature of world history: "How admirably interwoven the thread of world-history is!" (NA 18/2: 95).[67] The theme of rupture is also present, however, especially in his characterization of Gustav Adolphus. "A situation which one simply did not take into consideration—Gustav's heroic greatness—rent the web of this deceitful state's politics" (NA 18/2: 100).[68] Unlike in the early writings, the theme of rupture is now employed in order to promote moral justice and humanity. Its function is to tear the web of deceit that insulates the sphere of politics.

Turning now to Schiller's drama of history *Wallenstein,* I define "history" as the sum total of all human action, reaction, and non-action. This later dramatization of history opens on the troops which are assembled around the great commander Duke Albrecht von Wallenstein in Pilsen, Bohemia. I suggest that the major theme of the first part of the trilogy, *Wallenstein's Camp* [*Wallensteins Lager*], is war and the effects of war. The drama addresses not only the devastating Thirty Years War (the historical material) but also Schiller's own time, namely the Coalition Wars. As the Sergeant-Major says, "For war is the password now on earth" ("Denn Krieg ist jetzt die Losung auf Erden") (L 190; l. 428; NA 8: 27). Because middle-class social life has been ravaged by war, we are introduced to the so-called fourth estate of common soldiers, peasants, and canteen women. Disharmony rules the day. The frivolity, bawdiness, and promiscuity displayed by some of the soldiers in the early running of the drama underscore the suspension of social mores and values. As if compensating for the loss of center, i.e., social stability, the soldiers propagate a myth of the invincible commander who not only leads them, but who evokes in them a sense of order, or centeredness. Wallenstein thus seems to be the stable center of an otherwise chaotic world. The First Curassier, for instance, insists that the army should stand united and root themselves within Bohemia's borders (l. 830). The Second Trooper propounds the belief that, by virtue of belonging to Wallenstein's army, a man is protected by special powers (ll. 350–51). At the same time, however, there is something demonic about Wallenstein's unique power. For the same trooper senses that the commander has summoned the help of a devil out of the depths of Hell (l. 353). Part of the mythification of Wallenstein owes to his transfiguration as a second Faust. "Yes, he's sold his soul to the prince of hell; / That's why his troops can live so well," the Second Trooper remarks (L 188; ll. 353–54; NA 8: 24).[69]

Perhaps it is because of the affinity between Wallenstein and the demonic, the devilish, and the Faustian that the writer introduced the voice of moral condemnation in the dramatic figure of the Capuchin Friar (l. 597f.). In the final analysis, Wallenstein is an unstable, even dangerous center. Motifs prevalent in Baroque literature are appropriated in Schiller's writing to underscore the loss of stability: the transitoriness of life, vanity, *carpe diem*, and the reference to Fortuna dispensing her gifts or misfortunes as she wills. Life outside society is subject to the game of chance. In short, with the suspension of order, caused by war, the human being cannot be in control of one's destiny. As the chorus of soldiers at the end of *Wallenstein's Camp* makes clear, the soldiers' pledge of allegiance to Wallenstein is a call for a center to their otherwise nomadic and capricious lives. As the reader/ audience discovers, this seemingly great man is not really in control of history. Hence, the drama of history discloses the very loss of center.

In retrospect, Schiller's Wallenstein is not simply a victim of history. He is also a victim of his own character flaws. Hence, the loss of center in the drama is also attributable to the lack of development (*Bildung*) in the human being.

The three texts comprising this major dramatic writing continue to develop the central metaphor of the stringed instrument. They also rework motifs of flight and metaphors of enchainment. Near the very center of *Wallenstein's Death* [*Wallensteins Tod*, act 3, scene 4] the Duchess encourages her daughter Thekla to play the zither for her troubled father. It is not only a critical moment in their relationship but also a central turning point in the dramatic action. Wallenstein: "A gracious spirit dwells upon your lips, / Your mother speaks of your accomplishments / With praise, and tells me that a delicate / And sweet harmonious voice is yours, that charms / The soul. Just such a voice as this it is / I need to drive the evil demon from me, / That beats his dusky wings about my head" (L 376; ll. 1470–74; NA 8: 239–240).[70] Dieter Borchmeyer has appreciated the melancholic state in which Wallenstein swoons, but he does not relate this back to Schiller's medical writings; nor does he address the General's need for healing.[71] This is clearly denoted by the couple's expectation that their daughter play the stringed instrument. Wallenstein recognizes the power of Thekla's gift of harmonizing. Given her knowledge of her father's exploits, she cannot oblige.

> Spare me, I beg you —Sing now, when my soul
> With fear and dread is laden —sing to him—
> When he will send my mother to her grave![72]
>
> (L 376–77; ll. 1480–82; NA 8: 240)

Trembling, Thekla forsakes her father. The stage directions illuminate the crisis. [*She takes the instrument with trembling hands, her soul wrestling violently within her, and at the moment when she should begin to sing shudders convulsively, throws down the instrument and hurries off*] (L 377; NA 8: 240).[73] To which her mother responds: "My child—she is not well!" ("Mein Kind—o sie ist krank") (L 377; l. 1486b; NA 8: 240). The scene carries greater significance than heretofore recognized when viewed in the light of Schiller's previous writings.

Wallenstein's assessment of the world is unrealistic. His wife is not afraid to tell him: "let us not strive to fly / Too high, or else too great will be our fall" (L 378; ll. 1514b–15; NA 8: 242).[74] Her words anticipate the warning Faust and Helena issue to their son Euphorion shortly before his wings fail him in Goethe's *Faust Part II* (11.9737, 9739–40). The Duchess continues: "You must always build / Into the clouds, you build and build and do / Not stop to ask whether such narrow base / Can bear the giddy towers of your work" (L 379; ll. 1535b–37; NA 8: 243).[75] The truth is that the General has already been relieved of his command. Thekla's unwillingness to play the stringed instrument, that is to create harmonious, melodic music, which might soothe the hero's soul, underwrites the tragic element of the dramatic writing: the downfall of the mistaken hero, in whose presence there can be no restoration of order.[76] The very absence of music means the loss of harmony with Nature, the loss of center. Hence, the wings battering the melancholy hero about the head can only be dark in a world devoid of harmonious tension.

Wallenstein's tragic error consists not so much in trusting in the stars; though, to be sure, by doing so he turns his gaze from the historical world. Rather, it lies in the mistaken belief that he is invincible. Egotism and a lack of love combine to become his hamartia. As we recall from the early essay "Julius's Theosophy," a lack of love means rupture and chaos, i.e., a loss of center.

An example of this is Wallenstein's conversation with the lance corporal (*der Gefreite*), Heinrich Mercy, in act 3, scene 15. Still believing that he can save the world from strife and restore peace, the once great General passionately asserts: "All in dispute, and none to be / Their judge! Where will it end? Who can unravel / This tangled knot, that grows upon itself / And never stops? It must be cut asunder. / I feel I am the man that fate has chosen" (L 379; ll. 1985b–89; NA 8: 264–65).[77] Wallenstein is under the mistaken belief that he is capable of disentangling the knotted cords of life. Schiller's drama of history shows how the labyrinthine nature of history entangles even the most powerful of individuals and not simply by itself, as some sort of autonomous transcendent power, but always in conjunction with the human nature of the individual. In the end, history itself helps deconstruct the seemingly autonomous individual that was built up in the course of *Wallenstein's Camp.* Perhaps it was this aspect of Schiller's drama that prompted Hegel's criticism.

In the light of the internal development of the writer Friedrich Schiller, it is apparent in this later work that the historian of the Thirty Years War scanned the limits of his poetic-utopian inclinations as a writer of drama. Indeed, the historian seems to have won out over the dramatist.

In *Wallenstein,* the theme of war is juxtaposed to the theme of love. It is a curious fact that the only example of love in the trilogy is that of Max and Thekla. Both of these non-historical characters represent the realm of aesthetics. Max's death and Thekla's departure for Neustadt, where she will visit her lover's grave, indicate that there is simply no room for love (or beauty) in history as such. This tragic element of the drama constitutes a moral statement. As will become clear from our reading of the important series of letters *The Aesthetic Education of the Human Being,* which preceded the writing of *Wallenstein* by several years, the realization of the moral-rational State is unthinkable without training in aesthetics and the *sensus communis* it requires. In this light then, perhaps we discover a harmonious tension between the dramatist-aesthetician and the historian in the writer of *Wallenstein.*

Concerning my usage of key terminology, I will again define "history" as the sum total of all human action, reaction, and non-action. From this perspective, Wallensteins' *Gedankenspiel* (toying with ideas), itself a journey through the labyrinth of the mind, leads the supposed hero to the mistaken belief that his mind can shape history. The ensuing portrayal serves to highlight the writer's own skepticism concerning the merits of Idealism. We will explore this central issue of scholarship in more detail in the next chapter.

In *Wallenstein,* the connection to the writer's early work is quite apparent. In the monologue of the fourteenth scene of the same act, Wallenstein, now dressed in full armor, feels he is the same man he was years before. "And still I feel myself the same as ever! / The spirit shapes the body for its dwelling, / And Friedland soon will fill his camp about him" (L 391; ll. 1812–14; NA 8: 258).[78] Another source of Wallenstein's tragic error is his underestimation of the influence of the body (matter) on the mind (spirit).

His actions thus work against the harmonious balance between mind and body. Rather ironically, Wallenstein's own words raise this central issue: "Part the head and limbs, / and you will see in which the soul was dwelling" (L 391; ll.1817b–18; NA 8: 258).[79] The declaration refers to more than the soldiers who may still join him. Not having appreciated the healing power of harmonious tension between all things, Schiller's hero must suffer a tragic end.

A preliminary conclusion is that Schiller's "hero" collapses as much from within (physiology) as he does from forces outside his person, namely history. At the crossroads of physiology and history, Wallenstein's aspirations constitute merely an idea. Wallenstein's ideas have no regulative function, primarily so because they are centered only in the self.

Concerning the metaphysical dimension of the play, Wallenstein's rejection of religion as an urge that all animals obey ("der Tiere Trieb") (l. 1678; NA 8: 251)—a distant echo of Franz von Moor—leaves little hope for salvation. To be sure, Schiller's drama is no martyr-play and to speak of salvation in this dramatization of history may seem beside the point. However, given the writer's own upbringing, the influence of Swabian pietism on his thinking, and his preoccupation with the nature of death (the metaphysical dimension of his writings), the issue of salvation is still relevant. The several references in the texts alluding to Wallenstein's alleged pact with the Devil and union with the forces of Hell (Wallenstein-Faust, or Wallenstein-Mephistopheles) also raise the question of salvation. For the writer Friedrich Schiller, as we shall see, the means to salvation is found in the play-drive of art.

I have intimated that the very heart of the dramatic events of Schiller's *Wallenstein* is the love relationship between Max and Thekla. This warrants closer examination. Since both characters are not historical, they represent the aesthetic sphere. It is not coincidental that the lovers' relationship should unfold near the center of *Die Piccolomini,* in act 3, scene 5. Of the two companions, Thekla is the one who is familiar with the deceptive and deceitful politics of the nobility. To Max, she pleads that he should trust no one but her at the court, not even her father. Max misunderstands Wallenstein. His tragic error consists, perhaps, of mistaking Wallenstein for himself: "He shall decide my fortune, he is frank / and undeceiving, hates their crooked ways. / He is good and noble" (L 279; ll. 1700–1702b; NA 8: 127).[80]

Though he has lived with Wallenstein for ten years, Max perceives in his mentor only attributes native to himself. All his hopes and aspirations seem to be tied up with the seemingly invincible leader; that is, they are housed in someone other than himself. This too is merely an idea, the shattering of which will seal Max's tragic fate.

Piccolomini 3.6 calls for the following staging: "(*MAX tears himself from her embrace and goes out, the COUNTESS accompanying him. THEKLA at first lets her eyes follow him, then paces the room in agitation before*

standing still lost in thought. She picks up a guitar which is lying on the
table, and after playing a melancholy prelude, begins to sing" (L 282; NA
8: 129).[81] In act 3, scene 7, Thekla sings to the sounds of a stringed instrument. She laments:

> The world so empty, so dead my heart's fire,
> No more can there be to delight my desire,
> Thou holy one, call back thy child to thy breast,
> I have tasted earth's joys, and now I would rest,
> For life, ah! and love I have known.[82]
>
> (L 282; NA 8: 130)

Thekla accepts the facts of history. She is in no way naive. In this way she
resembles Luise Miller in *Intrigue and Love,* who recognizes the impossibil-
ity of love in a cunning and deceitful world, as well as Lady Milford, whose
experiences testify to this fact. Thekla's lamentation is also reminiscent of
Amalia's complaint in the garden scene in *The Robbers.*

There is little question that Thekla's character is stronger than Max's.
The younger Piccolomini decries and defies the enchainment of the body to
the physical world. For Thekla, however, "Our own heart's prompting is the
voice of fate" ("Der Zug des Herzens ist des Schicksals Stimme") (L 285;
l. 1840; NA 8: 133). As in the dramatic literature of the German Enlightenment, the trust in the ability of the human heart and intellect to assume
responsibility for one's own destiny replaces the ancient belief in the gods
of fate. "I can be his alone. It is his gift / To me, this fair new life that now
I live. / He has a right to what he has created. / For what was I, before his
love inspired me?" (L 285; ll. 1841–44; NA 8: 133).[83] Clearly, Thekla is
rooted in herself and, to that extent, is an enlightened character. In this
respect she also resembles Goethe's liberated heroine of *Iphigenia on Tauris*
[*Iphigenie auf Tauris*] (1787).

> That I may claim to own myself, I know now.
> I am acquainted with the strength of will,
> Indomitable, here in my breast,
> And for the highest I can stake my all.[84]
>
> (L 285; ll. 1850–53; NA 8: 133)

As we discover, however, it is not only the individual but also history that
plays a key role in determining the series of dramatic events. Somewhat
like Luise Miller, Thekla acknowledges her position within the labyrinth of
history. In her monologue in 3.9, she sees that "here but the dismal clang
of war resounds" ("Nur dumpfes Kriegsgetöse rasselt hier") (L 287; l. 1896;
NA 8: 135). She believes that she is being dragged by "fate" (read: history)
into an abyss.

Bearing me onward with its mighty storm [lit. divine might]
To the abyss, I cannot bid it stay.[85]

(L 287; ll. 1905–1906; NA 8: 135)

Instead of the intrigues of the early dramatic writings, secrets seem to drive the dramatic action of Schiller's later drama. In the light of the metaphorical level of the writer's language, secrets of the heart form a net, in which all the characters of the play become entangled. Octavio Piccolomini explains the dilemma to his son precisely in these terms. "Till now I could entrust you to your heart, / To your own judgement and your innocence. / But when I see them spread their fatal nets / To snare that very heart—the secret which / [*Staring pointedly at him*] You keep from me makes me disclose my own" (L 306; ll. 2309–14; NA 8: 157).[86] Like strings, however, nets can also be torn apart.

The metaphor of chains is employed at this point to underscore Wallenstein's apparent act of emancipation from the bonds of loyalty to the Emperor. "Broken is every bond / That binds the captain to his Emperor" (L 307; ll. 2347c–49b; NA 8: 159).[87] Max cannot bear hearing the truth. His loyalty to his surrogate father binds. As Octavio is given to say, "Your heart feels stronger love for Wallenstein, / For since you were a boy, a mighty bond / Of trust and reverence has drawn you to him" (L 311; ll. 2487–89; NA 8: 164).[88] Max's tragic error consists in his overconfidence in the dictates of the human heart and his unconditional (unenlightened) trust in Wallenstein, i.e., someone else, to help realize his dreams. To his biological father, Max exclaims, "Your judgment may speak false, but not my heart" ("Dein Urteil kann sich irren, nicht mein Herz") (L 313; l. 2547; NA 8: 166). Later, in 3.21, Max realizes: "Too great the trust I placed in my own heart" ("Zu viel vertraut ich auf das eigne Herz") (L 409; l. 2283; NA 8: 277), by which we infer that he has placed too much faith in Wallenstein. As a result, Max states, "I stand in doubt, do not know what to do" ("Ich stehe wankend, weiß nicht, was ich soll") (L 409; ll. 2284; NA 8: 277).

The reciprocal cooperation of heart and reason, thought and emotions, mind and body required for sound, moral judgment is nowhere in evidence. Max's overemphasis on the heart is juxtaposed to Wallenstein's overconfidence in the mind. The creative recurrence of the mind-body paradigm in Schiller's Wallenstein is thereby disclosed. It is not surprising then, that the absence of the harmonious tension between the two should contribute to the tragic downfall of both Max and Wallenstein.[89]

Near the end of his account of Wallenstein in *The History of the Thirty Years War,* Schiller concluded that the "colossal" talents of the ruler and hero General Wallenstein needed to be tempered by the gentler virtues of the human being.[90] The historian's description of Wallenstein elicits both admiration for and criticism of the military leader. The ruler and hero in the historical person, however, lacked humanity. In the dramatic trilogy,

Wallenstein's early history is described, by Gordon, as "Bent only upon greatness, like a man's" ("Auf große Dinge nämlich nur gerichtet") (L 420; l. 2551; NA 8: 288). As Gordon sees, however, Wallenstein "danced upon the swaying rope of life" (l. 2570), trodding "the way of greatness / With swift and gallant step" (L 420; l. 2572b–73a; NA 8: 289).[91] Here, too, Wallenstein is referred to as a dictator ("Diktator"; l. 2374c). Juxtaposed to these descriptions of Wallenstein stands Max's declaration, expressed in a biblical tone in 3.21: "Let / Us not seek greatness, but humanity" ("Nicht das Große, nur das Menschliche geschehe") (L 411; ll. 2327c–28; NA 8: 279).

If these traits—greatness and humanity—had been combined in one or the other of Schiller's central dramatis personae, perhaps that character would have approximated the model suggested by the historian's description in *The History of the Thirty Years War*. But that is speculative. The thematics of Schiller's dramatic writing is most telling. Not only does *Wallenstein* call up the question of the relation between greatness and humanity. It also addresses the relation, first suggested in the early essay "Julius's Theosophy," between love (Max/Thekla) and egotism (Wallenstein).

As I have suggested, the web of deceit caused by secrets is especially noticeable in Schiller's drama of history. Naively, perhaps, Max wishes to divulge the truth to Wallenstein. The writer's language in *Piccolomini* 5.3 is representative of the problem of political entanglement. "I go to find the Duke. This very day / I shall demand he clears his name before / The world, and with a plain, straight forward step / Breaks through the net your guile has set to snare him" (L 316; ll. 2610–13; NA 8: 170–71).[92] The direct and honest conveyance of truth, Max thinks, will sever the artificial web of political intrigue and restore harmony. But, as Thekla knows, the straight and narrow path is Max's manner, not Wallenstein's. In fact, the more Wallenstein approaches his secret goal, the tighter the web of deceit becomes.

When Max finally confronts Wallenstein in act 2, scene 2, of *Wallenstein's Death*, the motif of the straight path is repeated. To Wallenstein, Max insists on making "a choice between my heart and you" ("eine Wahl / zu treffen zwischen dir und meinem Herzen") (L 348; ll. 717c–18; NA 8: 205). Shattered by the realization that his friend has not been truthful with him, Max bewails the rift within his own heart, that is, between his physical and intellectual natures. "Oh! what a rift you open in my heart! / The native impulse of my old respect, / The sacred custom of obedience / That I have paid your name, must I deny?" (L 349; ll. 736–39; NA 8: 206).[93] And: "My senses still are bound in thrall to you, / Although my bleeding soul tears itself free!" (L 349; ll. 743–44; NA 8: 206).[94] For Wallenstein, the world ("Welt") is narrow and the mind ("Geist") expansive. While thoughts stand in close relation to each other, he is given to say, in the space of life matter constantly collides with matter. Wallenstein, too, acknowledges the consequences of the breach in their relationship. "The bond of love shall thus be torn apart, / Not gently loosed, and you will make this rent / That is so painful, yet more painful still" (L 413–14; ll. 2380–82; NA 8: 282).[95] As the concluding stage directions to this scene indicate, Max experiences painful emotional turmoil (the sensuous), while Wallenstein is lost deep in thought (the intellectual). It would seem that the fates of Wallenstein and Max, like Mary Stuart and Elizabeth, are mysteriously conjoined. Perhaps, then, these pairs of characters should be considered as two parts of a greater whole, the harmonious tension of each pair, however, is tragically lacking.

Relations with the Emperor are referred to at least three times in act 2, scene 6, alone as malice, or, literally, malady ["Kränkung" (l. 1145; NA 8: 223)]. In *The History of the Thirty Years War,* the historian characterized Wallenstein in similar terms: "His ambition was limitless, his pride unshakeable, his domineering spirit / mind incapable of tolerating a malice [malady?]" (NA 18: 132).[96] There, also, he referred to Wallenstein as a criminal ("Verbrecher"). The perceived insult or offense is a motivating factor behind Wallenstein's alleged treason. Octavio tells Butler that it was the Duke who tried to tear him away ("Losreißung") from the Emperor (l. 1147a; NA 8: 223). Consequently, Octavio encourages Wallenstein's allies to dissociate themselves ("trennen") from their leader.

Still reeling from the pain of having been betrayed, Max launches one last verbal attack against his father in act 2, scene 7. It is apparent that he still clings to the idea that truth could have vanquished all. Disillusioned, Max despairs—"My trust, my faith, my hopes, all are destroyed, / For everything I valued was a lie" (L 366; ll. 1214–15; NA 8: 227).[97] Still, there is one last thing that endures: the binding power of love. "Our love, the only pure spot that yet remains / Still undefiled in all humanity" (L 366; ll. 1220–21; NA 8: 227).[98] The physical, historical world having crumbled, there is still hope in the metaphysical realm, which binds the world to Nature, tapping the power of the universe.

The motif of the loving but suffering heart is fully developed. It is hardly coincidental that the motif should be combined with references to sound. Max laments having to leave Thekla, i.e., love: "No, she must see my suffering, my pain / Hear the lament of my dismembered soul, / And shed her tears on my account—Oh! men / Are cruel, but she is like an angel; From raging grief and hideous despair / My soul she will deliver, ease this pain / Of death with gentle comfort and lament" (L 367; ll. 1237–43; NA 8: 228).[99] Still, Max insists on trusting the dictates of his heart. Reminiscent of Thekla's words, he faults Octavio for not following "the voice of the heart" ("des Herzens Stimme") (l. 1262b; NA 8: 229). Though the scene ends with father and son embracing each other, they are directed to leave the stage from different ends. In other words, the natural bond between them has been permanently ruptured.

The exchange between the Duchess (mother) and Thekla (daughter) in act 3 also discloses the problem of rupture. Of her life with the great commander, the Duchess exclaims: "I lived with him a life of anxious dread, /

And always to the brink of the abyss, / As if to fall, his dizzy footsteps led"
(L 373; ll. 1382–84; NA 8: 236).[100] This widening gulf in the relationship
between Wallenstein and his wife is what Thekla laments when she refuses
to help recuperate her father's spirit with the aid of the harmonious, i.e.,
healing strains of music.

By act 3, scene 18, Max knows that his relationship with Thekla cannot
endure. Even Wallenstein declares, "The time / Of love and tender gentleness is gone" (L 402; ll. 2077c–78; NA 8: 269).[101] The motif of the fetters
and enchainment surfaces once again as love is eradicated from history. In
Max's words, "One wicked action follows on the other / Like close-forged
links within a hideous chain" (L 403; ll. 2133–34; NA 8: 271).[102] Rather
than attribute the cause to an other-worldly force (fate), Max ascribes his
lamentable situation to the feud between the fathers. For, in this cultural
environment, the rupture in the fathers' relationship also means that Max
and Thekla will have to sever theirs as well. Schiller reworks the metaphor
by assigning Wallenstein the following analogy:

> A net of love I spun and wound about you,
> Break from it if you can—to me you are,
> Bound fast by every tender bond of spirit,
> By every tie of natural affection.[103]
>
> (L 404; ll. 2166–2170; NA 8: 272)

Struggling to retain Max's allegiance, Wallenstein insists:

> You were planted in me, I am your Emperor,
> Belonging to me, obeying me, *that*
> Is your honor, your natural law.[104]
>
> (L 404; ll. 2183–2185; NA 8: 272)

The rift within Max's heart, that is, within human nature, is drawn out
especially well in act 3, scene 21. Recognizing the Faustian dilemma of two
competing souls in his breast, Max confesses: "Too great the trust I placed
in my own heart, / I stand in doubt, do not know what to do" (L 409; ll.
2283–84; NA 8: 277).[105] Max now tries to give himself over to Thekla: "Here,
upon this heart, / So holy, pure, infallible, I will / Rely, your love shall be
my oracle" (L 410; ll. 2302b–4; NA 8: 278).[106] As we have seen, Max divorces
himself from greatness ("Das Große") and advocates the divinely human
sphere ("das Menschliche"). Though aware that their relationship must end,
Thekla insists that while fate (read: history) may separate them, their hearts
will remain united. The scene ends with a plastic image of the two lovers
embracing motionless for one last time while the cry "Vivat Ferdinandus!"
rings out to the accompaniment of martial instruments ("kriegerischen In-
strumenten") (L 412; NA 8: 280). The embrace of love stands as a symbol
of hope over and against the crippling intervention of history.

The critical climax of the play comes in 3.23 where Max takes leave of Wallenstein. The highly expressive language employed at this moment of departure exhibits, both thematically and metaphorically, one of the predominant aspects of Schiller's work. We have cited part of the exclamation, but it is important at this point to cite the entire passage. "The bond of love shall thus be torn apart, / Not gently loosed, and you will make this rent, / That is so painful, yet more painful still. / You know that I have not yet learnt to live / Without you—to the wilderness I go / Alone, and everything that I hold dear / Stays here behind" (L 414; ll. 2380–86a; NA 8: 282).[107] Wallenstein's refusal to grasp Max's outstretched hand is a visible sign of the final breach in their relationship. It is not coincidental that the martial trumpets should sound. Wallenstein now blocks Max's path to his daughter as well. The writer's several direct uses of the verb *reißen* demonstrate the finality of the rupture. History seems to triumph over the culture of love as Max dies, willingly, on the battlefield. As the Hauptmann narrates later in act 4, scene 10, Max and his companions fought bravely, like animals, to the very end. "Like savage tigers now they fight" ("Gleich wilden Tigern fechten sie") (L 439; l. 3057a–b; NA 8: 312).

The binary opposition constituting the idealist-realist paradigm, which was first worked out most consequentially in Schiller scholarship by Ernst Stahl,[108] breaks down in the light of the dramatic action and of the writer's characterizations of both Max and Thekla. The fact is that Max's heart dictates he follow a different course than the one prescribed by the times. He may well have been sheltered. To Wallenstein, Max had admitted that he had not yet learned to live without him (ll. 2383). But this confession hardly reflects a naive attitude about the nature of reality. Thekla recognizes what history means for those who espouse the (moral) principles of love and humanity. In 3.9 of *Piccolomini,* she noted: "Fierce struggles lie before us" ("Uns drohen harte Kämpfe") (L 287; l. 1891b; NA 8: 135). Still, there is hope that the divine power of love will one day transform reality: "O love, O power divine, give us your strength!" ("Du, Liebe, gib uns Kraft, du göttliche!") (L 287; l. 1892; NA 8: 135). For his part, Max struggles with reconciling his former image of Wallenstein, a reflection of his own hopes and aspirations, with the knowledge that the General is not the champion of right. Wallenstein's hard words to Max in *Death* 3.18 express the ugly truth: "The time. Of love and tender gentleness is gone, / Revenge and hatred come to take their turn. / I can forget I am a man, as he [the Emperor] does" (L 402; ll. 2077c–80; NA 8: 269).[109]

At this point, Schiller the writer draws both upon the Faust-legend and the history of the Laocoön group. Like the traditional Dr. Faustus, Schiller's Wallenstein asserts unashamedly: "Who can stand / Against the might of hell!" ("Wer vermag, / Der Hölle Macht zu widerstehn") (L 402–3; ll. 2108c–9; NA 8: 270). Like Laocoön, Max feels himself being entwined by snakes. Unlike the Laocoön group, however, Wallenstein lacks the loving concern of a true father who would forsake his own interests and risk his life to save his son. Max Piccolomini is tormented by the idea of both fathers' "guilt and wickedness" ("Doppelschuld und Freveltat"), which "entwine / Us like serpent pair in loathsome knot?" ("Uns gräßlich wie ein Schlangenpaar umwinden?") (L 403; ll. 2138–39; NA 8: 271). Why is it, he gasps, should their fathers' unreconciled hate for each other "Sunder us too, and rend our bond of love?" ("Auch uns, die Liebenden, zerreißend scheiden?") (L 403; l. 2141; NA 8: 271). Clearly, it is self-interest and power politics that deride the humanity which both Max and Thekla espouse. If there are any progressive heroes or heroines in Schiller's *Wallenstein,* then they are Max and Thekla, not Wallenstein or Octavio. In the end, however, it is precisely the idea of progress in history that the writer problematicizes by way of Max's death and Thekla's departure.[110]

In retrospect, the rift between Wallenstein, Octavio, and Max is greater than scholars have admitted. For, if Max represents the race or the writer's aspirations for humanity and Wallenstein and Octavio the political variations within history as given, then the drama dicloses the gap between the idea of humanity and the human condition. Max's death may then be interpreted as a protest against the nature of historical reality and of the intrigues and entanglements of power politics. Deciding against Wallenstein in *Death* 3.23, Max points out the gross disparity between the way things are and the way things should be. At the same time, however, he recognizes that, though duties clash ("Pflichten streiten Pflichten"; l. 724), as in history, he must remain true to his heart, that is to his true self. Though innocent of wrongdoing, there is a deeper-lying connection here between the character Max Piccolomini and the early dramatic and prose figures Karl von Moor and Christian Wolf, both of whom established their identity by coming to terms with their personal histories.

Thekla's question in her monologue in act 4, scene 12—"What is this life when starved of love's sweet breath?" ("Was ist das Leben ohne Liebes-glanz?") (L 443; l. 3163; NA 8: 317)—posits a predicament for more than one age, perhaps. Indeed, "All beauty on this earth fate thus reproves!" ("Das ist das Los des Schönen auf der Erde!") (L 443; l. 3180; NA 8: 318). Max's death and Thekla's journey to Neustadt suggest that, in history as given, there is no place for the culture of love they represent. The idea of love as the gravitational center of life is not realized in the drama. The characterization of love in the relationship between Max and Thekla underscores the ineluctable nature of historical reality, which carries this work beyond the early drama *Intrigue and Love.* As non-historical figures, that is, aesthetic constructs, the lovers function as a sign of hope and an improved future while thematizing the problem of a world without love.

While critics have endeavored to establish a direct line between the writing of *Wallenstein* and the essay *Concerning Naive and Sentimental Poetry,* I think it is more appropriate to appreciate the thematic continuity between the later dramatic writing and the series of letters *Concerning the Aesthetic Education of the Human Being*. For in that writing Schiller had articulated the centrality of a middle state of aesthetic freedom in the transition from a condition of passive suffering to an active state of thinking and willing. As beautiful forms of aesthetic freedom both Max and Thekla point beyond themselves, thus signaling the direction history should pursue. Unlike Wallenstein, the ideas they espouse perform a regulative function.

Before closing this part of our discussion, let us take a closer look at Schiller's characterization of Wallenstein. Of Max, Wallenstein says: "[He turned] all harsh reality to dream, / And weaving vapours of a golden dawn / About the common clarity of things.— / Fired by the passion of his warm affection, / Life's dull and everyday creations seemed, / To my astonishment, to rise ennobled" (L 455; ll. 3446–51; NA 8: 333–34).[111] Max's absence evokes in Wallenstein more than a sense of loss. It is as if part of him had died. The writer's reference to organic nature at this point in his characterization of Wallenstein is especially apt.

> The blossom has been plucked out from my life,
> And cold and colourless I see it lying.[112]
> (L 455; ll. 3443–44; NA 8: 333)

Wallenstein and Max represent poles of human experience. In the end, Wallenstein, like Queen Elizabeth in *Mary Stuart,* stands alone. His departure from history underscores the folly of thinking that a human being, no matter how powerful or successful, is somehow insulated from the movement of history.

On the basis of the foregoing analysis, we conclude that, in *Wallenstein,* the writer traced the limits of the play of his own ideas. His cognitive-rational, i.e., critical faculty and knowledge of history informed, as it was, by his writings on history in 1789 and the early 1790s, as well as by the social-historical context of the aftermath of the French Revolution, tempered the activities of his imagination. Indeed, this grand dramatic trilogy may well be the most intricately woven product of the harmonious tension between criticism (reason) and creativity (imagination) in Friedrich Schiller's experience as a writer.

A Critique of Hegel's Criticism of *Wallenstein*

As much as the great German philosopher Georg Wilhelm Friedrich Hegel admired Friedrich Schiller's work, he was deeply disappointed in the dramatization of history in *Wallenstein*. In his short assessment "Concerning Wallenstein" ["Über Wallenstein"], the philosopher complained that, in Schiller's writing death triumphs over life. In his experience, Hegel was left with the "pathetic silence concerning the case of a powerful human being under a silent and deaf fate."[113] The philosopher desired a strong, positive hero, one who fights mightily both with and against the forces of history. According to his own dramatic theory in the *Aesthetics* [*Ästhetik*], Hegel insisted that tragic heroes must be active in order for the collision required of any tragedy to reach its axis.[114] Only through collision—that common denominator of history and tragedy alike—can the suspension ("Aufhebung") of the mutual destruction of two powerful characters representing two commanding worldviews be attained. Only at that moment can the truth of the historical content of tragedy be revealed to the recipient.

But the philosopher has a specific image of the historical Wallenstein in mind. He perceives in the once great commander a powerful ("mächtig") and great ("groß") man. Instead, Schiller has created a character who runs aground on history and is consumed by it. According to Hegel, in this case, there can be no reconciliation of the dramatic conflict. Hegel was correct when he asserted that the drama does not end as a theodicy.[115] That is precisely the point. History, that sum total of all human action, reaction, and non-action, in all its complex manifestations, proves to be more powerful than even the greatest human being. Clearly, then, Schiller's dramatization of history in *Wallenstein* flies in the face of Hegel's idealistic conception of the world-spirit ("Weltgeist"). It is important to note that Hegel had the younger, victorious crusader in mind, whereas Schiller's drama focuses on the later Wallenstein, the fallen hero. In the final analysis, Schiller's Wallenstein merely plays with ideas—"I took my pleasure in the thought alone" ("In dem Gedanken bloß gefiel ich mir") (L 329; *Death* 1.4; l. 148; NA 8: 183). His lack of action has already damned him.[116]

In retrospect, the myth of the powerful warrior has been deconstructed in the course of the dramatic writing. The audience cannot rest easy after such a dramatic performance. For, as Hegel sees, this kind of tragedy "tears the mind apart, from which we are unable to leap with a lightened heart!"[117] Rather than value this negatively, as does Hegel, I perceive this to be a positive sign of Schiller's abilities as a writer of dramatic literature. Furthermore, I find Hegel's employment of the metaphor of tearing or wrenching especially appropriate given the nature of Schiller's style of writing. If Hegel is correct about the dramatic effect of the piece, the fact that the recipient cannot experience a catharsis discloses a break with the requirements of ancient, Aristotelian tragedy, a split which the German philosopher implicitly bewails. Hence, Schiller's *Wallenstein* may be viewed as a positive, new beginning in the course of the history of drama, and not simply as a culmination point of Aristotelian dramatic theory.

In the final analysis, the candid confrontation with historical reality in Schiller's dramatization of history calls up the need for a better future. Perhaps, then, the practical value of studying world history is that it instills hope. Against Hegel, I redirect our attention to the benediction from *Wallenstein's Death:* "Nicht / Das Große, nur das Menschliche geschehe" ("Let / Us not seek greatness, but humanity") (L 4110; ll. 2327c–28; NA 8: 279).

5

The Tasks of Culture: Beauty and the Aesthetic Education of the Human Being

I. Immanuel Kant's *Critique of the Power of Judgment*

In the original introduction to his *Critique of the Power of Judgment* [*Kritik der Urteilskraft*] (1790), Immanuel Kant insisted that, if we did not assume the fundamental unity of all things, all reflection would be blind. Without presupposing unity, we would not be able to account for the nature of things.[1] The principle of reflection demands that empirically determined concepts be assigned to all natural objects. In short, in order to make the world intelligible, we must assume a form for all products of Nature. Kant advocates that the principle of the reflecting power of judgment is simply ("bloß") a principle for the logical use of judgment. It says to regard Nature a priori, *as if* it comprised a logical system of diverse objects ("Mannigfaltigkeit") operating according to empirical laws.[2]

Kant argued that the possibility of regarding experience as a system was also necessary. For without this assumption, we could never hope to come to terms with a labyrinth of diverse objects ("Labyrinth der Mannigfaltigkeit") of possible, yet specific laws.[3] With the aid of the power of judgment ("Urteilskraft"), we are able to think of the particular as subsumed under the general according to a particular principle.[4] In this way, our minds prescribe purposiveness ("Zweckmäßigkeit") to the manifold nature of things.[5] Still, Kant admits that this idea of the finality of Nature is simply reflected ("bloß reflektiert").[6]

The Königsberg philosopher held that the ground of determination ("Bestimmungsgrund") of the aesthetic power of judgment ("ästhetische Urteilskraft") is sensation ("Empfindung"). Hence, aesthetic judgment is conditioned by feelings of pleasure and displeasure ("Lust" and "Unlust"). This type of judgment is constitutive, and not regulative, since it assesses things according to a rule and not with regard to concepts. It is the agreement of the form of an object with the cognitive faculty without there being any connection in fact between that form and a particular concept. A purely

subjective ("bloß subjektiv"), i.e., aesthetic, judgment precedes the enjoyment of the same and is the basis of this kind of pleasure in the harmony of
the faculty of knowledge.[7] Kant's emphasis on the purely subjective, aesthetic judgment and the faculty of knowledge will become a serious point
of contention in Schiller's response to the third critique. For Kant, the type
of pleasure associated with aesthetic judgment is purely contemplative
("bloß kontemplativ"). It evokes no interest in the object.[8] The source of
this type of pleasure is simply the consciousness of the purely formal purposiveness of the activity in the play of the subject's powers of knowledge.[9]
According to Paragraph Nine of the *Critique of the Power of Judgment,* the
powers of knowledge ("Erkenntniskräfte") that are set into motion ("ins
Spiel gesetzt") in a judgment of taste are in a state of free play ("in einem
freien Spiele") precisely because they are not restricted to a particular rule
of knowledge by a specific concept.[10]

Later in my discussion of Jürgen Habermas, I will investigate Kant's
conclusion that, though subjective, a judgment of taste must be communicable on a general or universal level ("allgemein mitteilbar"). Here it is important to note that the eighteenth-century philosopher is interested solely
in defining the nature of a "pure" judgment of taste and only in the forms
(which are generally communicable) and not in the content of beautiful
objects (which, by extension of his argument, are not).

Schiller's Personal Copy of Kant's *Critique of the Power of Judgment*

Dieter Henrich was the first to draw attention to the existence of Schiller's
personal copy of Kant's third critique. It is part of the permanent collection
of Schiller's works at the Schiller National Museum adjacent to the German
Archive for Literature (Deutsches Literaturarchiv) in Marbach am Neckar.
The title page reads: *Critik der urtheilskraft* von Immanuel Kant. Berlin und
Libau bey Lagarde und Friedrich 1790.[11] In early February 1991, I compared
Schiller's copy to the allegedly complete register of the marginal notations
by Jens Kulenkampff.[12] The results of this research are interspersed through-
out this and subsequent chapters as well as the footnotes.

For Kant, beauty consists in the agreement of the form of an object with
the laws of sensousness. He argues that the nature of aesthetic satisfaction
with respect to laws is the same in all human beings. Aesthetic judgment
refers to the intuitively apprehensible (*anschaulich*) form of an object.[13]
From Schiller's marginal notations to the third critique, it is clear that the
writer was especially intrigued by Kant's point that beauty is a quality of
the "Gestalt," i.e., the form *of an object,* which is *given* in the apprehension
of beauty. Schiller underlined this point repeatedly in his copy of Kant's
treatise. One of the central ideas Kant developed concerning the judgment
of taste is the nature of pleasure. Paragraph Twelve includes one of the many
references to the object behind the beautiful appearance.

The consciousness of merely formal purposiveness in the play of the subject's powers of cognition attending a representation, whereby an object is given, is pleasure itself because it contains a determining ground of the subject's activity in respect of the revival of its cognitive powers, that is an internal causality (which is purposive) but without being limited to a particular cognition, [and] consequently containing a mere form of the subjective purposiveness of a representation in an aesthetic judgment.[14]

As indicated above, Schiller underlined Kant's point that an object—and not simply an appearance—is present in the beautiful form. Jens Kulenkampff did not note that Schiller underlined the word "Lust" (pleasure) twice in the complete passage quoted, in part, above.

Schiller corrected the ending of the accusative indefinite article, as shown, and then added the third-person verb form "einfält" vs. "enthält."[15] Elsewhere, Kulenkampff fails to note that the writer double underlined the words "Spiel" (play) and "Einbildungskraft" (imagination). This is a serious oversight since only these three key words, namely "pleasure," "play," and "imagination" are underscored in this way and each of them figures prominently in Schiller's aesthetic theories. In a passage concerning the idea that an object is given in a judgment of taste, Schiller underlined the word "Spiel" twice and added the following marginal notation: "Veränderung und Bewegung" ("change and motion").[16] Both of these words were also underlined in this way. Schiller's addendum to Kant's argument is especially significant since it provides a probable answer to why the writer underscored the three key words "pleasure," "play," and "imagination." Each of these terms connotes motion and, if motion, then, in all likelihood, change. Surely, the nature of play is such that it does not remain stationary. The game changes. It is indeed significant that Kant did not draw the connection that may well have intrigued the writer Friedrich Schiller. The notation concerning change and motion and the connection established thematically through double-underlining complement Schiller's much later underscoring of Kant's words concerning "perpetually progressing culture" ("*immer fortschreitende Kultur*").[17] As we know, this point is central to Schiller's argument in *Concerning the Aesthetic Education of the Human Being in a Series of Letters.*

Schiller's discussion of the nature of beauty in the *Kallias* letters mirrors Kant's interest in the nature of a pure judgment of taste. However, unlike Kant, Schiller was not satisfied with the exclusively subjective basis of the experience of beauty; rather, he sought to determine an objective ground to this phenomenon. The search may well have been sparked by Kant's repeated statement that an object is given whose form is apprehended as beautiful, as suggested by Schiller's own notations in his personal copy of the *Critique of the Power of Judgment*. Before turning to the *Kallias* letters, however, let us lay out the rest of Kant's general argument.

When our conception or idea ("Vorstellung") of an object is accompanied by a feeling of pleasure and we ascertain that this experience should evoke pleasure in all subjects observing the same object, then, *and only then,* have we formed an aesthetic judgment. We term the object of this experience beautiful and the faculty of this universal power of judgment, taste. Such a judgment is no longer simply subjective, but to a degree objective, since the object is considered to be beautiful by all subjects. Common assent *(sensus communis)* is a precondition of judgments of taste for Kant, and such judgments take into account similar judgments of all other human beings. Since aesthetic judgment is a subset of the power of judgment, its assessments cannot be mere expressions of subjectivity in the narrow sense, i.e., purely subjective responses. Rather, aesthetic judgment appropriates to itself a rule of the upper faculty of knowledge which, in light of the a priori conditions of reflection, is law-giving. As Kant makes clear, "this autonomy, however, is not . . . objective, i.e., by way of concepts of things or possible actions, but valid only subjectively ("bloß subjektiv") *for judgment based on feeling,* which, when capable of making a claim to universal validity ("Allgemeingül- tigkeit"), proves its origin, one that is based a priori on principles."[18] This law-giving force Kant names *heautonomy* since the power of judgment is derived from neither Nature nor freedom but gives itself its own law.[19]

In sum, Kant recognized clearly that the special conception of a whole proceeding from the possibility of parts is a mere idea ("eine bloße Idee"). When understood as the ground of causality, this idea is called purpose ("Zweck").[20] Kant ends the introduction to the third critique by defining beauty as "die Zweckmäßigkeit der Form in der Erscheinung" (the purpos- iveness of form in appearance) and taste as "das Beurteilungsvermögen derselben" (the faculty of judgment of the same).[21]

In concluding this section, I wish to underscore a point that the Königsb- erg philosopher made in the introduction to the first edition of the *Critique of the Power of Judgment* of 1790. For Kant, the faculty of taste (as the aesthetic power of judgment) was to be investigated only ("bloß") transcen- dentally and *not* in the light of the cultivation and culture of taste ("nicht zur Bildung und Kultur des Geschmacks").[22] In the light of Schiller's letters on the aesthetic education of the human being, there can be little doubt that this statement became one of the main provocations for Schiller's ultimate departure from the major tenets of Kant's philosophy.

II. Concerning the Nature of Beauty

A. (He-)autonomy

In a letter of February 23, 1793, addressed to his friend Christian Körner, Schiller conveyed some of his most original thoughts concerning the quality of beauty. The letter forms the cornerstone of the *Kallias* Letters.[23]

According to Schiller's letter, the nature of the technical form of any given object is indistinguishable from all other objects because of its own unique structure ("Oeconomie"). When an object is deemed beautiful, this technical form *appears* to be determined by the very nature of the thing itself. The technical form of a beautiful object thus appears to be self-contained, i.e., autonomous. When the technical form of an object in any way reflects the impact of external forces, something foreign ("etwas Fremdes") is said to have affected it. Once affected, the object can no longer be true to its own existence ("Existenz").[24] Schiller was exploring the Kantian proposition that beauty originates entirely from within the object itself. The technical structure of the thing in question is both necessary ("nothwendig") and inherent ("angebohren"). Should the object be shaped in any way from the outside, its technical form is simply given ("gegeben") and contingent ("zufällig").[25] In order for an object to be beautiful, then, its appearance must suggest freedom from external determination or, to state the matter positively, freedom of self-determination. This understanding of the nature of autonomy is the connecting link between the *Kallias* Letters and the letters *Concerning the Aesthetic Education of the Human Being*, which I explore further in part III. Before taking a closer look at this connecting link, let us explore the *Kallias* Letters from a new perspective.

B. The Example of the Musical Instrument and Schiller's Integrative Style

S. S. Kerry criticized Schiller for introducing the example of a musical instrument into his discussion of beauty and autonomy. Comparing Schiller to Kant, the problem is that "Schiller attributes . . . a separate noumenal reality to an inanimate, inorganic object, a pure artifact."[26] Kerry argues that, in order to be consistent with his own argument, the writer should have referred only to natural objects. Though Kerry appreciates the "more valid challenge" Schiller's position presents to Kant's idea of intellectual beauty,[27] it is illuminating that he should find in the example of the musical instrument further evidence of the writer's "naive vision intruding in the systematic argument."[28] We recall that the same kind of criticism was leveled against the writer by members of his dissertation committee when the candidate employed the metaphor of Nature's great lute to illustrate a point in the field of physiology.[29] To be sure, something else is clearly at work in this series of letters that complements the elaboration of a philosophical thesis.

Heinrich Mettler has suggested that Schiller's example of the musical instrument stands out against Immanuel Kant's conception of the perfection of Nature. The teleological power of judgment is at work in the art of the producer ("Mechanikus"). Hence, the purposiveness of the musical instrument (technical aspect) is underlined. Unlike humanmade objects, however, natural objects possess a self-creative power. They are organized products of Nature in which everything is purpose and, reciprocally, also the means.[30]

With beautiful objects of art, the inherent purposiveness or perfection of the thing comes into appearance. In the case of a natural object, however, the self-determined and self-determinate quality of an object or inner necessity of form ("die innere Notwendigkeit der Form"), as Schiller states, is the primary feature of its appearance.[31] In effect, then, Schiller transferred Kant's distinction between autonomy and heautonomy over to his description of the difference between natural and humanmade objects of beauty.[32] The writer clearly differentiates these types of objects by degree and substance.

In short, in the *Kallias* Letters, Schiller was not so much interested in the technical form of the object as he was in the freedom the object exudes. "*Freedom* alone," the writer asserts, "is the basis of the beautiful; technique is only the basis of our conception of freedom. . . . Technique . . . contributes to beauty only insofar as it serves to arouse the conception of freedom."[33]

The example of the musical (stringed) instrument is also an essential component of the *Kallias* Letters. To be sure, as a human-made object the musical instrument cannot fashion itself. Still, it too can be a beautiful object. We should give the writer credit for having noted that, unlike beautiful natural objects, "this technical form [of the instrument] is something external" and "that it has been forcefully imposed upon it by the understanding of the artist."[34] Most important, the example of the musical instrument serves as an analogy for the way *both* natural objects and those of human construction are in their "*aesthetic significance*" ["ästhetischer Bedeutung"]. Already at this point, then, the writer was moving one step ahead in his argument to a consideration of the social function of art as found in the series of letters *Concerning the Aesthetic Education of the Human Being*.[35]

Developing further the idea of independent action and the intimate association of beauty and morality, i.e., freedom, Schiller submitted that, for any beautiful object, including the moral human being, form and existence [content] must comprise the thing entirely. Concerning the major facilitator of what Schiller will call aesthetic education, it is expected "that even the forms of art must agree with the existence of the wholly shaped entity if they are to make a claim to the highest beauty."[36] We will return to this central point in our discussion of the published version of the correspondence between Schiller and Prince Christian of Schleswig-Holstein-Sonderburg-Augustenburg.

It should be pointed out that the core of Schiller's discussion in his correspondence with Christian Körner is preceded by references to the animal world. "A bird in flight is the most pleasant depiction of the material overcome by form, of gravitation overpowered by energy."[37] Indeed, when taking flight, a bird seems to defy the limitations of gravity.[38] The writer observes "that the ability to conquer gravitation is often used as a symbol of freedom."[39] His language is rich in some of the central metaphors he had already developed up to this point in his career. "We express the freedom of imagination by giving it wings; we allow Psyche to raise itself above the earthly with the wings of butterflies when we want to describe its freedom from the chains of matter."[40] But by appearing to transcend its technical, i.e., physical composition, a bird in flight can no longer be a beautiful, but is rather a sublime, manifestation of Nature. However, Schiller does not make this distinction between the beautiful and the sublime in his letter to Körner. Rather, as he had done in his early medical writings, he draws an analogy between gravity and human inclination. "Gravity maintains itself approximately like the lively power of the bird, as inclination—in the case of pure determinations of the will—maintains itself with law-giving Reason."[41] By associating free flight and the excursions of reason, the writer calls up the question of freedom.

Considering, for a moment, the historical context of the letters, it is indisputable that Schiller's interest in the problem of human freedom was sparked by the execution of Louis XVI, news of which horrified the writer. This reaction occurred one month before the writing of the letter under consideration, namely in January 1793.[42] The fact of Schiller's own tenuous state of health, i.e., the agonizing power of the body that sometimes disturbed the writer's mental concentration, was no doubt an additional reason for Schiller's interest in the sublimity of flight, that is freedom from gravity. From his letters and many other sources, it becomes clear that Schiller struggled with the problem of restriction even while advocating freedom from limitation.

It is a widespread scholarly opinion, advanced primarily by professional philosophers, that Schiller's argument concerning the nature of beauty and freedom is wanting in philosophical rigor and systematic development. S. S. Kerry found Schiller's reflections lacking in philosophical sophistication even though, as he notes, Schiller registered his own doubts concerning his commitment to this project in rigid philosophy.[43] Though initiating a philosophical discussion, Schiller's letter to Körner hardly constitutes a philosophical treatise. Rather, the letter evidences the merging of various intellectual activities. In this form, the writer did not and, perhaps, could not restrict himself to one topic, problem, or approach. In the light of Schiller's multidisciplinary activities, it is good to note S. S. Kerry's observation that "the philosophical and poetic modes are here so intertwined in the very texture of the language that either could be taken as the essence of the thing."[44] However, I am not partial to Kerry's reduction of Schiller's activities to the poet-philosopher anymore than I am to Benno von Wiese's, for Schiller was, I submit, first and foremost a writer.

Schiller's theory of an objective principle of beauty, though certainly incomplete, may well be "an ingenious account of the subjective conditions determining the experience of beauty."[45] At the same time, it is a theory that is "interrelated with thinking of a different order."[46] I submit that this thinking of a different order owes to the writer's comprehensive approach to reality. From this perspective, Kerry's observation that, in Schiller's style of argumentation, there are "opposed pronouncements, each of which has its validity in the mode of experience to which it refers"[47] has considerable merit. In his challenging comments on the traditional approach to the *Kallias Letters*, J. M. Ellis did not give Kerry his due.[48] Kerry was the first to draw attention to the "interaction" of various processes "in Schiller's thought and imagination."[49] For all his criticism of Schiller's general approach, Kerry could still appreciate the fact that "the special virtue" of Schiller's argument consists in "a mode of visualizing the world of objects which suspends the known enslavement of things to a general causality."[50] Perhaps the fundamental characteristic of the letters to Körner is that the writer develops his arguments by cognitive analogy. In sum, through the integration of diverse sources of knowledge, Schiller's writings traverse not only the traditional bounds of established fields of inquiry but also all those approaches to his work that are themselves bound by the specialized discipline to which they adhere.[51]

C. Beauty as "Freedom in Appearance"

Perhaps the most astute article by a professional philosopher on the nature of Kant's and Schiller's ideas on beauty is Dieter Henrich's essay "The Concept of Beauty in Schiller's Aesthetics" ("Der Begriff der Schönheit in Schillers Ästhetik," *Zeitschrift für philosophische Forschung* 11 [1957]: 527–47). It has been translated into English and included in a volume titled *Essays in Kant's Aesthetics*.[52]

Though calling Schiller's "philosophical" writings on aesthetics a "failure,"[53] as S. S. Kerry was to do a few years later, the German philosopher could still appreciate Schiller's daring attempt "'to move beyond [Kantian subjectivity and abstractness of thought] by intellectually grasping unity and reconciliation as the truth,'" as Hegel once said.[54] "Consequently," Henrich wrote, "we should not simply confirm the presence of contradictions and discrepancies in Schiller's philosophy; they should be understood as the results of such a process of thinking pointing beyond its own original foundations."[55] I submit that this process of thinking is attributable to the writer's multifaceted approach to reality. As Henrich has suggested, "the pressure of his [Schiller's] thought against the limits of his Kantianism, constantly constrained by the concepts of this system" was also "the source of what is fruitful and progressive in them [Schiller's philosophical writings]."[56] In the final analysis, perhaps it is the critical-creative nature of Schiller's writings that should command our attention.

This playful, creative-critical quality of Schiller's thinking distinguishes his thoughts on the nature of beauty from those of Immanuel Kant. Whereas Kant was drawn to a discussion of beauty by reflecting on the nature of theoretical reason, practical reason was Schiller's major point of departure. As Dieter Henrich noted, Schiller was not really interested in Kant's preoccupation with the problem of a transcendental theory of the possibility of knowledge.[57] For all its merits, the limits of Henrich's exclusively philosophical approach to Schiller's writings are exposed by the philosopher's undervaluation of the writer's anthropology as well as by his overemphasis on "Schiller the artist."[58] Schiller's emphasis on education (*Bildung*), cultivation, especially aesthetic education, clearly transcends the limits of Kant's philosophical writings.[59] In these writings, Schiller seemed preoccupied with the practical value of beauty for the progressive development of humankind.

In the *Letters Concerning the Sensations,* Moses Mendelssohn's Euphranor had argued that too much conceptual clarification of feelings will destroy emotion.[60] Dewhurst and Reeves have stated the case for beauty succinctly. "The appreciation of beauty requires an element of non-conceptual feeling: we sense the perfection behind beauty but cannot define it" (D/R, p. 121). Beauty escapes conceptualization. In short, it takes more than the powers of knowledge (Kant's "Erkenntniskräfte") to fully comprehend this quality. Perhaps the most intriguing aspect of beauty is that, though it cannot be compressed into a single concept, its existence is undeniable. Both sense and reason combine forces to create knowledge of beauty.

Unlike Mendelssohn and Kant, however, Schiller believed he had determined an objective ground for the knowledge of beautiful objects. Henrich explains: "In beautiful form and in the work of art the ground of our moral being, which otherwise discloses itself only to the reflective understanding, is supposed to confront us in intuitive form. 'Freedom' here means to be completely self-determined, to develop according to inner necessity independent of external influences,"[61] but also, I would add, in accordance with what Schiller terms our unchangeable determination ("unveränderliche Bestimmung") as human beings. Thus, "the beautiful appearance confronts us as a form freely taking its own course, without hindrance, a form in which all its parts make up a harmonious whole resting on a single ground."[62] By emphasizing the autonomy of self-determination, Schiller went beyond British empiricist aesthetics, specifically Edmund Burke.[63] At the same time, however, by emphasizing the role of sensuousness, Schiller transcended the limits of the rational-objective aesthetics of Christian Wolff.[64] Indeed, already Schiller's early aesthetics were, as he characterized it, "sensous-rational" ("sinnlich-vernünftig") in nature. In the light of Schiller's sensuous-rational aesthetics, we can more fully appreciate the interconnection between the writer's early anthropology and his later writings.

Precisely because the writer has not argued in a philosophically rigorous manner, that is, as a (traditional) professional philosopher, perhaps the true nature of his argument lies elsewhere. The example of the musical instrument in the letter of February 23, 1793, exhibits at least two things: 1) the strong influence of the metaphor of the stringed instrument as a symbol of the harmony—and now beauty—of the universe and its problematization in the *Kallias* Letters; and 2) the importance of the idea of the aesthetic education of the human being, which the writer was beginning to formulate simultaneously with the composition of his letters to Christian Körner.

In retrospect, the one-sided view of Schiller's classical essays that form and beautiful appearance are somehow detached from physical circumstances and, yet, the highest good, namely the conception of Schiller as Platonist,[65] overstates the "idealist" components of Schiller's writings. Idea is in no way detached from the sensuous-material world in Schiller's works. Indeed, the early tension between anthropolology (physiology) and metaphysics (theosophy) works against the longstanding view of Schiller as an idealist.[66] For Schiller, morality does not stem from the conflict between the human being's rational and sensuous natures, as Kant had maintained, but, rather, from the harmonious, i.e., beautiful tension between them.

III. A Closer Look at the Concept of Autonomy

The proceedings of the October 1988 symposium on "Autonomous Literature in Germany During the Age of the French Revolution," which was held at the State University of New York (Albany), form an important contribution not only to our understanding of German literature and theory of the late eighteenth century but also to the expanding field of international German studies. Most participants at the SUNY-Albany symposium tended to see in the development of the concept of aesthetic autonomy a critical response to the Reign of Terror following the French Revolution.[67] A great deal of the discussion revolved around Schiller's concept of autonomy, in particular the letters *Concerning the Aesthetic Education of the Human Being*. It is on these debates in particular that I focus our attention for a moment.

It is a curious fact that, despite the appearance in Germany of studies like Wolfgang Riedel's *Die Anthropologie des jungen Schiller* in 1985, the Albany conference did not include any discussion of the possible influence of Schiller's physiology on his later concept of heautonomy. Perhaps this has to do with the nature of German *Germanistik* in America. At one point in the deliberations, for instance, Wittkowski admitted "that German Germanistics is so strongly philosophically and ideologically conditioned and that we [Germanists] here all come from so many different backgrounds."[68] Part of the reason is certainly cultural, especially when we recall that the first serious investigation of the impact of Schiller's medical writings on his later works was conducted by Anglo-Saxon scholars, namely Kenneth Dewhurst and Nigel Reeves. Another reason may well be that *Germanistik* is still dominated by the close alliance between the study of poetry and the study of philosophy, which tends to exclude other fields of inquiry such as anthropology and medicine. A prime example of this is Benno von Wiese's long-standing book on Schiller.

In the introductory essay to the volume *Revolution und Autonomie: Deutsche Autonomieästhetik im Zeitalter der Französischen Revolution,* Wolfgang Wittkowski maintains that current debates concerning the autonomy of art owe, in large part, to the critical reception of German/Weimar classicism.[69] To be sure, the University of Wisconsin Workshop on the *Klassik-Legende*[70] was a turning point in contemporary interpretations of German classicism. One of the central issues of that workshop concerned the problem of aesthetic autonomy. Yet, the debate in this century over that question was fueled already by Herbert Marcuse and several other thinkers of Marxist persuasion. In the volume under consideration, for instance, one scholar cites Marcuse's provocative essay on the affirmative character of culture, "Über den affirmativen Charakter der Kultur."[71] In the postscript it will become clear just how deeply embedded the roots of this debate in the twentieth century really are. In the light of the debate between Marxists and non-Marxists, over the years, one of the reasons for the dispute over the question of autonomy in the volume under consideration is ideological in nature. Let us take a closer look.

Klaus Berghahn, also a participant in the Wisconsin Workshop, read-dresses the apparent problem of "Schiller's and Goethe's turn away from contemporary reality and their de-politicization of art" in his polemical contribution to the Albany conference.[72] Berghahn in the late 1980s attributes the "negation of reality" to Schiller (a point Herbert Marcuse had made long ago). This is not completely as abstract or worldless ("weltlos") as it may seem since the writer cultivates the ideal.[73] Berghahn writes: "Autonomous art acts critically toward deprived reality in the hope of keeping a more humane world alive. It withdraws from prescribed functionalization, (and) chooses the circuitous route [detour] of an aesthetic education in order to presentify the ideals of humanity in the appearance(s) [Vorschein] of art."[74] As we will see in chapter ten, Berghahn's thesis is reminiscent of Herbert Marcuse: "For Schiller, aesthetic appearance [Schein] is radically divided from reality. . . . Autonomy as the negation of reality is the presupposition of true art which relies on the help of ideas for its aesthetic practice [Praxis]."[75] The debate concerning autonomy thus tends to turn on the positive or negative reception of Marxist critics such as Ernst Bloch, Georg Lukács, and Herbert Marcuse, and the work of the musico-sociologist Theodor Adorno, though Berghahn does not refer to any of these thinkers directly.

The general consensus among participants at the Albany symposium, however, was that, for Schiller, an autonomous art performs a practical role in society. The more difficult question is how aesthetics and politics are ultimately related, but not simply in the revolutionary manner in which Marcuse and others have understood. Since Walter Sokel's contribution on the political function of a message-less art[76] stands at the far end of the spectrum of opinions expressed at the Albany symposium, let us juxtapose Sokel's essay to Klaus Berghahn's paper.

Walter Sokel advances the idea that Schiller's program of aesthetic education anticipates Sigmund Freud's theory of sublimation. According to Freud, the sublimation of desire is not synonymous with repression, but means instead to change one's goal, or to redirect one's drives.[77] Sokel's thesis is encapsulated in the following statement: "Also with Schiller, the redirection of drive from the goal of egoistic satisfaction to pleasurable identification with the law of the morality of reason is, in the broadest sense, the political task of art. It removes the contradiction that exists between both basic principles of the State of Reason: on the one hand, the absolute claim of Law, and, on the other hand, the freedom of the individual from external and internal force."[78] Sokel's elaboration of Schiller's example of the statue of Juno Ludovisi[79] is convincing. To recognize that the woman of this sculpture is, in the final analysis, only an appearance is to recognize that she cannot be the goal of a drive but simply the appearance of an object of desire which the viewer cannot possess.[80] In this case, the effect of art is to distance oneself from the egocentric compulsion toward more emotional satisfaction. With this realization, the individual becomes more selfless and open to other people. Hence, Sokel can claim that, for Schiller, "art has a de-selfing effect."[81]

In his own contribution to the discussion of Sokel's paper, Berghahn charges that his American colleague, whom he calls "der Superschiller,"[82] overemphasized the role of form (vis-a-vis sense/material). It is really the moral content which Sokel seems to ascribe to Schiller's concept of autonomy that disturbs Berghahn the most. "One should not bring provinces [the moral and the aesthetic] so closely together that, in the end, art exercises moral obligations."[83] The fact that the Romantics made fun of Schiller's depiction of women, to which Berghahn refers in his attempt to criticize the writer, does not detract in the least from Sokel's insights into Schiller's writing. In point of fact, the role of the sense-drive is quite compatible with Sokel's thesis. For, "Sublimation is not the expulsion of sensuous energy but a change in direction [goal]. Sensuous energy is turned toward a nobler goal than the satisfaction of the I-drive."[84] The Freudian concept of sublimation should not be equated with suppression. It simply redirects the sense-drive.

For Schiller, as Sokel makes clear, it is not a question of the poetics of creation ("Schaffenspoetik") but of the aesthetics of effect ("Wirkungsästhetik").[85] Viewed from this perspective, Schiller could not have used the term "Autonomie" in the absolute sense. Thus, Sokel is correct to emphasize the fact that the *goal* of Schiller's program of aesthetic education is not primarily aesthetic, but, rather, moral, i.e., rational. I agree with Sokel's conclusion: "With Schiller, the aesthetic [realm] is not completely autonomous."[86] As much as I appreciate Walter Sokel's insights into the possible effect of art for Schiller, I understand the overall function of his writing somewhat differently.

Let us begin with Sokel's question: What function can a message-less or purposeless art possibly have? According to Kant's concept of autonomy, with which Schiller was very familiar, the work of art (in contradistinction to Kant's judgment of Taste) should not transmit specific contents—moral, political, or otherwise—at least not directly. Given the central role the writer assigns to the aesthetic education of the individual for the development of the state, it is evident that, with regard to the immediate effect of art, the individual human being must decide the "true" content of the work for him or herself. Art advances the process of humanization required for the actualization (*Aktualisierung*) of the moral-rational state, only in a general, non-specific way. Through the appreciation of art, we become more sensitive not only to our own needs or interests but, simultaneously, to the needs and interests of others. This experience fosters a spirit of mutual cooperation. In this regard, Jürgen Habermas is correct to observe that the function of art in Schiller's theory of aesthetic education is primarily as a form of communication ("Form der Mitteilung") and that Schiller assigns to it "the task of bringing about 'harmony in society.'"[87] But we will return to this issue in chapter ten.

Interpretations of Schiller's published letters on aesthetic education have not emphasized the central importance of developing one's own human nature, namely the sensuous and rational components of one's being. To be sure, one of the central aspects of the concept of autonomy developed in the late eighteenth century among German writers, including Schiller, was the freedom of self-determination (*Selbstbestimmung*). In general, scholarly discussions of the writing *Concerning the Aesthetic Education of the Human Being* have dwelled on the first part, and forgotten the second part, of Schiller's title, namely "of the Human Being." Indeed, the ultimate work of art, we could say on Schiller's behalf, is the human being, the aesthetic education of which will necessarily transform the nature of society.

The formative process of aesthetic education thus entails shaping and reshaping one's own nature. The cultivation of the faculty of sensation ("die Ausbildung des Empfindungsvermögens") (Letter 8 of *Concerning the Aesthetic Education of the Human Being*) is the means and not the end of aesthetic education. Only by experiencing an autonomous work of art can one hope to truly refine one's own aesthetic sensibilities. The ultimate purpose of art, then, is to cultivate the human being by recapturing and fine-tuning the harmonious tension between the sensuous and rational natures embodied in one's person. Whenever the harmonious tension between body and mind/spirit is achieved that person helps cultivate a healthy state. The true end of Schiller's program of aesthetic education, then, is to reunite or re-wed the faculty of reason with the newly refined faculty of sensation. In

order to achieve this goal, the play-drive ("Spieltrieb") must be fully activated. For that human being is truly human who *plays* with beauty. The
Spieltrieb is not unique to the artist. It is a common human characteristic.
Thus, by activating the *Spieltrieb* one cultivates harmonious tension between the *Formtrieb* (reason) and the *Stofftrieb* (sense).

Viewed from this perspective, art or aesthetics (including aesthetic autonomy) provides us with the means not to perfection or happiness, but rather
to our final completion and true freedom as sensuous-rational beings. Having been educated in the German Enlightenment, Schiller knew from Leibniz, Lessing, Herder, Kant, and Moses Mendelssohn, that the truly
enlightened education of the human species was a never-ending task, i.e.,
"merely an idea" ("bloß eine Idee"), at most, a regulative idea. Schiller
seems to have agreed with Lessing's point in *A Defense [Eine Duplik]* (1778)
that the real value ("Wert") of being human lay in the process, i.e., the very
striving toward a seemingly unattainable goal. I believe that Schiller saw in
the autonomous nature of art an opportunity for human beings to achieve
wholeness, no matter how momentary, by activating the harmonious tension
between the sensuous and the rational components of our natures. Perhaps,
then, the final completed state of reason/morality can be experienced, if
only momentarily in an aesthetic state (Zustand).

To recap, experiencing autonomous art, at which moment one is granted
the freedom to shape oneself without being instructed, the individual human
being experiences the wholesome benefits of the process of *Bildung* for
oneself. Similar to Aristotle in the *Nicomachean Ethics,* Friedrich Schiller
believed in the freedom the individual human being possesses to develop
(perfect) one's own character, i.e., the freedom to cultivate morality.[88]

At this point in Schiller's writings, physiology (anthropology) and metaphysics (ontology) conjoin to actualize the even greater harmonious tension
between human nature and Nature in general. To appreciate not simply the
analogy but the real connection between human nature and Nature was one
of Schiller's unstated goals, one that was realized in practice in his last
completed dramatic work, *William Tell.*

IV. The Tasks of Culture: A New Reading of the Series of Letters
Concerning the Aesthetic Education of the Human Being (1793–95)

While in the course of exchanging letters with Christian Körner, Schiller
began an even longer and more significant correspondence with Prince
Friedrich Christian von Schleswig-Holstein-Sonderburg-Augustenburg. He
drafted the first important communique to the North German monarch two
weeks before his letter of February 23, 1793, to Körner. On February 9,
1793, the writer referred to the knot ("der Knoten") in the problem of feeling
when judging according to principles, which he maintained even Kant himself was incapable of untangling.[89] This knot, I believe, is formed when,

Duke Friedrich Christian von Schleswig-Holstein-Sonderburg-Augustenburg. From a painting in the Royal University in Copenhagen.

in contemplating the nature of beauty, we make a judgment of experience ("Erfahrungsurteil") in the very absence of a clear concept.[90]

To Prince Christian, Schiller stated his intention of lending the investigation of the philosophy of the beautiful a freer form (than Kant). For one thing, he was interested in individualizing and energizing his exposition. One of the hallmarks of Schiller's writings is his concern for the practical. This interest in the practical also influenced the writing of *Concerning the Aesthetic Education of the Human Being in a Series of Letters* between 1793 and 1795. In the important letter of July 13, 1793, addressed to the Prince, the writer underscored the differences between his own style and Kant's. "The strict purity and the scholastic form, in which they are set up, lend some Kantian propositions a harshness and peculiarity that is foreign to their contents, and when stripped of this layer, then appear as the limited claims of general Reason."[91] Developing a fluid style, and rejecting stiff and rigid argumentation, the writer came to the novel idea that philosophical truths must be found in a different form and disseminated in still another.[92] There can be little doubt that Schiller was critical of the inelasticity of systematic philosophy. The writer never lost sight of his artistic talent, which he combined with practically every activity in which he was engaged. The human being, then, is capable of creating beauty—not only in the work of art but, more important, within oneself. I will attempt to show that this simultaneously moral and political task lies at the center of the published series of letters.

Schiller's call for aesthetic education ["ästhetische Bildung"] clearly separates him from Kant. The (Kantian) conception of bridging Nature (sense) and reason through aesthetics finds its correlate in the (Schillerian) idea of the wholeness of the sensuous-rational human being. Specifically, Schiller advocates the *cultivation* of feeling in the spirit of universal assent (*sensus communis*).

I wish to underscore not only the writer's later efforts to develop an idealizing ("idealisierende") art[93] but also his equally strong interest in politics. One avenue of contemporary scholarship characterizes Schiller's *Concerning the Aesthetic Education of the Human Being* as a political aesthetics.[94] While sympathetic to the political nature of Schiller's writing, I stray somewhat from this direction in scholarship to the extent that I see in this published series of letters a cultural broadsheet (*Kampfschrift*). While composing the work, Schiller was writing primarily as a social critic and a cultural historian at one and the same time. In the final analysis, Schiller's writing strongly suggests that the political problem is, at bottom, a cultural or spiritual-intellectual one. For the writer of *Concerning the Aesthetic Education of the Human Being,* cultural and political issues are inextricably bound. For to attain freedom culturally presupposes the expansion of freedom in the political domain.

The Form of the Series of Letters

Judging by the first letter in this series, it is clear that Schiller had bene-
fited from writing the *Kallias* Letters. For one thing, he recognizes that his
new writing is based on the experience of self rather than on systematic
philosophy. Though he acknowledges that his propositions are based on
Kantian principles, Schiller develops his own arguments largely in accordance with his knowledge of Nature.[95] Most important, and quite unlike Kant,
Schiller explores the possibility of the coexistence of aesthetics and ethics
while appealing to the reader's sensibilities. "Your own feeling will provide
me with the material on which to build, your own free powers of thought
dictate the laws according to which we are to proceed" (NA 20: 310).[96] There
is no question that the writer appeals to the reader ("der Leser") for assent.
This attention to the enlightenment of the reader distinguishes Schiller's
writings from those of Immanuel Kant.[97]

It is instructive to foreground the differences between the extant letters
written to Prince Christian and the published series of letters.[98] Though
there are numerous verbatim references from the letters addressed to the
Prince in the completed manuscript, there are far more variations. In order
to appreciate the differences, I align a central paragraph from the important
letter of July 13, 1793, on the left, with the appropriate one from the Second
Letter of Schiller's published work. The series of statements contained in
these paragraphs comprise an essential part of Schiller's main argument.

The course of events in the political and the course of the human mind in the literary sphere has given the spirit of the age such a direction, which removes it more and more from idealizing art. This kind of art must abandon actuality, and soar with a certain bold-ness above the wants and needs of our present time; for Art is a daughter of Freedom. At this time, however, need rules, and the pressure of the physical situation, the depend-ency of the human being on a thousand relationships, which cast him/her in fetters, and entangle one more and more in non-ideal reality, restricts free flight into the region of the Ideal. Speculative	The course of events has given the spirit of the age a direction which threatens to remove it ever further from the art of the Ideal. This kind of art must abandon actuality, and soar with becoming boldness above our wants and needs; for Art is a daughter of Freedom, and takes her orders from the necessity inherent in minds, not from the exigencies of matter. But at the present time material need reigns supreme and bends a degraded humanity beneath their tyrannical yoke. *Utility* is the great idol of our age, to which all powers are in thrall and to which all talent must pay homage. Weighed in this cruel balance,

reason itself is wresting ["entreißt"] from the imagination one province after another; and the borders of art contract, the more science expands its own.[99]

the insubstantial merits of Art scarce tip the scale, and, bereft of all encouragement, she shuns the noisy marketplace of our century. The spirit of philosophical inquiry itself is wresting from the imagination one province after another, and the frontiers of art contract the more the boundaries of science expand.[100]

It becomes quite clear by juxtaposing these letters that the writer strove to attain a higher level of generalization in the published version. "Idealizing art," for instance, becomes "the art of the ideal," while the "need of the present" is equated with "need" or material necessity in general. The significant change from "speculating reason" to the "philosophical mind of investigation," which expresses greater freedom of thought, is coupled with a criticism of the expansion of the limits of science and the concomitant contraction of the province of art. The expansion of science and the contraction of art disclose a crisis in eighteenth-century German culture. When viewed in the light of Schiller's medical dissertations, the struggle between the two cultures of science and art calls up the problem of an unhealthy political state and the need for healing.

In the published letters, as well as the letters to Prince Christian, the writer addresses the problem of political freedom and the modern state, stressing the importance of an education in culture *before* reason and morality can be fully activated. In the light of the historical context of the letters, the appeal to the aesthetic sensibilities of the human being constitutes a criticism of the Reign of Terror. It is also a criticism of the extreme emphasis on reason that characterized the philosophical direction of the European Enlightenment. "Reason has accomplished all that she can accomplish by discovering the law and establishing it. Its execution demands a resolute will and ardour of feeling" (W/W 49: Letter 8: NA 20: 330).[101] The writer declares the age to be enlightened but only quantitatively, that is in terms of the accumulation of knowledge. To be sure, he recognizes that Reason has exposed the illusions, falsehoods, fanaticism and deceit of previous ages. But he also asks why, at times, modern human beings still tend to act like barbarians.

The writer underscores the development of character, through which process the enlightenment of the understanding is revitalized "since the way to the head must be opened through the heart" ["weil der Weg zu dem Kopf durch das Herz muß geöffnet werden"] (W/W 53; NA 20: 332). Not the expansion of the forces of knowledge but the expansion of the faculty of sensation ("Ausbildung des Empfindungsvermögens") (NA 20: 332) is the greatest need of the age. Wilkinson and Willoughby translate the German here as "the development of man's [read: the human being's] capacity for feeling" (W/W 53). Comparing this letter to the letter of July 13, 1793, to Prince Christian, we discover another source: Moses Mendelssohn's *Letters Concerning the Sensations* (Euphranor). Schiller: "It [the age] cannot achieve enlightenment of concepts alone, for from the head there is still a long way to the heart, and by far the greatest number of people is propelled to action by sensations."[102]

This fundamental difference between Schiller and Kant is not compromised in the course of the letters. For as late as the twenty-seventh letter, the writer reasserts the need for a cultural revolution while criticizing the merely natural human being. "Chained as he is to the material world, man subordinates semblance to ends of his own long before he allows it autonomous existence in the ideal realm of art. For this latter to happen a complete revolution in his whole way of feeling is required, without which he would not even find himself *on the way* to the ideal" (W/W 205; NA 20: 405).[103] And how is this to be achieved? The answer is through the cultivation of the beautiful human being. "Wherever, then, we find traces of a disinterested and unconditional appreciation of pure semblance, we may infer that a revolution of this order has taken place in his nature, and that he has started to become truly human" (W/W 205; NA 20: 405).[104] In short, the path to the completion of humanity is the active beautification of one's being ("*Verschönerung* seines Daseins").[105]

At this fundamental level of the writer's work, we also discover the practical application of ideas developed, almost simultaneously, in the *Kallias* project. Whereas Immanuel Kant had asserted that the beautiful evokes in the human subject "disinterested satisfaction" ("interesseloses Wohlgefallen") Schiller combines a "disinterested free appreciation" ("uninteressierte freie Schätzung") with the apprehension of pure appearance ("reinen Schein"). To cultivate and refine the human being's capacity to apprehend and appreciate beautiful objects, that is, to educate the human being in cultural enlightenment becomes the chief means to the political transformation of society. As the writer states in letter nine, "All improvement in the political sphere is to proceed from the ennobling of character" (NA 20: 332).[106] Near the end of the second letter, the writer had already asserted that "if man [read: the human being] is ever to solve that problem of politics in practice he will have to approach it through the problem of the aesthetic, because it is only through Beauty that man makes his way to Freedom" (W/W 9; NA 20: 312).[107] To sum up, the political task of culture stems from the idea that the beautiful representation of Nature through art will improve the quality of life by first transforming the consciousness of individual human beings, and, if individuals, then political society at large. Contrary to the opinions of some scholars and critics, Schiller did not circumvent practical problems of political life. Reformulating the question in various ways, the writer was well aware of problems created by the savage inclinations of the human being, especially by self-interest (egotism), *and* a "barbarian" Constitution (the State).

In letter five, the writer condemned the depravity extending from narrow self-satisfaction. "Proud self-sufficiency contracts the heart of the man [or woman] of the world, a heart which in natural man still often beats in sympathy; and as from a city in flames each man seeks only to save from the general destruction his own wretched belongings" (W/W 27; NA 20: 320).[108] It is now becoming clear that the problem of self-interest is a recurrent theme in Schiller's writings from "Julius's Theosophy" to *Wallenstein,* and beyond.

In the third letter the writer explored this problem further. The historian in Schiller is now fully engaged. The letter begins with a short overview of human history. "Nature deals no better with Man [the human being] than with the rest of her works: she [it] acts from him as long as he is as yet incapable of acting from himself as a free intelligence" (W/W 11; NA 20: 313).[109] At the same time, the writer assumes that the human being is endowed with the ability ("Fähigkeit") to transform the work of necessity ("das Werk der Noth") into a work of his or her own free choice, that is, to elevate physical necessity to the moral sphere (NA 20: 313). Schiller's argument recalls the outline of human history in the essay *Something Concerning the First Human Society:* "Awakening out of one's sensuous slumber, [the human being] comes to oneself, recognizes that she/he is a human being, looks about, and finds oneself—in the State" (NA 20: 313).[110] Prior to exercising freedom of choice, the force of need ("Zwang der Bedürfnisse") threw ("warf") the individual into the state. As a moral person ("moralische Person"), however, the human being is dissatisfied with the natural state of affairs and soon forsakes "the dominion of blind necessity" ("die Herrschaft einer blinden Nothwendigkeit") (W/W 11; NA 20: 313). The path from common ("gemein") to noble character lies in developing a state of Nature as idea ("einen Naturstand in der Idee"). This (imagined) state does not yet exist in reality ("Erfahrung"). It exists only in the consciousness of one's rational determination ("Vernunftbestimmung"). Cultivating the idea of a higher destiny, a "people grown to maturity" ("mündig gewordene[s] Volk") (W/W 13) is capable of transforming the natural state into a truly moral ("sittlich[]"), i.e., human one.

Like every political body ("jeder politische Körper"), the natural state contradicts the aspirations of the moral human being since it owes its existence to the arbitrary play of forces and is not yet constituted by laws. Schiller juxtaposes the moral individual ("der sittliche [Mensch]") to the physical human being ("der physische Mensch"). Reason suspends ("hebt . . . auf") the natural state. In doing so, it risks ("wagt") the physical human being for the "problematic", i.e., moral human being, as it does the current social state for "a merely possible (even though morally necessary) ideal of society" (NA 20: 314).[111]

The writer recontextualizes the paradigm of the medical dissertation at this point in order to underscore a central feature of his critique of modern-day (revolutionary) society. Reason instills in the human being something that he or she actually possesses with something one should possess. Hence, the moral human being will one day abolish the natural state. R. D. Miller has seen clearly that art, for Schiller, is concerned with "freeing man [the human being] from the forces of crude nature."[112] "And if in so doing she [it] should have counted on him for more than he can perform, then she would, for the sake of a humanity which he still lacks—and can without prejudice to his mere existence go on lacking—having deprived him of the means of that animal existence which is the very condition of his being human at all. Before he has had time to cleave unto the Law with the full force of his moral will, she would have drawn from under his feet the ladder of Nature" (W/W 13; NA 20: 314).[113] The analogy the writer introduces here is illuminating. For the work of fashioning the physical human being caught in *time* into a moral human being freed in *idea* is similar to the idea of the "artist" ("Künstler") who, in order to repair a clock, lets the inner mechanism of the wheels run down; "but," the writer insists, "the living clockwork of the State must be repaired while it is still striking, and it is a question of changing the revolving wheel while it still revolves" (W/W 13; NA 20: 314).[114] The employment of the metaphor of the clockwork is especially significant. Recalling the tension between the older mechanistic worldview and the new organic conception of the universe in Schiller's medical dissertations and early poetic and dramatic writings, the metaphor of the clockwork, in this context, represents the modern-day, bureaucratic state (Prussia). The writer as social critic has now taken over for the cultural historian. By representing the modern German state with the aid of the metaphor of the clock, the writer counters the mechanism of the dominant form of political governance in the German states in the eighteenth century. This use of the clockwork metaphor demonstrates quite clearly that, in the final analysis, the cultural project is a political one.

Schiller's call for the re-formation of society is primarily linguistic and cultural. It is not overtly revolutionary in the political sense. However, I believe that the reason for this posture has as much to do with the interdisciplinary nature of Schiller's writings as it does with the writer's reflections on the aftermath of the French Revolution and the Reign of Terror. By spanning various fields of inquiry, the writer transforms the dictates of acquired knowledge, and, in this way, contributes further to the development (*Bildung*) of the reader's consciousness.

Schiller also encouraged political change by avoiding the violence of the natural, i.e., merely physical human being. To be sure, Schiller attributed free will to human beings. In letter four, he wrote that the will of the human being "stands completely free between duty and inclination," indeed, that it is the "sovereign right of his/her personality" (NA 20: 216).[115] Depending on the responses of individuals to this general project, the doctrine of the free will either strengthens or undermines the writer's aspirations for humankind. For, the individual may elect to follow one's sensuous inclinations rather than the dictates of reason. A further complication is that reason may also manifest itself differently in each unique individual human being. Still, the free will, for Schiller, if truly free is also the *moral* will, which agency strives for common assent. Perhaps the most basic assumption here is that, as a social being, the individual will not elect to act alone.

Schiller noted his indebtedness to Fichte at this point in his argument when declaring that every single person carries within oneself a pure ideal human being whose proper task it is to bring all one's changes into agreement (harmony) with the unchanging unity of one's being. This type of human being substitutes, momentarily at least, for the true state, the condition of which is "the objective and, as it were, canonical form in which all diversity of individuals and individual subjects strive to unite" (NA 20: 316).[116] In this (beautiful) form, the individual becomes the state and the human being in *time* is ennobled as the human being in *idea* (NA 20: 316). In this way, reason (which requires unity) *and* Nature (which requires diversity) are combined in consciousness ("Bewußtsein") *and* feeling ("Gefühl").

This point is indispensable to an understanding of Schiller's *Gesamtwerk* not only because it builds up a general schema but because the writer focuses clearly on the role of human nature and the value of individual human beings in their totality. Schiller states the matter clearly. "The State should not only respect the objective and generic character in its individual subjects; it should also honour their subjective and specific character, and in extending the invisible realm of morals take care not to depopulate the sensible realm of appearance" (W/W 19; NA 20: 317).[117] Though rarely acknowledged, Schiller's statement conveys respect for individuals as vital parts of society and a concept of the whole of the state which is composed of individuals. In accordance with this view, the state will form ("bildet") itself. But it can only be shaped with the unique contributions and active involvement of individual members who are engaged in the process of education (*Bildung*).

The true state, then, will resemble a healthy, living organism, for it is enlivened by the harmonious tension between the particular (the individual) and the general (the state). The writer insists that the individual begin the process of re-forming society by re-shaping oneself. "Once man [the human being] is inwardly at one with himself, *he will be able to preserve his individuality however much he may universalize his conduct,* and the state will be *merely* the interpreter of his own finest instinct, a clearer formulation *of his own sense of what is right*" (W/W 21; NA 20: 318) [emphasis mine].[118] Hence, progress in society will depend on how seriously and to what degree the individual is engaged in this process. If the process is successful, then autocratic forms of governance will necessarily vanish.

Vociferous critics of Schiller have overemphasized the writer's perpetuation of a purely human domain (*das Allgemeinmenschliche*). As we have seen, it is not true that the restructuring of society must come at the cost of the individual. On the contrary, by participating in this common enterprise, the individual will preserve oneself as one actively cultivates oneself and, by extension, thereby help improve the state. "Consequently, whenever Reason starts to introduce the unity of the moral law into any actually existing society, she [it] must *beware of damaging the variety of Nature*. And whenever Nature endeavours to maintain her variety within the moral framework of society, moral unity must not suffer any infringement thereby"; for, "*removed alike from uniformity and from confusion*, there abides the triumph of form" (W/W 21/23; NA 20: 318) [emphasis mine].[119] Thus Schiller registers the hope that "wholeness of character" ("*Totalität des Charakters*") will enact the exchange of the state of necessity with the state of freedom (End of letter four).

The Fashioning of Ideas and the Polypoid Nature of the State

I have suggested that the new organic science of the eighteenth century may have shaped some of Schiller's main ideas. The writer's reference to the "polypoid" nature of the ancient Greek city-states in the letters *Concerning the Aesthetic Education of the Human Being* evidences this fact.[120] "That polypoid character of the Greek States, in which every individual enjoyed an independent existence but could, when need arose, grow into the whole organism, now made way for an ingenious clock-work, in which, out of the piecing together of innumerable but lifeless parts, a mechanical kind of collective life ensued" (W/W 35; NA 20: 323).[121] One result was that modern political life, anchored as it was in a mechanized bureaucratic structure, was virtually torn apart ("auseinandergerissen"). Once again, we can appreciate the impact of organic science on German culture, which in the eighteenth century was gradually replacing the older mechanistic worldview. The writer seems to be arguing that, in order for there to be genuine change, the state must function naturally, that is, in consonance with the lives of individual human beings. Despite claims to the contrary, Schiller's vision is not related to the Rousseauian doctrine of the return to an original state of Nature.[122] For as Schiller, the historian, states clearly, the original state of Nature was one of violence, in which condition human nature was enslaved by savage instincts. It is for this reason that the writer fears for his own day. "For society, released from its controls, is falling back into the kingdom of the elements, instead of hastening upwards into the realm of organic life" (W/W 27; NA 20: 319).[123]

The construction of the central typology of the savage and the barbarian complements the writer's insight that the modern state can lapse into violence. The point warrants consideration here not only because it is a major theme of this and subsequent writings, but also because it helps identify the writer's understanding of the limits of social behavior. Whereas the feelings of the savage ("der Wilde") rule one's principles, the principles of the barbarian ("der Barbar") destroy feelings (NA 20: 318). Clearly, Schiller wished to avoid both extremes.

We may then conclude that the healthy individual strives to maintain the harmonious tension between principles and feelings. Culture ("Kultur") becomes the primary vehicle by which the human being can mediate between extremes. The cultured human being ("der gebildete Mensch") "makes a friend of Nature, and honours her [its] freedom whilst curbing only her caprice" (W/W 21; NA 20: 318).[124] The goal is not to purge Nature from oneself but, rather, to arrest its power and help reshape one's own nature in accordance with rational-moral knowledge.

In retrospect, it is apparent that Schiller's writing of *Concerning the Aesthetic Education of the Human Being* was informed by the kind of typologizing common to eighteenth-century natural science.[125]

The Metaphor of Enchainment

Returning, in letter five, to the drama of his own time (NA 20: 319), that is, to contemporary political realities, Schiller notes that the two extremes of human decline—savagery ("Verwilderung") and lethargy ("Erschlaffung")[126]—occupy one space of time. The metaphor of enchainment represents the sustained violence of uncultured nature in modern times. The writer's purview of contemporary politics recalls the discussion of the animal nature of the human being in the third medical dissertation. "Among the lower and more numerous classes we are confronted with crude, lawless instincts ["Triebe"], unleashed with the loosening of the bonds of civil order, and hastening with ungovernable fury to their animal satisfactions" (W/W 25; NA 20: 319).[127] Some scholarly and critical opinions to the contrary, Schiller does not limit his criticism to the lower classes.[128] For his criticism is used as a rhetorical strategy to inform the members of the higher classes of their own moral deficiencies. At times, however, the point is stated directly and sharply. "The cultivated classes, on the other hand, offer the even more repugnant spectacle of lethargy, and of a depravation of character which offends the more because culture itself is its source" (W/W 27; NA 20: 320).[129] The rhetorical strategy indicts representatives of the higher classes for not having assumed their responsibility as the guardians of not simply their own political system but of culture.

A second example taken from the same letter foreshadows Schiller's call, in letter eight, for the cultivation of the capacity for feeling, or faculty of sensation ("Ausbildung des Empfindungsvermögens" vs. "Erkenntniskräfte"). For he launches a sharp criticism of the rationalistic side of the Enlightenment marked, in the German states, by the philosophical tradition extending from Christian Wolff to Immanuel Kant. "That Enlightenment of the mind [the understanding], which is not altogether a groundless boast of our refined classes, has had on the whole so little of an ennobling influence on feeling and character that it has tended rather to bolster up depravity by providing it with the support of precepts" (W/W 27; NA 20: 320).[130] Once refined, aesthetic sensibility will also produce greater sensitivity in the governance of human beings. Given the fact that this series of letters was originally written to a regent, Schiller's writing serves as a means to further educate the German aristocracy, especially about the value of democratic ideals.[131]

In sum, there can be little question that the letters *Concerning the Aesthetic Education of the Human Being* address the needs of the individual and that they assail the mistreatment of individuals by representatives of the German states.[132] Concerning the practical application of the ideas generated in the course of writing this series of letters, Schiller insists that the modern state must first meet the material needs of its members. He states clearly that people must first be freed from "the yoke of material necessity" ("von dem Joch der Bedürfnisse") (NA 20: 332) if they are to be open to the development of civilization. For, "The majority of men [human beings] are far too wearied and exhausted ("abgespannt") by the struggle for existence to gird themselves for a new and harder struggle against error" (W/W 51; NA 20: 331).[133] To be sure, Schiller did not state, as would Bertolt Brecht in the early twentieth century, "Erst kommt das Fressen, dann kommt die Moral" (Eating comes first, then morality), and he did not address the problem again while working out his theory of aesthetic education. However, his statements here certainly suggest that he knew that something had to be done for the people to better equip them materially, and not only intellectually or spiritually, both for their own *Bildung* as well as for the sake of society. It is a need that is evidenced also in Schiller's financial struggles.[134]

The Fragmentary Nature of Modern Society

Schiller openly criticized the fragmentation of modern society, the primary cause of which, he maintains, is "the all-dividing Intellect" ("der alles trennende Verstand") (W/W 33; NA 20: 322). On the one hand, overemphasizing intellect leads to "sharper divisions between the sciences." On the other hand, "the increasingly complex machinery [clockwork] of the State" necessitates "a more rigorous separation of ranks and occupations" (both quotations are from W/W 33; NA 20: 322). The earlier and later works are linked on the metaphorical and general thematic levels of Schiller's language. The fragmentation of society, caused both by science and by politics, is construed as nothing less than a transgression against Nature. In the light of the central symbol of the stringed instrument as a representation of Nature, it is consistent with his general argument that the writer should have employed the metaphor of rupture in this context: "thus the inner unity of human nature was severed too, and a disastrous conflict set its harmonious powers at variance" ("so zerriß auch der innere Bund der menschlichen Natur, und ein verderblicher Streit entzweyte ihre harmonischen Kräfte") (W/W 33; NA 20: 323).

In modern society, intuitive and speculative understanding battle for supremacy. As a result, each guards its own borders with mistrust and jealousy. The cultural problem of defending borders is highlighted by the motif of enslavement. "Everlastingly chained to a single little fragment of the Whole, man [the human being] himself develops into nothing but a fragment; everlastingly in his ear the monotonous sound of the wheel that he turns, he never develops the harmony of his being, and instead of putting the stamp of humanity upon his own nature, he becomes nothing more than the imprint of his occupation or of his specialized knowledge" (W/W 35; NA 20: 323).[135] In parentheses, the writer asks why a person would permit oneself to entrust one's freedom to "a mechanism [clockwork] so intricate and so fearful of light and enlightenment" (W/W 35; NA 20: 323).[136] A major component of Schiller's cultural criticism is the idea that neither a highly specialized science nor a political machine possesses sufficient strength to save the human species from fragmentation and eventual dissolution. Neither science nor politics in themselves, but the cultivation and refinement of feeling, together with the exercise of enlightened reason in pursuit of the common good (=culture), is the primary source for possible realization of the truly rational-moral state. At the same time, however, those who exercise the harmonious tension between the mind and the body in effect already actualize the state in time, that is, the here and now.

The writer's appreciation of the (imagined) unity of form and content in the natural state of ancient Greek culture undergirds the cultural-historical perspective. Ancient Greek culture is at once a rival to and a model for modern society. "In fullness of form no less than of content, at once philosophic and creative, sensitive and energetic, the Greeks combined the first youth of imagination with the manhood of reason in a glorious manifestation of humanity" (W/W 31; NA 20: 321).[137] Rather than take this description too literally as an example of what Schiller thought was characteristic of ancient Greek culture in fact, perhaps we should appreciate the emphasis the writer places on the values of form and fullness, philosophy and education, imagination and reason, all of which are recommended to the modern human being. Taken together, these forms of thinking and experiencing form a collective knowledge which every truly moral human being seeks to enact.

The Role of Imagination and the Instrument of Culture

In *Concerning the Aesthetic Education of the Human Being,* as well as the essay on universal history, imagination is assigned a central role in the process of historical change. "We know that the sensibility of the psyche [mind] depends for its intensity upon the liveliness, for its scope upon the richness of the imagination" (letter six) (W/W 39; NA 20: 325).[138] However, both in the light of imagination and social *Bildung,* two types of individuals in modern society impede progress toward the goal of the truly enlightened state. They are the speculative, or abstract thinker ("der spekulative Geist" / "der abstrakte Denker") and the practical spirit, or businessperson ("der Geschäftsgeist" / "der Geschäftsmann"). Seeking imperishable possessions in the sphere of ideas, the speculative mind estranges itself from the material world. The practical-minded individual, however, represents the opposite extreme. This type of individual restricts oneself to a monotonous circle of objects which blinds it to the freedom of the whole. The former attempts to shape the actual ("das Wirkliche") according to what is comprehendible, raising "the subjective conditions of its own perpetual and conceptual faculty into laws constitutive of the existence of things" (W/W 39; NA 20: 325).[139] The opposite extreme ("das entgegenstehende Extrem") fragmentizes the whole of experience by seeking "to make the rules of its own occupation apply indiscriminately to all others" (W/W 325; NA 20: 325).[140] In other words, the business mind utilizes its ingenuity to erect boundaries between multifarious fields of activity so as to reduce the wide range of human experience to its own interest.

In retrospect, the imbalance ("Übergewicht") of the analytic faculty robs the imagination of its power and "fire," thus trivializing the rich panorama of the world of objects in their totality. Whereas the abstract thinker has a cold heart, "since he dissects his impressions, and impressions can move the soul only as they remain whole" (W/W 39; NA 20: 325–26),[141] the businessperson has a narrow heart, "since his [or her] imagination, imprisoned within the unvarying confines of his own calling, is incapable of extending itself to appreciate other ways of seeing and knowing" (W/W 39; NA 20: 326).[142] As much as the writer laments these detrimental directions, he also sees their necessity. For, without such tension, the species ("die Gattung") would make no progress. "This antagonism of faculties and function is the great instrument of civilization [culture]—but it is only the instrument; for as long as it persists, we are only on the way to becoming civilized [cultured]" (W/W 41; NA 20: 326).[143] At bottom, the very "conflict with the truth of things" ("Widerstreit mit der Wahrheit der Dinge") (W/W 41) necessitates the common sense ("Gemeinsinn") or understanding required for lasting progress and the eventual realization of the rational-moral state (NA 20: 326).

On Politics, Culture, and the Shaping of Reality

At the very beginning of the ninth letter, Schiller reiterates his central thesis that all improvement in the political sphere is to proceed from the ennobling of human character (NA 20: 332). At the same time, he readdresses a central problem: "how under the influence of a barbarous constitution is character ever to become ennobled?" (W/W 55; NA 20: 332).[144]

According to Schiller, the human being is endowed with a divine drive or impulse ("der göttliche Bildungstrieb" [NA 20: 335]) by means of which he or she is able to shape reality. The term *Bildungstrieb* seems to have originated in discussions about human physiology. It was encoded by Johann Friedrich Blumenbach in his *Über den Bildungstrieb und das Zeugungsgeschäft* which appeared one year after Schiller completed his medical dissertation. For Schiller, this divinely creative formative force is inherent in the human being, though it attains its highest degree of development in the artist. Its task is to transform both necessity and the eternal into an object of the pure moral impulse ("der reine moralische Trieb"; NA 20: 335). At this point, Schiller offers some advice to citizens of the state which is reminiscent of Christ's words to the people concerning Caesar. "Live with your century; but do not be its creatures. . . . Without sharing their [one's contemporaries'] guilt, yet share with noble resignation in their punishment, and bow your head freely beneath the yoke which they find as difficult to dispense with as to bear" (W/W 61; NA 20: 335–36).[145] Like Martin Luther, the writer recommends "steadfast courage" ("standhaften Muth" [NA 20: 336]). Schiller's argument suggests that spiritual, or mental freedom is fashioned within the bounds (yoke) of the body. The same is true of the relationship between the individual and the body politic. We will return to this important point in chapter seven in our analysis of *Mary Stuart*.

In the ninth letter, the writer expresses his confidence in the power of both the artist and the human being to shape reality. The development of a historical perspective is again in evidence when Schiller reflects back on ancient Roman times. His words relate more directly, however, to the revolutionary state of affairs in his own days. "Humanity has lost its dignity; but Art has rescued it and preserved it in significant stone. Truth lives on in the illusion of Art, and it is from this copy, or after-image, that the original image will once again be restored" (W/W 57; NA 20: 334).[146] Not only the artist, but also the individual human being can dissociate oneself from the mere opinions of the time in which one is living. The writer encourages the reader to foster and cultivate the higher goals of dignity and law rather than fortune and everyday need since, he argues, the former values are infinite, or universal, whereas the latter are merely temporal, or contingent. Schiller sees, however, that individuals who actively seek this ideal can proceed too quickly and, expecting too much too soon, become disillusioned. He reminds the reader that the pure moral impulse is directed at the unconditional, for which time does not exist. Its present is the future (NA 20: 335). In the final analysis, it is up to the individual to decide whether one will cultivate the values of dignity and law or seek fortune and the fulfillment and gratification of everyday need. The choice is the reader's.

Schiller recommends a form of sublimation to help direct one's "animal" instincts. "Banish from their pleasures caprice, frivolity, and coarseness, and imperceptibly you will banish these from their actions and, eventually, from their inclinations too. Surround them, wherever you meet them, with the great and noble forms of genius, and encompass them about with the symbols of perfection, until Semblance conquer Reality, and Art triumph over Nature" (W/W 61; NA 20: 336).[147] Moving ahead, momentarily, to the tenth letter, it is instructive to juxtapose Schiller's description of the human being without form to the conception articulated in this letter. "A man [human being] who has himself no form will despise any grace of speech as bribery and corruption, any elegance in social intercourse as hypocrisy, any delicacy or distinction of bearing as exaggeration ["Ueberspannung"] and affectation" (W/W 65; NA 20: 337).[148] In *Concerning the Aesthetic Education of the Human Being* the primary means of salvation for humanity is not religion but culture. All of the diverse forms of culture are to be enlisted into service before the natural and artificial states of modern society can be transformed into a vibrant and beautiful state of reason and morality: "In a single word, Beauty would have to be shown to be a necessary condition of Human Being" (W/W 69/71; NA 20: 340).[149]

Concerning Human Nature

In the eleventh letter, Schiller offers an original answer to the perennial question of the nature of human existence. "Not because we think, will, or feel, do we exist; and because we exist, do we think, will or feel. We are because we are; we feel, think, and will, because outside of ourselves something other than ourselves exists too" (W/W 73; NA 20: 341–42).[150] The writer seeks to come to terms with the existence of both the phenomenal and noumenal worlds. Unlike Descartes's "I think, therefore I am," for Schiller, human character is transformed by the reciprocal cooperation between being and becoming. "Only inasmuch as he [the human being] changes does he *exist;* only inasmuch as he remains unchangeable does *he* exist" (W/W 75; NA 20: 343).[151] The eleventh letter surely reflects the profound influence of Johann Georg Fichte's philosophical insights, for Fichte's concepts of person and condition are said to be mutually complementary.[152] At the same time, however, the main thesis of Schiller's early anthropology is still in operation. For at the end of the same letter, he links Fichte's idea of those "two contrary challenges to man" (absolute Reality and absolute Formality) with his own thesis of the "two fundamental laws of his sensuous-rational nature" (W/W 77; NA 20: 344).[153] The vital link between medicine and aesthetics in Schiller's later writings is now apparent.

It is significant that the writer should have rejected Descartes's distrust of appearance and the concomitant argument that sense perception always entails deception. Among eighteenth-century French thinkers, Schiller shared the most in common, perhaps, with d'Alembert. For it was d'Alembert who rejected the mechanism and materialism of de La Mettrie and Holbach as the main principles of explanation for the natural operation of things. Unlike d'Alembert, however, Schiller retained his interest in metaphysics.

The Three Impulses of Sense, Form, and Play

In the twelfth letter, Schiller introduced his famous schema of the sense-drive ("Stofftrieb"), form-drive ("Formtrieb"), and play-drive ("Spieltrieb"). A central passage in the twelfth letter discloses the symbol of the stringed instrument. "When we strike a note on an instrument, only this single note, of all those it is capable of emitting, is actually realized; when man [the human being] is sensible of the present, the whole infinitude of his possible determinations is confined to this single mode of his being" (W/W 79; NA 20: 344–45).[154] Sensuous experience of the present moment alone resembles a note played in isolation. The analogy of the fruitful enchainment of the mind to the material world is also further developed.

> With indestructible chains it [the sense-drive] binds the ever-soaring spirit to the world of sense, and summons abstraction from its most unfettered excursions into the Infinite back to the limitations of the Present (W/W 81; NA 20: 345).[155]

The second drive, the form-impulse ("Formtrieb"), proceeds from the absolute nature of the human being, that is, from one's capacity to reason. It strives to bring "harmony into the diversity of his [the human being's] manifestations" and, "among all his changes of Condition," helps to establish one's person ("Person") (W/W 81; NA 20: 345–46).[156] With the aid of the form-impulse, borders are transcended and one is elevated to the level of the "unity of ideas" ("*Ideen-Einheit*"), under which the entire realm of appearances is subsumed (NA 20: 347). Here, we are no longer limited by time. Time is "in us." It is our creation. In the former state, we are merely individuals; in the latter, members of the human genus ("Gattung").

A third impulse—the play-drive ("Spieltrieb")—mediates between the sense- and form-drives. The structure of Schiller's argument resembles the first medical dissertation *Philosophy of Physiology,* according to which a transmutative force ("Mittelkraft") is required in order to mediate between the sensuous and intellectual natures of the human being.

The Task of Culture

Returning now to the thesis that the political problems of Schiller's time were fundamentally cultural in nature, the writer asserts that the task of culture ("die Aufgabe der *Kultur*") is to develop each of the three impulses of sense, form, and play to its full potential within the limits imposed upon them by Nature. This ongoing, never-ending process of mutual limitation is similar in structure to the interactionist theory developed in the revised medical dissertation of 1780. We recall that, according to the early medical writing, the healthy, harmonious tension of human physiology consists in the mind reminding the body of its limitations and the body holding the mind within its bounds. I have already suggested that such a relationship relativizes the binary opposition of the ideal and the real, thus robbing the dichotomy of its significance. Let us examine these points more closely while exploring the submerged parts of Schiller's text.

The thirteenth letter contains two lengthy footnotes. The first note clarifies the writer's point that the material-impulse and the form-impulse are *not* opposed by Nature (NA 20: 347f.). Countering the idea that these basic impulses are antagonistic, Schiller criticizes one of the main tenets of the transcendental philosophy of his day. "In the Transcendental method of philosophizing, where everything depends on clearing form of content, and obtaining Necessity in its pure state, free of all admixture with the contingent, one easily falls into thinking of material things as nothing but an obstacle, and of imagining that our sensuous nature, just because it happens to be a hindrance in *this* operation, must of necessity be in conflict with reason" (W/W 87; NA 20: 348).[157] Under these conditions, the only way to preserve unity is to subordinate the sensuous impulse to the rational faculty. As will become even clearer in chapter six, Schiller's appreciation of the harmonious tension between the sensuous and rational natures of the human being contradicts the overemphasis placed on *Geist* by proponents of German Idealism, especially by Schiller's colleague at the university in Jena J. G. Fichte.

Fichte's *Fundamental Principles of the Complete Theory of Knowledge* [Grundlage der gesamten Wissenschaftslehre] appeared in Leipzig, in 1794 and 1795, when Schiller was writing *Concerning the Aesthetic Education of the Human Being*. Schiller concluded the first footnote to letter thirteen by maintaining that it was *not* in the spirit of Kant's philosophical system to subordinate the sensuous to the rational, though he concedes this idea may inhere in its letter (NA 20: 348). To a certain extent, then, Schiller defended Kant against Fichte. To be sure, the writer was enamored of Fichte's concept of reciprocity ("Wechselwirkung"). However, we have seen that Schiller had already set a precedent for this interest when working out the interactionist theory of the third medical dissertation long before his encounter with Fichte. In the later writing, however, both principles, the material as well as the formal impulses, are "at once subordinated to each other and co-ordinated with each other, that is to say, they stand in reciprocal relation to one another: without form no matter, and without matter no form" (W/W 85; NA 20: 348).[158] The harmonious tension between these two impulses is facilitated by the play-impulse.

In the second footnote to the thirteenth letter, Schiller augmented his discussion of the interplay between the active and passive forces ("tätige Kraft" and "leidende [Kraft]") in human nature. He cautions against the detrimental influence of a domineering sensuality on thinking and human actions. The pernicious effect of a domineering rationality on our knowledge and behavior is less obvious (NA 20: 349–50), though no less serious. As in the third, revised dissertation of 1780, the later writer still seeks the middle line of truth.

It has been overlooked that Schiller was critical of the tendency within the natural sciences to privilege teleological judgment over the direct obser-vation of nature. "However strong and however varied the impact made upon our organs by nature, all her manifold variety is then entirely lost upon us, because we are seeking nothing in her but what we have put into her; because, instead of letting her come *in upon us,* we are thrusting ourselves *out upon her* with all the impatient anticipations of our reason" (W/W 89; NA 20: 350).[159] Consistent with his manner of argumentation, Schiller's pre-cautionary word is accompanied by a reference to harmony and sound.

> This premature hankering [striving] after harmony before we have even got to-gether the individual sounds which are to go to its making, this violent usurping of authority by ratiocination in a field where its right to give orders is by no means unconditional, is the reason why so many thinking minds fail to have any fruitful effect upon the advancement of science; and it would be difficult to say which has done more harm to the progress of knowledge: a sense-faculty uname-nable to form, or a reasoning faculty which will not stay for a content(W/W 89; NA 20: 350).[160]

This is a crucial passage. The writer cautions against the egotism that stems from the one-sided exercise of reason. Schiller's declaration functions at once as a criticism of the aftermath of the French Revolution and a general principle. The writer advocates the education of the whole person, which, as we now observe, can be achieved only when reason and sensuousness are trained to interact, while at the same time keeping the other within its bounds. This is how the writer configures his concept of unity and harmony: not as the fusion of two opposites, but as the tense, harmonious interplay of two competing, yet cooperating forces. "If we are to become compassionate, helpful, effective human beings, feeling and character must unite, even as wide-open senses must combine with vigour of intellect if we are to acquire experience" (W/W 89; NA 20: 350).[161] The idea of forming character ("*einen Menschen formieren*") is an essential part of Schiller's program of enlightenment, "and, that, even in the best sense of the word, where it implies the cultivation of the inner, and not merely of the outer, man [human being]" (W/W 91; NA 20: 351).[162] The truly excellent character adheres to the maxim "Severity with oneself combined with leniency toward others" ("Strenge gegen sich selbst mit Weichheit gegen andre verbunden" [W/W 91; NA 20: 351]). The opposite is true of "the most contemptible character of all" (NA 20: 351), for whom no higher goals exist other than to react to what the present moment dictates.

Schiller's careful attention to the placement of selected words in key passages has been overlooked. Here, the writer submits that the exercise of both the sense-impulse and the form-impulse requires restriction ("Einschränkung") and relaxation ("Abspannung") (thirteenth letter; NA 20: 352). Schiller is careful to note that, for the sensuous drive, relaxation ("Abspannung") does not mean the dulling of sensations anymore than it does for the form impulse; it means laxity of the rational powers of thinking. The natural law of delimitation is again in force. Concerning the form impulse, Schiller wrote: "It must, if it is to be at all praiseworthy, spring from abundance of feeling and sensation. Sense herself must, with triumphant power, remain mistress of her own domain, and resist the violence which the mind, by its usurping tactics, would fain inflict upon her" (W/W 93; NA 20: 352).[163] The proper relationship between the sense- and form-impulses would thus seem to be harmonious tension.

Consistent with the early mind-body paradigm, one impulse proves to be indispensable to the other. Not the dualistic clash of inherently antithetical entities (a central feature of traditional scholarship on Schiller) but reciprocal, yet taut interaction becomes the chief characteristic also of Schiller's later theoretical writings. Both forces—together—create a state of healthy tension when they properly perform their respective activities. In *Concerning the Aesthetic Education of the Human Being,* the play-impulse taps the creative potential of this type of activity.

Living Form

The true object of the play-impulse, in which both the sense- and the form-impulses work together ("vereinigt wirken") is *"lebende Gestalt"* (living form), or beauty (Letter 15; NA 20: 355). Scholars have suggested that this is a new definition of beauty. What is new, however, is not so much the definition, which was present already in the *Kallias* Letters, as it is the application of the definition to the writer's concept of the ultimately political task of culture. At the same time, scholarship has not yet appreciated Schiller's conscious awareness of the limits of his own theorizing. At the beginning of letter fourteen, for instance, we read: "Such reciprocal relation between the two drives is, admittedly, but a task enjoined upon us by Reason, a problem which man [the human being] is only capable of solving completely in the perfect consummation of his existence. It is, in the most precise sense of the word, the *Idea of his Human Nature,* hence something Infinite, to which in the course of time he can approximate ever more closely, but without ever being able to reach it" (W/W 95; NA 20: 352–53).[164] This point will be explored in more detail in chapter six.

Furthermore, Schiller's insight, that even a block of marble, though lifeless and constant, can still become living form in the hands of the architect and sculptor, has not been addressed. From this vantage point, the example of the musical instrument introduced in the *Kallias* project takes on even greater significance. Though confusing natural and humanmade objects in the exchange of letters with Körner, the employment of a similar example in this series of letters demonstrates, at the very least, the general consistency of Schiller's argument. Even more important, living form ("lebende Gestalt") is comprehended as the product of the reciprocal cooperation between the sense- and form-impulses in human nature. Recalling the writer's point that not only the artist but all human beings are endowed with the play-impulse, the primary task of humankind now is arresting this creative power and turning it into a positive force for social interaction.[165] In this way, the individual human being can—and should—become beautiful. "Only when his [the human being's] form lives in our feeling and his life takes on form in our understanding, does he become living form; and this will always be the case whenever we adjudge him beautiful" (W/W 101; NA 20: 355).[166] Neither thinking, nor feeling in themselves can achieve this. So the gateway to the actualization of beauty in the individual and society is culture. "Let there be a bond of union between the form-drive and the material drive; that is to say, let there be a play-drive, since only the union of reality with form, contingency with necessity, passivity with freedom, makes the concept of human nature complete" (W/W 103; NA 20: 356).[167]

The proper function of the *Spieltrieb* (play-impulse) is to maintain the creative tension between the form- and material-impulses. The essential point here is that the play-drive discloses ("entfaltet"; literally, unfolds) the bifold nature ("doppelte Natur") of the human being (NA 20: 358). This central idea establishes a fundamental link between this series of letters and the medical dissertations. Indeed, in the fifteenth letter, Schiller reintroduces the original paradigm of his early anthropology. "Man [the human being], as we know, is neither exclusively matter nor exclusively mind" ("Der Mensch, wissen wir, ist weder ausschließend Materie, noch ist er ausschließend Geist" (W/W 103; NA 20: 356). Only at this stage in his development did Schiller conceive of beauty as the very consummation of human nature and of humanity ("Consummation seiner Menschheit"; NA 20: 356).

In sum, I do not believe that Schiller argues for a true synthesis of the sense- and form-impulses. For the writer's recognition of the relaxing and tightening effect of beauty, and the idea of the consummation of one's nature in beauty (i.e., living form), resembles the kind of harmonious tension that

Moses Mendelssohn had ascribed to the nervous system of the healthy human being.

Qualifications

Unlike Immanuel Kant, the writer Friedrich Schiller imparts knowledge of the personal and social value of beauty. The often quoted statement— "man [the human being] only plays when he is in the fullest sense of the word a human being, and *he is only fully a human being when he plays*"— actually depends on the preceding statement for its full meaning: "With beauty man [the human being] shall *only play,* and it is *with beauty only* that he shall play" (W/W 107; NA 20: 359).[168] As outlined in the sixteenth letter, the task of aesthetic beauty is "to make beauty out of a multiplicity of beautiful objects" ("aus Schönheiten Schönheit zu machen") (W/W 107; NA 20: 361), the ultimate goal of which is the truly moral human being. Elizabeth Wilkinson, L. A. Willoughby, and even their critic R. D. Miller, among numerous other scholars on both sides of the Atlantic, have sidestepped the fact that, in the so-called classical writings, Schiller qualifies his ideal of the most perfect union and equilibrium of reality and form which stems from the reciprocally cooperative relationship between sense and form. The fact that critics have not come to terms with the writer's qualifiers has a great deal to do with the fact that such self-reflexive gestures work against the image of Schiller as an idealist. For, as the writer states in clear, non-rhetorical terms: "This equilibrium, however, remains no more than an Idea ("immer nur Idee"), which can never be fully realized in actuality" (W/W 111; NA 20: 360).[169] But, why not? "For in actuality we shall always be left with a preponderance of the one element over the other, and the utmost that experience can achieve will consist of an *oscillation* between the two principles, in which now reality, now form, will predominate" (W/W 111; NA 20: 360).[170] Schiller's honest recognition of the limits of theorizing has significant ramifications for the writer's formation of the concept of beauty as well as for his later work.

Beauty, Harmonious Tension, and the Fragmented Ideal

In the sixteenth letter, Schiller followed up on his earlier insight that the beautiful ("das Schöne") exhibits both a releasing ("auflösende") and a tensing ("anspannende") effect. In various places throughout his writings, he interchanged the terms "abspannend" and "auflösend" to capture the relaxing or releasing characteristic of beautiful forms, which he understood to be a basic phenomenon of Nature. In short, beautiful forms exhibit harmonious tension. The writer's discussion of the nature of beauty in this context thus calls up the central symbol of the stringed instrument.

Beauty is never static. On the contrary, it is perpetually active. The releasing effect of beauty is required in order to keep both the material- and the form-impulses within their borders. On the other hand, the function of the tightening effect is to keep them "at full strength" ("in ihrer Kraft") (W/W 111). With beauty in idea, however, both activities cooperate. "Beauty is to release by tensing both natures uniformly, and to tense by releasing both natures uniformly" (W/W 111; NA 20: 361).[171] In his discussion of beauty, Schiller posited a law of cooperative, but tense interaction ("Wechselwirkung"). The writer added that experience affords us with no example of such a perfect relationship. In history, there is either an excess or a lack in one or the other impulses which impedes the attainment of the beautiful ideal. As a result, ideal beauty and beauty in experience ("Schönheit in der Erfahrung") are forever divorced. I am convinced that it was the historian's knowledge of the eternal rift between these phenomena that led him to qualify so many of his pronouncements concerning the attainment of the ideal. In the light of the writer's form of Schiller's argumentation, then, perhaps it is best to speak of his fragmented ideal.

In retrospect, Schiller chose not to characterize the dynamics of beauty in the spatial terms of contraction and expansion, that is in terms germane to physics, but rather in terms that are more appropriate to both music and medicine, especially as they address the tensing and releasing effect of the nerves. The subsequent distinction between energetic beauty ("energische Schönheit") and mellifluous or melting beauty ("schmelzende Schönheit") relates intimately to music (song, tone, and voice). Energetic beauty can no more repel the vestiges of savagery and hardness ("Überrest von Wildheit und Härte")—we note the historian at work here—than mellifluous beauty can protect against a certain degree of effeminacy and enervation ("Weichlichkeit und Entnervung").

In the light of Schiller's early medical studies, the selection of the word "Entnervung" at this point in his discussion is especially illuminating. The fact that the writer wishes to guard against complete "de-nerving"(lit.) recalls Mendelssohn's reflections on physiology. Schiller applies the two categories of beauty to the human species ("Gattung"). For he is eager to test the effects of mellifluous beauty on the taut ("angespannten") human being and the effects of an energetic beauty on the relaxed ("abgespannten") individual. Schiller's hope is to dissolve ("auszulöschen") these seemingly unrelated kinds of beauty in the unity of ideal beauty ("[das] Idealschöne"). The function of ideal beauty is analogous to the manner in which the two opposite forms of humanity tend to be absorbed into the unity of the ideal human being (" [der] Ideal-Mensch[]") (NA 20: 363). We may conclude, then, that the function of beauty, as suggested especially by Schiller's later writings, is to foster an awareness of the practical value and importance of harmonious tension within and between individual human beings, whose relationships will effect positive social changes.

Continuously scanning the limits of speculation, the writer turns, in the seventeenth letter, from the ideal realm of beauty to the stage of reality ("Schauplatz der Wirklichkeit"), where the individual human being is found in a particular historical situation and encounters numerous limitations. The tension between tightening and relaxing is especially acute on the plane of experience. Schiller holds that, at any particular moment, the human being finds oneself either in a condition of tension ("Anspannung") or relaxation ("Abspannung"). One of the practical values of beauty, then, consists in restoring harmony to the overly tense individual and energy to the wholly relaxed individual (NA 20: 364). Energy and harmony stand in complementary distribution. One's condition is grounded in the unconditional, in the light of which the human being constitutes a "whole perfect in itself" ("[ein] in sich selbst vollendete[s] Ganze") (W/W 119; NA 20: 364). This new paradigm—tense human being and languid human being—is surely one of the most innovative in Schiller's writings (see also the essay *Concerning Grace and Dignity* [*Über Anmut und Würde*] [1793]).

The principle of reciprocally cooperative activity is also addressed in the opening paragraph of the eighteenth letter. "By means of beauty sensuous man [human being] is led to form and thought; by means of beauty spiritual man is brought back to matter and restored to the world of sense" (W/W 123; NA 20: 365).[172] Despite the discussion of various topics, Schiller remains true to his conviction that the individual must strive to achieve a reciprocally cooperative relationship between one's sensuous and intellectual activities. Unlike his early theoretical writings, however, the letters concerning aesthetic education are distinguished by a more acute knowledge of the limits of theory as well as by a more sophisticated style of argumentation.

Schiller now claims to know the string ("Faden") that threads the entire labyrinth of aesthetics ("das ganze Labyrinth der Ästhetik") (NA 20: 366). He elaborates by outlining two prominent conceptions of beauty advanced by his contemporaries. The first is that beauty connects two antithetical conditions which can never be united. For Schiller's part, however, beauty ties those two opposed conditions together and cancels their opposition.[173] He also assails those philosophers who trust the guidance of their feelings, but who can never develop a *concept* of beauty. They are unable to distinguish anything individual in the image of totality which beauty impresses upon the senses. Conversely, those who enlist intellect as their sole guide can never arrive at a concept of *Beauty* because they are unable to appreciate anything but the individual parts of the totality presented by the beautiful object. For them, mind ("Geist") and matter ("Materie") are forever divorced ("geschieden") (NA 20: 367). The desired equilibrium between feeling and intellect is expressed in the footnote concluding this letter.

Limiting Reality

The nineteenth letter contains one of the most cogent descriptions of the path of culture. It begins with the proposition that the human being possesses a limitless capacity for being determined ("eine Bestimmbarkeit ohne Grenzen") *before* any determination ("Bestimmung") takes place. The infinity of space and of time is presented to the human imagination for its free employment. This condition of interminability ("Bestimmungslosigkeit") is called empty infinity ("leere Unendlichkeit") (NA 20: 368). First, the human senses are stirred ("gerührt"). From the infinite set of possible determinations only a single one will attain actuality ("Wirklichkeit"), and only when there is sense perception can we develop an idea or conception ("Vorstellung"). What, previously, was an empty capacity (or infinity) now becomes an active power ("wirkende Kraft"). Through a sensuous act of intellectual awakening, this new power appropriates a content, that is, it assigns a reality to what appeared to be an infinite expanse. Thus, in order to begin to describe a form ("Gestalt") in space, we must first limit limitless space. In order to represent ("vorzustellen") any change in time, the mind first divides the totality of time. Schiller's conclusion commands our attention. "Thus it is only through limits that we attain to reality, only through *negation* or exclusion that we arrive at *position* or real affirmation, only through the surrender ("Aufhebung") [cancellation (or suspension)] of our unconditional determinability that we achieve determination" (W/W 129; NA 20: 369).[174] Only by limiting reality, that is excluding the infinite range of possibilities, can we account for an infinite universe.

In the final analysis, then, negation is a positive act to the extent that it helps determine the nature of reality. The essence of Schiller's concept of *Aufhebung* consists in raising something to a higher consciousness. When entity arises from non-entity and something positive is produced by negation, the mind is actively engaged in judging or thinking ("urtheilen," the result of which is thought ["der *Gedanke*"]) (NA 20: 369). Becoming aware of the infinite expanses of the universe, the human senses are moved and the mind is activated. The objects of Nature are perceived by the senses, but first given shape by the mind. Schiller, the philosopher, has now joined hands with Schiller, the cultural historian and social critic.

The writer concludes: "We do then, admittedly, only reach the whole through the part, the limitless only through limitation; but it is no less true that we only reach the part through the whole, and limitation only through the limitless" (W/W 131; NA 20: 369).[175] Unity in diversity, diversity in unity—both concepts complement each other in Schiller's writing. The whole and the part, the part and the whole seem to form a harmoniously taut relationship. Schiller's conclusion certainly does not preclude the fact that individual human beings perceive this relation differently, if only partially. It does presuppose, however, that individuals think universally, that is, globally.

Filling in the Gaps

Along the path of culture, the beautiful ("das Schöne") prepares the way for humankind to achieve the transition from sensation ("Empfinden") to thought ("Denken"). In order to fill in the gap a wholly new and independent faculty is required, which is endless ("unendlich"; NA 20: 369) and without which the universal ("Allgemeines") could not arise out of the particular. Thought ("der Gedanke") is the immediate act ("Handlung") of this absolute faculty. Though dependent on sense impression to express itself ("sich zu äußern") in the first place, thought presents itself to the senses *only* through opposition ("Entgegensetzung"). Declaring its independence, it excludes all external influences, through which act it secures for the intellectual faculties the freedom to express themselves in accordance with their own laws. Beauty is thus capable of leading the human being from matter to form, from sensations to laws and from a conditional state of existence to absolute being (NA 20: 370).

Even the finite mind, then, is endowed with the power to shape reality, and "only of him who is conscious of himself can we demand Reason, that is, absolute consistency and universality of consciousness; prior to that he is not a human being at all, and no act of humanity can be expected of him" (W/W 135; NA 20: 372).[176] Without reason, *human* life is impossible. Skeptical of what the metaphysician and the physicist on their own are able to ascertain about the nature of Reality, the writer contends: "Neither philosophical abstraction nor empirical method can ever take us back to the source from which our concepts of Universality and Necessity derive: their early manifestation in time veils it from the scrutiny of the empirical observor, their supersensuous origin from that of the metaphysical inquirer" (W/W 135/137; NA 20: 372).[177] What is undeniable, however, is self-consciousness ("Selbstbewußtseyn"): "and once its immutable unity is established, there is also established a law of unity for everything which is there *for* man [the human being], and for everything which is to come about *through* him, i.e., for all his knowing and for all his doing" (W/W 137; NA 20: 372).[178] But by underscoring self-consciousness, the writer also circumscribes the limits of both philosophy and science.

Schiller now returns, again as historian, to his original thesis. "The sensuous drive awakens with our experience of life (with the beginning of our individuality); the rational drive, with our experience of law (with the beginning of our personality); and only at this point, when both have come into existence, is the basis of man's [the human being's] humanity established" (W/W 137; NA 20: 373).[179] While it may appear that freedom originates in the opposition of two "necessities" ("Nothwendigkeiten"; NA 20: 373), Schiller's argument still presupposes the taut interaction between sense and reason.

The Question of Freedom

In the twentieth letter, Schiller concludes that freedom inheres in Nature. It is not, first and foremost, a work of the human being (NA 20: 373). Indeed, human freedom is possible only when we recognize that sensation precedes consciousness. As a product of Nature, freedom is tapped by the human mind, by virtue of which it is then transferred to social life. The free will of the human being chooses between the sensuous and the formal impulses. The historian and physiologist in Schiller cooperate. For as the human species progresses, a more rational period replaces the Age of Sensuousness ("Alter der Sinnlichkeit"). Unlike the mainstream of German Enlightenment thinking, progress does not constitute a straight, teleological line of development. Occasionally, a step backwards ("*einen Schritt zurückthun*") is required "since only through determination being annulled ("aufgehoben") again can a contrary determination take its place. In order to exchange passivity for autonomy [self-activity], a passive determination for an active one, man [the human being] must therefore be momentarily *free of all determination whatsoever,* and pass through a state of pure determinability" (W/W 139/141; NA 20: 374).[180]

The middle disposition, through which the mind ("das Gemüt") passes from sensation to thought, creates a zone in which sensuousness and reason are active simultaneously ("*zugleich* tätig sind"): "precisely for this reason, however, they cancel each other out [are suspended] ("aufheben") as determining forces, and bring about a negation by means of an opposition" (W/W 141; NA 20: 375).[181] The writer now offers a clear definition of the aesthetic. The middle disposition ("mittlere Stimmung") is described as one "in which the psyche [mind] is subject neither to physical nor to moral constraint, and yet is active in both these ways" (W/W 141; NA 20: 375). As the condition of real and active determinacy mediating between physical (or sensuous) and logical-moral (or rational) determination, the aesthetic is then free.[182] Only in a state of aesthetic experience can we know freedom. Still, the writer reminds the reader, in the light of history, the aesthetic state is intermediary to the realization of a wholly rational-moral state in which not only we as individuals but the whole of society will be truly free.

In the accompanying footnote, and in sum, Schiller points out that among all the objects of education (health, understanding, morality, and taste), the process of education to beauty cultivates "the whole complex of our sensual and spiritual powers in the greatest possible harmony" ("das Ganze unsrer sinnlichen und geistigen Kräfte in möglichster Harmonie"; W/W 143; NA 20: 376).

The Aesthetic Condition and the Reshaping of History

According to the twenty-first letter, the aesthetic condition creates a plane of existence where there is no individual purpose, truth, or duty. In aesthetic culture ("ästhetische Kultur"), a human being's personal worth or dignity ("Würde") remains undetermined. What is made possible, however, "by the grace of Nature" (W/W 147), or on account of it ("*von Natur wegen*"), is

the opportunity to fashion oneself according to one's own moral will. With
the aid of aesthetics, the human being actualizes the freedom to be what
one ought to be ("die Freiheit, zu seyn, was er seyn soll"; NA 20: 378). In
this way, humanity regains what it had lost through the onslaught of time.
From this perspective, we can better understand why the writer is able to
claim that beauty is "our second Creator" ("unsre zweyte Schöpferin"; NA
20: 378), the original creator being Nature.

The historian is again at work when Schiller states that the aesthetic
constitutes a whole in itself ("ein Ganzes in sich selbst") because it unites
the conditions of our origin, our continuing existence, and our future desti-
nation. As we discover in the twenty-second letter, rupture is a necessary
part of this process. "Here alone do we feel reft out ["gerissen"] of time,
and our human nature expresses itself with a purity and *integrity,* as though
it had as yet suffered no impairment through the intervention of external
forces" (W/W 151; NA 20: 379).[183]

Drawing upon the harmonious tension of beauty, we are able to become
masters of ourselves, turning, as we will, to play and seriousness, rest and
motion, compliance and resistance, abstract thinking and intuitive contemplation ("Anschauung") (NA 20: 380). The genuine work of art assists the
recipient by generating a mood ("Stimmung") of lofty serenity and freedom
of mind combined with power and vigor (NA 20: 380–81). This is, perhaps,
the major criterion that Schiller employs in his evaluations of the quality
and value of works of art. It also complements his activities as an art critic
and reviewer of books.

Schiller appreciated each of the arts for its own unique contribution to
culture. He describes their effects as follows: "We leave a beautiful piece
of music with our feeling excited, a beautiful poem with our imagination
quickened, a beautiful sculpture or building with our understanding awak-
ened" (W/W 153; NA 20: 381).[184] As time progresses, the arts develop ever
closer ties to one another.[185] Music, for instance, must become form ("Gestalt"); the plastic and pictorial arts must become music; and, poetry, like
musical art, will overpower us; yet, like the plastic arts, poetry surrounds
us with quiet clarity (NA 20: 381). Over time, each art form will develop
the power to extend beyond its original limitations. Perhaps this is one of
the theoretical origins of Richard Wagner's concept of the *Gesamtkunstwerk*
(the total work of art).[186]

With respect to aesthetic autonomy, Schiller insists that it is not the
content but the form of art that secures true aesthetic freedom ("wahre
ästhetische Freyheit"; NA 20: 381). The secret of the master of art ("Kunst-
geheimnis des Meisters") consists in having the form consume the material
(*"daß er den Stoff durch die Form vertilgt"*; NA 20: 382). Only in this way
can the recipient's mind be set free and made inviolate. Indeed, one of
the major effects of the beautiful is freedom from passions ("Freyheit von

Leidenschaften") (NA 20: 382), that is, from enslavement to one's sensuous nature.

Schiller summarizes his main thesis in the twenty-third letter: "The transition from a passive state of feeling to an active state of thinking and willing cannot, then, take place except via a middle state of aesthetic freedom" (W/W 161; NA 20: 383).[187] "In a word, there is no other way of making sensuous man [human being] rational except by first making him [or her] aesthetic" (W/W 161; NA 20: 383).[188] From one's unrefined physical-sensuous nature, the human being progresses through an aesthetic-cultural condition to a truly rational-moral state. Thought and form mean nothing without their counterparts, however. Considering the determinability of the sensuous human being, "were he merely to lose the passive determination, he would at the same time lose the possibility of an active one, since thought needs a body, and form can only be realized in some material" (W/W 163; NA 20: 384).[189] Though momentarily autonomous, art is not completely autonomous since the task of culture is ultimately political.

Once the difficult step from the physical to the aesthetic state is initiated, "the aesthetically tempered [tuned] man [human being] will achieve universally valid judgments and universally valid actions, as soon as he [or she] has the will to do so" (W/W 163; NA 20: 385).[190] Though this statement creatively reenacts Kant's concept of *sensus communis,* beauty is still the chief instrument in the reshaping of history. "It is, therefore, one of the most important tasks of education [culture] to subject man [the human being] to form, even in his purely physical life, and to make him aesthetic in every domain over which beauty is capable of extending her [its] sway; since it is only out of the aesthetic, not out of the physical, state that the moral can develop" (W/W 165; NA 20: 385).[191]

The footnote to letter twenty-three addresses the process of ennoblement which human beings experience when refining their sensibilities. "We call that form noble which impresses the stamp of autonomy [independence] upon anything which by its nature merely *serves some purpose* (is a mere means)" (W/W 167; NA 20: 386).[192] Schiller recaptures the essential characteristic of beauty which he discovered while in the process of writing the *Kallias* Letters. "Beauty is the only way that freedom has of making itself manifest in appearance" (W/W 167; NA 20: 386).[193]

In the twenty-fourth letter, however, the writer qualifies his ideas when asserting that the state of brute nature is "purely an Idea ["bloß Idee"], but an idea with which experience is, in certain particulars, in complete accord" (W/W 173; NA 20: 389).[194] For, even in the modern age, human beings have not been completely successful in controlling their "animal" instincts. As we noted earlier, the writer's critical self-reflection alerts him to moments of savagery even in the most cultivated states of development. It is on this score that Schiller's criticism of the Reign of Terror is most effective.

As in the essay on universal history, the writer wrestles with the idea that the vestiges of the past are never totally eradicated. Thus, the complete realization of the final state of true rationality via culture assumes the status of a beautiful idea. Points such as these disclose the limits of the letters *Concerning the Aesthetic Education of the Human Being*. For, if the human being is incapable, even over time, of controlling one's animal instincts, that is of reverting back to one's original state, then the goal of a perfect balance between mind and body as fostered by multiple forms of culture will never be achieved. It seems inevitable, then, that at some point the state will have to intervene on the behalf of the individual. This, I believe, is the most difficult, unresolved problem in Schiller's cultural-political program of aesthetic education.

Bearing in mind the writer's account of the gradual actualization of wholeness between the individual and society, we come to appreciate one of the writer's central theses. "On the wings of fancy [imagination], man [the human being] leaves the narrow confines of the present in which mere animality stays bound, in order to strive towards an unlimited future. But while the infinite opens up before his reeling imagination, his heart has not yet ceased to live in the particular or to wait upon the moment" (W/W 175; NA 20: 390).[195] Even on the wings of imagination, however, the human being does not leave present reality. One transcends only the narrow confines of reality. So, "in the midst of one's animality" ("Mitten in seiner Thierheit") the human being is overwhelmed by the compulsion to seek the absolute (NA 20: 390–391).

Education/Development/Cultivation ("Bildung")

The topic of the *Bildung* (education, development, or cultivation) of the human species was widely discussed in eighteenth-century German culture. Anna Louisa Karsch's poetry, Lessing's *The Education of the Human Race* [*Die Erziehung des Menschengeschlechts* (1780)], Sophie von La Roche's and C. M. Wieland's novels of education (*Erziehungsromane*), Johann Georg Herder's *Also a Philosophy of History for the Education of Humanity*, and Goethe's *Faust*,[196] among many other works underscored the indispensability of self-development in the general education of society. Thus, Schiller's *Concerning the Aesthetic Education of the Human Being* codifies one of the major currents of late eighteenth-century German culture. Perhaps for this reason this writing has received the widest reception among Schiller's theoretical works. What warrants special attention is that Schiller did not try to conceal the problems inherent in his own program of aesthetic education. Rather, he sought to disclose them through a process of critical self-reflection.

Unconvinced of Immanuel Kant's concept of moral necessity, Schiller perceived that, with its first appearance in the sensual world, the moral law—that "[which] is most sacred [the divine] in the human being" ("das

Heilige im Menschen")—cannot escape periodic adulteration (NA 20: 392). Misled, at times, by the interests of sensuous self-love, one "merely feels the fetters which Reason lays upon him [the human being], not the infinite liberation which she [it] is capable of affording him" (W/W 179; NA 20: 392).[197] Rather than sense the dignity of the lawgiver within ("die Würde des Gesetzgebers in sich"), the human being senses only constraint and becomes only a submissive subject ("Untertan") rather than an active citizen.

The political dimension of the letters on aesthetic education is revealed by the writer's choice of words. Time and again in one's physical condition, the impulse to live ("der Trieb des Lebens") dominates the form impulse (NA 20: 393). Though Schiller advances the idea that to be a human being "Nature is not meant to rule him exclusively, nor Reason to rule him conditionally" (W/W 181; NA 20: 393),[198] his recognition of the periodic resurgence of the bestial nature of the human being even in the rational human being remains an unresolved problem for the theorist. Still, Schiller continued to advocate freedom. The writer's language at this point is politically charged. "Contemplation (or reflection) is the first liberal relation which man establishes with the universe around him" (W/W 183; NA 20: 394).[199] In this state of contemplation, the world becomes an object. Because the human being is able to lend form to matter, one proves one's freedom by forming the formless.

The problem of sensuousness becomes acute when Schiller readdresses the nature of beauty. "Beauty, then, is indeed an *object* for us, because reflection is the condition of our having any sensation of it; but it is at the same time a *state of the [perceiving] subject,* because feeling is a condition of our having any perception of it. Thus beauty is indeed form, because we contemplate it; but it is at the same time life, because we feel it. In a word: it is at once a state of our being and an activity we perform" (W/W 187; NA 20: 396).[200]

Contrary to some scholarly opinions, Schiller's doctrine of the necessity of beautiful culture does not encourage inwardness (*Innerlichkeit*). Most certainly, the process of the enculturation and ennobling humankind begins with the individual subject. As is made plain in the twenty-sixth letter, "Not where man [the human being] hides himself, a *troglodyte,* in caves, eternally an isolated unit, never finding humanity *outside himself;* nor yet there where, a *nomad,* he roams in vast hordes over the face of the earth, eternally but one of a number, never finding humanity *within himself*—but only there, where, in his own hut, he discourses silently with himself and, from the moment he steps out of it, with all the rest of his kind, only there will the tender blossom of beauty unfold" (W/W 191; NA 20: 398).[201] This is certainly unlike Goethe's Werther or Schiller's own Ferdinand von Walter, both of whom demand the realization of their own self-interest from the privileged location of either the cottage (*Hütte*) or the court (*Hof*).

Two of Schiller's fundamental assumptions contradict the claims of mere subjectivity. The first is that the human mind is naturally inclined toward an aesthetic disposition, and the second, the idea that the freedom of the will does not amount so much to freedom of choice as it does to the freedom to will what is divine, namely the true, the good, and the beautiful. The proper vehicle for the activation of this noble aspiration is aesthetic culture. Throughout his writing, Schiller reiterates his hope that the appreciation and apprehension of beautiful forms and the cultivation of beauty, i.e., culture, will not simply guide the human being through the perilous labyrinth of historical existence, but will help the individual transform one's social environment and, if one's society, then history as well.

The (moral) will is inner necessity, i.e., natural. This idea is predicated on the assumption that human beings "delight in *semblance*, and a propensity to *ornamentation* and *play*" ("die Freude am *Schein*, die Neigung zum *Putz* und zum *Spiele*") (W/W 193; NA 20: 399). However, Schiller asserts that, once the sensuous human being contemplates the nature of beautiful objects, one is necessarily torn from a state of apparent tranquility ("gerissen") (NA 20: 399). This implies, on the one hand, that many are not persuaded by the merits of beauty. On the other hand, no civilized or cultured individual wills to be a savage ("ein Wilder"). One is compelled by inner necessity to will the good and the true which reason dictates. According to the writer, this is what all genuinely human beings wish for themselves and for each other.

Moving Toward a Conclusion

The last in this series of letters, the twenty-seventh, is especially rich not only in its summary of the main points of Schiller's treatise as a whole but also in the use of the metaphors and motifs we have been examining. The paradigm of the sensuous and intellectual nature of the human being in the early medical dissertations is here united with several fundamental precepts of Kantian philosophy. It is a further indication of the fact that the writer's multidisciplinary activities helped shape each of his major writings.

For instance, the writer asserts that Nature itself has given to the animal world more than the bare necessities of life. To a limited extent, animals also play. Clearly, Schiller's views here are based on observations of the animal world, i.e., Nature and not simply on ideas. For example, "with what enjoyment of life do insects swarm in the sunbeam" (W/W 207; NA 20: 406).[202] What we discern in the melodious warbling of the songbird is not simply the cry of desire. Like human beings, animals know work and play. Schiller: "An animal may be said *to be at work*, when the stimulus to activity is some lack; it may be said *to be at play*, when the stimulus is sheer pleni-tude of vitality, when superabundance of life is its own incentive to action" (W/W 207; NA 20: 406).[203] But even in that condition, the chains of mere sensuousness or animality are cast off. "Thus does Nature, even in her material kingdom, offer us a prelude of the Illimitable, and even here remove in part the chains which, in the realm of form, she casts away entirely" (W/ W 207; NA 20: 406).[204] The path of culture leads from the dire earnestness of the need for physical and aesthetic play. In this free movement ("freie Bewegung"), the human being already experiences some of the exalted freedom of the beautiful ("hohe Freiheit des Schönen") that breaks the chains of every specific end.

In a footnote, Schiller stressed the emancipatory power of the feeling (and play) of a free sequence of ideas ("Gefühl der freien Ideenfolge"). It is assumed that we take pleasure in the independence of the mind. But it is only with the aid of imagination that we are able to tear ourselves from everyday reality. "Only by tearing itself free from reality does the formative power raise itself up to the idea; and before the imagination, in its productive capacity, can act according to its own laws, it must first, in its reproductive procedures, have freed itself from alien laws" (W/W 209; NA 20: 407).[205] In its attempt to attain free form, the imagination takes a leap ("Sprung") to aesthetic play. Another agency, the legislative faculty of law-giving mind ("der gesetzgebende Geist"), now subjects the arbitrary process of imaging to its unity, imposing upon the infinite set of images its own self-dependence. In this state, the aesthetic play-impulse ("der ästhetische Spieltrieb") is hardly recognizable since crude taste ("rohe[r] Geschmack") will first grasp what is new and startling, colorful, adventurous and bizarre and avoid simplicity and tranquility. Fashioning grotesque forms, loving swift transitions and striking contrasts, the beautiful is simply what excites the human being. Even in the earliest stage of cultural development, the individual has learned something of importance. For by shaping the material world, a remarkable alteration has taken place in the very form of one's judgment. The source of pleasure now is no longer mere need but the laws of one's own legislative faculty (mind) working on the images created by one's imagination. No longer content with what is necessary or merely material, the freer play-impulse ("der freiere Spieltrieb") tears itself from ("losreißt") the chains of exigency, thus making beauty the object of its striving. Hence, one literally breaks into a new state of human being through the self-transformation of consciousness, and this act is one of free, moral election.

Even the writer's description of the transformation of the inner human being contains some of the major metaphors we have been tracking. "Uncoordinated leaps of joy turn into dance, the unformed movements of the body into the graceful and harmonious language of gesture; the confused and indistinct cries [sounds = Laute] of feeling become articulate, begin to obey the laws of rhythm, and to take on the contours of song" (W/W 213; NA 20: 409).[206] Schiller's language complements several of the main metaphors, motifs, and topics of his entire oeuvre at this point: "Released from its dark bondage, the eye, less troubled now by passion, can apprehend the form of the beloved; soul looks deep into soul, and out of a selfish exchange of lust there grows a generous interchange of affection. Desire widens, and is exalted into love" (W/W 213; NA 20: 409).[207]

The writer's choice of words in his concluding letter tends to unify his previous arguments. I will therefore cite the entire passage. "The dynamic State can merely make society possible, by letting one nature be curbed by another; the ethical State can merely make it (morally) necessary, by subjecting the individual will to the general; the aesthetic State alone can make it real, because it consummates the will of the whole through the nature of the individual. Though it may be his needs which drive man [the human being] into society, and reason which implants within him the principles of social behaviour, beauty alone can confer upon him a *social character*. Taste alone brings harmony into society, because it fosters harmony in the individual. All other forms of perception divide man, because they are founded exclusively either upon the sensuous or upon the spiritual part of his being; only the aesthetic mode of perception makes of him a whole, because both his natures must be in harmony ("zusammenstimmen") if he is to achieve it" (W/W 215; NA 20: 410).[208]

Concluding Remarks

In Schiller's later theoretical writings, beauty is enlisted as the major instrument in the cultural re-formation of society. For it alone creates an experience of freedom through the interplay of imagination and understanding. "Beauty alone do we enjoy at once as individual and as genus, i.e., as *representatives* of the human genus" (W/W 217; NA 20: 411).[209] And "beauty alone makes the whole world happy, and each and every being forgets its limitations while under its spell" (W/W 217; NA 20: 411).[210] The writer does not say that as individuals we should forsake our individuality or uniqueness. Such an understanding would contradict Schiller's belief in the proper functioning of the individual within the whole of society. Rather, through beauty, we are freed of our sense of limitation. By extension, the experience of beauty affords us the means to achieve wholeness without forsaking our uniqueness as individuals, precisely because it is up to us to fill the beautiful forms of art with our own content.

The kingdom of beautiful appearance ("Reich des schönen Scheins") is not the ethereal province some scholars and critics of Schiller's text have charged. Though reconstituting the province of reason, this new kingdom also reaches down to where natural impulse still holds sway over the individual and form has not yet been conceived. Perhaps, it is for this reason that the development of taste becomes such a critical task for the human species. For, "From within the Mysteries of Science [R. D. Miller: Truth], taste leads knowledge out into the broad daylight of Common Sense, and transforms a monopology of the Schools into the common possession of Human Society as a whole" (W/W 217; NA 20: 412).[211] One of the most important points here is that, by traversing the limits of established knowledge, taste contributes to the realization of a wholly human society.

Once again, the writer juxtaposes the metaphors of the fetters and the wings. In this context, however, the motif of flight underscores the liberating effect of the beautiful in the practical sphere of social life. "On the wings of taste even that art which must cringe for payment can lift itself out of the dust; and, at the touch of her wand, the fetters of serfdom fall away from the lifeless and the living alike" (W/W 219; NA 20: 412).[212] This is the full textual context for the following important claim:

> In the Aesthetic State—everything—even the tool which serves—is a free citizen, having equal rights with the noblest; . . . Here, therefore, in the realm of Aesthetic Semblance, we find that ideal of equality fulfilled. (W/W 219; NA 20: 412)[213]

In the end, the aesthetic, the ethical, and the political spheres are intimately connected in Friedrich Schiller's ruminations on the nature of aesthetic education.

It has been alleged that Schiller's treatise is elitist in nature because of his suggestion that, in fact ("der That nach") and not simply in need ("dem Bedürfniß nach"), the state of beautiful appearance ("Staat des schönen Scheins") might ("möchte") be found in "some few chosen circles" ("einigen wenigen auserlesenen Zirkeln") (NA 20: 412).[214] Let us cite the entire passage and allow the reader to judge for oneself in the light of the foregoing reading if this allegation holds. "But does such a State of Aesthetic Semblance really exist? And, if so, where is it to be found? As a need, it exists in every finely attuned soul; as a realized fact, we are likely to find it, like the pure Church and the pure Republic, only in some few chosen circles, where conduct is governed, not by some soulless imitation of the manners and morals of others, but by the aesthetic nature we have made our own; where men [human beings] make their way, with undismayed simplicity and tranquil innocence, through even the most involved and complex situations, free alike of the compulsion to infringe the freedom of others in order to assert their own, as of the necessity to shed their Dignity in order to manifest Grace" (W/W 219; NA 20: 412).[215] Did Schiller really encourage the formation of an elitist group? Or is the inquiring writer maintaining that, in the late eighteenth century, there were only very few who could appreciate the ultimately practical value of trying to actualize the rational-moral state? To draw upon Kant's essay "What is Enlightenment?" (1784), for Schiller, the late eighteenth century was but a first phase of Enlightenment and not the Age of Enlightenment. There can be no doubt here that all human beings are encouraged to join in the great task of culture. For the State of Beauty in Appearance, which in view of the *Kallias* Letters must be the practical realization of freedom in appearance, already exists in "every finely tuned soul" ("in jeder feingestimmten Seele"; NA 20: 412). Perhaps the idea of elitism is not generic to Schiller's writing but simply superimposed upon it.[216]

In concluding this chapter, it is helpful to recall that the adjective "feingestimmt" (fine-tuned) was implicit in the employment of various tropes developed already at the time of the early medical dissertations. In Schiller's writings, the central symbol of the stringed instrument is not only a sign of harmonious tension but also a symbol of health.[217] Therefore, the harmonious State is also the truly healthy State. In *Concerning the Aesthetic Education of the Human Being,* politics and physiology converge. In this work, the task of culture is to perpetually reactivate the creatively productive tension between sensuousness and reason in the human being. In order to be politically responsible, one must first be cultured (*gebildet*). And it is only through the universal communicability of the experience of Beauty (the aesthetic state) that individuals are capable of actualizing their humanity in the here and now of history. Finally, Schiller did not envision a future state of perfection, as had Lessing in *The Education of the Human Species.* Nor did he agree with Immanuel Kant's retention of the idea of providence ("Vorsehung") in his creative reworking of the eschatological tradition in *Religion Within the Bounds of Reason Alone (Die Religion innerhalb der Grenzen der bloßen Vernunft).*[218] More like Johann Gottfried Herder in the *Ideas Concerning the Philosophy of the History of Humankind,* Schiller sought to cultivate a common sense of humanity. In his own unique way, namely through the writing and dissemination of *The Aesthetic Education of the Human Being in a Series of Letters,* the writer promoted the actualization of the rational-moral state in the hearts and minds of free, yet interdependent human beings in and throughout history.[219] Perhaps Schiller would have agreed with Herder's conclusion in the *Ideas:* "the human being is in need of a long education."[220]

6

"Merely an Idea": The Later
Theoretical Essays

SCHILLER'S essay *Concerning Naive and Sentimental Poetry* [*Über naive und sentimentalische Dichtung*] (1795) has been viewed, time and again, as a major contribution to the German and European romantic movements. Though only part of a much older and longer debate, the classic example of the supposed agreement between Schiller and the romantics is the astonishing affinity between Schiller's work and Friedrich Schlegel's *Concerning the Study of Greek Poetry* [*Über das Studium der griechischen Poesie*] (1795). These important essays were written simultaneously, yet independently of each other, and form parts of a widespread debate between the moderns and the ancients.[1] More recent scholarship on this subject, however, has moved away from the historical significance of the assumed intellectual affinity between Schiller and Schlegel. It has engaged, instead, their ideological warfare.[2] A close assessment of this disagreement, and Schiller's relationship to various writers of the time, proves important for an understanding of Schiller's critical distance from the German romantic movement and German idealism. Let us begin by reexamining Schiller's essay *Concerning Naive and Sentimental Poetry*.

At the outset of his essay, the writer defines Nature in a twofold sense. First, there are the plant, mineral, animal, and "ecological" parts of Nature. Secondly, there is human nature ("menschliche Natur"). The highest developed, or cultured human being ("jeder feinere Mensch") knows of a higher interest ("Interesse") which the "contemplation of simple/naive nature" ("Anblick der einfältigen Natur") instills. At the beginning of the essay, Schiller expresses his interest in "naive" Nature, which stands apart from art and "shames" it (NA 20: 413). But what are the characteristics of this type of Nature?

In this way of looking at things, Nature is nothing other than voluntary existence [Dasein], the existence [Bestehen] of things through themselves, Existence [Existenz] by its own and immutable laws (NA 20: 413).[3]

193

The idea that Nature is unchangeable and that it functions in accordance with immutable laws is found in Schiller's writings as early as 1786, in the prose writing *Criminal Out of Infamy*. "Naive" Nature is essentially moral, at least to the extent that the moral "delight in Nature" which one experiences is mediated by an idea, the idea of humanity in harmony with Nature.

Schiller asks what makes the tweeting of birds and the humming of bees such a pleasant experience. What is it about such moments that claims our love ("Liebe")? His answer indicates that the writer has abandoned the search for the objective ground of beautiful objects, which was the chief enterprise of the *Kallias* Letters. For it is not the objects in themselves but the represented idea that now claims the reader's attention: "existence according to its own laws; . . . the eternal unity with itself" ("das Dasein nach eignen Gesetzen, . . . die ewige Einheit mit sich selbst") (NA 20: 414). As in Kant's critical philosophy, the human mind constructs unity with Nature. For Schiller, however, the task of ordering and reshaping reality is possible only as long as the human being remains sensitive to "naive" Nature, i.e., seeks harmony. But this state of mind is more characteristic of the condition of the ancient Greeks than it is of the vast majority of moderns.

> They [the ancient Greeks] *are* what we *were;* they are what we *should become* again (NA 20: 414).[4]

Cognizant of cultural differences, the writer acknowledges that the modern condition differs radically from the natural state of the ancients.

> We [moderns] were Nature, as they were, and our culture should lead us back to Nature on the path of Reason and Freedom (NA 20: 414).[5]

What, then, do the ancients mean for the moderns? The ancients represent the lost childhood of the moderns, a condition that fills moderns with melancholy.

> They are, at the same time, representations of our highest perfection in the ideal, which is why they set us into [a state of] sublime emotion (NA 20: 414).[6]

Since, however, the historical break between ancient and modern times renders the ideal of the highest completion unachievable, either melancholy or sublime emotion become the primary sensuous response.

Neither the ancients nor the moderns in themselves are divine because "We are free and they are necessary; we change, they remain one" (NA 20: 415).[7] The "divine or the ideal" (NA 20: 415) can be realized only by conjoining the two directions: "when the will follows the law of necessity freely and, with every shift of fantasy, Reason asserts its rule" (NA 20: 415).[8] Well aware of the fact that the process is one of infinite progression, the moderns seek to approximate original Nature.

Schiller's indebtedness to Immanuel Kant on this point is confirmed by the first footnote to the essay, where the writer refers directly to the chapter on the intellectual interest in the beautiful in the *Critique of the Power of Judgment*. Why are the ancients important for us moderns? They "furnish us with the sweetest enjoyment of our humanity as idea" (NA 20: 415).[9] Naive Nature, then, is equivalent to the idea of an original condition of harmony with Nature. Our "interest" in Nature ("Interesse für Natur") is based on an idea (NA 20: 415).[10] But this interest, as the writer stated clearly at the outset of his essay, is evident only in individual dispositions or minds ("Gemüter") that are receptive to rational-moral ideas. Here, Schiller makes one of his grand leaps of faith. For he assumes that, on the most general level, the "predisposition toward the moral" ("Anlage zum Sittlichen") is common to all people "without difference" ("ohne Unterschied") (NA 20: 415).

While exploring the naive way of thinking ("das Naive der Denkart"; NA 20: 422f.), the writer expands his concept of genius when he asserts that every true genius possesses childlike unity with Nature. A prime example of this type of understanding, for Schiller, is Christopher Columbus: "coming up with the right things [through inspiration] is typical of every ingenious decision" (NA 20: 424).[11] Surely, when Columbus finally departed Europe in search of India and headed West, he defied all scientific knowledge of the world. Had he listened to the scientists of his day (whose voices were clearly audible), he would never have set sail. At the same time, however, without their technology, he would never have been able to realize his ingenious idea.

It is important to note that Friedrich Schiller and Johann Wolfgang Goethe interpreted Columbus's deed as a product, not of science but of imagination and intuition. Early in his career in the essay "Julius's Theosophy," Schiller stated "He [Columbus] found this island on paper, and his calculation was correct" (NA 20: 127).[12] The sentence preceding this statement establishes a close affinity between the essay on universal history (1789), the early essay, and *Concerning Naive and Sentimental Poetry* (1795). "Columbus, the world discoverer, enters the questionable wager with an untraversed ocean with recourse to the infallibility of his calculation, to seek out the missing [second] half of the known hemisphere, the great island of Atlantis, which was supposed to fill in the gap on his geographical chart" (NA 20: 127).[13] Hence, it was more than God and gold that motivated Columbus to navigate the great Sea of Darkness. The will to undertake the voyage was sparked just as much by the seafarer's imagination. His true compass, then, was intuition and imagination, not certain knowledge (science). With geniuses such as Columbus, simplicity of thought triumphs over technical knowledge. "It [his genius] proceeds not according to acknowledged principles but according to notions and feelings" (NA 20: 424).[14]

For the writer Friedrich Schiller, a genius expresses oneself "freely and naturally" ("frey und natürlich") in consonance with the "innocence of the heart in lively 'company'"("Unschuld des Herzens im lebendigen Umgang") (NA 20:426). It is important to note that this category of individuals transcends time. The writer includes within this group Sophocles and Hippocrates in ancient times and, "from more modern times," Dante, Tasso, Dürer, Cervantes, Shakespeare, Fielding, and Sterne, together with several others (NA 20:425). It is crucial to note that Schiller's formulation of the genius as type now begins to override his earlier diachronic distinction between ancient and modern times. The genius's naive way of thinking is accompanied, in practice, by "a naiveté of expression in (social) contact" ("ein Naives des Ausdrucks im Umgang"), which, like the behavior of a child, consists in naming things by their name and dealing with matters "via the shortest path" ("auf dem kürzesten Wege") (NA 20: 426). According to this definition of the naive disposition ("Naive der Gesinnung") and "unadulterated Nature" ("die reine Natur") (NA 20: 427), and, in retrospect, Max Piccolomini would seem to qualify as a naive genius.[15]

Scholarship has overlooked the fact that, as much as he extolled the merits of the naive genius, Schiller also acknowledged the tendency of genius to exaggerate or even ignore the true nature of the world. Concerning this latter problem, the writer submits that naive people forget "out of one's own beautiful humanity that they must live in a corrupt world" (NA 20: 422).[16] There was a tendency among people Schiller knew personally to conduct themselves at the courts of kings, as he says, "with an ingenuity and innocence as we find them only in a pastoral world" (NA 20: 422).[17] This is a forceful criticism of his times, one that counteracts the idea that Schiller was an elitist who was somehow unconcerned about the needs of individuals.[18] It also constitutes a form of self-criticism. For Schiller's realistic assessment of human existence is informed by the fact that, while at the Hohe Carlsschule, he had been trained for diplomatic service. We have been informed that even Goethe marveled at Schiller's talent in aristocratic circles.[19] Though admiring the pure nature of the genius-type, Schiller perceived that, in the case of poetic genius, there is a tendency to transcend rather than to harmonize with it: "but through an effect of the poeticizing imagination, it is often transferred from the rational to the irrational" (NA 20: 427).[20] The critical posture vis-à-vis untempered imagination in this writing also complements Schiller's activities as a book reviewer.[21]

In *Concerning Naive and Sentimental Poetry* Schiller makes it abundantly clear that in the modern age the human being is free, but only at the expense of the states of happiness and completeness experienced by the children of Nature ("Naturkinder"). In modern times, we "have lost both" (NA 20: 427). The early anthropological paradigm of the medical dissertations is also operative in this essay. For as "the sensuous human being" ("der sinnliche Mensch") laments the loss of happiness, "the moral human being" ("der moralische [Mensch]" decries the loss of perfection (NA 20: 427–28). I think it important that we accept the writer's recognition that the original condition of Nature has indeed been lost to the past.[22] For it is a distinguishing feature of the relationship between Schiller and Schlegel.

Perhaps while thinking of his friend Johann Wolfgang Goethe, the mature writer conducted a dialogue with the naive genius, which he characterizes as a "sentimental friend of Nature" ("empfindsamer Freund der Natur") (NA 20: 428). The Stoic tradition is clearly evident since we are informed that the naive genius never complains about the difficulties, inequities, and pressures of life: "you must subjugate under you all maladies of culture with voluntary resignation" (NA 20: 428).[23] One of the central theses of his late theoretical works complements the cultural-political program of *Concerning the Aesthetic Education of the Human Being:*

> Do not be afraid of the confusion outside you but of the confusion within; strive for unity, but do not seek it in uniformity; seek peace, but through balance, not through the cessation of your activity (NA 20: 428).[24]

Unity and tranquility are not states of rest. Rather, they manifest the harmonious tension of activities. To be sure, for Schiller, striving to attain such a condition begins within oneself. It is clear that the interactionist theory of the third and final medical dissertation *Concerning the Connection of the Animal and Spiritual/Intellectual Natures of the Human Being* has informed this central point of the essay *Concerning Naive and Sentimental Poetry.*

Schiller offers the following advice to the naive genius. "Forsaken by the ladder that carried you, you no longer have any choice but to grasp the law with free consciousness and will or to fall hopelessly into the bottomless pit" (NA 20: 447).[25] The writer's description recalls the pitfalls encountered both by Christian Wolf in the narrative *Criminal Out of Infamy,* as well as by Karl Moor in the drama *The Robbers.* Furthermore, in its treatment of the loss of the original state of Nature and the relative freedom of the modern human being in a life of reason, the central thesis of *Something Concerning the First Human Society According to the Proscriptions of the Mosaic Testament* forms a thematic bridge between the earlier and later writings, which also undergirds the historical dimension of the essay under discussion.

A distinguishing feature of the later theoretical essays comes to light through the mature writer's advocation of a more highly developed sense of humanity. Cultivate the feeling of the value and honor of the most majestic humanity, he states, "but receive it [humanity] within yourself and strive to wed its endless advantage with your own boundless prerogative and to produce, from both, the divine" (NA 20: 429).[26]

With the later writings, Schiller introduced a new motif: the wedding of seemingly disparate elements. With the aid of the wedding motif, the writer begins to create several new associations. The principle of reciprocal cooperation ("gegenseitige Wechselwirkung") informing the interactionist theory of human anthropology surfaces time and again throughout his writings. Cultivating humanity is a perpetual exercise. For the naive genius is instructed to constantly reignite "the flame of the ideal, which is so easily extinguished in the storms of life," i.e., history (NA 20: 429).[27] Constantly, throughout this and other essays of the 1790s, the writer remains conscious of the harmonious tension between the ideal and the real. Rather than characterize the work of Friedrich Schiller in conventional terms, then, such as the binary opposition between the real and the ideal, perhaps we should appreciate the integrative nature of his writings and the tensions that inhere in them.

Compared to ancient Greek culture, life in the modern age is marked by disunity and rupture. The ancient Greek was "one with oneself and happy in the feeling of humanity," whereas we moderns are "at variance with ourselves and unhappy in our experiences of humankind" (NA 20: 431).[28] Referring directly to Goethe's sensational novel *The Sorrows of Young Werther,* the writer characterizes the modern situation (the sentimental) as follows: "Our feeling for Nature resembles a sick person's desire for health" ("Unser Gefühl für Natur gleicht der Empfindung des Kranken für die Gesundheit") (NA 20: 431). Hence, the merger of the study of medicine and the reading of literature, which characterizes Schiller's earliest writings (especially the third medical dissertation), also marks the later essay *Concerning Naive and Sentimental Poetry.* I wonder to what extent Johann Wolfgang Goethe's controversial characterization of the classical as the healthy and the romantic as the sick might have been influenced by his friend's statement in this important essay. In any event, it is certainly likely that the category of the sentimental evolved not simply out of Schiller's studies of the ancients but also proceeded from his own struggles with illness and the knowledge of the tendency of the mind ("Geist") to compensate, sometimes to the extreme, for the limitations of the body.

Whether naive or sentimental, all poets are "the guardians of Nature" ("die *Bewahrer* der Natur") (NA 20:432). In this capacity, they resemble doctors. For to preserve and cultivate Nature also implies healing. Very near the midpoint of his essay, the writer constructed various types of poets as well as a historical timeline. Poets, he states, will either be Nature, or they will seek lost Nature (NA 20: 432). Though Homer and Shakespeare are separated in time and were different persons, they are united, in their own natures, in one respect. "As the Godhead stands behind the world structure, so he [the poet] behind his work; He is the work and the work is He" (NA 20:433).[29] The poet's function as a creative-productive writer is analogous to the activities of God. The writer's text seems to resemble the text of the universe. For the inscriber of Nature produces a work that is both an extension of and something more (and different) than oneself. At the same time, the writer is also embodied in one's own work. The act of writing would thus seem to be self-constituting.

Referring specifically to individual human beings and the humanity one shares with the poet, the writer underscores the close relationship between morality and poetry: "should the human being immediately distance oneself from the simplicity, truth and necessity of Nature through the freedom of one's imagination and understanding, not only does the path to the same always remain open, but a powerful and indestructible drive—the moral impulse—propels him/her perpetually back to her [it], and precisely through this drive the faculty of poetry stands in the closest connection [with it]" (NA 20: 436).[30] As in the earlier dramatic and prose works, aesthetics and ethics are intricately interwoven. Of increasing importance for the later writer, however, is the insight that the "right" path is the one closest to Nature, by which is also meant one's own nature. One is expected, then, to cultivate the harmonious tension within one's own nature in particular and between oneself and Nature in general. The final step is to extend this outwardly to the society of which one is a vital part. Once the human being has accomplished this task, he and she will have attained freedom. In chapter nine I will argue that the writer succeeded in working out this central idea in his last completed dramatic writing, *William Tell*.

Unlike the ancient writer who felt one with Nature, the modern writer re-presents the idea of unity in his or her work, cultivating in particular a sense of common humanity. Both essays *Concerning Naive and Sentimental Poetry* and *Concerning the Aesthetic Education of the Human Being* thematize the idea of the social, i.e., practical value of art. The special task of poetry consists in giving "humanity its fullest possible expression" ("*der Menschheit ihren möglichst vollständigen Ausdruck zu geben*") (NA 20:437). This declaration complements the ending of the series of letters on aesthetic education, where the writer calls for the harmonizing of grace ("Anmut") and dignity ("Würde") in the interest of the cultural advancement of the state. Later on in the essay *Concerning Naive and Sentimental Poetry*, Schiller submitted that the common task of *both* the naive and sentimental poets is to give the most complete expression to human nature ("Der menschlichen Natur ihren völligen Ausdruck zu geben") (NA 20: 473), without which they could not rightfully be called poets. In the footnote addressed to "the scientifically critical reader" ("de[m] wissenschaftlich prüfenden Leser"), the writer drew out their necessary connection and subsumed them under a "third category." Of the two, however, the naive poet is closest to sensuous reality, which the sentimental poet can only strive to obtain (NA 20: 474).

In short, the naive and the sentimental are related as sensuous reality is related to the intellectual, which is further evidence of the sustained operation of the paradigm of the interaction between body and mind.[31] Here, too, the writer distinguishes between "actual nature" ("wirkliche Natur") and "true Nature" ("wahre Natur"), the latter of which requires "an inner necessity of existence" ("eine innere Nothwendigkeit des Daseyns") (NA 20: 476). The distinction also calls up the direction Schiller foresees for a history born of humanity, namely oneness with Nature. As I have suggested, this goal is to be attained by first cultivating the harmonious tension within one's own nature.

It is not coincidental, then, that Schiller should propose that, in a state of natural simplicity ("Zustande natürlicher Einfalt"), the human being still acts ("wirkt") in harmonious unity ("harmonische Einheit") with all of one's powers (NA 20: 437). In the "condition of culture" ("Zustande der Kultur"), however, that harmonious interaction of one's whole nature ("harmonisches Zusammenwirken seiner ganzen Natur") constitutes "merely an idea" ("bloß eine Idee"; NA 20: 437). For the modern, sentimental [vs. modern, naive] poet the proper object of one's work is the elevation of reality to the ideal or, what amounts to the same thing, the representation of the ideal (NA 20: 437). Whatever the merits of this endeavor, it is important to acknowledge the writer's recognition of the limits of not only the sentimental poet's enterprise but, in the light of our own times, the limits of modernity. For without the naive, it would seem, the sentimental in itself is incapable of overcoming the rupture between past and present and, to adopt Kant's formulation, reason and Nature. It is clear from Schiller's early anthropology that the real work of humankind is to cultivate the harmonious tension of and between all things. By doing so, history will move forward in the direction of humanity and not backward to savagery and barbarity. If there is a moral point to Schiller's writings, then, it is to be found in contemplation and the productive activation of the harmonious tension that inheres in all of Nature.

Whatever the quality of the ideas advanced either by the naive or the sentimental poet, the poetic genius ("der poetische Genius") subsumes them all under a higher concept, namely the "idea of humanity" ("Idee der Menschheit") (NA 20: 437). This is the full textual context of the often cited passage: "Nature makes him/her [the human being] one with oneself; art divides and turns one against oneself; through the ideal s/he returns to unity" (NA 20: 438).[32] There is an essential thematic link here to the series of letters on aesthetic education which develops the idea that the path of culture leads from the original state of Nature through aesthetics to the rational-moral state.

But the text does not end here. As so often occurs in his mature writings, Schiller qualifies his statement. "But because the ideal is an endless one that one can never attain, the cultivated human being can never become complete in one's own unique way, as the natural human being is capable of becoming in one's own state" (NA 20: 438).[33] Whereas in the naive state, Nature takes precedence over art, in modern history, aesthetic culture is deemed even more essential than Nature—at least for the time being. For, while the value of the former lies in the absolute attainment of limited greatness, the latter achieves its full value by approximating infinite greatness. The individual who is engaged in the process of culture is never determinable (NA 20: 438). Choosing between the naive and the sentimental, the writer opts for the latter, not simply because the sentimental is more characteristic of his times, but primarily because the endless approximation of an ultimately unattainable goal is preferable to resigning oneself to reality as given.

In further delineating the natures of naive and sentimental poets, Schiller readdressed his early anthropology. In poetic works of art, the ancients are unsurpassable in the simplicity of forms and "in that which is capable of representation sensuously and corporeally," whereas the moderns are superior in the richness of their material, "in that which cannot be depicted or expressed" (NA 20: 440). In a footnote to this part of the essay, Schiller adds that the impression created by naive poetry is "always joyful, always pure, always peaceful" ("immer fröhlich, immer rein, immer ruhig"), whereas, sentimental poetry creates impressions that are "always serious and tense" ("immer etwas ernst und anspannend") (NA 20:441). Modern poetry (the sentimental) is thus characterized by tension.[34] Since, at some point in time, the sentimental is to be conjoined with the naive, the ultimate task is to present that tension as harmonious through one's art.

Let us turn for a moment to Friedrich Schlegel's essay *Concerning the Study of Greek Poetry* in order to disclose the nature of the philologist's anthropology. It has not been noted that, in this early phase of his career, Schlegel's anthropology is similar to, but certainly not identical with, that of Friedrich Schiller. In the essay of 1795, Schlegel returns to Haller's, Platner's, and Schiller's general definitions of the human being as part animal and part spirit or mind, and then adds: "The human being is a mixture of one's own pure self and a strange being."[35] Later in the same essay, Schlegel will submit that sensuousness and spirituality are "so closely interwoven" ("so innig verwebt") in the human being while, at the same time, advocating the need for "genuine aesthetic lifeforce" ("echte ästhetische Lebenskraft"), especially passion ("Leidenschaft") and charm ("Reiz").[36] Vestiges of the Enlightenment tradition are still present in the younger Schlegel's work when he declares that understanding ("der Verstand") is the organ that ensures that "wrong concepts" ("verkehrte Begriffe") are brought back onto track as "correct concepts" ("richtige Begriffe").[37] In his *Speech on Genius,* Schiller's instructor in philosophy, J. F. Abel, had argued in favor of developing correct concepts.[38]

As in his essays on the sublime (*Vom Erhabenen* and *Über das Erhabene*), Schiller distinguishes, in this essay, between "the sublime character" ("erhabener Charakter") and the "beautiful heart" ("schönes Herz"). This differentiation complements the paradigm of the naive and the sentimental. Whereas a beautiful heart creates "a complete picture of itself" ("ein vollendetes Bild von sich selbst"), sublime character manifests itself "only in individual victories over the resistance of the senses, only in certain instances of momentum and momentary strain" ("nur in einzelnen Siegen über den Widerstand der Sinne, nur in gewissen Momenten des Schwunges und einer augenblicklichen Anstrengung") (NA 20: 444). In the beautiful soul ("schöne Seele"), the ideal functions as Nature, that is, uniformly. Its distinguishing quality is the state of peace or tranquility ("Zustand der Ruhe") (NA: 20: 444) it generates.

Schiller as literary critic found evidence of the sentimental in the poetry of some of his contemporaries—Albrecht von Haller, Ewald von Kleist, and Friedrich Gottlieb Klopstock. The one German poet receiving Schiller's highest praise in this area was the musical poet ("musikalische[r] Dichter") Klopstock. In a footnote, Schiller records his impressions of Klopstock's work and defends his choice of terminology. In the main text he describes Klopstock's manner of writing as follows: "His sphere is always the realm of ideas, and he knows how to transport everything he treats into the infinite" (NA 20: 457).[39] The writer draws upon the mind-body paradigm (physiology) to enhance his literary criticism. Concerning Klopstock, "One is inclined to say that he extracts the body from everything he treats in order to make it spirit [Geist], as other poets clothe everything spiritual with a body" (NA 20: 457).[40] And: "His poetic muse is chaste, celestial, uncorporeal ["unkörperlich"], [and] sacred like his religion" (NA 20: 457).[41] The literary critic in Schiller maintains that all those feelings which the poet knows how to evoke "so deeply and so powerfully in us" "stream forth out of supersensuous sources" (NA 20: 457). But the state of the sublime clearly generates tension, as is evident in his reference to "this perpetual tension of the [modern] mind" ("diese immerwährende Spannung des [modernen] Gemüths") (NA 20:457).

The writer's central thesis discloses the symbol of the stringed instrument. "Capable of every energy and master of the whole range of sentimental poetry, he [the German poet] can shake us one moment through the highest pathos and, the next, cradle us in heavenly sweet sensations; but his heart inclines mainly toward lofty ingenious melancholy, and as sublime as his harp, his lyre may sound, the melting tones of his lute still sound truer, deeper, and are more moving" (NA 20: 458).[42] Creating harmoniously with all the powers of one's soul and senses, the sentimental poet is perpetually active. In the work of the sentimental writer, the harmonious tension of the strings creates mellifluous sounds. The three literary works Schiller refers to in order to illuminate his point are all by young Goethe: *The Sorrows of Young Werther, Torquato Tasso,* and *Faust* (NA 20:459–60).

In contemplating to what extent Friedrich Schiller was a romantic,[43] we must note the writer's clear awareness of that "dangerous extreme" ("gefährliche Extrem") in the material with which the genius may be dealing (NA

20: 459). "A person who embraces an ideal with burning sensation and flees reality in order to achieve an infinite without being; who searches unceasingly outside oneself, and constantly destroys what is in him; to whom only his dreams are the real and his experiences eternally only barriers; who, finally, in his own being [Dasein] sees only one barrier, and even this, as is proper, still tears apart in order to penetrate true reality" (NA 20: 459).[44] In Goethe's *Werther*, Schiller locates not only the sentimental but also the dangerous tendency to languish in the extremes of "fanciful, unrequited love, sentimentality for Nature, religious exuberance, philosophical, contemplative mind" and even "the gloomy, formless, melancholic world of Ossian" (NA 20: 459).[45] Finally, for all his admiration of Klopstock's *Messias*, Schiller cautioned against the expression of an overly active imagination. For the way in which the German poet had represented the angels, gods, and satans (i.e., Heaven and Hell) in that seminal work is the product of an imagination which is much too freely constituted ("viel zu sehr frey gestellt") (NA 20: 456).

Unlike the sentimental writer, the naive type of poet willingly subjugates oneself to "all Nature's fetters" ("allen Fesseln der Natur") (NA 20: 463). By chaining oneself to Nature, he or she makes use of its freedoms, and thereby furthers the cause of humanity ("Humanität") (NA 20: 463). On this point, the 1795 essay *Concerning Naive and Sentimental Poetry* recalls the poem "The Artists" (1788–89), in which we first discerned a shift in emphasis from the limitations to the freedoms represented by the chains of Nature. It is now clear that the naive and the beautiful are more intimately related to Schiller's concepts of the sentimental and the sublime than has hitherto been acknowledged.

In sum, Schiller's writing of 1795 presupposes the eventual wedding of the sentimental and the naive, a union characterized by harmonious tension. The mood which the sentimental poet evokes is defined both in terms of the writer's early anthropology and the symbol of the stringed instrument. For, with the aid of an active drive ("einen lebendigen *Trieb*"), the sentimental poet evokes a sense of harmony which he has felt to make a whole out of himself and, in oneself, bring humanity to a completed expression ("die Menschheit in sich zu einem vollendeten Ausdruck zu bringen") (NA 20: 474). "Therefore," Schiller adds, "the [sentimental] mind is here [in its present state] in motion; it is tense [and] vacillates between conflicting feelings; since there [in a perfected state of harmony], it is peacefully disbanded, one with itself, and completely gratified" (NA 20: 474).[46] Once again, the basic paradigm of the third medical dissertation returns. For the writer draws out the limitations of the sensuous (naive) and the intellectual (sentimental) components of human nature when referring to the naive poet as suffering under the limits ("Schranken") of reality, while thought ("der Gedanke") is said to be endless ("grenzenlos") (NA 20: 474). The same structure also informs the nature of Schiller's definitions of the beautiful and the sublime in the 1790s.

Schiller and the Idealists and Romantics of His Day[47]

As I intimated at the beginning of this chapter, Schiller's relationship to proponents of German romanticism and idealism warrants more thorough critical analysis and more exacting differentiation.[48] We discover one of the essential differences between Schiller and the romantics and the idealists when contemplating the role of imagination. Elsewhere I have advanced the thesis that the tension-filled relationship between the freedom of imagination and the necessity of understanding, for Schiller, produces the higher concepts ("Begriffe") of art (see n. 21). For one thing, it is important to distinguish between Schiller's sensuous-rational aesthetics and Friedrich Schlegel's later understanding of the "Romantic" of 1800 as "the depiction of a sentimental content in a fantastic form."[49] The reader will seek in vain for a concept of the fantastic in Schiller's writings. Neither is there any evidence of romantic irony.[50]

Though also highly complimentary of Schiller's work, Friedrich Schlegel criticized the writer for the incurably "ruined health of imagination" ("zerrüttete Gesundheit der Einbildungskraft") in his critical review of the *Poetic Annals for the Year 1796* [*Musenalmanach für das Jahr 1796*] in the Berlin journal *Germany* [*Deutschland*].[51] Somewhat later, Schlegel would define imagination as a supernatural power. "The essence of imagination is the perception of infinite abundance. Imagination is a supernatural faculty, is always revelation, enthusiasm and inspiration. Intoxication, dream, and wit all belong to imagination."[52] The conclusion of Schiller's provocative essay *Concerning Naive and Sentimental Poetry* underscores the essential disagreement between the two writers, despite the generally enthusiastic reception of the work by Friedrich Schlegel himself in his book *Greeks and Romans* [*Griechen und Römer*] (1797).[53] For Schiller concludes his essay by collapsing ancient and modern poetry. The uneasy tension between the idealist and the realist types remains.

It has often been overlooked that the writer ended his essay indicting the dreamer or visionary ("Phantast"). This "false" idealist, the writer submits, leaves nature behind "in order to be able to surrender all the more to the willfulness of his desires and the humours of the power of the imagination" (NA 20: 503).[54] Clearly, the pronouncement amounts to a moral indictment of the limitlessness of imagination. It is important to recognize that this criticism is not motivated by some preconceived idea of morality or by decrees formulated and disseminated by institutions such as the church or state. It is not a religious doctrine. Rather, Schiller's moral credo evolved out of his own anthropology.

Schiller and Fichte

Schiller's disagreements with Schlegel and his critical encounter with the German philosopher Johann G. Fichte highlight the differences between himself and the new schools of romanticism and Idealism, respectively. As we know, these directions in thought were developing not only in the very same town, but at the very same university where Schiller was holding lectures on history and aesthetics—in Jena.

In his essay *Concerning the Necessary Limits in the Use of Beautiful Forms* [*Über die nothwendigen Grenzen beim Gebrauch schöner Formen*] (1795), Schiller advanced the idea that the imagination, when left to itself, will react arbitrarily ("ungebunden und regellos"). It will spring from one intuitive perception to another, without establishing the necessary connection between the perceptions derived only by understanding ("Verstand"). Individual insights into the essence of things ("Anschauungen") in themselves betray "the entire disorder of an opalescent imagination obeying only itself" (NA 21: 9).[55] Though, at first, maintaining a good personal relationship, Schiller grew increasingly critical of Fichte's idea of the self-sufficiency of imagination.

In his *Theory of Knowledge* [*Wissenschaftslehre*] of 1794, Fichte asserted that the power of imagination consists in uniting the irreconcilable, namely the Ego ("Ich") and the Non-Ego ("Nicht-Ich"). "The power of imagination is a faculty that hovers in the middle between determination and the infinite."[56] In his *Critique of the Power of Judgment,* Immanuel Kant defined the power of imagination as a transmutative force ("Mittelkraft") that mediates between understanding and sensibility. For Fichte, however, the condition of hovering is the essential characteristic of the power of imagination and the key to reconciling the irreconcilable.[57] *Geist* (mind) forms its own unique space that undercuts the bounds of external reality—for *Geist* shapes reality.[58] In the light of the essay "Julius's Theosophy," it is quite probable that Schiller also objected to the egoism of Fichte's theory of the subject.[59] For, in Fichte's philosophy, the I or Ego (*das Ich*), understood as the highest principle, contemplates and attempts to account for the primacy of its existence.

It is illuminating to discover that Schiller was skeptical of Fichte's *Theory of Knowledge* even before the work appeared.[60] Schiller indicated to his friend Johann Benjamin Erhard: "Everything is quiet in our residence of the muses, and Fichte is still working hard to complete his basic philosophy. I am convinced that it will be up to him to play a leading role in philosophy, and to bring it quite a big step forward. But the path leads past an abyss, and all vigilance will be required not to fall into it. The purest speculation borders so closely on empty speculation, and keen perception on nitpicking. What I understand about his system up to now has my complete approval, but there is still a great deal about it that is unclear; and this is not simply my reaction, but everyone else's whom I have asked about it" (September 8, 1794; NA 27: 41).[61] The fact that Carl Reinhold would eventually be persuaded by Fichte's arguments and give up his professorial chair to Fichte upon his retirement shows that Schiller's sense of the importance of Fichte's work was correct.[62] Still, accusations of confusion and lack of clarity persisted. As evidenced by the first sentence of Fichte's later response to Schiller in the letter of June 27, 1795, as well as a letter six days earlier to Goethe, Fichte was deeply troubled by the accusations.

Well into the year 1795, however, the personal relationship between Schiller and Fichte remained congenial. Schiller was so impressed by the philosopher's essay *On Stimulating and Increasing the Pure Interest in Truth* [*Ueber Belebung und Erhöhung des reinen Interesses für Wahrheit*] that he included it as the fourth contribution in the inaugural issue of his periodical *The Horae* [*Die Horen*] in 1795. As in his relationship with Friedrich Schlegel, however, Schiller's meetings with Fichte became more and more unsettling.

In my reading, Fichte's essay is unique in its creative rewriting of Kant's moral categorical imperative. Though he does not name Kant in this essay, the philosopher arrives at the following dictum: "judge in such a manner that you could think of the manner of your current judgment as an eternal law for your entire judgment" (*The Horae* 1: 89).[63] The philosopher's stance seems to assume the individualization of the power of judgment. The most important question for Fichte is whether or not we think in agreement with the dictates of our own reasoning ("ob wir mit uns selbst übereinstimmend denken") (*Graces* 1: 89). Unlike Schiller, Fichte was not interested in the universal assent of Kant's *sensus communis*. Fichte was more radical. All intelligent beings share the same *Geist:* "and thus, as we should think, so also all rational beings should think."[64] Though *Geist* manifests itself differently in individual human beings, according to Fichte, all friends of truth are endowed with the same *Geist*. There is no evidence of this central postulate of German Idealism in Schiller's writings.

Schiller rejected Fichte's essay *Concerning the Spirit and Letter in Philosophy* [*Über Geist und Buchstab in der Philosophie*] for inclusion in *The Horae*.[65] The philosopher was incensed and lashed out in the letter of June 27, 1795, which contains the noteworthy accusation: "You chain the power of imagination—which can only be free—and want to force it to think— which it cannot do."[66] Despite the expression of outrage, Fichte's declaration is a fairly apt characterization of the difference between Schiller's and Fichte's understandings of the role of imagination. As James Engell has suggested, to Fichte's understanding, "the imagination is a key to the act of philosophizing, the highest of endeavors."[67]

With respect to Schiller, however, Engell construes Schiller's concept of the play-impulse ("Spieltrieb"), developed in *Concerning the Aesthetic Education of the Human Being,* far too broadly as "the highest level of the imagination."[68] On the one hand, he argues that Schiller favored this concept because "he was deterred by the use of *Einbildungskraft* [the power of imagining, or imagination] in Kant, Fichte, and Maimon."[69] On the other hand, he asserts that the concept of the play-impulse "In its total capacity . . . effectually serves the same *kind* or purpose as *Einbildungskraft* does in Kant, Schelling, Fichte, and Goethe, or as 'imagination' does in Coleridge."[70] Furthermore, he claims that Schiller's view of aesthetic imagination "paved the way for Schelling."[71] Engell's blurring of distinctions notwithstanding, the debate between Schiller and Fichte turns on the question of the proper role of imagination. For Schiller, *Geist* (mind) can only be productive if it is tied to the object ("Gegenstand"). Imagination aids the formation of concepts and ideas. According to Fichte's philosophy, *Geist* transcends the limits of the material world. Though forming a reciprocally cooperative relationship, imagination and reason comprise an autonomous whole which, in the final analysis, hovers above and beyond the limits of the objective world.

In retrospect, comparing Schiller's concept of the play-impulse ("Spieltrieb") in the series of letters on the aesthetic education of the human being to Fichte's concept of the "aesthetic impulse" ("ästhetischer Trieb") in the *Theory of Knowledge,* we discover that Fichte's concept carries its value within itself. Unlike Schiller's understanding, imagination for Fichte has nothing to do with correspondences to things outside itself.[72] However, as Peter Baumanns notes, for Fichte, "The human being is only completely human where one goes beyond the beautiful play of one's imagination to theoretical knowledge of truth and the self-satisfaction of morally ("sittlich") prescribed action."[73] For the idealist, the primary task of the philosopher is to account fully for the self-positing subject. For Schiller, the *Spieltrieb* is not only the vehicle by which the human being realizes one's own potential, it is the most essential means by which one is empowered to contribute actively to the creative restructuring of society in consonance with the dictates of one's free, moral will.

In sum, perhaps one of the reasons for the collapse of the *Horae* project is attributable to its design. Initially, the publication was to include historical accounts, philosophical essays and various contributions on poetry and aesthetics, "everything that can be treated with Taste."[74] However, as he was to convey on September 8, 1794, to his friend Johann Benjamin Erhard, the leading Jacobin thinker in Nürnberg, Schiller would not be dealing with either political or religious issues (NA 27: 41). Perhaps these omissions were indeed a mistake given the cultural climate of Schiller's day. In any case, the decision worked against the writer's own multidisciplinary interests.

Schiller's Concept of Imagination in the Book Review of Matthisson, with a Note on Bürger

The heart of Schiller's more mature concept of imagination is found in his review of Friedrich Matthisson's poetry. This book review was written

one year before the appearance of the essay on beautiful forms, in 1794, the
year in which both Goethe's novel *Wilhelm Meister's Apprenticeship* [*Wilhelm Meisters Lehrjahre*] (1794) and Fichte's *Theory of Knowledge* were
nearing completion. Schiller praised Matthisson for the skillful combination
of imagination and reason in the writing of poetry. "The imagination appears
here in its full emancipation from chains and yet, in that condition, in the
most beautiful agreement with the idea which is to be expressed" (NA 22:
280).[75]

This positive assessment of the quality of Matthisson's poetry is consistent with the writer's description of a beautiful style of writing in the essay
Concerning the Necessary Limits in the Use of Beautiful Forms, a work
that originated at the time of Schiller's writing of the twenty-sixth letter of
Concerning the Aesthetic Education of the Human Being. The essay was
also fueled by the quarrels with Fichte. The work is also remarkable for its
further development of some of the central motifs and metaphors of Schiller's earlier writings. The "magical power of beautiful diction" ("Zauberkraft
der schönen Diktion"), the writer contends, arises out of the successful
relationship between external freedom and inner necessity.

> By representing the race through an individual and depicting a general concept
> in a particular case, we release the chains imposed by the understanding on
> imagination ("Phantasie") and give it full authority to prove itself creatively. Always striving for the completion of its determinations, it now obtains and uses
> its right to expand, enliven, and reshape the given image as it wishes, [and] to
> follow it in all its connections and transformations. For a moment, it may forget
> its subservient role and act as its own free master since through its strict inner
> connection adequate care has been taken to ensure that it can never completely
> escape the reins of understanding (NA 21: 9–10).[76]

In the poetry of Friedrich Matthisson, Schiller rediscovered the proper
balance between the interests of the imagination and the interests of the
understanding. In the essay *Concerning the Necessary Limits in the Use of
Beautiful Forms,* Schiller posited the point at which diction is most beautiful. "As much as these two interests [imagination and understanding] appear
to conflict with each other, between both there is still a point of unity.
Finding this point is the task of beautiful diction (NA 21: 8)."[77] The writer
then addressed the question of the nature of imagination directly, when
he added:

> In order to satisfy the imagination, speech must have a material part or body.
> This is comprised by intuitions, by which the understanding isolates the individual
> features or concepts; for as abstractly as we may also wish to think, there is still
> always something sensuous that underlies our thinking (NA 21: 8).[78]

The writer warns of the inherent tendency of imagination to spring randomly from one perception or intuition to another, which points up "the entire disorder of an imagination that simply plays and obeys only itself" ("die ganze Unordnung einer spielenden und bloß sich selbst gehorchenden Einbildungskraft") (NA 21: 9). For Schiller, this is a danger that Friedrich Matthisson had avoided. In the post-1789 essay *Concerning the Necessary Limits in the Use of Beautiful Forms,* the writer insisted that the truly beautiful ("das wahrhaft Schöne") is grounded in strict determination, the most exact differentiation, and the greatest inner necessity, which is achieved not by force, but proceeds naturally from the artistic mind. "The highest [degree of] regularity must be present, but it must appear to be Nature" ("Die höchste Gesetzmäßigkeit muß da seyn, aber sie muß als Natur erscheinen"; NA 21: 13).

Schiller's review of Gottfried August Bürger's poetry sparked a controversy over which scholars are still divided.[79] Schiller asked "how it was possible to overlook the fact that the poet's enthusiasm is not seldom lost to the bounds of madness ("Wahnsinn") [and] that a fire often becomes a fury."[80] It may indeed be surprising that, for all his flair for the dramatic, Schiller could not at least appreciate the drama of Bürger's ballads. Whatever the personal or political nature of our assessment of Schiller's disparaging remarks concerning Bürger's poetry may be, they are consistent not only with the writer's call for the art of idealization ("Idealisierkunst"), in the ancient sense, but also with his later statements on the nature of beautiful diction and his exploration of the freedom and limits of imagination, even if the writer overestimates the aesthetic value of Matthisson's work.

Before returning to Schiller's review of Friedrich Matthisson's poetry, I draw our attention to a statement Schiller made in passing in his critical review of Bürger. "With his sonnets, models in their own right, which are transformed on the lips of the orator into song, we wish along with him that they would find no imitator who, like him and his splendid friend Schlegel, cannot play the lyre of the Pythian god."[81] August Wilhelm Schlegel was deeply hurt by Schiller's cutting remark. As we know, August Wilhelm's talent lay not in the writing of poetry but, rather, in the articulation of theoretical issues, especially those pertaining to drama in particular and Western literature in general. For our purposes here, the intriguing aspect of this critical remark is the analogy the writer makes to the playing of the lyre. The Pythian god was Apollo. The Pythian games that were organized at Delphi to honor the god of poetry, music, and manly beauty consisted primarily of musical and gymnastic competitions. The cultural core of the cult was the Pythian *nomos* (custom, law) in which Apollo's battle with the dragon Python was represented. Once again, the metaphor of the lyre is employed, only this time to denounce the strains of Bürger's poetry as well as of those who supported his cause.

Schiller maintained that Friedrich Matthisson had mastered a particular genre, "Landschaftsdichtung," or idyllic poetry. Of the various forms of poetry, Schiller perceived that it was this genre that lent itself perhaps all too easily to "free fictions of the imagination" ("freie Fiktionen der Einbildungskraft") (NA 22: 280). But being the "very successful painter of sensations" he was ("ein sehr glücklicher Maler von Empfindungen"), Matthisson made his work appear as if the imagination had been emancipated when, in fact, it was tied to the cultivation of a specific idea. Bürger's expressed intention of writing his now famous *Lenore* in a popular mode ("volksmäßig") meant that he would accentuate the emotional response, i.e., sensuousness, to the detriment of the understanding. Whereas, in the case of the romantics, Schiller was concerned about granting the imagination too much freedom, in the case of Bürger, he worried that the senses would override reason. To be sure, Schiller seriously underestimated the ballad writer's sensitivity to form. He also failed to recognize Bürger's indebtedness to one of his own mentors, J. G. Herder.[82]

The apparent flight from the difficult exigencies of life is indicative of idyllic poetry. Here, Schiller reintroduced the analogy of tensing and relaxing.

> Should the poet wish to draw us out of the jostling of the world into his [world of] seclusion, then it must not be the need for relaxation ("Abspannung") but for tension ("Anspannung"), not the demand for peace and tranquility ("Ruhe") but for harmony ("Harmonie") that makes art weary and Nature attractive to him (NA 22: 282).[83]

Schiller maintains that the reader's aesthetic sense is delighted and one's moral sense gratified when experiencing the "tender harmony of figures, tones, and light ("liebliche Harmonie der Gestalten, der Töne und des Lichts") found, for example, in Matthisson's poetry. The metaphor of the finely tuned instrument also informs this discussion when, for instance, he submits that the artistic representation achieved by the German poet becomes "a natural symbol of the inner correspondence of the mind ("Gemüt") with itself and of the moral ("sittlichen") connection of actions and feelings; and in the beautiful posture of a picturesque or musical piece [of art] there is painted the even more beautiful one of a morally ("sittlichen") tuned soul" (NA 22: 273).[84] The fact that the romantics rejected Matthisson's poetry and favored Bürger's provides additional evidence of the difference between Schiller and several of the German romantics such as the Schlegel brothers; though, in the end, Schiller was more kindly disposed to August Wilhelm than he was to Friedrich.

Schiller and Schelling

Another revealing example of an original affinity and subsequent disagreement between Schiller and his fellow contemporaries stems from Schiller's essay on the nature of ancient and modern poetry and the work of the Swabian philosopher of Idealism F. W. J. Schelling. In his early work *Concerning the Ego as a Principle of Philosophy; or, the Absolute in Human Nature* [*Vom Ich als Prinzip der Philosophie oder das Unbedingte im menschlichen Wesen*] (1795), Schelling approved of the structure of Fichte's idea of the mutual relationship between ego and non-ego which, together, form the absolute. In the *System of Transcendental Idealism* [*System des tranzendentalen Idealismus*] (1800), Schelling would draw upon Fichte's concept of the hovering of imagination in order to characterize the relationship between the ego and the non-ego.[85] This is the basis of that "preestablished harmony" between the conscious and the unconscious which the recipient is said to visualize in the work of art. According to Schelling, the genius who creates with the power of imagination is actually the "cause of everything objective."[86]

Like Friedrich Schlegel, Schelling found Schiller's essay on naive and sentimental poetry to be rich in ideas.[87] Though working with Schiller's conceptual pair in his lectures on the *Philosophy of Art* [*Philosophie der Kunst*] (1802–5), Schelling's main disagreement with the writer concerns the nature of naive genius. "The character of the naive genius is complete— imitation, not also, as Schiller stated, but much more attainment of reality."[88] Among modern poets, including Shakespeare, Schiller's countryman asserts, what is missing is the "complete indifference of the naive and the sentimental" ("vollkommene Indifferenz des Naiven und Sentimentalen").[89] At the most basic level of his critique, Schelling rejects the diachronic distinction between naive and sentimental, tracing both forms of poetry back to their synchronic amalgamation in the absolute. Paragraph 68 of his work calls up one of the essential differences between the writers.

Poetry in its absolute state is, in itself, neither naive nor sentimental.[90]

However, Schelling does draw upon Schiller's examples of the mixture of the sentimental and the naive in some ancient as well as modern poets in order to elucidate his idea of the primal unity of both in the absolute nature of poetry.

Unlike Schiller's concepts, Schelling's ideas on art are informed by a specific philosophy of Nature. Since Nature is a fully active principle,[91] the true artist will imitate by creatively reproducing the internal forces of Nature rather than represent its external manifestations. This Nature is objectified in the work of art primarily through the activation of the creative power of imagination. The beautiful work of art surpasses ("übertrifft") external reality because it embodies the life processes at work in Nature.[92] The absolute shimmers through the work of art (beauty). Hence, the work of art, for Schelling, is an ontological structure of the essence of the universe. In Schiller's writings, in turn, the beautiful work of art functions much the same way as do regulative ideas in their relation to the material world. The writer describes the work of art historically, culturally and politically, namely as a formative force in the restructuring of consciousness and as a vehicle for the refashioning of society. The work of art seeks to transform original human nature into a more beautiful, morally responsible, and ever more active humanity. In effect, Schiller assigns to the imagination a specific, moral-practical, and cultural-political function. Unlike Schelling, Schiller grounds the work of art not so much in ontology as in history, society, and personal experience. In short, for Schiller, the ultimate goal of reintegrating the human being and Nature on a higher plane is achieved through the auspices of art/culture by activating the play-impulse within the individual.

Up until his move to Weimar in 1799, Schiller was in close personal contact with many leading writers of the time such as Friedrich Schlegel, Friedrich von Hardenberg (Novalis), Fichte, Schelling and the foremost Kantian scholar of his day, Carl Reinhold. The small city of Jena, where Schiller and German romantics and idealists lived, seems to have encouraged a close intellectual affinity. As we have seen, however, despite the close cultural affinities, there were considerable differences in temperament and outlook that worked against the development of close personal relationships, with the possible exception of that between Schiller and Novalis. In retrospect, unlike the romantics, Schiller checked the free play of imagination with the aid of understanding. Unlike the German Idealists, Schiller did not subsume the whole of reality under the operations of the mind. Unlike his compatriot F. W. J. Schelling, Schiller did not comprehend reality in terms of an undifferentiated whole wherein, in the final analysis, subject and object are not simply identical but indistinguishable. Like Immanuel Kant, Schiller appreciated the fact that we cannot know things in themselves. What we can know, however, is ourselves; hence, the dictum: "Dare to be wise!" ("Erkühne Dich, weise zu sein!").

Toward a Conclusion

Considering the history of intellectual thought and literary history, perhaps it is best to position the work of Friedrich Schiller between G. E. Lessing and the German romantics, that is, between Enlightenment and romanticism.[93] Despite the apparent continuity between Enlightenment and romanticism posited by James Engell and by German scholars before him,[94] the disagreements between Schiller and Schlegel, Schelling, and Fichte demonstrate the writer's generally critical distance from the founders of what we now term German romanticism and Idealism. In particular, by clipping the wings of imagination, Schiller created equal room for the play of understanding (Verstand) and the cooperative interaction between the spiritual-intellectual and material-corporeal worlds.

In the sixteenth letter of his famous work on the aesthetic education of the human being, Schiller insisted on the "equilibrium of reality and form" ("*Gleichgewicht* der Realität und der Form") (NA 20: 360). As we have noted, the harmonious tension between the material-drive and the form-drive is first activated by the play-drive. The writer states unequivocally that such an ideal state of equilibrium "remains, however, always only idea, which can never be fully attained" (NA 20: 360).[95] While exploring the nature of progress and the possibility of the perfectibility of the human species, Schiller charted the limits of his own theorizing. As I have intimated, the often repeated phrase—"bloß eine Idee" (merely an idea)—is not simply a rhetorical strategy.[96] Given his acute knowledge of the limits imposed upon the life of reason by the body, Schiller imposed limits on the life of the *Geist* while, at the same time, extolling its merits. Already at the very beginning of his career as a writer, namely in the *Philosophy of Physiology,* Schiller set up a noble ideal—"Equality with God is the destiny of the human being" ("Gottgleichheit ist die Bestimmung des Menschen")—only to add that the mind/spirit ("Geist), while developing eternally, will never attain that state ("aber es niemals erreichen") (NA 20: 10). But what would have led Schiller to become skeptical of Immanuel Kant's idea of the infinite progression of the human species, for instance?

I believe that the writer's act of self-critical enlightenment tempered the man's personal longing to transcend the confines of physical reality, especially the restrictions imposed upon him by his own body. The philosopher's act of charting the limits of his own theorizing is analogous to the limitations the historian imposed on the aspirations of the poet-dramatist in the writing of *Wallenstein.* In the essay *Concerning Naive and Sentimental Poetry,* Schiller came to grips with the rupture between Nature and reason. For while shaping the concept of the sentimental poet, he did not lose sight of the indispensable value of the naive. Once again, then, terms such as dualism and dialectical synthesis cannot capture the real dynamics of Schiller's work. Perhaps, instead, we need to appreciate the harmonious, yet tense interplay of the multidisciplinary activities that conjoin to create the inter-disciplinary texture of Schiller's writings.

A Final Note

Thomas Carlyle's tendency to romanticize Schiller in his book *Life of Friedrich Schiller* (1825) actually helps situate the writer between Enlightenment and romanticism. While speaking of Schiller's poetry, for instance, the English romanticist came to the following conclusion: "It was not the 'lean and flashy song' of an ear apt for harmony, combined with a maudlin sensibility, or a mere animal ferocity of passion, and an imagination creative chiefly because unbridled; it was, what true poetry is always, the quintessence of general mental riches, the purified result of strong thought and conception, and of refined as well as powerful emotion."[97] Surely, Carlyle was one of the first modern day writers to acknowledge the multifarious activities that inform the work of Friedrich Schiller: "In his writings, we behold him a moralist, a philosopher, a man of universal knowledge."[98]

Like Wilhelm von Humboldt, however, the English romantic writer glided over Schiller's battle with illness and his knowledge of the restrictions the body imposes on the activities of the mind, thereby idealizing his accomplishments. Carlyle writes concerning Schiller: "On the whole, we may pronounce him happy. His days passed in the contemplation of ideal grandeurs. . . . It is true, he had no rest, no peace; but he enjoyed the fiery consciousness of his own activity, which stands in place of it for men like him."[99] How often has contemporary scholarship on Schiller also repeated this lovely, all too lovely refrain.

7

At the Crossroads of Physiology and Politics:
Mary Stuart

I. *Mary Stuart*

MARY *Stuart* was completed in 1800. The idea for this tragedy ("Trauer-spiel") originated in the idyllic setting of Bauerbach in the Thuringian forest in the early 1780s. The relative compactness of the dramatic structure and the refined language point to the writer's heightened awareness of form. At the same time, there is also a clearer focus on Nature.

Schiller's depiction of the conflict between Queen Elizabeth and Mary Stuart discloses the operations of Nature. Already in act 1, scene 7, Mary Stuart informs Elizabeth's High Treasurer Lord Burleigh that Nature is responsible for the struggle between herself and Elizabeth: "Nature herself / Cast both of these two fiery rival peoples / Upon the one plank in the sea, gave them / Unequal shares, and bade them fight for it."[1] Differences in physical nature, then, also underlie the cultural differences between the two monarchs. It is apparent that Nature has distributed its gifts unevenly. As we now know, this idea has its origin in Schiller's earliest works, the *Philosophy of Physiology, The Robbers,* and *Criminal Out of Infamy.*

In *Mary Stuart* the writer captured the tension between appearance and being, politics and morality, sensuousness and rationality. Since scholarship has focused mainly on Mary Stuart's character, I wish to highlight the struggle within Queen Elizabeth and then assess its value for a new reading of the dramatic writing. Discussions of both Mary's characterization and Schiller's essay on the nature of the sublime will follow.[2]

In her conversation with Bellievre, in act 2, scene 2, Elizabeth bemoans the pressures of her office. "Kings are no more than slaves of their condition. / They are not free to follow their own hearts" (SW 45; NA 9: 45).[3] She interprets the people's expectations to be a form of enslavement. Questioning the call to marriage, she wrestles with the demands of political expediency and moral freedom. The metaphor of fetters is again well integrated into the text. Taking a ring from her finger, the Queen declares: "The same enslavement—wedlocks made with rings, / And rings when interlocking, make a chain . . . / It is *not* yet a chain, binds me *not yet,* / But can become

215

a circle that will bind" (SW 47; NA 9: 46).[4] Elizabeth seems to be most concerned with the even greater imprisonment of whatever free will she may still have at this point. She had intimated this shortly before when lamenting what the people expect of a female monarch, namely that she bear a child. "Their [my subjects'] present happiness is not enough, / I must be immolated to their future / And sacrifice my virgin liberty, / My highest good, to satisfy my people; / Now I must have a master forced on me. / They let me know that in their eyes I am / Only a woman, though I had believed / I governed like a man, and like a king" (SW 45; NA 9: 45).[5] Schiller's selection of the material for his drama of history was not coincidental.

From the vast array of historical material, the writer chose to dramatize certain themes, topics, and problems that were not unique to his own time. In *Mary Stuart,* he chose the clash of interest between two female monarchs. The rivalry between them, I will argue, is animated by the writer's earlier examination of the proper relationship between mind and body.

In order to illuminate the conflict within Schiller's Queen Elizabeth, I raise the question of the relationship between women and men in this drama. In act 3, scene 3, for instance, when Shrewsbury reminds the Queen of her freedom, he states that "woman is a weak and fragile thing" ("ein gebrechlich Wesen ist das Weib") (SW 53; NA 9: 52). For that reason, Talbot implies, Elizabeth should have compassion for Mary. Elizabeth recoils immediately, exclaiming: "A woman is not always [read: not] weak. Strong souls / Are found in women. In my presence, Sir, / Let no one speak of woman's weaknesses" (SW 53; NA 9: 52).[6] Elizabeth's sense of identity is underscored by the strength she exhibits as a politically powerful individual. But her declaration is as much a reminder to herself. Viewed within the body of Schiller's writings, the exclamation also constitutes a profound challenge to the contents of a poem like "Women's Dignity" ("Würde der Frauen"). For it is also a reminder to the writer himself of the strengths and limitations of human beings of both genders.

To Elizabeth's right and left stand Burleigh, the voice of political expediency, and Talbot, the voice of moral action. To Burleigh's declaration, "Her life is death to you, her death your life!" (SW 50; NA 9: 49),[7] Talbot responds: "As inclination changes, so opinion / Rises and falls, a variable tide. / Oh, do not say that you are subject to / Necessity, and to your people's will / At any moment, when you wish, you can / Prove to yourself your will is free indeed" (SW 51–52; NA 9: 50).[8] Hence practical politics and human compassion inform Elizabeth's personal dilemma. This deeper conflict within Elizabeth is suggested by her words: "wisdom which cries out for blood / I cannot but abhor with all my soul" (SW 50; NA 9: 49).[9] With such self-knowledge, Queen Elizabeth is a worthy rival, one whose characterization begins to fuel the dramatic conflict.

Schiller acknowledged that at any point in history, there is struggle. In

Mary Stuart, the recipient is presented with a myriad of interconnected and competing circumstances in which even the most powerful individuals are necessarily entangled. In the later dramatic writings, such as *Wallenstein,* it becomes increasingly apparent that physiology, history, and nature form a labyrinth of complex interrelationships, which on a more fundamental level points to the complexities of human existence.

In *Mary Stuart,* one of the central tensions of Schiller's writings is animated through the metaphors of chains and fetters, the metaphor of wings, and the motif of flight. At the beginning of act 3, Mary races through the park enjoying her physical freedom. She is no longer imprisoned—or, so it seems. To be sure, Mary's chains have been cast off. Kennedy says: "you move on wings, my Lady; wait for me!" (SW 81; NA 9: 79).[10] (They are the first words to be spoken in act 3.) Mary rejoices in having been freed from the narrow confines of her prison. For the first time in the play, her words call up the question of the sublime. "Am I not sheltered by this vaulting sky? / Unchecked, untrammeled, my delighted eyes / Can roam and measure all infinity" (SW 82; NA 9: 79–80).[11] The sights she beholds are described in the German as "frei und fessellos" (free and unfettered) (NA 9: 79). The fact that Kennedy must remind the Queen that she has simply escaped the prison and not the wall that still encircles them would seem to suggest that freedom is conditional.

It is a striking fact that, upon her release from prison, Mary's language changes. Through a more lyrical language, she begins to reconstitute her world. The following lines form a poetic stanza in the text, indicating that Mary has taken flight on the wings of imagination: "Swift, fleeting clouds, you ships of the air! / Oh, to be drifting and sailing up there! / Take my dear love to the land of my youth. / I am a captive here, chained foot and hand, / No other envoys are at my command; / You can move freely up there in the blue, / That evil queen has no hold upon you" (SW 82; NA 9: 80).[12] The poetry of these and similar lines underscores one of the major themes of Schiller's writings: the tension between confinement and liberation in life. As we have seen, this theme recurs on many levels within Schiller's works: the physical-intellectual, political-moral, individual-historical, anthropological-metaphysical/religious. The recurrent and creatively reconceptualized themes cutting across the borders of traditional classifications of genre clearly enhance the work of the modern writer Friedrich Schiller.

Somewhat like Elizabeth, Mary wills not to be a "heartless" prisoner of her surroundings. By defying the Queen of England, she may bewail the historical circumstances in which she is caught, but she cannot escape her natural tie to her cousin. Mary may well defy history, but the very act of turning Elizabeth into the object of her resentment, hatred, jealousy, and scorn demonstrates just how strong the natural bond to her relative actually is. Like Elizabeth, the dynamics of Mary's character reside in her own

Charlotte von Lengefeld Schiller. From a painting by Ludovike Simanowitz.

nature, namely between the dictates of the head and the heart, that is, between the rational and sensuous components of her being.

Considering the main characters of Schiller's *Mary Stuart* in the light of
the medical dissertations and subsequent writings, it becomes clear that
Elizabeth and Mary exhibit, both in themselves and taken together, the
creative recurrence of the mind-body problem. At the same time, they also
represent the tension between politics and morality, which was so central
to the concerns of German middle-class writers of the eighteenth century.
Furthermore, with the introduction of the idea of the sublime, the metaphor
of rupture undergoes a positive transformation.

Schiller's characterizations of both Mary and Elizabeth reflect the struggle between sensuousness and rationality. On the level of human nature,
they represent the tense interrelationship between the body and the mind.
On another level, the battle within these characters exhibits the socio-
historical conflict of the split ("Spaltung") between the political and the
moral spheres of influence.[13] In short, Schiller's later dramatic writing *Mary
Stuart* explores the problems of physiology and politics.

On the one hand, Elizabeth recognizes clearly what she must do as monarch of England. On the other hand, she laments this obligation on several
occasions. Thus, both the political and the moral dimensions also help animate the conflict within Elizabeth's character. I will argue here that as the
play progresses Elizabeth tends more and more to the corporeal, whereas
Mary gravitates to the spiritual-intellectual domain. Though she is imprisoned in body politically, Mary demonstrates sublimity of character through
which she exudes a sense of freedom of will. Because Elizabeth becomes
weaker in spirit and a prisoner of not only her own body but also of the
body politic and Mary less so, perhaps we should see in Elizabeth and Mary
two parts of a greater whole.

	(Beginning)		(Middle)	(End)
Elizabeth	–	Mary	Rupture	Elizabeth < – > Mary
(body + mind)	–	(body + mind)	act 3, scene 4	(body) < – > (mind)

Mary Stuart is beautiful in outward appearance. In her state of sublimity,
however, she transcends the limits of her beauty (physiognomy). Politically,
i.e., physically enchained, Mary is morally free. For her part, however, Elizabeth is politically strong as queen, but a prisoner of her office. Still, as a
person, Elizabeth wrestles with the problem of moral freedom. One source
of Elizabeth's jealousy is that Mary not only voices, but is actually capable
of attaining moral freedom. The fierce rivalry between the two female monarchs transcends political issues. Their battle of words in act 3, scene 4,
forms more than a dramatic crisis point.[14] And Mary's exclamation—"It is
the fate / Of kings that their dissensions split the world, / Unleashing all the
furies of disruption" (SW 91; NA 9: 88) [15]—raises a more fundamental

question than the problem of politics. For the true crisis is brought about
by the rupture within the central characters' own natures as well as the
natural split between them. Mary's momentary victory in the battle of words
not only comes at the cost of political defeat. It means that the harmonious
tension between the rational and sensuous natures of the human being has
been short-circuited. This crisis point has tragic consequences.

The signing of the death warrant, for instance, illustrates Elizabeth's inclination to imprison the body. Both the sequence of events following the
verbal climax in act 3, scene 4, and the stage directions in act 4, scene 10,
make it plain that the signing is an act of sensuousness. Having discovered
that Leicester has betrayed her, Elizabeth directs all her wrath at the woman
who had wounded her spirit in Fotheringay Park. At first attributing her
situation to the nature of her office ("What slavery is to serve the people"
(p.129) ["O Sklaverei des Volksdiensts! Schmähliche / Knechtschaft"]) (NA
9: 127), she quickly turns Mary into her "nemesis, fated to plague / My life
relentlessly" (p.130) ("die Furie meines Lebens! Mir / Ein Plagegeist vom
Schicksal angeheftet") (NA 9: 128). The rupture in her relationship to Mary
is underscored by the metaphor of tearing: "She [Mary] tears from me my
lover, / Snatches my bridegroom" (p.130) ("Sie entreißt mir den Geliebten, /
Den Bräutigam raubt sie mir!") (NA 9: 128). Jealousy gives rise to rage and
the desire for vengeance. Following a short silence, Elizabeth rails against
her competitor.

> With what contempt her eyes looked down on me,
> As though her lightning glance could strike me down.
> Impotent fool! My weapons are much better;
> They hit their mark, and you are gone forever!
> (*goes quickly to the table and seizes the pen*)[16]
>
> (SW 131; NA 9: 129)

The choice of words may remind the reader of act 3, scene 4, where Mary
had called Elizabeth a bastard.

> *Elizabeth:* I am a bastard, am I? Luckless wretch!
> I am a bastard while you live and breathe. . . .
> As soon as England has no choice, the bed
> Where I was born will be legitimate.
> (*She signs with a swift, firm stroke, then drops
> the pen and steps back with an expression of fright.*)[17]
>
> (SW 131; NA 9: 129)

To be sure, the actual signing of the death warrant is a political act that
satisfies the will of the people, especially the will of her closest counsel
Burleigh. But Elizabeth's act is also personal and sensuous, i.e., utterly
corporeal in the sense that her deed is divorced from reason altogether. Her

act of retribution is a purely emotional response. Only when she steps back in dread is rational reflection reinstated. At this critical moment in the drama, Elizabeth does not act as a queen. She *reacts* as a sensuous and revengeful individual. As she says to Burleigh concerning Leicester: "love's dead, revenge is all" (SW 115; NA 9: 113). In short, as the drama progresses, Schiller's Elizabeth moves toward the merely corporeal side of the mind-body paradigm. At the same time, by signing the death warrant, she ostracizes herself completely from the moral sphere and abandons herself to the political realm. From this perspective, Elizabeth becomes the prisoner not only of her body but also of the body politic. Given this series of events, the Queen's manipulation of Davison exhibits her lack of moral responsibility. Glancing back at act 4, scene 10, the intersection of physiology and politics in Schiller's *Mary Stuart* becomes quite apparent. The simultaneous operation of the writer's multidisciplinary activities would seem to be evident in his late as well as early writings.

The scenes where Mary confesses her sins in the presence of Melvil (act 5, scenes 6–7) are punctuated with references to flight and the breaking of chains: "My misery is in sight, my chains will fall, / My prison open, and my gladdened soul / May rise on angels' wings toward endless freedom" (SW 143; NA 9: 142). Though her physical body is held captive, Mary's *Geist* (spirit/mind) is free. It has been overlooked that, for the writer, death can also be a source of healing. In Mary's words: "A healer and a balm to me is death, / My solemn friend! With his black pinions he / Will gently hide all my humiliations. / Man's [the human being's] death restores nobility to man [the human being], / No matter how degraded was his life" (SW 143; NA 9: 142).[18] Unlike *Wallenstein,* in which the black pinions may well represent the central character's state of melancholy,[19] in *Mary Stuart* the pinions are the wings of death which Mary now interprets as a source of healing from the limitations of the material world.

Reminiscent of Schiller's early literary practice, Mary feels that she is standing at a precipice—"Upon the brink of all eternity" (SW 147) ("Ich stehe an dem Rand der Ewigkeit"; NA 9: 145). In this seemingly precarious situation, she accepts fully (sublimely) the rift between temporality and eternity, which is overcome by death. The wing metaphor captures the freedom of Mary's spirit: "the soul grows wings and mounts / To highest heaven" (SW 147–48; NA 9: 146).[20] In Mary's case, the writer associates the metaphor of rupture with the sublime. Rupture has become a sign of liberation from the confinement of earthly concerns: "my last earthly tie has now been torn" (SW 150) ("Zerrissen ist das letzte irdische Band") (NA 9: 149). By this time in Schiller's career, the implicitly negative connotation of the rupture metaphor in the early writings has been infused with a new, positive meaning.

The difference between the literary conceptions of death in Schiller's early and later writings should now be apparent. Death is no longer a chasm or abyss to be feared. It is a means of merging the visible, finite world with the as yet unseen world of the infinite. Viewed in the light of Mary's development, the world appears as a sickly body in need of spiritual healing. This is underscored also by Elizabeth's anti-*Bildung*. It is here, I believe, that the truly tragic element of the dramatic work resides.

In the first two numbers of the *Hamburg Dramaturgy* [*Hamburgische Dramaturgie*], Gotthold Ephraim Lessing maintained that Christian martyr plays are not, in effect, tragic, because the martyr is saved in the end. He or she receives a reward in Heaven. Similarly, Schiller's Mary Stuart, largely because of her confession and absolution in act 5, scene 7, gains spiritual-intellectual strength, moral fortitude and the hope of salvation. The display of sublime character cannot be tragic.[21] Rather, the real tragedy lies in Elizabeth's inability to exercise her free, moral will. Her moral ineptitude is underscored by her self-imposed imprisonment in the narrow confines of both her sensuous being and her political office. In the end, her embodiment of the will of the people, now her will as well, leaves the Queen isolated and alone. Burleigh is dismissed. Shrewsbury resigns. From a minor character, Kent, a messenger of sorts, we learn that Leicester has gone into exile in France. At the very end of the drama, then, Elizabeth sits all alone, in virtual isolation. The spiritual-intellectual, as represented now by Mary, has departed her. On a fundamental level, mind (Mary) and body (Elizabeth) have been completely ruptured. Therein, perhaps, lies the full tragic effect of the dramatic writing, *Mary Stuart*.

II. The Essay "Concerning the Sublime"

The essay "On the Sublime" ["Vom Erhabenen"], which appeared in 1793 in *New Thalia* [*Neue Thalia*], demonstrates the impact of both Immanuel Kant's critical philosophy and Moses Mendelssohn's *Letters Concerning the Sensations*. The exact date of origin of the subsequent writing "Concerning the Sublime" ["Über das Erhabene"] is uncertain, though it may have originated as early as 1793. The fact, however, that it did not appear until 1801 among Schiller's *Shorter Prose Writings* [*Kleinere prosaische Schriften*] places it in closer proximity to the writing of *Mary Stuart* than the earlier essay. The work also exhibits greater intellectual independence and maturity of thought than the former writing.

The essay "Concerning the Sublime" poses the question: How can the human being attain freedom? The answer lies in the process of moral-aesthetic *Bildung*. As in earlier writings, Schiller maintains that the human being is endowed by nature with a "sensuous-rational" ("sinnliche vernünftige"), or "aesthetic propensity" ("ästhetische Tendenz"). He emphasizes the indispensable role of feeling in his discussions of the beautiful and the sublime. Both sensations, he sees, are capable of engendering freedom. "We feel free in beauty because the sensuous drives harmonize with the law of reason; we feel free in the sublime because the sensuous drive has no influence on the legislation of reason, because the mind acts here as if it stood under no laws other than its own" (NA 21: 42).[22] Beauty is described in terms of harmony, and the sublime in terms of autonomy as if the mind were divorced from the sensuous or material components of reality. However, the sublime state is conditional, for the writer introduces the Kantian "als-ob" (as if). The window to the realm of the sublime is opened when contemplating the infinite. "We enjoy the sensuous-infinite because we can think what the senses no longer understand and the understanding no longer comprehends" (NA 21: 43).[23] In short, the sublime is a condition of pure reason.

The mind-body paradigm is also at work in Schiller's discussions of the sublime. For the feeling of the beautiful is described as a "condition of our sensuousness" ("Zustand des Sinnes"), whereas sublime feeling is a "condition of our mind" ("Zustand unsers Geistes") (NA 21: 42). When experiencing the beautiful, we accept "the fetters of necessity" ("die Fesseln der Notwendigkeit") and become willing prisoners of the world of sense ("die Sinnenwelt"). In this sensuous state, we harmonize with Nature.[24] Experiencing the sublime, the human being transcends the "earthly wing" ("irrdische[n] Flügel") of the beautiful, "[elevating] us above the power of Nature and, if only momentarily, [releasing] us from all influence of the body" (NA 21: 41).[25] In a state of sublimity, physical and moral culture are sharply divided. The magic ("Zauber") of sublime feeling consists in the "contradiction" ("Widerspruch") between the dictates of reason and the claims of sensuality, and this captures the full attention of our mind ("Gemüt") (NA 21: 43).

Sublime experience is especially compelling, perhaps, because it illuminates the paradox that the human being is by nature determined, yet free; free, yet determined. This conclusion is attained when appreciating the play of the interaction between mind and body. The power of the sublime, however, is that it evokes in the human being a sense of freedom from limitation, thereby instilling the hope of progress. As such, the sublime becomes one of the driving forces of history which can propel us beyond the confines of the present. At this point, Schiller's essays on the sublime and the essay on universal history intersect.

I submit that, for Schiller, the special function of the beautiful is to capture and preserve the harmonious tension between things, especially the relationship between the human being and Nature. It is not coincidental, then, that the writer should refer to the "beautiful harmony of the natural impulses" in terms of music. If the human being wishes to progress, then one should ("soll") be torn away from the state of harmony with Nature, at least momentarily, so as not to allow beauty to imprison us. The special function of the sublime is to break the chains beauty imposes on sensuous nature. "The sublime thus creates an exit point out of the sensuous world wherein the beautiful would always gladly hold us prisoner" (NA 21: 45).[26] Mary's beautiful outward appearance enchains her to the physical world, as seen in Mortimer's and Leicester's attempts to possess her, as well as in Shrewsbury's infatuation with Mary's beauty. Mary's sublimity of mind, however, propels her beyond the limits of her beautiful, corporeal nature.

Yet, Schiller's language connotes more than this since it reminds the reader of the arachnean web of existence. For, "Not gradually . . ., but suddenly, and through a shock [to the nerves], it [the sublime] tears the independent mind away from the net with which refined sensuousness entangled it [the mind], and binds it all the tighter, the more transparently it is spun" (NA 21: 45).[27] The writer draws a close analogy between the metaphor of rupture and his theory of the sublime. For sublime emotion ("erhabene Rührung") rends the "seductive veil of intellectual beauty" ("[die] verführerische Hülle des geistigen Schönen")—"thus, often a single sublime emotion is enough to tear this web of deceit, to suddenly give back to the enchained spirit its full elasticity, to endow it with a revelation about its true determination, and to impose a feeling of one's dignity, at least momentarily" (NA 21: 45).[28] Schiller seems to encourage the fullest expression of the human being in a state of sublimity and the concomitant idea of the progressive advancement of the human species. As a side note, the writer further developed the metaphors of rupture, spinning, and tearing in his later works.

Schiller's account of the ancient story of Calypso develops the idea of the sublime even further. "Beauty, in the form of the goddess Calypso, has bewitched the courageous son of Ulysses and, by the power of her charms, and for a long period of time, holds him captive on her island. For a long time, he believes that he is paying homage to an immortal divinity since he is lying in the arms of sensuality—but a sublime impression in the figure of Mentor suddenly seizes him. He remembers his higher calling, throws himself into the wave, and is free" (NA 21: 45).[29] Tearing oneself loose from the imprisonment of the body requires a conscious act of willing ("der selbstherrschende Wille"), the will to moral freedom. The innate capacity to experience sublimely sets the individual's "pure daemon" ("reine[n] Dämon") into action. This type of critical engagement helps further the process of aesthetic education.[30]

Schiller offers several examples of situations in which the individual may be tested. One of these is the individual's ability to cope with illness. Only in moments of crisis, it seems, can the human being judge the quality of those virtues with which the beautiful person is naturally endowed. Whereas the beautiful marks the attainment of a healthy state of harmonious tension, the sublime presupposes rupture. Schiller's physiology plays a vital role in the later theoretical and dramatic works. Only now, the mind (*Geist*) transgresses, at least momentarily, the limits imposed upon it by corporeal reality.

In order to realize one's fullest potential as a human being, the writer argues, one should be placed in a state other than "the physical world order," "by which, to be sure, reason flies with its ideas, but [which] the understanding is unable to comprehend with its concepts" (NA 21: 45).[31] Only by freeing oneself from the material world with the aid of reason, if only momentarily, can the human being activate one's "absolute moral capacity" (NA 21: 45). The writer qualifies this, however, when he admits that the seed ("Keim") for the capacity to feel ("Empfindungsfähigkeit") both the beautiful and the sublime is apportioned unevenly among individual human beings. Time and again throughout his writings, Schiller notes the importance of the uniqueness of the individual, albeit within the context of the identity of the species.

The historian Friedrich Schiller is also at work in the essay "Concerning the Sublime." Reminiscent of the 1789 essay "Something Concerning the First Human Society According to the Proscriptions of the Mosaic Law," the writer distinguishes between the human being in one's natural versus rational state. The main part of the essay traces the development of the human species out of the original state, wherein "free [or, unimpaired] observation" ("die freie Betrachtung") is juxtaposed to "the blind drive of the powers of Nature" ("de[m] blinden Andrang der Naturkräfte") (NA 21: 46). Schiller conceives of world history ("die Weltgeschichte") as a sublime object insofar as history itself informs the outcome of the conflict of the powers of Nature ("der Konflikt der Naturkräfte untereinander selbst") as well as the tug-of-war between those powers and freedom (NA 21: 49). As a general concept, world history transcends the narrow limits circumscribed by particular historical events. Historical occurrences and world history thus form a connection that is analogous to the relationship between the particular (*das Besondere*) and the general (*das Allgemeine*).

It is important to note that Schiller repeatedly qualifies his optimism concerning the course of history. "If one approaches history only with great expectations of insight and knowledge—how often one finds oneself disillusioned" (NA 21: 49).[32] Progress is limited. The "lessons of experience" ("Aussagen der Erfahrungen") tell a different story than the force of philosophical or theoretical argumentation: "how unbridled it [Nature] tears the reins away in the realm of freedom, wherein the spirit of speculation would very much like to lead it into imprisonment!" (NA 21: 50).[33] With the aid of the metaphor of imprisonment, the writer once again draws a connection between the sublime and the beautiful. Whereas the bounds of beauty are determined by Nature, the extreme of the sublime consists in the captivity of pure speculation. As we have seen, this precaution was registered by Schiller in his critique of Fichte's *Theory of Knowledge*. In both the earlier and later writings, Schiller sought to determine the "middle line of truth." For extremes actually limit one's freedom the more they draw us away from the truth of our bifold nature.

"Blessed, then, is the person who has learned to bear what one cannot change and to accept with dignity what one cannot save" (NA 21: 51).[34] As

Schiller states in the essay on the sublime: "The highest ideal, which we struggle to attain, is to remain in good spirits with the physical world, as the protector of our happiness, without feeling compelled to break with the moral world, which determines our dignity" (NA 21: 50).[35] The pathetic ("das Pathetische") is seen as the central means of encouraging "the independent principle in our minds" ("das selbstständige Prinzipium in unserm Gemüte") (NA 21: 51). Through this means, the human being gains and maintains absolute independence ("absolute Independenz") as a moral being (NA 21: 51). The earlier interactionist theory of the relationship between mind and body has undergone a significant shift of emphasis. "The more often, then, the mind renews this act of self-activity, the more this act becomes a capacity—thereby, one gains a greater lead over the sensuous drive" (NA 21: 51).[36] In the sublime feeling of transcendence over physical nature, the individual experiences "the highest flourish of human nature" ("der höchste Schwung der Menschennatur") (NA 21: 51).

Only by encountering danger and accepting the crises in life can there be healing ("Heil") for humankind. To this end, "the terribly majestic drama of all-destroying and re-creating, and again destructive change helps us" (NA 21: 52).[37] This, too, is at the basis of Nature; hence, the symbolic significance of those "pathetic portraits of a humanity wrestling with its fate" ("pathetische Gemählde der mit dem Schicksal ringenden Menschheit" [NA 21: 52]). All possible perils and pitfalls in life are not only represented, but explored in and transmitted through the creative imitation and pathos of tragedy, which not simply exposes the limitation but champions the potentiality of the human spirit. Endowed with reason and imagination the human being is empowered by sublime feeling to creatively transform reality in consciousness and, in the process, transcend the narrow confines of the material world, if only for the moment.

Scholarship has not emphasized the fact that Friedrich Schiller postulated the *unity* of the sublime and the beautiful in the essay "Concerning the Sublime" and that this unity became one of the major tasks of the aesthetic education of the human being: "hence, the sublime must meet the beautiful in order to make of aesthetic education a complete whole, and to expand the capability of the sensation of the human heart according to the entire range of our determination and, therefore, also escape the world of sense" (NA 21: 52).[38] The feeling of the beautiful is indispensable, since without it we would not be able to reconcile our determination in Nature ("Naturbestimmung") with our determination in reason ("Vernunftbestimmung") (NA 21: 53). The feeling of the sublime is likewise essential, for without it "beauty would make us forget our dignity" ("würde uns die Schönheit unsrer Würde vergessen machen") (NA 21: 53). To return to the beginning of the essay, in the sublime experience two feelings are mixed, a feeling of sorrow and a feeling of happiness ("Wehsein" and "Frohsein"). This connecting of two (seemingly) contradictory sensations ("Empfindungen") into a single feeling is the source of moral independence ("moralische Selbständigkeit") (NA 21: 42).

Both senses of the beautiful and the sublime comprise essential parts of "our unchangeable determination" ("unsre unveränderliche Bestimmung") (NA 21: 53). Ultimately, then, both must be conjoined if the human being is to feel complete. It is especially fitting that the writer should have employed the metaphor of marriage to capture this idea. "Only when the sublime is wed with the beautiful, and our receptiveness of both has been developed in equal measure, are we complete citizens of Nature without, for that reason, being its slaves and without forfeiting our citizenship in the intelligible world" (NA 21: 53).[39] The metaphor of marriage is especially well chosen because of the distinct, yet *interdependent* operations of the beautiful and the sublime. In reality, two different natures ("Naturen") are being conjoined within us. The ideal relationship between the beautiful and the sublime, then, can only be one of harmonious tension. In effect, the writer has preserved the concept of the whole without sacrificing the uniqueness of the particular.

A Glance Back at *Mary Stuart*

Reconsidering Schiller's later dramatic writing, we discover that the symbol of the stringed instrument does not seem to be developed. Already at the very beginning of the play (act 1, scene 1), we learn that Elizabeth has confiscated Mary's lute. Kennedy says, "Her harmless lute was taken from her, too." Paulet responds, "Because she would play wanton songs on it" (3; NA 9: 5).[40] Perhaps the stringed instrument has been removed from her prison chamber so that its beautiful strains will not entice those that hear them to be drawn to Mary: the stringed instrument as a potential political weapon! I interpret the relative absence of metaphors relating to the stringed instrument as a sign of the writer's preoccupation with the incorporation of the sublime into his dramatic practice. For the strings that produce beautiful, harmonious music have been ruptured. Indeed, with the one exception of the sounds of hunting horns, one of the outstanding characteristics of Schiller's *Mary Stuart* is the relative absence of music. By comparison, both *Wallenstein* and *William Tell* are much richer acoustically. As we have seen, metaphors of enchainment and imprisonment and the motif of flight abound in *Mary Stuart,* in which writing the metaphor of rupture plays a central role. Given the nature of Schiller's language, the choice of metaphors in the later play accords quite well with the theory of the sublime.

The fact that Melvil calls Mary a "transfigured angel" ("verklärter Engel") complements the emphasis on sublime feeling. In this play, perhaps more than any other dramatic writing aside from *The Maid of Orleans* [*Die Jungfrau von Orleans*], we witness a dramatic shift away from the physical to the spiritual-intellectual. Mary's statement in line 3838—"Now I have nothing more on earth" ("Jetzt hab ich nichts mehr auf der Erden") (157; NA 9: 155)—suggests that the mind or spirit (*Geist*) has transcended the confines of the body. Interaction is no longer possible, either within Mary or between Mary and Elizabeth. Mary shows no sign of fear, either of Elizabeth's political might or of death itself. Rather, she accepts her situation completely. Hers is an act of independent, moral freedom, that is, of moral will. Hence, Schiller's *Mary Stuart* is a powerful testimony to the strength of the human spirit.

By having one of the central characters achieve sublimity, however, the writer transcends the limits of conventional tragedy. By accepting death fearlessly, the heroine seems to triumph even over death itself. I hasten to add that this is also a characteristic of dignity ("Würde"), as articulated in the essay *Concerning Grace and Dignity* [*Über Anmut und Würde*]. With this trait, "the mind presents itself in the body as the ruler" (NA 20: 296).[41] The mind-body paradigm informs that essay as well. We recall that it was this type of fearlessness in the face of death that characterized the early drama *The Robbers* and the prose work *Criminal Out of Infamy*.

It has often been overlooked that the play *Mary Stuart* does not end with Mary but, rather, with Elizabeth. Having avenged herself, Elizabeth manipulates Burleigh's original idea that the people force her to carry out the demands of her office. By signing the death sentence, however, she forsakes the moral sphere of action and listens only to the dictates of her own sensuous need, that is, her body, which is now indistinguishable from the body politic. In the end, Elizabeth's life is ignoble because she has become merely the instrument of power politics and her own sensuousness. Without her moral or spiritual-intellectual counterpart (Mary Stuart), she abandons herself to a life of servitude to politics. With that, the drama of seemingly opposed, yet interdependent forces draws to its inevitable tragic-pathetic conclusion.

8

The Later Poetic Writings

THERE is a gap of approximately ten years between the time of the completion of the early poetic writings and the resurgence of Schiller's poetry in 1795. Two very important exceptions are "The Gods of Greece" ["Die Götter Griechenlands"] and "The Artists" ["Die Künstler"]. Both poems appeared in Christoph Martin Wieland's *Teutscher Merkur,* in the March issues of 1788 and 1789, respectively.[1] Compared to the early poetry, the later writings exhibit far greater sensitivity to the force of history. There is also considerably more emphasis on the power of the creative mind.[2] At the same time, however, many of the metaphors, themes, and problems explored in the early poetry resound throughout the later writings. Images of a melodic universe and the symbol of the stringed instrument, for instance, are still essential constituents of Schiller's later poetry.

In "The Gods of Greece" the more mature poet-historian juxtaposes the modern world to ancient times, acknowledging the great differences between the past and the present.[3] Whereas, in ancient times, the beauty and truth of poetry flowed through Creation, exuding a sense of the fullness of life ("Lebensfülle"), by the eighteenth century the sun rotates "soullessly" ("seelenlos") through the solar system. Science has left an indelible mark.

The reader or listener also perceives the sounds of pain and lament. In ancient times, we are told, fire flowed from Pindar's proud hymns and Arion's lyre.[4] The seventeenth strophe begins with the qualifier "but" ("aber"), denoting the fact that the times have changed. Its infusion highlights the poet's lament concerning the loss of the past. As the writer makes clear, however, the past is "lost, never to return" ("ohne Wiederkehr verloren").[5]

Schiller continues to foreground the regenerative, creative power of Nature. Although, for the time being, its "golden trace" ["goldne Spur"] can be discovered "only in the fairyland of songs" ["nur in dem Feenland der Lieder"], this does not mean that it must remain a fable. It is not the case that the modern writer is unable to locate the gods of the past. He is simply not interested in seeking them. Rather, human beings are encouraged to tap the power of one's own nature, without reliance on the gods. In order to recreate the world, the individual human being must develop the harmonious tension within oneself, i.e., within one's own nature. Only then will one rediscover the divine element of human *being*. This is a major impetus behind the writer's lament concerning "godless Nature" ("die entgötterte Natur"). For, in a soulless universe, godless Nature (or godless humanity) slavishly serves the law of gravity ("knechtisch dem Gesetz der Schwere").

We recall that, in Schiller's earlier critical reception of Sir Isaac Newton, the writer had subjugated the physical law of gravity to the metaphysical law of love. In "The Gods of Greece," the soulless nature of the modern world, an effect of the one-sided scientific exploration of reality, is compared to "the hollow [literally: dead] stroke of a pendulum clock" ("Gleich dem toten Schlag der Pendeluhr").[6] Perhaps this interpretation best explains the last two lines of the final version of 1800:

> Was unsterblich im Gesang soll leben
> Muß im Leben untergehn.

> [What should live immortally in song
> Must perish in life.]

(NA 2: 367)

Given the historical perspective the writer has developed, there is no real separation of art and life, as some scholars have maintained. By deleting the last three strophes of the first version of the poem and adding several more, the writer simply strengthened the idea that science *alone* cannot permeate the deeper realities of the universe. In no way, however, should this be construed as a rejection of science.

Klaus Berghahn has seen in this poem an example of "Schiller's mythological symbolism."[7] He recognizes that it constitutes considerably more than philosophical poetry: "more distinct implications of words and images; bold metaphors and leaps of thought . . . , where we expect logical stringency."[8] In his reading, the poem highlights the sentimental poet, who not only desires, but must realize the ideal poetically.[9] We should bear in mind, however, that the poem was written seven years before (and, in revised form, five years after) the essay *Concerning Naive and Sentimental Poetry*. My concern here is more with the writer's presentation of Nature in general and human nature in particular without sustained discussion of the creative transformation and anthropomorphizing of ancient mythology.[10]

I suggest that the writer's later occasional statements in the theoretical essays concerning the (possible) transcendence of the material world through ideas should be comprehended in full view of the writer's life-long development. It seems to me that we should take seriously Schiller's repeated qualification of ideas, the recognition of the power of the body and the material world, and the honest assessment of the limits of history per se, as well as the potential of universal history as a regulative theoretical construct.

As I have suggested, in "The Gods of Greece" the writer does not bemoan the passing of the gods. Rather, he lamented the extinction of a soul-filled universe that results from the uncritical adoption of a purely mechanistic and/or materialistic view of life. It should now be apparent that the author of "Julius's Theosophy" is still very much at work in this later poem. For he is interested in recreating a soulful and happy existence. The world, he sees, is enlivened by feeling and emotion. Through this poem, Schiller disseminates the idea of the indispensability of sensitive knowledge in the determination and creative transformation of reality, an activity that complements the theoretical work *Concerning the Aesthetic Education of the Human Being*.

The very first line of "The Artists" extols the beauty of the human being in all one's splendor. Thematically, the poem may be understood as a companion piece to "The Gods of Greece." Unlike the earlier poem, however, "The Artists" begins on a triumphant note. It heralds the great accomplishments of the modern human being, who is "free through reason" ["frei durch Vernunft"], "great through gentleness" ["Durch Sanftmut groß"], and "master of Nature, which loves your [Nature's] fetters" ["Herr der Natur, die deine Fesseln liebet"] (strophe 1). The human being's greatest power, perhaps, consists in the creative production of art, in and through which she or he shapes and reshapes the world. On the eve of a new century, the modern individual has emerged as a new, cultivated human being, one, it is hoped, who has transcended the barbarism ("Verwilderung") of the past. The transformation from savagery and barbarism to humanity is brought about primarily by advancements in the arts, and it is precisely this development that the writer describes in terms of the sounds of a stringed instrument.

> Was bey dem Saitenklang der Musen
> Mit süßem Beben dich durchdrang,
> Erzog die Kraft in deinem Busen,
> Die sich dereinst zum Weltgeist schwang.
>
> [What, with the muses' sound of strings,
> Moved you with sweet vibrato,
> Trained that power in your soul,
> Which once swayed to the world-spirit.]
>
> (End of strophe 3; NA 1: 202; 2: 384)

In and through the act of writing poetry, Friedrich Schiller actively worked out some of the major tenets of his later theories of aesthetic education and the naive and sentimental. Though primarily concerned with the rhetorical components of Schiller's art, Gerd Ueding has observed that the content of "The Artists" transmits the aesthetic conviction of the author concerning the meaning and task of art in the education of the human species, as well as the influence of art on the process of civilization. For, as Schiller wrote: "Nur durch das Morgenthor des Schönen / Drangst du in der Erkenntniß Land" [Only through the morning gate of beauty / did you enter the world of Knowledge] (NA 1: 202; 2: 384).[11] Addressing the nature of Schiller's art, Terence J. Reed disclosed an intimate connection between this poem and the later essay *Concerning the Aesthetic Education of the Human Being*. "Art was the foreplay of reason, the only means by which primitive humanity could absorb to good effect what it was destined one day to know abstractly and with full awareness. 'What we have here perceived as beauty / Will one day come to meet us as the truth.'"[12] In recognizing this point, we should also acknowledge the influence of Schiller's earliest theoretical writings, especially the medical dissertations, on his later works.[13] For, in this poetic writing, the capacity to produce art is said to distinguish the human being from the animals.

As in "The Gods of Greece," Schiller's differentiation between ancient and modern times in "The Artists" exhibits his interest in history. But rather than underscore the rupture between the present and the past, the poem reflects a more contiguous timeline. The contribution of artists, both ancient and modern, to the enrichment and progress of civilization in history is acknowledged. Whereas, in earliest times, uncultivated barbarians were chained to mere desire, i.e., slaves of the material world, artists are capable of capturing the "beautiful soul of Nature" ("schöne Seele der Natur") through the "beautiful power of imaging" ("schöne Bildkraft"). The artistic human being perceives the melodic sounds of Nature and creates them anew for humankind. It is essential to note that the cultivation of humanity is first activated by communing with Nature.

Toward the end of this famous poem, the writer lays primary stress on "die seelenbildende Natur" [soul-building Nature], i.e., "die vollendende Natur" [perfecting Nature] (ll. 394b–c and 396b–c; NA 2/1: 394). In touch with one's own nature, the individual human being cultivates the interplay of mind and body. The more one exercises the art of playing the instrument of one's body and soul (the *Saitenspiel*), the more the individual becomes a vibrant and even more vital part of the world. In this way, the individual begins to transform society.

Thematically, the two poems "The Gods of Greece" and "The Artists" intersect at this point. Not surprisingly, in the latter poem, "the singer's lyre" is the means by which the melodic strains of beauty, order, and harmony are not simply restored, but created anew. Another tie to the theoretical program of *Concerning the Aesthetic Education of the Human Being* is now transparent. For the soulful artist is capable of transforming barbarians into cultivated social beings. He or she is empowered, through creative, i.e., productive genius, with the ability to establish new worlds. "Doch höher stets, zu immer höhern Höhen / Schwang sich der schaffende Genie. / Schon sieht man Schöpfungen aus Schöpfungen erstehen, / Aus Harmonien Harmonie" [Yet higher still, to ever greater heights / The creating genius did leap. / Already one sees creations arising from creations / (And) harmony from harmonies] ("The Artists"; NA 2: 390). As in Schiller's early Laura poems, tropes referring to music and harmony abound in "The Artists." Analogies to sound and song proliferate. The singer-artist's mouth, for instance, is fully inspired ("beseelt"). Whatever flows from it is melodic, and this encourages harmony. Through poetry, souls are bound together. In the light of these developments, aesthetic culture forms a new source of knowledge. "Der fortgeschritt'ne Mensch trägt auf erhob'nen Schwingen / Dankbar die Kunst mit sich empor, / Und neue Schönheitswelten springen / Aus der bereicherten Natur hervor" [The (culturally) advanced human being carries up art / Gratefully on raised wings / And new worlds of beauty spring forth / From enriched Nature] (NA 2: 390). Through art, the nature and character of the human being can be ennobled and improved. Knowledge transcends the limits imposed upon it by scientific understanding ("Des Wissens Schranken gehen auf"). The spirit ("Geist") realizes its full potential. The human mind, especially that of the artist, is capable of infusing harmony into history through the sights, sounds, and beautiful forms of his or her craft.

> In selbstgefäll'ger jugendlicher Freude
> Leiht er [der Geist] den Sphären seine Harmonie,
> Und preiset er das Weltgebäude,
> So prangt es durch die Symmetrie.
>
> [In self-satisfied youthful joy
> It [the mind] lends the spheres its harmony,
> And when praising the structure of the universe,
> It becomes resplendent through its symmetry.]
>
> (Strophe 20; NA 2: 391)

At this point in the writer's career, we note a close affinity between Schiller's imagery and the Pythagorean idea of the harmony of the spheres. I will return to this interesting connection in my concluding remarks.

Various other tropes are employed in order to underscore the emancipating power of aesthetic culture. Several key references to liberation from enchainment, especially the limitations of animal-like behavior are evident; and the metaphors of the fetters and the yoke again play essential roles.

David Pugh has underscored the intimate connection between the writing of "The Artists" and the letters addressed to Prince Christian von Augustenburg. Observing a "curious pattern in the poem's imagery," Pugh isolates "the different purpose" of metaphors in this work. The metaphor of chains, for instance, draws out "the poems' ethical implications."[14] Schiller has also developed a historical dimension, since the human being "is in the chains of sensuality, but after the artists have released him, he is free to enjoy nature's beautiful soul."[15] Pugh perceives that the employment of the same metaphor in two other passages creates a different effect. As we have already observed in the case of some of Schiller's earlier writings, the modern human being is the master of Nature who loves its chains.[16] Pugh sees in this analogy the non-menacing "enchainment of nature by reason."[17] "Nature assents to the enchainment of sensuality (which is the dark side of nature), because that is the way to *un*chain its 'beautiful soul.' In spite of the imagery, therefore, all these passages assert a harmony between reason and nature, or at least a part of nature."[18] The scholar maintains, however, that art "merely creates the illusion of releasing [the human being] from the chains of reason [and its attendant moral obligations.]"[19] Moral freedom, it is concluded, is "the cause of unfreedom vis à vis our natural character."[20] Hence, both the natural *and* the rational human being must be "released from chains of a different kind."[21] In sum, "contrary ethical viewpoints," in "The Artists," are expressed by means of the single metaphor of chains.[22] Pugh then draws the important conclusion that "for all his adherence to the principle of aesthetic autonomy, he [Schiller] regards ethics and aesthetics as intertwined."[23]

My main reservation about Pugh's lucid interpretation concerns the idea that, for Schiller, art somehow transcends the world as we know it. It seems that Pugh has not taken Schiller's early medical writings into account. By tracing the impact of the writer's early anthropology on his later writings, we discover not the release of art into some ethereal sphere somehow detached from life as we know it, but rather the very tension between the writer's metaphysical inclinations (especially the Platonic strain) and knowledge of human nature (anthropology). The forms of art are signposts that mark the path to the further improvement of the human species. That path, however, does not lead away from but toward greater development and refinement of the instrumentation of mind *and* body.

Pugh attributes to Schiller's "mind" "a superb grasp of the dynamics of drama, but one that, in philosophical writing, is more adept at the exploration of dilemmas than at their resolution."[24] Unlike Pugh, I do not categorize Schiller's writings according to genre, primarily because they are the product of one "mind." Too narrowly conceiving of "Schiller's role" in the historical development of his time as "a transmitter of the Neo-platonic tradition to the younger Romantic generation," Pugh does speak of "the poem's wealth of fruitful philosophical tensions."[25] But surely this latter statement suggests that there is more at work in Schiller's writings than the traditional literary-historical understanding of the writer's place in Western literature can tolerate.

Unlike the early poetic writings, the liberated human being ("der entjochte Mensch") of "The Artists" loves the fetters of Nature. Thus the tension between the freedom of the mind and the containment of the body would seem to be rooted in Nature itself. The artist seeks to cultivate and safeguard humanity. Capable of transforming the world, the "divine magic of poetry" ("Der Dichtung heilige Magie"; NA 1: 213; 2: 395) serves a higher and wiser purpose. The writer's plan guides the beautiful forms of poetry, gently and quietly, "to the ocean of the great harmony [of all things]" ("zum Ozeane / Der großen Harmonie") (NA 1: 213; 2: 395). As we know from the early poetic writings, this harmonious ocean is characterized by endless circles of activities. The image of the whirlpool in Schiller's poetic writings thus discloses the creative power of the universe.

The Poetry of Life ("Poesie des Lebens")

Between 1788 and 1795, Friedrich Schiller devoted himself mostly to timely theoretical-philosophical issues and the study of history. At the same time, however, he did not lose sight of the problems he had explored in his early poetic writings. As before, many of the poems written after 1785 exude confidence in the transformative power of healthy, actively creating Nature.[26]

Even though it did not appear in print until 1798, the poem "Poetry of Life" ["Poesie des Lebens"] is one of the pivotal centers of Schiller's poetic writings. It was the first poem that Schiller wrote after the hiatus in lyrical production. This writing is composed of a dialogue between one voice criticizing the value of art and another exposing the negative effects of such an attitude. In effect, the poetic writing constitutes a defense of art, albeit *ex negativo.*

The first voice desires nothing but the naked (prosaic) truth, seeing in art only a veil or mere illusion, a flight from reality. The voice responding to a friend ("Du") underscores the centrality of the metaphor of the stringed instrument. But the rejection of all appearance can only despiritualize the world, turning it into mere stone. The concept of cancellation, or suspension (*Aufhebung*) is present, though negatively, since turning something to stone ("Versteinerung") eliminates both love ("Liebe") and joy ("Freude"). The writer builds up the image of Apollo breaking the golden lyre in order to capture the potentially negative impact of a merely factual (narrowly scientific) understanding of the world.

> Apoll zerbricht die goldne Leyer,
> Und Hermes seinen Wunderstab,
> Des Traumes rosenfarbner Schleier
> Fällt von des Lebens bleichem Antlitz ab
> Die Welt scheint was sie ist, ein Grab.

> [Apollo tears the golden lyre asunder,
> And Hermes his magic wand,
> Dream's rose-colored veil

Falls away from the pale countenance of life
The world appears to be what it is: a grave].

(ll. 23–27; NA 1: 433; 2: 416)

Without the soulful music of the spheres, there is only silence and emptiness; in short, not life but death. In no way, then, do these lines suggest
that art is distinct from life; on the contrary, art first animates life.

On the whole, "Poetry of Life" signals the indispensability of poetry and
celebrates its rebirth in the human soul. Even in the coldest regions of the
globe, "Whatever lives wishes to be delighted" ("was lebt, will sich er-
freuen") (l. 22). And, in the same poem, whatever Nature embues with life,
is splendid and true ("Glänzend ists und ewig klar" [l. 28]). The later poem
"Punch Song, to Sing in the North" ["Punschlied. Im Norden zu singen"]
(1803) complements the thematic content of "Poetry of Life" by glorifying
the strength of human character: "Was der Mensch sich kann erlangen / Mit
dem Willen und der Kraft" [What the human being can achieve / With will
and power] (ll. 47–48). Like Nature, art is a divine gift ("Himmelgabe"; l.
31). In the final analysis, the beautiful forms of art, which constitute aesthetic culture, produce and transmit images of a strong and determined, yet
always sensitive humanity.

The poems "Expectation" ["Die Erwartung"] (1799) (included among the
Tabulae votivae) and "Yearning" ["Sehnsucht"] (1802) (in the *Taschenbuch
zum geselligen Vergnügen 1803* [Pocketbook for Social Entertainment])
demonstrate the value the mature writer placed on both the visual and
auditory capacities of human experience. The first poem focuses on the
auditory perception of the harmonious flow of all things. The first person
form of *hören* (to hear) begins the poem. The verb is repeated at the very
center of the work. One of the most important lines recalls the Pythagorean
doctrine of the harmony of the spheres. "Mein Ohr umtönt ein Harmonieen-
fluß" [A river of harmonies sounds 'round my ear] (l. 29; NA 2: 201). The
complimentary poem "Yearning" stresses the importance of visual experience. Even in the most labyrinthine regions of the earth, the poetic I catches
sight of beautiful hills (l. 5; NA 2: 197). Still, the deeper harmonies of the
universe are audible. "Harmonien hör ich klingen, / Töne süßer Himmels-
ruh" [I hear harmonies sounding, / Sounds of the sweet peace of Heaven"]
(ll. 9–10; NA 2: 197). The recurrent allusions to music complement the
metaphor of the stringed instrument. The visible products of the harmony
of the spheres are described as "golden fruits" ("Goldne Früchte") which the
poetic I "sees . . . glowing" (l. 13; NA 2: 197). All in all, the complementation
between the harmony of the universe and the beauty of earthly nature leads
to the soul-filled experience of "the beautiful wonderland" ("das schöne
Wunderland") of Nature (l. 32; NA 2: 197).

The Ballads

Schiller's ballads number among the finest and most moving in German literature. The dramatic quality of the form captures the dynamics of life's struggles. The activities of the dramatist and the poet are here united.

In one of his most masterful ballads "The Cranes of Ibycus" ["Die Kraniche des Ibykus"], written in 1797 for the *Poetic Annals for the Year 1798* [*Musen-Almanach für das Jahr 1798*], the writer recreated the perilous, legendary journeys of the Greek poet.[27] Apollo had granted this friend of the gods "the gift of singing, / the sweet mouth of songs" ("des Gesanges Gabe, / Der Lieder süßen Mund"; ll. 5b–6; NA 1: 385; 2: 245). A "swarm" of cranes accompanies him to Poseidon's pine grove, where they forsake him for the warm climate of the South. On a narrow bridge in the very middle of the forest ("des Waldes Mitte"; NA 1: 385; 2 :245), two murderers ("Mörder") kill the sojourner. In Schiller's rendition of the legend, Ibycus perishes not simply because he is defenseless, but because he does not lay hold the power of the tense harmony of the universe. Carefree ("munter") and unprepared for battle, Ibycus's hand "has tightened the tender strings of the lyre, / But never the power of the bow" ("hat der Leyer zarte Saiten, / Doch nie des Bogens Kraft gespannt") (ll. 31–32; NA 1: 385; 2: 245). This moment marks an important turning point in Schiller's writings from the metaphor of the musical stringed instrument to the stringed weapon of the crossbow in *William Tell*. For Ibycus possesses only the power of song and art but not of combat. The poem and the later drama are united thematically through their common exploration of the theme of justice. Perhaps there is also a moral here. Totally cut off from the world, i.e., wholly autonomous, art is rendered ineffectual and perishes.

An atmosphere of vengeance and lamentation begins to pervade the scene, as represented by "the afeared melody of the chorus" ("Des *Chores* grauser Melodie"; l. 96; NA 1: 387; 2: 247). Snakes and vipers, "des Hymnus Weise, / Der durch das Herz zerreißend dringt" [the awful hymn of the Furies, / That penetrates the heart and rends it asunder] (ll. 114b–115), appear to coil themselves around the criminals. When violated, Nature itself seeks justice. We will encounter this theme again in *William Tell*. In this context, the analogy to coiled strings, i.e., knots of retribution suggests the means by which justice is to be sought. The experience of guilt proves too much for one of the murderers, who is then motivated to confess his crime. For, "between deceit and truth wavers / Doubting, every heart and quavers, / And pays homage to the terrible might, / Which judging, awakens, in the hidden recesses [of the soul], / Which impenetrably, unfathomably, / Entwines the dark, knotted ball of fate, / Announcing itself in the depths of one's heart, / Yet it flees from the light of the sun" ("zwischen Trug und Wahrheit schwebet / Noch zweifelnd jede Brust und bebet, / Und huldiget

der furchtbarn Macht, / Die richtend im Verborgnen wacht, / Die unerf-
orschlich, unergründet, / Des Schicksals dunkeln Knäul flicht, / Dem tiefen
Herzen sich verkündet, / Doch fliehet vor dem Sonnenlicht"; strophe 19;
NA 1: 389; 2: 249).

Like Karl Moor in *The Robbers,* the murderer of "The Cranes of Ibycus"
calls for his own arrest, i.e., to be enchained by the law and, like both Karl
Moor and Christian Wolf of *Criminal Out of Infamy,* to face the consequences. As in his early writings, the later writer Friedrich Schiller underscores the triumph of the free, moral will of the human being. Perhaps the
most significant aspect of this development is that such an act seems to be
inherent in human nature. Justice need not always be administered from the
outside. Indeed, it is internal to the world and a natural consequence of
one's moral determination. Perhaps it is helpful to recall that young Schiller
had studied law (and religion) before changing his major field of study to
medicine. In any case, the idea that nemesis is not so much an aspect of
history as it is of Nature will prove to be of crucial importance for an
understanding of *William Tell.*

In this poem, the employment of the wing motif and the return of the
cranes both underscore the theme of justice. "Und glaubt er [der Frevler]
zu entspringen, / Geflügelt sind wir da, die Schlingen / Ihm werfend um den
flüchtgen Fuß, / Daß er zu Boden fallen muß" [And if he (the criminal/
sinner) thinks he has escaped, / We are there on wings with slings / To throw
around his fleeting foot, / So that he must fall at last] (ll. 129–32; NA 1: 388;
2: 248). In this creative transformation of the Laocoön legend, the strings
of the instrument represent the coils of justice. In the context of retribution
and punishment, however, no harmonious, i.e., beautiful, chord may be
struck. "Besinnungraubend, Herzbethörend / Schallt der Erinnyen Gesang, /
Er schallt des Höreres Mark verzehrend, / Und duldet nicht der Leier
Klang" ["Taking away his senses, beguiling his heart, / The furies song
resounds [rings out], / It rings out, frightening the listener to the marrow of
his bones, / And it will not tolerate the lyre's song"] (NA 1: 388; 2: 248).
Indeed, it is the music of the lyre that creates an atmosphere "as if the
Godhead were near" ["Als ob die Gottheit nahe wär"] (l. 140; NA 1: 389;
2: 249).

In retrospect, the key to unraveling "the dark, knotted ball of fate" lies
within the human breast (strophe 19; NA 1: 389), which ordinarily "hovers
between deceit and truth." The metaphor of the stringed instrument and
the wing motif are related since the cranes of Ibycus signify the liberating
power of justice. It is purposeful, then, that they should return to help
avenge evil.

The forum of spectators thus becomes a tribunal. It is a stage on which
the offenders of Nature are violently punished. "Man reißt und schleppt
sie vor den Richter, / Die Szene wird zum Tribunal; / Und es gestehn die
Bösewichter, / Getroffen von der Rache Strahl" [Before the judge they force

and drag them, / The scene becomes a tribunal; / And the culprits confess, / Struck by the beam of vengeance] (ll. 181–84; NA 1: 390; 2: 250). Already in the early theoretical essay, subsequently titled *The Stage Considered as a Moral Institution* [*Die Schaubühne als moralische Anstalt betrachtet*], young Schiller had conceived of the stage as a tribunal, i.e., as an ethical world of justice.[28] To simply equate the metaphor of the tribunal with Schiller's activities as a dramatist, as Benno von Wiese and others have done, however,[29] though establishing further continuity, is not sensitive enough to Schiller's development as writer. In this later phase of writing, Schiller had transformed the legend of the cranes of Ibycus from a symbol of poetic justice into a sign of natural justice. This is an important turning point in the thematics of Schiller's writings, one which will be of great importance for an understanding of *William Tell*.

In his later writings, Schiller concentrated more and more on the powerful forces of Nature that animate life in the universe. These same forces are present also in both the human soul and history. Hence, the metaphysical, anthropological, and historical dimensions of Schiller's writings are fully integrated.

Metaphors of enchainment and rupture as well as the pilgrim motif are redeveloped in "The Battle with the Dragon" ["Der Kampf mit dem Drachen"] (1798). One of the most captivating aspects of this poem is the depiction of a spirit resembling evil, or destruction. "Die Schlange, die das Herz vergiftet, / Die Zwietracht und Verderben stiftet, / Das ist der widerspenst'ge Geist / Der gegen Zucht sich frech empöret, / Der Ordnung heilig Band zerreißt, / Denn der ist's, der die Welt zerstöret" [The snake that poisons the heart, / That causes discord and corruption, / That (person) is the unruly spirit / Who with impudence defies discipline and rends the sacred bonds of order"] (ll. 271–76; NA 1: 416; 2: 296). The battle with the dragon is as much a battle with oneself as it is with an external enemy. The threat of destruction is averted, however, by cultivating a state of harmonious tension. As in *Concerning the Aesthetic Education of the Human Being*, one begins this process with oneself. For by actively shaping one's own nature, one necessarily establishes a closer tie to Nature in general.

In "The Song of the Bell" ["Das Lied von der Glocke"] (1799), the bell was forged out of the earth. It is an instrument that has been shaped both by imagination and the ardent toil of human hands. Following its construction, "From the dome, / Slow and deep, / The bell tolls / The death-knell. / Sadly its peals of sorrow accompany / The wanderer on his last journey" ("Von dem Dome, / Schwer und bang, / Tönt die Glocke / Grabgesang. / Ernst begleiten ihre Trauerschläge / Einen Wandrer auf dem letzten Wege"; ll. 244–49; NA 2: 234). The change in meter (2-beat lines) signals the "musical" toll of death. The bell also sounds when important developments unfold. For instance, in this poem, there are several allusions to the French Revolution. "Das Volk, zerreissend seine Kette, / Zur Eigenhilfe schrecklich greift! / Da zerret an der Glocke Strängen / Der Aufruhr, daß sie heulend schallt, / Und, nur geweiht zu Friedensklängen, / Die Losung anstimmt zur Gewalt. / Freiheit und Gleichheit! hört man schallen, / Der ruh'ge Bürger greift zur Wehr" [The people, tearing their chains, / Grasp frightfully at self-help! / Rebellion tugs at the bell's cords / So that it rings out discordantly / Once dedicated only to the sounds of peace, / The bell now tolls for war. / "Freedom and Equality!" rings out, / And the peaceful citizen prepares for battle] (ll. 356–63; NA 2: 237). Imagery representing the animal-like tendencies of the human being discloses the problem of physical violence. "Verderblich ist des Tigers Zahn, / Jedoch der schrecklichste der Schrecken, / Das ist der Mensch in seinem Wahn" [Pernicious are the tiger's fangs, / Still the most terrible of terrors, / Is the human being in one's rage] (ll. 375–77; NA 2: 237). Understood also in light of the earlier writings, Schiller's position should now be graphically clear: the cooperative exercise of both the emotions and reason first produces a healthy state of being.

The focus changes quickly, however, to the healing and unifying power of joy, when the bell is named "*Concordia*." In contradistinction to "discord," namely, "a chord satisfying in harmonic effect and not requiring resolution,"[30] the word "concord" has a specific meaning. "Und dies sei fortan ihr Beruf, / Wozu der Meister sie erschuf!" [And this is, henceforth its calling, / To which end the master created it] (ll. 396–97; NA 2: 238), namely to create harmony, but the kind of harmony that does *not* require resolution, that is, the taut yet dynamic equilibrium produced by harmonious tension.

The politically charged ballad "The Count of Habsburg" ["Der Graf von Habsburg"] (1803) also contains metaphors of song. All earthly things lie at the Emperor's disposal: "Doch den Sänger vermiß ich, den Bringer der Lust, / Der mit süßem Klang mir bewege die Brust / Und mit göttlich erhabenen Lehren" [And, yet, I miss the singer, the bearer of pleasure, / Who moves my soul with sweet sounds / And divinely sublime teaching] (ll. 25–27; NA 2/ I: 277). Once again, the writer employs the metaphor of the stringed instrument to underscore the potential power of poetry in proclaiming the merits of goodness and conciliation. "Süßer Wohllaut schläft in der Saiten Gold" [Sweet harmony is latent in the golden sounds of the strings] (l. 35; NA 2: 277). "Und der Sänger rasch in die Saiten fällt / Und beginnt sie mächtig zu schlagen:" [Swiftly the singer takes to the strings / And begins to strike them mightily] (ll. 51–52; NA 2: 278).[31] In addition to the political dimension of the ballad, the poetic writing conveys the idea of the involvement of the body with its senses and not simply the mind. It would seem that both auditory and visual perception are required in order to gain understanding.[32] "Jetzt daß er dem Sänger ins Auge sah, / Da ergreift ihn der Worte Bedeuten" [Now that he looked the singer in the eye, / He is struck by the meaning of his words] (ll. 113–14; NA 2: 279). Only through the development of aesthetic sensibility and the refinement of sensitive knowledge can one appreciate "the divine workings" ("das göttliche Walten"; l. 120; NA 2: 279) of Nature.

Anthropology and metaphysics are once again conjoined in Schiller's later poetic writings.

The Elegies

Among German elegies, two poems are especially noteworthy. Both "The Walk" ["Der Spaziergang"] and "The Dance" ["Der Tanz"] were written in 1795 near the beginning of the resurgence of Schiller's writing of poetry. Both poems develop the image of the knot-like nature of life. Next to the metaphor of the wings and the motif of flight stand numerous analogies to winding, twisting, and even tearing. In "The Walk,"[33] a "twisting [serpentine] path" ("ein schlängelnder Pfad") leads the writer upwards (l. 24; NA 2: 309). Nature is vibrant. "Aber plötzlich zerreißt der Flor" [But suddenly the flora splits apart] (l. 27a; NA 2: 309) and, "in freieren Schlangen durchkreuzt die geregelten Felder" [in freer snake-like patterns traverses the ordered fields"] (l. 43; NA 2: 309). The sounds of Nature are everywhere discernible.[34] "Vielfach ertönt der Herden Geläut im belebten Gefilde, / Und den Wiederhall weckt einsam des Hirten Gesang" [Frequently the herds' ringing resounds through the enlivened fields, / And the echo awakens the lonely song of the herdsman] (ll. 47–48; NA 2: 309). This same image of Nature is recreated in the opening scene of *William Tell*.

The ancient-modern topos of the fates spinning the thread of life now complements the metaphor of the stringed instrument, and together they create a new image: "Durch die Saiten des Garns sauset das webende Schiff" [The weaver's shuttle passes through the threads of the fabric] (l. 110; NA 2: 311). Imagery such as this indicates a concerted attempt on the writer's part to combine the ancient and the modern and not simply dissociate one from the other. "The Walk" is more a classical than a romantic gesture on the part of the writer. Written in 1795, it seems to be a response to both Schiller's essay *Concerning Naive and Sentimental Poetry* and the early German romantic movement.

As we have witnessed elsewhere, the attempt to bridge the gap, that is to overcome rupture, is a trademark of Schiller's later writings.[35] It is a curious fact that this gesture of healing occurred at a time when Schiller's body was rapidly deteriorating and the rift between body and mind was widening. At the same time, however, the aftermath of the French Revolution and the beginning of the Coalition Wars also impacted Schiller's writing such that, as in *Mary Stuart,* the reader/spectator would again be led to the crossroads of physiology and politics.

"The Dance" (1795) underscores the knotted nature of life. The dancing couples are described in terms of hovering. At times, they resemble the motion of waves. The metaphor of the stringed instrument, the motif of rupture, and references to the corporeal world are all intricately interwoven. "Säuselndes Saitengetön hebt den ätherischen Leib. / Jetzt, als wollt es mit Macht durchreißen die Kette des Tanzes / Schwingt sich ein muthiges Paar dort in den dichtesten Reihn" [Rustling sounds of strings propel the ethereal body, / Now—as if wishing to forcefully rend the dance's chain / One bold couple swings into the widest rows"] (ll. 8–10; NA 2: 299).[36] Their wild gesticulations upset this world in motion (l. 14). Thus, when the knot of life is disentangled, or unraveled ("der Knoten entwirrt sich" [l. 15c]), a feeling of joy is reinstated. Easing the dramatic tension, the writer prepares the reader for a moral lesson.

> Nur mit verändertem Reiz stellet die Regel sich her.
> Ewig zerstört, es erzeugt sich ewig die drehende Schöpfung,
> Und ein stilles Gesetz lenkt der Verwandlungen Spiel.
>
> [Only with changed appeal is the rule established.
> Only by perpetually destroying can revolving Creation
>   be produced eternally,
> And a quiet law directs the play of change.]

> > > > > > > > > > > (ll. 16–18; NA 2: 299)

Still, the poet asks why "forms oscillate restlessly from anew, and calm [peace] evolves from moving form?" [daß rastlos erneut die Bildungen schwanken; / Und die Ruhe besteht in der bewegten Gestalt?] (ll. 19b–20; NA 2: 299). On this thematic level, "The Dance" intersects with Schiller's theoretical work. For, in *Concerning the Aesthetic Education of the Human Being,* as well as in the *Kallias* Letters, the writer was actively engaged in the process of defining beauty as "lebende Gestalt" (living form). Hence, in Schiller's writings, beauty, like harmony, is a perpetually dynamic process, not a tranquil or static state of being.

But what restores the wild leaps to a convivial and socially acceptable dance? "Es ist des Wohllauts mächtige Gottheit" [It is the powerful divinity of harmony] (l. 23b). We should note here that the word "Wohllaut" (pleasant sound), as a compound word (the very one deleted in the revised poem "The Walk"), can be understood literally as a sound that effects healing, a *Wohl-Laut.* Music and medicine are thus interrelated. The golden reins of rhythm guide foaming inclination, wild emotion is tamed (l. 26), and justice, as signalled by the rhythm of the universe, prevails. In this way, the knotted nature of life, both the *Knoten* (knot) and the *Knäul* (ball [of thread]), is disentangled and unraveled, and peace, order, and joy are restored.[37]

The unnamed "du" ([personal] you), to whom the writer refers, is criticized for not adhering to the rhythm of the celestial spheres. "Und dir rauschen umsonst die Harmonieen des Weltalls, / Dich ergreift nicht der Strom dieses erhabnen Gesangs, / Nicht der begeisternde Takt, den alle Wesen dir schlagen, / Nicht der wirbelnde Tanz, der durch den ewigen

Raum / Leuchtende Sonnen schwingt in kühn gewundenen Bahnen? / Das du im Spiele doch ehrst, fliehst du im Handeln, das Maß" [And, for you, the harmonies of the universe sound in vain, / Does not the current of this sublime song move you, / Not the enlivening beat that all creatures impart / Not the swirling dance which through infinite space / Swings bright suns [shining planets] in boldly bounded paths? / (And) though you still honor moderation in play, you flee it in action] (ll. 27–32; NA 2: 299). The ancient (Pythagorean) conception of the harmony of the spheres still informs Schiller's later writings. At the same time, the writer's attention is directed to the modern (Copernican) preoccupation with revolution. For, in "The Dance," there is an unmistakable parallel between the art of dance and the physical law of planetary motion. Given the tense fusion of ancient philosophy and modern science we can better comprehend why the modern writer Friedrich Schiller so often reemployed the metaphor of the stringed instrument and thematized the problem of world order, especially rupture. Whereas in *The Robbers* love and gravity (metaphysics and physics) are interrelated, in Schiller's later poetic writings philosophy and science are interwoven.

The last of the great elegies is "Fortune" ["Das Glück"], which appeared in the *Poetic Annals for the Year 1799*. While lauding the stamina of the human being, the writer also addresses the limitations of the human spirit by adding the qualifier "aber" [but]. True strength of character is won by listening to the poet who possesses "die Gabe des Lieds" [the gift of song] (l. 51; NA 2: 301), which is a gift of Heaven. And because the poet is "der Glückliche" [the happy individual], "you" can be "der Selige" [the blessed individual] (l. 54; NA 2: 301). There is cause for joy. The moral underscores the cultivation of organic processes. Much like Goethe, Schiller writes: "Alles Menschliche muß erst werden und wachsen und reifen, / Und von Gestalt zu Gestalt führt es die bildende Zeit, / Aber das Glückliche siehest du nicht, das Schöne nicht werden, / Fertig von Ewigkeit her steht es vollendet vor dir" [Everything human must first develop and grow and mature, / And from form to form it is led by shaping time, / But you do not see happiness, or the beautiful developing, / Finished already from the beginning of time it stands completed before you"] (ll. 59–62; NA 2: 301). By virtue of the fact that completion is a characteristic of Nature, the potential for completion must also lie within human nature. For that reason, the writer of *Concerning the Aesthetic Education of the Human Being* and many other essays of the early 1790s reiterated the need to educate oneself and to take the practical step of extending one's knowledge outward to society as a whole, that is into history. But without self-formation (*Selbstbildung*), there can be no re-formation of society. In the end, the *Bildung* (cultivation) of Humanity depends on the participation of the individual in the never-ending process of self-education and the perpetual education of the species.

"The Feminine Ideal. To Amanda" ["Das weibliche Ideal. An Amanda"], which first appeared in the *Poetic Annals for the Year 1787* [*Musenalmanach für das Jahr 1797*], also underscores the idea of the music of the soul, for "Auch dein zärtester Laut ist dein harmonisches Selbst" [Even your most tender sound is your harmonious self] (l. 10; NA 1: 287). In "Task" ["Aufgabe"] (in *Tabulae Votivae*), the writer suggested that one must understand, i.e., be in tune with oneself, while emphasizing the uniqueness (difference) of individuals. "Keiner sey gleich dem andern, doch gleich sey jeder dem höchsten. / Wie das zu machen? Es sey jeder vollendet in sich" [No one is like another, but everyone is equal in the face of the highest. / How this is to be accomplished? Everyone is complete in oneself] (NA 1: 298). One of the major themes of the *Votive Tablets* [*Votivtafeln*] is best expressed in the title "Beautiful Individuality" ["Schöne Individualität"], the last two lines of which read: "Stimme des Ganzen ist deine Vernunft, dein Herz bist du selber, / Wohl dir, wenn die Vernunft immer im Herzen dir wohnt" [Your reason is the voice of the whole, your heart is your Self, / when Reason resides always in your heart] (NA 1: 298; 2: 318). In sum, true freedom is first attained when one has tapped the harmonious tension that conjoins all things.

Other Poetic Writings

"The Ideal and Life" ["Das Ideal und das Leben"] (1804; "Das Reich der Schatten" [1795]) figures prominently among the so-called philosophical poems. Two often-quoted lines capture the tension of human existence: "Zwischen Sinnenglück und Seelenfrieden / Bleibt dem Menschen nur die bange Wahl" [Between the pleasure of the senses and the peace of the soul / The human being is given but the fearful choice] (ll. 7–8; NA 1: 247; 2: 396).[38] At the same time, we detect a significant change in the writer's disposition. To be sure, the poem contains the frequently cited lines: "Wollt ihr hoch auf ihren [der Gestalt] Flügeln schweben, / Werft die Angst des Irdischen von euch, / Fliehet aus dem engen dumpfen Leben / In des Ideales Reich!" [Should you want to hover high on [the] wings [of form], / You must forsake the fear of earthly things. / Flee from narrow, muffled life / Into the realm of the ideal] (ll. 26–30; NA 2: 397; ll. 37–40; NA 1: 248).[39] Contrary to some critical opinions, this poetic writing does not encourage flight from reality. Though the rays of perfection emanate from the realm of the ideal, the realities of life prove to be more pressing. Indeed, one does not have a choice. Life is greater and more powerful than any one individual.

> Mächtig, selbst wenn eure Sehnen ruhten,
> Reißt das Leben euch in seine Fluten,
> Euch die Zeit in ihren Wirbeltanz.

> [Powerfully, even when your tendons [chords] rested,
> Life cast you into its tides,
> And time into its whirling dance.]

(ll. 44–46; NA 2: 397–98)

Yet, the writer immediately qualifies such moments of apparent helplessness:

> Aber sinkt des Muthes kühner Flügel
> Bei der Schranken peinlichem Gefühl,
> Dann erblicket von der Schönheit Hügel
> Freudig das erflog'ne Ziel.

> [But should the bold wings of courage droop
> With the humbling feeling of finitude,
> Then, from the hills of beauty, joyfully behold
> The goal you have attained (by flying)].

(ll. 47–50; NA 2: 398)

Biographically, the poem may be read as a response to Schiller's own state of health. Much more than that, however, it is also an integral part of the writer's conception of the general task of culture. Concerning the multidisciplinary interplay of Schiller's writings, several lines reestablish the connection between the author's poetry and the early medical dissertations. There are also some traces of the influence of Moses Mendelssohn's *Letters on the Sensations*. "Wenn, das Todte bildend zu beseelen, / Mit dem Stoff sich zu vermählen, / Thatenvoll der Genius entbrennt, / Da, da spanne sich des Fleisses Nerve, / Und beharrlich ringend unterwerfe / Der Gedanke sich das Element." [When, while reenlivening what is lifeless and giving it shape, / So that it can be wed to matter, / Genius flares up to act, / That is when the nerve of diligence is tightened, / And persistently striving, thought conquers the elements] (ll. 71–76; NA 2: 398). It has been overlooked that, when considering the work of the genius, the writer appreciates the knot-like, tension-filled nature of creative production.[40] We may now conclude that, for Schiller, harmonious tension is required for the greatest possible completion of all things and that it is at the center of all creatively productive forms of endeavor.

In the title of the poem "The Ideal and Life," the coordinating conjunction "and" suggests that there is a tense relationship between thought and matter.[41] In poetic practice, there is a tense relationship between the ideal and life. "Reality," for Schiller, may be defined as the sum total of the taut associations between all the elements of life and between life and any and all ideals. As much as Schiller might have desired to transcend mere reality, the images his later poetic writings project capture the tensions inherent in all aspects of life. In the first version of the poem, "The Realm of Shadows" ["Das Reich der Schatten"], the writer drew out these tensions with recourse to Winckelmann's and Lessing's discussions of the artistic depictions of the Laocoön legend. "Wenn der Menschheit Leiden euch umfangen, / Wenn Laokoon der Schlangen / Sich erwehrt mit Namenlosem Schmerz, / Da empöre sich der Mensch! Es schlage / An des Himmels Wölbung seine Klage / Und zerreisse euer fühlend Herz! / Der Natur furchtbare Stimme siege, / Und der Freude Wange werde bleich, / Und der heilgen Sympathie erliege / Das Unsterbliche in euch!" [Whenever the sufferings of humankind envelop you, / When Laocoön fends off the snakes with unspeakable pain, / Let the human being be filled with indignation! / May his lament strike against the dome of heaven / And let it break your feeling heart! / May the dreadful voice of Nature triumph, / And joy's cheek [also: stringboard] be paled, / And the immortal in you / Succumb to sacred sympathy] (strophe 15; NA 1: 250).[42] The imagery of the knotted nature of life recurs only occasionally throughout Schiller's early poetry and dramatic practice. It is especially pronounced, however, in the later poetic writings, such as "The Cranes of Ibycus" and "The Ideal and Life." Feeling, especially sympathy and understanding, and the idea of active self-determination in consonance with the rhythm of one's own nature, remind the reader of the need to develop one's fullest potential as a human being, not only in one's own self-interest, but most important, in the interest of humanity. In the end, attributes such as these will sever ("zerreiße[n]") the knots of physical and emotional pain and free humankind from all forms of political enslavement. Once again, the path of freedom is charted by cultivating the qualities embedded in human nature.

As I have suggested, "The Ideal and Life" has been misunderstood, at times, as encouraging flight from reality. "Aber flüchtet aus der Sinne Schranken / In die Freiheit der Gedanken, / Und die Furchterscheinung ist entflohn, / Und der ew'ge Abgrund wird sich füllen; / Nehmt die Gottheit auf in euren Willen / Und sie steigt von ihrem Weltenthron. / Des Gesetzes strenge Fessel bindet / Nur den Sklavensinn, der es verschmäht, / Mit des Menschen Widerstand verschwindet / Auch des Gottes Majestät" [But flee the confines of the senses / Into the freedom of thoughts, / And you have escaped the semblance of fear, / And the eternal abyss will be filled; / Make divinity a part of your will / And it will descend from its world throne. / The tight shackle of the law binds / Only the slave's mentality, who scorns it. / When one's resistance disappears / So also God's majesty" (strophe 11; NA 2: 399). But neither the sensuous world nor the law of necessity are to be abandoned. On the contrary, they are to be more fully integrated into human experience. In point of fact, it is only the "Furchterscheinung" (the semblance of fear) of enslavement to matter that is to be overcome. Once the individual fully appreciates the harmonious tension of all things, the "eternal abyss" or gap created by enslavement to material reality is "filled" and one experiences a state of freedom. With the aid of understanding, suffering is also transcended, albeit momentarily. "Aber in den heitern Regionen, / Wo die reinen Formen wohnen, / Rauscht des Jammers trüber Sturm nicht mehr. / Hier darf Schmerz die Seele nicht durchschneiden, / Keine Thräne fließt hier mehr dem Leiden, / Nur des Geistes tapf'rer Gegenwehr. / Lieblich, wie der Iris Farbenfeuer / Auf der Donnerwolke duft'gem Thau, / Schimmert durch der Wehmuth düstern Schleier / Hier der Ruhe heitres

Blau" [But in those cheerful regions, / Where pure forms reside, / The cloudy storm of misery sounds no more. / Here, pain is no longer allowed to pierce the soul, / Here, no more tears that from suffering flow, / Only the mind's (spirit's) brave fortitude. / Charmingly, like the colorful fire of the iris / On the sweet dew of the thundercloud, / Shimmering through the forboding veil of melancholy, / Here, too, the delightful blue of peace] (strophe 13; NA 2: 400).

In the poem "Pegasus in Service" ["Pegasus in der Dienstbarkeit"] (1795), later retitled "Pegasus Bound" ["Pegasus im Joche"], the writer juxtaposed the metaphor of the yoke and the motif of flight. "Das edle Tier wird einges-pannt. / Doch fühlt es kaum die ungewohnte Bürde, / So rennt es fort mit wilder Flugbegierde" [The noble animal is harnessed. / Yet it hardly feels the unusually heavy load, / Still continuing to run with the wild desire of flying] (ll. 22–24). The tug-of-war between Pegasus and the new owner, who wishes to have the winged horse serve as a beast of burden, activates the poem's dramatic tension. The alliterative oxymoron of a "Winged horse on the plow" ["Flügelpferd am Pfluge"] (l. 56b; NA 1: 231; 2: 114) evokes a sense of the tense relationship between the enchainment of the body and the freedom of the mind.

Out of frustration and anger over Pegasus's lack of obedience as a beast of burden, the owner draws a whip. The threat of violence is countered by a merry lad who happens to be playing a stringed instrument—a zither. The boy points out the contradiction of joining a "bird" and an ox to the same rope ("Seile"), which is unnatural: "Ich bitte dich, welch ein Gespann" [I beg of you, what an (unusual) team] (l. 78). The alliterative association be-tween the verb *spannen* and the substantive *Gespann* is hardly coincidental. Indeed, the German verb carries the double meaning of "to tighten" or "tauten" *and* "to hitch up" or "harness." Soon released from the reins' bondage, Pegasus feels his new master's hand: "So knirscht es in des Zügels Band, / Und steigt, und Blitze sprühn aus den beseelten Blicken" [Hence, it gnashes the reins' band, / And ascends, and thunderbolts fly out of its soul-filled glances] (ll. 85–86; NA 1: 232; 2: 115). Now depicted as "a spirit, a God" ["ein Geist, ein Gott"] (l. 88a), the winged horse ascends "to the blue heights" ["zu den blauen Höhen"] of the heavens (l. 92b), where freedom is realized.

"The Division of the Earth" ["Die Teilung der Erde"] and "The Power of Singing" ["Die Macht des Gesanges"], both of which were written in 1795, depict the poet as the eyes and ears of the universe. Whereas in Schiller's first published poem "Evening," the poet prayed that God would grant him the gift of song and inspiration, these two later poetic writings convey the idea that the poet was present already at the very beginning of Creation. The harmony of Nature is thus transmitted through the music of poetry. The poet's song is endowed with the potential to heal. Lines 39–40 of "Eve-ning" read: "Es schwinden jedes Kummers Falten, / Solang des Liedes

Zauber walten" [Every fold of sorrow disappears, / As long as the magic of song prevails] (NA 1: 226). References to the dynamic workings ("walten") of terrestrial and extraterrestrial forces of the universe were present already in Schiller's early poetic writings.

A central moral is transmitted through one of the most moving poems of the later period, "The Veiled Image at Sais" [Das verschleierte Bild zu Sais] (1795). The first part of a twofold moral comes quickly: "Nimm einen Ton aus einer Harmonie, / Nimm eine Farbe aus dem Regenbogen, / Und alles, was dir bleibt, ist Nichts, solang / Das schöne All der Töne fehlt und Farben" [Take one sound away from a harmony, / Take one color out of the rainbow, / And everything that remains is nothing, so long as / The beautiful universe of sounds and colors is missing] (ll. 14–17; NA 1: 254). The second moral concerns the "sin" of desiring the naked truth and the fatal consequences of beholding what is reserved only for God ("das Heilige"). Unlike Lessing's decision in "Concerning Truth" ["Über die Wahrheit"] (Eine Duplik) to continue searching for the truth rather than possess it, the young man of Schiller's poem is anxious to know the truth. But peering behind the veil to behold the truth brings sorrow, not joy, and premature death. The moral here seems to be tied to the poetic confessions of the poem "Ideals" ["Die Ideale"].

In "Ideals" (1795), the reemployment of the metaphor of the extinguishing sun indicates what I term the crisis of idealism. "Erloschen sind die heitern Sonnen, / Die meiner Jugend Pfad erhellt, / Die Ideale sind zerronnen, / Die einst das trunkne Herz geschwellt" [Extinguished (are) the cheerful suns [planets], / Which brightened the path of my youth, / Those ideals have faded away, / Which once swelled my intoxicated heart]. The lament expresses more than the simple loss of past innocence or youth's vitality. At this later date in the writer's career, the imagery of the sun functions as a sign of skepticism regarding the ideas and ideals of the new school of German thinkers, idealists and romantics alike.

The following four lines of the eight-line strophe in the first version read: "Die schöne Frucht, die kaum zu keimen / Begann, da liegt sie schon erstarrt! / Mich weckt aus meinen frohen Träumen / Mit rauhem Arm die Gegenwart" [The lovely fruit which just began to sprout / There it lies turned to stone! / Waking me from my happy dreams / With its rugged arm—the present] (NA 1: 234). The first sign of organic growth is claimed by the first frost. The singer's hopes and dreams have been seized by the austere realities of his time. It is an important indication of the writer's development between 1795 and 1800 that Schiller should have replaced the lines just cited with the following for inclusion in his Poems [Gedichte] (1800): "Er ist dahin, der süße Glaube / An Wesen, die mein Traum gebar, / Der rauhe Wirklichkeit zum Raube, / Was einst so schön, so göttlich war" [Gone, the sweet belief / In creatures that encouraged my dream, / Given over to harsh reality now, / What once was so fair, so divine] (NA 2: 367).[43] A comparison of the two versions of the poem "Ideals" suggests that, between 1795 and 1800, the crisis of idealism in Schiller's writings actually intensified. It is helpful to recall at this point that both Max Piccolomini (*Wallenstein*) and Mary Stuart must perish. With the aftermath of the French Revolution, as well as with the writer's failing health, perhaps the hope of realizing ideals in history had indeed been merely an idea ("bloß eine Idee"). Rather than despair, however, the writer seems to have striven even harder to effect change.

As the poem continues, "Ideals" begins to complement the inspired insights of "The Ideal and Life." Now embracing Nature with "loving arms" ("Liebesarmen"), the young man of the poem gains new insights into life. References to music and organic nature abound once again. "Und theilend meine Flammentriebe, / Die Stumme eine Sprache fand, / Mir wiedergab den Kuß der Liebe / Und meines Herzens Klang verstand; / Da lebte mir der Baum, die Rose, / Mir sang der Quellen Silberfall, / Es fühlte selbst das Seelenlose / Von meines Lebens Wiederhall" [And, joining in flaming desires (drives), / The mute one found a language, / Giving back to me the kiss of love / And understanding the sound of my heart; / Thus the tree, the rose, came alive, / The silvery cascade of springs sang to me, / And even emptiness (literally soulless things) divined / The echo of my life] (strophe 4; NA 2: 368).

In addition to the innumerable references to music, the motif of flight and the metaphor of wings continue to play essential roles in Schiller's later writings. "Wie sprang, von kühnem Mut beflügelt, / Beglückt in seines Traumes Wahn, / Von keiner Sorge noch gezügelt, / Der Jüngling in des Lebens Bahn. / Bis an des Aethers bleichste Sterne / Erhob ihn der Entwürfe Flug, / Nichts war so hoch und nichts so ferne, / Wohin ihr Flügel ihn nicht trug" [How the youth sprang, with wings of bold courage, / Made happy by his dream's illusion, / Not yet restricted by any care, / Into the path of life. / Well to the palest stars of the ether / The flight of his ideas and plans carried him, / Nothing was so high and nothing so far, / Where their wing was not able to carry him] (strophe 6). As in several poems written in 1795, the writer celebrates emancipation from enchainment to the material world. His goal, however, is not to escape or transcend reality but to transform it. This is to be accomplished by drawing upon the powers of Nature.

Even with the suspension of time in "Konfusius's Saying" ["Spruch des Konfuzius"], Schiller continued to underscore the ceaseless activity of the universe. The first of three descriptions of space enhances this idea: "Rastlos fort ohn Unterlaß" [Restlessly forth without respite"] ([2], l. 2; NA 2: 413). In consonance with the rhythm of the universe, the human being remains active. "Rastlos vorwärts mußt du streben, / Nie ermüdet stille stehn, / Willst du die Vollendung sehn" [Restlessly forward you must strive, / Never tired or standing still, / You will see completion" ([2], ll. 7–9; NA 2: 413). It would seem, then, that the individual must strive to develop the harmonious tension within oneself and the activity such tension presupposes in order to live in true harmony with Nature. To this end, self-determination, clarity of vision, and the search for truth are all required.

> Nur Beharrung führt zum Ziel,
> Nur die Fülle führt zur Klarheit,
> Und im Abgrund wohnt die Wahrheit.

> [Only perseverance leads to the goal,
> Only fullness leads to clarity,
> And in the abyss resides the truth.]

(ll. 14–16)

In Schiller's dramatic and prose writings, the central heroes encounter the truth about their own being only by experiencing the world.

As the romantic movement in Jena developed, Friedrich Schiller became increasingly skeptical of the notion of a golden age of completion. Surely, he had his good friend Friedrich von Hardenberg (Novalis) in mind when, in 1798, he added the following lines to his poem "Hope" ["Hoffnung"]: "Es reden und träumen die Menschen viel / Von bessern künftigen Tagen, / Nach einem glücklichen goldenen Ziel / Sieht man sie rennen und jagen" [People talk and dream much / Of better future days, / After a happy golden goal / One sees them running and chasing] (ll. 1–4; NA 1: 401; 2: 409). These are critical lines. For the writer's skepticism about yearning for a golden age is unmistakable. This is juxtaposed, instead, to the imperishable hope one possesses within one's heart. The third, and final strophe reads:

> Es ist kein leerer schmeichelnder Wahn,
>   Erzeugt im Gehirne des Thoren,
> Im Herzen kündet es laut sich an:
>   Zu was besserm sind wir gebohren!
> Und was die innere Stimme spricht,
> Das täuscht die hoffende Seele nicht.

> [It is not an empty, flattering illusion,
>   Produced in the head of a fool,
> Loudly, in the heart, it is made known:
>   We are born (created) for something better!
> And what our inner voices speak,
>   Will never deceive the trusting soul.]

(ll. 13–18) (NA 1: 401; 2: 409)

The musical metaphors in "Words of Illusion" ["Die Worte des Wahns"] (1800) also elicit criticism of the romantic movement. Given Schiller's and the romantics' common interest in music, the poem becomes an even more powerful form of criticism. The golden age was one of the three words heard at the turn of the century. But all three words (golden age, happiness, understanding), the writer adds, "schallen vergeblich, ihr Klang ist leer" [ring in vain, their sound is empty] (l. 3; NA 2: 371). The metaphor of tearing is employed in order to advance the moral, "Drum, edle Seele, entreiß dich dem Wahn / Und den himmlischen Glauben bewahre! / Was kein Ohr vernahm, was die Augen nicht sahn, / Es ist dennoch, das Schöne, das Wahre! / Es ist nicht draußen, da sucht es der Tor, / Es ist *in* dir, du bringst es ewig hervor" [Therefore, noble soul, tear yourself away from illusion / And maintain your divine faith! / What no ear perceives, what no eye sees, / It is still the beautiful, the true! / It is not outside; the fool searches for it there, / It is *in* you; you create it yourself] (strophe 5, ll. 25–30; NA 2: 371). Only when cultivating the harmonious tension of body and mind can the individual human being tap the harmonizing power of Nature. Each individual heart contains the seeds of harmony as well as the strength to transform the world. The further development (*Bildung*) of culture reshapes political society because it derives its power from the harmonious tension that inheres in all of Nature.

One of the great poetic testaments to the meaningfulness and purposefulness of the universe is Schiller's "The Words of Faith" ["Die Worte des Glaubens"] (1797). Fittingly, a large print of this poem hangs on an upstairs wall of the Schiller residence in Marbach on the Neckar River. The historian is again at work. Though born into slavery to the material world, we are told, the human being is created free (ll. 7–8). While the human will may oscillate, there is a God whose divine will ("heiliger Wille") weaves ("webt") all things together "high above time and space" (strophe 4, l. 3; NA 2: 370). It seems that, as the faith of the later Schiller increases, so also does his hope in a better world. But rather than call upon ideas, the writer endeavors to harness the power of Nature. This is evidenced most clearly, perhaps, in the dramatic writing *William Tell.*

In Schiller's later poetic writings, the universe is depicted as a grand tapestry, the individual threads of which have been woven together by a supreme being. This modern image corresponds to the ancient Greek image of the universe as a stringed instrument though, as we have seen, it is infinitely more problematic. In "The Words of Faith," ancient, pagan, and modern Christian elements are fused. The gap between ancient and modern times seems to have been bridged. Recalling the major theme of the earlier essay *Something Concerning the First Human Society According to the Introduction of the Mosaic Testament,* in the poem "The Elysian Festival" ["Das Eleusische Fest"] (1798), for instance, the writer laments the fall of humankind. Nevertheless, the rift between God and the human being is bridged by the expressed hope in the infinite approximation to Nature. This process of development (*Bildung*) becomes fruitful by cultivating the original divinity of the human being, he and she who were created in God's own image.

At the same time as the writer was investigating the Christian tradition in "The Elysian Festival," he drew an analogy to the Pythagorean view of the harmony of the spheres. Recognizing that one's true home is the Earth, the human being is afforded a glimpse of the harmonious tension that animates all living things. "Daß der Mensch zum Menschen werde, / Stift' er einen ew'gen Bund / Gläubig mit der frommen Erde, / Seinem mütterlichen Grund, / Ehre das Gesetz der Zeiten / Und der Monde heil'gen Gang, / Welche still gemessen schreiten / Im melodischen Gesang." [So that the human being may become a human being, / S/he must establish an eternal union / Trustingly, with the good Earth, / His motherly ground, / Honor the law of times / And the sacred motion of the moons, / Which calmly and softly proceed / In melodious song] (strophe 7; NA 2: 377). The harmonious, melodic strains of Apollo's lyre counteract the threat of Zeus, who hurls "the jagged bolt of lightning" [den gezackten Blitz] and "thunder from the blue heights (of heaven)" [Donnern aus den blauen Höhen] (ll. 100b and 99, respectively; NA 2: 379). This point, too, is qualified. "Aber aus den goldnen Saiten / Lockt Apoll die Harmonie / Und das holde Maß der Zeiten / Und die Macht der Melodie. / Mit neunstimmigem Gesange / Fallen die Kämonen ein, / Leise nach des Liedes Klange / Füget sich der Stein zum Stein" [But from golden strings / Apollo entices harmony / And the sweet measure of times / And the power of melody. / With nine-voiced song / The Camenas fall in, / Softly according to the sound of the song / Stone joins stone in harmony] (strophe 22; ll. 169–79; NA 2: 381). As a result, new citizens ("die neuen Bürger") are led "with harmonies" ("mit Harmonieen") by a choir of gods to the open door of Heaven (ll. 193–96; NA 2: 382). And all enter its portals ("Flügel") to laud Ceres, "the mother of the world who brings happiness to all" ("Die beglückende Mutter der Welt") and who is exalted by "our song" ("Unser Gesang"; l. 215a; NA 2: 382).

Unlike in the early poetic writings, references to Ceres, the Roman goddess of grain and fertility, appear fairly frequently in Schiller's later poems. In "The Favor of the Moment" ["Die Gunst des Augenblicks"] (1803), for instance, one of the writer's final poems, the goddess appears in the context of exploring the creativity and fulfillment of the moment. The poem serves, perhaps, as a final comment on "The Elysian Festival." For all the momentary experiences of fulfillment and of beauty must pass away. As we learn from "The Favor of the Moment," "So ist jede schöne Gabe / Flüchtig wie des Blitzes Schein, / Schnell in ihrem düstern Grabe / Schließt die Nacht sie wieder ein" [Thus is every beautiful gift / As transitory as the light of a bolt of lightning, / Quickly, in its gloomy grave, / The night envelops it once again] (strophe 9; NA 2: 415). This is hardly an idealistic view of life in the world. Read together with other more optimistic poetic writings, Schiller's vacillation between idealism and realism, optimism and pessimism, and hope and skepticism betrays a deeper lying tension that enlivens the writer's entire oeuvre. One of my central theses is that this same tension displaces the apparent binary opposition between dualistic or antithetical aspects of Schiller's work.

On a final note, there is a connection between "The Favor of the Moment" and the ironic, elegiac "Victory Festival" ["Siegesfest"], which was also written in 1803. The eleventh strophe of this poem is the only one to repeat the very same lines preceding the refrain. The repetition leads us to the very heart of the poem. A tearful Hecuba exlaims: "Trink ihn [den Becher] aus dem Trank der Labe, / Und vergiß den großen Schmerz, / Wundervoll ist Bacchus' Gabe, / Balsam fürs zerrißne Herz!" ["Drink it [the cup] from the refreshing draught, / And forget the great pain, / Marvelous Bacchus's gift, / Balsam for the battered heart!"] (strophe 11; ll. 129–32; NA 2: 192). Ironically, perhaps, the atmosphere of mourning conflicts with the final exclamation: "Therefore, let us live (it up) today!" [Darum laßt uns heute leben!]. In the end, the poem works against the spirit of merriment conveyed by the *carpe diem* tradition. As the depiction of the returning Greek soldiers in "Das Siegesfest" ["Victory Festival"] makes clear, mourning and loss will occur even in victory. In the end, a torn heart cannot be healed merely by satisfying the desires of the body. A sense of perpetual renewal and ever-active harmony can only be achieved when one appreciates, accepts and actively cultivates the healthy tension between the spiritual/intellectual and corporeal spheres of reality. Perhaps, this is the most fundamental level at which Schiller's writings operate.

9

William Tell, or Natural Justice

I<small>N</small> view of Schiller's interest in music, it is neither coincidental, nor unique that in *William Tell* the writer should have the fisher-boy, the herdsman, and the alpine hunter sing from the lake, the mountains and the cliffs, respectively. Music is an intimate part of the seemingly idyllic, poetic-dramatic setting.[1] Yet, as the stage directions indicate, music is audible even before the dramatic events begin. "Even before the curtain rises, one hears the cowherd's tune and the harmonious ringing of the herd-bells, which even continues a while yet after the scene has begun" (NA 10: 131).[2] Hermann Fähnrich has observed that the song of the fisher-boy is a symbol of untouched, peaceful Nature which, however, also signals demonic perils.[3] Music performs a practical function, since, by stirring the soul, it is capable of influencing sensuous nature and, therefore, has the potential to shape reality. Schiller had once written to Goethe about the power of music when discussing the nature of opera. "Opera tunes the mind ('Gemüt'; also 'disposition') to a more pleasant reception through the power of music and a freer, harmonious stimulation of the senses (lit. 'sensuousness'); here, a freer play is really present even in pathos itself because music accompanies it and the Wonderful, which is now tolerated, must necessarily be more apathetic toward the material."[4]

Unlike the fisher-boy and the herdsman, who both behold the sights and sounds of Nature, the alpine hunter's view is obscured. "Only through the rift of the clouds / Does he catch sight of the world" (K 8; ll. 33–34; NA 10: 132).[5] The scene changes quickly: "one hears a dull cracking from the mountains; shadows of clouds pass over the region" (K 8; NA 10: 132).[6] The dramatic change in Nature draws Ruodi from his hut. Werni descends the cliffs, and as the shepherd Kuoni arrives, Werni draws attention to the fact that a storm is gathering (l. 45b). The cows begin to stir and their bells sound. Turmoil within Nature seems to give rise to turmoil on the human level of existence. From the very beginning of the play, there is tension— and dire need. Konrad Baumgarten, a fellow countryman, suddenly invades the stage, begging those assembled to save him from the governor's horsemen. Within a very short time, the audience's attention has been turned from the tranquility of Nature to the relative chaos of history and political society. The initial composure of the author's style is offset by the quick series of dramatic events.

Schiller's hero William Tell makes his initial appearance in the very first scene. He is already carrying a crossbow, symbolically resembling the bow of a violin. Though not a stringed musical instrument, Tell's weapon serves as a stringed instrument of justice. As a stringed instrument, the crossbow also serves as a sign for Nature. Showing concern for Baumgarten, Tell encourages the ferryman to navigate the raging lake by trusting in God and helping save the "oppressed" (l. 140). The man responds that Tell is his "savior" and "angel" (l. 154). Indeed, Schiller's hero is a blend of Robin Hood and Jesus Christ, of legend and ecclesiastical history. From the outset of the play, he appears to be a superhuman individual. And once the hut is torn down and burned—itself a sign of the intervention of history in Nature—one of the characters (Ruodi) calls out for divine justice. The cry for divine justice has a relatively long history in German affairs. It is at least as old as the peasant revolts under Thomas Münzer at the time of the German Reformation.[7] Already in the very early running of his play, then, the writer poses the question of the relationship not only between history and Nature but, more specifically, between revolution and reform.

It is easy to overlook Tell's remark that, though he can help Baumgarten escape the governor's troops, only another can protect them "from the tempest's perils" ("Aus Sturmes Nöten") (K 13; l. 156a). The dynamics of Tell's character and the forthrightness of his actions evidence the harmonious tension between the anthropological, metaphysical-religious, and historical dimensions of life. Unlike in *Wallenstein,* the central hero of Schiller's last completed drama does not undergo a process of de-mythification. Whereas General Wallenstein appeared to be the one constant in the chaos of war, Tell becomes the one positive force in the vacillating series of dramatic events. Unlike Wallenstein, Tell is not overcome by history. On the contrary, Tell becomes a prime mover of the historical events in this writing. Unlike Wallenstein, who was preoccupied with politics, Tell acts according to the dictates of Nature. For as bearer of the crossbow, he is also the instrument of what I will term natural justice. This point should become clearer as our reading of the play continues.

In the second scene, Stauffacher's wife Gertrud draws out the threat Geßler poses. The metaphor of the yoke is especially pronounced. In Urner Land, the people are tired of the hard yoke ("des harten Jochs") of political dominance (K 18; l. 280c; NA 10: 144). The third scene opens with the toil of building a fortress and the recognition that "everything is in (a state of) movement and work" ("Alles ist in Bewegung und Arbeit") (K 20; NA 10: 147). The unsympathetic taskmaster refers to the workers as "a bad people, good for nothing but milking the cows" ("ein schlechtes Volk, / Zu nichts anstellig als das Vieh zu melken") (K 20; ll. 361c–362; NA 10: 147). He names the place "Keep Uri" ("Zwing Uri"), "for under this yoke one will humble you" ("Denn unter dieses Joch wird man euch beugen") (K 20; ll. 370b and 371; NA 10: 148). For Stauffacher, however, Uri is a land of freedom. Tell is clearly aware of the difference between what the human being is capable of doing and what God is able to accomplish. Pointing to the mountains, i.e., Nature, Tell admires "that house of freedom God has established for us" (K 22; l. 388; NA 10: 149).[8] The fact that Schiller's Tell is a deeply religious person should not be ignored. Through the sequence of events, he strives to maintain the tense equilibrium between the physical and metaphysical realms of existence.

In sum, Schiller's *William Tell* testifies to the fundamental unity of the universe. In his last completed play, the heart inspires words, which are then translated into action. Mere rhetoric has vanished. Tell acts by drawing upon his intuitive and natural sense of justice. He also cherishes the value of self-initiative: "Each (and every) one can count safely on himself only" (K 24; l. 435; NA 10: 151).[9] Unlike the earlier works, the self-development theme is especially pronounced here.[10] The autocratic political system of the time is symbolized by the precarious structure of the castle under construction. Act 1, scene 3, ends with the collapse of a scaffolding and the death of a common worker, a mason. Perhaps this is symbolic of the fact that, for Schiller, the human heart is a greater source of security than any political system.

Act 1, scene 4, is related to the first scene insofar as Melchthal, like Baumgarten before him, has blood on his hands. He is tired of being a prisoner ("ein Gefangner"). Later, he complains of the tyrannous yoke ("Tyrannenjoch") that binds them all. The scene is important because it constitutes a call to avenge injustice in the name of ancient right (*altes Recht*).[11] Melchthal asks if they are defenseless. The answer he receives unshrouds one of the main currents of Schiller's writings. "For what purpose did we learn to bend [lit. tighten] the bow and wield the heavy weight of the battleaxe?" (K 30; ll. 643b–45b; NA 10: 160).[12] Clearly, the taut crossbow must stand for justice.

Here, too, several other major metaphors and themes employed in Schiller's writings resurface. In this context, each of these metaphors underscores the fact that every living creature was given some means of self-defense. "The chamois drags the hunter into the abyss. The plow-ox himself, the gentle household companion of man that has meekly bent the enormous strength of his neck beneath the yoke, springs up, (when) aroused, whets his powerful horn, and hurls his enemy towards the clouds (K 30; ll. 649–54; NA 10: 160).[13] The first act concludes with the swearing of an oath of solidarity. A future day of freedom may not be visible but, as Melchthal submits: "You shall hear it . . . bring glad tidings to your ear" (K 33; ll. 746a–b, and 750; NA 10: 164).[14] Sound and song do not simply evoke pleasure. The messages they convey constitute knowledge of the workings of Nature. This was foreshadowed in the writer's early interest in musical-lyrical production and theosophy. Here, music represents the intimate connection between the human being and Nature. At the same time, the writer's appreciation of the metaphysical realm of love and music is anchored in his knowledge of human anthropology. Once again, the spiritual-intellectual and material-sensuous dimensions of human existence are fundamentally interrelated.

Whereas act 1 of *William Tell* opened on a natural setting and the common inhabitants of Switzerland (Nature), act 2 takes place at the court of the Freiherr von Attinghausen, a man of eighty-five years who, in his own words, is but a shadow of his former self (l. 764). The political sphere is now juxtaposed to the realm of Nature. Unlike his uncle, the Freiherr, Ulrich von Rudenz, however, longs for battle. The writer's awareness of history is signaled when Rudenz complains that his helmet and shield are rusting away and that "the spirited clanging of the war trumpet" ("Der Kriegstrommete muthiges Getön") no longer pervades the valley (K 36; l. 834; NA 10: 168). "Nothing but the cowherd's tune and the herd bell's monotonous ringing do I note here" (K 36; ll. 837–38; NA 10: 168).[15] Attinghausen warns Ulrich by countering that the strange, false world is not intended for him. For at the Emperor's Court his loyal heart would soon be betrayed. Whereas power politics corrupts, humanity ennobles the human spirit. Closeness to Nature, especially to one's own nature, empowers the individual. By ascribing to the human being the power to reshape reality through the various forms of art and aesthetic education, the writer helps empower the sensitive reader, encouraging the individual to revitalize, i.e., humanize the society of which one is a part.[16] As we witnessed in the letters *Concerning the Aesthetic Education of the Human Being*, not more and more critical reason but greater and greater sensitivity to the needs of humanity, together with rational discernment (in short, a process of re-spiritualization through the multifarious forms of culture), can ultimately transform the world of politics.[17]

The challenge that *William Tell* presents to the idea of humanity is that violent action seems to be required at times in order to promote justice. One of the central debates in Schiller scholarship is how this realization is to be reconciled with morality and the program of cultural action delineated in the letters *Concerning the Aesthetic Education of the Human Being*.[18] The answer, I believe, lies in the writer's sensitive awareness of natural justice. Because William Tell lives in concord with Nature, his actions will be just. It is important to realize that Schiller's dramatic hero embraces no one specific political program or ideology.[19] He simply listens to Nature. By listening to his own nature, and by cultivating the harmonious interaction between his own sensuous and rational natures, Tell does what is right. In tune with Nature, Tell also gains freedom of action.[20]

Rudenz's actions illuminate the predicament of political enchainment, since he resigns himself, at least momentarily, to the arbitrary rule of the Emperor. "The world belongs to him. Shall we alone be willfully stubborn and obstinate in breaking that chain of lands of his which he has so powerfully drawn around us?" (K 37; ll. 870–73; NA 10: 169).[21] The themes of "Freiheit" (freedom) and "Knechtschaft" (slavery or bondage) are especially strong at this point. The events are also complicated by the metaphor of the net, which underscores the entangled nature of political life. "We are surrounded all about and enclosed by his lands as with a net" (K 37; ll. 877–78; NA 10: 169).[22] Attinghausen admonishes Rudenz not to betray his homeland. "Get to know this race of shepherds, boy! . . . Let them come to force a yoke upon us! That we are resolved not to tolerate! Oh, learn to feel of what race you are!" (K 38; ll. 909, 912–14; NA 10: 170).[23] The close affinity between Nature and politics is captured by the metaphor of chains. "Join tightly the natural ties. Attach yourself to your native land, to the dear land (of your fathers). That (you should) grasp firmly with your whole heart!" (K 38; ll. 921–23; NA 10: 170).[24] The disagreement between Attinghausen and Rudenz is especially significant in the light of our discussion. For, whereas Rudenz believes he is bound ("Ich bin gebunden" [l. 931c]), Attinghausen maintains that his nephew is bound only by the rope of love ("Gebunden bist du durch der Liebe Seile!" [l. 934]). Rudenz is tied to the court by his sensual-sensuous love for Berta von Bruneck, who, in Attinghausen's words, "chains" him "to the Emperor's service" ("dich . . . an des Kaisers Dienst [fesselt]" [l. 937b–c]). Attinghausen also conveys to Rudenz the fact that the Imperial Court wishes to enchain the man and claim him as its subject.

Schiller underscores the lure of strange or foreign things ("das Fremde"). Attinghausen: "The strange spell tears away (from me and) over our mountains the young man with his mighty aspirations. Oh, unhappy hour when strange things came into this quiet and happy valley to destroy the innocent simplicity of our lives!" (K 39; ll. 947–51; NA 10: 171).[25] In the next scene, Melchthal's remarks develop the theme of separation even further with the aid of the metaphor of the extinguishing sun. "[I] have drunk in (a) glowing feeling of revenge from the sunshine of his glance, (a sunshine now) extinguished" (K 41; ll. 990–91; NA 10: 174).[26] The tyrannical enemy is characterized as one who lurks behind the bulwarks of the mountain embankments and plunders the land, and whose stare resembles an extinguished sun. Equating Geßler with the Devil, the writer mythifies the enemy in the minds of the characters as well as of the recipients. The apocalyptic undertones are unmistakable. According to Rösselmann, right is on the side of those who know God. "Yet God is in every place where one administers justice and we are standing beneath His Heaven" (K 45; ll. 1114c–16; NA 10: 179).[27] Konrad Hunn adds: "Even if the old books are not at hand, they are engraved in our hearts" (K 45; ll. 1121–22; NA 10: 179).[28] As in the Protestant tradition, as well as in the writer's own essay *Concerning the Aesthetic Education of the Human Being,* the human heart (wherein conscience is rooted) is the source of right. In this context, however, it is apparent that the human heart is rooted in Nature. On the Rütli, under a starry sky, the people seal a new-old alliance ("Bund"). They insist that they, the people, must now rule themselves, both in consonance with a universal concept of inalienable rights and their own cultural heritage.[29]

In *William Tell*, divine justice and democratic principles of self-governance combine to form an especially powerful appeal for political freedom based on the democratic principle of popular consensus. The theme of freedom from the yoke ("Joch") of tyranny recurs throughout the drama. Rather than accept political enslavement by other people ("fremdes Joch" [l. 1205c]), the Swiss, like their forefathers, maintain their ancient right of self-rule.[30] Their commitment is underscored by the chorus (which includes everyone): "We are one people and we shall act as one" (K 47; l. 1204; NA 10: 182).[31] The importance of unanimity and solidarity of purpose is underscored at the very end of act 2 where Stauffacher speaks out against self-initiative born of wrath or vengeance for the good of a common, political cause (ll. 1465–68; NA 10: 192). In operatic fashion, "the orchestra comes in with a splendid flourish" (K 55; NA 10:192).[32] The dawn of a new day is mirrored in the symbol of the sun, which now causes the icy fields of Switzerland to glisten.[33]

Act 3, the structural center of the drama, takes place in Tell's hometown (society). Father and son are both playing with a small crossbow. Young Walter sings a type of folk song: "With the arrow (and) the bow / Through mountain and valley / The archer comes (walking) along / Early in the morning" (K 56; ll. 1466–70; NA 10: 193).[34] The lyrics suggest that there is a more profound source of justice. The string to Walter's crossbow has snapped, however. "My string is broken. Fix it, father" ("Der Strang ist mir entzwei. Mach mir ihn, Vater") (K 56; l. 1478; NA 10: 193). William insists that the lad repair it himself. In addition to the self-development theme, we find several key passages that place Tell in very close association with Nature. Tell's wife, Hedwig, even grows fearful that her husband will not return, that he will make a false step and fall to his death, that the chamois, leaping backwards, will drag him into the abyss, or that he will be buried by an avalanche (K 57; ll. 1497–1508; NA 10: 194). In spite of her fear, however, she sees clearly that "(literally) Something is being spun against the governors" ("Es spinnt sich etwas / Gegen die Vögte") (K 58; ll. 1517b–18a; NA 10: 195). Tell and the crossbow now appear to be one and the same: "I'm missing my (right) arm when I'm missing my weapon" (K 58; l. 1537; NA 10: 196).[35]

With Rudenz, the writer continues the analogy to the abyss in scene 2. "Abysses shut us in all around" ("Abgründe schließen rings umher uns ein") (K 61; l. 1587; NA 10: 199). The thematics turn to love and politics, at which point the problem of the relationship between the human being and Nature surfaces. Despite her love for the people, Bertha insists that the Swiss are the ones who enchain the country and cause her pain: "you are the ones who hurt and grieve me [literally: make me ill]. I must force my heart not to hate you" (K 62; ll. 1627–28; NA 10: 200).[36] "They [the people] have thrown a net about your head" (K 62; l. 1634; NA 10: 200).[37] "There [at the Imperial Court] the chains of a hateful marriage await me. Love alone, your (love), can save me!" (K 63; ll. 1671–72; NA 10: 202).[38] For his part, Rudenz desires that the people fulfill their love in the narrower confines of the quiet valley, that is, in Nature, where they can renounce "earth's glamor" (l. 1680b–c). "Then may these rocks all around us, which extend (their) strong walls impenetrably, and this secluded, happy valley, be open and clear to heaven alone!" (K 64; ll. 1686–89; NA 10: 202).[39] Later, Rudenz will come to grips with the fact that he had left his blood relatives and his people: "all ties of nature I tore asunder in order to attach myself to you" ("alle Bande der Natur / Zerriss ich, um an euch mich anzuschließen") (K 76; ll. 2012b–13; NA 10: 218). Bertha is convinced that Rudenz must remain where he is. For it is his natural habitat. He is encouraged to sever ("Zerreiße") the noose (rope) of tyranny that drags him along. And the scene ends with a call to freedom. "Fight for the fatherland (and) you fight for your love! One enemy it is before whom we all tremble and one (advance towards) freedom makes us all free!" (K 65; ll. 1728c–31; NA 10: 204).[40]

Act 3, scene 3, marks the pivotal center of the play. Tell is forcibly taken prisoner. Though the three countrymen promise they will help, Tell counters by saying, "I'll help myself" ("Ich helfe mir schon selbst") (K 70; l. 1846a–b; NA 10: 210). Still, the people challenge the arrest and are willing to fight for Tell's release. Upon his arrival, Geßler orders Tell to shoot an apple from his own child's head. Should he not hit the mark with the first shot, he will be killed. One of the tyrant's most criminal acts is that he is insensitive to the natural pleas of a loving father. It is an unnatural act. Ironically, perhaps, it is a representative of the Imperial Court (Bertha) who not only acknowledges this, but who expresses the greatest concern: "It is inhuman to trifle thus with a father's anguish" (K 73; ll. 1922n–23; NA 10: 214).[41] Thus, even within courtly circles, there are people who respond to the call of humanity.

Young Walter is not simply innocent; he is also brave. Refusing to be bound to the tree, he asserts his independence and trusts in his father's skill, holding still, like a lamb ("wie ein Lamm"). In short, he is a willing sacrifice to justice. It is a tense moment, the main crisis point in the dramatic action. As Tell tightens the string, so also the emotions (sensuous natures) of the people observing the event become tautly strung. Though Tell is, at first, unable to release the arrow, Geßler demands that he try. Geßler's remarks are less taunting than they are telling. "Why, you can do (anything and) everything, Tell! The rudder you handle like the bow. No storm frightens you if it means saving (someone). Now, savior, help yourself! You're always saving people" (K 75; ll. 1989–90; NA 10: 217).[42] The writer draws a close association between the bow and the rudder that had successfully navigated Nature (the lake). It should be noted that Geßler's words also echo the voice of one of the soldiers at the foot of the cross, the one who mocked Jesus Christ.

Standing "in the most violent excitement" [literally: state of great tension] ("in der heftigsten Spannung") Rudenz implores Geßler to stop his cruel game. "Severity, pushed too far, fails to its sage design and the bow snaps (if it's) all too tightly drawn" (K 75; ll. 1994–96; NA 10: 21).[43] Rudenz understands his relationship to the court well and is not afraid to confront Geßler. It is a moment of insight for Rudenz, one which, at the precipice of an emotional-sensuous and potentially deadly abyss, promotes personal development (*Bildung*). Like the descriptions of Christian Wolf in the early novella, *Criminal Out of Infamy,* and Mary Stuart of the later drama, Rudenz observes: "Shuddering, I see myself led to a precipice" ("Schauderned / Seh ich an einen Abgrund mich geführt") (K 76; ll. 2016c–17; NA 10:218). At this point of decision, Rudenz declares his freedom from Geßler: "I'm born (as) free as you" ("Frei bin ich / Wie ihr gebohren") (K 76; ll. 2022c–23b; NA 10: 218). His voice also echoes the words of both Karl Moor (*The Robbers* [1782]) and Max Piccolomini (*Wallenstein* [1799]).

As Rudenz threatens to apply physical force to combat Geßler's injustice, Stauffacher announces that the arrow has already hit its mark. Given the battle of words between Rudenz and Geßler at the very moment of Tell's concentration on the target, the apple shot scene means that Rudenz's remarks have also had an effect. At this moment, Rudenz, like Tell, frees himself from enchainment to the tyrant. Perhaps it is rather humorous that, having been diverted by Rudenz, Geßler was deprived of witnessing the event. Still, he is able to admire the master shot ("Meisterschluß"). Asking why a second arrow had been readied, Tell replies, "I would have shot (clean) through you, if I had hit my darling child" (K 78; ll. 2060–61; NA 10: 221). With that threat, Tell is bound. But, as Stauffacher notes, "With you [Tell], we are all (now) bound and tied" ("Mit Euch / Sind wir gefesselt alle und gebunden!") (K 79; ll. 2090c–91; NA 10: 222). Leaving with the troops, Tell trusts that God will help him.

Like the first act of the play, act 4 opens on the Vierwaldstättensee (Nature). Only now, the community receives the report that Tell has been bound and taken prisoner: "the arm that was to save (us) is bound" ("Der Arm, der retten sollte, ist gefesselt!") (K 81; l. 2126; NA 10: 225). Fittingly, an innocent lad (Knabe) notes how Nature is now responding to Tell's arrest. "Hear how the abyss rages (and) the whirlpool roars" ("Hört, wie der Abgrund tost, der Wirbel brüllt") (K 81; l. 2137; NA 10: 225). At this moment, a bell tolls, signaling a boat in distress. Nature seems to be responding to the injustice of Tell's capture. The governor's boat, with Tell aboard, is being tossed about on the lake. Only if (politically) unchained, however, does Tell have any hope of saving the ship.

While the people wonder what has happened to him, Tell appears, miraculously, before them. He is carrying his crossbow. Schiller's hero attributes his liberation from the shackles and the storm to "God's gracious providence" ("Gottes gnädge Für[Vor]sehung") (l. 2211a–b; NA 10:22a). Narrating the story of the escape, Tell relays how he had been asked by the governor himself to pilot the boat and save the passengers. Standing at the helm and rowing steadily on despite the threat of destruction, Tell appears to be one with the forces of Nature. "Thus am I here, saved from the storm's fury and from man's (which was even) worse" (K 85; ll. 2269–2270; NA 10: 230).[44] The comparison is significant. One of my theses is that the more the people of Uri live in accord with the laws of Nature, the more they are protected against those who defy Nature. Schiller's hero thus appears to be the perfect embodiment of Nature, which no human being or political system can enchain. We recall that Tell's release resulted from a natural event which secured his freedom. In this state (*Zustand*), he is empowered to administer natural justice, i.e., to carry out the justice inherent in Nature. Hedwig's fearful vision seems to complement this interpretation: "I should forever be seeing my boy standing bound, his father aiming at them and (still) the arrow would forever be flying at my heart" (K 88; ll. 2325b–27; NA 10: 234).[45] Hedwig's portrayal stands as a powerful symbol of the precarious and always taut relationship between the forces of Nature.

In the dialogue between Stauffacher, Attinghausen, and Walter Fürst, the reinstitution of the alliance and the holy oath presuppose an apocalypse. Melchthal notes that the ground beneath the tyrants is hollow and that the days of their rule are numbered. For the Swiss people, however, a new day is dawning. Thinking back on the moment of the apple shot, Attinghausen declares an end to the old regime: "The old order is collapsing, the time(s) are changing, and (a) new life flourishes from the ruins" (K 91; ll. 2425–26; NA 10: 238).[46] Stauffacher understands that the passing of history does not mean the extinction of Nature ("Erlöschen der Natur") but, rather, the beam ("Stra[h]l") of a new life (ll. 2428–29). In short, the Freiherr von Attinghausen's death and Rudenz's transformation of character coincide with the hope of the dawn of a new day. Rudenz recaptures his original identity by returning to his natural habitat. It is not coincidental that this act should entail rupture, the opposite, however, of the kind marking Schiller's early writings. For he freely enchains himself to Nature. "I have torn asunder forever all foreign ties. I am restored to my people. I am a Swiss" (K 93; ll. 2467c–71b; NA 10: 239–40).[47] He accepts the fact that his loved one has been torn away from him ("Geraubt, entrissen" [l. 2531a]). Through it all, he has learned something important about life. "Out from under the ruins of the tyrant's might alone can she be dug. Every stronghold must we subdue (to see) if we (can) penetrate her prison" (K 95; ll. 2543–46; NA 10: 242).[48] One result of his self-enlightenment is that he can now join the chorus of voices, which exclaims: "and bring down [literally break to pieces] the structure of tyranny!" ("Und brecht den Bau der Tyrannei zusammen") (K 96; l. 2559; NA 10: 243).[49] The natural has become political.

According to the stage directions to one of the most critical moments, act 4, scene 3, rocks enclose the landscape (K 96; NA 10: 243). The first part of the scene consists of Tell's controversial monologue. Carrying his crossbow, he declares that the moment is ripe. He hopes that the one arrow will be able to hit the mark in the narrow path lying before them. And he is aware that there is a God of justice, whose instrument he has now become.[50] The symbol and instrument of justice is the stringed crossbow, which is characterized by tension: "To defend you [future generations] (and) to protect your sweet innocence from the revenge of the tyrant, he will now bend [literally: taughten] his bow for (an act of) murder" (K 98; ll. 2632b–33; NA 10: 245).[51] Earlier he had hoped that the bow would not forsake him: "And you, trusty bowstring, that so often has served me faithfully in joyous sports, do not desert me in this (moment of) frightful seriousness!" (K 97; ll. 2601c–4; NA 10: 244–45).[52] Fritz Martini once traced Tell's sense of inner freedom back to the "purely human" realm ("das Rein-Menschliche"), i.e., "the self-assertion of the mind/spirit" ("die Selbstbehauptung des Geistes"), i.e., to an intellectual construct of freedom.[53] Given the close association between the crossbow and Nature, however, Schiller's text suggests that Tell is acting in accordance with the dictates of natural justice. What occurs at this juncture in the text is a wholly natural development. Consistent with Schiller's writing, the moment is marked by tension. The hunter (Tell) awaits his prey (Geßler). At the same time, "One hears from afar (a) gay music which is (gradually) approaching" (K 98; A 10: 246)—the music of a wedding procession. Today, Tell says, he wishes to take the true master's shot ("*Meisterschuß*"). It is consistent with our thesis concerning natural justice that Tell should sense that the mountains (Nature itself) are shaking.

Geßler's entrance in act 4, scene 3, shows that he has learned nothing. For he is utterly determined to enslave the Swiss people. To Rudolf der Harras's claim that the people do have certain rights, Geßler counters that the people are simply "a stone in our way" ("ein Stein im Weg") (K 102; l. 2730c; NA 10: 250). Armgard pleads for mercy, but her cry falls on deaf ears. The stage directions read that Armgard "pulls her children to the ground and throws herself (along) with them in his way" (K 103; NA 10: 252).[54] Something significant is about to transpire, to which the acoustic level of the play attests. "One hears the music from before (once) again on the top of the pass, but (now it has) softened" (K 103; NA 10: 252).[55] Geßler insists: "I will destroy it, this stubborn mood (of theirs); the bold spirit of freedom will I bend (and break). I will proclaim a new law in these cantons" (K 103; ll. 2783–85; NA 10: 252)[56]—at which moment Tell's arrow runs Geßler through the heart. We may conclude that the tyrant wills the political enslavement of the people, while Nature does not. At this point in Schiller's career, "enslavement" to Nature is actually an act of freedom.

In the foreground, the wedding processional and the music continue, but only until the participants realize that the tyrant is dead. Rushing to the site of the execution, "the whole wedding party stands around the dying man with a dread devoid of feeling" (K 105; NA 10: 254).[57] Natural justice has been executed. Stüssi announces the people's newly won freedom: "The tyrant of the land has fallen. We'll tolerate no further violence. We are free men" (K 105; ll. 2818c–20; NA 10: 255).[58] Six Brothers of Mercy appear who form a half-circle around the victim while the chorus sings:

> Death approaches man [the human being] quickly;
>   No respite is given him
> He is overthrown in the midst of his career;
>   He is hurried away from the fullness of life.
> Prepared (to go) or not, he must station himself
>   before his judge![59]
>
> (K 106; ll. 2833–38; NA 10: 255)

The fourth act closes not only on the theme of death, one of the most pervasive topics in Schiller's entire oeuvre, but also on the theme of natural justice.

Concerning the contested issue of Tell's act, though Tell commits murder, the audience may have the resounding feeling that justice has been done. Perhaps, the act is morally defensible. In any case, Geßler's death seems to be the natural consequence of events. Whatever Tell's actual motives may be, Marie-Luise Waldeck is correct in her observation that "Here, right triumphs over evil and restores the ethical order."[60] I would add that it is an act of Tell's free, moral will. However, our moral sensibilities may still be offended, for the content of a central line is not wholly resolved: "Schrecklich immer, auch in gerechter Sache, ist Gewalt" (l. 1320; NA 10: 187) [Always terrible, even for the sake of good, is violence].

The final act of *William Tell* bears some resemblance in location and acoustic dimension to act 1, scene 3, and the very beginning of the play. The fortress Keep Uri still stands. Bells are ringing, only this time from various distant locations.[61] Considering themselves free at last, the country people decide to tear down the castle, which has stood as a symbol of the injustice of tyranny. In fact, this structure is referred to directly as the "tyrant's castle" ("Tyrannenschloß" [l. 2843c; NA 10: 256]). Steinmetz exclaims: "Shall the yoke stand that wanted to keep us down? Up! Tear it down!" (K 107; ll. 2845–46b; NA 10: 256). By dismantling the castle, the people have not only destroyed the tyrannical political order, they have established an intimate relationship with Nature and have realized their power to create (and destroy), i.e., to construct and deconstruct the world around them. As the Stonemason declares: "We have erected it [the castle]; we know how to destroy it" ("Wir habens aufgebaut / Wir wissens zu zerstören") (K 108; ll. 2862b–63; NA 10: 257).

Suddenly hearing Bertha's cry for help from within the structure, Melchthal and Rudenz hasten to save this last representative of the tyrannical social order.[62] Whereas, in the opening scenes of this play, the life of a countryman was lost to the construction of the castle, here, in the end, a life, the life of a nobleperson, is saved. Children "[hurry across the stage with pieces of scaffolding]. Freedom! Freedom! [The horn of Uri is blown mightily]" (K 110; NA 10: 260).[63] With the partial destruction of the castle, "The peasants, men, women and children, some standing and some sitting on the beams of the shattered scaffolding, (are) picturesquely grouped around in a semicircle" (K 110; NA 10: 260).[64] Formally, the technique of portraiture in drama—the blending of literature and the visual arts—is an essential characteristic of Schiller's *William Tell,* as it was in the more mature dramatic and prose works of Goethe.

Near the end of the play, we learn that Duke John of Swabia has killed the Emperor. Given Schiller's earlier background, it is interesting to note that the writer had incorporated the history of a Swabian into his writing. Stauffacher exclaims: "The greatest enemy of freedom has fallen" ("Gefallen ist der Freiheit größter Feind") (K 113; l. 3019; NA 10: 264). Melchthal refers to the "people, freed from anxiety" ("angstbefreites Volk") (K 116; l. 3079b-c; NA 10: 266). Stauffacher credits Tell with having done most of the work: "bid hail to the savior of us all" ("rufet Heil dem Retter von uns allen") (K 116; l. 3086; NA 10: 267). On the metaphysical level of the dramatic writing, the Christlike figure of William Tell defeats the personification of the Devil, i.e., evil (Geßler). Instead of fear and suffering, one can now exercise love. Melchthal: "He who wants to reap tears must sow love" ("Wer Thränen ärnten will, muß Liebe säen") (K 116; l. 3181; NA 10: 266). And love, like gravity, holds all things together. Having restored the harmony between his community and nature, the central hero no longer needs his crossbow. When Walter asks what his father had done with the instrument of justice, Tell responds that it has been enshrined. "It is put away in (a) holy place. From now on it will serve the hunt no more" (K 119; ll. 3138–39; NA 10: 270).[65]

Tell and Parricida (John of Swabia) encounter each other in the next scene. As controversial as this episode has become in the secondary literature, it has not been noted that it is similar in structure and significance to the encounters between Luise Miller and Lady Milford in *Intrigue and Love* and Mary Stuart and Elizabeth in *Mary Stuart.* The difference between Tell's and Parricida's act is that Tell has avenged "sacred Nature" ("die heilige Natur") (l. 3182b).[66] Whereas Parricida has willfully committed murder, even of his own kin (his uncle), Tell has defended the natural community of which he is a part. Despite some scholarly opinions to the contrary, there is an important qualitative difference between the two acts. Whereas Parricida has transgressed the natural order, Tell has defended it. Tell rejects Parricida's plea to stay with them, primarily because it is not his homeland.

It is as much a cultural consideration as it is a moral one. To receive absolution (a religious rite), however, Tell suggests that Parricida journey to Rome and seek the Pope's forgiveness for his serious transgression against the Empire. But he is forewarned, since "The path goes by (the edge of) the precipice and many crosses . . . mark it" ("Am Abgrund geht der Weg und viele *Kreuze* / Bezeichnen ihn") (K 123; ll. 3245–46a; NA 10: 275). Because he is genuinely prepared to come to terms with his own guilt, Parricida appears to be unafraid of the "terrors of Nature" ("Schrecken der Natur") (K 123). And, in this, there is hope.

Like Karl Moor, Christian Wolf, Mary Stuart and Ulrich von Rudenz, Parricida's path to his true self leads down the path of self-knowledge. Only from this perspective do Tell's directions and advice make sense: "then you'll come to the bridge (literally: that scatters spray). If it does not give way beneath your guilt, (and if) when you have left it safely behind you, a black gateway in the rock(s) then opens suddenly—no day as yet has brightened it (then) through there you go. It leads you into a gay valley of joy. But with hasty step(s) you must hurry past (it) (for) you dare not tarry where peace dwells" (K 123; ll. 3255–62; NA 10: 275).[67] The path of understanding is also one of self-activity and insight informed by experiencing life. Perhaps through his characterization of Duke John of Swabia, the writer Friedrich Schiller was also holding up the liberation of Switzerland as a model for his home state of Württemberg.

The play ends with a portrait of solidarity—Tell's countrymen and women are "grouped" together in front of his home; it also ends as it had begun— with music. "All" form a chorus which, in unison, praise the man and his work: "Long live Tell, the archer and the savior (of our country)." ("Es lebe Tell! der Schütz und der Erretter!") (K 124; l. 3281; NA 10: 277). It is significant that, once again, the music should come from the mountain, that is, from Nature, as it had even before the beginning of the dramatic action. With Rudenz's act of freeing his bondsmen,[68] the play ends on a triumphant note: "As the music promptly begins anew, the curtain falls" (K 125; NA 10: 277).[69]

In conclusion, Schiller's last completed dramatic writing, *William Tell*, is, quite literally, a *Schau-Spiel* (visual play) as the subtitle states. As such, it transcends the limits of traditional drama. Form and content are wholly integrated. In no other work by this German writer is the relation between Nature (as represented also by music) and human action so tightly interwoven. In the final analysis, Schiller's Tell is neither an aesthetic human being nor a political one. He is, quite simply, the representation of a natural man whose actions are wholly consistent with his being as a sensuous-rational ("sinnlich-vernünftig") human being. As a consequence, what we witness is not the reinstatement of the ancient, medieval state, but rather the realization of the moral-rational state of the future.[70] Unlike his previous writings, Schiller had now succeeded in demonstrating that a "naive," or "beautiful" hero can be as compelling as a "sentimental," or "sublime" one (Mary Stuart). In his last completed play, then, the split (*Entzweiung*) between art and Nature seems to have vanished. Despite the author's untimely death, *William Tell* may therefore be understood as the culmination point of Friedrich Schiller's career as a writer.[71]

Conclusion

THOUGH the traditional view of Friedrich Schiller as an idealist is well-preserved in the scholarly literature, few scholars today recreate the glossy picture of the writer that Wilhelm von Humboldt had portrayed nearly two hundred years ago. In 1982, Norbert Oellers advanced the thesis that Schiller's change in direction ("Wende"), following a severe illness in 1791,[1] informed the writer that a political revolution ("eine Revolution mit der Faust") was no longer possible and that the only remaining alternative was an intellectual one ("eine Revolution des Geistes").[2] He maintained that "physical collapse removed Schiller from the physical, the historical world and distanced him from his lectern, namely his active professorship in Jena."[3] The latter statement, however, seems contradictory. How was it possible for Schiller to distance himself from the physical world if, indeed, he was suffering from a physical ailment? In the present study, I have tried to show that it was not only the aftermath of the French Revolution, namely the Reign of Terror (1791–92f.), it is not only politics, but also the writer's own recognition of the limitations of the body and, by extension, the corporeal-material world—well before the advent of the French Revolution, namely his study of physiology—that helped shape the nature of Schiller's writings in the so-called classical period.

Rather than distance himself from his own corporeality, Friedrich Schiller was acutely aware of the limitations of both the body and the intellect. This awareness led the writer to qualify his most idealistic intellectual insights by repeatedly introducing the phrase "merely an idea" ("bloß eine Idee") throughout the later essays. Given the fact of his schooling in the German Enlightenment, especially his experiences at the Carlsschule in Stuttgart, Schiller's conscious recognition of the limits of his own theorizing reflects an arresting, self-critical posture over and against the free, creative operations of his own mind.

In this study, I intimated that scholars have glided over those passages in Schiller's writings that work against his assumed affiliation with German Idealism, specifically G. W. F. Hegel, and the Platonic idealist tradition. While drawing, more and more, on the power of the mind for inspiration and insight in the later period, the writer recognized, time and again, the limits of the new schools of romanticism (F. Schlegel and Novalis) and Idealism (J. G. Fichte and F. W. J. Schelling). His repeated qualifications concerning the realization of the goal of humanity in history lead me to

268

conclude that the ideals that Schiller built up in the course of his writings are either shattered, or at best fragmented. This is one reason why the central symbol of the stringed instrument as a model of Nature proves to be so powerful.

On the one hand, for Schiller, states of harmonious tension mark a healthy condition. On the other hand, rupture remains an imminent possibility. Perhaps it was Schiller's personal experience of the rupture between sense and reason and history and thought that makes the work of this, the first modern German writer, so dynamic. But rather than apply terms like "classical," or "naive," "romantic," or "sentimental" to Schiller and his work, as even contemporary scholarly research is prone to do, perhaps we should appreciate the deeper-lying tension that stems from the writer's knowledge of the limits which corporeal and historical reality impose on the seemingly infinite possibilities of the intellect. Schiller's multidisciplinary activities as a physiologist, historian, philosopher, and writer of both literature and letters may well disclose the writer's dissatisfaction with the claims of any one discipline or any single approach to the discernment of reality. One of the most intriguing aspects of Schiller's writings is the problematization of the various roles of the human being not only with respect to oneself but also with regard to one's location and situation within a society, as well as within history and Nature as a whole. In retrospect, the formal attributes and recurrent thematics of the vast majority of Schiller's writings complement the writer's overall search for unity and harmony and the concomitant knowledge of discontinuity and rupture.

In his book *Philosophy Beside Itself: On Deconstruction and Modernism* (1986), Stephen W. Melville characterized the structure of "radical self-criticism" as holding oneself in a "condition of being at stake."[4] The situation of being at risk assumes "neither the positive guarantee of that self's inviolable autonomy nor the negative guarantee of its nonexistence; and this means that self-criticism is radically and inevitably critical."[5] From this perspective, we can better appreciate the intersection of Schiller's writings with current contemporary thinking. In the act of expressing his creative talents, the writer also monitored his activities with the aid of critical reason. Viewed in this light, there can be no real negation, as is sometimes attributed to Schiller (e.g., Herbert Marcuse). Rather, what we discover is a truthful encounter with the nature of reality in all its manifold appearances. Where Schiller's critical, self-critical reflexes dissected and separated, his creatively productive mind unified and harmonized. I have argued that the ongoing, simultaneous activity of creating and analyzing evident in Schiller's writings stems from the writer's appreciation for the harmonious tension between mind and body. Furthermore, the texture of Schiller's manifold writings was informed largely by the multidisciplinary activities that came to bear on his consciousness while he was engaged in the act of writing.

Friedrich Schiller strove to account for the seemingly labyrinthine nature of the world and its inherent problems in several different, yet thematically related forms, that is intertextually. In short, there could be no simple, straightforward answers to the questions raised by the encounter of the human mind with a corporeal-material world. The primary task remained the perpetual cultivation (*Bildung*) of the harmonious tension of one's own nature as a sensuous-rational being. While engaged in this mission, one would also develop a closer working relationship with Nature.

Most important, Schiller saw that the problem of modernity, namely the rupture of the original harmony between the human being and Nature, could not be overcome by intellect alone. For the cultivation of sensation ("die Ausbildung des Empfindungsvermögens"), as articulated in the eighth letter of *Concerning the Aesthetic Education of the Human Being,* must first accompany the exercise of reason. The ultimate goal of a wholly rational, moral, and aesthetic state of moral integrity and mutual respect was to be achieved by reuniting reason and sense, the sublime and the beautiful, dignity and grace. But, for Schiller, this could be accomplished only by developing one's aesthetic sensibilities, namely with the aid of art.

In sum, knowledge of the world and the creative transformation of society through culture entail far more than rationality alone. It is for this reason that I am critical of the philosophies of Jürgen Habermas and Hans-Georg Gadamer, both of whom privilege reason over sense. For Friedrich Schiller, however, knowledge of the world requires the full participation and simultaneous operation of all of the human being's capacities. Schiller's appreciation of the interrelatedness of all knowledge is also reflected in the interdisciplinary character of his writings.

Schiller's collected works suggest that Nature is not so much sacred (*heilig*) as it is healing (*heilend*). Indeed, it is usually only after a moment of crisis that healing (or death) occurs. In the early literary practice, Karl Moor and Christian Wolf decide in favor of what is right only after experiencing the world and by coming to terms with the criminality of their personal histories. Self-criticism, then, would also seem to be an essential part of the process of (moral) enlightenment. As in the process of healing, wherein fever fights fever, or a virus combats another virus, many of Schiller's literary heroes exhibit a dire struggle with their own natures. Once the battle between sense and reason has run its course, there is often moral insight (e.g., Karl Moor and Mary Stuart). We recall that, in the second medical dissertation on fevers, young Schiller had argued that Nature, in its innumerable attempts to burst through the blockages in the pulmonary vessels— which process threatens the very life of the body—produces certain crisis situations in which disorder and even destruction must occur in order to acquire health and restore the original harmonious tension of the nervous system. For this idea, Schiller drew on Moses Mendelssohn's *Letters on the Sensations.* At the same time, the writer turned the physiological and historical facts of tension and rupture into a dynamic source of criticism against the political order of his day. For his ultimate goal was the truly rational-moral state. Though the historical attainment of such a government remained "merely an idea," the substance of such a state, for Schiller, could be actualized daily through the cultivation of the harmonious tension between the rational and sensuous components of human nature. Within this process, the primary function of art is not to afford the individual a safe haven of autonomy, nor to construct merely beautiful symbols for contemplation or mere speculation, but rather to assist the human being in developing a fine-tuned soul and morally responsible behavior. Perhaps it was Schiller's hope that the training of the faculty of sensation, once reunited with reason, would furnish society not only with examples of wholeness of being, both individual and social, but even more so with self-activated individuals who would be working, naturally and dynamically à la William Tell, perhaps, toward the realization of the moral-rational state. However, the true crisis of Schiller's writings may well reside in the seemingly irresolvable conflict between the desirability of the goal of completion and the knowledge of its unattainability. To the extent that Schiller was the first German writer to recognize the problem, his writings appear to be quite contemporary. The fact, however, that the writer set up a goal or an ideal only to deconstruct it, may be perceived as either a flawed attempt and an ultimate failure, or a hermeneutic process of self-critical reflection which in the light of history would situate the writer between Enlightenment and romanticism.

Schiller's last completed dramatic writing, *William Tell,* demonstrates that the writer had taken his earlier work to a profound level. For while fighting to preserve and actualize the moral integrity of the people whom he represents, Schiller's Tell acts instinctively in harmony with Nature. The harmonious tension between the human being and Nature is illustrated in Tell's struggle to do what is, at bottom, required of his natural inclinations as a moral being. The killing of Geßler, the embodiment of evil, while an act which scholars and critics have had such a difficult time reconciling with Tell's character, appears to be both a natural and moral act, that is, a product of Nature healing itself and a product of human reason. It may not be necessary to share Jeffrey Sammons's ideology in order to appreciate his point, that Geßler's killing would be similar, in effect, to the act of assassinating Adolf Hitler: "an act of moral surgery, the effect of which is not catharsis but relief and gratification,"[6] or, from my perspective, an act of healing. Rather than interpret Schiller's play solely from a narrow political perspective, perhaps Geßler's murder should be understood as a natural act of justice to the extent that Nature, in Schiller's writings, also exhibits a certain violence which, at times, functions as a necessary corrective when things get out of control.[7]

In *William Tell,* both the natural and the ethical orders thus seem to be mutually cooperative. I cite a passage by Schiller which Jeffrey L. Sammons translated and included in his 1988 essay on this topic. Schiller had warned that "in moral matters one does not without danger depart from rational, practical feeling in order to ascend to general abstractions, that a human being much more securely trusts the intimations of his [or her] heart or the already present and individual feelings of justice and injustice than the dangerous guide of universal rational ideas that he [one] has artificially created for himself [oneself]—for nothing leads to the good that is not natural (NA 22: 172)."[8]

In order to capture both the possibility of harmony and the fact of rupture in the modern world, Schiller reinscribed the ancient, pre-Socratic symbol of the stringed instrument. As we have noted, this reinscription of the ancient tradition occurs in almost all of Schiller's major writings. The founding of scientific astronomy, the scientific study of music, number theory, and the philosophy of the harmony of the spheres have all been traced back to the pre-Socratic Pythagorean School.[9] The school which Pythagoras (570/560–480 B.C.) founded in Croton in the southern part of ancient Italy after his exile from Greece was a religious-philosophical community that was engaged with political issues. Hans Schavernoch describes this school as a nursery ("Pflanzschule") of piety and moral stringency, of moderation, and courage. That early order reminds us of Carl Eugen's Military Academy ("Pflanzschule") where Friedrich Schiller received his primary education.[10] According to the oral tradition of the teachings of Pythagoras, the goal of human existence is to attain agreement with the divine will and the divine world order.[11] For Friedrich Schiller, the human being's ultimate goal was unity with Nature in a wholly rational-moral state. As I have suggested, this state was made possible only by cultivating the harmonious tension between the intellectual and sensuous components of one's human nature through the auspices of art and the concomitant fine-tuning of one's aesthetic sensibilities. For the modern writer, then, art, not religion, became the means of salvation for the human condition.

In the Pythagorean School, connections between the realm above and the province below were first established numerically. Through analogical thinking in general and numerical associations in particular, the human being was able to connect the divine cosmos with the earthly realm. The first general image of these ties was the vision of the heavenly lyre.[12] To my knowledge, pre-Socratic and ancient Greek images of the lyre, while attentive at times to the phenomenon of tension, show no evidence of the possibility of rupture. Clearly, this aspect separates the modern writer Friedrich Schiller from the ancient Greek world.

Already long before Epicurus, followers of Pythagoras believed that the soul was imprisoned in the body. Because of this original condition, it was necessary for the human being to engage in various purification rites in order to prepare oneself for the reception of wisdom.[13] Whereas the body was to be purged by a disciplined and cultivated lifestyle (the seeds of Gnosticism are clear), the soul was to be purified through music and the study of philosophy.[14] For Friedrich Schiller, the eighteenth-century science of physiology had suggested that the healthy human being was the one who cultivated the harmonious tension between mind and body.

However, in the light of the advent of history as depicted in Schiller's essay, *Something Concerning the First Human Society According to the Proscriptions of the Mosaic Law,* the original bond between God and the human being had been severed. Having been thrown back on one's own native talents and abilities the human being was forced to cultivate first sense, then reason. Though, well after the Fall, human reason became the primary source of knowledge. By the time of the aftermath of the French Revolution, it was apparent that the development (*Bildung*) and refinement of the human senses was first necessary before the original harmony between reason and sense could be restored. Friedrich Schiller's creative reinscriptions of the ancient symbol of the stringed instrument represent the operations of the universe. However, in the light of the problem of modernity, Schiller's writings register an acute awareness that, when properly tuned, the strings of a musical instrument can produce melodic, i.e., beautiful music and, when improperly tuned, lassitude or rupture.

According to the classical philologist Leonid Zhmud (St. Petersburg, Russia), whose specialty is the science of Greek antiquity, the Pythagorean School comprehended the harmony of the spheres physically since the seven celestial bodies emit sounds that are discernible (and, by analogy, communicable) only on a seven-string lyre.[15] From this perspective, we can better understand Hans Schavernoch's claim that, for the pre-Socratics, the seven strings originally stood for the totality of the universe.[16] According to the Pythagoreans, sounds emanate from the movement of the seven celestial bodies. I wish to suggest that, for Friedrich Schiller, the stringed instrument symbolized the taut relationships between all things. According to Schiller's third medical dissertation, in order for harmony between mind and body to exist, the strings must first be plucked. In the final analysis, then, it is incumbent upon the individual to play and, if possible, master the instrument of one's own body and mind. The assumption is this: the more one engages in the work of culture on a personal level, the more one furthers the goals (political and moral) of rational-moral society as a whole.

Hans Schavernoch points out that the divine (melodious) sound ("Wohlklang") or heavenly symphony, which ancient religious healers ("Heilbringer") were able to discern, was known as the music of the angels in the Christian world.[17] Through music, the powers of the soul ("Seelenkräfte") would be restored to their original, harmonious balance.[18] Thus, in the ancient world, music was appreciated for its magical, healing power. In Schiller's writings, we have also found substantial evidence of the healing power of art. But, with the modern German writer, art serves not only as the means for cultivating aesthetic sensibility in the individual but also for promoting the interests of the rational, moral, and aesthetic state that mark the completion of history. In the end, however, this goal remains an eternal hope, or, as Schiller states repeatedly, merely an idea ("bloß eine Idee").

Contrary to Hans Schavernoch's short account of Schiller and Pythagoras, the harmony of the spheres, for Schiller, is not simply ("nur") "the work of transference of the inner harmony of the human being to the heavenly province."[19] For the primary mission of culture, for Schiller, was to encourage the health and healing of both body and mind by tapping and cultivating the power of the harmonious tension in the hope of actualizing the rational-moral state.

In the light of Schiller's consistent employment of the ancient symbol of the lyre in his writings, it is a curious fact that, on June 7, 1805, at a memorial service held in the Hamburg German Theater, Johann Friedrich Schink and others should have reintroduced the symbol in their choral eulogy for the writer. The first four lines of the eighth strophe read:

Wer wird, wie er, die Leyer wieder schlagen?
Mit seinem Zauber, seiner Geisteskraft,
Ihm gleich, den Flug in's Land der Dichtung wage,
Nie, seit er reist', im Adlerschwung' erschlafft!

[Who, but he, will be able to strike the lyre like that again?
With his magic, his power of mind,
[Who], like him, will dare undertake the flight into the land of poetry;
Never, since he began his journey, and his wings rested!][20]

Though not great poetry, these lines highlight the importance of the symbol of the stringed instrument for an understanding of Schiller's oeuvre.

Finally, Schiller's gesture toward the ancient Greeks should not be mistaken as a sign of Jean Jacques Rousseau's philosophy of the return to nature. For the writer makes it plain that unity in spirit between the ancients and "us" moderns is first necessary for the (historical) advancement of culture. Such an agreement, he implies, will propel us beyond the present moment. The qualification Schiller makes near the beginning of his essay *Concerning Naive and Sentimental Poetry* bears repeating. "We perceive, perpetually, in them [the ancient Greeks] that which recedes from us [moderns], but toward which we are required to struggle, and which we are allowed to hope to approximate even if we can never attain it, save in infinite progression" (NA 20: 415).[21] In spite of my reservations of his provocative and polemical criticisms of the writer's work, Klaus Berghahn stated the matter well when he professed that the writer sought "the present in the past in order to give shape to the future."[22]

Postscript

On the way back to Schiller's residence from a lecture sponsored by the Natural Scientific Society (Naturforschende Gesellschaft) in Jena, Goethe wrote the word "Urpflanze" (prototype of all plants) down on a piece of paper. Goethe's account of this moment provides us with a deeper appreciation of the contours of the partnership between Goethe and Schiller. Goethe: "We arrived at his house, the conversation [we were having] enticed me to enter; there I recited, in a lively manner, the 'Metamorphosis of Plants' and, with some characteristic strokes of the pen, let a symbolic plant emerge before his eyes. He [Schiller] perceived it and observed all of this with great interest ("mit großer Anteilnahme") [and] with decisive power of comprehension ("mit entschiedener Fassungskraft"). When I stopped, however, he shook his head and said: That's not an experience; it's an idea."[23] Though Goethe then remarked that, like a learned Kantian ("ein gebildeter Kantianer"), Schiller's statement exhibited the very point that separated them, namely idea ("Idee") versus experience ("Erfahrung"), it is ironic that Schiller's response was intended to remind his friend that the conception of such a prototype was merely an idea! The question arises, then, as to who, Goethe or Schiller, at that moment, was more in touch with the reality of Nature. It is apparent that Schiller's depiction of the dualistic relationship between himself and Goethe, i.e., between analysis and organic re-creation in the important letter of August 23, 1794, should not be taken literally.

In the historical section of his work *Toward a Theory of Colors,* which was completed five years after Schiller's death, Goethe paid his friend a remarkable tribute. Recalling the lively intellectual engagement which his "irreplaceable Schiller" had demonstrated whenever they discussed his interests, Goethe wrote: "With great naturalness of genius, he [Schiller] not only comprehended quickly the main points we were discussing; but, when I sometimes hesitated on my contemplative path ("auf meinem beschaulichem Wege"), he forced me to forge ahead by way of his reflective power and, at the same time, drove me to the goal I was seeking."[24] Goethe's remembrances and notes of thanks provide posterity with a loving testimony to the native speed of Schiller's intellect, the thoroughness of his studies, and the soundness of his judgment.

Appendix:
Conversations with Hans-Georg Gadamer and Jürgen Habermas: A Chapter on the Reception of Friedrich Schiller in the Twentieth Century

Hans-Georg Gadamer

I met Hans-Georg Gadamer on February 13, 1991, at the Karl Ruprecht University in Heidelberg.[1] Our encounter was neither an interview nor a one-sided monologue. It was a truly engaging and enriching conversation.

Gadamer mentioned just having returned from a conference on the problem of form at the university in Göttingen. Immediately, he turned to Kant's *Critique of the Power of Judgment* and to ancient Greek philosophy. It was the opening of a discussion. I shared with him my experience of working with Schiller's personal copy of Kant's work, which he found especially interesting. We would return, near the end of our exchange, to a discussion of the marginal notations and the significance of the work for an understanding of the writer. There is no doubt that Gadamer is interested, almost exclusively, in Friedrich Schiller the philosopher, and that, by his own admission, he knows nothing about Schiller's poetry.

It was clear to me that Gadamer wished to be challenged, but he also wanted to instruct. His paternal approach to discussing important issues reminded me of the form of the Socratic dialogues. However, I detected no great desire on his part to entwine me in my own line of argumentation. Indeed, throughout the entire session, I detected a genuine sense of humanity in the man. Still, he was the one in control of the exchange of ideas. Perhaps because his love of wisdom was so clearly in evidence, the one and one-half hours passed almost without notice.

My idea of writing a chapter on the reception of Schiller in the twentieth century met with enthusiasm. Indeed, Gadamer seemed very interested in cooperating. He agreed that Schiller's ideas do play an important role in his own writings. The first impetus ("Anregung"), he thought, came from Ernst Cassirer (*Freiheit und Form*). He also mentioned the influence of Nicolai Hartmann on his thought. The encounter with Martin Heidegger was, for him, nothing short of inspirational ("inspirierend"). Still, his own ideas concerning the nature of the work of art, he insisted, have far less to do with Heidegger than with Hölderlin's poetry—and that of Rilke and the Stefan George Circle. Concerning his own education and encounter with the work of Schiller, Gadamer's understanding of the philosophical writer is informed by the Neo-Kantian Marburg School, in particular by its critique of Idealism.

A. Ernst Cassirer on Schiller

Gadamer's first serious encounter with the philosophy of Friedrich Schiller was Ernst Cassirer's book *Freedom and Form* [*Freiheit und Form*] (1923). The final chapter on Schiller is conditioned by the philosopher's approach. In the 1920s and 1930s, *Geistesgeschichte* [the history of the mind, or ideas] was driven by the resurgence of the *Geisteswissenschaften* (human and humanistic "sciences") in the work of Wilhelm Dilthey. In Hegelian fashion, Cassirer focused on the "life of the spirit/mind" ("Leben des Geistes"),[2] especially on "the German life of the spirit/mind" ("das deutsche Geistesleben").[3] In Dante, for instance, Cassirer perceived "the greatest domineering person ("Herrschernatur") which the history of world-literature has known" and an individual who comprehended the world "as a unified and unbroken lawful order."[4] Cassirer's pre-understanding on this point emerged again somewhat later in the text when he declared: "'Reality' is not an incoherent complex of particulars but a whole whose structure can be expressed in general principles, from which the peculiarity of being and individual objects are determined in progressive determination."[5]

Cassirer privileges subjectivity (*Subjektivität*) over concrete historical and political realities. This becomes transparent in his account of the Renaissance and the rise of humanism. "The I discovers itself in its control over the world—no matter whether this power represents itself in the form of historical-political reality or is cloaked in more complex intellectual-ideal forms."[6] Like both Schiller and Goethe, Cassirer reveres the development of personality; only in Cassirer's case this emphasis leads to a different conclusion: "Nothing is, in and of itself, good or bad, desirable or regrettable ("lust—oder leidvoll"), but everything depends on what I make of it."[7] The idea that the ego has its center of being within itself and obeys its own innate law sets the stage for the philosopher's discussion of Schiller. From this orientation, it is understandable why Cassirer's exposition should have revolved around the central issues of freedom and the autonomy of art.

During the turbulent times of the Weimar Republic, we detect ever increasing emphasis on individual and artistic autonomy by leading German intellectuals such as Ernst Cassirer. Thinking about the rather rapid development of the natural sciences in his time, Cassirer was convinced that "autonomy within the individual fields had to be won before its new intellectual connection could be tied and truly substantiated."[8] Later in his writing, Cassirer isolates "that general tendency of the German life of the spirit/mind," namely "that the individual fields complete their growth and their intellectual justification at the same time and alongside each other."[9] From the perspective of German *Geistesgeschichte,* the cultivation of autonomy is mirrored in the classical German epoch of literature, of which Cassirer remarks: "aesthetic reflection and criticism becomes the productive condition for the creative process."[10] For Cassirer, the correspondence between Goethe and Schiller is highly representative of this development.

Perhaps the clearest example of the tendency toward autonomy in the 1920s and 1930s was the Stefan George Circle of friends. Of this circle, Gadamer noted in his *Philosophical Apprenticeship* [*Philosophische Lehrjahre*]: "It was a circle of young people who formed something like a church: *extra ecclesiam nulla salus.* I myself stood outside [the circle], and, as someone told me later, forbidden to associate with the disciples."[11] As much as Gadamer appreciated Max Kommerell as a friend,[12] he was influenced far less by Kommerell's essays, including the portrayal of Schiller in *The Poet as Leader in German Classicism* (*Der Dichter als Führer in der deutschen Klassik*] (1928]), than he was by Ernst Cassirer. But, then, Kommerell appreciated the psychologist and not so much the philosopher in Schiller. Furthermore, Gadamer was Heidegger's disciple and Kommerell Stefan George's.

Cassirer denigrates Schiller's intense study of Nature by overemphasizing the writer's interest in subjectivity, i.e., the *Geist*. Since his point of departure is the life of the German mind, Cassirer assumes that Schiller was a precursor to German Idealism.[13] According to the twentieth-century philosopher, Schiller's early dramas capture the spirit of the writer's work. A psychological reaction to the harsh discipline and sheer force of will of Duke Carl Eugen and Schiller's early resistance to that orientation in the name of the "purity of moral personality" ("Reinheit der sittlichen Persönlichkeit") are reasons the philosopher generates to explain the nature of the young writer's work.[14] Cassirer's Hegelian terminology and purely philosophical interest lead him to a dramatic conclusion concerning Schiller: "Nature, for him [Schiller], is the conflict and the antithesis to the idea of freedom."[15] Rather than emphasize Schiller's interest in the world of ideas, I have sought to disclose the writer's appreciation of Nature. Though the early writer was well aware of the potential breach between world *(Welt)* and spirit/mind *(Geist)* within Nature *(The Philosophy of Physiology)*, the goal of maintaining the harmonious tension between the corporeal and the mental was one of Schiller's most fundamental objectives since the time of the third medical dissertation. We have seen that this taut equilibrium remains the primary goal throughout the later writings as well, though, in that period of his life, Schiller tended to compensate for the limitations of the body with the power of the mind. This is disclosed, in particular, by the writer's preoccupation with the concept of the sublime as well as by the writing of *Mary Stuart*. According to Cassirer, however, young Schiller demanded of the artist, as well as the philosopher and the poet that, "in that happy moment of the ideal," they "really are the great and good human beings whose image they depict."[16] But Cassirer lifts this statement from the essay "Julius's Theosophy" without appreciating the writer's awareness of the fragmentation of the ideal in modern times.

Cassirer's account of Schiller is overpowered by the conviction that the minds of Schiller and Goethe form polar opposites. In fact, the philosopher begins his chapter on Schiller by differentiating sharply between the two writers, a juxtaposition that takes the form of an antithesis encountering a thesis and the hope of achieving synthesis. "When it became a habit early for the one [Goethe] to consider even hostile forces of life and individuals as 'wholly real,' objectively determined beings of Nature, then, with Schiller, everywhere there ruled the passionate indignation against everything that is merely given and fixed externally."[17] Our discussion of the early prose work *Criminal Out of Infamy,* with its emphasis on immutable natural laws, and the morally responsible decision of Christian Wolf (as well as the decision of Karl in *The Robbers*) strongly suggests that there was a different reason for the affinity between Schiller and Goethe, namely their common interest in Nature. But, whereas Goethe dealt more extensively than Schiller with natural science, Schiller was more concerned with physiology. In any case, both writers were interested in determining the relation between human nature and Nature in general. This common interest in the collaborative endeavors of the two writers has been buried beneath the narrowly philosophical preoccupation with Hegelian dialectics. To be sure, Cassirer is correct to observe that, for Schiller, reflection remains an active element ("aktives Element") in the formation of his total view ("Gesamtansicht"): "in its continual development, the theory of form constitutes ("bildet") a necessary component in the construction of the concrete world of form itself."[18] For Cassirer, this is the intellectual center of Schiller's poetry and philosophy.[19] However, it is not only further reflection (reason) but also the cultivation of the faculty of sensation which, according to Schiller's own writings, is equally necessary for the development of humankind. Hence, by overemphasizing Schiller's attention to form, Cassirer bypasses the role of sense education in aesthetic culture. Both the rational form-impulse (*Formtrieb*) and the sensuous material-drive (*Stofftrieb*) first become creative (or *bildend*) in and through the auspices of the play-impulse (*Spieltrieb*). To be sure, Schiller does state, in the fourteenth letter, that the reciprocal cooperation ("Wechselverhältnis") of both drives is "simply" a task of reason. Yet, it is a task which the human being is first able to accomplish in the process of completing his/her being.

It is in the most precise sense of the word *the Idea of his [or her] Human Nature*, hence something Infinite, to which in the course of time he can approximate ever more closely, but without ever being able to attain it (W/W 95).

[Es ist im eigentlichsten Sinne des Worts die Idee seiner Menschheit, mithin ein Unendliches, dem er sich im Laufe der Zeit immer mehr nähern kann, aber ohne es jemals zu erreichen. (NA 20: 352–353)]

The ultimate task of culture ("Aufgabe der *Kultur*") is the cultivation (*Bildung*) of both the faculty of feeling ("Ausbildung des Gefühlsvermögens") and the faculty of reason ("Ausbildung des Vernunftvermögens") and their tense, yet fruitful remarriage.

According to the *Aesthetic Education of the Human Being,* the true aesthetic condition is rooted in a middle mood ("mittlere Stimmung") in which the mind is pressured neither physically nor morally and yet remains active in both capacities (letter 20). A productive aesthetic mood is attained when, through the cooperative opposition ("Entgegensetzung") of both the form and the material impulses, the relative negation ("Negation") of both is realized, no matter how momentarily. This new aesthetic state is the condition of real and active determinacy ("Zustand der realen und aktiven Bestimmbarkeit"). Therefore, the aesthetic state is achieved only through the activity of the play-impulse (*Spieltrieb*), in and through which the human being enters the realm of freedom.

The play-drive, in consequence, as the one in which both the others act in concert, will exert upon the psyche at once a moral and a physical constraint; it will, therefore, since it annuls all contingency, annul all constraint too, and set man [the human being] free both physically and morally (W/W 97).

[Der Spieltrieb also, als in welchem beyde (der Formtrieb und der sinnliche Trieb) verbunden wirken, wird das Gemüth zugleich moralisch und physisch nöthigen; er wird also, weil er alle Zufälligkeit aufhebt, auch alle Nöthigung aufheben und den Menschen, sowohl physisch als moralisch in Freiheit setzen. (NA 20: 354)]

Cassirer's sharp distinction between art and reality undoubtedly influenced the work of Hans-Georg Gadamer. Though Cassirer recognizes that, for Schiller, entering the realm of ideas with beauty does not mean leaving the world of sense,[20] the value of this process, for him, consists in canceling out the "change between doing and passivity," that is, between "work and enjoyment," which is the essence of all practical action.[21] Aesthetic humanity consists not in treating Nature as a restriction but in restricting its arbitrariness ("Willkür"). Though referring directly to Schiller's statements concerning the two fundamental laws of our nature and the idea that the human being "should externalize everything inward and form everything external," Cassirer maintains that, in the moment of aesthetic humanity, "we cast aside ["beseitigen"] the world in order to draw the world to us; here we stand opposite the world in the freedom of reflection and pure contemplation, though we are completely imbued with its content. Beauty is at once our condition and our deed."[22] But rather than appreciate the harmonious tension inhering in beauty, Cassirer says of living form ("lebende Gestalt") that it does not comprise a whole of heterogenous components "but, rather, a synthesis in which the difference is at once retained and canceled ["aufgelöst"]."[23] In the end, Cassirer blurs the distinction between poetry and philosophy seeing in both the very same principle of origin, namely the basic antinomy between freedom and form which is then brought to a resolution ("Lösung"). [24]

B. Gadamer on Play

Hans-Georg Gadamer elucidates the nature of play ("Spiel") at the beginning of part 2 of his *Truth and Method* (1960). Almost immediately, it becomes apparent where the difference between the twentieth-century philosopher and the eighteenth-century writer lies. According to Gadamer, the conception of play found in Kant and Schiller is rooted in subjectivity. By contrast, Gadamer focuses on "the mode of being of play" ("Seinsweise des Spiels").[25] The phenomenon of play also determines the mode of being of the work of art. Hence, the concept of play is ontologically conditioned. It is a basic characteristic of being in the world.

Gadamer is not interested in the "freedom of a subjectivity engaged in play, but the mode of being of the work of art itself."[26] Since Gadamer considers play ontologically, he can argue that we cannot know anything about the nature or essence of play by considering only the subjective reflection of the player. No subject that plays can be held hostage. "The play is the occurrence of the movement as such."[27] When we say that something is in play, we do not mean the subject, that is, ourselves necessarily, but that something is in motion. Something is happening. All play is something that is being played ("ein Gespieltwerden," or an "Etwas-Spielen").[28] In short, Gadamer prioritizes the phenomenon of play rather than the consciousness of playing.[29]

Concerning certain selective affinities between Schiller and Kant, Gadamer sees in Schiller's concern for the moral freedom of the player a turning point ("Wendepunkt") away from Kant's transcendental idea of taste.[30] Schiller's new imperative reads: "Live aesthetically!"[31] What Schiller has done is to transform Kant's theoretical-methodical procedure into a practical-moral task. Gadamer sees that Schiller's practice of moral freedom was indebted not to Kant, but to Fichte,[32] and he submits that Schiller understood play "anthropologically in terms of Fichte's theory of impulses: the play impulse was to harmonize the form impulse and the matter impulse."[33] Gadamer then insists that the cultivation of the play-impulse was "the end of aesthetic education" for Schiller.[34] In the final analysis, the "subject" of playing is "not the player but instead the game itself."[35] It is with these last two points that I must take exception with Gadamer.

Nonetheless, there are at least two structural affinities between Gadamer and Schiller. First, Schiller's turn from Kant is akin to Gadamer's own turn from the Königsberg philosopher. As Schiller turned to Fichte, so Gadamer turned to Heidegger, though in the case of the former the eventual break with the German idealist was complete, whereas, in Gadamer's case, Heidegger has remained the main inspiration. Like Heidegger, Gadamer is concerned primarily with the ontological study of being.

At this point, I would like to draw attention to a common thread in the intellectual development of Schelling and Heidegger. With the appearance of the *System of Transcendental Idealism* [*System des transcendentalen Idealismus*] (1800) and *The Origin of the Work of Art* [*Der Ursprung des Kunstwerkes*] (1935), Schelling and Heidegger alike lifted the work of art to the highest pedestal of human achievement.[36] For both philosophers, at this point in their respective careers, the work of art, not the philosophical treatise (Hegel), embodies and radiates truth. For Schelling, this is the truth concerning the underlying reality of the universe, the objectivization of the fundamental identity of all things. For Heidegger, however, the truth is "the disclosing or revelation of the Being of existing Reality,"[37] which he calls an event ("Geschehnis").[38] In *Truth and Method,* Gadamer wanted to demonstrate just "how much there is of *event* effective in all *understanding.*"[39] For Gadamer, however, unlike the more mature Schelling and Heidegger, philosophy and not art is still the highest form of truth. Hence, Gadamer tacitly rejects Schelling's earlier prioritizing of art over philosophy and follows Hegel's insistence that philosophy stands higher than art at least with respect to knowledge.

Literature, for Gadamer, "is a function of being intellectually preserved and handed down, and therefore brings its hidden history into every age."[40] Literature is the playing field "where art and science merge."[41] There is "nothing so strange, and at the same time so demanding, as the written word."[42] For, "The written word and what partakes of it—literature—is the intelligibility of mind transferred to the most alien medium."[43] Therefore, "Nothing is so purely the trace of the mind as writing, but nothing is so dependent on the understanding mind either."[44] Gadamer's conclusion is especially insightful:

> Just as we were able to show that the being of the work of art is play and that it must be perceived by the spectator in order to be actualized ("vollendet"), so also it is universally true of texts that only in the process of understanding them is the dead trace of meaning transformed back into living meaning.[45]

As Gadamer takes great pains to demonstrate, it is a text's power to express ("Aussagekraft") a truth that enamors the reader to the written word.

For Schelling, beauty comprehended as "the infinite finitely presented"[46] is synonymous with the true work of art. The converse is also true: "without beauty there is no work of art."[47] However, for Schelling, beauty is a by-product of the resolution of an infinite contradiction between conscious and unconscious activity that characterizes the work of art. In the final analysis, for Schelling, as for Gadamer, beauty is of secondary importance to the transmission of the truth of the underlying identity of reality which the work of art reflects.

Even for Martin Heidegger, beauty is "appearance that has been placed into the work" ("das ins Werk gefügte Scheinen").[48] For Gadamer's mentor, as well, beauty conveys truth or, to be exact, a truth. In the "Nachwort" to *The Origin of the Work of Art (Der Ursprung des Kunstwerks),* for instance, Heidegger describes the relationship between beauty and truth as follows: "When(ever) truth is placed into the work, it [beauty] appears. This coming into appearance—as this being of truth in the work and as the work—is beauty. Thus the beautiful belongs in the occurring [happening] of truth."[49] Beauty, then, is only one way in which truth reveals itself: "Beauty is a way in which truth is present as unconcealment" ("Schönheit ist eine Weise, wie Wahrheit als Unverborgenheit west").[50]

Let us now return to Gadamer's concept of play before critiquing his understanding of Schiller. In *Truth and Method,* Gadamer maintained that play "clearly represents an order in which the to-and-fro motion of play follows of itself."[51] He asserts that the "ease of play—which naturally does not mean that there is any real absence of effort ("Fehlen der Angestrengheit") but refers phenomenologically only to the absence of strain—is experienced subjectively as relaxation ("Entlastung").[52] However, while it may be that strain is absent, tension is still very much part of the game of playing. The Dutch philosopher Johann Huizinga (*Homo Ludens: Vom Ursprung der Kultur im Spiel),* whom Gadamer cites, refers to the fact that "through the contest arises the tense ("spannungsvolle") to-and-fro movement from which the victor emerges."[53] Unlike Huizinga (and Schiller), however, Gadamer attempts to deny that tension inheres in play. "A person playing is, even in his play, still someone who comports himself, even if the proper essence of the game consists in his disburdening himself of the tension ("Anspannung") he feels in his purposive comportment."[54] In the final analysis, however, the human being who plays "cannot enjoy the freedom of playing himself out without transforming the aims of his purposive behavior into mere tasks of the game."[55] For Gadamer, then, it is not so much the purpose of the game to solve the task as it is to order and shape the movement of the game itself.[56]

Yet, "first and foremost, play is self-presentation,"[57] and this is itself "a universal ontological characteristic of nature."[58] Gadamer thus differs from Schiller in that, for him, "the self-presentation of human play depends on the player's conduct being tied to the make-believe goals of the game."[59] In the end, however, "the 'meaning' of these goals does not in fact depend on their being achieved,"[60] whereas, for Schiller, the ultimate completion of the rational-moral state depends completely on the degree of success of the aesthetic education of human beings.

Clearly, Friedrich Schiller's theory of play has had a tremendous impact on Western thought in the twentieth century. Even Jacques Derrida, no intellectual companion of Gadamer's, but an individual who, willingly or self-deniably, has learned much from Heidegger, has also developed a distinct concept of play. In his important essay "Structure, Sign and Play in the Discourse of the Human Sciences,"[61] for instance, we note the need, especially of deconstructionist thought, to privilege play. For it is precisely play or, rather, "the *play* of the structure" which keeps the presence or fixed origin of the center from closing.[62] In other words, play is the term naming the open-ended activities of a decentered universe. As a result, "the reference to play is always caught up in tension."[63] As we have now seen in the case of Friedrich Schiller, one of the central "classical problem[s]" is, as Derrida also perceives, the very "tension with history."[64] Furthermore, "Besides the tension between play and history, there is also the tension between play and presence," since, for the French philosopher, "play is the disruption of presence," or "play of absence and presence," though, to be sure "play must be conceived of before the alternative of presence and absence."[65] Before we transcend the bounds of the present study, however, let us return to Gadamer's account of Friedrich Schiller.

C. Toward a Critique of Gadamer's Understanding of Schiller in *Truth and Method*

Gadamer was quite right to underscore "Schiller's call for aesthetic freedom against mechanistic society", and to see in the writer one of the "forerunners of the protest against modern industrial society, one who advocated living feeling [form]"[66] against the cold insensitivity of pure reason. However, in *Truth and Method*, Gadamer assailed what he called "The Dubiousness [Fragwürdigkeit] of the Concept of Aesthetic Cultivation (Bildung)." By transforming Kant's transcendental idea of taste into a moral demand, Gadamer contends, Schiller assigned a content to the universality of aesthetic judgment. Gadamer maintains that, when Schiller spoke of art as the practice of freedom, the writer was referring more to Fichte's theory of drives than to Kant.[67] Gadamer assumes, however, that where art rules, the boundaries of reality are transcended. He maintains, in the *Aesthetic Education of the Human Being in a Series of Letters*, that Schiller had advocated that individual human beings comport themselves aesthetically. This means that they not only educate themselves *"through* art but also *for* art," that is, that they inhabit an ideal realm rather than the real community in which they live.[68] "But since reality, moral, social, and scientific, has now been ceded to the un-ideal realm of non-art, art itself undergoes a corresponding change. It comes to be seen as artifice, appearance, and unreality."[69] As provocative as this latter position may be, I have argued, in effect, that Schiller's writing does not suggest a sharp "contrast" between the appearances of art and harsh reality, primarily because of the writer's high regard for the indispensability of experience and the cultivation of aesthetic sensibility. In the end, Gadamer's account of Schiller is consistent with idealist readings of Schiller's writings. It is hardly coincidental, then, that Gadamer should see in Helmut Kuhn's study *Die Vollendung der klassischen deutschen Ästhetik durch Hegel* such an "excellent account."[70]

For the writer of *Concerning the Aesthetic Education of the Human Being*, however, aesthetics is grounded in the experience (and sensuousness) of the individual members of a particular society and not in some ideal world. Schiller's practical maxim is: "Dare to be wise!" ("Erkühne dich, weise zu sein"). Surely, in light of sensitive knowledge, aesthetics is related to human nature, i.e., reality. The intersection between the later aesthetics and early physiology must then alter the view that has dominated narrative descriptions of Schiller's program of aesthetic education in the twentieth century. In this study, I have striven to show that Schiller appreciated the complementation between art and Nature and that, contrary to Gadamer, they were not simply "contrasted as appearance and reality."[71] It is for this reason that Schiller's program of enlightened self- and social development is no longer "dubious," as the contemporary German philosopher contends.

Still, Gadamer insists that, with the concept of aesthetic education, art "becomes a standpoint of its own and establishes its own autonomous claim to supremacy."[72]

For him, "an education by art becomes an education to art. Instead of art's preparing us for true moral and political freedom, we have the culture of an 'aesthetic state,' a cultured society ("Bildungsgesellschaft") that takes an interest in art."[73] But "cultivating the play impulse," as Gadamer contends, is *not* "the end of aesthetic education."[74] Schiller may well have wanted "to embrace everything of quality, from all cultures and all times,"[75] thereby promoting universality, but what kept him from merely abstracting reality was his respect for the further development and unique contributions of individuals and of specific cultures. Most likely, this posture developed out of his study of Johann Gottfried Herder's *Also a Philosophy of History for the Development of Humankind [Auch eine Philosophie der Geschichte zur Bildung der Menschheit]* (1774) as well as from his own knowledge of history.[76] Most important, however, the true goal of aesthetic education, for the writer of *Concerning the Aesthetic Education of the Human Being,* is the cultivation of a truly moral-rational state wherein, with the aid of aesthetics, sensation is reunited with reason. In short, twentieth-century readings of Schiller's work by prominent German philosophers and some outstanding scholars of literature have not appreciated the writer's profound understanding of the task of culture.

One of the fundamental problems of Gadamer's philosophy with respect to Friedrich Schiller, as well as in the scholarly literature on the writer (e.g., Klaus Berghahn), is the assumption, conditioned, as it is, by Hegel's generally positive reception of Schiller, that Schiller was an early proponent of German Idealism. It is significant that Gadamer would have been quick to tell me that he "knows nothing" about Schiller's poetry ("Dichtung"). This helps to explain why Gadamer uncritically accepts Hegel's appropriation of Schiller in the mainstream of German Idealism. Furthermore, in addition to aligning Schiller with the tradition of German Idealism, Gadamer may well have been influenced by Marcuse's positive reception of Schiller, a topic to which we will return in our discussion of Jürgen Habermas. The relation of Friedrich Schiller to German Idealism is an intriguing problem. Gadamer was most interested in my account of Schiller's relationship to Fichte and the writer's suggestions to Wilhelm von Humboldt that he—Schiller—was never convinced by the arguments advanced by what have come to be known as the German Idealists.[77] Indeed, when I asked him about the writer's repeated employment of the phrase "merely an idea" ("bloß eine Idee"), Gadamer immediately carried this back to the mind-body problem and Schiller's encounter with corporeality ("Leiblichkeit"). Perhaps as a natural extension of the problem of the body which he himself was experiencing at the moment, he characterized Schiller as "ein Arzt seines Selbstes" (his own physician).

I shared with Gadamer Wolfgang Riedel's formulation of the field of tension between metaphysics and anthropology ("Spannungsfeld zwischen Metaphysik und Anthropologie") in Schiller's works. He thought that this was on the right track ("auf der richtigen Spur"). For him, it also helped clarify Schiller's special interpretation of Kant's concept of duty (*Pflicht*), which, as he was quick to insist, demands more insight ("Einsicht") than repression ("Verdrängung")—"as you Americans understand it" ("wie Sie Amerikaner es verstehen"!). On this point, Gadamer's respect for tradition was most glaring.

In concluding the discussion, I mentioned my plans to visit Jürgen Habermas. Among other things, Gadamer was happy to share with me the fact that he had helped secure a position for Habermas at the very beginning of his career. We will have an opportunity to explore this fascinating connection between the two German philosophers in the section on Habermas.

Transition

The introduction to Hans-Georg Gadamer's *Truth and Method* (1992) [*Wahrheit und Methode*] (1960) contains numerous references to one of the two words for "experience" in German. The editors of the most recent English edition of this commanding work have done an excellent job of determining the meanings of key words employed by Gadamer to elucidate his ideas on hermeneutics. Joel Weinsheimer and Donald G. Marshall distinguish clearly between the personal experiences (*Erlebnisse*) which we "have" and the experience (*Erfahrung*) we "undergo." In the moment of personal experience, "subjectivity is overcome and drawn into an 'event' (*Geschehen*) of meaning."[78] This latter meaning of experience (hereafter: Experience) has nothing to do with momentary events but with "an ongoing integrative process" in which our horizon of understanding is widened and where we gain insight into the limitations of a particular perspective. In my experience, the widening of the horizon of understanding unlocks the door to reflection which, by virtue of the insight's location in Experience, would also seem to encourage self-criticism. In Experience, then, reason becomes intersubjective. Herein, I believe, lies the Gordian knot between Gadamer's philosophical hermeneutics and Habermas's theory of communicative action. The emphasis on experience and intersubjective communication also relates to Friedrich Schiller's *Concerning the Aesthetic Education of the Human Being,* the one work by Schiller about which both contemporary German philosophers are most conversant.

To the extent that Gadamer seeks to account for the tradition or transmission ("Überlieferung") of "the classical heritage"[79] into the present, and given his belief in the "truth" of the experience ["Erfahrung"] of art[80] (which cannot be attained "in any other way" [*Truth and Method,* p. 80]), there is, quite clearly, a deeper-lying affinity between the twentieth-century philosopher and the work of Friedrich Schiller. Indeed, the interest in the collaborative work of philosophy and art underlies and, I think, forms the major impetus behind the project of modern hermeneutics which Gadamer tracks in *Truth and Method.* In the foreword to the second edition, for instance, Gadamer acknowledged that the section on experience in his work (part 2, II.3.B.) "takes on a systematic and key position in [his] investigations."[81] This interest in the nature and role of experience intersects with Gadamer's chief interest in *Truth and Method.* For, "together with the experience of philosophy, the experience of art," Gadamer writes, "is the most insistent admonition to scientific consciousness to acknowledge [recognize] its own limits."[82] "Hence these studies on hermeneutics, which start from the experience of art and of historical tradition, try to present the hermeneutic phenomenon in its full extent."[83]

In the foreword to the second edition of *Truth and Method,* Gadamer asserts "that everyone who experiences a work of art incorporates this experience wholly within himself: that is, into the totality of his self-understanding, within which it means something to him."[84] This idea is closely related to Schiller's expressed belief in the power of art to shape consciousness and, with the thought of revolutionizing "the modes of perception," also human action, at which point art becomes socially relevant, indeed a creative force in the restructuring of society itself.

It is important to reiterate the fact that hermeneutics, for Gadamer, does not constitute a methodology. It is, rather, "a theory of the real experience that thinking is."[85] This also presupposes that modern-day, philosophical hermeneutics is not an art of interpretation. It is, rather, a cognitive process of observation, critical self-reflection, and understanding. There is a point in *Truth and Method* where Gadamer's writings intersect with the work of, and disclose something of essential importance to the philosopher Friedrich Schiller. For, according to the twentieth-century philosopher, "The philosopher, of all people, must . . . be aware of *the tension* between what he claims to achieve and the reality in which he finds himself" [emphasis mine].[86] Perhaps this is why, in our conversation of February 13, 1991, Gadamer was struck by the possibility of Schiller's enlightened self-criticism of the limits of his own theorizing.

Jürgen Habermas

I met Jürgen Habermas in his office in the philosophy department at the Johann Wolfgang Goethe University in Frankfurt on April 22, 1991. He was on time and rather surprised that I had actually showed up to speak to him. I was invited into his office almost immediately. There was no sense of being rushed, and I was made to feel welcome.[87]

Habermas is *menschlich* (humane), but he is not as warm as Gadamer. Like Gadamer, he is a good or, rather, an acute listener. The personal differences between the two men are also fairly reliable signs of the differences in their intellectual outlooks: Habermas's belief in the merits of critical, communicative reason and social-political engagement versus Gadamer's application of self-reflecting, self-critical reason and the pursuit of common understanding in and through dialogue. Whatever form their inquiries may take, however, both philosophers are committed to the articulation, communication and refinement of ideas.

Despite their philosophical differences, Gadamer and Habermas possess an undying respect for each other. Habermas gladly confirmed the fact that Gadamer had been instrumental in securing a position for him at the very beginning of his career, at which time he was carrying his dissertation around with him from one university to the next. In fact, Gadamer had invited Habermas to lecture on Schelling. There is little question that the real subject of that lecture was the relation between art and philosophy. I found it curious that, somewhat later in our conversation, Habermas would suggest that I compare Schiller and Schelling.

I did not convey to Habermas Gadamer's assessment of this moment in Habermas's career. Gadamer told me that Max Horkheimer and "Ted" (Theodor) Adorno, who otherwise agreed on everything else, it seemed, had disagreed about the substance and quality of Habermas's dissertation and that this disagreement was a sign that his contribution must be of real importance. Gadamer added that this was precisely what had led him to support Habermas and his work.[88] I wonder if Habermas was aware of this before he was invited to lecture on Schelling. In any case, Gadamer was very impressed with Habermas's lecture.[89] Despite the comparatively more conservative ideology underlying his philosophy, it was clear to me that Gadamer is tolerant of controversial ideas. It would seem then, that Gadamer subsumes all ideas, irrespective of their import, under the more general heading of the pursuit of understanding.

Unlike the dialogue with Gadamer, I was asked to begin the conversation. I find it curious that, after having been asked how long I had conversed with Gadamer, Habermas allowed me the very same amount of time to discuss my project. At first, the social philosopher resisted the idea that his own writings constitute a kind of subchapter in the reception of Schiller's ideas. The short excursus in *The Philosophical Discourse of Modernity* was clear to him, of course, but he still did not think that the German writer had been that important to his own thinking. I began to cite quite a few examples from his own works, beginning with *The Structural Transformation of the Public Sphere* [*Strukturwandel der Öffentlichkeit*] (1989) of 1962. Still somewhat reluctant to embrace Schiller, Habermas began recounting some aspects of his own "Bildungsgeschichte" (history of education), as he termed it. He reflected on how Hegel's and Marx's philosophies had impacted the development of his own ideas. His reading of Schiller, he thought, was informed most profoundly by the young Georg Lukács.

Interlude 1: Young Lukács on Schiller, and Habermas

In the central chapter on reification ("Verdinglichung") in *History and Class Consciousness* [*Geschichte und Klassenbewußtsein*] of 1923, the more radical Lukács claimed that Schiller's analysis of the play-impulse (the aesthetic principle) "contains very valuable insights into the question of reification, as is indeed true of all his aesthetic writings."[90] By pushing the concept of the play instinct far beyond the bounds of aesthetics per se, Schiller offers a modern-day classical philosophy. For the play-impulse is the agency that will restore the "socially destroyed, fragmented and divided" human being to wholeness.[91] The perpetual process of open-ended play (aesthetics), for the young Lukács, becomes a means to salvage the contents of life "from the deadening effects of the mechanism of reification."[92]

It is interesting that Habermas should have referred me to this aspect of his own history of education since it is here, in the context of Schiller's aesthetic ideas, that Lukács launched one of his most aggressive assaults on the notion of subjectivity (*Subjektivität*). The alleged objectivity of critical (Kant) and dialectical (Hegel) philosophy is, in reality, an objectivity within the bounds of subjectivity since, according to Lukács, these grounds are derived solely from the dogma of rationality (that is, without consideration of the material base of reality). The subjective principle of Kantian and Hegelian philosophy becomes conscious of itself within "the narrow confines of its own validity."[93]

The fact that Habermas should have recalled and recommended this chapter is also interesting in the light of his own theories of intersubjectivity and communicative reason in his *Theory of Communicative Action* [*Theorie des kommunikativen Handelns*] (1981f.). For it is in that work that Habermas explores the idea that the early Lukács and Critical Theory "conceived of reification as rationalization." Also in the *Philosophical Discourse of Modernity* Habermas maintained that the Hegelian Marxists (Lukács, Horkheimer, Adorno), with the help of Max Weber, "translated the *Capital* back into a theory of reification and re-stablished the interrupted connection between economics and philosophy."[94]

Next, Habermas directed me to his exchange of ideas with Herbert Marcuse on the nature of art and its function in contemporary society. In particular, he seemed taken by Schiller's idea of art in *Concerning the Aesthetic Education of the Human*

Being as the means to overcome the division ("Entzweiung") between Nature and reason.

Interlude 2: Herbert Marcuse and Habermas on Aesthetics

In his conversation with Herbert Marcuse in 1977, Habermas asked if Marcuse and Adorno had not reversed Hegel's emphasis on philosophy and, in effect, reinstated art as the sensuous appearance of the idea, that is, as the most direct means of creating and conveying concepts of a better life. We recall the value that Schelling had assigned to art. Marcuse argued that art is privileged because its unique language means a break with everyday reality. "The language of art carries on the subversion of everyday experience, an alienation from 'normality.'"[95] By subverting both consciousness and the unconscious, art emancipates the human being from the dominating principle of reality. Hence, the values encoded in everyday language are put into question—and examined, both rationally and affectively.

Habermas then charged that Marcuse had changed his opinion about the *affirmative* character of culture, especially the possibility of the suspension ("Aufhebung") of art. The joy Marcuse had once appreciated in beautiful appearances (a tie to Schiller's "Ode to Joy") had been dampened by the deep concern he felt when experiencing the burning of the books in Nazi Germany. At that moment, the Marxist critic believed he had witnessed one of the dangers of the culture of late capitalism, namely the integration of art into life, the attempt to reconcile life and art and, thus, according to Marcuse, to subvert the revolutionary power of the language of art. Once pushed, however, Marcuse suggests that had he had to write the same essay in the 1970s, he would have to weaken the idea of the affirmative character of art and foreground its "critical-communicative character."[96] In short, he concedes to Habermas.

Marcuse effectively counters Habermas's retelling of the (Hegelian) thesis of the end of art, however. According to this philosophy of the history of art, the rise of middle-class society brought with it the tendency to insulate art within a sphere of autonomy. Once middle-class society has run its course, then this type of art dissipates. According to Marcuse, however, the language of art always constitutes a break with everyday reality, irrespective of time. Precisely because it obeys its own laws and not the laws of existing reality, art continues to produce ever newer forms, thus creating a sphere that constantly challenges, and often criticizes, the existing status quo. Hence, Marcuse, somewhat like Friedrich Schiller, comprehended art as the "aestheticization of [social] contents" ("Ästhetisierung von Inhalten").[97] Unlike Schiller, however, Marcuse states the matter negatively: "When one surrenders the aesthetic form, one has surrendered art itself."[98] The sensuousness ("Versinnlichung") of the idea or concept in art is suspended or terminated only in transformation. This opens up a new way of seeing and/or hearing, which leads to knowledge ("Erkennen").[99] In the end, the truth of art is the result of "the inner connection of eros and beauty,"[100] captured in the imperative: "Es soll (muß) Friede sein, Erfüllung, Glück."[101] For Schiller, Eros does not play a central role in art; rather, beauty and sublimity are the primary agencies in the moral transformation of the human being in the direction of the fully rational-moral state. Unlike Marcuse, a utopia of happiness and fulfillment is not an essential element of Schiller's writings. Where the work of Marcuse and Schiller intersects, however, is on the point of the regenerative and transformative power of the forms of art. The essence of art, for Marcuse (and here we may add: for Schiller), as for the ancient Greeks, is beauty. Marcuse defines beauty "not" as "the object of art, but rather of the aesthetic form in which the object is re-presented."[102] Though Schiller states the matter positively, this definition comes very close to the eighteenth-century writer's search, in the *Kallias* Letters, for an objective ground of beauty.[103] Again, it would seem that the notion of the autonomy of art is, at best, relative though, in the final analysis, it remains socially and politically engaged.

When Habermas asserted that there can be no grounding ("Begründung") of normative contents, Marcuse countered that those normative contents would, according to his own system, be those of Eros and drive ("Trieb") in their fullest dynamic. He makes it abundantly clear that art should not take the place of a renounced ("abgedankte") reason as a protector of norms and, primarily so, because he is convinced that reason (like art) will outlive its middle-class form of appearance. The type of reason to which theory and art are committed, then, is not the narrow, middle-class concept thereof. Though there is an attempt, on Marcuse's part, to mediate the discussion, Habermas pushes the Marxist critic on the point that reason is anchored in the drive nature of the human being and that, when all is said and done, aesthetics is the true enlightening force. Clearly, Habermas rejects what is, originally, Fichte's theory of the drives, a theory that influenced the writing of Schiller's *Concerning the Aesthetic Education of the Human Being*.[104]

Habermas's Excursus on Schiller in *The Philosophical Discourse of Modernity*

Ten years after his dialogue with Herbert Marcuse, in the essay "Philosophy as Stand-In and Interpreter" (1987), Habermas called for the reenhancement of "the interplay between the cognitive-instrumental, moral-practical, and aesthetic-expressive dimensions that has come to a standstill today."[105] There is a link here to the excursus on Schiller, which Habermas embeds in his analysis of Hegel in the *Philosophical Discourse of Modernity* [*Der philosophische Diskurs der Moderne*] (1985). In his challenge to "post"-modernist thinking, Habermas approves of the emphasis Schiller seems to place on "the communicative, community-building and solidarity-giving force of art," namely "its *public character*," without, however, embracing what he thinks is the writer's "aesthetic utopia."[106]

Before proceeding, it is important to determine the context of the contemporary philosopher's remarks. To Habermas's understanding, Schiller's text *Concerning the Aesthetic Education of the Human Being* is "the first programmatic work toward an aesthetic critique of modernity."[107] This critique anticipates the philosophical analysis of modernity by those (Swabian) friends in Tübingen, namely Schelling, Hegel, and Hölderlin. Hence, the twentieth-century philosopher assigns Schiller's writings an important place within a tradition of German intellectual history that includes his own critique of the as yet unresolved problem of modernity. In effect, Habermas rallies the forces of the German intellectual tradition, specifically Kant, Hegel, Marx, and their successors, to combat the a-, or irrational influence of our "post"-modern era. It is an engaging battle, one that has put contemporary neo-structuralists, feminists, Marxists, and Derridians on the defensive, and perhaps has contributed, albeit indirectly, to the advancement of the New Historicism today.

In his rereading of Schiller, Habermas sees clearly that the writer had replaced religion with art as the chief means of transforming society. Because of his understanding of the bifold nature of history (the then and now), Habermas rewrites key aspects of Schiller's work into his own philosophical system. A key example is the following. Presumably, art, for Schiller, is effective as a unifying power ("vereinigende Macht") "because it is understood to be a 'form of communication' that enters into the intersubjective relationships between people."[108] Schiller, we are informed, comprehended art as "a communicative reason" ("eine kommunikative Vernunft") which, in the future, will be actualized in the aesthetic state.[109] However, given the historical context in which Schiller was living, the writer was exploring the paradigm of critical reason presented to him and his contemporaries by Kant's critical philosophy. Though his writings may suggest that art is a form of communicative reason, this does not mean that Schiller's representation of the function of art is wholly compatible with the contemporary philosopher's interpretation. Most important, however, Habermas recognizes the potential of Schiller's aesthetics for the eventual political transformation of society: "art itself is the medium for the education ["Bildung"] of the human race to true political freedom."[110] Hence, the appropriation of this part of Schiller's work among German philosophers today is still a vital part of our "post"-modernist age.

In the end, Habermas understands the goals of Schiller's "aesthetic utopia" to reside not in the "aestheticization of living conditions" ("Ästhetisierung der Lebensverhältnisse") but in "revolutionizing the conditions of mutual understanding" ("Revolutionierung der Verständigungsverhältnisse" [*PDM*, p.63]). The image Habermas conveys in his seminal work compels us to place into serious doubt a common notion disseminated by Schiller scholars at least since the early 1970s, namely Schiller's supposed aestheticization of the political (e.g., Klaus Berghahn).

Toward a Critique of Jürgen Habermas's Account of Schiller

Acknowledging the fact that Habermas enlisted Schiller into service to his own philosophy, we see that the type of reason he attributes to the writer is the ultimate goal and not the primary means of achieving the final state of completion. Here we should take seriously the writer's words in the eighth letter of *Concerning the Aesthetic Education of the Human Being,* that "the more pressing need of [modern, post-revolutionary] times" is not *more* reason but, rather, the "education ["Ausbildung"] of the faculty of sensation."[111] In order to be consistent with Schiller, the "revolutionizing of the conditions of mutual understanding" central to Habermas's program of communicative action must also be rooted in the sensuous nature of the human being. But it is precisely this aspect of Schiller's work that Habermas wishes to discredit, as we recall from his conversation with Marcuse.

It is important to acknowledge the fact that Schiller's concern with the vital role of sensuous experience and the refinement of sensuality through art distinguishes him from the philosophy of Immanuel Kant. It is a distinguishing aspect of the Gadamer-Habermas debates around 1970. Though overstated, perhaps, David Couzens Hoy (*The Critical Circle*) has suggested: "Gadamer fears that Habermas is another Robespierre, preaching an abstract, rational morality. He reminds us that the hour eventually comes when society must be freed from such a reign of reason."[112] Recalling the historical context in which Schiller was writing, however, it was precisely this concern about the Reign of Terror which prompted the writing of the letters *Concerning the Aesthetic Education of the Human Being*. As the writer argued, not more reason but greater refinement ("Bildung") of human sensibility was the most pressing need of the times in which Schiller was living.

As we saw in the Habermas-Marcuse debate of 1977, Habermas has yet to come to terms with the role of sensuous experience. Albeit in passing, Habermas perceives that "the emancipation of consciousness must be rooted in the emancipation of the senses."[113] Ironically, he does not acknowledge the greater significance of Schiller's insistence on the development of the faculty of sensation. For, like Kant, though from the perspective of intersubjectivity, Habermas insists on the transcendental regulation of the agency of reason in conducting all human affairs in the public/social arena. Like Habermas today, Immanuel Kant maintained his trust in the ultimately redemptive power of the faculty of reason ("Erkenntniskräfte"), whereas, for Schiller, the cultivation and refinement of aesthetic sensibility and judgment, in conjunction with the operation of reason, is the true means to the effective re-formation of society both regionally and globally, that is, in the cosmo-political domain of human affairs.

Despite the possible link between Schiller and Karl Marx, as proposed by Habermas and others, Marx's call for the "revolution in the modes of production and exchange" in the *Communist Manifesto* [*Kommunistisches Manifest*] (1848)[114] must be distinguished from Schiller's call for a revolution in the mode of perception. In short, Schiller's discussion seeks to mediate between subjectivity (*Subjektivität*) and the objective, material world. In the final analysis, the ultimate goal of Schiller's *Concerning the Aesthetic Education of the Human Being* is the humanization of reason.

Most important for Habermas, perhaps, Schiller's writings form an early response to the problem of modernity.[115] "Whereas modernity becomes ever more deeply entangled, as reason advances, in the conflict between the unleashed system of needs and the abstract principles of morality, art can 'confer on' this dichotomized totality a 'social character' because it shares in both legislations."[116] Art, as Schiller had indeed written, generates a "middle disposition, in which our nature is constrained neither physically nor morally and yet is active both ways."[117] Schiller's answer to the *moral* question, however, is simple and direct. The individual human being must decide to act according to the dictates of one's own free moral will. For Schiller, art presents and supports the possibility of moral decision (e.g., Karl Moor, Christian Moor, Mary Stuart, William Tell).

In retrospect, Habermas includes Schiller in both the German idealist tradition of thought and in at least one of the two traditions of Marxian theory, the one shaped by Max Weber, Georg Lukács and the Critical Theory of the Institute for Social Research. However, Habermas admits that Schiller "was more modest" than either Schelling or Hegel, who made the mediating power of reflective judgment the bridge to an intellectual intuition "that was to assure itself of absolute identity."[118] Because Schiller "held on to the restricted significance of aesthetic judgment in order to make use of it for a philosophy of history,"[119] Habermas's statement actually has the unexpected effect of dissociating Schiller from the mainstream of German Idealism. It is for this reason that Habermas's response to my question regarding the writer's employment of phrases like "bloß eine Idee" (merely an idea) proves to be so interesting.

Finally, Habermas attributes to art some practical value since art "operates as a catalyst, as a form of communication, as a medium within which separated moments are rejoined into an uncoerced totality."[120] Statements such as these disclose the impact of Schiller's aesthetics on Habermas's philosophy of communicative reason. So it is from the perspective of art as *one* of the forms of intersubjective communication that Habermas is able to appreciate Schiller's theory of aesthetic education.

In effect, then, both Gadamer and Habermas recommend the work of Friedrich Schiller for consideration in the playing field of the modernist-postmodernist age. Within late twentieth-century German philosophical discourse, Schiller's *Concerning the Aesthetic Education of the Human Being* is remembered as the modern voice of social reintegration through art and the language of aesthetic judgment.

Concluding the Conversation with Habermas

One of the most significant outcomes of the conversation with Habermas concerned the multidisciplinary quality of Schiller's writings. Thinking aloud, Habermas suggested that this aspect of Schiller's thought may well provide a stronger basis of analysis than any single approach (external or internal) to his writing. He then suggested that it may well have been the multidisciplinary nature of Schiller's writings that kept the writer from becoming a full-fledged proponent of German Idealism. In particular, he found the explanation of Schiller's recurrent statement in the classical essays—"Aber das ist bloß eine Idee"—"einleuchtend" (illuminating) and was quite intrigued about the possibility that this may help explain the problem of integration ("das Problem der Integration") in Schiller's work. Like Gadamer, Habermas agreed that Schiller's repeated qualifier cannot be understood simply as a rhetorical strategy; indeed, it constitutes a self-reflective qualification of his own ideas, exhibiting, in my words, an enlightened, self-critical exploration of the limits of his own theorizing. As much as he may have wanted to, Habermas added, Friedrich Schiller was simply unable to take the final leap into Idealism.

Concluding Remarks

For Habermas, unlike Gadamer, then, it is not so much the mind-body problem (physiology) as it is the interdisciplinary texture of Schiller's writings that helps explain why Schiller did not embrace the German idealist movement. The mind-body problem and the question of the integrative nature of knowledge thus stand in complementary distribution to each other in Schiller's writings, a fact that still recommends the writer's work to us today.

I was surprised. The Habermas I had feared worked cooperatively with me in exploring the possibilities of my thesis. The combativeness of critical reason I had expected was rarely in evidence. Rather, communicative reason was fully operative. What I experienced in those ninety minutes was the mutual exploration of a single idea—a common pursuit of understanding. This formal characteristic, I believe, is what unites Habermas and Gadamer on the most fundamental level, despite the differences in the content of their philosophies. A clear example of this quest for understanding is found in *The Philosophical Discourse of Modernity,* where Habermas runs a trace on his own approach to the question of "post"-modernity. Here, he understands himself to be "taking up the ordinary perspective of a participant who is recalling the course of the argument [of modernity] in its rough features for the sake of searching out in each of the three positions [of the discourse of modernity] their inherent difficulties."[121] Habermas's critical self-awareness unites him, fundamentally, with the spirit of Gadamer's philosophical hermeneutics. Of his own procedure, Habermas writes: "This path will not lead us out of the discourse of modernity, but it will perhaps allow its theme to be better understood."[122]

In Habermas's orientation there seems to be an unreconciled tension between his respect for Gadamer's hermeneutics and his own *praxis* as a vocal social philosopher and politically engaged citizen. In this light, Habermas both critiques and contributes to the philosophical discourse of modernity. Perhaps part of Habermas's critique of "post"-modernism is driven by his commitment to what one critic has termed the "habit of mind" that hermeneutics fosters, one "that is reflexive, perspectival, and insistent on the value of cooperation rather than combat in intellectual endeavors."[123] Indeed, this habit of mind is diametrically opposed to the general mission of "post"-modernism, which, in the opinion of John McGowan [*Postmodernism and Its Critics*] (1991), is to attack, and ultimately destroy humanist philosophies such as the one developed by Hans-Georg Gadamer.[124]

If anything, then, the Gadamer-Habermas debate of the late 1960s and early 1970s should be reread in the light of the undying respect the two men have had for each other.[125] According to Gadamer, Habermas is "sehr ideenreich" (full of ideas), and despite Habermas's disagreements with Gadamer, most notably with one of the traditions Gadamer embraces, namely the work of Martin Heidegger, there is gratitude and a profound sense of indebtedness.

Notes

Preface

1. Benno von Wiese, *Friedrich Schiller* (1959; Stuttgart: J.B. Metzler, 1978).

2. E.g., Wolfgang Riedel, "Der Spaziergang," *Ästhetik der Landschaft und Geschichtsphilosophie der Natur bei Schiller* (Würzburg: Königshausen and Neumann, 1989).

3. As noted by Helmut Koopmann, *Schiller-Forschung. 1970–80. Ein Bericht* (Marbach a.N.: Deutsche Schiller-Gesellschaft, 1982), p. 8. In the 1980s, we find instead the collected essays of Klaus Berghahn, *Schiller: Ansichten eines Idealisten* (Frankfurt a.M.: Athenäum, 1986) and Hans Mayer, *Versuche über Schiller* (Frankfurt a.M.: Suhrkamp, 1987).

4. Lesley Sharpe, *Friedrich Schiller: Drama, Thought and Politics* (Cambridge: Cambridge University Press, 1991). See also her book *Schiller and the Historical Character: Presentation and Interpretation in the Historiographical Works and in the Historical Dramas* (Oxford: Oxford University Press, 1982) and T. J. Reed, *Schiller* (Oxford/New York: Oxford University Press, 1991). Among German scholars, see Helmut Koopmann, *Schiller: Eine Einführung* (München/Zürich: Artemis, 1988) and Gert Ueding, *Friedrich Schiller* (München: C. H. Beck, 1990). The last three contributions are more general, introductory accounts of the life, works, and times of the writer, unlike Lesley Sharpe's more detailed study.

5. Von Wiese, *Friedrich Schiller,* p. 355. To be sure, von Wiese admitted: "Dabei lassen sich Philosophie, Geschichtsschreibung und Dichtung nicht trennen, sondern deuten ständig wechselseitig, aufeinander hin und ergänzen sich gegenseitig" (pp. vii–viii).

6. Kenneth Dewhurst and Nigel Reeves, *Friedrich Schiller: Medicine, Psychology and Literature with the first English edition of his complete medical and psychological writings* (Oxford: Sandford, 1978; Berkeley/Los Angeles: University of California Press, 1978). References to Schiller's medical writings are from this translation (Sandford), hereafter marked by D/R and the appropriate page number in the main body of the text. I have included the original German in the notes, or, where appropriate, in bracket notation in the main body. In n. 1, Dewhurst and Reeves note that Benno von Wiese's book on Schiller contains but a few pages on the medical writings, while Gerhard Storz said nothing at all. Caught up in beautiful prose, Friedrich Burschell glided over the deeper-lying connections between literature and physiology in *Friedrich Schiller* (Reinbek bei Hamburg: Rowohlt, 1968). Burschell refers to Schiller's *Philosophie der Physiologie,* Schiller's first dissertation, only once and disparagingly as a naive study ("kindliche[r] Versuch") (p. 326). Though some work has been accomplished in this area subsequent to D/R's pioneering book of 1978, their point is still well taken: "we have seriously to consider whether medicine did not play a vital part in the foundation of his [Schiller's] intellectual development" (p. 1). The British scholars determined that psychology was not only central to Schiller's dramatic writing, but that the work of medical theorists and popular philosophers of his time "laid a foundation for his later theories of art

and tragedy that remained firm even after the encounter with Kant" (p. 136). Scholarship of the later 1980s and early 1990s has devoted more attention to Schiller's physiology.

7. Though slower to develop than in the United States, the impact of interdisciplinary studies on the concept of literature has been felt in Germany (e.g., Wolfgang Martens, ed., *Bibliographische Probleme im Zeichen eines erweiterten Literaturbegriffs* [Weinsheim: V. C. H. Acta humaniora, 1988]).

8. See, for instance, Julie Thompson Klein, *Interdisciplinarity: History, Theory and Practice* (Detroit: Wayne State University Press, 1990). This study contains an excellent bibliography that cuts across and unites major fields of inquiry. An outstanding study example is John A. McCarthy's award-winning book *Crossing Boundaries: A Theory and History of Essay Writing in German, 1680–1815* (Philadelphia: University of Pennsylvania Press, 1989).

9. Rene Wellek, *The Attack on Literature and Other Essays* (Chapel Hill: University of North Carolina Press, 1982), p. 15.

10. Koopmann, *Schiller-Forschung,* n. 3, p. 8.

Introduction: Portraits of Schiller's Life and Intellectual Development: The Writings of Wilhelm von Humboldt and Caroline von Wolzogen

1. Wilhelm von Humboldt, "Über Schiller und den Gang seiner Geistesentwicklung," in Bernhard Zeller, *Schillers Leben und Werk in Daten und Bildern* (Frankfurt a.M.: Insel, 1966), p. 27.

2. Ibid.

3. Ibid., p. 28.

4. Ibid., p. 37.

5. Christian Garve demanded "die harmonische Übereinstimmung von Empfindungskraft und Vernunft," and Thomas Abbt the "Zusammenstimmung der Seelenkräfte," in Jakob Friedrich Abel, *Rede über das Genie. Werden grosse Geister geboren oder erzogen und welches sind die Merkmale derselbigen? Mit einer Wiedergabe des Original-Titelblattes,* Walter Müller-Seidel, ed. (Marbach a.N.: Schiller Nationalmuseum, 1955), n. 21.

6. Ibid., p. 7.

7. Ibid., p. 34. Alexander Gerard in his essay on genius (*Versuch über das Genie,* trans. Christian Garve [Leipzig: Weidmanns Erben und Reich, 1776]) advocates that the true artistic genius always possesses a well-developed sense of taste (pp. 390–409). "Das Genie erfordert zweytens eben so viel Regelmäßigkeit als Reichthum der Einbildungskraft" (p. 62). Indeed, the proper function of taste, for Gerard, is to make genius "regelmäßig und correct" (p. 394). And the philosophical doctor Johann Georg Zimmermann seems to have sought a balance between the exercise of imagination and that of the understanding in true genius when he asserted: "Also ist die Einbildungskraft in ihrer größten Stärke, und der Verstand in seiner ganzen Grösse das Genie" (*Von der Erfahrung in der Arzneykunst,* new ed. [Zürich: Orell, Geßner, Fueßli and Compag., 1787], p. 277).

8. Von Wiese, *Friedrich Schiller,* p. 291.

9. Ibid., p. 291.

10. Caroline von Wolzogen, *Schillers Leben,* verfaßt aus Erinnerungen der Familie, seinen eignen Briefen und den nachrichten seines Freundes Körner, 2 parts in 1, vol. 1 (Stuttgart/Tübingen: J. G. Cotta, 1830), pp. 23–24.

11. Ibid., vol. 1, p. 209.

12. Ibid., p. 264.

13. Ibid.
14. Ibid., p. 330.
15. Ibid., vol. 2, p. 57.
16. Ibid., p. 78.
17. Ibid., p. 64.
18. Ibid.
19. Ibid.
20. Ibid., p. 83.
21. Ibid.
22. Ibid., p. 77.
23. Ibid., p. 78.
24. Ibid., p. 278.
25. Von Wolzogen's portrait is diametrically opposed to the National Socialist image of the writer, e.g., Hans Fabricius, *Schiller als Kampfgenosse Hitlers. Nationalsozialismus in Schillers Dramen* (Bayreuth: N. S. Kultur-Verlag, 1932). A second edition of this work appeared in 1934 with the Verlag Deutsche Kultur-Wacht in Berlin-Schöneberg. Joseph Goebbels, who received a doctorate in German literature, opened the Schiller-Gedächtnisfeier in Weimar on November 10, 1934, with the following declaration: "Had Schiller lived in this time, he would undoubtedly have become the great poetic champion of our revolution." His speech is printed in Georg Ruppelt, *Schiller im nationalsozialistischen Deutschland. Der Versuch einer Gleichschaltung* (Stuttgart: J. B. Metzler, 1979), p. 154. See, also, the critical review of Ruppelt's study by Lesley Sharpe, "National Socialism and Schiller," *German Life and Letters* 36 (1982–83): 156–65.
26. Von Wolzogen, *Schillers Leben*, vol. 2, p. 302.
27. Ibid., p. 304.
28. Ibid., p. 307.
29. Ibid.

Chapter 1. "Harmonious Tension" and the Field of Tension Between Anthropology and Metaphysics

1. As noted by Jost Hermand, "Schillers Abhandlung *Über naive und sentimentalische Dichtung*," *Publications of the Modern Language Association* 79 (1964): 428. D/R remark that Mendelssohn's *Letters on the Sensations* remained a "constant source of stimulation" for Schiller (D/R 120).
2. Moses Mendelssohn, *Schriften zur Philosophie und Ästhetik*, ed. Fritz Bamberger 81. Schiller consulted a copy of *Moses Mendelssohns Philosophische Schriften*, improved version, part 1 (Berlin: Christian Friedrich Voss, 1777), p. 77.
3. Moses Mendelssohn, *Schriften zur Philosophie und Ästhetik*, p. 82; *Moses Mendelssohns Philosophische Schriften* part 1, 79. Translations of Mendelssohn are my own. With few exceptions, I will supply the original German only for Schiller's writings in the notes. Jakob Minor (*Schiller. Sein Leben und seine Werke*, 2 vols. [Berlin: Weidmann 1890]) was one of the first to appreciate the impact of Mendelssohn's *Letters* on Schiller. He assigned primary importance to the fifth and twelfth letters, however, thereby overlooking the significance of the tenth letter for a broader understanding of Schiller's writings.
4. *Schriften zur Philosophie und Ästhetik*, p. 82; *Moses Mendelssohns Philosophische Schriften*, part 1, p. 80. Mendelssohn was also aware of the consequences of a breakdown in the nervous system. "Wenn nervigte Theile, die natürlicher Weise vereinigt seyn sollten, aus ihrer Verknüpfung gerissen werden; so erstrecken sich die traurigen Wirkungen davon auf das gantze organische Gebäude. Der Ton wird

verändert, es äussert sich eine Mißstimmung in allen Sennadern; die Lebensbewegungen sind entweder träge oder im vollen Aufruhr. Die Nerven verkündigen diese Unordnung unverzüglich dem Gehirne" (*Schriften zur Philosophie und Ästhetik*, p. 84).

5. Johann Heinrich Zedler, *Grosses vollständiges Universal- Lexikon Aller Wissenschaften und Künste*, vol. 44 (Leipzig/Halle: Johann Heinrich Zedler, 1745) 1184.

6. Ibid., vol. 44, p. 1186.

7. *Schillers Werke. Nationalausgabe. Historisch-kritische Ausgabe*, ed. Julius Petersen and Friedrich Beißner/Lieselotte Blumenthal and Benno von Wiese/Norbert Oellers (Weimar: Böhlau, 1943f.), vol. 20, p. 3f. Hereafter referred to as NA, followed by the appropriate volume and page number in the main body of the text and the notes. In his discussion of the metaphysics of love, the young writer described love as the mediating force between two antagonistic inclinations ("Gegenneigungen"), virtue ("Tugend") and vice ("Untugend"). The pupils greatly admired the countess, who appeared as a paragon of virtue in contradistinction to their lusty monarch. A passing remark by the philosophical doctor Johann Georg Zimmermann characterizes the Duke as follows: "Ein Eugen ist an Ludwigs Hofe ein verachteter Knabe . . ." (*Von der Erfahrung in der Arzneykunst*, cited in Introduction, n. 7, p. 89).

8. "What I enjoy, I call melodic and beautiful; what I dislike, ugly and discordant" (D/R, p. 164) [Was mich ergötzt, nenn ich melodisch und schön, heßlich und unmelodisch, was mich verdrießt] (NA 20: 29).

9. "Wenn ich zwei Klaviere neben einander stelle und auf einem derselben eine Saite rühre, und einen Ton angebe, so wird auf dem andern Klavier die nehmliche Saite und keine andere, ohne mein Zutun zittern und eben den Ton, freilich matter, angeben" (NA 20: 24).

10. "Soviel Saiten sind in der sinnlichen Welt, als Objecte. Soviel Fibern im Denkorgan, als Saiten in der sinnlichen Welt. Und beide, die Welt und das Denkorgan, und die Saiten in jener und die Fibern in dieser sich eben so genau entsprechend, als die beiden Klaviere, als ihre Saiten sich entsprochen haben" (NA 20: 24).

11. The full title of the original publication, a copy of which I have consulted, is: *Versuch über den Zusammenhang der thierischen Natur des Menschen mit seiner geistigen. Eine Abhandlung welche in höchster Gegenwart Sr. Herzoglichen Durchlaucht während den öffentlichen akademischen Prüfungen vertheidigen wird Johann Christoph Friedrich Schiller*, Kandidat der Medizin in der Herzoglichen Militair-Akademie Stuttgart, gedruckt bei Christoph Friedrich Cotta, Hof-und Canzlei-Buchdruker [1780]. For accounts by German scholars of the historical significance of Schiller's ideas on medicine in the light of eighteenth-century science, see, for instance, Wolfgang Riedel, *Die Anthropologie des jungen Schiller* (Würzburg: Königshausen und Neumann, 1989), and Irmgard Müller, "'Die Wahrheit . . . von dem Krankenbett aus beweisen . . .' Zu Schillers medizinischen Studien und Bestrebungen," in *Schiller. Vorträge aus Anlaß seines 225. Geburtstages*, eds. Dirk Grathoff and Erwin Leibfried (Frankfurt a.M./Bern/New York/Paris: Peter Lang, 1991), pp. 112–32.

12. "Wenn man eine Saite auf dem einen rühret, und einen gewissen Ton angibt, so wird auf dem andern eben diese Saite freiwillig anschlagen, und ebendiesen Ton nur etwas schwächer angeben. So wekt, vergleichsweise zu reden, die fröhliche Saite des Körpers die fröhliche in der Seele, so der traurige Ton des ersten den traurigen in der zweiten" (NA 20: 63–64).

13. "Das war der erste Stoß, der erste Lichtstrahl in die Schlummernacht der Kräfte, tönender Goldklang auf die Laute der Natur" (NA 20: 50).

14. An article by Dorothea Kuhn directed my thinking here: "Versuch über Mod-

elle der Natur in der Goethezeit," in her *Typus und Metamorphose. Goethe Studien* (Marbach am Neckar: Deutsche Schillergesellschaft, 1988: 159–76). Though Ilse Graham examined the metaphor of the strings as a symbol of love, she did not appreciate the general significance of the stringed instrument as a sign of the operations of Nature (*Schiller's Drama: Talent and Integrity* [London: Methuen, 1974]).

15. " . . . so machte er [der Körper] ihm die Welt interessant und wichtig, weil er sie ihm unentbehrlich machte" (NA 20: 54).

16. In *Andreas Streicher. Schillers Flucht von Stuttgart und Aufenthalt in Mannheim von 1782 bis 1785* (Stuttgart: Reclam, 1968: 59).

17. See n. 19. Peter Michelsen, *Der Bruch mit der Vater-Welt. Studien zu Schillers Räubern* (Heidelberg: Carl Winter, 1979). The first part of this seminal study appeared in *Jahrbuch der Deutschen Schillergesellschaft* 8 (1964): 57–111. Michelsen demonstrated conclusively Schiller's indebtedness to the stage of his day, especially to Italian opera, thus disproving R. Buchwald's contention: Schiller's "dichterischer Weg ging nicht von frühen Bühneneindrücken aus" (*Schiller. Leben und Werk,* vol. 1, 124; cited by Michelsen, *Der Bruch mit der Vater—Welt,* p. 15). See also chapter 3, n. 25 for more details.

18. Carl Dahlhaus determined that Schiller's writings contain only a few, scattered reflections of a direct nature on musical-aesthetic matters ("Formbegriff und Ausdrucksprinzip in Schillers Musikästhetik," in *Schiller und die höfische Welt* [Tübingen: Max Niemeyer, 1990], pp. 156–57). See also Rey M. Longyear, *Schiller and Music* (Chapel Hill, N.C.: University of North Carolina Press, 1966) and Hermann Fähnrich (*Schillers Musikalität und Musikanschauung* Hildesheim: Gerstenberg, 1977). Ludwig Finscher ("Was ist eine lyrische Operette? Anmerkungen zu Schillers *Semele*" in *Schiller und die höfische Welt,* pp. 148–55) warns of the unreliability of some of Longyear's work (p. 153, n. 10). According to Fähnrich, however, both Longyear's study and Albert Schaefer's *Historisches und systematisches Verzeichnis sämtlicher Tonwerke zu den Dramen Schillers, Goethes, Shakespeares, Kleists und Körners unter besonderer Berücksichtigung der Zwischenaktmusik* (Leipzig: Merseburg, 1866) give us "ein klares Bild, wie Bühnenmusik zur Schillerzeit aufgeführt wurde" (p. 186). Fähnrich is primarily concerned with analyzing the impact of opera and instrumental music on Schiller's writings. Making no reference to Longyear, Michelsen, or even Fähnrich, Dahlhaus draws the puzzling conclusion "Daß Schiller, in Übereinstimmung mit Kant, den Eindruck von Musik als 'bloß transitorisch' empfand und nicht erkannte, daß sich in der Imagination aus den in der Zeit vergehenden Teilen ein der Zeit enthobenes Ganze aufbauen läßt, ist nicht allein der Begrenztheit seiner musikalischen Erfahrung zur Last zu legen, sondern auch dem äußerlichen Umstand, daß die zum Formverständnis von Instrumentalmusik notwendige Wiederholung von Aufführungen noch nicht zur Regel geworden war" (p. 166).

19. Streicher wrote that Schiller "durch Anhören trauriger oder lebhafter Musik außer sich selbst versetzt wurde, und daß es nichts weniger als viele Kunst erforderte, durch passendes Spiel auf dem Clavier, alle Affecte in ihm aufzureizen" (*Schillers Flucht von Stuttgart,* p. 102; also cited by von Wiese, *Friedrich Schiller,* pp. 133–34).

20. Goethe was irritated by Schiller's "Tic bei Musik sprechen zu lassen." Cited by Michael Mann *Sturm-und-Drang Drama. Studien und Vorstudien zu Schillers "Räubern"* (Bern/München: Francke, 1974), p. 89.

21. Fähnrich maintains that Schiller could neither sing, nor play an instrument (*Schillers Musikalität,* p. 8). Unlike Fähnrich, I am most interested in the representation of music in Schiller's writings.

22. Jakob and Wilhelm Grimm, *Deutsches Wörterbuch* (München: Deutscher Taschenbuch, 1984), vol. 10, 484.

23. Ibid., vol. 10, 485.

24. Johann George Sulzer, *Allgemeine Theorie der Schönen Künste* 4 parts (Leipzig: Weidmann, 1792), part 2, p. 473.

25. *Deutsches Wörterbuch,* vol. 10, 484.

26. A related question is: What is the relationship between rupture and harmony in Schiller's writings? David Vaughn Pugh's dissertation *Conflict and Harmony: A Study of Schiller's Philosophical Writings* (University of Toronto, 1986) tends in this direction, though it is limited to a discussion of the later theoretical essays.

27. *Deutsches Wörterbuch,* vol. 16, 1915.

28. *Ibid.,* vol. 10, 485. The Grimms' definition makes a connection between Schiller and Pythagoras plausible, when they state: ". . . the Pythagorean conception of the harmony of the spheres is used frequently by our poets either in stricter or freer expression" (Ibid., vol. 10, 485).

29. "Dieses Zittern pflanzt der Nervengeist biß in das Denkorgan fort" (NA 10: 24).

30. "Ihr Verlust hat einen Riß zwischen Welt und Geist gemacht. Ihr Daseyn lichtet, wekt, belebt alles um ihn—Ich nenne sie *Mittelkraft*" (NA 20: 13).

31. "Dann wann ich diesen verleze, so ist das Band zwischen Welt und Seele dahin" (NA 20: 16).

32. *Grosses vollständiges Universal-Lexikon,* vol. 31 (1724), 1741. Here we must be careful to distinguish between the various uses of the word *Riß* in the eighteenth century. The word appeared both by itself and with the prefixes *Ab-* and *Um-,* both of which denoted a plan or design, i.e., not rupture.

33. Ibid., vol. 31, 1741.

34. Walter Müller-Seidel pointed to the possible influence of Georg Friedrich Gaus's *Gebetbuch aus dem Herzen* (Stuttgart : 1775) on Schiller's religious sensibilities. In his prayer book, Gaus conceived of God as "das Urbild der Vollkommenheit der Seele." At the same time, however, he also employed the metaphor of the abyss to characterize the nature of the world. The following pronouncement may well have struck young Schiller: "Alles ist voll Klippen und Abgründe . . . die ganze Welt ist eine beständige Versuchung" (cited by Müller-Seidel the "Gaus"—article *Deutsche Vierteljahrhsschrift für Literaturwissenschaft und Geistesgeschichte* 26 [1952]: 84).

35. *Deutsches Wörterbuch,* vol. 8, 1045.

36. Reinhart Koselleck, *Critique and Crisis: Enlightenment and the Pathogenesis of Modern Society* (Cambridge, Mass.: MIT Press, 1988), p. 103, n. 15. The original definition in German reads: "Scheidung und Streit, aber auch die Entscheidung, im Sinne eines endgültigen Ausschlags oder eines Urteilsspruches oder einer Beurteilung überhaupt" (*Kritik und Krise. Eine Studie zur Pathogenese der bürgerlichen Welt* [Freiburg/München: Karl Alber, 1959], p. 197, n. 155).

37. Koselleck, *Critique and Crisis,* p. 198.

38. In *Friedrich Schiller. Medizinische Schriften. Eine Buchgabe der Deutschen Hoffmann—La Roche AG aus Anlaß des 200. Geburtstages des Dichters 10. November 1959* (Miesbach/Obb.: Wilhelm Friedrich Mayr, 1959), p. 69.

39. "Auf dem tätigen Vorgehen der Natur gegen den Krankheitsstoff beruht die Krankheit und die Schwere der Krankheit" (*Medizinische Schriften,* p. 70).

40. "Hüten uns daher, daß wir uns nicht zu eigenwillig bei den Erklärungen der Begriffe Kochung und Krisis festlegen und unsere Lehrmeinungen sich nicht von der Natur der Krankheiten unterscheiden! Ich wenigstens bin durch verschiedene Gaukelwege des Irrtums endlich zu der Ueberzeugung geführt worden, daß so die Ordnung in der Natur der Dinge nicht sei, wie wir sie in unseren Lehrbüchern zurechtlegen: Es gibt mehr Dinge in Himmel und Erde als erträumt werden in unserer Wissenschaft" (*Medizinische Schriften,* p. 71).

41. Koselleck detected that Zedler had assigned the same meaning to "crisis" and "critic" (*Critique and Crisis*, p. 104, n. 15).

42. "Schon mehrere Philosophen haben behauptet, daß der Körper gleichsam der Kerker des Geistes sey, daß er solchen allzusehr an das Irrdische hefte, und seinen sogenannten Flug zur Vollkommenheit hemme. Wiederum ist von manchem Philosophen mehr oder weniger bestimmt die Meinung gehegt worden, daß Wissenschaft und Tugend nicht sowohl Zwek, als Mittel zur Glükseeligkeit seyen, daß sich alle Vollkommenheit des Menschen in der Verbesserung seines Körpers versammle" (NA 20: 40).

43. Riedel believes that Schiller sought to overcome the Platonic and Epicurean ideal of perfectibility by comprehending blending ("Vermischung") as perfection ("Vollkommenheit") (*Die Anthropologie des jungen Schiller*, p. 112).

44. "Da aber gewöhnlicher Weise mehr darinn gefehlt worden ist, daß man zu viel auf die eigene Rechnung der Geisteskraft, in so fern sie ausser Abhängigkeit von dem Körper gedacht wird, mit Hintansezung dieses leztern geschrieben hat" (NA 10: 40–41).

45. This was suggested already in my book *On Imitation, Imagination and Beauty: A Critical Reassessment of the Concept of the Literary Aritist During the Early German "Aufklärung"* (Bonn : Bouvier, 1977), p. 3. At that time, I also pointed out that Mendelssohn's *Letters Concerning the Sensations* attempted to attain such a synthesis (p. 3).

46. René Descartes had also conceived of the human body as a machine, as noted by Dorothea Kuhn: "nach Descartes ist wie der tierische so auch der menschliche Körper eine durch Gott geschaffene Maschine, die analog zur Weltmaschine eingerichtet ist" ("Versuch über Modelle der Natur in der Goethezeit," cited in chapter 1, n. 14, p. 162).

47. "Experience and observation should therefore be our only guides here." And: "they alone have laid bare to us those springs [of life] hidden under the external integument which conceals so many wonders from our eyes;" in Aram Vartanian, *LaMettrie's L'Homme Machine: A Study in the Origins of an Idea*, p. 151.

48. "wirken, und in einander wirken, gleich Saiten eines Instruments tausendstimmig zusammenlautend in eine Melodie" (NA 20: 10).

49. "von allen jenen dunkeln Fühlungen des Mechanismus umnachtet wird" (NA 20: 67).

50. "Die Seele befindet sich in der Illusion einer angenehmen Empfindung, weil sie einer lang anhaltenden schmerzhaften los ist" (NA 20: 67).

51. "Sie ist schmerzenfrei, nicht weil der Ton ihrer Werkzeuge wiederhergestellt ist, sondern weil sie den Mißton nicht mehr empfindet. Die Sympathie hört auf, so bald der Zusammenhang wegfällt" (NA 20: 67). Pointing to Abel's *De phaenomenis sympathiae in corpore animali conspicuis* (1779), with which Schiller was well familiar, Jakob Minor defined "Sympathie" as follows: "Wenn ein entfernter Teil unseres Körpers heftig von einem Gegenstand bewegt wird, so pflanzt sich diese Bewegung durch die Nerven bis zum Gehirn fort und geht auf die Seele über (sinnliche Vorstellung): wird dann aber durch eine innere oder seelische Ursache dieselbe Bewegung im Gehirn wieder hervorgerufen, dann geht sie in umgekehrter Ordnung wieder auf den Körper über" (*Schillers Leben und seine Werke*, p. 277). See also Bernhard Zeller, "Jakob Friedrich Abel. 1751–1829," *Heimatbuch für Schöndorff und Umgebung. Festschrift zum 75. Geburtstag von Dr. Reinhold Maier* (Schöndorff: Herman Schmid, 1964): 87–89.

52. Julien Offray de La Mettrie, *Man a Machine*, edited by Gertrude Carman Bussey (Chicago/London: Open Court, 1927), p. 24. Hereafter: *Man a Machine*.

53. Ibid., p. 45.

54. Ibid., pp. 48–49.

55. Ibid., p. 55.

56. Ibid., p. 57. Dewhurst and Reeves have noted that Consbruch approved of the work of Georg Ernst Stahl (*Theoria medica vera* [1707]) (D/R, pp. 95 and 97). He may also have introduced it into the curriculum for his own classes. Stahl's position was diametrically opposed to de La Mettrie's inasmuch as he found mechanistic explanations inadequate to account for the interaction between mind and body and mental illness. Abel actually favored Stahl over Haller (D/R, p. 97). De La Mettrie vociferously opposed Stahl's non-chemico-mechanistic explanation of human anatomy. Thinking that he could disprove Stahl's concept of the *anima*, the vital life force that exercises seemingly conscious election of means in the achievement of its goals, the French scientist refers to the example of a violinist. Impressed with the quickness of response in that musician's fingers, whose responses are practically invisible, de La Mettrie attempts to reinstate the idea of the "independent motion of organic substances," which Stahl had denied. The Frenchman's choice of words when criticizing Stahl is especially noteworthy: "The soul wills, and the springs play, contract and relax" (*Man a Machine*, p. 58).

57. Though devoting considerable space to the concept of imagination, de La Mettrie curbed the operation of too much imagination in scientific inquiry—"if the imagination be trained from childhood to bridle itself and to keep from being carried away by its own impetuosity . . . and to check, to restrain, its ideas . . . then the imagination, ready in judgment, will comprehend the greatest possible spheres of objects, through reasoning" (*Man a Machine*, p. 32). Schiller's personal response to illness was also much different than de La Mettrie's. In Frederick the Great's eulogy on de La Mettrie, the Prussian king recalled the Frenchman's bout with violent fever. Frederick records that during de La Mettrie's convalescence the Frenchman "boldly bore the torch of experience into the night of metaphysics; he tried to explain by the aid of anatomy the thin texture of understanding, and he found only mechanism where others had supposed an essence superior to matter" (*Man a Machine*, p. xiv).

58. As found especially in the poetry of North German poets of the early eighteenth century. See, for instance: Uwe-K. Ketelsen, *Die Naturpoesie der norddeutschen Frühaufklärung* (Stuttgart: J. B. Metzler, 1974).

59. There is no doubt that the young Schiller was influenced by Leibniz's monadology, especially by his theory of preformation, as explored, for instance, in the seventy-fourth paragraph of *Die Monadologie*. There is, likewise, little doubt that Schiller would have agreed with Leibniz's conception of God as the author of Nature (paragraph 65). However, Schiller's employment of the symbol of the stringed instrument, together with his interactionist theory, overrides Leibniz's transference of the Cartesian image of the clockwork and the theory of parallelism between world and soul.

60. One of the four propositions concerning the relationship between mind and body is the so-called interactionist dualism. This has been outlined by Keith Campbell, *Body and Mind*, second edition (Notre Dame: University of Notre Dame Press, 1984), p. 14f., and esp. 50f. "In action, changes in one item cause changes in another. In interaction, the process is mutual" (p. 25).

61. "Thierische Natur bevestiget die Thätigkeit des Geistes" (NA 20: 41). ("Man's [the human being's] animal nature strengthens the operation of his [one's] spirit [mind]"; D/R, p. 257).

62. As suggested by Riedel, *Die Anthropologie des jungen Schiller*, p. 31.

63. "Alle diese Wirkungen erfolgen aus einem wundervollen mechanischen Triebe, bevor sich noch der denkende Theil des Menschen in das Spiel mischt"

(*Schriften zur Philosophie und Ästhetik,* p. 83; *Moses Mendelssohns Philosophische Schriften,* p. 80).

64. "Vollkommenheit des Menschen ligt in der Uebung seiner Kräfte durch Betrachtung des Weltplans; und da zwischen dem Maase der Kraft, und dem Zwek, auf den sie wirket, die genaueste Harmomie seyn muß, so wird Vollkommenheit in der höchstmöglichen Thätigkeit seiner Kräfte, und ihrer wechselseitigen Unterordnung bestehen" (NA 20: 41).

65. The idea of a world plan complements the beginning of the *Philosophy of Physiology.* "Just as the omnipotent influence of divine power transformed the design [of the universe] into reality, and all its forces act both alone and together with others like notes from a thousand-stringed instrument sounding a single melody, so the human mind, ennobled with divine powers, is destined to discover from particular effects their cause and purpose, from the connection between causes and purposes the grand design of the whole and to recognise from that design the Creator and to love and glorify Him" (D/R, p. 150). [So wie es izt durch den allmächtigen Einflus der göttlichen Kraft aus dem Entwurffe zur Wirklichkeit hinrann, und alle Kräfte wirken, und in einander wirken, gleich Saiten eines Instruments tausendstimmig zusammenlautend in eine Melodie: so soll der Geist des Menschen, mit Kräften der Gottheit geadelt, aus den einzelnen Wirkungen Ursach und Absicht, aus dem Zusammenhang der Ursachen und Absichten all den grosen Plan des Ganzen entdeken, aus dem Plane den Schöpfer erkennen, ihn lieben, ihn verherrlichen] (NA 20: 10). In both the medical dissertations and the essay "Julius's Theosophy," the problem of rupture seems to be of major concern to the writer.

66. "Aber die Thätigkeit der menschlichen Seele ist . . . an die Thätigkeit der Materie gebunden. Die Veränderungen in der Körperwelt müssen durch eine eigene Klasse mittlerer organischer Kräfte, die Sinne modifizirt, und so zu sagen verfeinert werden, ehe sie vermögend sind in mir eine Vorstellung zu erweken; so müssen wiederum andere organische Kräfte, die Maschinen der willkührlichen Bewegung, zwischen Seele und Welt treten, um die Veränderung der erstern auf die leztere fortzupflanzen; so müssen endlich selbsten die Operationen des Denkens und Empfindens gewissen Bewegungen des innern Sensoriums korrespondiren. Alles dieses macht den Organismus der Seelenwirkungen aus" (NA 20: 41–42).

67. "Aber die Materie ist ein Raub des ewigen Wechsels, und reibt sich selbst auf so wie sie wirket, unter der Bewegung wird das Element aus seinen Fugen getrieben, verjagt und verloren" (NA 20: 42).

68. Quoting Riedel, *Die Anthropologie des jungen Schiller,* p. 27. Ernst Platner (1714–1818) was Professor of Medicine and Philosophy in Leipzig and one of Jean Paul Richter's instructors. Riedel notes that it was Abel who developed the idea of reciprocal effect (p. 27). Here, I cannot agree with Heinrich Schipperges ("Der Medicus Schiller und das Konzept seiner Heilskunde" in *Schiller und die höfische Welt,* p. 145), who sees in this very definition only the idea of unity ("Einheitsgedanke"). The blending of elements causes tension.

69. "Diß ist die wunderbare und merkwürdige Sympathie, die die heterogenen Principien des Menschen gleichsam zu Einem Wesen macht, der Mensch ist nicht Seele und Körper, der Mensch ist die innigste Vermischung dieser beiden Substanzen" (NA 20: 64).

70. "Der Mensch ist weder Körper noch Seele allein; er ist die Harmonie von beyden" (Cited by Riedel, *Die Anthropologie des jungen Schiller,* p. 16).

71. "Da nun die Annehmlichkeit eines Klanges ohne Zweifel aus dieser harmonischen Vermischung oder Vereinigung mehrerer Töne entsteht; warum sollte man diesem Wink der Natur nicht folgen, und den Gesang nicht vielstimmig machen, wie die Natur jeden einzeln Ton gemacht hat?" Sulzer, *Allgemeine Theorie der Schönen*

Künste, part 2, 473. This work, which enjoyed further printings in 1786–87 and 1792–94, was directed against the so-called geniuses of the Storm-and-Stress movement.

72. Heinrich Wagner, *Geschichte der Hohen Carls-Schule. Mit Illustrationen von Carl Alexander von Heideloff.* 2 vols. (Würzburg : C. Etlinger, 1856–57). These documents were translated into English for the first time by D/R.

73. "daß der Verfasser sich manchmal zu viel von seiner Einbildungskraft fortreißen läßt. Daher jene poetische Ausdrücke, welche so offt den ruhigen Gang des philosophischen Styls unterbrechen" (Wagner, *Geschichte der Hohen Carls-Schule,* vol. 2, 280, appendix XI).

74. The reception of the *Philosophy of Physiology* also supports this point. Where Christian Reuß objected to the combination of physiological inquiry and philosophical observations and found the candidate's style "frei und schwülstig," Duke Carl Eugen, while accepting the committee's decision, admitted "daß der junge Mann viel schönes darinnen gesagt—und besonders viel Feuer gezeigt hat" (Wagner, *Geschichte der Hohen Carls-Schule,* vol. 2, 280) [that this young man has written many fine things in it—and shown much mettle] (D/R, p. 168). Still, out of respect for the committee's judgment, the Duke suggested that Schiller's "fire" be "dampened" (D/R, p. 168).

75. In his insightful essay "Schillers philosophische Rhetorik" (in *Schiller. Festschrift des Euphorion* 53 [1959]: 313–50), Herman Meyer submitted: "In dieser Einheit von Verstand und Einbildungskraft, von Begriff und Bild, drückt sich die Totalität des Menschlichen aus, die Schiller als Natur bezeichnet" (p. 126). Rather than the unity, first and foremost, Schiller appreciated the harmonious tension at work within Nature. Thus, we could substitute the word *Spannung* for "Einheit" in Meyer's formulation and capture the essence of Schiller's work.

76. "Tönender Wohlklang auf die grosse Laute der Natur." The Nationalausgabe records "Goldklang" instead of "Wohlklang." The statement was precipitated by the writer's discussion of the origination of thought out of bodily pain. "Das war der erste Stoß, der erste Lichtstrahl in die Schlummernacht der Kräfte, tönender Goldklang auf die Laute der Natur" (NA 20: 50).

77. D/R maintain that Consbruch was Schiller's favorite instructor, but that he was most influenced by Abel. In fact, Abel interested Schiller in the psychopathology of the criminal mind (D/R, p. 37).

78. "Die Thätigkeiten des Körpers entsprechen den Thätigkeiten des Geistes; d.h. Jede Ueberspannung von Geistesthätigkeit hat jederzeit eine Ueberspannung gewisser körperlicher Aktionen zur Folge, so wie das Gleichgewicht der erstern, oder die harmonische Thätigkeit der Geisteskräfte mit der vollkommensten Uebereinstimmung der leztern vergesellschaftet ist. Ferner: Trägheit der Seele macht die körperlichen Bewegungen träg, Nichttätigkeit der Seele hebt sie gar auf" (NA 20: 57).

79. Hans-Jürgen Schings, "Philosophie der Liebe und Tragödie des Universalhasses," *Jahrbuch des Wiener Goethe-Vereins* 84–85 (1980–81). Wolfgang Riedel (*Die Anthropologie des jungen Schiller*), who is indebted to Schings on this point, believes that the theme of love in this essay ties the last three of the five sections of the work together.

80. A section of Riedel's book (*Die Anthropologie des jungen Schiller*) is titled "Das Spannungsfeld zwischen Metaphysik und Anthropologie." I follow Mareta Linden's definition of the term "anthropology" in the eighteenth century as the "Lehre vom Menschen" [the theory of the human being]. Mareta Linden, *Untersuchungen zum Anthropologiebegriff des 18. Jahrhunderts* (Bern/Frankfurt a. M.: Herbert und Peter Lang, 1976). Riedel comprehends anthropology as psycho-physiological knowl-

edge of the human being or the theory of the nature of the human being. He does not mean ethnology, Blumenbach's comparative-anatomical anthropology or Kant's pragmatic anthropology. But Riedel limits his discussion to Schiller's medical dissertations and the *Philosophische Briefe* [*Philosophical Letters*] (1786). Linden deliberately leaves out the question of theology or religion. Though modern anthropology offers an explanation for religion, it does not engage in metaphysical inquiry or speculation. Since Schiller did explore metaphysical issues in his writings, it is meaningful to speak of a field of tension between anthropology and metaphysics in his case. Unlike Riedel, I focus primarily on the tension between the human being, who believes he or she is protected by a Creator-God overseeing even the seemingly apocalyptic developments in the world and the human being who, as half animal, half angel, strives for self-perfection.

81. Gerhard Kaiser, *Vergötterung und Tod. Die thematische Einheit von Schillers Werk* (Stuttgart: J. B. Metzler, 1967), p. 7. Riedel adds: "Liebe ist wie Erkenntnis für Schiller ein Modus der Vervollkommnung, ein Weg, Gott ähnlicher zu werden" (*Die Anthropologie des jungen Schiller*, p. 200).

82. "Bestimmung des Menschen zur Göttlichkeit." Acknowledged by Riedel, *Die Anthropologie des jungen Schiller*, p. 157, n. 17.

83. "denn er [Schiller] sieht den Tod in einer Weise, die sich im Barock vorbereitet—nicht eigentlich christlich als der Sünde Sold, sondern als den großen Riß der Welt, in dem alle ihre Fragwürdigkeit offenbar wird, als Schranke und Prüfstein des Menschen" (Kaiser, *Vergötterung und Tod*, p. 8). Though they do not cite Kaiser's study, Dewhurst and Reeves follow this type of argumentation in their analysis of Schiller's concern with death in the medical writings.

84. "Wie kann der Mensch Gott gleich sein, wo doch der Tod eine letzte Realität ist?" (Kaiser, *Vergötterung und Tod*, p. 8).

85. "unglükseliger Widerspruch der Natur—dieser freie emporstrebende Geist ist in das starre unwandelbare Uhrwerk eines sterblichen Körpers geflochten, mit seinen kleinen Bedürfnissen vermengt, an seine kleinen Schicksale angejocht—dieser Gott ist in eine Welt von Würmern verwiesen" (NA 20: 112); cited also by Kaiser, *Vergötterung und Tod*, p. 8.

86. "alle streben nach dem Zustand der höchsten freien Aeußerung ihrer Kräfte, alle besizen den gemeinschaftlichen Trieb, ihre Thätigkeit auszudehnen, alles an sich zu ziehen, in sich zu versammeln, sich eigen zu machen, was sie als gut, als vortreflich, als reizend erkennen" (NA 20: 117).

87. "In dem Augenblike, wo wir sie [the true, the beautiful, and the good,] uns denken, sind wir Eigenthümer einer Tugend, Urheber einer Handlung, Erfinder einer Wahrheit, Inhaber einer Glükseligkeit. Wir selber werden das empfundene Objekt" (NA 20: 117).

88. "Welchen Zustand wir wahrnehmen, in diesen treten wir selbst" (NA 20: 117).

89. "Welche Schönheit, welche Vortreflichkeit, welchen Genuß ich außer mir hervorbringe, bringe ich in mir hervor, welchen ich vernachläßige, zerstöre, vernachläßige ich mir" (NA 20: 119).

90. "Die ganze Schöpfung zerfließt in seine Persönlichkeit" (NA 20: 121).

91. "Die Philosophie unsrer Zeiten—ich fürchte es—widerspricht dieser Lehre" (NA 20: 121).

92. "Seid vollkommen, wie euer Vater im Himmel vollkommen ist, sagt der Stifter unsers Glaubens" (NA 20: 125).

93. "Also Liebe . . . ist die Leiter, worauf wir emporklimmen zur Gottähnlichkeit" (NA 20: 124).

94. "Liebe findet nicht statt unter gleichtönenden Seelen, aber unter harmonischen" (NA 20: 121).

95. "Alle Vollkommenheiten im Universum sind vereinigt in Gott" (NA 20: 123).

96. It is for this reason that I cannot agree with Riedel's point that Schiller's Julius advocates a belief in the unlimited perfection of the human being (*Die Anthropologie des jungen Schiller*, p. 158).

97. "Liebe ist die mitherrschende Bürgerin eines blühenden Freistaats, Egoismus ein Despot in einer verwüsteten Schöpfung" (NA 20: 123).

98. "Ein Geist, der sich allein liebt, ist ein schwimmender Atom im unermeßlichen leeren Raume" (NA 20: 122).

99. "Würde die Liebe im Umkreis der Schöpfung ersterben—wie bald—wie bald würde das Band der Weesen zerrissen seyn, wie bald das unermesslich Geisterreich in anarchischem Aufruhr dahintoben, eben so als die ganze Grundlage der Körperwelt zusammenstürzen, als alle Räder der Natur einen ewigen Stillstand halten würden, wenn das mächtige Gesez der Anziehung aufgehoben worden wäre" (NA 20: 32).

100. Both Riedel (*Die Anthropologie des jungen Schiller*) and Schings ("Philosophie der Liebe und Tragödie des Universalhasses," cited n. 79) have underscored this point while exploring the possible influence of Friedrich Christoph Oetinger, i.e., a part of the hermetic-pietistic tradition, on Schiller's thinking. We will explore the writer's emphasis on love, to which both Schings and Riedel refer, again in the next chapter. Riedel makes the important point that poetic metaphors do not serve the same function as rhetorical decoration (pp. 182–83). Rather, in the case of love, the metaphor has to do with a real analogy. God created both the "Geisterwelt" and the "Körperwelt" according to a single principle. However, neither Riedel nor Schings account for the potential crisis of rupture, despite brief mention by Riedel of what would happen without love (p. 183).

101. "Alles in mir und außer mir ist nur Hieroglyphe einer Kraft die mir ähnlich ist. Die Geseze der Natur sind die Chiffern, welche das denkende Wesen zusammenfügt, sich dem denkenden Wesen verständlich zu machen—das Alphabet, vermittelst dessen alle Geister mit dem vollkommensten Geist und mit sich selbst unterhandeln" (NA 20: 116).

102. *Albrecht Haller, First Lines of Physiology . . . A Reprint of the 1786 Edition*, p. xxxv.

103. "Die Analogie verbindet eine Menge besonderer und wohl unterschiedener Erscheinungen unter sich und mit andern durch gewisse allgemeinere Sätze" (Johann Georg Zimmermann, *Von der Erfahrung in der Arzneykunst*, p. 293).

104. Zimmermann, *Von der Erfahrung in der Arzneykunst*, p. 293.

105. "daß eine jede Empfindung, welcher Art sie auch immer seye, also gleich eine andere ihrer Art ergreiffe, und sich durch diesen Zuwachs vergrössere" (NA 20: 72).

106. "Nun ist, wie wir wissen, jede geistige Empfindung mit einer ähnlichen thierischen vergesellschaftet, d.i. mit andern Worten: jede ist mit mehr oder wenigern Nervenbewegungen verknüpft, die sich nach dem Grad ihrer Stärke und Ausbreitung richten. Also: so wie die geistigen Empfindungen wachsen, müssen auch die Bewegungen im Nervensystem zunehmen" (NA 20: 72).

107. "Jeder Zustand der menschlichen Seele hat irgendeine Parabel in der physischen Schöpfung, wodurch er bezeichnet wird" (NA 20: 116).

108. "daß sogar das künftige Schicksal des menschlichen Geistes im dunkeln Orakel der körperlichen Schöpfung vorher verkündigt liegt" (NA 20: 116).

109. "Ich bespreche mich mit dem Unendlichen durch das Instrument der Natur, durch die Weltgeschichte—ich lese die Seele des Künstlers in seinem Apollo" (NA 20: 116).

110. "Unsre Gedanken von diesen Dingen sind nur die endemische [*sic*] Formen, worinn sie uns der Planet überliefert, den wir bewohnen—unser Gehirn gehört diesem Planeten, folglich auch die Idiome unsrer Begriffe, die darinne aufbewahrt liegen" (NA 20: 127).

111. "die Kraft der Seele ist eigenthümlich, nothwendig, und immer sich selbst gleich" (NA 20: 127).

112. "das Willkührliche der Materialien, woran sie sich äußert, ändert nichts an den ewigen Gesetzen, wornach sie sich äußert . . . so lang das Zeichen dem Bezeichneten durchaus treu bleibt" (NA 20: 127).

113. Riedel remarks that Bonnet was "der Biologe des 18. Jahrhunderts, der das Konzept einer Stufenleiter das Wesen am konsequentesten durchzuführen sucht" (*Die Anthropologie des jungen Schiller*, p. 114, n. 56), one extending from the plant world to the inhabitants of other planets.

114. This thesis is worked out in Charles Bonnet's *La palingénésis philosophique; ou, Ideés sur l'etat passé et sur l'etat futur des etres vivans.* 2 vols. (Geneva: C. Philbert, 1769).

115. Karl S. Guthke, "Are We Alone? The Idea of Extraterrestrial Intelligence in Literature and Philosophy from Copernicus to H. G. Wells," in *Utopian Vision. Technological Innovation and Poetic Imagination*, eds. Klaus L. Berghahn and Reinhold Grimm (Heidelberg: Carl Winter, 1990), pp. 94–95.

116. In his *Phaedon oder über die Unsterblichkeit der Seele in drey Gesprächen* 4th ed. (Berlin: Nicolai, 1776), Moses Mendelssohn presented a case for the indestructibility of the soul, as had Plato before him. Riedel suggests that Mendelssohn's writing was a critical response to Voltaire's satire *Candide* (1759) with its criticism of theodicy, optimism, and the perfectibility of the human being (*Die Anthropologie des jungen Schiller*, p. 161).

117. I disagree somewhat with D/R's interpretation here. The inclusion of Haller's now famous definition in the third dissertation did come at the urging of his committee members because of the candidate's alleged disrespect for the great physiologist (Stahl/Reuß). In fact, this idea of the twofold nature of the human being as part animal, part spirit has a long tradition in the Western world, dating back at least to the time of St. Augustine. In this context, the definition serves to draw out the tension between anthropology and metaphysics in Schiller's writings.

118. "und so schwebe ich, als eine Zwitterart, zwischen dem Begriff und der Anschauung, zwischen der Regel und der Empfindung, zwischen dem technischen Kopf und dem Genie" (NA 27: 32). According to Helmut Koopmann ("Denken in Bildern," *Jahrbuch der Deutschen Schillergesellschaft* 30 [1986]: 218–50), this was an unfortunate formulation. It is unfortunate to the extent that it has led scholars to distinguish far too sharply between Goethe and Schiller. Anni Carlsson, for instance, favors Goethe's "reichere . . . dichterische Kraft" based on "Anschauung" over Schiller's "Spekulation" (*Die deutsche Buchkritik: Von den Anfängen bis 1850* [Stuttgart: Kohlhammer, 1963], vol. 1, p. 97). S. S. Kerry: "Goethe has, as it were, natural rights and interests over a wider terrestrial area than Schiller" (p. 5); and: "The natural world which is available to Schiller is available only in fragmentation" (p. 6); finally: "Schiller's poetic enthusiasm is generated a priori—before and independently of that contact with the earth which fructifies the naive imagination" (p. 6). Carlsson further disseminated the notion of Schiller as an idealist ("der Idealist Schiller"; p. 100). I believe that Schiller's statement helps explain the harmonious tension of his writings.

119. "leider aber, nachdem ich meine moralischen Kräfte recht zu kennen und zu gebrauchen angefangen, droht eine Krankheit, meine physischen zu untergraben. Eine große und allgemeine Geistesrevolution werde ich schwerlich Zeit haben in mir

zu vollenden, aber ich werde tun, was ich kann, und wenn endlich das Gebäude zusammenfällt, so habe ich doch vielleicht das Erhaltungswerte aus dem Brande geflüchtet" (NA 27: 32).

120. Dorothea Kuhn, "Der naturwissenschaftliche Unterricht an der Hohen Karlsschule," *Medizin historisches Journal* 11 (1976): 331. This important article underscores just how intense the study of nature was at the Carlsschule, especially after the founding of the medical faculty in Stuttgart in 1775. On a more general level, Kuhn explains: "Die Affinität der Aufklärung zum naturwissenschaftlichen Denken rückte die Naturwissenschaften in die innere Sphäre der Bildungsbestrebungen" (p. 327). Professor Kuhn is, however, less enthusiastic about Schiller's involvement with natural science than I. She cautions that we should know which natural-scientific studies and textbooks Schiller actually studied before generalizing. The fact, however, that no one seems to know where the library of the Carlsschule is, preempts determining this with certainty. We are aware of Goethe's influence on Schiller in this area after 1794. Still, a study of Schiller's language does not preclude the possibility of the impact of natural-scientific study. On the contrary, but this specific topic awaits a separate, more detailed study.

121. Dewhurst and Reeves note that this book became "a standard work, going into several editions" (D/R, p. 12).

122. Cited by Reinhard Buchwald in his portrait of Schiller in *Schwäbische Lebensbilder,* eds. Hermann Haering and Otto Hohenstatt (Stuttgart: W. Kohlhammer, 1940), vol. 1, p. 484.

Chapter 2. The Early Poetic Writings

1. "Noch einmal also: der Mensch mußte Thier seyn, eh er wußte, daß er ein Geist war, er mußte am Staube kriechen, eh er den Newtonischen Flug durch das Universum wagte" (NA 20: 56). For the poetry, I include the original German in the main body of the text together with as literal of a translation as possible. Line and page numbers are from the Nationalausgabe.

2. Kuhn, "Der naturwissenschaftliche Unterricht an der Hohen Karlsschule," cited in chapter 1, n. 120, p. 327. Schiller's father Johann Caspar noted the uniqueness of the Academy. "Der Herzog führt das wissenschaftliche und polizeiliche Ruder zugleich, was allem schon die Akademie zu einem Originale macht." Quoted by Ernst Müller, *Der junge Schiller* (Tübingen/Stuttgart: Rainer Wunderlich, 1947), p. 33.

3. *Dr. Sulzers Abgekürzte Geschichte der Insecten Nach dem Linaeischen System* 2 parts (Winterthur: H. Steiner u. Comp., 1776), p. 23. Schiller may also have consulted Charles Bonnet's *Abhandlungen aus der Insektologie. Aus dem Französischen übersetzt und mit einigen Zusätzen hrsg. von Joh. August Ephraim Goeze* (Halle: J. J. Gebauers Witwe und Joh. Jac. Gebauer, 1773). One of the most noteworthy studies of insects in the eighteenth century was written by Bonnet's mentor René-Antoine Ferchault de Réaumur. The six-volume work is titled *Mémoires pour servir a l'histoire des insectes* (1734–1742).

4. *Sulzers Abgekürzte Geschichte der Insecten,* p. 23.

5. Ibid.

6. Ibid., p. 24.

7. Wolfgang Düsing, "Kosmos und Natur in Schillers Lyrik" *Jahrbuch der Deutschen Schillergesellschaft* 13 (1969): 201. Hans-Jürgen Schings is too harsh in his negative review of Düsing's contribution as poeticizing, metaphorizing subjectivism ("Philosophie der Liebe and Tragödie des Universalhasses," cited in chapter 1, n. 79, p. 86).

8. As suggested by Düsing, p. 199. I note here that, for Barthold Heinrich Brockes, the sun was "der Lebens-Gluth / Entflammter Mittelpunkt" ("Der Abend," ll. 39b–40a, in *Hrn. B. H. Brockes. Harmonische Himmels-Lust im Irdischen, oder auserlesene, theils neue, theils aus dem Irdischen Vergnügen genommene, und nach den 4 Jahres-Zeiten eingerichtete Musicalische Gedichte und Kantaten. Mit einer Vorrede zum Druck befördert von B. H. Brockes.* Second edition. Hamburg: Conrad König, 1744, p. 81; and God is "Der Sonnen-Sonne" [l. 77] [83]). Johann Georg Zimmermann once recalled how the ancients conceived of the sun. "Pythagoras, sagte ein alter Philosoph, siehet die Sonne mit anderen Augen an als Anaxagoras, jener als einen Gott, dieser als einen Stein" (*Von der Erfahrung in der Arzney-kunst,* p. 90).

9. *Schwäbisches Magazin von gelehrten Sachen auf das Jahr 1776,* Balthasar Haug, ed., Stuttgart: Erhardische Schriften. Sechstes Stück, 436 (III. "Gelehrte Neuigkeiten und Anzeigen"). Jakob Minor characterized the journal as "eine Art von württembergischer Litterarhistorie" (*Schiller. Sein Leben und seine Werke,* vol. 1, p. 495).

10. *Dr. Albrecht Hallers Versuch Schweizerischer Gedichte,* third edition (Bern: Niclaus Emanuel Haller, 1743), p. 152.

11. Ibid., p. 153.

12. In *Klopstocks Oden* (Leipzig: Georg Joachim Göschen, 1798), vol. 2, p. 246.

13. Düsing, "Kosmos und Natur in Schillers Lyrik," cited in n. 7, p. 206.

14. Dorothea Kuhn observes: "Aber bei dem Wort 'Kreislauf' zögert man, es der Maschinenwelt zuzuordnen, weil es ebenso im Sinn des Planetenlaufes wie in dem der Blutzirkulation gebräuchlich war" ("Versuch über Modelle der Natur in der Goethezeit," cited in chapter 1, n. 14, p. 164).

15. Fähnrich has seen that the most frequently employed metaphor in Schiller's early poetry is that of the stringed instrument (Schillers Musikalität, pp. 34–35).

16. See chapter 1, n. 19.

17. Suggested by Düsing, "Kosmos und Natur in Schillers Lyrik," p. 198.

18. "Der Abend" appeared in the October 1776 issue of the *Schwäbisches Magazin von gelehrten Sachen auf das Jahr 1776,* Zehentes Stück, pp. 715–19.

19. Ueding, *Friedrich Schiller,* p. 67f.

20. Düsing, "Kosmos und Natur in Schillers Lyrik," p. 4.

21. E.g., Kaiser, *Vergötterung und Tod.* The religious dimension of much of Schiller's earliest poetic writings testifies to the importance of such instruction in the writer's education (e.g. Brastberger's book of devotions) and the influence of Swabian pietism (Oetinger et al.). A generally reliable, and certainly very helpful study of the impact of Swabian pietism on the young Schiller is Arthur W. McCardle's *Friedrich Schiller and Swabian Pietism* (New York/Berne/Frankfurt a.M.: Peter Lang, 1986). At times, however, the reader may wonder how well founded the assumed influences are. It is the same question I have when reading Riedel's *Die Anthropologie des jungen Schiller.* While on the topic of religion and Schiller, I must take issue with Wolfgang Martens's claim that, for the later Schiller, "Gebildetes Ästhetentum macht christliche Religiosität überflüssig . . . Schiller hat es in einem Brief an den Prinzen von Augustenburg ähnlich gesehen . . . Die Religion also nur noch ein Zufluchtsort der Amusischen, der zur Wahrnehmung der heiligen Kunst Unfähigen!" ("Officiana Diaboli. Das Theater im Visier des Halleschen Pietismus," in *Literatur und Frömmigkeit in der Zeit der frühen Aufklärung* [Tübingen: Max Niemeyer, 1989], p. 47).

22. As much as I appreciate David Pugh's contribution "Schiller as Platonist" *Colloquia Germanica* 24 (1991): 273–95, the Platonic tradition is only one of many

strains of Schiller's writings. When bearing in mind the other dimensions of his writings, we arrive at a much broader understanding of the man and his work.

23. Von Wiese, *Friedrich Schiller,* p. 132.

24. "Schillers Metaphorik dient der Versinnlichung des Abstrakten und seiner dialektischen Spannungen. Die zwischen Elysium und Tod gespannte Existenz des Menschen muß immer erneut widerspruchsvoll werden" (Von Wiese, *Friedrich Schiller,* p. 130).

25. Düsing, "Kosmos und Natur in Schillers Lyrik," p. 201.

26. Ibid., p. 203.

27. Schiller accentuates the reciprocity of reason and imagination in the creative production of literary works in his book reviews. See my article "Shaping the Imagination: Friedrich Schiller's Book Reviews," in *The Eighteenth-Century German Book Review,* edited by Herbert Rowland and Karl J. Fink. (Heidelberg: Carl Winter, 1995), pp. 137–50.

28. Dewhurst and Reeves were the first to sketch the possible impact of the medical writings on some of Schiller's poetic, philosophical, and dramatic works ("Chapter 7. The Intellectual Legacy of Medicine and Psychology" [D/R, p. 307f.]).

29. NA 1: 47 records "Sennen," which must be a printing error. Only "Sinnen" makes sense in this context.

30. Riedel, *Die Anthropologie des jungen Schiller,* p. 182f.

31. Drawing upon the work of Hans-Jürgen Schings, Riedel points to this connection between the essay and the speech (p. 182).

32. "Die Anziehung der Elemente brachte die körperliche Form der Natur zu Stande. Die Anziehung der Geister in's Unendliche vervielfältigt und fortgesetzt, mußte endlich zur Aufhebung jener Trennung führen, oder . . . Gott hervorbringen. Eine solche Anziehung ist die Liebe" (NA 20: 124).

33. On this point, Riedel (*Die Anthropologie des jungen Schiller*) does not take issue with Gert Ueding's book *Schillers Rhetorik. Idealistische Wirkungsästhetik und rhetorische Tradition* (Tübingen: Max Niemeyer, 1971), a study that overemphasizes the writer's employment of [Florentine] rhetoric. However, the omission may well be intentional. In addition to the close association between poetry and rhetoric in eighteenth-century German literature, aesthetics and poetology (for the latter, see my *On Imitation, Imagination, and Beauty*), we should keep in mind the emphasis eighteenth-century thinkers such as Johann Jacob Breitinger (*Critische Dichtkunst* [Zürich: Orell, 1740]) placed on the use of metaphor "as a remedy of sorts for the arbitrary nature of signs, for it is the vividness of the metaphorical expression that allows us to see the relationship between things and the words that describe them" (Jill Anne Kowalik, *The Poetics of Historical Perspectivism: Breitinger's "Critische Dichtkunst" and the Neoclassic Tradition* [Chapel Hill/London: University of North Carolina Press, 1992], p. 115). In *The Birth of Tragedy Out of the Spirit of Music,* Friedrich Nietzsche understood that "Metaphor, for the authentic poet, is not a figure of rhetoric but a representative image standing concretely before him in lieu of a concept" (*Friedrich Nietzsche: "The Birth of Tragedy" and "The Genealogy of Morals,"* trans. Francis Golffing [New York/London: Doubleday, 1956], p. 55). Recently, Jonathan Culler advanced the idea "that today metaphor is no longer one figure among others but the figure of figures, a figure for figurality" (*The Pursuit of Signs: Semiotics, Literature, Deconstruction* [Ithaca, New York: Cornell University Press, 1983], p. 189). Other valuable studies on metaphor include: Terence Hawkes, *Metaphor* (London/New York: Methuen, 1972), J. J. A. Mooy, *A Study of Metaphor* (Amsterdam: North Holland Publishing Co., 1976), and Paul Ricoeur, *The Rule of Metaphor,* trans. Robert Czerny, et al. (Toronto: University of Toronto Press, 1977). An interdisciplinary conference on metaphor was held, in 1978, at the University of

California at Davis. See also: James Fernandez, *Beyond Metaphor: The Theory of Tropes in Anthropology* (Palo Alto: Stanford University Press, 1991), which challenges this direction in scholarly research.

34. Riedel, *Die Anthropologie des jungen Schiller*, p. 183.

35. "Ein Geist, der sich allein liebt, ist ein schwimmender Atom im unermeßlichen *leeren* Raume" (NA 20: 122).

36. Karl S. Guthke, *The Last Frontier: Imagining Other Worlds, from the Copernican Revolution to Modern Science Fiction*, trans. Helen Atkins (Ithaca/London: Cornell University Press, 1990b), pp. ix–x. Translated from: *Der Mythos der Neuzeit. Das Thema der Mehrheit der Welten in der Literatur—und Geistesgeschichte von der kopernikanischen Wende bis zur Science Fiction* (Bern/München: Francke, 1983), to which I also refer.

37. Guthke, *The Last Frontier*, p. 213; *Mythos*, p. 190.

38. Ibid.

39. Guthke, *The Last Frontier*, p. 322; *Mythos*, p. 283.

40. As pointed out by Von Wiese, *Friedrich Schiller*, p. 125.

41. Arthur O. Lovejoy, *The Great Chain of Being: A Study of the History of an Idea*, tenth edition (Cambridge, Massachusetts: Harvard University Press, 1971).

42. Guthke, *The Last Frontier*, p. 215; *Mythos*, p. 192.

43. Guthke, *The Last Frontier*, p. 54; *Mythos*, p. 56.

44. Also noted by Guthke, *The Last Frontier*, p. 218; *Mythos*, p. 195.

45. *Carl Friedrich Drollinger. Gedichte*, Faksimiledruck nach der Ausgabe von 1743, kommentiert von Uwe-K. Ketelsen (Stuttgart: J. B. Metzler, 1972), p. 115.

46. Karl Richter quotes this passage from Drollinger's poem only from a different angle in his *Literatur und Naturwissenschaft. Eine Studie zur Lyrik der Aufklärung* (München: Wilhelm Fink, 1972). See also his important article "Die kopernikanische Wende in der Lyrik von Brockes bis Klopstock," *Jahrbuch der Deutschen Schillergesellschaft* 12 (1968): pp. 132–69.

47. Richter, *Literatur und Naturwissenschaft*, p. 92.

48. Ibid., p. 92.

49. Ibid.

50. Ibid.

51. Gerhard Storz, "Gesichtspunkte für die Betrachtung von Schillers Lyrik," *Jahrbuch der Deutschen Schillergesellschaft* 12 (1968): 259–74. The theses Storz advances in this article indicate an about-face from his earlier book on Schiller, *Der Dichter Friedrich Schiller* (Stuttgart: Ernst Klett, 1959).

52. Storz, "Gesichtspunkte für die Betrachtung von Schillers Lyrik," p. 260.

53. Fritz Wagner, *Zur Apotheose Newtons. Künstlerische Utopie und naturwissenschaftliches Weltbild im 18. Jahrhundert* (München: Verlag der Bayerischen Akademie der Wissenschaften, 1974), p. 10.

54. Hans Blumenberg, *Die kopernikanische Wende* 46.

55. For a study of the transdisciplinary character of eighteenth-century thought, see Barbara Stafford, *Body Criticism: Imaging the Unseen in Enlightenment Art and Medicine* (Cambridge, Massachusetts: MIT Press, 1991). Her interest in metaphorology is related structurally to the work of Hans Blumenberg, though she does not refer to the German scholar directly.

56. Hayden White investigated the tropes that characterize historical writings in the nineteenth century in his *Metahistory: The Historical Imagination in Nineteenth-Century Europe* (Baltimore/London: Johns Hopkins Press, 1973). A defense of the scientific nature of historical writing was then offered by Maurice Mandelbaum, *The Anatomy of Historical Knowledge* (Baltimore: Johns Hopkins Press, 1977).

57. Blumenberg, *Die kopernikanische Wende*, p. 37.

58. Düsing, "Kosmos und Natur in Schillers Lyrik," cited in n.7, pp. 201–02.
59. Anonymous, *Klopstock und Schiller. Oder: Kritische Versuche über einige lyrische Gedichte des Letztern, in poetischer und moralischer Absicht* (Ellwangen/ Gmünd: Ritter, 1821), p. 87.
60. Anon., *Klopstock und Schiller*, p. 88.
61. Ibid., p. 89.
62. Ibid.

Chapter 3. The Thematic Unities of *Criminal Out of Infamy* and the Early Dramatic Texts

1. My interpretation of Schiller's story differs markedly from Lesley Sharpe, "*Der Verbrecher aus verlorener Ehre*: An Early Exercise in Schillerian Psychology," *German Life and Letters* 33 (1980): 102–10.
2. "Die Natur hatte seinen Körper verabsäumt" (NA 16: 10). Translations are my own.
3. E.g., Gerhard Kaiser, *Von Arkadien nach Elysium. Schiller Studien* (Göttingen: Vandenhoeck und Ruprecht, 1978). Kaiser asserts "daß die Gesellschaft als Ordnung einzelner den Sonnenwirt bei größerer Anteilnahme vielleicht hätte retten können, ehe die Justiz ihn verschlingen mußte" (p. 56). What troubles me most about Kaiser's interpretation is that he does not account for the fact that Christian Wolf commits murder. In approaching the work of Friedrich Schiller, one should look not only at the writer's aesthetics but also his sense of ethics.
4. "Er wollte ertrotzen, was ihm verweigert war" (NA 16: 10).
5. "Drückendes Gefühl des Mangels gesellte sich zu beleidigtem Stolze, Not und Eifersucht stürmen vereinigt auf seine Empfindlichkeit ein, der Hunger treibt ihn hinaus in die weite Welt, Rache und Leidenschaft halten ihn fest" (NA 16: 11).
6. "Ich will alles um mich her ausrotten, was mich einschränkt daß ich nicht *Herr* bin. *Herr* muß ich seyn, daß ich das mit Gewalt ertrotze, wozu mir die Liebenswürdigkeit gebricht" (NA 3: 20). Translations of *Die Räuber* are from *Friedrich Schiller: The Robbers. Wallenstein*, trans. and introd. F. J. Lamport (London: Penguin, 1979). Hereafter: L; followed by the appropriate page number in the main body of the text.
7. "Mit einem Wort: der Zustand des grösten Seelenschmerzes ist zugleich der Zustand der grösten körperlichen Krankheit" (NA 20: 59).
8. In the Löffler edition, which was authorized only pro forma by the author, Franz speaks of the "Joch des Mechanismus" and adds: "Leidenschaften mißhandeln die Lebenskraft" (II:1). The edition is included in Volume III of the *Nationalausgabe*. This expanded version of Schiller's play actually strengthens the thematic unity between the drama and the medical dissertation.
9. "Diese Spinnweben von Systemen zerreißt das einzige Wort: Du mußt sterben!" (NA 3: 122).
10. "So kann man denn mit Recht behaupten, daß der übertriebene Vigor der physischen Aktionen den Tod so sehr beschleunigt als die höchste Disharmonie oder die heftigste Krankheit" (NA 20: 73, para. 25).
11. "Ich wollte Böses tun . . . Ich wollte mein Schicksal verdienen" (NA 16: 14).
12. An important discussion of this aspect of the narrative is found in the response to Hildburg Herbst's presentation "Zur Sprache des Sonnenwirts in Schillers Erzählung 'Der Verbrecher aus verlorener Ehre,'" in *Friedrich Schiller. Kunst, Humanität und Politik in der späten Aufklärung. Ein Symposium*, ed. Wolfgang Wittkowski (Tübingen: Max Niemeyer, 1982), pp. 48–58.
13. Hans-Jürgen Schings has seen that Schiller was critical of the extremes of

melancholy and sanguine behavior in his book *Melancholie und Aufklärung. Melancholiker und ihre Kritiker in Erfahrungsseelenkunde und Literatur des 18. Jahrhunderts* (Stuttgart: J. B. Metzler, 1977), esp. p. 256f. His study actually situates Schiller more firmly within the German Enlightenment.

14. "Zwischen einem Leben voll rastloser Todesfurcht und einer gewaltsamen Entleibung war mir jetzt eine schreckliche Wahl gelassen, und ich *mußte* wählen. Ich hatte das Herz nicht, durch Selbstmord aus der Welt zu gehen und entsetzte mich vor der Aussicht, darin zu bleiben" (NA 16: 17).

15. "Am schroffen Absturz eines Felsen, der sich in eine tiefe Kluft hinunterbückte" (NA 16: 20).

16. "Ich sah in den Schlund hinab, der mich jetzt aufnehmen sollte; es erinnerte mich dunkel an den Abgrund der Hölle, woraus keine Erlösung mehr ist" (NA 16: 21).

17. *"Was hat ein Mörder zu wagen?"* (NA 16: 21).

18. Kaiser offers a close analysis of Wolf's association with the robbers (*Von Arkadien nach Elysium*, cited in n. 3, p. 53), but he fails to appreciate the effect of this alliance on the moral development (*Bildung*) of Wolf's character.

19. "Verlassen von der Leiter, die dich trug, bleibt dir jetzt keine andere Wahl mehr, als mit freyem Bewußtseyn und Willen das Gesetz zu ergreifen oder rettungslos in eine bodenlose Tiefe zu fallen" (NA 20: 428).

20. "Neid, Argwohn und Eifersucht wüteten im Innern dieser verworfenen Bande" (NA 16:23).

21. "Sein natürlich guter Verstand siegte endlich über die traurige Täuschung" (NA 16: 24).

22. "Jetzt fühlte er, wie tief er gefallen war . . . Er wünschte mit Tränen die Vergangenheit zurück; jetzt wußte er gewiß, daß er sie ganz anders wiederholen würde . . . Auf dem höchsten Gipfel seiner Verschlimmerung war er dem Guten näher, als er vielleicht vor seinem ersten Fehltritt gewesen war" (NA 16: 24).

23. "Meine Hinrichtung wird ein Beispiel sein für die Welt, aber kein Ersatz meiner Taten. Ich hasse das Laster, und sehne mich feurig nach Rechtschaffenheit und Tugend" (NA 16: 25).

24. Lesley Sharpe distrusts the judge's sincerity ("Der Verbrecher aus verlorner Ehre," cited in n.1). But she cites only the last two phrases of the following passage: "Den Morgen darauf überlegte der Oberamtmann, der Fremde möchte doch wohl unschuldig sein; die befehlshaberische Sprache würde nichts über seinen Starrsinn vermögen, es wäre vielleicht besser getan, ihm mit Anstand und Mäßigung zu begegnen" (NA 16: 28). I detect no insincerity on the magistrate's part. In fact, the use of the subjunctive form reflects his concern for the proper course of action given the present circumstances. Hence, he appears to be a rational-moral individual, "ein edler Mann" (an honorable man), as Christian perceives. Furthermore, it is only Christian's attempt to flee which makes him look suspicious. As the judge observes, only the appearance ("Schein") of wrongdoing incriminates the newcomer. It is also clear that the townspeople have no idea who this individual is even though his actions indict him. In light of these facts, Christian's disclosure of his true identity constitutes a bold moral decision. Here, I agree with Sharpe that the magistrate's behavior "in no way detracts from the moral quality of his [Christian's] response" (p. 109, n. 1). Still, we must question the British scholar's point that "Wolf's apparent moral rebirth is based on a mistaken perception of the situation" which she makes in her insightful book *Schiller and the Historical Character: Presentation and Interpretation in the Historiographical Works and in the Historical Dramas* (Oxford: Oxford University Press, 1982), p. 86.

25. "Und ist nicht der körperliche Schmerz, der jedes Übermaas begleitet, ein Fingerzeig des göttlichen Willens?" (NA 3: 17).

26. Also suggested by Michelsen (*Der Bruch mit der Vater-Welt*, p. 39) and D/
R. To be sure, the characters "wüten, toben, wimmern, klagen und seufzen durch
die fünf Akten hindurch" (Michelsen, p. 42), but the experience is also auditory and
the representation is symbolic in nature. Michelsen argues "Daß der pathetische
Geist der Oper die szenische Wirklichkeit auch der *Räuber* prägt" (p. 20).
Michelsen argued convincingly how strongly the opera had influenced the writing of Schiller's
dramas. He put to rest Reinhard Buchwald's earlier claim: "Auch in der Mannheimer
Zeit hat Schiller für die Oper als Kunstform nur Spott übrig gehabt" (*Schiller* [Leip-
zig: Insel, 1937], vol. 1, p. 124). Michelsen refers back to Charles Batteux's depiction
of music and its effect on the sensations and passions. Yet, he concentrates more
on the "Gebärdensprache" (which is said to constitute a "seelisches Geschehen"
[p. 32]) than on the music and the musical analogies. However, he completely overlooks Schiller's creative employment of the stringed instrument as metaphor and
symbol. Still, Michelsen does perceive "Die Spannung, Über-Spannung, der Schillerschen Sprache" (p. 105). Hans-Jürgen Schings ("Schillers *Räuber:* Ein Experiment
des Universalhasses," in *Friedrich Schiller. Kunst, Humanität und Politik*) also refers
to the "Explosionen der großen Geister" in the "Experimentierraum" of the drama.
Their "Aufschwünge, Entzückungen, Höhenflüge, Gewalttaten" belong "in ein[em]
festumrissene[n] Koordinatensystem" (p. 1). Michelsen, however, understands Schiller's intentions to be largely those of a rhetorician: "durch Einflußnahme auf ele-
mentare Triebschichten die Zuhörer in einen Zustand leidenschaftlich-emotionaler
Erregtheit zu versetzen" (p. 12). Michelsen underscores the operatic conventions of
Schiller's drama vs. natural expression. In n. 20, he goes so far to assert that opera
is opposed to the operations of Nature (p. 14). But though such conventions certainly
surprise the audience, is not Nature also capable of surprising the observer, such as
in sublime moments? Does not Karl Moor's change (*Wandlung*) in nature surprise
the audience? Gloria Flaherty (*Opera in the Development of German Critical
Thought* [Princeton, N.J.: Princeton University Press, 1978]) also recognized that
Schiller had learned a great deal from the operatic stage (p. 297). In advance of
Friedrich Nietzsche, Schiller was confident that "a new, more ideal tragic form could
develop out of opera just as Greek tragedy had developed out of the Dionysian
chorus" (p. 297). Owing, perhaps, to his Marxist orientation, Klaus Scherpe
("Friedrich Schiller. 'Die Räuber'" in *Dramen des Sturm und Drang. Interpretationen* [Stuttgart: Reclam, 1987]) criticized the "Herzreißende und Sentimentale" of
the opera-like ("opernhafte") premiere performance (p. 12). For him, this evidences
"die Widersprüchlichkeit eines aufs Revolutionäre zielenden Stücks, das in sich doch
die Möglichkeit der Revolution energisch bestreitet" (p. 14). According to Andreas
Streicher, the applause at the premiere performance in Mannheim was so rousing
that Schiller, himself surprised by the response, stood up and bowed to the audience
(*Schillers Flucht von Stuttgart*, p. 195). One of the strengths of Michael Mann's
study, by contrast, is his attempt to account for the religious, moral, psychological,
and philosophical dimensions of the dramatic writing (p. 101f.). Schings's understanding of the drama as an "experimentellen Generalangriff auf das Konzept der 'chain
of love'" (p. 8) is most perceptive. The warring brothers, he argues, are *both* engaged
in a frontal attack on society and world order (p. 9). He asks if "mit dem ganzen
Instrumentarium der Anthropologie und Metaphysik, die Labyrinthe, die 'ineinand-
ergedrungenen Realitäten' der großen Verbrecher angegangen werden?" (p. 9). Somewhat like Von Wiese, Helmut Koopmann, Dieter Borchmeyer, and Michelsen,
however, Schings conceives of the brothers reacting against the patriarchal order
represented by their father. But father Moor is pale and weak. Schiller's own reference ("die Privaterbitterung gegen den unzärtlichen Vater wütet in einen Univer-
salhaß gegen das ganze Menschengeschlecht aus" [NA 12: 120]), which is Schings's

point of departure, is not convincing given the father's very weak constitution—and death. In actuality, the relationship between self-enlightenment and worldly experience seems most central. Karl's tragic error consists in his having trusted the contents of his brother's letter containing his father's *apparent* condemnation. He simply accepts the authority of the written word when he declares that the letter "sprengt den Kosmos der Sympathie" (p. 12). No, Karl's unenlightened, i.e., uncritical, acceptance of the authority of the written word is the true source of his tragic downfall. Finally, though Schings states that he would not like to see the pupil, the philosopher, man of medicine, and dramatist divided (p. 24), he does not really incorporate the content of the medical dissertations into his reading of the play. Whatever one's reservations concerning his ideas, the strength of Schings's studies is that he takes Schiller's early writings seriously by relating them to a wider cultural context.

27. "Soll sich mein hochfliegender Geist an den Schneckengang der *Materie* ketten lassen?" (NA 3: 38).

28. "Philosophen und Mediziner lehren mich, wie treffend die Stimmungen des Geistes mit den Bewegungen der Maschine zusammenlauten. Gichtrische Empfindungen [= Krämpfe] werden jederzeit von einer Dissonanz der mechanischen Schwingungen begleitet—Leidenschaften *mißhandeln* die Lebenskraft—. . . den *Körper* vom *Geist* aus zu verderben—ha! ein Originalwerk!—wer das zu Stand brächte!" (NA 3: 38–39).

29. Noted also by Riedel, *Die Anthropologie des jungen Schiller*, p. 164.

30. Jürgen Schlunk submits that the recipient overlooks the "Explosionskraft" of *The Robbers* "wenn man in ihrer größeren Harmonie nicht auch den Kern einer schrillen Dissonanz erkennen würde" ("Vertrauen als Ursache und Überwindung tragischer Verstrickung in Schillers 'Räubern,'" *Jahrbuch der Deutschen Schillergesellschaft* 27 [1983]: 197).

31. "Große Gedanken dämmern auf in meiner Seele! . . . Verfluchte Schlafsucht! . . . Die bisher meine Kräfte in Ketten schlug, meine Aussichten sperrte und spannte; ich erwache, fühle, wer ich bin—wer ich werden muß!" (NA 3: 24).

32. "Mein Geist dürstet nach Thaten, mein Athem nach Freyheit,—*Mörder, Räuber!*" (NA 3: 32).

33. "Warum ist dieser Geist nicht in einen Tyger gefahren, der sein wütendes Gebiß in Menschenfleisch haut? Ist das Vatertreue? Ist das Liebe für Liebe? Ich möchte ein Bär seyn, und die Bären des Nordlands wider dis mörderische Geschlecht anhezen" (NA 3: 31).

34. "Ein reissend Thier hat Joseph zerrissen!" (NA 3: 52).

35. "Ach, sie stimmten so harmonisch zusammen, ich meynte immer, wir müßten Zwillinge seyn!" (NA 3: 36).

36. "Seine Küsse—paradiesisch Fühlen!—/ Wie zwo Flammen sich ergreiffen, wie / Harfentöne in einander spielen / Zu der himmelvollen Harmonie" (NA 3: 74).

37. "Er ist hin . . . und alle Lust des Lebens / Wimmert hin in ein verlornes Ach!" (NA 3: 74). Gerhard Kluge raises the character of Amalia to an equal level with the feuding brothers ("Zwischen Seelenmechanik und Gefühlspathos," *Jahrbuch der Deutschen Schillergesellschaft* 20 [1976]: 184–207). Hans Schwerte ("Schillers 'Räuber'" in *Der Deutschunterricht* 12 [1960]: 18–41) had assigned Amalia only the third level in the constellation of Karl-Franz-Amalia (22f.). It is significant that Kluge should describe her character in terms of dissonance and rupture. "Amalias Seelenzustand ist disharmonisch, dissonantisch." Unable to reconcile her sensuous inclinations and intellectual knowledge, Kluge argues, "so entsteht die Disharmonie in ihrem Seelenleben, den Riß zwischen Gefühlswahrheit und faktischer Wirklichkeit" (p. 189). He also underscores the "Verwirrung, Spannung zwischen der sinnlichen und geistigen Komponente ihrer Liebe" (p. 193). Already before Dewhurst/Reeves,

Kluge observed "daß der Dualismus in der Konzeption der frühen Figuren eindeutig auf Schillers medizinische Schriften verweist" (p. 193). He also perceived that some insights recorded in the third medical dissertation apply to Amalia as well, for "Amalia ist aufs tiefste gekränkt und entrüstet, der Seelenschmerz überträgt sich, gemäß Schillers Auffassung vom Zusammenhang der tierischen mit der geistigen Natur des Menschen, demzufolge 'die geheimsten Rührungen der Seele auf der Aussenseite des Körpers geoffenbahrt' werden (NA 20: 68) in körperliche Aktionen" (p. 196). He asserts that part of Amalia's character exhibits the capacity for freedom, but one that "für alle gewichtigen Figuren in Schillers Jugenddramen in der Spannung zwischen Fatalismus und Freiheit kennzeichnend bleibt" (pp. 203–4). Drawing upon Adolf Beck's important article "Die Krisis im Drama des jungen Schiller" (*Euphorion* 49 [1955]), Kluge speaks of "existentielle[n] Krisen, in die Schillers Figuren gebracht werden" (p. 195) instead of medical crises at this point. For Kluge, Amalia is "dadurch ausgezeichnet, daß sie das Ganze der menschlichen Natur in seinem spannungsreichen Antagonismus von Beginn an sichtbar werden läßt, 'das Bedürfniß des Thiermenschen' und das 'Bedürfnis des Geistes'" (p. 206). Whereas Franz is representative of the animal and Karl of the spiritual-intellectual side of human nature, Amalia, according to Kluge, is the one who reflects "das Ganze der menschlichen Natur in seinem spannungsreichen Antagonismus von Beginn an" (p. 206). Rachid Jai Mansouri suggests, however, that though Amalia is the only character who openly confronts Franz (whereby she asserts her independence) she is actually "das begehrte Objekt von Franz," "das zum Bruderkonflikt führt" (*Die Darstellung der Frau in Schillers Dramen* [New York/Berne/Frankfurt a/M/Paris: Peter Lang, 1988], p. 8). Most important, Gerhard Kluge appreciates the necessity of human action which not only reminds one of the limitations of trying to shape the world but, also, of the strength of human, i.e., moral character in a world that is often not amenable to the personal restructuring of reality. "Schillers Drama ist das Drama des handelnden Menschen, der durch Taten seine Freiheit . . . verliert, in Schuld und krisenhafte Situationen gerät, in denen seine Menschlichkeit auf die Probe steht" (p. 204).

38. Mann, *Sturm-und-Drang Drama,* pp. 89 and 125. I see no evidence of "Amalias Resignation" here, as Mann claims (p. 126).

39. As maintained by Mann, Ibid., p. 126.

40. See *Herzog Karl Eugen von Württemberg und seine Zeit,* ed. vom Württembergischen Geschichts- und Altertums-Verein. 2 vols. (Eßlingen a.N: Paul Neff [Max Schreiber], 1907), vol. 1, 558f. Noted also by Michelsen, *Der Bruch mit der Vater-Welt,* and Mann, *Sturm-und-Drang Drama.*

41. As noted by Michael Mann, *Sturm-und-Drang Drama,* p. 125.

42. The song was originally part of the fourth act. In a letter to W. H. von Dalberg of October 6, 1781, Schiller wrote how, with the encouragement of his friends, he finally placed it in the third act (NA 23: 22). Detlef Brennecke examined the possible sources of Schiller's interest in Walhalla ("'Schön wie Engel, voll Walhallas Wonne.' Altnordisches bei Schiller," *Germanisch-Romanische Monatsschrift* 35 [1985]: 224–27). He refers to the Germanic myth which appeared in translation in 1777 by Jacob Schimmelmann (*Die isländische Edda in Stettin*) and the Balder-myth in the "Edda"-poem to "Balders Träume" in J. G. Herder's *Volkslieder.* Brennecke is certainly correct that the lyrical rhythm of the third act is not, as Benno von Wiese had maintained, simply a "wehrlose[s] Stillehalten." But he goes too far on the basis of just one partial strophe when he sees in the song the "ersten[n] Schritt zu einer rüstigen Attacke gegen den Bruder des Liebsten" (p. 225).

43. "Amalia, *Im Garten, spielt auf der Laute*" (NA 3: 73).

44. "Meere und Berge und Horizonte zwischen den Liebenden" (NA 3: 102).

45. "Ja, eine Welt, wo die Schleyer hinwegfallen, und die Liebe sich schröcklich

widerfindet—*Ewigkeit* heißt ihr Name" (NA 3: 102). Günter Hess considered the
"*Fracta Cithara* oder Die zerbrochene Laute. Zur Allegorisierung der Bekehrungsgeschichte Jacob Baldes im 18. Jahrhundert," in *Formen und Funktionen der Allegorie,* ed., Walter Haug (Stuttgart: J. B. Metzler, 1979), pp. 605–31. In the case of
Jacob Baldes the emblem had to do with his conversion through the curative musica
caelestis, i.e., spiritual music and poetry after having broken the zither or cithara
(as "res significans der Musica mundana") (p. 618). In short, everything remained in
the spiritual realm. Noted also by Peter Michelsen, "Ordnung und Eigensinn. Über
Schillers 'Kabale und Liebe,'" *Jahrbuch des Freien Deutschen Hochstifts 1984:* 208,
n. 10.
     46. Mann called Zumsteeg "der erste Vertoner Schillers" (*Sturm-und-Drang
Drama,* p. 129).
     47. *200 Jahre Schillers 'Räuber'. Die Entstehung des Werks, Uraufführung und
Inszenierungen am Nationaltheater Mannheim,* ed. Wilhelm Herrmann (Mannheim:
Städtisches Reiss-Museum, 1982), p. 17. The project was funded, in part, by the
Schiller Nationalmuseum in Marbach a.N. According to the anonymous author of
Johann Rudolf Zumsteeg (Berlin: Hayn, n.d.), Zumsteeg wrote interlude music to
Klopstock's famous ode "Die Frühlingsfcier" for dramatic performances as well as
music to Bürger's *Lenore* [!] (pp. 39 and 42).
     48. Ludwig Finscher, "Was ist eine lyrische Operette? Anmerkungen zu Schillers
Semele," in *Schiller und die höfische Welt,* p. 151f. See also Christa Vaerst-Pfarr,
"Semele—Die Huldigung der Künste," in *Schillers Dramen. Neue Interpretationen,*
ed. Walter Hinderer (Stuttgart: Reclam, 1979), pp. 294–315.
     49. Finscher, "Was ist eine lyrische Operette? Anmerkungen zu Schillers *Sem-
ele,*" p. 155.
     50. Carl Dahlhaus, "Formbegriff und Ausdrucksprinzip in Schillers Musikäs-
thetik," in *Schiller und die höfische Welt,* p. 167.
     51. "Spielt, befehl ich!—Musik muß ich hören, daß mein schlafender Genius
wieder aufwacht" (NA 3: 210).
     52. "Verworrene Labyrinthe—kein Ausgang—kein leitendes Gestirn" (NA 3:
109).
     53. "Aber wofür der heisse Hunger nach Glückseligkeit? Wofür das Ideal einer
unerreichten Vollkommenheit?" (NA 3: 109).
     54. "Es ist doch eine so göttliche Harmonie in der seelenlosen Natur, warum
sollte dieser Mißklang in der vernünftigen seyn?" (NA 3: 109).
     55. "*Zeit* und *Ewigkeit*—gekettet aneinander durch ein einzig Moment!" (NA
3: 109).
     56. "Sei wie du willst *namenloses Jenseits*—bleibt mir nur dieses mein *Selbst*
getreu" (NA 3: 110).
     57. "Und soll ich für [vor] Furcht eines quaalvollen Lebens sterben?—Soll ich
dem Elend den Sieg über mich einräumen? Nein! Ich wills dulden. *Er wirft die
Pistole weg*" (NA 3: 110).
     58. "Siehe, die Menschheit erschlapft unter *diesem* Bilde, die Spannkraft des
Endlichen läßt nach, und die Phantasey, der muthwillige Affe der Sinne gaukelt
unserer Leichtgläubigkeit seltsame Schatten vor" (NA 3: 109–10).
     59. "Ich würde dann die schweigende Oede mit meinen Phantasien bevölkern,
und hätte die Ewigkeit zur Muße, das verworrene Bild des allgemeinen Elends zu
zergliedern" (NA 3: 110).
     60. "Diese Spinnweben von Systemen zerreißt das einzige Wort: du must ster-
ben!" (NA 3: 122).
     61. "Ich habs immer gelesen, daß unser Wesen nichts ist als Sprung des Geblüts,
und mit dem lezten Blutstropfen zerrinnt auch Geist und Gedanke. Er macht alle

Schwachheiten des Körpers mit, wird er nicht auch aufhören bey seiner Zerstörung? nicht bey seiner Fäulung verdampfen? Laß einen Wassertropfen in deinem Gehirne verirren, und dein Leben macht eine plözliche Pause, die zunächst an das Nichtseyn gränzt, und ihre Fortdauer ist der Tod . . . Empfindung ist Schwingung einiger Saiten, und das zerschlagene Klavier tönet nicht mehr" (NA 3: 121).

62. Gerhard Sautermeister, "Aufklärung und Körpersprache. Schillers Drama auf dem Theater heute," in *Klassik und Moderne. Die Weimarer Klassik als historisches Ereignis und Herausforderung im kulturgeschichtlichen Prozeß. Walter Müller Seidel zum 65. Geburtstag,* eds. Karl Richter and Jörg Schönert (Stuttgart: J. B. Metzler, 1983). Sautermeister sees that body language and enlightenment "bilden ein vielgliedriges Spannungsverhältnis" (p. 624).

63. Ibid.

64. Ibid., p. 625.

65. Ibid.

66. "Müssen denn aber meine Entwürfe sich unter das eiserne Joch des Mechanismus beugen?" (NA 3: 38). As much as I admire his scholarship, John Neubauer ("The Freedom of the Machine: On Mechanism, Materialism, and the Young Schiller," *Eighteenth-Century Studies* 15 [1982]: 275–90) puts the cart before the horse when he applies statements contained in *Concerning the Aesthetic Education of the Human Being in a Series of Letters* to the work of young Schiller without appreciating the historical development of and changes in Schiller's writings.

67. As I first suggested in "Friedrich Schiller's *Der Verbrecher aus verlorener Ehre,* or the Triumph of the Moral Will," *Sprachkunst* 18 (1987): 2–3.

68. "Soll sich mein hochfliegender Geist an den Schneckengang der *Materie* ketten lassen?" (NA 3: 38).

69. In *Friedrich Schiller. Die Räuber. Eine Bild-Dokumentation zur Entstehungs—und Wirkungsgeschichte,* ed. Doris Maurer (Dortmund: Harenberg Dokumentation, 1983), p. 131.

70. *Langenscheidts Enzyklopädisches Wörterbuch der Englischen und Deutschen Sprache. "Der Große Muret-Sanders,"* ed. Otto Springer. 4 vols. 5th ed. (Berlin/München/Wien/Zürich/New York: Langenscheidt, 1990) 2/2: 1422–23.

71. Concerning the problem of the deceived deceiver in German drama of the time, see my article "The Cunning of Deceit in Lessing's Major Works," *Lessing Yearbook* 14 (1982): 99–118.

72. Hans-Jürgen Schings sees in Franz a "Verbrecher aus verlorener Liebe" ("Schillers *Räuber,*" cited in n.26, p. 15). Of Karl, Dieter Borchmeyer ("Die Tragödie vom verlorenen Vater . . ." in *Friedrich Schiller. Angebot und Diskurs. Zugänge/Dichtung/Zeitgenossenschaft,* ed. Helmut Brandt [Berlin/Weimar: Aufbau-Verlag, 1987]) says: "Das Gravitationsgesetz der Liebe ist erloschen" (p. 168). Following Schings, Borchmeyer concludes: "Und so richtet Karl gegen den Kosmos der universalen Sympathie die Gegenordnung des Universalhasses entgegen, das Räubersein" (p. 168). Peter Michelsen had already spoken of the "Riß in seinem [Franz's] Fundament," namely between the body and the mind (*Der Bruch mit der Vater-Welt,* p. 80).

73. "*Reißt seine goldene Hutschnur ab, und erdrosselt sich*" (NA 3: 126).

74. "Wohin hat sich die Bestie verkrochen?" (NA 3: 126).

75. "Hier liegt er wie eine Kaze verrekt" (NA 3: 127).

76. "Kann denn ein grosser Sünder noch umkehren? Ein grosser Sünder kann nimmermehr umkehren, das hätt' ich längst wissen können" (NA 3: 133).

77. Dieter Borchmeyer explored the possible significance of the original title for an understanding of the play. "Die Tragödie vom verlorenen Vater" in *Friedrich Schiller. Angebot und Diskurs.* Already in 1959, von Wiese claimed that, in this play, "Der eine Vater steht also hier für alle Väter" (*Friedrich Schiller,* p. 148). According

to Koopmann (*Drama der Aufklärung. Kommentar zu einer Epoche* [München: Winkler, 1979]), "Nicht der Konflikt der Brüder ist das dramatische Thema, sondern die gestörte Vaterordnung" (p. 145). Michelsen also follows this general line of interpretation, for whom father Moor constitutes "das Zentrum des Stückes" ("Der Bruch mit der Vater-Welt," p. 72). In father Moor, Michelsen sees the "Abbild" of the "empfindsam-temperierte Tugend der bürgerlichen Epoche, das unheroische Ideal des Biedermannes, des 'mittleren Charakters'" (p. 93), and tries to distinguish between Schiller's work and Storm-and-Stress drama. Whereas the Storm and Stress advocated the "Zerreißen der Bindungen" within the family as a means of change, for Schiller, the dissolution of familial ties is "das Werk des Verbrechers" (p. 81). "Sein [Franz's] Zerreißen der Vaterbande ist zugleich ein Sich-Lösen von der religiös sanktionierten väterlichen Ordnung; und das ist sein eigentliches Verbrechen: das Sich-auf-sich-selbst-Stellen-dieEmanzipation des Teils"—"Die Verabsolutierung des Teils" (p. 81). But the play reflects more a decentered order than a structured universe. Indeed, Schiller's writing strongly suggests that, because of his frailty, father Moor is incapable of performing the role of father as in the biblical story of the prodigal son. Thus father Moor cannot be the representative of patriarchal authority or of the traditional social order in eighteenth-century Germany.

78. "Da steh ich am Rand eines entsezlichen Lebens, und erfahre nun mit Zähnklappern und Heulen, daß *zwei Menschen wie ich den ganzen Bau der sittlichen Welt zu Grundrichten würden*" (NA 3: 135).

79. Wolfgang Wittkowski's response to Hans-Jürgen Schings's interpretation of *The Robbers* in *Friedrich Schiller. Kunst, Humanität und Politik* echoes the traditional nemesis theory as applied to Schiller's dramatic practice. Wittkowski argues that the moral order cannot be destroyed. "Vielmehr wendet die Ordnung sich gegen den Kläger, klagt ihn an und vernichtet ihn durch ihn selbst. Es ist das erste und einzige Stück Schillers, das diesen Zusammenhang als Nemesis bezeichnet" (p. 25). To reiterate, Karl Moor's act is one of free moral decision. He is not forced to accept his situation. The traditional theodicy is actually inverted. For this reason, it is difficult to subscribe to Benno von Wiese's long-standing study of theodicy in eighteenth-century German tragedy (*Die deutsche Tragödie von Lessing bis Hebbel* [Hamburg: Hoffmann und Campe, 1948]), a tradition that has been continued by F. J. Lamport in *Lessing and the Drama* (Oxford: Clarendon, 1981). For a critical response to Lamport's interpretation, see my review in *Eighteenth-Century Studies* 18 (1984–85): 300–302.

80. In his contribution "'Der Tod kann kein Übel sein . . .' Zu Schillers 175. Todestag am 9. Mai 1980," *Jahrbuch der Deutschen Schillergesellschaft* 24 (1980): 68–86, Benno von Wiese could not appreciate Karl's free, moral act.

81. Jürgen E. Schlunk's suggestion that Karl's desire to return to his father is also a return to God ("Vertrauen als Ursache und Überwindung tragischer Verstrickung in Schillers *Räubern*. Zum Verständnis Karl Moors," *Jahrbuch der Deutschen Schillergesellschaft* 27 [1983]: 187) is not borne out by the text. Clearly, the emphasis is on the individual's coming to terms with oneself and one's own history. For that reason, Karl's final actions reflect the attainment of sublime moral character. Once again, this development works against the idea of theodicy in drama (see n. 79).

82. *Bilddokumentation,* p. 131.

83. Ibid.

84. It would seem, then, that the binary pair idealist-realist breaks down with the illustration of ethical behavior.

85. "Daß die unsichtbare Hand der Vorsicht, auch den Bösewicht zu Werkzeugen ihrer Absicht und Gerichte brauchen, und den verworrensten Knoten des Geschicks zum Erstaunen auflösen könne" (Ibid., p. 131).

86. "Eh will ich mit meiner Geig auf den Bettel herumziehen, und das Konzert um was Warmes geben—eh will ich mein Violinzello zerschlagen, und Mist im Sonanzboden führen, eh ich mirs schmecken laß von dem Geld, das mein einziges Kind mit Seel und Seligkeit abverdient" (NA 5: 7). I refer to the 1971 translation of the play by Charles Passage, reprinted in *Friedrich Schiller: Plays. "Intrigue and Love" and "Don Carlos,"* ed. Walter Hinderer, 2 vols. (New York: Continuum, 1983), p. 5. Hereafter: P, followed by the page number in the main body of the text.

87. "Der Himmel und Ferdinand reißen an meiner blutenden Seele" (NA 5: 11–12).

88. "*Sie sinkt entfärbt und matt auf einen Sessel*" (NA 5: 13).

89. "Wer kann den Bund zwoer Herzen lösen, oder die Töne eines Akkords auseinander reißen?" (NA 5: 14).

90. "Mein Ideal von Glück zieht sich genügsamer in mich selbst zurück. In meinem Herzen liegen alle meine Wünsche begraben" (NA 5: 21). The repeated use of the personal pronoun raises the question of egotism. It is not coincidental that Ferdinand's words should stand in close affinity to Goethe's Werther, who, in his letter of May 22, wrote: "Ich kehre in mich selbst zurück und finde eine Welt!" (*Die Leiden des jungen Werthers*, in: *Johann Wolfgang Goethe. Sämtliche Werke nach Epochen seines Schaffens. Münchner Ausgabe*, ed. Karl Richter, et al. vol. 1.2 *Der junge Goethe 1757–1775*, ed. Gerhard Sauder (München: Carl Hanser, 1987: 203). But the tragic consequences in *Intrigue and Love* are perhaps more riveting than in Goethe's novel, for in the play the so-called hero kills his lover. In the lively discussion following Helmut Koopmann's contribution, "Loss of the Past?" on *Intrigue and Love* in the 1984 symposium on the topic in Albany, New York, Wolfgang Wittkowski made the following observation about eighteenth-century German tragedy: "Bei tragischen Helden geht es in dieser Zeit immer darum, zuletzt eine Entscheidung gegen das eigene Interesse zu fällen. Darin besteht die sittliche Leistung" (in *Verlorene Klassik? Ein Symposium*, ed. Wolfgang Wittkowski [Tübingen: Max Niemeyer, 1986], p. 305). It is a valid point, one that recurs with Karl Moor and Christian Wolf, among many other protagonists.

91. "Egoismus und Liebe scheiden die Menschheit in zwei höchstunähnliche Geschlechter, deren Grenzen nie in einander fließen" (NA 20: 122–23). Michelsen sensed this as well when he asserted: "Auch das geliebte Gegenüber [Luise] ist ihm weniger eigenständiges Subjekt als Objekt seines Eigensinns: Eigentum" ("Ordnung und Eigensinn," *Jahrbuch des Freien Deutschen Hochstifts* [1984]: 210). A similar relationship exists between Karl (and also Franz) Moor and Amalia in *The Robbers*.

92. "Egoismus errichtet seinen Mittelpunkt in sich selber; Liebe pflanzt ihn außerhalb ihrer in die Achse des ewigen Ganzen. Liebe zielt nach Einheit, Egoismus ist Einsamkeit. Liebe ist die mitherrschende Bürgerin eines blühenden Freistaats, Egoismus ein Despot in einer verwüsteten Schöpfung" (NA 20: 123). Rainer Gruenter ("Despotismus und Empfindsamkeit. Zu Schillers *Kabale und Liebe*," in his *Vom Elend des Schönen*) submitted that the real despot, Duke Carl Eugen, plays the main role in Schiller's piece without, to be sure, appearing as an individual character. "Er ist omnipräsent. Seine Allgegenwart ist in den Personen, den Dialogen, den Handlungen spürbar. Der Präsident handelt und befiehlt im Namen des Herzogs" (p. 72).

93. It is primarily for this reason that I find it difficult to subscribe to various interpretations highlighting the unconditionality of love (Benno von Wiese, *Friedrich Schiller*) either as a new secularized theology of love (Karl S. Guthke, "Tragödie der Säkularisation. Schillers *Kabale und Liebe*" in K. S. G., *Das Abenteuer der Literatur. Studien zum literarischen Leben der deutschprachigen Länder von der Aufklärung bis zum Exil* [Bern/München: Francke, 1981], pp. 210–41 and his "Kabale und

Liebe" in *Schillers Dramen. Neue Interpretationen,* pp. 58–86), or as an act of the enlightened self-determination of the individual (Helmut Koopmann, "'Kabale und Liebe' als Drama der Aufklärung," in *Verlorene Klassik?,* pp. 286–303). According to Guthke's astute reading, love in this play is a form of secularized religion. He credits Luise with self-determination. Her decision to renounce Ferdinand, however, amounts to a rejection of Ferdinand's theology of love (*Das Abenteuer der Literatur,* p. 216). On a deeper level, then, the tragedy owes to the "Gegeneinander des Gottes der säkularen Religion und des Richtergottes des Christentums" (p. 218). Koopmann sees that attempts at self-determination in this play do not succeed. For him, the drama is "eine Tragödie des . . . gebrochenen Vertrauens" (p. 295). Already in his book *Das Drama der Aufklärung,* Koopmann called this play a human tragedy that dealt with the collapse of the family. The "Experiment der individuellen Autonomie" (p. 150), he stated, does not succeed and the "Autonomieanspruch des Einzelnen," though originally positive, actually ends in the severing of the ties between the generations (p. 151). Hans Peter Herrmann and Martina Herrmann (*Friedrich Schiller: Kabale und Liebe.* 4th ed. [Frankfurt a.M.: Moritz Diesterweg, 1988]) are of the opinion: "Die aus der Autonomie des Ich geborene und als Selbstverwirklichung bewußt ergriffene Liebe ist das zentrale Thema des Stücks" (p. 57). In his contribution "Musikmeister Miller, die Emanzipation der Töchter und der dritte Ort der Liebenden" (*Jahrbuch der Deutschen Schillergesellschaft* 8 [1984]: 223–47), Hans Peter Herrmann speaks of the "doppelte[n] Scheitern des Autonomiepostulats" (p. 247). "Die erhabene Geste, in der das Individuum seinen Anspruch auf Selbstbestimmung bewährt und zugleich sich einer allgemeineren Gesetzhaftigkeit individuellen Selbstdefinition macht: diese Geste, mit der die 'Räuber'—wirkungsvoll abgeschlossen hatten und an deren Ausarbeitung der Klassiker Schiller später all seine Kraft setzt—in 'Kabale und Liebe' will sie Schiller nicht gelingen" (p. 247). See also Rolf-Peter Janz's provocative essay "Schillers 'Kabale und Liebe'—als bürgerliches Trauerspiel," *Jahrbuch der Deutschen Schillergesellschaft* 20 (1976): 208–28. According to Janz, Miller's sense of morality simply reflects his own materialistic-economic interests. Thus, he simply transforms Luise into the object of her father's code of morality. "Da der Vater ökonomisch Herr über die Tochter ist, ist er auch Mitbesitzer ihres Herzens, des Inbegriffs ihrer Individualität" (p. 223). Such a position, however, does not take into account the possibility that Luise's renunciation of Ferdinand is based not on passivity but on a conscious, i.e., rational, and possibly even enlightened decision. I find her decision to be utterly realistic given her knowledge of the limits of her society. If there is a capitalist in this play, then it is Ferdinand, for whom Luise is but the object of his "love," i.e., desire, something to which he, as an autocrat, feels he has a right and which he wishes to possess. Perhaps it was in this direction that the writer aimed his sharpest criticism. In the scholarly research, Michelsen recognized: "Auch das geliebte Gegenüber [Luise] ist ihm [Ferdinand] weniger eigenständiges Subjket als Objekt seines Eigensinns: Eigentum" ("Ordnung und Eigensinn," cited in n. 91, p. 210). To extrapolate, there can be little doubt that the writer Friedrich Schiller was acutely interested in political matters. Where scholars on both sides of the Atlantic seem to quarrel most (though it is often unstated) is over the desirability or practical nature of Schiller's approach.

94. "*Mein* bist du, und wärfen Höll und Himmel sich zwischen uns" (NA 5: 39).

95. "Was hat diess Lamm getan, daß Sie es würgen?" (NA 5: 40).

96. "Aber ich will seine [his father's] Kabalen durchbohren—durchreißen will ich alle diese eiserne Ketten des Vorurteils—Frei wie ein Mann will ich wählen, daß diese Insektenseelen am Riesenwerk meiner Liebe hinaufschwindeln" (NA 5: 40).

97. "Doch aufs äußerste treibt's nur die *Liebe*—Hier Luise! Deine Hand in die

meinige. *Er faßt diese heftig.* So wahr mich Gott im letzten Hauch nicht verlassen soll!—Der Augenblick, der diese zwo Hände trennt, zerreißt auch den Faden zwischen *mir* und der *Schöpfung*" (NA 5: 41).

98. "Wenn Sie sich selbst lieben, keine Gewalttätigkeit" (NA 5: 44).

99. Christoph Bruckmann, "'Freude! sangen wir in Thränen, Freude! in dem tiefsten Leid.' Zur Interpretation und Rezeption des Gedichts *An die Freude* von Friedrich Schiller," *Jahrbuch der Deutschen Schillergesellschaft* 35 (1991): 99.

100. "Ja! es auf ewig zu trennen! auf ewig diese schändliche Ketten zu brechen!" (NA 5: 27–28).

101. "Die Wollust der Großen dieser Welt ist die nimmersatte Hyäne, die sich mit Heißhunger Opfer sucht" (NA 5: 109).

102. "Hatte Braut und Bräutigam zertrennt—hatte selbst der Ehen göttliches Band zerrissen" (NA 5: 34).

103. "Ich stellte mich zwischen das Lamm und den Tiger" (NA 5: 34).

104. "Walter, ich habe Kerker gesprengt—habe Todesurteile zerrissen, und manche entsetzliche Ewigkeit auf Galeeren verkürzt" (NA 5: 35).

105. "Ich *zuerst* zerriß ihrer Unschuld goldenen Frieden—wiegte ihr Herz mit vermessenen Hoffnungen, und gab es verräterisch der wilden Leidenschaft preis" (NA 5: 36).

106. "Er führt mich da vor einen entsetzlichen Abgrund" (NA 5: 48).

107. "Den Herrn Major umspinnen wir mit List" (NA 5: 49).

108. "Das Geweb ist satanisch fein" (NA 5: 50).

109. "Vater und Mutter ziehen gelindere Saiten auf, und durch und durch . . . erkennen sie's noch zuletzt für Erbarmung, wenn ich der Tochter durch meine Hand ihre Reputation wieder gebe" (NA 5: 50).

110. "Das die Fugen der Bürgerwelt auseinandertreiben, und die allgemeine ewige Ordnung zugrund stürzen würde" (NA 5: 57).

111. "*Ich* bin die Verbrecherin—mit frechen törichten Wünschen hat sich mein Busen getragen—mein Unglück ist meine *Strafe*" (NA 5: 57).

112. "FERDINAND *hat in der Zerstreuung und Wut eine Violine ergriffen, und auf derselben zu spielen versucht—Jetzt zerreißt er die Saiten, zerschmettert das Instrument auf dem Boden, und bricht in ein lautes Gelächter aus*" (NA 5: 57–58). Ilse Graham's reading of "Passions and Possessions in *Kabale und Liebe*" (*Schiller's Drama: Talent and Integrity* [London: Methuen, 1974]) notes the importance of "the image-pattern of music" for the development of the theme of love, but maintains that "as the tragedy unfolds, the images from the sphere of music, with all their attendant associations of harmony and fulfillment, become transferred from the figure of Luise's lover to that of her father" (p. 111). She sees that Miller threatens to break his violin over his wife's back and even refers to Ferdinand's shattering of the violin. Still, she relates this only to the theme of possessive love. Similarly, Peter Michelsen (1984) reduces the incident of Ferdinand's smashing of the violin to a dramatic device, seeing in it only "ein Zug der Heftigkeit und Gewaltsamkeit im Bild Ferdinands" (p. 209).

113. "Kalte Pflicht gegen feurige Liebe!" (NA 5: 58).

114. "Sie sind verschanzt eure Großen—verschanzt vor der Wahrheit hinter ihre eigene Laster" (NA 5: 62).

115. "Das ist tyrannisch o Himmel! Strafe Menschen menschlich, wenn sie dich reizen, aber warum mich zwischen zwei Schröcknisse pressen? Warum zwischen Tod und Schande mich hin und her wiegen? Warum diesen blutsaugenden Teufel mir auf den nacken setzen?" (NA 5: 63–64).

116. "O du weißt allzugut, daß unser Herz an natürlichen Trieben, so fest als an Ketten liegt" (NA 5: 64).

117. "Ich führe dich wie irgendein seltenes Murmeltier mit mir. Wie ein zahmer Affe sollst du zum Geheul der Verdammten tanzen, apportieren und aufwarten" (NA 5: 69).

118. "An meine Blume soll mir das Ungeziefer nicht kriechen, oder ich will es . . . so und so und wieder so durcheinander quetschen" (NA 5: 69).

119. "Wie eine Verbrecherin zittre ich, die Glückliche zu sehen, die mit meinem Herzen so schrecklich harmonisch fühlt" (NA 5: 72–73).

120. "Wer sollte sich träumen lassen, daß Lady Milford ihrem Gewissen einen ewigen Skorpion halte" (NA 5: 76).

121. "Ich hatte einen ewigen Anspruch auf die Freuden der Welt zerrissen" (NA 5: 77).

122. "Fühlt sich doch das Insekt in einem Tropfen Wassers so selig, als wär es ein Himmelreich, so froh und so selig, bis man ihm von einem Weltmeer erzählt, worin Flotten und Walfische spielen!" (NA 5: 77).

123. "Felsen und Abgründe will ich zwischen euch werfen; eine Furie will ich mitten durch euren Himmel gehn; mein Name soll eure Küsse wie ein Gespenst Verbrecher auseinanderscheuchen" (NA 5: 78).

124. "Sie haben den Himmel zweier Liebenden geschleift, voneinandergezerrt zwei Herzen, die *Gott* aneinanderband" (NA 5: 79).

125. "Lady! Ins Ohr des Allwissenden schreit auch der letzte Krampf des zertret-tenen Wurms" (NA 5: 79).

126. "Noch o Himmel! noch zerreißen sie mein Ohr die fürchterlichen mich ver-dammenden Worte: *Nehmen Sie ihn hin!*" (NA 5: 79).

127. "*Beschämen* läßt sich Emilie Milford—doch *beschimpfen* nie! Auch ich habe Kraft, zu entsagen" (NA 5: 80).

128. "Zerbrochen alle Bande zwischen mir und dem Herzog, gerissen aus meinem Busen diese wütende Liebe!—In deine Arme werf ich mich, Tugend . . . Groß, wie eine fallende Sonne, will ich heut vom Gipfel meiner Hoheit heruntersinken, meine Herrlichkeit sterbe mit meiner Liebe, und nichts als mein *Herz* begleite mich in diese stolze Verwesung" (NA 5: 80).

129. "Ich verabscheue Gunstbezeugungen, die von den Tränen der Untertanen triefen" (NA 5: 82).

130. "Der Kampf ist entschieden. Vater! man pflegt unser Geschlecht zart und zerbrechlich zu nennen. Glaub Er das nicht mehr" (NA 5: 84).

131. "Vor einer Spinne schütteln wir [Frauen] uns, aber das schwarze Ungeheuer *Verwesung* drücken wir im Spaß in die Arme" (NA 5: 84–85).

132. "Eide, Vater, binden wohl die Lebendigen, im Tode schmilzt auch der Sakra-mente eisernes Band" (NA 5: 85).

133. "Ein Bubenstück ohne Beispiel zerriß den Bund unsrer Herzen, aber ein schröcklicher Schwur hat meine Zunge gebunden . . . ich weiß einen *dritten* Ort, wo kein Eidschwur mehr bindet" (NA 5: 85).

134. "Das Brot unsers Herrgotts wächst überall, und Ohren wird er auch meiner Geige bescheren" (NA 5: 89).

135. "An dünnen unmerkbaren Seilen hängen oft fürchterliche Gewichte" (NA 5: 93).

136. "Unglückseliges Flötenspiel, das mir nie hätte einfallen sollen" (NA 5: 93).

137. "daß ich die Natter zertrete, ehe sie auch noch den Vater verwundet" (NA 5: 94).

138. "Wir machen aus diesem verdrüßlichen Duett eine Lustbarkeit, und rächen uns mit Hilfe gewisser Galanterien an den Grillen der Liebe" (NA 5: 99).

139. "Komm in deiner ungeheuren Furchtbarkeit, Schlange, spring an mir auf, Wurm—krame vor mir deine gräßliche Knoten aus, bäume deine Wirbel zum Him-

mel—So abscheulich als dich jemals der Abgrund sah-Nur keinen Engel mehr—Nur jetzt keinen Engel mehr—es ist zu spät—Ich muß dich zertreten, wie eine Natter, oder verzweifeln—Erbarme dich!" (NA 5: 101).

140. "Und die süße melodische Stimme—Wie kann so viel Wohlklang kommen aus zerrissenen Saiten? *Mit trunkenem Aug auf ihrem Anblick verweilend.* Alles so schön—so voll Ebenmaß so göttlich vollkommen!" (NA 5: 101).

141. "Die zärtliche Nerve hält Freveln fest, die die Menschheit an ihren Wurzeln zernagen; ein elender Gran Arsenik wirft sie um" (NA 5: 103).

142. "Fein und bewundernswert, ich gestehs, war die Finte, den Bund unsrer Herzen zu zerreißen durch Eifersucht—Die Rechnung hatte ein Meister gemacht, aber schade nur, daß die zürnende *Liebe* dem Draht nicht so gehorsam blieb, wie deine hölzerne Puppe" (NA 4: 105).

143. Walter Pape, "'Ein merkwürdiges Beispiel produktiver Kritik,'" *Zeitschrift für Deutsche Philologie* 107 (1988): 205.

144. Ibid., p. 205.

145. As noted by Pape, ibid.

146. See Norbert Oellers, *Schiller—Zeitgenosse aller Epochen. Dokumente zur Wirkungsgeschichte* (Frankfurt a.M.: Athenäum, 1970) and Gert Ueding, *Friedrich Schiller.*

147. See the listings in *Schaubühne. Schillers Dramen 1945–84. Eine Ausstellung des Deutschen Literaturarchivs und des Theatermuseums der Universität zu Köln,* ed. Bernhard Zeller (Marbach a.N.: Schillernationalmuseum, 1984) and Ferdinand Piedmont's *Schiller spielen. Stimmen der Theaterkritik. 1946–1985. Eine Dokumentation* (Darmstadt: Wissenschaftliche Buchgesellschaft, 1990) as well as the most recent issues of *Theater heute* for further evidence.

148. "Unsre Geisteskräfte müssen wie die Saiten eines Instruments durch Geister gespielt werden" (NA 23: 67).

149. "Daß es vielleicht einen Riß in meinem ganzen künftigen Schiksal zurükläßt" (NA 23: 73).

150. "Einsamkeit, Misvergnügen über mein Schiksal, fehlgeschlagene Hoffnungen, und vielleicht auch die veränderte Lebensart haben den Klang meines Gemüths, wenn ich so reden darf, verfälscht, und das, sonst reine, Instrument meiner Empfindung verstimmt" (NA 23: 76).

151. "Die schönen Tage in Aranjuez / sind nun zu Ende" (ll. 1–2a; NA 6: 9). I refer to the translation by A. Leslie and Jeanne R. Willson in *Friedrich Schiller: Plays,* ed. Walter Hinderer, 2 vols. (New York: Continuum, 1983). Hereafter: W, in the main body of the text.

152. "In dieser Umarmung heilt mein krankes Herz" (NA 6: 15).

153. "Ein unnatürlich Rot / Entzündet sich auf Ihren blassen Wangen, / Und Ihre Lippen zittern fieberhaft" (NA 6: 16).

154. "Der löwenkühne Jüngling . . . zu dem / Ein unterdrücktes Heldenvolk mich [Posa] sendet" (NA 6: 16).

155. "Laß mich weinen, / An deinem Herzen heiße Tränen weinen, / Du einz'ger Freund. Ich habe niemand- niemand- / Auf dieser großen weiten Erde niemand" (NA 6: 17).

156. "Ich weiß ja nicht was Vater heißt—ich bin / Ein Königssohn" (NA 6: 18).

157. " . . . und unsrer Seelen zartes Saitenspiel / am Morgen unsres Lebens gleich bezog" (NA 6: 18).

158. "Daß die schaffende Natur / Den Roderich im Carlos wiederholte" (NA 6: 18).

159. "Warum an den mich mahnen! . . . Unheilbar, / auf ewig rissen zwischen mir und ihm / die demantstarken Bande der Natur" (NA 6: 22).

160. "Zweifelnd ringt / Mein guter Geist mit gräßlichen Entwürfen; / Durch laby-rinthische Sophismen kriecht / Mein unglücksel'ger Scharfsinn, bis er endlich / Vor eines Abgrunds gähem Rande stutzt" (NA 6: 24).

161. "Daß Gebärdenspäher und Geschichtenträger / Des Übels mehr auf dieser Welt getan, / Als Gift und Dolch in Mörders Hand nicht konnten" (NA 6: 12).

162. "Dies schöne Band der Ewigkeit zu knüpfen. / Nie hat zwei schönre Herzen die Natur / Gebildet füreinander—nie die Welt, / Nie eine Wahl so glücklich noch gepriesen" (NA 6: 37).

163. "Sie waren mein—im Angesicht der Welt / Mir zugesprochen von zwei großen Thronen, / Mir zuerkannt von Himmel und Natur, / Und Philipp, Philipp hat mir Sie geraubt" (NA 6: 43).

164. "Hat er / Ein fühlend Herz, das Ihrige zu schätzen?" (NA 6: 43).

165. Paul Böckmann investigated the significance of the incest motif for an under-standing of the dramatic structure of Schiller's play in his speech *Strukturprobleme in Schillers 'Don Karlos'*, vorgetragen am 24. Januar 1981 (Heidelberg: Carl Winter, 1982). According to Böckmann, who cites Duke Carl August's concerns, the thematic connection of the dramatic action revolves, from beginning to end, around this motif (pp. 30 and 32). He admits, however: "Das Motiv der verbotenen Leidenschaft wird nun mehr auf indirekte Weise dramatisch fruchtbar" (p. 32). Still, the theme helps heighten the tragic effect. It is also central to the dialogue, as Böckmann observes: "Diese Dialogführung gewinnt eine dialektische Spannung, je mehr sie die Aussagen der Dialogpartner in ein Spiegelungsverhältnis zu anderen Dialogpartien und damit vor andre, von den Beteiligten unbeachtete Horizonte bringt" (p. 34). Perceiving the play's dramatic-tragic "Rückspiegelung im Raum der Geschichte" (p. 36), Böckmann sees in *Don Carlos* "ein entscheidener Wendepunkt" in Schiller's creative activity in the direction of a classical ideal of the art of personal responsibility (p. 37). Friedrich Kittler ("Carlos als Carlsschüler. Ein Familiengemälde in einem fürstlichen Hause," in *Unser Commercium* [1984], pp. 241–73) posits a connection between the Queen and the triangle of the Princess of Hohenheim, Duke Carl Eugen and the student Friedrich Schiller and "die Erfindung einer Mutterimago, in der die Wünsche von Despot und Untertanen zusammenfallen" (p. 258). In this way, Kittler retains Schiller's original idea that *Don Carlos* is a "Familiengemälde in einem fürstlichen Hause" (p. 259). Unlike Böckmann ("Schillers 'Don Karlos,'" in *Friedrich Schiller. Kunst, Humanität und Politik*, p. 45), however, Kittler foregrounds the political strat-egy behind Carlos's interest in the Queen rather than the transgression against Na-ture (p. 270). Like Böckmann, Kittler sees in the writing of *Don Carlos*, the beginning of Schiller's classical period (p. 273). Assuming that courtly politics ignores the interests of the individuals affected by its decisions, Klaus-Detlef Müller argues that the institution of marriage in such circles lent itself to incestuous relationships ("Die Aufhebung des bürgerlichen Trauerspiels im 'Don Karlos,'" in *Friedrich Schiller. Angebot und Diskurs*, p. 223). Again, because of the fact that the Queen is Carlos's stepmother, I do not find the problem of incest to be terribly acute.

166. "O in diesem / Gefühl liegt die Hölle. Hölle liegt im andern, / Sie zu besitzen" (NA 6: 47).

167. "Weh! Ich faß es nicht, / Und meine Nerven fangen an zu reißen" (NA 6: 47).

168. "Ich fürchte viel von Carlos' heißem Blut, / Doch nichts von seinem Herzen" (NA 6: 55).

169. "Hier ist die Stelle, wo ich sterblich bin" (NA 6: 4).

170. "Es ist die höchste Zeit. Ein schauerndes / Exempel soll die Irrenden bekeh-ren" (NA 6: 55).

171. "Will mächtig reißen an dem Vaterherzen, / Bis dieses Zweifels felsenfeste Rinde / Von diesem Herzen niederfällt" (NA 6: 67).

172. "Daß unsre Freude fremde Wangen rötet, / Daß unsre Angst in fremden Busen zittert, / Daß unsre Leiden fremde Augen wässern!" (NA 6: 68).

173. "Zu heftig braust das Blut in deinen Adern. / Du würdest nur zerstören" (NA 6: 70).

174. "Dies Amt / Will einen Mann und keinen Jüngling" (NA 6: 71).

175. "Solche Kranke / Wie du, mein Sohn, verlangen gute Pflege / Und wohnen unterm Aug des Arzts. Du bleibst / In Spanien" (NA 6: 74).

176. Karen Beyer traces the regent's search for truth ("die Wahrheitssuche des Regenten") only to determine that he lapses back into his former self: "die Rekonstruktion des Königs vollzieht sich als Destruktion des Menschen" ("Höfisches Leben im 'Don Carlos,'" in *Schiller und die höfische Welt,* p. 375). The question remains why Schiller would have done this other than to show: "das gesellschaftliche *Sein* bestimmt unmittelbar das moralische *Sollen*" (p. 377). Lesley Sharpe sees in Philipp "something of a monster, lacking any human qualities" (*Friedrich Schiller,* p. 85).

177. As recognized recently by Wolfgang Wittkowski, "Höfische Intrige für die gute Sache. Marquis Posa und Octavio Piccolomini," in *Schiller und die höfische Welt,* pp. 378–97.

178. Noted also by Denis Jonnes, "Pattern of Power: Family and State in Schiller's Early Drama," *Colloquia Germanica* 20 (1987): 145.

179. This would seem to add greater textual support to Klaus Bohnen's thesis: "es ist hier eben gerade nicht die Frage nach zwei alternativen Staatssystemen, sondern die Frage nach einer neuen gesellschaftlichen Organisation" ("Die Politik im Drama. Anmerkungen zu Schillers *Don Carlos,*" *Jahrbuch der Deutschen Schillergesellschaft* 24 [1980]: 30). The fact that Posa dies and Carlos is turned over to the inquisition is indicative not so much of a pessimistic attitude toward the future, as it is of a realistic assessment of the practical obstacles besetting the realization of an egalitarian state. It is important to note here that Klaus Bohnen captured well the nature of Schiller's interest in politics in this article. "Politik ist für Schiller— auch hier steht er in der Tradition Lessings—nicht eine Frage staatlicher Alternativlösungen und auch nicht eine von Klassenkämpfen, sondern eine Frage des Einsatzes für die größtmögliche Sicherung der Individualrechte des Einzelnen gegenüber Machtansprüchen staatlicher Instanzen und Institutionen" (p. 21). "In dieser Aufspaltung von Staat und Gesellschaft liegt der besondere deutsche Weg durch die Krise oder der Bewältigung der Krise [healing?]" (p. 31). Oskar Seidlin stated the matter eloquently. "Was mir aber als die wahrhaft erregende und einmalige Essenz des Schillerschen Werkes erscheint, ist seine Erkenntnis und Darstellung der unlöslichen Verstrickung, des subtilen Ineinandergreifens von menschlichem Gefühlsleben und seinen politischen Überzeugungen und Ideen" (Schillers 'Don Carlos'—nach 200 Jahren," *Jahrbuch der Deutschen Schillergesellschaft* 27 [1983]: 482).

180. "Ich höre / Auf einer—Laute jemand spielen—War's / Nicht eine Laute? *Indem er sich zweifelhaft umsieht.* / Recht! dort liegt sie noch— / Und Laute—das weiß Gott im Himmel!—Laute, / Die lieb ich bis zur Raserei. Ich bin / Ganz Ohr, ich weiß nichts von mir selber, stürze / Ins Kabinett, der süßen Künsterlin, / Die mich so himmlisch rührte, mich so mäßchtig / Bezauberte, ins schöne Aug zu sehen" (NA 6: 97).

181. "Die Arie, Prinz Carlos, werd ich wohl / Noch einmal spielen müssen, Ihre Strafe / Soll sein, mir zuzuhören" (NA 6: 98).

182. "Der schönste Text in diesem schönen Munde; / Doch freilich nicht so wahr gesagt, als schön" (NA 6: 99).

183. "*Sie ergreift diesen Augenblick, ihn zu sich auf den Sofa zu ziehen.* / Sie

brauchen Ruhe lieber Karl-Ihr Blut / Ist jetzt in Aufruhr—setzen Sie sich zu mir— / Weg mit den schwarzen Fieberphantasien!" (NA 6: 101).

184. "Einen nur / Wird meine Liebe glücklich machen-einen- / Doch diesen einzigen zum Gott. Der Seelen / Entzückender Zusammenklang-ein Kuß— / Der Schäferstunde schwelgerische Freuden- / Der Schönheit hohe, himmlische Magie / Sind *eines* Strahles schwesterliche Farben, / Sind *einer* Blume Blätter nur. Ich sollte, / Ich Rasende! ein abgerißnes Blatt / Aus dieser Blume schönem Kelch verschenken?" (ll. 1784c-93; NA 6: 108).

185. "Süßes, seelenvolles Mädchen! / Anbetungswürdiges Geschöpf!-Ich stehe / Ganz Ohr–ganz Auge–ganz Entzücken–ganz / Bewunderung" (NA 6: 109).

186. "An diesem Hof bist du / Die Würdigste, die einzige, die erste, / Die meine Seele ganz versteht" (NA 6: 110).

187. "Ich liebe / Die Menschheit, und in Monarchieen darf / Ich niemand lieben als mich selbst" (NA 6: 181). Perhaps, Oskar Seidlin was too harsh when he asked, "Ist der politische Idealist—und dies ist Schillers bohrendste Frage im *Dom Carlos*— der so leidenschaftlich und unbeirrbar für die ganze Menschheit kämpft, nicht selber ein menschlicher Versager?" ("Schillers 'Don Carlos'—nach 200 Jahren," *Jahrbuch der Deutschen Schillergesellschaft* 27 [1983]: 489).

188. "Das Jahrhundert / Ist meinem Ideal nicht reif. Ich lebe / Ein Bürger derer, welche kommen werden" (NA 6: 185).

189. "Da Sie den Menschen / Zu Ihrem Saitenspiel herunterstürzten, / Wer teilt mit Ihnen Harmonie?" (NA 6: 187).

190. "(Bei Gott, / Er greift in meine Seele!)" (NA 6: 187).

191. "Daß Menschen nur—nicht Wesen höhrer Art— / Die Weltgeschichte schreiben!" (NA 6: 189).

192. "Geben Sie, / was Sie uns nahmen, wieder. Werden Sie / von Millionen Königen ein König" (NA 6: 191).

193. "Der Mensch ist mehr, als Sie von ihm gehalten. / Des langen Schlummers Bande wird er brechen, / Und wiederfordern sein geheiligt Recht" (NA 6: 191). Paul Böckmann appreciated the multiple layers of a literary text when he said of *Don Carlos:* "Durch diese Mehrschichtigkeit gelingt es, die politischen Zwecke mit ihren menschlichen Folgen zu konfrontieren und damit Sinn und Aufgabe des politischen Handelns in seiner [Schillers] Dramatik vorzuführen" (*Schillers Don Karlos*, p. 488).

194. "Wer ist der Mensch, der sich vermessen will, / Des Zufalls schweres Steuer zu regieren, / Und doch nicht der Allwissende zu sein?" (NA 6: 266).

195. "Gehört die süße Harmonie, die in / Dem Saitenspiele schlummert, seinem Käufer, / Der es mit taubem Ohr bewacht? Er hat / Das Recht erkauft, in Trümmern es zu schlagen, / Doch nicht die Kunst, dem Silberton zu rufen, / Und in des Liedes Wonne zu zerschmelzen. / Die Wahrheit ist vorhanden für den Weisen, / Die Schönheit für ein fühlend Herz. Sie beide / Gehören füreinander. Diesen Glauben / Soll mir kein feiges Vorurteil zerstören" (NA 6: 272).

196. "Nichts-nichts-kein Ausweg-keine Hülfe-keine / Im ganzen Umkreis der Natur! Verzweiflung / Macht mich zur Furie, zum Tier-ich setze / Den Dolch auf eines Weibes Brust—Doch jetzt-/ Jetzt fällt ein Sonnenstrahl in meine Seele" (NA 6: 295).

197. "Der Menschheit Bande sind entzwei. Du selbst / Hast sie zerrissen, / Sire, in deinen Reichen" (NA 6: 301).

198. "Dies feine Saitenspiel zerbrach in Ihrer / Metallnen Hand. Sie konnten nichts, als ihn / Ermorden" (NA 6: 303).

199. "Hier entsag ich allem, / Was mich auf dieser Welt erwartet. Suchen / Sie unter Fremdlingen sich einen Sohn— / Da liegen meine Reiche-" (NA 6: 304). The exclamation undergirds Denis Jonnes's point that, by challenging paternal authority, Carlos (as well as Franz Moor and Ferdinand) would see himself as being fatherless

("Pattern of Power: Family and State in Schiller's Early Dramas," *Colloquia Germanica* 20 [1987]: 145).

200. "Er [Carlos] hatte einen Freund, der in den Tod / Gegangen ist für ihn—für ihn! Mit mir / Hätt er ein Königreich geteilt!" (NA 6: 318).

201. Gerhard Kluge in *Friedrich Schiller. Werke und Briefe in zwölf Bänden*, eds. Klaus Harro Hilzinger et al. (Franfurt a.M.: Deutscher Klassiker, 1988f), p. 1156. Klaus-Detlef Müller, albeit from a much different perspective, maintains: "Schiller ist Realist genug, um die Pläne Posas vorab an der Hellsichtigkeit der verdinglichten Gewalt in der Politik der Inquisition zu widerlegen und ihnen keine wirkliche Chance einzuräumen" ("Schiller und das Mäzenat. Zu den Entstehungsbedingungen der Briefe *Über die ästhetische Erziehung des Menschen*," in *Unser Commercium. Goethes und Schillers Lliteraturpolitik*, eds. Wilfried Barner, Eberhard Lämmert, and Norbert Oellers [Stuttgart: J. G. Cotta], p. 232). He suggests that Schiller postulated not only humanity, but also showed the real obstacles standing in the way of its realization, the analysis of which he then continued in *Concerning the Aesthetic Education of the Human Being* (p. 232).

202. Gerhard Kluge in *Friedrich Schiller. Werke und Briefe*, p. 1161.

203. "Das Seil, an dem / Er flatterte, war lang, doch unzerreißbar" (NA 6: 327).

204. "Nichts hör ich, als die fürchterliche Glocke, / Die uns zur Trennung lautet" (NA 6: 338). It is a curious fact that Duke Carl Eugen was a Catholic regent in a Protestant land. To return for a moment to the question of politics, the idea that Schiller's *Don Carlos* is a non-political play is still prevalent. Gerhard Kluge maintains this when pointing out that the "Familiengemälde" was a popular dramatic form in Mannheim. Rather than justify the family order, however, as was often done in plays performed in Mannheim, Schiller's *Don Carlos* reflected, instead, the "Auflösung und Zerstörung dieser Ordnung" (in *Friedrich Schiller. Werke und Briefe*, 3: 1024). On this point, Kluge follows Helmut Koopmann's general thesis in *Das Drama der Aufklärung* concerning the gradual dissolution and disintegration of the family in eighteenth-century German drama, even though Koopmann charts a concomitant rise in claims to individuality and stops short of considering *Don Carlos*. Hans-Georg Werner draws out the apparent contradiction between the private and the public spheres in "Die Vergegenwärtigung von Geschichte in Schillers *Dom Karlos*" in *Friedrich Schiller. Angebot und Diskurs*, pp. 235–49. Klaus Bohnen sees in *Don Carlos* the "Politisierung des Moralischen," in "Politik im Drama. Anmerkungen zu Schillers *Don Carlos*," *Jahrbuch der Deutschen Schillergesellschaft* 24 (1980): 29. "Das Drama ist politisch, nicht weil es das politische Intrigen—und Konfliktspiel von Staatsmännern entwirft, sondern weil es im Aufriß der Kluft von Gesellschaft [Moral] und Staat [Politik] zwei heterogene Politikkonzeptionen aufeinander prallen läßt und in der Konfrontation zweier Grundmuster von Gesellschaftsgefügen den politischen Nerv der Zeit trifft" (p. 29). See also: Wilfried Malsch, "Moral und Politik in Schillers *Don Karlos*" in *Verantwortung und Utopie. Zur Literatur der Goethezeit. Ein Symposium,* ed. Wolfgang Wittkowski (Tübingen: Max Niemeyer, 1988).

205. The concept of morality undergoes a decisive transformation in the works of Lessing, Schiller, and Goethe. The moral individual is one who remains true to one's nature while cognizant of the fact that one is a social being. For Schiller, this idea would be conveyed in the form of a maxim: "Erkühne dich, weise zu sein" (*Concerning the Aesthetic Education of the Human Being*, letter 8). From Schiller's collected works, it is clear that the reciprocal cooperation ("gegenseitige Wechselwirkung") between *Sinnlichkeit* and *Sittlichkeit,* perhaps the most essential characteristic of concepts of *Humanität* in the eighteenth century, generates true moral character.

206. Following his quarrel with what he calls the "im Irrgarten der Gattungsbestimmung herumtaumelnden Novellenforscher," Gerhard Kaiser views Schiller's *Eine*

großmütige Handlung, aus der neuesten Geschichte (1782) and *Der Verbrecher aus verlorener Ehre* as novellas (*Von Arkadien nach Elysium,* p. 45). There is substantial evidence that the form of Schiller's narrative marks the birth of the German novella. In my view, this is the encounter with the apparition and the descent into the abyss. Scholarship on Schiller's narrative continues to be divided on the question of the determination of the genre. An example of the continued blurring of distinctions is Gerhard Neumann's "Die Anfänge deutscher Novellistik" in *Unser Commercium,* pp. 433–60. In n. 2, Neumann refers to Schiller's "Erzählung," while, in n. 9, he classifies the work under "Novellen" (pp. 434 and 439, respectively). My interpretation of Schiller's novella calls into question John Ellis's point (based, as it is, on previous secondary literature) that "character is less important in the Novelle, and there is little or no development of character" (*Narration in the German Novelle: Theory and Interpretation* [Cambridge: Cambridge University Press, 1974], p. 3).

207. From the essay *Concerning the Sublime* [*Über das Erhabene*] (NA 21: 38). In this last important theoretical work on the nature of tragedy and the theatrical experience, Schiller referred again to the unchangeable (moral) determination of the human species ("unsre unveränderliche Bestimmung"). In the light of our later discussion of *William Tell,* it is important to note here already that, in this essay, the writer envisioned human beings in their final state of being, i.e., as "vollendete Bürger der Natur" (NA 21: 53).

208. On this point, Schiller's work resembles *Der Prokurator* from the *Unterhaltung deutscher Ausgewanderten.* Goethe called his novella a "moralische Erzählung." In his view, this form shows "daß der Mensch in sich eine Kraft habe, aus Überzeugung eines Bessern selbst gegen seine Neigung zu handeln" (quoted by Kaiser, *Von Arkadien nach Elysium,* pp. 46–47). Kaiser concludes, "Die Novelle hebt sich zögernd aus dem Feld der moralischen Erzählung heraus" (p. 47). I am unsure what Kaiser means by "zögernd," however. In Schiller's case, the two forms are intimately connected. Jürgen Bolten opens up another window on the eighteenth century in his analysis "Zur Genese des bürgerlichen Selbstverständnisses im ausgehenden 18. Jahrhundert" (*Germanistik-Forschungsstand und Perspektiven. Vorträge des Deutschen Germanistentages 1984,* ed. Georg Stötzel, 2.Teil: Ältere Deutsche Literatur. Neuere Deutsche Literatur [Berlin/New York: Walter de Gruyter, 1985]). He suggests that the anchoring of the contemporary consciousness of crisis in the plot structures of Schiller's early dramatic works reveals that the responsibility for the existing social situations was seen not so much in the political domain as it was "in dem zweischneidigen Tugendverständnis der bürgerlichen Individualität" (p. 499).

209. Klaus Berghahn draws out a few aspects of the contemporary relevance of Schiller's works in his "Schiller und die Tradition" in *Friedrich Schiller—zur Geschichtlichkeit seines Werkes,* ed. Klaus Berghahn (Kronberg/Ts.: Scriptor, 1975), pp. 9–24.

210. On this point, Schiller's novella foreshadows the classical drama *Mary Stuart.* Kaiser has drawn a connection between the two works which bears repeating. "Gefangengenommen, gesteht er [Wolf] doch frei . . . frei im Schillerschen Sinne, wie er sich ähnlich bei Maria Stuart zeigt: nicht, indem er etwas wählt, was er auch vermeiden könnte, sondern indem er sein Schicksal akzeptiert, die irdische Gerechtigkeit mit allen ihren Gebrechen als Stellvertreterin der himmlischen Gerechtigkeit annimmt" (*Von Arkadien nach Elysium,* p. 57).

211. "Aber in diesem Kampfe allein konnte er seine Vernunft und Sittlichkeit ausbilden" (NA 17:401).

212. In n. 18 of his article "Interpretation and Misinterpretation of Schiller's *Kabale und Liebe,*" *German Life and Letters* 38 (1984): 448–61, G. A. Wells takes

Ilse Graham (*Schiller's Drama: Talent and Integrity*) to task for seeing in Miller's statement in V, 1 ("Ich setze die Geschichte deines Grams auf die Laute") "the culminating metaphor of the whole pattern" of music imagery in this play (p. 460). However, both overlook the fact that the stringed, musical instrument is the central metaphor, or symbol of Schiller's writings considered as a whole.

Chapter 4. The Writing and Dramatization of History: The Essay on Universal History and *Wallenstein*

1. Ernst Cassirer, *The Philosophy of the Enlightenment,* trans. Fritz C. A. Koelln and James P. Pettegrove (Princeton: Princeton University Press, 1951), p. 198.
2. The essay was first presented as an inaugural lecture in two parts in late May 1789 shortly after Schiller's appointment as professor of philosophy at the university in Jena. It was revised slightly and received its widest exposure when it appeared as an essay in Wieland's *Teutscher Merkur* in November of the same year. All translations are my own.
3. In his controversial series of essays, *Blindness and Insight. Essays on the Rhetoric of Contemporary Criticism* 2. rev. ed. (Minneapolis: University of Minnesota Press, 1986), Paul de Man advanced the idea that "literary texts are themselves critical but blinded, and the critical reading of the critics tries to deconstruct the blindness" (p. 141). With Schiller's essay, it will become evident that the author aids the critical reader in the act of deconstructing the text precisely because he is aware of the limits of his own reasoning. This writing, among other theoretical essays by Schiller, discloses a process of hermeneutical reflection which accompanies the writer's own deconstruction of the text. To that extent, Schiller may well qualify as a kind of non-blinded author.
4. Koopmann, *Schiller-Forschung*, p. 167.
5. Von Wiese, *Friedrich Schiller,* p. 330. As von Wiese noted, both Richard Fester, the editor of Schiller's historical writings for the Säkularausgabe ("Vorstudien zur Säkularausgabe der historischen Schriften Schillers," *Euphorion* 12 [1905]: 78–142) and Heinrich (Ritter) von Srbik (*Geist und Geschichte vom deutschen Humanismus bis zur Gegenwart*. 2 vols. [München: F. Bruckmann, 1950–51]) should be credited with having elevated Schiller's standing in the course of historical thought.
6. Johannes Janssen, *Schiller als Historiker* (Freiburg: Herder, 1863).
7. Karl-Heinz Hahn, "Schiller und die Geschichte," *Weimarer Beiträge* 1 (1970): 49.
8. As disclosed by Hayden White in *Metahistory: The Historical Imagination in Nineteenth-Century Europe* (Baltimore/London: Johns Hopkins, 1973).
9. Harry Elmer Barnes maintained that the poet and dramatist in Schiller overpowered the work of the historian. He repeats the positivist bias that Schiller's work as a historian was "a contribution to great literature rather than to scientific history" (*A History of Historical Writing*. 2. rev. ed. [New York: Dover, 1962], pp. 168–69). But his orientation is informed by the nineteenth-century understanding of history as a social science.
10. Hinrich Seeba, "Historiographischer Idealismus?" in *Friedrich Schiller. Kunst, Humanität und Politik*, p. 239.
11. In his book *Schillers Rhetorik*, Gert Ueding maintained that Schiller's recourse to the ancient rhetorical-humanistic ideal of the development (*Bildung*) of the human being is the condition for his criticism of middle-class society (p. 31).
12. Theodor Schieder, "Schiller als Historiker," *Historische Zeitschrift* (1960): 36.
13. Ibid.

330   NOTES TO CHAPTER 4

14. Ibid., p. 38.

15. Ibid., p. 45.

16. The classic study that applies the idealist-realist paradigm to Schiller's works is E[rnst] L. Stahl, *Friedrich Schiller's Drama*. This paradigm is characteristic of Schiller scholarship of the 1960s and still lingers in some learned accounts of the writer's work today (e.g., Klaus Berhahn and Wolfgang Wittkowski). See, also, n. 108.

17. The most prominent, perhaps, being Helmut Kuhn, *Die Vollendung der Ästhetik durch Hegel* (Berlin: Junker und Dünnhaupt, 1931).

18. When employing the term *idealism,* I follow either the first or third definitions recorded in *Webster's Third International Dictionary:* "1a: a theory that regards reality as essentially spiritual or the embodiment of mind or reason esp. by reasserting either that the ideal element in reality is dominant (as in Platonism) or that the intrinsic nature and essence of reality is consciousness or reason (as in Hegelianism)"; 3: literary or artistic theory or practice that values ideal or subjective types or aspects of beauty more than formal or sensible qualities or that affirms the preeminent value of imagination as compared with faithful copying of nature—opposed to *realism*" (p. 1122). By *Idealism,* I mean the philosophies of Fichte, Schelling, and Hegel (up to the time he developed his mature dialectical philosophy). Here, Idealism emphasizes the primacy of consciousness over matter vs. materialism (which advocates the primacy of matter over consciousness). By *idealistic,* I mean either, the tendency to privilege consciousness over matter or the artistic impulse to compose and transmit ideal types as immediate products of the imagination. The view of Schiller as a representative of subjective idealism was disseminated by Wilhelm Dilthey in his essay "Die Typen der Weltanschauung und ihre Ausbildung in den metaphysischen Systemen" in *Gesammelte Schriften.* vol. 8: *Weltanschauungslehre. Abhandlungen zur Philosophie der Philosophie.* 4th ed. (Stuttgart: B. G. Teubner; Göttingen: Vandenhoeck und Ruprecht, 1968), pp. 75–118, esp. p. 110. For a clear definition of an *idealist* in the late eighteenth century see Carl Leonard Reinhold, *Versuch einer neuen Theorie des menschlichen Vorstellungsvermögens* (Prague/ Jena: C. Widtmann and I. M. Mauke, 1789). Drittes Buch, SS ** XXXIV, p. 551. Reinhold was the foremost Kantian of his time. He was professor of philosophy in Jena and knew Schiller very well. In fact, it was Reinhold who first suggested to Schiller that he consider an appointment as a professor in Jena. Reinhold was also C. M. Wieland's son-in-law. For an excellent discussion of the relation between the history of concepts and social history, especially German social history after 1770, see Reinhardt Koselleck, "Begriffsgeschichte und Sozialgeschichte," in his *Vergangene Zukunft. Zur Semantik geschichtlicher Zeiten* (Frankfurt a.M.: Suhrkamp, 1979), pp. 107–29.

19. Seeba, "Historiographischer Idealismus?" p. 237.

20. Eike Middell, *Friedrich Schiller: Leben und Werk* (Leipzig: Reclam, 1982), p. 174.

21. The work of Stephen Greenblatt at the University of California, Berkeley, has been instrumental in shaping this new direction of literary exegesis since the late 1980s. See the critical remarks by Edward Pechter, "The New Historicism and Its Discontents," *Publications of the Modern Language Association* 102 (1987): 292–303. See also: *The New Historicism,* ed. Aram H. Veeser (New York: Routledge, 1989).

22. David Couzens Hoy, *The Critical Circle: Literature, History, and Philosophical Hermeneutics* (Berkeley/Los Angeles/London: University of California Press, 1978), p. 120.

23. Wolfhart Pannenberg, "Hermeneutik und Universalgeschichte," *Zeitschrift für Theologie und Kirche* 60 (1963): 91.

24. For instance, like Schiller, Pannenberg addresses the problem of historical distance ("das Problem des historischen Abstandes"), p. 93. He offers a compelling criticism of Gadamer's understanding of the nature of the "Aussage" (statement, or expression) in *Truth and Method*, 2 rev. ed., translation revised by Joel Weinsheimer and Donald G. Marshall (New York: Crossroad, 1992). The work appeared in 1960 as *Wahrheit und Methode*. Pannenberg's thesis is: "Nicht der Text 'redet,' sondern der Ausleger findet einen sprachlichen Ausdruck, der die Sache des Textes mit dem eigenen Gegenwartshorizont zusammenfaßt" (pp. 111–12). It is not just the connection between "then" and "now" ("Damals und heute"), to which Gadamer directed his full attention, but, as Pannenberg suggests, also "mit dem Zukunftshorizont des gegenwärtig Möglichen" (with the future horizon of what is possible presently) (p. 116) that facilitates a complete understanding of a given text.

25. "Wo der Brodgelehrte trennt, vereinigt der philosophische Geist" (NA 17: 362).

26. J. Hillis Miller, "Presidential Address 1986," *Publications of the Modern Language Association* 102 (1987): 281–91.

27. Already in 1975, David H. Miles called for the merger of "Anglo-American empiricism" and "German theoretical insights" to help move German Studies "out of the doldrums and into stimulating and creative new territory" ("Literary Sociology: Some Introductory Notes," *German Quarterly* 48 [1975]: 31–32).

28. Geoffrey Hartman, *Criticism in the Wilderness: A Study of Literature Today* (New Haven, Connecticut/London: Yale University Press, 1980), p. 221.

29. In *Hans-Georg Gadamer: Philosophical Hermeneutics,* ed. David Linge (Berkeley/Los Angeles: University of California Press, 1977), p. 62.

30. "Die Quelle aller Geschichte ist Tradition, und das Organ der Tradition ist die Sprache" (NA 17: 370).

31. In *The Hermeneutics Reader: Texts of the German Tradition from the Enlightenment to the Present,* ed. Kurt Mueller-Vollmer (New York: Continuum, 1985), p. 100.

32. Hoy, *The Critical Circle,* p. 139.

33. Derec Regin examined the possible influence of Kant's essay on Schiller's inaugural lecture (*Freedom and Dignity: The Historical and Philosophical Thought of Schiller* [The Hague; M. Nijhoff, 1965]). Only in passing, however, did he mention what I think is the most decisive point. According to Regin, conjecture "is not an invention, but reasoning about human experience which is fundamentally the same throughout the ages" (p. 59).

34. *Immanuel Kant. Schriften zur Geschichtsphilosophie,* p. 67.

35. Ibid.

36. Russell B. Nye, "History and Literature: Branches of the Same Tree," in *Essays on History and Literature,* p. 157.

37. Ibid.

38. Ibid., 155.

39. Unlike Schiller, Kant, in his essay "Idee zu einer allgemeinen Geschichte in weltbürgerlicher Absicht," understood the greatest problem for the human species to lie in the attainment of a wholly just, middle-class constitution. Fünfter Satz, *Immanuel Kant. Schriften zur Geschichtsphilosophie,* p. 27. More deliberately than Schiller, Kant emphasized that the history of the human species is directed toward the complete realization of a hidden plan of Nature (Achter Satz 33), and that the justification of Nature rests on providence ("Vorsehung") (p. 38).

40. Hans-Georg Gadamer, "On the Problem of Self-Understanding," in *Philosophical Hermeneutics*, p. 58.

41. "Weil die Weltgeschichte von dem Reichthum und der Armuth an Quellen abhängig ist, so müssen eben so viele Lücken in der Weltgeschichte entstehen, als es leere Strecken in der Ueberlieferung giebt" (NA 17: 372).

42. "Es ist daher zwischen dem Gange der *Welt* und dem Gange der *Weltgeschichte* ein merkliches Mißverhältnis sichtbar" (NA 17: 372).

43. Abraham Kaplan addressed the problem of creating what he calls "linkages" in the absence of the "traces" of history (e.g., documents, coins, inscriptions) in his account of "Historical Interpretation" in *Philosophy of History and Action: Papers presented at the First Jerusalem Philosophical Encounter December 1974*, ed. Yirmiahy Yovel (Dordrecht/Boston: 1978), p. 29. I use the term "trace" in Kaplan's sense and not the metaphysical manner in which Nietzsche, Heidegger, and even Derrida employ it ("Spur"). In *Spurs, Nietzsche's Style/Eprons. Les Styles de Nietzsche*, introd. Stefano Agosti and trans. Barbara Harlow (Chicago / London: University of Chicago Press, 1979), Derrida employs the term "spur" ("eperon") as a mark, a signature which stands proxy, in a sense, for something which was once present and now absent (p. 39f).

44. "Indem er diese Bruchstücke durch künstliche Bindungsglieder verkettet, erhebt er das Aggregat zum System, zu einem vernunftmäßig zusammenhängenden Ganzen" (NA 17: 373).

45. Arthur O. Lovejoy, *The Great Chain of Being. A Study of the History of an Idea* 10th ed. (Cambridge, Massachusetts: Harvard University Press, 1971). But Lovejoy gave Schiller short shrift (pp. 299–303 and 184) and considered him, along with many English scholars, to be a romantic. The topic sentence of chapter six of Lovejoy's study reads: "It was in the eighteenth century that the conception of the universe as a Chain of Being, and the principles which underly this conception—plenitude, continuity, gradation—attained their widest diffusion and acceptance" (p. 183). Lovejoy maintains that Leibniz repeated certain "ancient theses," as, for example, that "in all the visible corporeal world we see no chasms or gaps" (p. 184). We have seen, however, that the modern writer Friedrich Schiller was well aware of the ramifications of gaps for an understanding of world order and the writing of history. See Karl Guthke's persuasive arguments against Lovejoy's conception in chapter two of this study.

46. "Es zieht sich also eine lange Kette von Begebenheiten von dem gegenwärtigen Augenblicke bis zum Anfange des Menschengeschlechts hinauf, die wie Ursache und Wirkung in einander greifen" (NA 17: 370).

47. "Je öfter also und mit je glücklicherm Erfolge er den Versuch erneuert, das Vergangene mit dem Gegenwärtigen zu verknüpfen; desto mehr wird er geneigt, was er als *Ursache* und *Wirkung* in einander greifen sieht, als *Mittel* und *Absicht* zu verbinden" (NA 17: 373).

48. "Warf er sich in das wilde Spiel des Lebens, machte er sich auf den gefährlichen Weg zur moralischen Freiheit" ("Etwas über die erste Menschengesellschaft nach Leitfaden der mosaischen Urkunde"; NA 17: 399).

49. "Liegt in der Gleichförmigkeit und unveränderlichen Einheit der Naturgesetze und des menschlichen Gemüths" (NA 17: 373).

50. "Die Methode, nach der Analogie zu schließen, ist, wie überall so auch in der Geschichte ein mächtiges Hülfsmittel: aber sie muß durch einen erheblichen Zweck gerechtfertigt, und mit eben soviel Vorsicht als Beurtheilung in Ausübung gebracht werden" (NA 17: 373).

51. Ricoeur, "History and Hermeneutics," cited in n. 43, p. 9.

52. Ricoeur, p. 9.

53. "Der nach Übereinstimmung strebt—der ihn unwiderstehlich reizt, alles um sich herum seiner eigenen vernünftigen Natur zu assimiliren, und jede ihm vorkommende Erscheinung zu der höchsten Wirkung die er erkannt, zum *Gedanken* zu erheben" (NA 17: 373).

54. "Er nimmt also diese Harmonie aus sich selbst heraus, und verpflanzt sie ausser sich in die Ordnung der Dinge, d.i. er bringt einen vernünftigen Zweck in den Gang der Welt, und ein teleologisches Prinzip in die *Weltgeschichte*" (NA 17: 374).

55. The entire passage reads: "aber so lange in der Reyhe der Weltveränderungen noch wichtige Bindungsglieder fehlen, so lange das Schicksal über so viele Begebenheiten den letzten Aufschluß noch zurückhält, erklärt er die Frage für *unentschieden,* und diejenige Meinung siegt, welche dem Verstande die höhere Befriedigung, und dem Herzen die größre Glückseligkeit anzubieten hat" (NA 17: 374).

56. "Eine Erscheinung nach der andern fängt an, sich dem blinden Ohngefähr, der gesetzlosen Freyheit zu entziehen, und sich einem übereinstimmenden Ganzen (das freylich nur in seiner Vorstellung vorhanden ist) als ein passendes Glied anzureyhen" (NA 17: 373).

57. *"Nur als der höchsten Kraft der Gegenwart dürft ihr das Vergangene deuten"* (*Friedrich Nietzsche. Werke,* ed. Karl Schlechta [München: Hanser, 1966], vol. 1, p. 250).

58. Pannenberg expressed something similar: "In seiner Fraglichkeit ist das gegenwärtige Sachverständnis bezogen auf Überlieferung, angesichts einer offenen Zukunft" ("Hermeneutik und Universalgeschichte," cited in n. 23, p. 119).

59. Jacques Derrida, "Structure, Sign and Play in the Discourse of the Human Sciences," in *Writing and Difference* 279, 281, and 289.

60. "Daß diese Folge von Erscheinungen, die in seiner Vorstellung soviel Regelmäßigkeit und Absicht annahm, diese Eigenschaften in der Wirklichkeit verläugne; es fällt ihm schwer, wieder unter die blinde Herrschaft der Nothwendigkeit zu geben, was unter dem geliehenen Lichte des Verstandes angefangen hatte eine so heitre Gestalt zu gewinnen" (NA 17: 373).

61. "Indem sie den Menschen gewöhnt, sich mit der ganzen Vergangenheit zusammen zu faßen, und mit seinen Schlüssen in die ferne Zukunft voraus zu eilen: so verbirgt sie die Grenzen von Geburt und Tod, die das Leben des Menschen so eng und so drückend umschliessen, so breitet sie optisch täuschend sein kurzes Daseyn in einen unendlichen Raum aus, und führt das Individuum unvermerkt in die Gattung hinüber" (NA 17: 375).

62. Among contemporary accounts of world history, Alfred Heuß appreciated what we have now discerned to be Schiller's recognition that the unity of a world-historical process based on teleology is actually an illusion ("Illusion"). Alfred Heuß, "Möglichkeiten einer Weltgeschichte heute," in his *Zur Theorie der Weltgeschichte* (Berlin: Walter de Gruyter, 1968), p. 2. But Heuß sidesteps the problem by embracing the "unity of the human race as a verifiable phenomenon" (p. 3). Contary to Heuß, the original meaning of the term "world, or universal history" understood as a history of the cosmos (at least since Augustine) does indeed involve certain presuppositions about the nature of the universe as evidenced here by Schiller's essay. Unlike Heuß, who focuses his attention on the question of the nature and direction of the human species ("Gattung"), Ernst Schulin, like Schiller in part, regards universal history as a special field of historical inquiry ("Individualgebilde"), one which is not so far removed from empirical research as has been assumed. Ernst Schulin, "Einleitung" to his volume of collected essays *Universalgeschichte* (Köln: Kiepenheuer und Witsch, 1974), pp. 11–65. Rather than constituting, first and foremost, "a unity in becoming" (*Saeculum Weltgeschichte* [Freiburg/Basel/Wien: Herder, 1965], vol. 1,

p. XI), "the inner continuum of humanity" (p. X), universal history, for Schulin, forms "a real connection to the world" (p. 13).

63. "Ein edles Verlangen muß in uns entglühen, zu dem reichen Vermächtniß von Wahrheit, Sittlichkeit und Freyheit, das wir von der Vorwelt überkamen und reich vermehrt an die Folgewelt wieder abgeben müssen, auch aus *unsern* Mitteln einen Beytrag zu legen, und an dieser unvergänglichen Kette, die durch alle Menschengeschlechter sich windet, unser fliehendes Daseyn zu befestigen" (NA 17: 376).

64. "Eine eben so anziehende als nützliche Beschäftigung" (NA 17: 374).

65. Hoy, *The Critical Circle,* p. 121.

66. Wolfhart Pannenberg argues that the thematics of hermeneutics is directed back to the problem of universal history, "weil ein Verstehen überlieferter Texte in ihrer historischen Differenz von der Gegenwart ohne ein universal-geschichtliches Denken, das freilich den Horizont einer offenen Zukunft und damit der Möglichkeiten gegenwärtigen Handelns miteinschließen muß, nicht in sachgerechter Weise methodisch durchführbar zu sein scheint" ("Hermeneutik und Universalgeschichte," cited in n. 23, p. 121).

67. "Bewundernswürdig verflochten ist der Faden der Weltgeschichte!" (NA 18/2: 95).

68. "Ein Umstand, auf den man allein nicht gerechnet hatte-Gustavs Heldengröße, zerriß das Gewebe dieser betriegerischen Staatskunst" (NA 18/2: 100).

69. "Daß der Friedländer einen Teufel / Aus der Hölle im Solde hält" (NA 8: 24).

70. "Es ist ein guter Geist auf deinen Lippen, / Die Mutter hat mir deine Fertigkeit / Gepriesen, es soll eine zarte Stimme / Des Wohllauts in dir wohnen, die die Seele / Bezaubert. Eine solche Stimme brauch / Ich jetzt, den bösen Dämon zu vertreiben, / Der um mein Haupt die schwarzen Flügel schlägt" (NA 1: 239–40). Translations are by F. J. Lamport, *Friedrich Schiller: The Robbers. Wallenstein* (London: Penguin, 1979).

71. Dieter Borchmeyer, *Macht und Melancholie. Schillers "Wallenstein"* (Frankfurt a.M.: Athenäum, 1988), pp. 87–89. Borchmeyer sees that one of the most widespread topoi of the tradition of melancholy is healing through music (p. 87).

72. "Verschont mich -Singen- jetzt- in dieser Angst / Der schwer beladnen Seele- vor ihm singen- / Der meine Mutter stürzt ins Grab!" (NA 8: 240).

73. "*Hält das Instrument mit zitternder Hand, ihre Seele arbeitet im heftigsten Kampf, und im Augenblick, da sie anfangen soll zu singen, schaudert sie zusammen, wirft das Instrument weg und geht schnell ab*" (NA 8: 240).

74. "Streben wir nicht allzuhoch / Hinauf, daß wir zu tief nicht fallen mögen" (NA 8: 242).

75. "Sie bauen immer, bauen / Bis in die Wolken, bauen fort und fort / Und denken nicht dran, daß der schmale Grund / Das schwindelnde schwanke Werk nicht tragen kann" (NA 8: 243).

76. Karl Guthke sees clearly that, for Wallenstein, Thekla is simply a means to an end, "Objekt von Wallensteins Ambitionen" ("'Wallenstein' als Spiel von Spiel," *Wirkendes Wort* 43 [1993]: 182). However, Guthke understands Schiller's text as a "Spiel von Spiel" (p. 195), wherein Wallenstein becomes the victim of his own playing/gaming (p. 185f.). Concerning Schiller's characterization of Wallenstein in the drama, I agree more with Hans-Georg Werner, who believes Schiller was indicting his hero. "Schiller verurteilte Wallenstein als einen auf seinen eigenen Vorteil bedachten Menschen, der selbst vor dem Verrat nicht zurückschreckt, um seine Interessen durchzusetzen" ("Ein Beitrag zur Deutung der Wallenstein-Trilogie Friedrich Schillers. Das Verhältnis des Dichters zur Geschichte," *Wissenschaftliche Zeitschrift* 10 [Halle, 1961]: 1043–57). Most critics would seem to agree that Wallenstein's main

problem is his limitless ego. "Wallenstein thinks only of his personal interest, of power and ambition" (R. D. Miller *Interpreting Schiller: A Study of Four Plays* [Harrogate: The Duchy Press, 1986], p. 104). Hence, he is loveless. Whereas Werner emphasized the moral import, Guthke appreciates the playfulness of Schiller's aesthetics. From my perspective, aesthetics and ethics are central to Schiller's concerns as a writer.

77. "Alles ist Partei und nirgends / Kein Richter! Sagt, wo soll das enden? Wer / Den Knäul entwirren, der sich endlos selbst / Vermehrend wächst-Er muß zerhauen werden. / Ich fühls, daß ich der Mann des Schicksals bin" (NA 8: 264–65).

78. "Noch fühl ich mich denselben, der ich war! / Es ist der Geist, der sich den Körper baut, / Und Friedland wird sein Lager um sich füllen" (NA 8: 258).

79. "Wenn Haupt und Glieder sich trennen, / Da wird sich zeigen, wo die Seele wohnte" (NA 8: 258).

80. "Er soll mein Glückentscheiden, er ist wahrhaft, / Ist unverstellt und haßt die krummen Wege, / Er ist so gut, so edel-THEKLA. Das bist du!" (NA 8: 127).

81. *Max reißt sich aus ihren Armen und geht, die Gräfin begleitet ihn. Thekla folgt ihm anfangs mit den Augen, geht unruhig durch das Zimmer und bleibt dann in Gedanken versenkt stehen. Eine Gitarre liegt auf dem Tische, sie ergreift sie, und nachdem sie eine Weile schwermütig präludiert hat, fällt sie in den Gesang* (NA 8: 129).

82. "Das Herz ist gestorben, die Welt ist leer, / Und weiter gibt sie dem Wunsche nichts mehr. Du Heilige, rufe dein Kind zurück, / Ich habe genossen das irdische Glück, / Ich habe gelebt und geliebet" (NA 8: 130).

83. "Ich bin die Seine. Sein Geschenk allein / Ist dieses neue Leben, das ich lebe. / Er hat ein Recht an sein Geschöpf. Was war ich, / Eh seine schöne Liebe mich beseelte?" (NA 8: 133).

84. "Daß ich mir selbst gehöre, weiß ich nun. / Den festen Willen hab ich kennenlernen, / Den unbezwinglichen, in meiner Brust, / Und an das Höchste kann ich alles setzen" (NA 8: 133).

85. "Es zieht mich fort, mit göttlicher Gewalt, / Dem Abgrund zu, ich kann nicht widerstreben" (NA 8: 135).

86. "Ich konnte dich der Unschuld deines Herzens, / Dem eignen Urteil ruhig anvertraun, / Doch deinem Herzen selbst seh ich das Netz / Verderblich jetzt bereiten—Das Geheimnis, (*ihn scharf mit den Augen fixierend*) / Das *du* vor mir verbirgst, entreißt mir *meines*" (NA 8: 157).

87. "Aufgelöst / Sind alle Bande, die den Offizier / An seinen Kaiser fesseln" (NA 8: 159).

88. "Der Wallenstein ist deinem Herzen teuer, / Ein starkes Band der Liebe, der Verehrung / Knüpft seit der frühen Jugend dich an ihn" (NA 8: 164).

89. Gert Ueding recaptures the traditional view of Max as "die Verkörperung schöner Humanität," a "'schöne Seele,'" or, even, "das utopische Gewissen Wallensteins," a "Paradigma für die Wirksamkeit des Schönen überhaupt" (*Friedrich Schiller*, p. 107); and, "der Repräsentant des utopischen Gedankens, der in ihm [Wallenstein] steckt" (p. 104).

90. "Die Tugenden des *Herrschers* und *Helden,* Klugheit, Gerechtigkeit, Festigkeit und Muth, ragen in seinem Charakter kolossalisch hervor; aber ihm fehlten die sanftern Tugenden des *Menschen,* die den Helden zieren, und dem Herrscher Liebe erwerben" (NA 18: 328). This description stands in juxtaposition to the characterization of Gustav Adolphus, who remained "auch in der Trunkenheit seines Glückes noch Mensch und noch Christ, aber auch in seiner Andacht noch Held und noch König" (NA 18: 139). Already in his *Geschichte des Abfalls der vereinigten Niederlande von der Spanischen Regierung* of 1788, Schiller had made it clear that he was

not interested in the exceptional deeds of colossal individuals found in the history of past ages. "Jene Zeiten sind vorbey, jene Menschen sind nicht mehr" (NA 17:11). For him, the Netherlandic people, with their "Mangel and heroischer Größe," were driven to action by the circumstances in which they found themselves.

91. "Lief er auf schwankem Seil des Lebens hin"; and, "Er ging der Größe kühnen Weg, Mit schnellem Schritt" (NA 8: 289).

92. "Ich geh zum Herzog. Heut noch werd ich ihn / Auffordern, seinen Leumund vor der Welt / Zu retten, eure künstlichen Gewebe / Mit einem graden Schritte zu durchreißen" (NA 8: 170).

93. "O! welchen Riß erregst du mir im Herzen! / Der alten Ehrfurcht eingewachsnen Trieb / Und des Gehorsams heilige Gewohnheit / Soll ich versagen lernen deinem Namen?" (NA 8: 206).

94. "Die Sinne sind in deinen Banden noch, / Hat gleich die Seele blutend sich befreit!" (NA 8: 206).

95. "Zerreißen soll das Band der alten Liebe, / Nicht sanft sich lösen und du willst den Riß, / Den schmerzlichen, nur schmerzlicher noch machen!" (NA 8: 282).

96. "Grenzenlos war sein Ehrgeitz, unbeugsam sein Stolz, sein gebietherischer Geist nicht fähig, eine Kränkung ungerochen zu erdulden" (NA 18: 132).

97. "Vertrauen, Glaube, Hoffnung ist dahin, / Denn alles log mir, was ich hochgeachtet" (NA 8: 227).

98. "Der einzig reine Ort ist unsre Liebe, / Der unentweihte in der Menschlichkeit" (NA 8: 227).

99. "Die Klagen hören der zerrißnen Seele, / Und Tränen um mich weinen—O! die Menschen / Sind grausam, aber sie ist wie ein Engel. / Sie wird von gräßlich wütender Verzweiflung / Die Seele retten, diesen Schmerz des Todes / Mit sanften Trostesworten klagend lösen" (NA 8: 228).

100. "Bracht ich ein angstvoll Leben mit ihm zu, / Und stets an eines Abgrunds jähem Rande / Sturzdrohend, schwindelnd riß er mich dahin" (NA 8: 236).

101. "Die Zeiten / Der Liebe sind vorbei, der zarten Schonung" (NA 8: 269).

102. "Und eine Frevelhandlung faßt die andre / In enggeschloßner Kette grausend an" (NA 8: 271).

103. "Ein Leibesnetz hab ich um dich gesponnen, / Zerreiß es, wenn du kannst,— Du bist an mich / Geknüpft mit jedem zarten Seelenbande, / Mit jeder heilgen Fessel der Natur, / Die Menschen aneinanderketten kann" (NA 8: 272).

104. "Auf *mich* bist du gepflanzt, ich bin dein Kaiser, / Mir angehören, mir gehorchen, *das* / Ist deine Ehre, dein Naturgesetz (NA 8: 272).

105. "Zu viel vertraut ich auf das eigne Herz, / Ich stehe wankend, weiß nicht, was ich soll" (NA 8: 277).

106. "Hier, auf dieses Herz / Das unfehlbare, heilig reine will / Ichs legen, deine Liebe will ich fragen" (NA 8: 278).

107. "Zerreißen soll das Band der alten Liebe, / Nicht sanft sich lösen und du willst den Riß, / Den schermzlichen, mir schmerzlicher noch machen! / Du weißt, ich habe ohne dich zu leben / Noch nicht gelernt—in eine Wüste geh ich / Hinaus, und alles was mir wert ist, alles / Bleibt hier zurück" (NA 8: 282).

108. In Chapter V of his book *Friedrich Schillers' Drama* titled "The Realist as Hero," Stahl asserted that Schiller had portrayed Wallenstein "as a realist who is compelled by ambition, yet is forced into a false position by the circumstances in which he finds himself" (p. 93). But the realist, according to Stahl's reading of Schiller's *Concerning Naive and Sentimental Poetry,* is one who sees in necessity a supreme law and the major motive behind human behavior. But this is not true of the Wallenstein of Schiller's texts. Among more recent interpretations of Max Piccolomini, Walter Müller-Seidel sees in Max an idealist who is detached from all

knowledge of the world ("Die Idee des neuen Lebens," in his *Die Geschichtlichkeit der deutschen Klassik. Literatur und Denkformen um 1800* [Stuttgart: J. B. Metzler, 1983], p. 131). This opinion is not informed by the fact that Max has known nothing but the Thirty Years' War. He is also praised for his heroism in battle. For Müller-Seidel, whatever Max and Thekla want, they represent the idea of humanity—and nothing more ("nur Verkörperungen dieser Idee—eines Ideals noch vor aller Wirklichkeit") (p. 133). Of Wallenstein, Müller-Seidel says, "Er ist Idealist und Realist zugleich" (p. 132). But, if this is the case, then the terms "idealist" and "realist" lose their meaning as signifiers. Müller-Seidel's interpretation is not free of logical confusion when, for instance, he characterizes Schiller's Wallenstein as both "ein revolutionär Idealist" and "the realist of political life" ("der Realist des politischen Lebens") (p. 131)! Whatever substance Wallenstein's vision may or may not have, there is little doubt that he is an egoist. For even when thinking about peace, he thinks about his own power and possessions. In short, he is decidedly self-interested. When contrasted to Schiller's essay "Julius's Theosophy," our understanding of the later "hero" receives added weight.

109. "Die Zeiten / Der Liebe sind vorbei, / der zarten Schonung, / Und Haß und Rache kommen an die Reihe. Ich kann auch Unmensch sein, wie er [der Kaiser]" (NA 8: 269).

110. Norbert Oellers sees in Max's and Thekla's downfall an indication of Schiller's loss of trust in the realization of the ideal and its experience on earth: "politisch enttäuscht, physisch zerstört, sieht er sich von jeder Art Idyll mehr und mehr abgedrängt, auch von persönlichen Hoffnungen, die einmal sehr stark waren" ("Idylle und Politik. Französische Revolution, ästhetische Erziehung und die Freiheit der Urkantone," in *Friedrich Schiller: Kunst, Humanität und Politik*, p. 128.

111. "Er macht mir das Wirkliche zum Traum, / Um die gemeine Deutlichkeit der Dinge / Den goldnen Duft der Morgenröte webend- / Im Feuer seines liebenden Gefühls / Erhoben sich, mir selber zum Erstaunen, / Des Lebens flach alltägliche Gestalten" (NA 8: 333–34).

112. "Die Blume ist hinweg aus meinem Leben, / Und kalt und farblos seh ichs vor mir liegen" (NA 8: 333).

113. "Trauriges Verstummen über den Fall eines mächtigen Menschen, unter einem schweigenden und tauben Schicksal" ("Ueber *Wallenstein*," in *Georg Wilhelm Friedrich Hegel. Werke*, vol. 15, *Vorlesungen über die Ästhetik III*, eds. Eva Moldenhauer and Karl Markus Michel [Frankfurt a.M.: Suhrkamp, 1970], p. 618).

114. See my study *Between Luther and Münzer: The Peasant Revolt in German Drama and Thought* (Heidelberg: Carl Winter, 1988), pp. 80–81, and the penetrating study by Helmut Pillau, *Die fortgedachte Dissonanz. Hegel Tragödientheorie und Schillers Tragödie. Deutsche Antworten auf die Französische Revolution* (München: Fink, 1981).

115. "Es endigt nicht als eine Theodicee" ("Über Wallenstein," *Werke*, vol. 1, p. 618).

116. Lesley Sharpe suggested that Wallenstein's role-playing actually works against him since he becomes the plaything of history (*Schiller and the Historical Character*, pp. 98 and 89, respectively). This last point is stressed by F. J. Lamport ("The Charismatic Hero," *Publications of the Englisch Goethe Society* 58 [1987–88]: 73f.). Lamport submits that, unlike Goethe's Egmont, Schiller's Wallenstein fails in the exercise of charismatic authority (p. 73). Sharpe sees clearly that Wallenstein "can control neither people nor events. While he thinks he is holding himself apart from the movement of events he is in fact being carried along by it" (p. 90). However, while the audience is aware of this, I am not convinced Wallenstein ever is. In the light of the dramatic irony, I cannot agree that "Wallenstein discovers that he cannot

stand outside history" (Sharpe, p. 90). Indeed, right before his downfall, the general suits up for battle, thinking that he can still act.

117. "Zerreißt das Gemüth, daraus kann man nicht mit erleichterter Brust springen!" ("Über Wallenstein," *Werke,* vol. 1, p. 620). Hegel's disappointment in Schiller's dramatization of history has been echoed in various ways in recent scholarship. E.g., Klaus Berghahn and Hans-Dietrich Dahnke. Lesley Sharpe contrasts the "historical optimism" of the later theoretical works with the "profoundly pessimistic view of a hostile world" in the "historical dramas" (*Schiller and the Historical Character,* p. 105). One of the strengths of her study is that it contradicts the many critics who admire the "idealist heroes" of Schiller's plays (p. 79f.).

Chapter 5. The Tasks of Culture: Beauty and the Aesthetic Education of the Human Being

1. *Immanuel Kant. Werkausgabe X: Kritik der Urteilskraft,* ed. Wilhelm Weischedel, 5th ed. (Frankfurt a.M.: Suhrkamp, 1981), p. 25. Hereafter: *KU.* Translations are my own.
2. Ibid., p. 27.
3. Ibid., p. 26.
4. Ibid., p. 27.
5. Ibid., p. 32.
6. Ibid., p. 33.
7. Ibid., p. 132.
8. Ibid., p. 137.
9. Ibid.
10. Ibid., p. 132.
11. In early February 1991 I shared my findings with the director of the Deutsches Literaturarchiv, Ulrich Ott, and my mentor Dorothea Kuhn.
12. Jens Kulenkampff, "Friedrich Schiller. Vollständiges Verzeichnis der Randbemerkungen in seinem Handexemplar der *Kritik der Urteilskraft,*" in *Materialien zu Kants "Kritik der Urteilskraft,*" ed. Jens Kulenkampff (Frankfurt a.M.: Suhrkamp, 1974). The vast majority of Schiller's entries are in brown ink, which the writer entered while preparing his lectures for the winter semester 1792–93 at the University of Jena. The penciled notations stem from his reading of the spring of 1791. There are also a few in black ink. The volume is in excellent shape. The leather jacket is still tightly bound and almost every page is still white with a slightly yellowish brown tint. There are very few water spots.
13. The first and third points here are adapted from Jens Kulenkampff, ed. *Materialien zu Kants "Kritik der Urteilskraft,*" p. 17.
14. *KU,* pp. 137–38.
15. Besides the double underlining, there are several omissions and/or errors in Kulenkampff's register. On p. 129 of Kulenkampff's copy, the first mention of a "Vorstellung" should be underlined, and not the second. There is no reference "144," as indicated by J. K. (p. 144). The marginal notations "90" on p. 100 and p. "5" on p. 139 of Schiller's personal copy, as well as a series of numbers on the backside of the very last page before the back cover of the text are not noted by Jens Kulenkampff.
16. *KU,* p. 141.
17. Ibid., p. 257.
18. Ibid., p. 39.
19. Ibid.
20. Ibid., p. 50.
21. Ibid., p. 65.

22. Ibid., p. 76.

23. The letter of January 25, 1793, opens with an expression of concern regarding the author's recurrent illness. "Ich bin zu Catarrhalischen Uebeln geneigt, welche der Winter vorzüglich herbeyführt, und meine 2 Entzündungsfieber sind catarrhalisch gewesen" (NA 26: 175). Despite the potentially fatal limitations of the body, it is evident that Schiller developed some of his most original ideas on the nature of beauty when ill.

24. NA 26: 206.

25. Denny McClelland has stated the matter well: "Beauty, as freedom in appearance, suggests that an object of art or an object in nature must not appear to an observor as if its form had been affected by something external. The object's appearance must give the suggestion of freedom. For example, a distorted tree might appear offensive because its appearance would seem contrary to nature. Something external would seem to have influenced its appearance" ("The Discrepancy Between Kant and Schiller," in *Friedrich von Schiller and the Drama of Human Existence*, ed. Alexej Urgrinsky [New York/Westport, Connecticut: Greenwood Press, 1988], p. 138).

26. S. S. Kerry, *Schiller's Writings on Aesthetics* (Manchester: Manchester University Press, 1961), p. 67.

27. Ibid., p. 38.

28. Ibid., p. 66.

29. Incidentally, Schiller ordered a guitar in Jena for his friend Christian Körner. It was made by Jakob August Otto. In a letter of April 7, 1797, Schiller notified Körner that he had sent it (NA 29: 383).

30. Heinrich Mettler, *Entfremdung und Revolution: Brennpunkt des Klassischen. Studien zu Schillers Briefen "Über die ästhetische Erziehung des Menschen" im Hinblick auf die Begegnung mit Goethe* (Bern/München: Francke, 1977), p. 92. J. M. Ellis puts the matter as follows: "The beautiful instrument is one which looks as though it was never actually designed as such but still has a shape which is directly related to its purpose" (*Schiller's 'Kalliasbriefe' and the Study of His Aesthetic Theory* [The Hague/Paris: Mouton, 1969], p. 114).

31. Mettler, *Entfremdung und Revolution*, p. 93.

32. Kerry and others have missed this important point. According to Mettler, it was Goethe who drew Schiller to the distinction with respect to organic "natures" (Mettler, p. 93). In general, however, Mettler fails to account for Schiller's own studies of Nature long before his friendship with Goethe.

33. "*Freiheit* allein ist der Grund des Schönen, Technik ist nur der Grund unserer Vorstellung von der Freiheit . . . Technick . . . trägt nur insofern zur Schönheit bey, als sie dazu dient, die Vorstellung der Freiheit zu erregen" (NA 26: 209).

34. "Daß diese technische Form [des Instruments] etwas Auswärtiges ist" and "daß sie ihm durch den Verstand des Künstlers gewaltthätig aufgedrungen worden" (NA 26: 207).

35. In his intellectually stimulating book *Autonomie und soziale Funktion der Kunst. Studien zur Ästhetik von Schiller und Novalis* (Stuttgart: J. B. Metzler, 1973), Rolf-Peter Janz took great pains to disclose the apparent contradictions in Schiller's attempt to conjoin Kant's concept of autonomy and the social function of art into one theory of the aesthetic education of the human being. However, he overlooks Schiller's early literary practice (see the preliminary conclusion to chapter three).

36. "Daß auch die Formen der Kunst mit der Existenz des geformten Eins ausmachen müssen, wenn sie auf die höchste Schönheit Anspruch machen sollen" (NA 26: 207).

37. "Ein Vogel im Flug ist die glücklichste Darstellung des durch die Form bezwungenen Stoffs, der durch die Kraft überwundenen Schwere" (NA 26: 205).

38. Ellis says, simply, "It is noticeable in the animal analogies that the emphasis is on gravity" (p. 111). The question, of course, is why.

39. "Daß die Fähigkeit über die Schwere zu siegen oft zum Symbol der Freiheit gebraucht wird" (NA 26: 205).

40. "Wir drücken die Freiheit der Phantasie aus, indem wir ihm Flügel geben" (NA 26: 205).

41. "Die Schwerkraft verhält sich ohngefehr eben so gegen die lebendige Kraft des Vogels" (NA 26: 205).

42. Mettler has suggested that Schiller understood the aftermath of the French Revolution as an apocalyptic event, one that had driven the natural intention ("Naturabsicht") of human development ad absurdum. The writer's experience of his times discloses what I call a culture crisis. In *Concerning the Aesthetic Education of the Human Being,* Schiller was fully aware of the political task of culture. Mettler's comments tend, at times, in this direction though, in general, he emphasizes the moral rather than the political goal of aesthetic education. "Die Entkräftung der zeitgenössischen Kultur der Aufklärung, die man mit dem modernen Begriff der Dekadenz bezeichnen könnte, hat schließlich die Entfesselung der urtümlichen, blinden Kräfte vor aller Kultur herausgefordert: die radikale Pervertierung des Anfangs—und des Endzustands der Menschheit ist für Schiller zur unumstößlichen Tatsache der eigenen Gegenwart geworden" (Mettler, *Entfremdung und Revolution,* p. 51). To be sure, Schiller's writings show that the author was concerned about both the moral and political ramifications and implications of the French Revolution. Where I part company with Mettler is in his uncritical transference of Rousseau's indictment of civilization to Schiller. As I suggest elsewhere, Schiller's vision is always future oriented, i.e., progressive, unlike Rousseau's reactionary position which calls for a return to Nature. Wolfgang Düsing fails to appreciate the political nature of Schiller's ruminations (*Friedrich Schiller: Über die ästhetische Erziehung des Menschen in einer Reihe von Briefen. Text, Materialien, Kommentar,* ed. Wolfgang Düsing [München: Hanser, 1981]). "Das Interesse am politischen Geschehen tritt zurück" (148). In general, Düsing treats Schiller's reaction to the French Revolution with ambivalence. His summarial statement reflects nothing new: "Es ging Schiller um die Realisierung des Humanitätsideals" (p. 149). Hans-Georg Pott, *Die schöne Freiheit. Eine Interpretation zu Schillers Schrift "Über die ästhetische Erziehung des Menschen in einer Reihe von Briefen"* (München: Wilhelm Fink, 1980), focuses on the politics of Schiller's concepts of the beautiful. "Der Weg zur Freiheit ist nicht angelegt wie ein schöner Park, nach dessen Durchquerung man durch das 'Morgentor des Schönen' in jenes ersehnte Reich eintritt. Das Woraus der Mensch die Freiheit nur ergreifen kann, muß selbst Freiheit sein: dies ist die Quintessenz der Lehre der 'Briefe'(p. 10). One of the strengths of Pott's study lies in his sensitivity toward what he terms Schiller's "Erfahrung der Zerrissenheit der bürgerlichen Gesellschaft" (p. 11). An important contribution to this discussion is Jeffrey Barnouw's article "'Freiheit zu geben durch Freiheit! Ästhetischer Zustand—Ästhetischer Staat," in *Friedrich Schiller. Kunst Humanität und Politik in der späten Aufklärung. Ein Symposium,* ed. Wolfgang Wittkowski (Tübingen: Max Niemeyer, 1982), pp. 138–61. See also Jürgen Bolten's *Schillers Briefe über die ästhetische Erziehung* (Frankfurt a.M.: Suhrkamp, 1984); and, Walter Hinderer, "*Republik oder Monarchie? Anmerkungen zu Schillers politischer Denkungsart,*" in *Literatur in der Demokratie. Für Walter Jens zum 60. Geburtstag,* eds. Winfried Barner et al. (München: Kindler, 1983), esp. p. 306.

43. Kerry, *Schiller's Writings on Aesthetics,* p. 29.

44. Ibid., p. 31.
45. Ibid., p. 11.
46. Ibid.
47. Ibid., p. 12.
48. Ellis is especially critical of Kerry's "traditional" approach to Schiller in *Schiller's "Kalliasbriefe" and the Study of His Aesthetic Theory*. Despite Ellis's generalizations about "the" traditional approach, Klaus Berghahn supports Ellis's indictment of the tradition ("Ästhetik und Politik im Werk Schillers: Zur jüngsten Forschung," *Monatshefte* 66 [1974]: 410f.).
49. Kerry, *Schiller's Writings on Aesthetics*, p. 13.
50. Ibid., p. 70.
51. I am skeptical about Ellis's reduction of knowledge to one or the other specific field of inquiry.
52. Further evidence of the importance of Henrich's contribution is supplied by Lesley Sharpe's *Friedrich Schiller*. In general, she echoes the main tenets of Henrich's essay. Sharpe describes the practical effect of Schiller's definition of beauty as freedom in appearance as "drawing together Kantian ethics and aesthetics in an attempt to prove the intuition that the beautiful touches the deepest part of our being by appearing to us to have the total serenity or composure which in Kantian ethics can come only from the realization of freedom in moral behavior" (p. 132). I disagree that, for Schiller, serenity or composure was at all a final goal. Sharpe's opinion on this point reflects the traditional notion of harmony as a tranquil state of completion and sustained equilibrium.
53. Henrich, "Beauty and Freedom: Schiller's Struggle with Kant's Aesthetics," trans. David R. Lachterman in *Essays in Kant's Aesthetics,* eds. Ted Cohen and Paul Guyer (Chicago/London: University of Chicago Press, 1982), p. 239.
54. Ibid.
55. Ibid.
56. Ibid., p. 250. Despite Schiller's lack of systematic unity, Henrich could still recommend the study of the theoretical part of his [Schiller's] work as "a worthy task of philosophy" (p. 257).
57. Ibid., p. 243.
58. Ibid.
59. Karl Vorländer was one of the first to examine the formal qualities of Kant's writings in his seminal work *Immanuel Kant. Der Mann und das Werk* 3rd ed. (Hamburg: Felix Meiner, 1992), p. 81f. See my review of the third edition of 1992 in *The Lessing Yearbook* 26 (1994): 165–66. For a more recent and detailed analysis of the writer Immanuel Kant, see Willi Goetschel, *Kant als Schriftsteller* (Wien: Passagen, 1990).
60. "Die Wahrheit stehet fest, kein deutlicher, auch kein völlig dunkler Begriff verträgt sich mit dem Gefühle der Schönheit" (*Schriften zur Philosophie und Ästhetik*, vol. 1, p. 50; *Moses Mendelssohns Philosophische Schriften*, vol. 1, p. 11).
61. Henrich, "Beauty and Freedom," p. 244.
62. Ibid.
63. Dieter Borchmeyer has offered a detailed analysis of Schiller's intellectual relationship to Burke in his article "Rhetorische und ästhetische Revolutionskritik: Edmund Burke und Schiller," in *Klassik und Moderne. Die Weimarer Klassik als historisches Ereignis und Herausforderung im kulturgeschichtlichen Prozeß. Walter Müller-Seidel zum 65. Geburtstag,* eds. Karl Richter and Jörg Schönert (Stuttgart: J. B. Metzler, 1983). "Entscheidend ist, daß Schiller wie Mendelssohn und die Popularphilosophen der Überzeugung ist, daß die theoretische Aufklärung allein den Fortschritt der Menschheit nicht fördert, sondern daß dazu praktische Maximen

erforderlich sind, die sich nicht aus rein vernünftigen Grundsätzen ableiten lassen-wird doch der Mensch in der Regel nicht durch 'Begriff, sondern 'durch Empfindungen' zum Handeln bestimmt" (p. 66). Borchmeyer suggests that this insight into the action-motivated role of feeling ties Schiller to the tradition of empiricist ethics and rhetoric (66). D. B. emphasizes Schiller's contributions to practical-aesthetic culture. He also underscores the writer's interest in the image rather than concept formation.

64. Jeffrey Barnouw has examined Schiller's indebtedness to the empiricist tradition in a series of articles. In his excellent contribution to *Friedrich Schiller. Kunst, Humanität und Politik* ("'Freiheit zu geben durch Freiheit'. Ästhetischer Zustand—Ästhetischer Staat"), Barnouw differentiated clearly between Kant and Schiller with respect to the issue of morality. "Wo Kant als Grundlage der Moralität eine Freiheit des Menschen *von* der Erfahrung aufstellt, behauptet Schiller, nur eine Freiheit, die *durch* die Erfahrung erhalten und ins Werk gesetzt wird, kann eine ethische Rationalität begründen" (p. 147). Joachim Schmidt-Neubauer offers a cogent description of Schiller's "sensuous-objective" aesthetics vis-à-vis the aesthetics of Burke ("sensuous-objective"), Kant ("subjective-rational"), and Baumgarten ("rational-objective") in *Tyrannei und der Mythos vom Glück. Drei Essays zu Lessing, Schiller und Goethe* (Frankfurt a.M.: Rita Fischer, 1981), pp. 73–74.

65. A one-sided view of Schiller's classical essays develops from the Platonic idea that form and beautiful appearance, as detached from physical circumstances, are the highest good. A considerable amount of British Schiller scholarship is conditioned by this view (e.g., as of late, Sharpe and F. J. Lamport). David Pugh continues this tradition in his thought-provoking article on Schiller as Platonist (1991).

66. Looking at the matter from the point of view of early nineteenth-century German thought, Ellis argued against affiliating Schiller (and Kant) with the German Idealists (*Schiller's "Kalliasbriefe,"* p. 143). The general conception that Schiller was an idealist (either in the Platonic or Hegelian sense) is seriously challenged by the presence of the tension between anthropology (physiology) and metaphysics (theosophy) in his writings and the writer's repeated qualifications ("bloß eine Idee") in the classical essays. By cultivating the Platonic tradition, some scholars have overemphasized the writer's interest in "ideal beauty," which is far more characteristic of the work of Johann Joachim Winckelmann. Despite the arguments advanced by Ellis (p. 143f.) against fashioning Schiller as an idealist, Schiller scholarship still continues to do so. In addition to Klaus Berghahn (*Schiller. Ansichten eines Idealisten*) and Denny McClelland ("The Discrepancy between Kant and Schiller," cited in n. 25, see Claudia Brodsky, "Freedom in Kant and Schiller: Criticism and Idealism," in *Friedrich von Schiller: The Drama of Human Existence*, pp. 129–33. For a challenging account, see Wolfgang Wittkoswki's "Introduction: Schiller's Idealism—How 'Idealistic' Is It?" in *Friedrich von Schiller*, pp. 1–9. Perhaps the first serious challenges to this direction of thought were Käte Hamburger's work on Sartre and Schiller and the problem of idealism. See especially her article "Zum Problem des Idealismus bei Schiller," *Jahrbuch der Deutschen Schillergesellschaft* 4 (1960): 60–71.

67. *Revolution und Autonomie. Deutsche Autonomieästhetik im Zeitalter der Französischen Revolution. Ein Symposium,* ed. Wolfgang Wittkowski (Tübingen: Max Niemeyer, 1990).

68. Ibid., p. 370.

69. See, for instance, the numerous references to Schiller in the "Einleitung. Zur Konzeption ästhetischer Autonomie in Deutschland," in *Revolution und Autonomie,* pp. 1–29.

70. University of Wisconsin Workshop on the *Klassik-Legende* (Frankfurt a.M.: Athenäum, 1971).

71. "Über den affirmativen, and charakter der Kultur" in *Zeitschrift für Sozialforschung* 6 (1937): 5–94.

72. *Revolution und Autonomie,* p. 218.

73. Ibid.

74. Ibid.

75. Ibid., p. 223.

76. Ibid., pp. 264–272.

77. Ibid., p. 266.

78. Ibid.

79. Ibid., p. 267f.

80. Ibid., p. 268.

81. Ibid.

82. Ibid., p. 274.

83. Ibid.

84. Ibid.

85. Ibid., p. 275.

86. Ibid., p. 276.

87. Schiller, *The Philosophical Discourse of Modernity,* 6th ed (Cambridge: MIT Press, 1992) p. 48.

88. The term "moralisch" (moral) as used by many prominent German writers of the eighteenth century referred mostly to the general process of the perfection of the human being and society, irrespective of the dictates of institutions such as the church and the state. Aristotle's *Nicomachean Ethics* exerted considerable influence at that time. A useful article on "The Noble" was written by John Casey for *Philosophy and Literature,* ed. Phillip Griffiths (Cambridge/London: Cambridge University Press, 1984), pp. 135–53. However, Casey denigrates the noble as a quality of character and leaves out of his discussion the play on the terms "edel" and "Edelmann" or "Edelfrau" by German writers of the eighteenth century. According to writers like Schiller, Wieland, and many others, a middle-class individual could be just as "edel" (noble) in character (if not more so) as any "Edelmann" (nobleman). Hence, for these middle-class writers, neither money nor means in general but character was considered most noble.

89. "Dies ist der Knoten, dessen Auflösung leider selbst Kant für unmöglich hält" (NA 26: 186). Like Dieter Henrich, though from the perspective of rhetoric, Todd Kontje has also appreciated the writer's "attempt to move beyond the systematic rigor of Kantian philosophy" (*Constructing Reality: A Rhetorical Analysis of Friedrich Schiller's "Letters on the Aesthetic Education of Man"* [New York/Berne/Frankfurt a.M./Paris: Peter Lang, 1987], p. 7).

90. Even in the philosophy of science and, recently, pre-theoretical mathematics (e.g., among knot theorists such as Ruth J. Lawrence), knots play an essential role. In his *Philosophy of Natural Science* (Englewood Cliffs, N.J.: Prentice-Hall, 1966), for instance, Carl Hempel characterized the concepts of science as "the knots in a network of systematic interrelationships in which laws and theoretical principles form the threads" (p. 94). And: "The more threads converge upon, or issue from, a conceptual knot, the stronger will be its systematizing role or its systematic import" (p. 94). Concerning science and metaphor, John Neubauer characterized both Goethe's and Novalis's "vision[s] of science and poetry" as "two forms of symbolic representation" ("Literature and Science" in *Yearbook of Comparative and General Literature* 32 [1983]: 70). He adds: "However the two modes of representation may differ, they are both symbolic or metaphoric apprehensions of the world that arise

from our inability to grasp anything directly" (p. 70). However, Neubauer is careful enough to note that "both science and literature operate with images and metaphors, but the status of representation is ultimately its congruency with observation" (p. 71). See also *Science and Metaphor: The Historical Role of Scientific Theories in Forming Western Culture,* ed. Richard Olson (Belmont, Ca.: Wadsworth, 1971). For the use of terms relating to knots in the later eighteenth century, see Edna Purdie, "Some Word-Associations in the Writings of Hamann and Herder," in *German Studies* [Festschrift for Leonard Ashley Willoughby] (Oxford: Basil Blackwell, 1952), pp. 144–58. Two examples from Schiller's early and later works are found in V, 7 of *Kabale and Liebe* and 11. 1986c-1988 of *Wallenstein* ("Wer / Den Knäuel entwirren, der sich endlos selbst / Vermehrend wächst—Er muß zerhauen werden").

91. "Manchen Kantischen Sätzen gibt die strenge Reinheit und die scholastische Form, in der sie aufgestellet werden, eine Härte und eine Sonderbarkeit, die ihrem Inhalte fremd ist, und von dieser Hülle entkleidet, erscheinen sie dann als die verjährten Ansprüche der allgemeinen Vernunft" (NA 26: 258).

92. "Philosophische Wahrheiten, habe ich oft bemerkt, müssen in einer andern Form gefunden, und in einer andern angewandt und verbreitet werden" (NA 26: 258).

93. Schiller's idea of an idealizing art ("idealisierende Kunst") is based largely on ancient Greek art. "Idealization—the attempt to capture the essence of a thing—was also fundamental to Greek art. But the ideal originated in the recognizable" (*Literature of the Western World.* volume 1: *The Ancient World Through the Renaissance,* eds. Brian Wilkie and James Hurt. 3rd ed. [New York: Macmillan, 1992], p. 6). Wilkie and Hurt also observe that "Greek art . . . is characterized by a direct, unblinking view of reality and a combination of passion and restraint that is the essence of classicism," which is "not to say that Greek art was "realistic" in the modern sense" (p. 6). In his review of Christian Körner's essay on "Charakterdarstellung in der Musik," which Körner submitted to Schiller already in January 1795 for inclusion in *Die Horen,* Schiller defined the term. He first distinguished between "idealisiren" and "veredeln," which Körner had done. Schiller: "Etwas idealisiren heißt mir nur, es aller seiner zufälligen Bestimmungen entkleiden und ihm den Charakter innerer Notwendigkeit beilegen" (NA 22: 293).

94. Dieter Borchmeyer: "So sehr Schiller in seiner letzten Lebenzeit aus einem tief verwurzelten Geschichtspessimismus und aus politischer Resignation angesichts des Verlaufs der Französischen Revolution den Rückzug ins Reich der Innerlichkeit angetreten zu haben scheint—auch die Räume des Herzens bleiben bei ihm, dem *poeta politicus* schlechthin, politische Kabinette" (*Macht und Melancholie,* p. 246). According to Borchmeyer, Schiller's goal was "die evolutionäre Überwindung des alten Staates, der las eine Notordnung äußerlich bestehen bleibt, bis eine Vernunftordnung an seine Stelle treten kann" (p. 162). In short, the final goal, for Schiller, is not the aesthetic state. Aesthetics is the means to a political end. For a series of inquiries into the nature of political aesthetics, see Friedrich Tomberg, *Politische Ästhetik. Vorträge und Aufsätze* (Darmstadt: Luchterhand, 1973).

95. In *A Study of Schiller's "Letters on the Aesthetic Education of Man"* (Harrogate: The Duchy Press, 1986) R. D. Miller critiques Elizabeth Wilkinson's and L. A. Willoughby's exhaustive edition of Schiller's letters on aesthetic education *Friedrich Schiller: On the Aesthetic Education of Man in a Series of Letters* (Oxford: Clarendon Press, 1967). Hereafter: W/W. I note my disagreements with the translation of certain terms either by substituting my own translation (as noted) or adding them to the footnotes. I place the word *human being* in brackets next to the first use of the word *man* in each of the quotations. I did not include he or she for "he" or his(him)/her(s) for "his"/"him" because it would become too cumbersome and interrupt the flow of the translation. However, I do make it clear that the correct

translation for the German *Mensch* is "human being" since the German noun is genderless. In response to critics' complaints that Schiller treated the term "Nature" paradoxically, Miller submits that "The paradox of Schiller's attitude to Nature is the paradox of Nature itself" (p. 2). Miller equates Schiller's reference to "pure Nature" with the "moral instinct" (p. 3), and then juxtaposes it to "crude Nature." Miller concludes: "It is Schiller's concept of pure or noble Nature, rather than Kant's rational-moral principle, which forms the main feature of the work, though this does not imply any denigration of Reason" (p. 3). Unlike W/W, Miller underscores the moral potential and strength of the human being. "Morality is the common denominator of crude nature raised to the level of pure Nature, and the rational-moral principle brought into association with Nature" (p. 9). But Miller fails to account for the role of Schiller's early physiology in this writing. This lacuna is also woefully apparent in W/W's gloss of the term "Natur" (W/W, pp. 322–26). In their helpful discussion of "Translators and Translation," W/W addresses the fact that Schiller's text makes "conflicting claims upon the translator" (p. 344). In particular, they debate the merits of a "philosophical" or "literary" translation, choosing to opt "now for the one, now for the other" (p. 345). Importantly, they see that "more than most philosophers, Schiller often exploits his linguistic medium in a way that only poets are wont to do" (p. 346). Hence, the poetic and philosophical discourses at work in Schiller's text must necessarily broaden our perspective of the nature of his writing. I take pains to show that the text is also enriched by thematic affinities to other and earlier texts by the same author as well as to other fields of knowledge.

96. "Ihre eigne Empfindung wird mir die Tatsachen hergeben, auf die ich baue, Ihre eigene freye Denkkraft wird die Gesetze diktiren, nach welchen verfahren werden soll" (NA 20: 310).

97. For a recent discussion of the nature of Kant's writing, see Willi Goetschel, *Kant als Schriftsteller* (Wien: Passagen, 1990).

98. The translation by W/W should be read together with Miller's often insightful remarks in *A Study of Schiller's "Letters on the Aesthetic Education of Man."*

99. "Der Lauf der Begebenheiten im Politischen, und der Gang des menschlichen Geistes im Litterarischen hat dem Genius der Zeit eine solche Richtung gegeben, die ihn je mehr und mehr von der *idealisirenden* Kunst entfernt. Diese muß die Wirklichkeit verlassen, und sich mit einer gewissen Kühnheit über das Bedürfniß der Gegenwart erheben, den*n* die Kunst ist eine Tochter der Freiheit. Jetzt aber herrscht das Bedürfniß, und der Drang der physischen Lage die Abhängigkeit des Menschen von tausend Verhältnissen, die ihm Fesseln anlegen, und ihn je mehr und mehr mit der unidealischen Wirklichkeit verstricken, hemmt freien Aufflug in die Regionen des Idealischen. Selbst die spekulirende Vernunft entreißt der Einbildungskraft eine Provinz nach der andern, und die Grenzen der Kunst verengen sich, je mehr die *Wissenschaft* die ihrigen erweitert" (NA 26: 259–60).

100. "Der Lauf der Begebenheiten hat dem Genius der Zeit eine Richtung gegeben, die ihn je mehr und mehr von der Kunst des Ideals zu entfernen droht. Diese muß die Wirklichkeit verlassen, und sich mit anständiger Kühnheit über das Bedürniß erheben; denn die Kunst ist eine Tochter der Freyheit, und von der Notwendigkeit der Geister, nicht von der Nothdurft der Materie will sie ihre Vorschrift empfangen. Jetzt aber herrscht das Bedürfniß, und beugt die gesunkene Menschheit unter sein tyrannisches Joch. Der *Nutzen* ist das große Idol der Zeit, dem alle Kräfte fronen und alle Talente huldigen sollen. Auf dieser groben Waage hat das geistige Verdienst der Kunst kein Gewicht, und, aller Aufmunterung beraubt, verschwindet sie von dem lermenden Markt des Jahrhunderts. Selbst der philosophische Untersuchungsgeist entreißt der Einbildungskraft eine Provinz nach der andern, und die

Grenzen der Kunst verengen sich, jemehr die Wissenschaft ihre Schranken erweitert" (NA 20: 311).

101. "Die Vernunft hat geleistet, was sie leisten kann, wenn sie das Gesetz findet und aufstellt; vollstrecken muß es der muthige Wille, und das lebenige Gefühl" (NA 20: 330).

102. "Aufklährung der Begriffe kann es allein nicht ausrichten, denn von dem Kopf ist noch ein gar weiter Weg zu dem Herzen, und bey weitem der größere Theil der Menschen wird durch Empfindungen zum Handeln bestimmt" (NA 26: 265). The call for the cultivation of the faculty of sensation as a response to the aftermath of the French Revolution has its origin in the third medical dissertation, the preface to which underscores the importance of both "Aufklärung des Verstandes" and the "Verfeinerung unserer Empfindungen" (NA 20: 40).

103. "An das Materielle gefesselt, läßt der Mensch diesen [den Schein] lange Zeit bloß seinen Zwecken dienen, ehe er ihm in der Kunst des Ideals eine eigene Persönlichkeit zugesteht. Zu dem letztern bedarf es einer totalen Revolution in seiner ganzen Empfindungsweise, ohne welche er auch nicht einmal *auf dem Wege* zum Ideal sich befinden würde" (NA 20:405).

104. "Wo wir also Spuren einer uninteressierten freyen Schätzung des reinen Scheins entdecken, da können wir auf eine solche Umwälzung seiner Natur und den eigentlichen Anfang der Menschheit in ihm schließen" (NA 20: 405).

105. W/W translate this as the "embellishing of one's being" (see n. 96, p. 205), which seems inappropriate in this context.

106. "Alle Verbesserung im politischen Bereich soll von Veredlung des Charakters ausgehen" (NA 20:332).

107. "Daß man, um jenes politische Problem in der Erfahrung zu lösen, durch das ästhetische den Weg nehmen muß, weil es die Schönheit ist, durch welche man zu der Freyheit wandert" (NA 20:312).

108. "Stolze Selbstgenügsamkeit zieht das Herz des Weltmanns zusammen, das in dem rohen Naturmenschen noch oft sympathetisch schlägt, und wie aus einer brennenden Stadt sucht jeder nur sein elendes Eigentum aus der Verwüstung zu flüchten" (NA 20: 320).

109. "Die Natur fängt mit dem Menschen nicht besser an, als mit ihren übrigen Werken: sie handelt für ihn, wo er als freye Intelligenz noch nicht selbst handeln kann" (NA 20: 313).

110. "Er [der Mensch] kommt zu sich aus seinem sinnlichen Schlummer, erkennt sich als Mensch, blickt um sich her, und findet sich—in dem Staate" (NA 20: 313).

111. "Ein bloß mögliches (wenngleich moralisch notwendiges) Ideal von Gesellschaft" (NA 20: 314). W/W translate "möglich" as "hypothetical" (see n. 96, p. 13), which is quite different than "possible."

112. Miller suggests that art, for Schiller, is concerned with "freeing man [the human being] from the forces of crude nature" (*A Study*, p. 5).

113. "Und hätte sie zuviel auf ihn gerechnet, so würde sie ihm für eine Menschheit, die ihm noch mangelt, und beschadet seiner Existenz mangeln kann, auch selbst die Mittel zur Thierheit entrissen haben, die doch die Bedingung seiner Menschheit ist. Ehe er Zeit gehabt hätte, sich mit seinem Willen an dem Gesetz fest zu halten, hätte sie unter seinen Füßen die Leiter der Natur weggezogen" (NA 20: 314).

114. "aber das lebendige Uhrwerk des Staats muß gebessert werden, indem es schlägt, und hier gilt es, das rollende Rad während seines Umschwunges auszutauschen" (NA 20: 314).

115. "Vollkommen frey zwischen Pflicht und Neigung"; " Majestätsrecht seiner Person" (NA 20: 316).

116. "Die objektive und gleichsam kanonische Form in der sich die Mannichfaltigkeit der Subjekte zu vereinigen trachtet" (NA 20: 316).

117. "Der Staat soll nicht blos den objektiven und generischen, er soll auch den subjektiven und specifischen Charakter in den Individuen ehren, und indem er das unsichtbare Reich der Sitten ausbreitet, das Reich der Erscheinung nicht entvölkern" (NA 20: 318).

118. "Ist der innere Mensch mit sich einig, so wird er auch bey der höchsten Universalisierung seines Betragens seine Eigenthümlichkeit retten, und der Staat wird bloß der Ausleger seines schönen Instinkts, die deutlichere Formel seiner innern Gesetzgebung seyn" (NA 20: 318).

119. "Wenn also die Vernunft in die physische Gesellschaft ihre moralische Einheit bringt, so darf sie die Mannichfaltigkeit der Natur nicht verletzen. Wenn die Natur in dem moralischen Bau der Gesellschaft ihre Mannichfaltigkeit zu behaupten strebt, so darf der moralischen Einheit dadurch kein Abbruch geschehen"; for, "gleich weit von Einförmigkeit und Verwirrung ruht die siegende Form" (NA 20: 318).

120. For a general overview, see Shirley A. Roe, *Matter, Life, and Generation: Eighteenth-Century Embryology and the Haller-Wolff Debate* (Cambridge/New York: Cambridge University Press, 1981). The first full discussion of the nature of polyps is contained in Abraham Trembley's *Philosophical Transactions* of 1743. In the absence of fresh water hydra, Charles Bonnet experimented with worms. For an interesting discussion, see Virginia P. Dawson, "The Problem of Soul in the 'Little Machines' of Réaumur and Charles Bonnet," in *Eighteenth-Century Studies* 18 (1985): 503–22.

121. "Jene Polypennatur der griechischen Staaten, wo jedes Individuum eines unabhängigen genoß, und wenn es not tat, zum Ganzen werden konnte, machte jetzt einem kunstreichen Uhrwerke Platz, wo aus der Zusammenstückelung unendlich vieler, aber lebloser, Teile ein mechanisches Leben im Ganzen sich bildet" (NA 20: 323). Cited also by Wilfried Malsch but in the context of Schiller-Herder (philosophy) and not in the light of the development of natural science in the eighteenth century. ("Schillers und Friedrich Schlegels Poesiebegriffe im Licht von Herders typologischer Griechenlanddeutung," in *Perspektiven der Romantik. Beiträge des Marburger Kolloquiums zum 80. Geburtstag Erich Ruprechts,* ed. Reinhard Görisch [Bonn: Bouvier, 1987]).

122. See esp. Bernd Bräutigam, "Rousseaus Kritik ästhetischer Versöhnung," *Jahrbuch der Deutschen Schillergesellschaft* 31 (1987): 137–55.

123. "Die losgebundene Gesellschaft, anstatt aufwärts in das organische Leben zu eilen, fällt in das Elementarreich zurück" (NA 20: 319).

124. "Macht die Natur zu seinem Freund, und ehrt ihre Freyheit, indem er bloß ihre Willkühr zügelt" (NA 20: 318).

125. On this point, Schiller's close study of Johann Gottfried Herder's *Ideen zur Philosophie der Geschichte der Menschheit* (Riga/Leipzig: Johann Friedrich Hartknoch, 1784–1791) may have been a contributing factor.

126. Miller insists that the proper translation of "Erschlaffung" in this context is "moral laxity" (*A Study,* p. 21). I see this rather as a sign of an overly relaxed state, the extreme opposite of overly tense. In either condition, the human being is unproductive.

127. "In den niedern und zahlriechen Klassen stellen sich uns rohe gesetzlose Triebe dar, die sich nach aufgelöstem Band der bürgerlichen Ordnung entfesseln, und mit unlenksamer Wuth zu ihrer thierischen Befriedigung eilen" (NA 20: 319).

128. E.g., Klaus Berghahn, "Volkstümlichkeit ohne Volk?" in *Popularität und*

Trivialität. Fourth Wisconsin Workshop, ed. Reinhold Grimm and Jost Hermand (Frankfurt a.M: Athenäum, 1974), pp. 51–75.

129. "Auf der andern Seite geben uns die civilisirten Klassen den noch widrigern Anblick der Schlaffheit und einer Depravation des Charakters, die desto mehr empört, weil die Kultur selbst ihre Quelle ist" (NA 20: 320).

130. "Die Aufklärung des Verstandes, deren sich die verfeinerten Stände nicht ganz mit Unrecht rühmen, zeigt im Ganzen so wenig einen veredelnden Einfluß auf die Gesinnungen, daß sie vielmehr die Verderbniß durch Maximen befestigt" (NA 20: 320).

131. The rhetorical strategy of trying to persuade German regents of the virtues (and informing them of the "threat") of Enlightenment is evident in other writings of that time, e.g., J. H. Tieftrunk, "Über den Einfluß der Aufklärung und Revolutionen" and others contained in the collection *A. Bergk, J. L. Ewald, J. G. Fichte u.a. Aufklärung und Gedankenfreiheit. Fünfzehn Anregungen, aus der Geschichte zu lernen,* ed. Zwi Batscha (Frankfurt a.M: Suhrkamp, 1977), pp. 195–205. Tieftrunk, for instance, constructed an enlightened type, *der Aufgeklärte,* who is both "ein guter Mensch" and "ein guter Bürger" (p. 200). Tieftrunk, among others, also constructed an ideal type of regent which they then disseminated through their writings among the reading public, which was both largely middle class and aristocratic.

132. See Georg Ruppelt, *Schiller im nationalsozialistischen Deutschland. Der Versuch einer Gleichschaltung* (Stuttgart: J.B. Metzler, 1979) and Lesley Sharpe's response "National Socialism and Schiller" *German Life and Letters* 36 (1982–83): 156–165.

133. "Der zahlreichere Theil der Menschen wird durch den Kampf mit der Noth viel zu sehr ermüdet und abgespannt, als daß er sich zu einem neuen und härtern Kampf mit dem Irrthum aufraffen sollte" (NA 20: 331).

134. In his book *'Jene Scheu vor allem Mercantilischen'. Schillers 'Arbeits-und Finanzplan'* (Tübingen: Max Niemeyer, 1984) Karl-Heinz Hucke reduces Schiller's work to a matter of financial need.

135. "Ewig nur an ein einzelnes kleines Bruchstück des Ganzen gefesselt, bildet sich der Mensch selbst nur als Bruchstück aus, ewig nur das eintönige Geräusch des Rades, das er umtreibt, im Ohre, entwickelt er nie die Harmonie seines Wesens, und anstatt die Menschheit in seiner Natur auszuprägen, wird er bloß zu einem Abdruck seines Geschäfts, seiner Wissenschaft" (NA 20: 323).

136. " . . . ein so künstliches und lichtscheues Uhrwerk" (NA 20: 323).

137. "Zugleich voll Form und voll Fülle, zugleich philosophirend und bildend, zugleich zart und energisch sehen wir sie die Jugend der Phantasie mit der Männlichkeit der Vernunft in einer herrlichen Menschheit vereinigen" (NA 20: 321).

138. "Wir wissen, daß die Sensibilität des Gemüths ihrem Grade nach von der Lebhaftigkeit, ihrem Umfange nach, von dem Reichthum der Einbildungskraft abhängt" (NA 20: 325).

139. "Die subjektiven Bedingungen seiner Vorstellungskraft zu konstitutiven Gesetzen für das Daseyn der Dinge" (NA 20: 325).

140. "Die Regeln *seines* Geschäfts jedem Geschäft ohne Unterschied anpassen zu wollen" (NA 20: 325).

141. "Weil er die Eindrücke zergliedert, die doch nur als ein Ganzes die Seele rühren" (NA 20: 325–26).

142. "Weil die Einbildungskraft, in den einförmigen Kreis seines Berufs eingeschlossen, sich zu fremder Vorstellungsart nicht erweitern kann" (NA 20: 326).

143. "Dieser Antagonism der Kräfte ist das große Instrument der Kultur, aber auch nur das Instrument; denn solange derselbe dauert, ist man erst auf dem Wege zu dieser" (NA 20: 326).

144. The entire passage reads: "Alle Verbesserung im politischen soll von Veredlung des Charakters ausgehen . . .—aber wie kann sich unter den Einflüssen einer barbarischen Staatsverfassung der Charakter veredeln?" (NA 20: 332).

145. "Lebe mit deinem Jahrhundert, aber sey nicht sein Geschöpf; . . . Ohne ihre Schuld getheilt zu haben, theile mit edler Resignation ihre Strafen, und beuge dich mit Freyheit unter das Joch, das sie gleich schlecht entbehren und tragen" (NA 20: 335–36).

146. "Die Menschheit hat ihre Würde verloren, aber die Kunst hat sie gerettet und aufbewahrt in bedeutenden Steinen; die Wahrheit lebt in der Täuschung fort, und aus dem Nachbilde wird das Urbild wieder hergestellt werden" (NA 20: 334).

147. "Verjage die Willkühr, die Frivolität, die Rohigkeit aus ihren Vergnügungen, so wirst du sie [ihre Maximen] unvermerkt auch aus ihren Handlungen, endlich aus ihren Gesinnungen verbannen. Wo du sie findest, umgieb sie mit edeln, mit großen, mit geistreichen Formen, schließe sie ringsum mit den Symbolen des Vortrefflichen ein, bis der Schein die Wirklichkeit und die Kunst die Natur überwindet" (NA 20: 336).

148. "Der Mensch ohne Form verachtet alle Anmuth im Vortrage als Bestechung, alle Freinheit im Umgang als Versellung, alle Delikatesse und Großheit im Betragen als Ueberspannung und Affektation" (NA 20: 337).

149. "Mit einem Wort: die Schönheit müßte sich als eine nothwendige Bedingung der Menschheit aufzeigen lassen" (NA 20: 340).

150. "Nicht, weil wir denken, wollen, empfinden, sind wir; nicht weil wir sind, denken, wollen, empfinden wir. Wir sind, weil wir sind; wir empfinden, denken und wollen, weil außer uns noch etwas anderes ist" (NA 20: 341–42). Schiller may well have had in mind J. G. Herder's essay of 1778 *Vom Erkennen und Empfinden der menschlichen Seele.*

151. "Nur indem er sich verändert, *existirt* er [der Mensch]; nur indem er unveränderlich bleibt, existirt *er*" (NA 20: 343).

152. Hans-Georg Pott has offered a penetrating analysis of the impact of Fichte's theory of drives on Schiller's work in his book *Die schöne Freiheit. Eine Interpretation zu Schillers Schrift "Über die ästhetische Erziehung des Menschen in einer Reihe von Briefen"* (München: Wilhelm Fink, 1980). Earlier accounts include Hubertus Lossow, *Schiller und Fichte in ihren persönlichen Beziehungen und in ihrer Bedeutung für die Grundlegung der Ästhetik* (Dresden: Risse, 1935). See also W. Hogrebe, "Fichte und Schiller. Eine Skizze," in *Schillers Briefe über die ästhetische Erziehung,* pp. 276–89. Wolfgang Riedel criticizes Hogrebe for blurring the distinction between Fichte and Schiller in their attitudes toward Rousseau in his book *"Der Spaziergang." Ästhetik der Landschaft und Geschichtsphilosophie der Natur bei Schiller* (Würzburg: Königshausen und Neumann, 1989). I agree with Riedel's point that Schiller opposed Kant's and Fichte's suppression of feeling, sensation, and sensuousness, i.e., "die Naturseite des Menschen" (p. 66, n. 9).

153. "Zwey entgegengesetzte Anforderungen an den Menschen"; . . . "zwey Fundamentalgesetze der sinnlich-vernünftigen Natur" (NA 20: 344).

154. "Indem man auf einem Instrument einen Ton greift, ist unter allen Tönen, die es möglicherweise angeben kann, nur dieser einzige wirklich; indem der Mensch das Gegenwärtige empfindet, ist die ganze unendliche Möglichkeit seiner Bestimmungen auf diese einzige Art des Daseyns beschränkt" (NA 20: 344–45).

155. "Mit unzerreißbaren Banden fesselt er den höher strebenden Geist an die Sinnenwelt, und von ihrer freyesten Wanderung ins Unendliche ruft er die Abstraktion in die Grenzen der Gegenwart zurücke" (NA 20: 345).

156. "Und ist bestrebt, ihn [den Menschen] in Freyheit zu setzen, Harmonie in

die Verschiedenheit seines Erscheinens zu bringen, und bey allem Wechsel des Zustands seine Person zu behaupten" (NA 20: 345–46).

157. "In einer Transzendental-Philosophie, wo alles darauf ankommt, die Form von dem Inhalt zu befreyen, und das Nothwendige von allem Zufälligen rein zu erhalten, gewöhnt man sich gar leicht, das Materielle sich bloß als Hinderniß zu denken, und die Sinnlichkeit, weil sie gerade bei *diesem* Geschäfte im Wege steht, in einem nothwendigen Widerspruch mit der Vernunft vorzustellen" (NA 20: 348).

158. "Zugleich subordinirt und coordinirt, d.h. sie stehen in Wechselwirkung; ohne Form keine Materie, ohne Materie keine Form" (NA 20: 348).

159. "Die Natur mag unsre Organe noch so nachdrücklich und noch so vielfach berühren—alle ihre Mannichfaltigkeit ist verloren für uns, weil wir nichts in ihr suchen, als was wir in sie hineingelegt haben, weil wir ihr nicht erlauben, sich *gegen uns herein* zu bewegen, sondern vielmehr mit ungeduldig vorgreifender Vernunft *gegen sie hinaus* streben" (NA 20: 350).

160. "Dieses voreilige Streben nach Harmonie, ehe man die einzelnen Laute beysammen hat, die sie ausmachen sollen, diese gewaltthätige Usurpation der Denkkraft . . . ist der Grund der Unfruchtbarkeit so vieler denkenden Köpfe für das Beßte der Wissenschaft, und es ist schwer zu sagen, ob die Sinnlichkeit, welche keine Form annimmt, oder die Vernunft, welche keinen Inhalt abwartet, der Erweiterung unserer Kenntnisse mehr geschadet haben" (NA 20: 350).

161. "Um uns zu theilnemenden, hülfreichen, thätigen Menschen zu machen, müssen sich Gefühl und Charakter miteinander vereinigen, so wie, um uns Erfahrung zu verschaffen, Offenheit des Sinnes mit Energie des Verstandes zusammentreffen muß" (NA 20: 350).

162. "Und zwar im beßten Sinne des Worts, wo es Bearbeitung des innern, nicht bloß des äussern Menschen bedeutet" (NA 20: 351).

163. "Fülle der Empfindungen muß ihre rühmliche Quelle seyn; die Sinnlichkeit selbst muß mit siegender Kraft ihr Gebiet behaupten, und der Gewalt widerstreben, die ihr der Geist durch seine vorgreifende Thätigkeit gerne zufügen möchte" (NA 20: 352).

164. "Dieses Wechselverhältniß beider Triebe ist zwar bloß eine Aufgabe der Vernunft, die der Mensch nur in der Vollendung seines Daseyns ganz zu lösen imstande ist. Es ist im eigentlichsten Sinne des Worts *die Idee seiner Menschheit,* mithin ein Unendliches, dem er sich im Laufe der Zeit immer mehr nähern kann, aber ohne es jemals zu erreichen" (NA 20: 352–53).

165. Anthony Saville relocated "the centre of Schiller's reflection as the beauty of man [the human being] rather than the beauty of natural objects of works of art" in his book *Aesthetic Reconstructions: The Seminal Writings of Lessing, Kant, and Schiller* (Oxford: Basil Blackwell, 1987), p. 215. I do not disagree so much with assigning Schiller an "ideally harmonious balance of his [the human being's] metaphysical constituents" which is then "manifested in appearance" (p. 214), as I do with the accompanying idea that, with the balance between forces of sense and reason, "all tension between them is resolved" (p. 214). I am suggesting that the cancellation or suspension ("Aufhebung") of which Schiller writes consists in the abolition of the extremes of the sense- and form-impulses and not the cessation of the tension between them. As we have seen, the cultivation (*Bildung*) of harmonious tension is also characteristic of Schiller's concept of beauty.

166. "Nur indem seine Form in unsrer Empfindung lebt, und sein Leben in unserm Verstande sich formt, ist er [der Mensch] lebende Gestalt, und dieß wird überall der Fall seyn, wo wir ihn als schön beurtheilen" (NA 20: 355).

167. "Es soll eine Gemeinschaft zwischen Formtrieb und Stofftrieb, das heißt ein Spieltrieb seyn, weil nur die Einheit der Realität mit der Form, der Zufälligkeit

mit der Nothwendigkeit, des Leidens mit der Freyheit den Begriff der Menschheit vollendet" (NA 20: 356).

168. "Der Mensch spielt nur, wo er in voller Bedeutung des Worts Mensch ist, und *er ist nur da ganz Mensch, wo er spielt*"; . . . "der Mensch soll mit der Schönheit *nur spielen,* und er soll *nur mit der Schönheit* spielen" (NA 20: 359). In his influential essay "'Das Pathetischerhabene'. Schillers Dramentheorie" in *Deutsche Dramentheorien. Beiträge zu einer historischen Poetik des Dramas in Deutschland,* ed. Reinhold Grimm (Frankfurt a.M.: Athenäum Verlag, 1971), pp. 214–44, Klaus Berghahn cited Schiller's definition of the human being as "weder ausschließend Materie, noch . . . ausschließend Geist" (NA 20: 356). He calls this "das wiederkehrende Thema seiner theoretischen Schriften und die vorherrschende Dialektik seiner Dramen" (p. 215), but without appreciating the fact of the true origin of this theory of the human being in the medical dissertations, i.e., Schiller's early anthropology.

169. "Dieses Gleichgewicht bleibt aber immer nur Idee, die von der Wirklichkeit nie ganz erreicht werden kann" (NA 20: 360).

170. "In der Wirklichkeit wird immer ein Übergewicht des *einen* Elements über das andere übrigbleiben und das Höchste was die Erfahrung leistet, wird in einer *Schwankung* zwischen beiden Prinzipien bestehen, wo bald die Realität bald die Form überwiegend ist" (NA 20: 360).

171. "Sie [die Schönheit] soll auflösen, dadurch daß sie beyde Naturen gleichförmig anspannt, und soll anspannen, dadurch daß sie beyde Naturen gleichförmig aufiöst" (NA 20: 361).

172. "Durch die Schönheit wird der sinnliche Mensch zur Form und zum Denken geleitet; durch die Schönheit wird der geistige Mensch zur Materie zurückgeführt, und der Sinnenwelt wiedergegeben" (NA 20: 365).

173. Concerning Schiller's concept of *Aufhebung* (cancellation, or suspension), Miller claims that Schiller uses the verb *aufheben* here in the bifold sense of to "put an end to" and to "preserve" ("beibehalten") (*A Study,* p. 112). "By putting an end to the opposition between the Form-impulse and the sensuous impulse, Beauty is able to 'preserve' them in their complementarity" (p. 112). According to the British scholar, Beauty as the "third condition" is "also a paradigm of the state of pure Nature which is the most important fruit of the aesthetic condition" (p. 112). Wilkinson and Willoughby also appropriate Hegel's concept of synthesis. "Schiller develops a process of the destruction of opposites, and their union in a new synthesis, to the point where *aufheben* is used in a double sense: 'to abolish *and* preserve' or 'preserve by destruction'" (W/W, p. 304). They refer to this as a "dialectical concept" (p. 304) and note that the double sense of the term was to become a key term for Hegel's dialectical method. Like Reginald Snell (*Friedrich Schiller: On the Aesthetic Education of Man in a Series of Letters,* ed. and trans. Elizabeth Wilkinson and Leonard A. Willoughby [Oxford: Clarendon Press, 1967]), W/W suggest that Hegel took his concept of *Aufhebung* from Schiller's letters on aesthetic education. They disagree with Snell's point, however, that Goethe sometimes used the term to mean "disappearance in a higher import" (p. 305). However, Schiller does not use the term "Synthese" (synthesis) to characterize what he has in mind about the relationship between opposed forces. It is vitally important to note that it is only the extremes in the opposites that are canceled or suspended (*augehoben*) and that these entities do not fuse into a higher synthesis wherein those entities would then become one wholly different entity. As in the case of beauty, especially melting beauty, tension is still present. The difference is that the nature of the tension is now harmonious. See also Vicky Rippere, *Schiller and "Alienation"* (Bern/Frankfurt a.M.: Peter Lang, 1981).

174. "Wir gelangen also nur durch Schranken zur Realität, nur durch *Negation*

oder Ausschließung zur *Position* oder wirklichen Setzung, nur durch Aufhebung unsrer freyen Bestimmbarkeit zur Bestimmung" (NA 20: 369).

175. "Wir gelangen also freylich nur durch den Theil zum Ganzen, nur durch die Grenze zum Unbegrenzten; aber wir gelangen auch nur durch das Ganze zum Theil, nur durch das Unbegrenzte zur Grenze" (NA 20: 369).

176. "Nur von demjenigen, der sich bewußt ist, wird Vernunft, das heißt, absolute Consequenz und Universalität des Bewußtseyns gefodert; vorher ist er nicht Mensch, und kein Akt der Menschheit kann von ihm erwartet werden" (NA 20: 372).

177. "Weder Abstraktion noch Erfahrung leiten uns bis zu der Quelle zurück, aus der unsre Begriffe von Allgemeinheit und Nothwendigkeit fließen; ihre frühe Erscheinung in der Zeit entzieht sie dem Beobachter, und ihr übersinnlicher Ursprung dem metaphysischen Forscher" (NA 20: 372).

178. "Und zugleich mit der unveränderlichen Einheit desselben ist das Gesetz der Einheit für alles, was *für den* Menschen ist, und für alles, was *durch ihn* werden soll, für sein Erkennen und Handeln aufgestellt" (NA 20: 372).

179. "Der sinnliche Trieb erwacht mit der Erfahrung des Lebens (mit dem Anfang des Individuums), der vernünftige mit der Erfahrung des Gesetzes (mit dem Anfang der Persönlichkeit), und jetzt erst, nachdem beyde zum Dasein gekommen, ist seine Menschheit aufgebaut" (NA 20: 373).

180. "Weil nur, indem eine Determination wieder aufgehoben wird, die entgegengesetzte eintreten kann. Er muß also, um Leiden mit Selbstthätigkeit, um eine passive Bestimmung mit einer aktiven zu vertauschen, augenblicklich *von aller Bestimmung frey seyn*, und einen Zustand der bloßen Bestimmbarkeit durchlaufen" (NA 20: 374).

181. "Eben deswegen aber ihre bestimmende Gewalt gegenseitig aufheben, und durch eine Entgegensetzung eine Negation bewirken" (NA 20: 375). W/W note that young Schiller conceived of the idea of a middle state in his 1784 essay "Die Schaubühne als moralische Anstalt betrachtet" (see n. 96, p. 257), but they fail to trace this back even earlier to the medical writings.

182. Referring back to his earlier discussion of Schiller's use of the term *aufheben* (see n. 156), Miller contends that the separateness of the two basic impulses is completely "done away with," and that they disappear (or dissolve) in a "'third condition' brought about by their complete union" (*A Study*, p. 125), which is beauty. The fact, however, that the writer now makes it even clearer that, in the aesthetic condition, both principles are still active ("tätig") works against Miller's seemingly uncritical acceptance of Hegel's concept of dialectical synthesis. The same criticism holds for W/W, as well as for Reginald Snell. With respect to Miller's central thesis that "a union" is "essential to the moral principle of pure or noble Nature" (p. 128), the essence of such a union need not constitute a genuine synthesis in the Hegelian sense. It can also consist of harmonious tension. For what is canceled or suspended is the *opposition* between two competing, yet ultimately inseparable forces and not their (sustained) *activity*. I also disagree with the idea that, in letter twenty-two, Schiller emphasized the educational function of the aesthetic condition "in presenting man [the human being] with an ideal image of the union of the two impulses" (p. 130). No such ideal image is necessary if we appreciate the harmonious tension rather than the complete synthesis of the two impulses since such harmonious tension is rooted already in the healthy state of cooperative interaction between the mind and the body. At the same time, I agree generally with Miller's central thesis, that, for Schiller, morality is "innate in Nature" (p. 141f.). However, the "contradiction" between Nature and reason is only apparent given the writer's early physiology. What is "resolved" at a higher level by the "synthesis" of noble Nature (p. 142) is, in actuality, the reinstatement on a higher plane of the original harmonious tension

between all things (Nature), of which the stringed instrument is a most fruitful symbol.

183. "Hier allein fühlen wir uns wie aus der Zeit gerissen; und unsre Menschheit äußert sich mit einer Reinheit und *Integrität,* als hätte sie von der Einwirkung äußrer Kräfte noch keinen Abbruch erfahren" (NA 20: 379).

184. "Wir verlassen eine schöne Musik mit reger Empfindung, ein schönes Gedicht mit belebter Einbildungskraft, ein schönes Bildwerk und Gebäude mit aufgewecktem Verstand" (NA 20: 381).

185. As the writer states: "es ist eine nothwendige und natürliche Folge ihrer Vollendung, daß, ohne Verrückung ihrer objectiven Grenzen, die verschiedenen Künste *in ihrer Wirkung auf das Gemüt* einander immer ähnlicher werden" (NA 20: 381).

186. In Schiller's own culture, the opera was understood as such a form. "So beschäftigt eine Oper den ganzen Menschen, weil uns alle Künste auf einmal bestürmen" (*Schwäbisches Magazin von gelehrten Sachen auf das Jahr 1775;* Zweites Stück, p. 131).

187. "Der Übergang von dem leidenden Zustande des Empfindens zu dem thätigen des Denkens und Wollens geschieht also nicht anders, als durch einen mittleren Zustand ästhetischer Freyheit" (NA 20: 383).

188. "Mit einem Wort: es giebt keinen andern Weg, den sinnlichen Menschen vernünftig zu machen, als daß man denselben zuvor ästhetisch macht" (NA 20: 383).

189. "Verlöre er bloß die passive Bestimmung, so würde er zugleich mit derselben auch die Möglichkeit einer aktiven verlieren, weil der Gedanke einen Körper braucht, und die Form nur an einem Stoffe realisirt werden kann" (NA 20: 384).

190. "Der ästhetische gestimmte Mensch wird allgemeingültig urtheilen, und allgemein gültig handeln, sobald er es wollen wird" (NA 20: 385).

191. "Es gehört also zu den wichtigsten Aufgaben der Kultur, den Menschen auch schon in seinem bloß physischen Leben der Form zu unterwerfen, und ihn, so weit das Reich der Schönheit nur immer reichen kann, ästhetisch zu machen, weil nur aus dem ästhetischen, nicht aber aus dem physischen Zustande der moralische sich entwickeln kann" (NA 20: 385).

192. "Edel heißt jede Form, welche dem, was seiner Natur nach bloß *dient* (bloßes Mittel ist), das Gepräge der Selbständigkeit aufdrückt" (NA 20: 386).

193. "Schönheit . . . ist der einzig mögliche Ausdruck der Freyheit in der Erscheinung" (NA 20: 386).

194. "Bloß Idee, aber eine Idee, mit der die Erfahrung in einzelnen Zügen aufs genaueste zusammen stimmt" (NA 20: 389).

195. "Auf den Flügeln der Einbildungskraft verläßt der Mensch die engen Schranken der Gegenwart, in welche die bloße Thierheit sich einschließt, um vorwärts nach einer unbeschränkten Zukunft zu streben; aber indem vor seiner schwindelnden *Imagination* das Unendliche aufgeht, hat sein Herz noch nicht aufgehört im Einzelnen zu leben, und dem Augenblick zu dienen" (NA 20: 390).

196. See, for instance, my article "Error and the Problem of 'Bildung' in Goethe's *Faust*," *Euphorion* 82 (1988): 104–15.

197. "Empfindet also bloß die Fesseln, welche die letztere [die Stimme der Vernunft] ihm anlegt, nicht die unendliche Befreyung, die sie ihm verschafft" (NA 20: 392).

198. "Die Natur soll ihn nicht ausschließend und die Vernunft soll ihn nicht bedingt beherrschen" (NA 20: 393).

199. "Die Betrachtung (Reflexion) ist das erste liberale Verhältniß des Menschen zu dem Weltall" (NA 20: 394).

200. "Die Schönheit ist also zwar *Gegenstand* für uns, weil die Reflexion die

Bedingung ist, unter der wir eine Empfindung von ihr haben; zugleich aber ist sie ein *Zustand unseres Subjekts,* weil das Gefühl die Bedingung ist, unter der wir eine Vorstellung von ihr haben. Sie ist also zwar Form, weil wir sie betrachten, zugleich aber ist sie Leben, weil wir sie fühlen. Mit einem Wort: sie ist zugleich unser Zustand und unsre That" (NA 20: 396).

201. "Nicht da, wo der Mensch sich *troglodytisch* in Höhlen birgt, ewig einzeln ist, und die Menschheit nie *außer sich* findet, auch nicht da, wo er *nomadisch* in großen Heermassen zieht, ewig nur Zahl ist, und die Menschheit nie *in sich* findet— da allein, wo er in eigener Hütte still mit sich selbst, und sobald er heraustritt, mit dem ganzen Geschlechte spricht, wird sich ihre liebliche Knospe entfalten" (NA 20: 398).

202. "Mit frohem Leben schwärmt das Insekt in dem Sonnenstrahl" (NA 20: 406).

203. "Das Thier *arbeitet,* wenn ein Mangel die Triebfeder seiner Thätigkeit ist, und es *spielt,* wenn der Reichthum der Kraft diese Triebfeder ist, wenn das überflüssige Leben sich selbst zur Thätigkeit stachelt" (NA 20: 406).

204. "So giebt uns die natur schon in ihrem materiellen Reich ein Vorspiel des Unbegrenzten, und hebt ·hier schon *zum Theil* die Fesseln auf, deren sie sich im Reich der Form ganz und gar entledigt" (NA 20: 406).

205. "Nur indem sie [die Phantasie] sich von der Wirklichkeit losreißt, erhebt sich die bildende Kraft zum Ideale, und ehe die Imagination in ihrer produktiven Qualität nach eignen Gesetzen handeln kann, muß sie sich schon bei ihrem reproduktiven Verfahren von fremden Gesetzen frei gemacht haben" (NA 20: 407).

206. "Der gesetzlose Sprung der Freude wird zum Tanz, die ungestalte Geste zu einer anmuthigen harmonischen Gebärdensprache, die verworrenen Laute der Empfindung entfalten sich, fangen an dem Takt zu gehorchen und sich zum Gesange zu biegen" (NA 20: 409).

207. "Aus ihren düstern Fesseln entlassen, ergreift das ruhigere Auge die Gestalt, die Seele schaut in die Seele, und aus einem eigennützigen Tausche der Lust wird ein großmüthiger Wechsel der Neigung. Die Begierde erweitert und erhebt sich zur Liebe" (NA 20: 409).

208. "Der dynamische Staat kann die Gesellschaft bloß möglich machen, indem er die Natur durch Natur bezähmt; der ethische Staat kann sie bloß (moralisch) nothwendig machen, indem er den einzelnen Willen dem allgemeinen unterwirft; der ästhetische Staat allein kann sie wirklich machen, weil er den Willen des Ganzen durch die Natur des Individuums vollzieht. Wenn schon das Bedürfniß den Menschen in die Gesellschaft nöthigt, und die Vernunft gesellige Grundsätze in ihm pflanzt, so kann die Schönheit allein ihm einen *geselligen Charakter* ertheilen. Der Geschmack allein bringt Harmonie in die Gesellschaft, weil er Harmonie in dem Individuum stiftet. Alle andre Formen der Vorstellung trennen den Menschen, weil sie sich ausschließend entweder auf den sinnlichen oder auf den geistigen Teil seines Wesens gründen; nur die schöne Vorstellung macht ein Ganzes aus ihm, weil seine beyden Naturen dazu zusammen stimmen müssen" (NA 20: 410).

209. "Das Schöne allein genießen wir als Individuum und als Gattung zugleich, d.h. als *Repräsentanten* der Gattung" (NA 20: 411).

210. "Die Schönheit allein beglückt alle Welt, und jedes Wesen vergißt seiner Schranken, so lang es ihren Zauber erfährt" (NA 20: 411).

211. "Aus den Mysterien der Wissenschaft führt der Geschmack die Erkenntnis unter den offenen Himmel des Gemeinsinns heraus, und verwandelt das Eigenthum der Schule in ein Gemeingut der ganzen menschlichen Gesellschaft" (NA 20: 412).

212. "Beflügelt durch ihn entschwingt sich auch die kriechende Lohnkunst dem Staube, und die Fesseln der Leibeigenschaft fallen, von seinem Staube berührt, von dem Leblosen wie don dem Lebendigen ab" (NA 20: 412).

213. "In dem ästhetischen Staate ist alles—auch das dienende Werkzeug ein freyer Bürger, der mit dem edelsten gleiche Rechte hat . . . Hier also in dem Reiche des ästhetischen Scheins wird das Ideal der Gleichheit erfüllt" (NA 20: 412).

214. Even in his more sympathetic reading, Dieter Borchmeyer claims that Schiller's political concerns gave way to the idea of a kingdom of beautiful appearance as the letters near their conclusion. In the end, however, Borchmeyer argues, the metaphorical reference to an "aesthetic state" that lies between a "dynamic" and "ethical" state forms "eine Insel der Seligen" ("Rhetorische und ästhetische Revolutionskritik," in *Klassik und Moderne*, p. 75). When juxtaposed to Jacobin interests, Schiller's work may appear to constitute a flight from reality, as Walter Grab has asserted in *Leben und Werke norddeutscher Jakobiner* (Stuttgart: Metzler, 1973), p. 25. However, in my reading of the times, the work of representatives of the liberal tradition such as Friedrich Schiller actually created various, albeit indirect political strategies in the hope of convincing not only educated readers but rulers of the need for social reform. Jeffrey Barnouw, for one, has correctly underscored Schiller's statement near the end of the second letter, "daß man, um jenes politische Problem in der Erfahrung zu lösen, durch das ästhetische den Weg nehmen muß, weil es die Schönheit ist, durch welche man zu der Freiheit wandert," and that Schiller meant political freedom and not just spiritual freedom when he spoke of the wholly rational-moral state. Jeffrey Barnouw, "'Freiheit zu geben durch Freiheit'. Ästhetischer Zustand—Ästhetischer Staat," in *Friedrich Schiller. Kunst, Humanität und Politik*, p. 152. See also n. 200. For a discussion of the differences between Schiller and Johann Benjamin Erhard, the Jacobin thinker in Nürnberg, later physician in Berlin, and friend of the Schiller's, see my article "Reason, Revolution, and Religion," in *History of European Ideas* 12 (1990): 221–26.

215. "Existiert aber auch ein solcher Staat des schönen Scheins, und wo ist er zu finden? Dem Bedürfniß nach existiert er in jeder feingestimmten Seele, der That nach möchte man ihn wohl nur, wie die reine Kirche und die reine Republik in einigen wenigen auserlesenen Zirkeln finden, wo nicht die geistlose Nachahmung fremder Sitten, sondern eigne schöne Natur das Betragen lenkt, wo der Mensch durch die verwickelsten Verhältnisse mit kühner Einfalt und ruhiger Unschuld geht, und weder nöthig hat, fremde Freiheit zu kränken, um die seinige zu behaupten, noch seine Würde wegzuwerfen, um Anmuth zu zeigen" (NA 20: 412).

216. The charge of elitism has been leveled against Schiller by several scholars, especially by Rolf Grimminger, "Die ästhetische Versöhnung. Ideologiekritische Aspekte zum Autonomiebegriff am Beispiel Schiller," in *Schillers Briefe über die ästhetische Erziehung in einer Reihe von Briefen*, ed. Jürgen Bolten (Frankfurt a.M.: Suhrkamp, 1984), pp. 161–84. It is also implicit in Wolfgang Düsing's compilation *Friedrich Schiller. Über die ästhetische Erziehung des Menschen in einer Reihe von Briefen*, p. 146. See Düsing 164–65, for a short overview of the secondary literature on this question prior to the SUNY Albany Symposium of 1988. Klaus Berghahn (1974) also criticizes Schiller for his allegedly elitist disposition. See also n. 129. For Alfred Doppler, this was the first of two possible readings of Schiller's writing. The second was to appreciate the "Spannung von Kunst und Politik" and Schiller's attempt to offer "dem entfremdeten Bürger des modernen Staates den Spielraum der Kunst als Heilung" ("Geschichtliche Situation und ästhetische Konzeption [Bemerkungen zu Schillers Briefen 'Über die ästhetische Erziehung des Menschen'])," in *Tradition und Entwicklung. Festschrift Eugen Thurnher zum 60. Geburtstag*, eds. Werner M. Bauer, Achim Masser and Guntram A. Plangg [Innsbruck: AMOE, 1982], p. 288).

217. In his *Abhandlung von der Fähigkeit der Empfindung des Schönen in der Kunst, und dem Unterrichte in Derselben* (Dresden, 1763), Johann Joachim Winckel-

mann recognized that all human creatures possess "the capacity of perceiving beauty, but in very varying degrees" (in *Winckelmann. Writings on Art,* ed. David Irwin [London: Phaidon, 1972], p. 89). He also maintained that the feeling of the majority of people with respect to beauty "is brief, like the tone of a taut string" (p. 89). This is in contradistinction to Schiller, for whom the sounding of a taut string meant the fine-tuning and potentially harmonious tension of human existence.

218. See Alice C. Kuzniar, "Philosophic Chiliasm: Generating the Future, or Delaying the End?" *Eighteenth-Century Studies* 19 (1985), esp. p. 8; and Steven D. Martinson, "Reason, Revolution and Religion: Johann Benjamin Erhard's Concept of Enlightened Revolution," *History of European Ideas* 12 (1990), esp. pp. 224–25. See also Josef Chytry, *The Aesthetic State: A Quest in Modern German Thought* (Berkeley/Los Angeles/London: University of California Press, 1989). While exploring some problems inherent in that "political document," *Concerning the Aesthetic Education of the Human Being,* Chytry embarks on an excellent discussion of Schiller's variance from Kant and attempts to show that Schiller "discards Kant" (p. 80).

219. I do not believe, therefore, that Schiller's aesthetic-ethical, rational-moral state constitutes a utopia versus Benno von Wiese, "Die Utopie des Ästhetischen bei Schiller," in his *Zwischen Utopie und Wirklichkeit. Studien zur deutschen Literatur* (Düsseldorf: August Bagel, 1963), pp. 81–101. Benjamin Bennet has suggested that it is not so much the goal as the path to freedom in which Schiller was most interested. "Der eigentliche Höhepunkt des Menschseins wird immer wieder in dem ästhetischen Zustand unendlicher Bestimmbarkeit erreicht; aber dieser Zustand existiert nur unter der Bedingung, daß wir ihn *nicht als Ziel denken,* sondern als 'Weg'" ("Trinitarische Humanität: Dichtung und Geschichte bei Schiller," in *Friedrich Schiller. Kunst, Humanität und Politik,* pp. 169–170).

220. "Der Mensch ist einer langen Erziehung bedürftig." *Johann Gottfried Herder. Ideen zur Philosophie der Geschichte der Menschheit,* ed. Martin Bollacher (Frankfurt a.M.: Deutscher Klassiker Verlag, 1989), p. 315.

Chapter 6. "Merely an Idea": The Later Theoretical Essays

1. Hans Eichner, "The Supposed Influence of Schiller's *Über naive und sentimentalische Dichtung* on F. Schlegel's *Über das Studium der Griechischen Poesie,*" *The Germanic Review* (1955): 262. In fact, "Schlegel had not yet read Schiller's essay when he completed the *Studiumaufsatz*" (p. 262). The notion of an influence is at least as old as A. Koberstein's *Grundriß der Geschichte der deutschen Nationalliteratur* of 1827. In 1920, Arthur Lovejoy ("Schiller and the Genesis of German Romanticism" *Modern Language Notes* 35: 1–10, and 136–46) argued that Schiller's essay was the very impetus behind Schlegel's adoption of the romantic, a transition that was completed with the writing of the Lyceum fragments (p. 138). Because of Schlegel's conversion to a new "aesthetic faith" with the writing of the *Lyceum* fragments, Lovejoy makes a leap in logic by calling Schiller "the spiritual grandfather of German Romanticism" (p. 140). Despite the sharp distinction between the writers, which Lovejoy himself draws at times, the philosopher claimed Schiller for romanticism (p. 146). This is still generally the case, especially in Anglo-Saxon scholarship. The present study should help correct Lovejoy's opinion that Schiller removed all the limitations of an object in order to idealize it (p. 145). Hans Heinz Borcherdt's assessment in *Schiller und die Romantiker. Briefe und Dokumente,* ed. Hans Heinz Borscherdt (Stuttgart: Cotta, 1948) is diametrically opposed to Lovejoy's. Borcherdt: "Die festgefügte Persönlichkeit Schillers und seine Stellung neben Goethe bleiben der Stein des Anstoßes für die Romantiker und ebenso stand Schiller der werdenden romantischen Literaturbewegung sehr skeptisch gegenüber" (p. 1). Although he sug-

gests that the concept of the sentimental united both Schlegel and Schiller, Borcherdt distinguishes sharply between them (p. 3). But he overemphasizes their "völlig verschiedene Beweggründe und Argumentationen" (p. 3). In general, Borcherdt is insensitive to Schillers' development as a writer, i.e., the evolving nature of his thinking. Alfred Doppler ("Schiller und die Frühromantik" Jahrbuch des Wiener Goethe-Vereins 64 [1960]: 71–91), who is likewise cognizant of the differences between Schiller and the early German romantics, makes the imporant point that the disparity or breach between the ancients and the moderns occupied the thinking of many of Schiller's and Schlegel's contemporaries, e.g., Wilhelm von Humboldt ("Über das Studium des Altertums und des Griechischen insbesondere").

Bearing in mind Hans Eichner's determination that Schiller's and Schlegel's essays were written independently of each other, Ernst Behler ("The Origins of the Romantic Literary Theory," Colloquia Germanica 2 [1968]: 109–26) was more cognizant of the differences between the two writers than Lovejoy. However, on a more general level, Behler tended to conflate their early work. "In his [Schlegel's] endeavor to unite the two antithetical aesthetics of nature and art, of Classicism and Romanticism, he parallels similar efforts made by Schiller" (p. 123). The same can be said of Goethe in the writing of Faust II. This fact, however, should remind us that terms like "classical" or "romantic" are useful as relative markers but not as absolute terms. Unlike Lovejoy, Behler found in Schlegel's writings "the roots of the program of European Romanticism" (p. 114). In his more recent scholarship, Behler foregrounded the differences between Schlegel and Schiller. In "Die Wirkung Goethes und Schillers auf die Brüder Schlegel" Unser Commercium. Goethe und Schillers Literaturpolitik, eds. Wilfried Barner, Eberhard Lämmert, and Norbert Oellers (Stuttgart: Cotta, 1984) for instance, he underscored the fact that the relationships between the Schlegel brothers and Schiller were marked by sharp prejudices (p. 567). Hans Eichner ("Der Streit mit Schiller" in Kritische Friedrich Schlegel Ausgabe 2, eds. Ernst Behler et al. [Paderborn/München/Wien: Ferdinand Schönigh; Zürich: Thomas Verlag 1967]) had also drawn out the strained relations between the writers. But Eichner cast Schlegel in a heroic light, namely as someone who could withstand criticism and still appreciate Schiller's greatness (p. XI). Leonard Wessell ("Schiller and the Genesis of German Romanticism," Studies in Romanticism 10 [1971]: 176–98) suggested that Schlegel "differed from Schiller in that he sought to bring objective (beautiful or simple) poetry and modern (characteristic or sentimental) poetry into a dynamic synthesis in which the two apparently antagonistic principles are reconciled" (p. 196). According to Wessell, Schiller treated sentimental and naive poets "in a disjunctive manner" (p. 197), a point that seems to support the idea of the basic tension between them. Wessell summed up the debate: "although Schiller's concept of sentimentality and Schlegel's interestingness have contradictory features in their concrete applications (as Richard Brinkmann [Deutsche Vierteljahrsschrift für Literaturwissenschaft und Geistesgeschichte 32 (1958): 344–71] has shown), they nevertheless, Lovejoy to the contrary notwithstanding, share the same 'infinity', only Schiller generally places emphasis on the orderly and lawful manifestations of super-sensuous freedom, while Schlegel stresses the rich creativeness of the same noumenal freedom" (p. 196). For Schiller, there is equivocation, not satisfaction, and this implies "disunity or tension in any attempted synthesis" (p. 197). For Schlegel, irony entails the simultaneous affirmation and negation of the object and "a self-distancing from it" (p. 198). As we will have opportunity to observe later, Schlegel's implicit call for hovering between the two forms of the sentimental and the naive in which the "longed-for harmony is hopefully attained" (p. 198) actually places him in closer contact with Fichte's concept of imagination than that of Schiller's. Doris Starr Guilloton ("Schiller and Friedrich Schlegel: Their Controversial Relationship," in *Friedrich von Schiller: The Drama of Human Existence,* pp. 148–54) does not engage in this important discussion in the secondary literature and thus fails to go beyond established knowledge on the subject. Wilhelm G. Jacobs ("Geschichte und Kunst in Schellings 'System des transzendentalen Idealismus,'" in *Früher Idealismus und Frühromantik* [Tübingen: J. G. Cotta, 1800]) offers a refreshing appraisal of Schlegel's essay by focusing on the actual study ("Studium") of the material, thereby highlighting the pedagogical nature of the work (pp. 202–5). His all-too-brief discussion deserves a separate, more detailed analysis.

2. Scholarship has emphasized the quarrel between the moderns and the ancients in this exchange; e.g., Hans Robert Jauss, "Schlegels und Schillers Replik auf die 'Querelle des Anciens et des Modernes,'" in H. R. J., *Literaturgeschichte als Provokation* (Frankfurt a.M.: SuhrKamp, 1970). Though trying to offer a balanced assessment, in the end, Ernst Behler is vociferous about Friedrich Schlegel's "victory" ("Sieg") over Schiller in the "higher" circles of *Germanistik* in his critical review of Emil Staiger's *Friedrich Schlegels Sieg über Friedrich Schiller. Vorgetragen am 13. Dezember 1980* (Heidelberg: Carl Winter, 1981) in *The German Quarterly* 57 (1984): 657–58. Perhaps it was the tone of Staiger's presentation ("Heute stehen die Kritiker . . . allem, was Regel und Muster sein will, was allgemeine Geltung beansprucht, ratlos, skeptisch, um nicht zu sagen mit unverhohlenem Spott gegenüber" [p. 5]) that motivated Behler to state: "Im übrigen zuckt man die Achseln, geht an Schiller vorüber oder deutet ihn nach modernen Bedürfnissen um. Noch immer befremden aber dieselben Züge seiner Gestalt, die schon für die Romantiker ärgerlich waren" (p. 424). In "Origins of Romantic Aesthetics in Friedrich Schlegel" (*Canadian Review of Comparative Literature* 7 [1980]: 47–66), Behler viewed the debate within the context of aesthetics today "when the occupation with the timeless value of a work of art in its classical sense of perfection has been all but replaced by the consideration of its function within society and when the classical model of the predominance of the work of art over its contemplator has been substituted by the pre-eminence of its experience through the recipient" (p. 52). Unfortunately, there is a deeper-lying bias that has marked the tradition of scholarship on this subject. For, already in 1920, Lovejoy referred to Schiller as "moralistic" (p. 142) and placed Schlegel on the side of "Fülle und Leben," i.e., amorality (p. 143). I hope that the present study in its own small way might serve as a corrective to untempered ideological warfare and the Germanic predilection for conquest in scholarship. In passing, we should note that Staiger's 1980 address in Heidelberg evolved out of his 1967 study of the writer. Already in his book *Friedrich Schiller* (Zürich: Atlantis, 1967), Staiger had bemoaned the fact "daß Friedrich Schlegel im neunzehnten und im zwanzigsten Jahrhundert über Schiller gesiegt hat" (p. 420), despite Goethe's attempt to mediate where he could. Already in 1967, Staiger asked: "Was ist an Friedrich Schlegels Sieg über Schiller . . . begrüßens-, was ist beklagenswert?" (pp. 424–25). I am not sure what such quibbling is intended to prove.

3. "Natur in dieser Betrachtungsart ist uns nichts anders, als das freiwillige Dasein, das Bestehen der Dinge durch sich selbst, die Existenz nach eignen und unabänderlichen Gesetzen" (NA 20: 413).

4. "Sie *sind,* was wir *waren;* sie sind, was wir wieder *werden sollen*" (NA 20: 414).

5. "Wir waren Natur, wie sie, und unsere Kultur soll uns, auf dem Wege der Vernunft und der Freyheit, zur Natur zurückführen" (NA 20: 414).

6. "Sie sind also zugleich Darstellung unserer verlornen Kindheit, die uns ewig das theuerste bleibt; daher sie uns mit einer gewissen Wehmuth erfüllen. Zugleich sind sie Darstellungen unserer höchsten Vollendung im Ideale, daher sie uns in einer erhabene [*sic*] Rührung versetzen" (NA 20: 414).

7. "Wir sind frey und sie sind nothwendig; wir wechseln, sie bleiben eins" (NA 20: 415).

8. "Wenn der Wille das Gesetz der Nothwendigkeit frey befolgt und bey allem Wechsel der Phantasie die Vernunft ihre Regel behauptet" (NA 20: 415).

9. "Sie verschaffen uns daher den süßesten Genuß unserer Menschheit als Idee" (NA 20: 415).

10. Schiller's "interest in Nature" is explored in some detail by Wolfgang Riedel in his book *Spaziergang,* pp. 63–80. In a footnote, Riedel remarks that Schiller employed the concepts of "naive" and "sentimental" not as literary-historical but as cultural-anthropological categories (p. 67, n. 13). He observes that Schiller's first essay "Über das Naive" was shaped not so much by the aesthetician as by the psychologist and anthropologist (p. 67).

11. "Das Ey des Kolumbus gilt von jeder genialischen Entscheidung" (NA 20: 424).

12. "Er fand sie, diese Insel seines Papiers, und seine Rechnung war richtig" (NA 20: 127).

13. "Auf die Unfehlbarkeit seines Kalkuls geht der Weltentdecker Kolumbus die bedenkliche Wette mit einem unbefahrenen Meere ein, die fehlende zwote Hälfte zu der bekannten Hemisphäre, die große Insel Atlantis zu suchen, welche die Lüke auf seiner geographischen Charte ausfüllen sollte" (NA 20: 127).

14. "Es verfährt nicht nach erkannten Prinzipien sondern nach Einfällen und Gefühlen" (NA 20: 424).

15. If so, then Schiller's Max is certainly more than the hopeless or mistaken idealist Rolf Linn (*Schillers junge Idealisten* [Berkeley/Los Angeles/London: University of California Press, 1973]) and others have seen in him.

16. "Aus eigener schöner Menschlichkeit, daß sie es mit einer verderbten Welt zu thun haben" (NA 20: 422).

17. "Mit einer Ingenuität und Unschuld, wie man sie nur in einer Schäferwelt findet" (NA 20: 422).

18. See, for instance, Klaus Berghahn, "Volkstümlichkeit ohne Volk," cited in chapter 5, n. 129.

19. Eike Wolgast, "Schiller und die Fürsten," in *Schiller und die höfische Welt,* eds. Achim Aurnhammer, Klaus Manger, and Friedrich Strack (Tübingen: Max Niemeyer, 1990), p. 17.

20. "Aber durch einen Effekt der poetisierenden Einbildungskraft wird es öfters von dem Vernünftigen auf das Vernunftlose übertragen" (NA 20: 427).

21. See my article "Shaping the Imagination: Friedrich Schiller's Book Reviews," in *The Eighteenth-Century German Book Review,* pp. 137–50.

22. Wilfried Malsch ("Schillers und F. Schlegels Poesiebegriffe," in *Perspektiven der Romantik. Beiträge des Marburger Kolloquiums zum 80. Geburtstag Erich Ruprechts,* ed. Reinhard Görisch [Bonn: Bouvier, 1987]) examined more closely than before the understanding of the term *Urbild* for the Greeks in the eighteenth century. According to Malsch, this meant "keine Wiederkehr des Gleichen, sondern typologische Entsprechung" (p. 12). Malsch's contribution is especially valuable for its reevaluation of both Schiller's and Schlegel's concepts of poetry in the light of J. G. Herder's typology of ancient Greek culture. He sees that two of Schiller's later central postulates "Idealisierung" and "Veredlung" were shaped by Schiller's experience of rupture ("Zerrissenheit") in the idea of the totality of the human being which owed, in part, to the aftermath of the French Revolution. I have striven to show, however, that the experience of rupture was present from the very beginning of Schiller's career as a writer. Another especially valuable article on the subject of Schiller and Rousseau is Bernd Bräutigam's "Rousseaus Kritik ästhetischer

Versöhnung," *Jahrbuch der Deutschen Schillergesellschaft* 31 (1987): 137–55. Malsch makes the important point that Schiller did not follow Rousseau's return to nature but, rather, that his vision was directed toward the future reassociation with Nature. This is also my position, one that becomes clear in my discussion of *William Tell* in chapter nine.

23. "Allen Übeln der Kultur mußt du mit freyer Resignation dich unterwerfen" (NA 20: 428).

24. "Fürchte dich nicht vor der Verwirrung außer dir, aber vor der Verwirrung in dir; strebe nach Einheit, aber suche sie nicht in der Einförmigkeit; strebe nach Ruhe, aber durch das Gleichgewicht, nicht durch den Stillstand deiner Thätigkeit" (NA 20: 428).

25. "Verlassen von der Leiter, die dich trug, bleibt dir jetzt keine andere Wahl mehr, als mit freyem Bewußtseyn und Willen das Gesetz zu ergreifen, oder rettungslos in eine bodenlose Tiefe zu fallen" (NA 20: 428).

26. "Aber nimm sie in dich auf und strebe, ihren unendlichen Vorzug mit deinem eigenen unendlichen Prärogativ zu vermählen, und aus beydem das Göttliche zu erzeugen" (NA 20: 429).

27. "Die Flamme des *Ideals,* die in den Stürmen des Lebens so leicht erlischt" (NA 20: 429).

28. "Einig mit sich selbst, und glücklich im Gefühl seiner Menschheit . . . uneinig mit uns selbst, und unglücklich in unsern Erfahrungen von Menschheit" (NA 20: 431).

29. "Wie die Gottheit hinter dem Weltgebäude, so steht er hinter seinem Werk; Er ist das Werk und das Werk ist Er" (NA 20: 433).

30. "Entfernt sich gleich der Mensch durch die Freyheit seiner Phantasie und seines Verstandes von der Einfalt, Wahrheit und Nothwendigkeit der Natur, so steht iħm doch nicht nur der Pfad zu derselben immer offen, sondern ein mächtiger und unvertilgbarer Trieb, der moralische, treibt ihn auch unaufhörlich zu ihr zurück, und eben mit diesem Triebe steht das Dichtungsvermögen in der engsten Verwandtschaft" (NA 20: 436).

31. Peter Szondi ("Das Naive ist das Sentimentalische," in his, *Schriften II,* eds. Jean Bollack et al. [Frankfurt a.M.: Suhrkamp, 1978], pp. 59–105) conflated both terms without appreciating the tension of their future "wedding."

32. "Die Natur macht ihn mit sich Eins, die Kunst trennt und entzweyet ihn, durch das Ideal kehrt er zur Einheit zurück" (NA 20: 438).

33. "Weil aber das Ideal ein unendliches ist, das er niemals erreicht, so kann der kultivierte Mensch in seiner Art, niemals vollkommen werden, wie doch der natürliche Mensch es in der seinigen zu werden vermag" (NA 20: 438).

34. Alfred Doppler observed "Was Schiller in seiner Schrift als 'Überspannung' bezeihnete, als Gefahr erkannte und zum Unterschied von 'idealisieren' 'schwärmen' nannte, das proklamierte Friedrich Schlegel als die Aufgabe der neueren Poesie" ("Schiller und die Frühromantik," cited in n. 1, p. 85). Doppler captured an essential aspect of Schiller's work: "Schiller begrenzte aber das Sentimentalische durch das Postulat der 'reinen Menschheit' und band das Poetische an das Moralische und an die sittliche Kultur" (p. 84).

35. "Der Mensch ist eine aus seinem reinen Selbst und einem fremdartigen Wesen gemischte Natur" (Friedrich Schlegel, *Über das Studium der Griechischen Poesie,* 28).

36. Ibid., p. 93.

37. Ibid., p. 100.

38. In his *Rede über das Genie,* Abel had proclaimed that the truly great mind or genius is at once a work of Nature and education ("ein Werk der Natur und der

Erziehung", p. 7). He postulated: "Im Genie erleuchtet ein strahlendes Feuer alle Teile des Gegenstandes, alles steht vor ihm in lebendiger Klarheit, alles bis zum lebenden Anschauen erhoben" (p. 26). He also proposed that imagination ("Einbildungskraft") and the understanding ("Verstand") are co-dependent in the genius (pp. 21 and 30), a posture that is especially significant in light of Schiller's later book reviews wherein Schiller insists on the cooperation of both faculties. Abel then states: "Die Richtigkeit der Begriffe ist oft Zeichen des Genies" (p. 33). We note, also, Abel's position with respect to genius and harmony: "Harmonie ist überhaupt beim Genie" (p. 34).

39. "Seine Sphäre ist immer das Ideenreich, und ins Unendliche weiß er alles, was er bearbeitet, hinüberzuführen" (NA 20: 457).

40. "Man möchte sagen, er ziehe allem, was er behandelt, den Körper aus, um es zu Geist zu machen, so wie andere Dichter alles Geistige mit einem Körper bekleiden" (NA 20: 457).

41. "Keusch, überirrdisch, unkörperlich, heilig wie seine Religion ist seine dichterische Muse" (NA 20: 457).

42. "Fähig zu jeder Energie und Meister auf dem ganzen Felde sentimentalischer Dichtung kann er uns bald durch das höchste Pathos erschüttern, bald in himmlisch süße Empfindungen wiegen; aber zu einer hohen geistreichen Wehmuth neigt sich doch überwiegend sein Herz, und wie erhaben auch seine Harfe, seine Lyra tönt, so werden die schmelzenden Töne seiner Laute doch immer wahrer und tiefer und beweglicher klingen" (NA 20: 458).

43. Wilfried Malsch offered a more general definition of the term that helps point up the difference between Schiller and the German romantics: "Romantisch bezeichnet hier keine neue Literatur, sondern die Fähigkeit unserer dichterischen Phantasie, Wünsche und Sehnsüchte in entrückten Bildern zu versinnlichen, noch ehe wir sie verstehen" (in *Die Klassik-Legende. Second Wisconsin Workshop*, eds. Reinhold Grimm and Jost Hermand [Frankfurt a.M.: Athenäum, 1971], p. 131).

44. "Ein Charakter, der mit glühender Empfindung ein Ideal umfaßt, und die Wirklichkeit flieht, um nach einem wesenlosen Unendlichen zu ringen, der, was er in sich selbst unaufhörlich ausser sich selbst suchet, dem nur seine Träume das Reelle, seine Erfahrungen ewig nur Schranken sind, der endlich in seinem eigenen Daseyn nur eine Schranke sieht, und auch diese, wie billig ist, noch einreißt, um zu der wahren Realität durchzudringen" (NA 20: 459).

45. "Schwärmerische, unglückliche Liebe, Empfindsamkeit für Natur, Religionsgefühle, philosophischer Contemplationsgeist, . . . die düstre, gestaltlose, schwermüthige Ossianische Welt" (NA 20: 459).

46. "Daher ist hier das Gemut in Bewegung, es ist angespannt, es schwankt zwischen streitenden Gefühlen; da es dort ruhig, aufgelöst, einig mit sich selbst und vollkommen befriedigt ist" (NA 20: 474).

47. The primary results of the research for this part of the chapter were presented at the Eighth International Congress on the Enlightenment in Bristol, England, in July 1991, titled "Schiller: Between Enlightenment and Romanticism." They have not been published previously and, in the interim, have undergone extensive revision. My ideas in this chapter were also fueled by the lively discussions of participants' papers at the Internationaler Kongreß der Eichendorff-Gesellschaft "Schiller und die Romantik," held in Marbach a.N. from July 5–8, 1990.

48. See chapter 4, n. 18 for a definition of Idealism. Concerning the genesis of romanticism in the German States, see Ernst Behler, "The Origins of the Romantic Literary Theory," *Colloquia Germanica* 2 (1968): 109–26, and his "Origins of Romantic Aesthetics in Friedrich Schlegel," *Canadian Review of Comparative Literature* 7 (1980): 47–66.

49. Cited by both Arthur Lovejoy, "Schiller and the Genesis of Romanticism," cited in n. 1, and Ernst Behler, "The Origins of the Romantic Literary Theory," p. 122. Behler detects that Schlegel's understanding is, in part, based on a concept of imagination as "infinite abundance." "Imagination is a supernatural faculty, is always revelation, enthusiasm and inspiration" (p. 122).

50. Leonard Wessel (1971) has seen that Schiller did not bridge the two different ways (sentimental and naive) of mirroring the infinite, as Schlegel had "through irony" ("Schiller and the Genesis of German Romanticism," *Studies in Romanticism* 10 [1971]: 198).

51. *Kritische Friedrich-Schlegel-Ausgabe* 2, eds. Ernst Behler et al. (Paderborn/München/Wien: Ferdinand Schönigh; Zürich: Thomas Verlag, 1958f), p. 8. Hans Eichner noted the fact that Schlegel continued his criticism of Schiller in his review of *Die Horen* and the *Musenalmanach auf das Jahr 1797* in the journal *Deutschland*.

52. Quoted by Behler, "The Origins of the Romantic Literary Theory"; cited in n. 48, p. 122.

53. Schlegel presented a signed copy of his book *Die Griechen und Römer* to Schiller's wife, Charlotte (von Lengefeld). I do not recall finding any marginal notations. Concerning its contents, Schiller recorded the following sentiment in a letter to Wilhelm von Humboldt of December 17, 1795: "In der Sache selbst hat er [Schlegel] mich nicht bekehrt" (NA 28: 134).

54. "Um dem Eigensinne der Begierden und den Launen der Einbildungskraft desto ungebundener nachgeben zu können" (NA 20: 503).

55. "Die ganze Unordnung einer spielenden und bloß sich selbst gehorchenden Einbildungskraft" (NA 21: 9).

56. Fichte's *Grundlage der gesammten Wissenschaftslehre als Handschrift für seine Zuhörer* (Leipzig: Christian Ernst Gabler, 1794) in: *Gesamtausgabe* I,2: *Werke 1793–1795* vol. 1, eds. Reinhard Lauth and Hans Jacob [Stuttgart/Bad Canstatt: Friedrich Frommann, 1964f], p. 359.

57. Hovering is a key concept for Fichte. Peter Baumanns observes: "Mit diesem Schweben der produktiven Einbildungskraft über der Bestimmbarkeit des Ichs durch die Subjekt-Objekt-Relation, in welchem Schweben sich das Ich als Substanz der Antithesis und Synthesis der Subjekt-Objekt-Relation Thesis zur Geltung" (*J. G. Fichte. Kritische Gesamtdarstellung seiner Philosophie* [Freiburg/München: Karl Alber, 1990], p. 87). Klaus Peter also acknowledges this in his appraisal of the similarities between Novalis and Fichte: "Beide, Novalis und Fichte, stimmen darin überein, daß die 'Realität' nicht ein Produkt des Denkens ist, sondern der Einbildungskraft oder Imagination. Nur die Einbildungskraft kann die Entgegengesetzten, Subjekt und Objekt, deren Einheit Realität konstituiert, verbinden. Beide, Novalis und Fichte, beschreiben diese Einheit als ein 'Schweben'" (*Stadien der Aufklärung. Moral und Politik bei Lessing, Novalis und Friedrich Schlegel* [Wiesbaden: Akademische Verlagsgesellschaft Athenaion, 1980], p. 96).

58. Baumanns: "Realität zu bilden, wird dieses Ich sich aber nicht als seine Leistung zurechnen, sofern es sich besinnt, da mit ihm das Bilden der Realität schon begonnen hat und es nur darauf, nicht aber auf die Ichform, ankommt" (*J. G. Fichte,* p. 338). This central insight conditions Fichte's concept of freedom. Baumanns: "Dies ist das Wesen sittlicher Freiheit: daß das Individuum sich erscheint als sich erhebend zur Erkenntnis der Prinzipheit der Erscheinung, als fortschreitend durch formale Freiheit zur Vollendung dieses fragmentarischen Bildes im Prinzipiat [= in der Natur] (mit beidem innerhalb der Erscheinung verbleibend), schließlich als die Erschei*nung* zum Erschei*nen* hin transzendierend" (p. 339). A key difference between Fichte and Schiller is that Schiller does not wish to tear himself either from his own nature or from Nature in general as does Fichte. Indeed, Fichte speaks of

the necessity of the act of "Sich-Losreißen." Wolfgang Riedel rightly criticizes W. Hogrebe ("Fichte und Schiller. Eine Skizze," in *Schillers Briefe über die ästhetische Erziehung*, ed. Jürgen Bolten, pp. 276–89) for placing Schiller and Fichte side by side in the latter's assault on Rousseau (*Spaziergang*, p. 65, n. 9). I agree that Schiller opposed both Kant's and Fichte's denigration of feeling, sensation, and sensuousness, i.e., "die Naturseite des Menschen" (Riedel, p. 66, n. 9). Peter Rohs: "Natur ist, so kann man kurz sagen, für Fichte nur die Naturseite von Freiheit" (*Johann Gottlieb Fichte* [München: C. H. Beck, 1991], p. 104).

59. For a cogent study on this topic, see Frederick Neuhouser, *Fichte's Theory of Subjectivity* (Cambridge/New York: Cambridge University Press, 1990).

60. Daniel Breazeale reminds us that Fichte first presented his ideas on the theory or science of knowledge in a series of lectures in both Zürich and Jena (*Fichte. Early Philosophical Writings*, trans. and ed. Daniel Breazeale [Ithaca, NY/London: Cornell University Press, 1988], pp. 16 and 18).

61. "In unserm Musensitze ist alles ruhig, und Fichte ist noch in voller Arbeit, seine Elementarphilosophie zu vollenden. Ich bin überzeugt, daß es nur bey ihm stehen wird, in der Philosophie eine Gesetzgebende Rolle zu spielen, und sie um einen ziemlich großen Schritt vorwärts zu bringen. Aber der Weg geht an einem Abgrund hin, und alle Wachsamkeit wird nötig seyn, nicht in diesen zu stürzen. Die reinste Spekulation gränzt so nahe an eine leere Speculation, und der Scharfsinn an Spitzfindigkeit. Was ich biß jetzt von seinem System begreife, hat meinen ganzen Beyfall, aber noch ist mir sehr vieles dunkel, und es geht nicht bloß mir, sondern jedem so, den ich darüber frage" (NA 27: 41). In the same letter, Schiller added the following interesting fact: "Mit meiner Gesundheit geht es weder besser noch schlechter, aber an Thätigkeit fehlt es mir nicht, und der Geist ist heiter" (NA 27: 41).

62. Breazeale (1988), p. 15.

63. In *Die Horen, eine Monatsschrift*, vol. 1, ed. [Friedrich] Schiller (Tübingen: J. G. Cotta, 1795–97), p. 89.

64. *Die Horen*, vol. 1, p. 89.

65. In part, Schiller's negative response owed to the fact that Fichte had submitted only an uneven and incomplete manuscript of his work, even though he had promised Schiller a completed work by the time of the deadline. Daniel Breazeale (1988) misses this important point in his defense of Fichte (n. to p. 396). On June 24, 1795, Schiller sent the manuscript back. In the second draft of a letter to Fichte, Schiller expressed the fact that he had done so not simply because he was dissatisfied with its length, but because he liked neither the content nor the treatment of it. In the third and final draft of the letter, Schiller asked Fichte to forgive the direct and honest manner in which he was conveying his sentiments. In particular, he complained that the first exhaustive part on *Geist* concerns only "Geist in den schönen Künsten" (*Gesamtausgabe* vol. 3, *Briefe*, vol. 1, p. 331) and he saw problems with its possible reception among the reading public. Three days later, Fichte complained that Schiller had misunderstood his work and that he had done him a disservice. "Zu welchem Stümper machen Sie mich! Sie müßen den Aufsatz sehr flüchtig gelesen haben" (p. 337). It is possible that Schiller did not understand Fichte's concept of the "Nicht-seyende." Fichte highlights what he perceives to be their differences in style. It is a highly interesting declaration given Schiller's criticism of G. A. Bürger's poetry. "Sie [Schiller] gehen gröstentheils analytisch, den Weg des strengen Systems; und setzen die Popularität in Ihren unermeßlichem Vorrath von Bildern, die Sie fast allenthalben Statt des abstrakten Begriffs setzen. Ich setze die Popularität vorzüglich in den Gang, den ich nehme. . . . Bei mir steht das Bild nicht *an der Stelle* des Begriffs, sondern *vor* oder *nach* dem Begriffe, als Gleichniß: ich sehe, darauf, daß es paße" (p. 339). After accusing Schiller of enchaining the imagination, Fichte goes

on to insult his erstwhile friend. Referring to the public's supposed reception of Schiller's philosophical writings, Fichte added: "Jeder lobt, so sehr er kann; aber er hütet sich wohl vor der Frage: was denn eigentlich darin stehe?" (p. 339). It is reasonable to assume that Schiller reacted negatively to Fichte's accusation. By way of contrast, on May 3, 1794, in a letter to Marie Johanne Fichte from Zürich, Fichte wrote: "Schiller gehört unter die ersten, geliebtesten, und berühmtesten Professoren von Jena" (p. 102). After the quarrel that summer, Fichte writes how he had just met Goethe, how much he admired the man, and how he "übertrifft Schiller darin um Vieles, der eigentlich in zwei Welten lebt, in der poetischen und dann und wann in der kantisch-philosophischen" (p. 182). Finally, I add two small corrections to Breazeale here. Schiller was appointed professor of philosophy and not of history, as the reception of his *Geschichte des dreissigjährigen Kriegs* by his colleague in history, Professor Heinrich, makes clear. Breazeale renders Schiller's name incorrectly as "Johann Cristoph [*sic*] Schiller" instead of Johann Christoph Friedrich Schiller. For a fine discussion of the Horen-Project and its reception, see: Wulf Koepke, ". . .'das Werk einer glücklichen Konstellation': Schillers *Horen* und die deutsche Literaturgeschichte," in *Friedrich Schiller. Kunst, Humanität und Politik,* pp. 366–82.

66. *Gesamtausgabe; Werke* I/2, p. 399. Translation by Breazeale p. 395. Ernesto Grassi has suggested that it was Fichte's commitment to the dualism in the division between art and philosophy, and image and concept, which was to be overcome, that led him to lash out at Schiller (*Die Macht der Phantasie. Zur Geschichte abendländischen Denkens* [Königstein/Ts: Athenäum, 1979], p. 41).

67. Engell, *The Creative Imagination,* p. 217. According to Engell, the idea of the imagination evolved at the time of the Enlightenment and the formation of this concept was an essential part of the Enlightenment's transforming itself into romanticism (p. 217). Engell goes too far, however, when he states: "The Enlightenment created the idea of the imagination" (pp. 3 and ix).

68. Engell, *The Creative Imagination,* p. 232. It is not true, as Elmar Dod asserts uncritically in following Engell, that Schiller did not use the concept of *Einbildungskraft* explicitly (*Die Vernünftigkeit der Imagination,* p. 105, n. 301). Schiller's book reviews clearly refute this assumption.

69. Ibid., p. 231.

70. Ibid., p. 232.

71. Ibid., p. 231. In general, Engell's thesis, which focuses on the continuity between Enlightenment and Romanticism (rather than the tension between them), calls up the need for more exacting differentiation given varying definitions of imagination in the writings of so many thinkers of the eighteenth and early nineteenth centuries. For a thought-provoking discussion of the relationship between Enlightenment and romanticism and a critical overview of the genesis of this debate, see Wolfdietrich Rasch, "Zum Verhältnis der Romantik zur Aufklärung," in *Romantik. Ein literaturwissenschaftliches Studienbuch,* ed. Ernst Ribbat (Königstein/Ts.: Athenäum, 1979). Elmar Dod (*Die Vernünftigkeit der Vernunft*) aligns Schiller with romanticism in his comparative study of Schiller and Shelley, thus cutting across the grain of traditional German literary scholarship (but not of Anglo-Saxon research). Dod's study fails to adequately engage the problem of comparing texts written independently of each other and in quite different cultural contexts. The New Historicism has alerted us to the importance of first appreciating the specific cultural context(s) in which a text was/is written. I find it specious to select one work by a writer, such as Schiller's *Concerning the Aesthetic Education of the Human Being* (no matter how seminal the work) and then maintain that that one work represents the entire oeuvre or thinking of the writer. Not only is such a position suspect historically, it

is also untenable on rational grounds. Finally, Dod fails to differentiate clearly between the distinct operations of *Verstand* (understanding) and *Vernunft* (reason) in eighteenth-century German literature and philosophy. Leonard Wessell has given us a lucid explanation. The concepts of *Verstand,* he submits, are "determinate, limited, conditioned and finite in content," whereas *Vernunft* is "the source for concepts such as unconditionality, infinity, and absolute totality" (p. 192).

72. This point was missed by Hans-Georg Pott (*Die schöne Freiheit*), who investigated the influence of Fichte's theory of drives in the *Vorlesungen* on Schiller's writing *Concerning the Aesthetic Education of the Human Being.* Though he traces this development back to an earlier tradition, Pott does not work this connection out in detail. His discussion of the possible influence of Karl Reinhold's *Briefe über die Kantische Philosophie* (1786–87) on Schiller (especially in the *Horen*) is helpful, which letters were well circulated and discussed at the time (see especially p. 34). Pott does not note, however, that Schiller's *Spieltrieb* shares nothing in common with the self-sufficiency of Fichte's "ästhetischer Trieb." For Schiller, the play impulse ultimately contributes to the creative restructuring of political society. For Fichte, the goal of *Trieb* is Idea; for Schiller, the reconstitution of the individual and society.

73. Baumanns, *J. G. Fichte,* pp. 166–67.

74. On June 12, 1794, Schiller wrote, with confidence, to Körner: "Unser Journal [*Die Horen*] soll ein Epoche machendes Werk seyn, und alles, was Geschmack haben will, muß uns kaufen und lesen" (NA 27:11).

75. "Die Einbildungskraft erscheint hier in ihrer ganzen Fessellosigkeit und dabei doch in der schönsten Einstimmung mit der Idee, welche ausgedrückt werden soll" (NA 22: 280).

76. "Indem wir die Gattung durch ein Individuum repräsentiren, und einen allgemeinen Begriff in einem einzelnen Falle darstellen, nehmen wir der Phantasie die Fesseln ab, die der Verstand ihr angelegt hatte, und geben ihr Vollmacht, sich schöpferisch zu beweisen. Immer nach Vollständigkeit der Bestimmungen strebend, erhält und gebraucht sie jetzt das Recht, das ihr hingegebene Bild nach Gefallen zu ergänzen, zu beleben, umzustalten, ihm in allen seinen Verbindungen und Verwandlungen zu folgen. Sie darf augenblicklich ihrer untergeordneten Rolle vergessen, und sich als eine willkührliche Selbstherrscherinn betragen, weil durch den strengen innern Zusammenhang hinlänglich dafür gesorgt ist, daß sie dem Zügel des Verstandes nie ganz entfliehen kann" (NA 21: 9–10).

77. "So sehr diese beyden Interessen mit einander zu streiten scheinen, so giebt es doch zwischen beyden einen Punkt der Vereinigung, und diesen auszufinden, ist das eigentliche Verdienst der schönen Schreibart" (NA 21: 8).

78. "Um der Imagination Genüge zu thun, muß die Rede einen materiellen Theil oder *Körper* haben, und diesen machen die Anschauungen aus, von denen der Verstand die einzelnen Merkmale oder Begriffe absondert; denn so abstrakt wir auch denken mögen, so ist doch immer zuletzt etwas sinnliches, was unserm Denken zum Grund liegt" (NA 21: 8).

79. Perhaps the strongest provocation against Schiller's negative review of Gottfried August Bürger's poetry came from Klaus Berghahn ("Volkstümlichkeit ohne Volk?" in *Popularität oder Trivialität*). His position was challenged by Helmuth Kiesel and Paul Münch in their account of the situation of the German author in the eighteenth century in *Gesellschaft und Literatur im 18. Jahrhundert. Voraussetzungen und Entstehung des literarischen Markts in Deutschland* (München: Beck, 1977, esp. p. 99). It is sheer polemics to assert, as Berghahn did, that Friedrich Schiller was an enemy of the public (57). The following historically based study provides us with a corrective to Berghahn's allegations: Horst Möller, "Wie bürgerlich war die Aufklärung, wie aufgeklärt der Bürger?" in *Vernunft und Kritik.*

Deutsche Aufklärung im 17. und 18. Jahrhundert (Frankfurt a.M.: Suhrkamp, 1986, esp. 297). See also Helmut Koopmann, "Der Dichter als Kunstrichter. Zu Schillers Rezensionsstragie," in *Jahrbuch der Deutschen Schillergesellschaft* 20 (1976): 229–46, Walter Hinderer, "Schiller und Bürger: Die ästhetische Kontroverse als Paradigma," in *Jahrbuch des Freien Deutschen Hochstifts* (1986): 130–54, and Arnd Bohm, "The Desublimated Body: Gottfried August Bürger," in *Subversive Sublimities: Undercurrents of the German Enlightenment,* ed. Eitel Timm (Columbia, S.C.: Camden House, 1992), pp. 12–26. Walter Hinderer sees "daß Schiller bei aller Zeitgenossenschaft einen eigenen Weg einschlägt, der schon in der Karlsschule beginnt. Dichtung . . . gehört für ihn von Anfang an in einen Zusammenhang, der von der Totalitätsidee des Menschen oder der 'Gottgleichheit' wie er in seiner Dissertation die anthropologische Bestimmung definiert, geprägt wird" (pp. 138–39).

80. "Wie es möglich war, zu übersehen, daß sich die Begeisterung des Dichters nicht selten in die Grenzen des *Wahnsinns* verliert, daß sein Feuer oft *Furie* wird" (NA 22: 256).

81. "Bei seinen Sonetten, Mustern ihrer Art, die sich auf den Lippen des Deklamateurs in Gesang verwandeln, wünschen wir mit ihm, daß sie keinen Nachahmer finden möchten, der nicht gleich ihm und seinem vortrefflichen Freund, *Schlegel,* die Leier des pythischen Gottes spielen kann" (NA 22: 257).

82. Though I am more sympathetic to Schiller than Arnd Bohm, I recommend his defense of Bürger, "Gottfried August Bürger: Texts of the Body," *Studies in Eighteenth-Century Culture* 23 (1994): 161–78.

83. "Will uns also der Dichter aus dem Gedränge der Welt in seine Einsamkeit nachziehen, so muß es nicht Bedürfnis der Abspannung, sondern der Anspannung, nicht Verlangen nach Ruhe, sondern nach Harmonie sein, was ihm die Kunst verliert und die Natur liebenswürdig macht" (NA 22: 282).

84. "Ein natürliches Symbol der innern Übereinstimmung des Gemüts mit sich selbst und des sittlichen Zusammenhangs der Handlungen und Gefühle, und in der schönen Haltung eines pittoresken oder musikalischen Stücks malt sich die noch schönere einer sittlich gestimmten Seele" (NA 22: 273).

85. As noted also by Claus Artur Scheier, "Die Frühromantik als Kultur der Reflexion," in *Früher Idealismus und Frühromantik. Der Streit um die Grundlagen der Ästhetik (1795–1805),* eds. Walter Jaeschke and Helmut Holzhey (Hamburg: Felix Meiner, 1990), p. 71.

86. On this point, I follow Werner Beierwaltes, "Einleitung" to *F. W. J. Schelling. Texte zur Philosophie der Kunst,* ed. Werner Beierwaltes (Stuttgart: Reclam, 1959), p. 13.

87. Ibid., p. 262. Werner Beierwaltes notes that Schelling does not accurately represent Schiller's statements (p. 264, n. 35). Furthermore, I wish to note that Schelling and Schiller wrote with different understandings of the nature of reality in mind. Whereas Schelling's reality was the reality of the mind, Schiller attended not simply to the formative power of *Geist* but also to the corporeal, material world and historical reality.

88. Ibid., p. 264.

89. Ibid., p. 263.

90. Ibid., p. 265.

91. Andrew Bowie defines Schelling's concept of Nature as follows: "Nature appears *both* as product in an analogous way to being conscious—in the constitution of organisms which 'give the law to themselves' as we do in practical reason—*and* as a blind mechanism it is an object of the understanding" (*Aesthetics and Subjectivity: From Kant to Nietzsche* [Manchester/New York: Manchester University Press, 1990], p. 88).

92. David Simpson has captured the essence of Schelling's view of the work of art: "Art is the visibly embodied and therefore communicable union of the Idea in nature with that in humanity" (*German Aesthetic and Literary Criticism: Kant, Fichte, Schelling, Schopenhauer, Hegel*, ed. David Simpson [Cambridge/London/ New York: Cambridge University Press, 1984], p. 2).

93. The *Propyläen Geschichte der Literatur IV: Aufklärung und Romantik 1700– 1830* (Berlin: Propyläen, 1983) uses the terms Enlightenment and Romanticism as historical markers. Storm and Stress and Classicism are stylistic terms. "Weimar Classicism" is both a geographical and a stylistic term, however (e.g., Dieter Borchmeyer, *Die Weimarer Klassik*). Though the Wisconsin Workshop may have gone too far in its claims, it is good to bear in mind the results of *Die Klassik-Legende*. I understand the terms Enlightenment and Romanticism to be historical signposts marking the two poles of Schiller's intellectual development (*Bildung*) as a writer. This includes Schiller's schooling in the Enlightenment (both before and at the time of his tenure at the Carlsschule), including the later encounter with Kant's critical philosophy and his own activities as a professor of philosophy in Jena, as well as his association with Goethe, the early German romantics and proponents of Idealism. Hence, historically, Schiller's writings stand *between* Enlightenment and Romanticism. Finally, I understand one of the major ambitions of the German Enlightenment (Lessing and Mendelssohn, for instance) to consist of unraveling or disentangling the knotted nature of life, whereas romanticism tended to accept those knots, thereby retaining the mystery of life.

94. James Engell (*The Creative Imagination*) does not refer to earlier accomplishments of German scholarship in this area. See, for instance, Helmut Schanze, *Romantik und Aufklärung. Untersuchungen zu Friedrich Schlegel und Novalis* (Nürnberg: Hans Carl, 1966) and Klaus Peter, *Stadien der Aufklärung*. Nor does he draw upon other contributions to the same topic written in English, e.g., my *On Imitation, Imagination, and Beauty: A Critical Reassessment of the Concept of the Literary Artist During the Early German "Aufklärung"* (Bonn: Bouvier, 1977). Perhaps this presents a good argument for the need for greater interdisciplinarity in scholarship.

95. "Bleibt aber immer nur Idee, die von der Wirklichkeit nie ganz erreicht werden kann" (NA 20: 360).

96. Exploring Schiller's use of metaphor, as I do, my thesis diverges from the fine studies by Gert Ueding (*Schillers Rhetorik* and *Friedrich Schiller*) and Todd Kontje (*Constructing Reality*), both of whom interpret Schiller's writings from the point of view of rhetorical devices (Ueding) and/or strategies (Kontje). Not wishing in any way to deny the influence of Florentine rhetoric on Schiller's writings, my main interest in the present study is to investigate the possible significance of central and recurrent metaphors/symbols in Schiller's works. As is evident from the preceding study, I cannot accept Kontje's explanation: "Schiller's skepticism only arises out of the pressure he exerts on his ideals in the attempt to demonstrate the possibility of their realization" (p. 101). I find his assumptions likewise unconvincing: "Only a visionary idealist could conceive of autonomous art leading society to a utopian state, and only a political revolutionary would become impatient with an ideal which can only be approximated or at best realized by some society in the distant future" (p. 101). For a fine study that explores the emphasis German writers of the early and "high" Enlightenment placed on metaphor, see Jill Anne Kowalik, *The Poetics of Historical Perspectivism: Breitinger's "Critische Dichtkunst" and the Neoclassic Tradition* (Chapel Hill, N.C./London: University of North Carolina Press, 1992).

97. Thomas Carlyle, *The Life of Friedrich Schiller: Comprehending and Examination of his Works* (London: Taylor and Hessey, 1825), p. 290.

98. Ibid.
99. Ibid., p. 306.

Chapter 7. At the Crossroads of Physiology and Politics: *Mary Stuart*

1. *Schiller: Mary Stuart. A Tragedy,* trans. Sophie Wilkins (Woodbury, N.Y./ London/Toronto/Sydney: Barron's, 1959), p. 31. Hereafter: SW, followed by page references in the main body of the text; ". . . die Natur / Warf diese beiden feurigen Völkerschaften / Auf dieses Brett im Ozean, ungleich / Verteilte sies, und hieß sie darum kämpfen" (NA 9: 32).
2. Andreas Mielke ("*Maria Stuart:* Hermeneutical Problems of 'One' Tragedy with 'Two' Queens," in *Friedrich von Schiller: The Drama of Human Existence,* pp. 49–61) sees that "in spite of Schiller's own continued interest in Elizabeth, old and new interpretations favor Maria Stuart" (p. 54). Ellen Finger perceives that Schiller's Elizabeth "shows signs of suffering a personal crisis no less severe than Maria's," and notes that, in preparing an early production of the play, the author "showed more concern for the difficult performance of Elisabeth's role than for Maria's" ("Schiller's Concept of the Sublime and Its Pertinence to *Don Carlos* and *Maria Stuart,*" *Journal of English and Germanic Philology* 79 [1980]: 176). Mielke takes note of Schiller's plans for the performance, where, among other things, he observes that the dramatist did not wish for Queen Elizabeth to be ugly or physically homely, but in every way "a person dramaturgically equal to Maria Stuart" (p. 52). As will become clear from the following analysis, there is good reason to doubt Jeffrey Sammons's opinion that the author reduced the Queen's role to "a missed opportunity of major dimensions" ("Mortimer's Conversion and Schiller's Allegiances," *Journal of English and Germanic Philology* 72 [1973]: 159). On the contrary, he capitalized on it. Ellen Finger declares that "Elisabeth's character is compromised by many flaws" (p. 176). However, I do not find Finger's alignment of Elizabeth and the sublime in any way convincing (pp. 177–78).
3. "Die Könige sind nur Sklaven ihres Standes, / Dem eignen Herzen dürfen sie nicht folgen" (NA 9: 45).
4. "Auf gleiche Dienstbarkeit—Der Ring macht Ehen, / und Ringe sinds, die eine Kette machen / . . . Es ist / Noch keine Kette, bindet mich noch nicht, / Doch kann ein Reif draus werden, der mich bindet" (NA 9: 46).
5. "Nicht genug, / Daß *jetzt* der Segen dieses Land beglückt, / Auch ihrem künftgen Wohl soll ich mich opfern, / Auch mein jungfräuliche Freiheit soll ich, / Mein höchstes Gut, hingeben für mein Volk, / Und der Gebieter wird mir aufgedrungen. Es zeigt mir dadurch an, daß ich ihm nur / Ein Weib bin, und ich meinte doch, regiert / Zu haben, wie ein Mann und wie ein König" (NA 9: 45).
6. "Das Weib ist nicht schwach. Es gibt starke Seelen / In dem Geschlecht— Ich will in meinem Beisein / Nichts von der Schwäche des Geschlechtes hören" (NA 9: 52).
7. "Ihr Leben ist dein Tod! Ihr Tod dein Leben!" (NA 9: 49).
8. "Wie sich / Die Neigung anders wendet, also steigt / Und fällt des *Urteils* wandelbare Woge. / Sag nicht, du müssest der Notwendigkeit / Gehorchen und dem Dringen deines Volks. / Sobald du willst, in jedem Augenblick / Kannst du erproben, daß dein Wille frei ist" (NA 9: 50–51).
9. "Diese Weisheit, welche Blut befiehlt, / Ich hasse sie in meiner tiefsten Seele" (NA 9: 49).
10. "Ihr eilet ja, als wenn Ihr Flügel hättet, / *So* kann ich Euch nicht folgen, wartet doch!" (NA 9: 79).

11. "Umfängt mich nicht der weite Himmelsschloß? / Die Blicke, frei und fessellos, / Ergehen sich in ungemeßnen Räumen" (NA 9: 79–80).

12. "Eilende Wolken! Segler der Lüfte! / Wer mit euch wanderte, mit euch schifften! / Grüßet mir freundlich mein Jugendland! / Ich bin gefangen, ich bin in Banden, / Ach, ich hab keinen andern Gesandten! / Frei in Lüften ist eure Bahn, / Ihr seid nicht dieser Königin untertan" (NA 9: 80).

13. As explored by Reinhart Koselleck in his *Critique and Crisis* (*Kritik und Krise*). Koselleck's thesis continues to influence recent Schiller scholarship. E.g., Wilfried Malsch (in *Verantwortung und Utopie. Zur Literatur der Goethezeit. Ein Symposium,* ed. Wolfgang Wittkowski [Tübingen: Max Niemeyer, 1988]) and Wolfgang Wittkowski (in *Zeitschrift für Germanistik* N.F. 2 [1992]: 31–50).

14. Arthur Henkel has taken a close look at the verbal duel between Elizabeth and Mary ("Wie Schiller Königinnen reden läßt" in *Schiller und die höfische Welt,* eds. Achim Aurnhammer, Klaus Manger, and Friedrich Strack [Tübingen: Max Niemeyer, 1990]) and maintains that the fundamental, psychological motive of the queens' rivalry owes to their gender ("im Geschlecht") (p. 401). At times, the rivalry is also erotic (p. 405). However, Henkel underscores the playfulness of their encounter and the formal-rhetorical devices that heighten the dramatic effect (esp. p. 404).

15. "Das ist das Fluchgeschick der Könige, / daß sie, entzweit, die Welt in Haß zerreißen, / Und jeder Zwietracht Furien entfesseln" (NA 9: 88). Unfortunately, these two central lines, as well as many other key passages, are missing from Eric Bentley's adaptation and Joseph Mellish's translation *Mary Stuart: A Tragedy. Friedrich von Schiller (1800)* (New York: Applause Theatre Book Publishers, 1959), p. 31.

16. "Mit welchem Hohn sie auf mich nieder sah, / Als sollte mich der Blick zu Boden blitzen! / Ohnmächtige! Ich führe beßre Waffen, / Sie treffen tödlich und du bist nicht mehr! *Mit raschem Schritt nach dem Tische gehend und die Feder ergreifend*" (NA 9: 129).

17. "Ein Bastard bin ich dir?—Unglückliche! / Ich bin es nur, so lang *du* lebst und atmest / . . . Sobald dem Briten keine Wahl mehr bleibt, / Bin ich im echten Ehebett geboren! *Sie unterschreibt mit einem raschen, festen Federzug, läßt dann die Feder fallen, und tritt mit einem Ausdruck des Schreckens zurück*" (NA 9: 129).

18. "—Wohltätig, heilend, nahet mir der Tod, / Der ernste Freund! Mit seinen schwarzen Flügeln / Bedeckt er meine Schmach—den Menschen adelt, / Den tiefstgesunkenen, das letzte Schicksal" (NA 9: 142).

19. As suggested by Dieter Borchmeyer in *Macht und Melancholie,* p. 88.

20. "Und beflügelt / Schwingt sich der Geist in alle Himmel auf" (NA 9: 146).

21. Thomas Diecks compared Schiller's work to dramatizations of the Mary Stuart material in seventeenth-century German literature in his article "'Schuldige Unschuld': Schillers *Maria Stuart*" in *Schiller und die höfische Welt,* pp. 233–46. He did not differentiate clearly enough, however, between Schiller's drama and August Adolph von Haugwitz's *Schuldige Unschuld Oder Maria Stuarda* (1683), which follows the model of Andreas Gryphius's martyr plays (p. 237). Among the differences he does address, Diecks says nothing about what is perhaps the major difference, namely the phenomenon of the sublime. He does see clearly, however, that the duel between Elizabeth and Mary in Schiller's writing is based largely on Elizabeth's personal resentment (p. 241).

22. "Wir fühlen uns frey bey der Schönheit, weil die sinnlichen Triebe mit dem Gesetz der Vernunft harmonieren; wir fühlen uns frey beym Erhabenen, weil die sinnlichen Triebe auf die Gesetzgebung der Vernunft keinen Einfluß haben, weil der Geist hier handelt, als ob er unter keinen andern als seinen eigenen Gesetzen stünde" (NA 21: 42).

23. "Wir ergötzen uns an dem Sinnlich-unendlichen, weil wir denken können, was die Sinne nicht mehr fassen, und der Verstand nicht mehr begreift" (NA 21: 43).

24. Jeffrey Barnouw's reflections in "The Morality of the Sublime: Kant and Schiller" (*Studies in Romanticism* 19 [1980]) complement one of my theses. He sees that "the effect of Schiller's ruminations is usually to undermine the fixed and determinate character of the conceptual oppositions he begins with, and he ends by treating feeling rather as a condition (state) or character of experience in which the opposition and even the separation of the other 'faculties' is resolved in their harmonious working" (p. 498). The American scholar makes several important distinctions between Kant and Schiller. Whereas Kant "insists on the separation and even the opposition of the sublime and the beautiful" (p. 500), for instance, Schiller's work implies the mutual "interdependence and interaction" of Kant's "disjunctive categories" (p. 500). Indeed, "In overcoming Kant's separations, Schiller in effect seeks to undermine and obviate the 'critical' philosophy" (p. 500). Barnouw's major contribution in this article lies in his exploration of the differences between Kant and Schiller with respect to "the morality of the sublime," where experience, for Schiller, is primary (p. 500f.). For Kant, "The experience of the sublime is meant to disrupt and transcend harmonious interaction at all levels" (p. 506). "Conversely, in the empirical psychology of his major 'esthetic' essay *On the Aesthetic Education of Man [the Human Being]*, Schiller never overrides or obscures the evident tensions and divisions within human experience in order to affirm its integrity. . . . But Schiller's characteristic way of working toward a grasp of the integration of functions by working—and playing—with given dualities and dualisms is apparent already in the medical dissertations, the 'Philosophy of Physiology' and 'Essay on the Connection between the Animal and Spiritual Nature of Man [the Human Being]'" (p. 507).

25. "Welche uns über die Macht der Natur erhebt und von allem körperlichen Einfluß entbindet" (NA 21: 41).

26. "Das Erhabene verschafft uns also einen Ausgang aus der sinnlichen Welt, worinn uns das Schöne gern immer gefangen halten möchte" (NA 21: 45).

27. "Nicht allmählig . . . , sondern plötzlich und durch eine Erschütterung, reißt es den selbstständigen Geist aus dem Netze los, womit die verfeinerte Sinnlichkeit ihn umstrickte, und das um so fester bindet, je durchsichtiger es gesponnen ist" (NA 21: 45). Ehrhard Bahr suggests something similar, though from a different perspective: "Schillers Geschichtsrealismus erweist sich nun darin, daß er den Durchbruch zum Erhabenen—trotz der Worte Kennedys—nicht plötzlich erfolgen läßt, wie theoretisch gefordert, sondern nur stufenweise und mit Rückfällen. Er unterläuft sozusagen die idealische Konstruktion seines Dramas" ("Geschichtsrealismus in Schillers dramatischem Werk," in *Friedrich Schiller. Angebot und Diskurs*, p. 289).

28. "So ist oft eine einzige erhabene Rührung genug, dieses Gewebe des Betrugs zu zerreissen, dem gefesselten Geist seine ganze Schnellkraft auf einmal zurückzugeben, ihm eine Revelation über seine wahre Bestimmung zu ertheilen, und ein Gefühl seiner Würde, wenigstens für den Moment aufzunöthigen" (NA 21: 45).

29. "Die Schönheit unter der Getalt der Göttinn Calypso hat den tapfern Sohn des Ulysses bezaubert, und durch die Macht ihrer Reizungen hält sie ihn lange Zeit auf ihrer Insel gefangen. Lange glaubt er einer unsterblichen Gottheit zu huldigen, da er doch nur in den Armen der Wollust liegt,—aber ein erhabener Eindruck ergreift ihn plötzlich unter Mentors Gestalt, er erinnert sich seiner bessern Bestimmung, wirft sich in die Wellen und ist frey" (NA 21: 45).

30. Among contemporary scholars, Lesley Sharpe (*Friedrich Schiller*) comes closest to recognizing a greater truth. Referring to the essay *Concerning the Pathetic [Über das Pathetische]*, she writes: "Only if the [dramatic] characters are seen to suffer can that experience be taken up into the sublime" (p. 30). This would seem

to characterize Mary Stuart's condition. A connecting link in Schiller's writings at this time is also found in the essay *Concerning Grace and Dignity* [*Über Anmuth und Würde*], where the writer maintained that dignity is required more in suffering and grace in one's demeanor, "for only in suffering can the freedom of the mind and, in action, the freedom of the body reveal themselves" [" . . . denn nur im Leiden kann sich die Freyheit des Gemüths, und nur im Handeln die Freyheit des Körpers offenbaren"] (NA 20: 297).

31. "Welche die Vernunft zwar mit ihren Ideen erfliegen, der Verstand aber mit seinen Begriffen nicht erfassen kann" (NA 21: 45).

32. "Nähert man sich nur der Geschichte mit großen Erwartungen von Licht und Erkenntniß—wie sehr findet man sich da getäuscht!" (NA 21: 49).

33. "So unbändig reißt sie [die Natur] im Reich der Freyheit den Zügel ab, woran der Spekulations-Geist sie gern gefangen führen möchte" (NA 21: 50).

34. "Wohl ihm also, wenn er gelernt hat zu ertragen, was er nicht ändern kann, und Preiß zu geben mit Würde, was er nicht retten kann!" (NA 21: 51).

35. "Das höchste Ideal, wornach wir ringen, ist, mit der physischen Welt, als der Bewahrerinn unserer Glückseligkeit, in gutem Vernehmen zu bleiben, ohne darum genöthigt zu seyn, mit der moralischen zu brechen, die unsre Würde bestimmt" (NA 21: 50).

36. "Je öfter nun der Geist diesen Akt von Selbstthätigkeit erneuert, desto mehr wird ihm derselbe zur Fertigkeit, einen desto größern Vorsprung gewinnt er vor dem sinnlichen Trieb" (NA 21: 51).

37. "Verhilft uns das furchtbar herrliche Schauspiel der alles zerstörenden und wieder erschaffenden, und wieder zerstörenden Veränderung" (NA 21: 52).

38. "So muß das Erhabene zu dem Schönen hinzukommen, um die *ästhetische Erziehung* zu einem vollständigen Ganzen zu machen, und die Empfindungsfähigkeit des menschlichen Herzens nach dem ganzen Umfang unsrer Bestimmung, und also auch über die Sinnenwelt hinaus, zu erweitern" (NA 21: 52). Jeffrey Barnouw ("The Morality of the Sublime," cited in n. 24) suggests that, unlike Kant, Schiller "treats the sublime as continuous with the beautiful (indeed it is a form of beauty)" (p. 501), but he does not address their difficult "marriage."

39. "Nur wenn das Erhabene mit dem Schönen sich gattet, und unsere Empfänglichkeit für beydes in gleichem Maaß ausgebildet worden ist, sind wir vollendete Bürger der Natur, ohne deswegen ihre Sklaven zu seyn, und ohne unser Bürgerrecht in der intelligiblen Welt zu verscherzen" (NA 21: 53).

40. Kennedy: "Selbst ihre Laute ward ihr weggenommen." Paulet: "Weil sie verbuhlte Lieder drauf gespielt" (NA 9: 5).

41. "Bey der Würde also führt sich der Geist in dem Körper als *Herrscher* auf" (NA 20: 296).

Chapter 8. The Later Poetic Writings

1. "The Gods of Greece" was completed in 1788 and extensively revised in 1800. "The Artists," also completed in 1788, was revised shortly thereafter, in 1789.

2. In her account of Schiller's poetry, Lesley Sharpe overemphasizes the impact of the Platonic tradition on Schiller's writing. Speaking of the writer's later poetry, she asserts: "Schiller was a poet whose deepest inspiration came from ideas" (*Friedrich Schiller*, p. 199). In the light of the problem of modernity explored by Schiller in the essay *Concerning Naive and Sentimental Poetry,* she gradually begins to modify her account, now stressing the tensions inhering in the writer's later poetry (pp. 200, 201, 202). There is a slight contradiction when the British scholar places Schiller "outside the tradition of *Erlebnisdichtung*" (p. 200) and then maintains:

"The personality and concerns, the aspirations and disappointments of the man [his experiences?] are there, and it is in the tension between the origin of the poem in the poet's experience and his desire to express a broader vision that we are struck by the emotional force of the poems" (p. 200). Her attempt to redefine and broaden the term "philosophical poetry" should have been accompanied by a redefinition of the term *Erlebnisdichtung*. But at that point, of course, the strict distinction between the two terms would have disappeared. I refer the reader to the salient remarks on this topic by Hans Mayer ("Skizzen zu einem Porträt," in his *Versuche über Schiller* [Frankfurt a.M.: Suhrkamp, 1987], esp. 171). In "Schillers Gedichte und die Traditionen deutscher Lyrik" (1959), Mayer had also appreciated the tensions in Schiller's poetry (see chapter 5 of *Versuche über Schiller,* pp. 130, 133, 137, 138, and 141). Unlike Mayer, I do not reduce the fact of tension in Schiller's writings to either the antithetical style of Baroque poetry or Hegelian dialectics. Instead, I explore it in what we know about the man, his writings, and the social-cultural context of the times in which he was living and writing.

3. Though conditioned by Marxist ideology, Hans-Dietrich Dahnke's thought-provoking article "Die Debatte um 'Die Götter Griechenlands'" in *Debatten und Kontroversen. Literarische Kontroversen am Ende des 18. Jahrhunderts,* eds. Hans-Dietrich Dahnke and Bernd Leistner (Berlin/Weimar: Aufbau, 1989) helps situate Schiller's poem within a specific, cultural context. Dahnke stresses the fact that the author of this poem was critical of mechanistic science, specifically the de-divination of the universe (p. 200). True to the ideological underpinnings of his investigation, however, Dahnke maintains that the writer radicalized the "anti-Christian" criticism of traditional conceptions of death and the afterlife (p. 201). He sees in the poem "der Ausdruck der inneren Zweispältigkeit und Ratlosigkeit [!] des Autors" (p. 204). He also stresses the impact of Greek mythology on the writer's work (p. 198). Dahnke's conclusion leaves much to be desired: "Im Gedicht ist einem subjektiven Befinden Sprache gegeben, das durch Disharmonie und Isolierung gekennzeichnet ist und in äußerstem Widerspruch zu grundlegenden Tatbeständen der gegenwärtigen Entwicklung steht. . . . Die tiefe Enttäuschung über die geschichtliche Entwicklung und die eigene Hilflosigkeit [!] demgegenüber schlugen sich in einem großen lyrischen Ausbruch nieder, der die unerfüllten Hoffnungen und Sehnsüchte in der Klage über einen verlorengegangen glücklicheren Lebenszustand und über die alle Befriedigung versagende Gegenwart zum Mittelpunkt macht" (p. 255). Perhaps this statement reveals more about the scholar's own situation and feelings at the end of the German Democratic Republic than it does about Schiller's experience. To that extent, Dahnke's study is, in part, "historical." Helmut Brandt, another former East German scholar of literature, maintained that the scholar's task was to draw out the possible significance of a writer's work for one's own time. Referring to the task of the Germanist today, Brandt argued: "Seine kritische Arbeit geht vonstatten inmitten heutiger Lebenskämpfe, sie ist selber ein Teil davon, und er weiß es—letztlich kann er über Schiller nur im Horizont seiner eigenen Zeit urteilen" ("Der bleibende Schiller," in *Friedrich Schiller. Angebot und Diskurs,* p. 11). I believe we should appreciate both aspects of "history," the past era that we study with the aid of the artifacts at our disposal and our general knowledge of that time from a number of different fields of inquiry as well as the developments and thinking in our own day. Both aspects of history, I would argue, need to be assessed critically.

4. This analogy is missing from the revised version of the poem (1800).

5. This strophe was deleted in the revised version.

6. The strophe was retained in the final version.

7. Klaus Berghahn, "Schillers mythologische Symbolik" in *Schiller. Vorträge aus Anlaß seines 225. Geburtstages,* eds. Dirk Grathoff and Erwin Leibfried (Frank-

furt a.M./Bern/New York/Paris: Peter Lang, 1991). Also in *Friedrich Schiller. Angebot und Diskurs*, pp. 361–81.

8. Berghahn, *Schiller: Vorträge aus Anlaß*, p. 29.

9. Ibid., p. 37.

10. Ibid., p. 43.

11. The connection between beauty and truth is indicative of the impact of the Platonic tradition not only on Schiller's writings but also on much British scholarship on Schiller. Referring to the poetry of this period (the mid-to-late 1780s), Terence J. Reed (*Schiller*) alerts us to the writer's "swings from grand assertion to negation," which calls up Schiller's apparent volatility. He notes: "Where a professional philosopher would settle for a position before making public utterance, Schiller captures the movement towards a position and between positions, confesses the tension between faith and doubt which is at least as much a reality of the intellectual life seriously lived as any stable 'philosophy' is" (p. 61). Like much traditional scholarship, Reed's position presupposes that Schiller the poet was mostly interested in ideas.

12. Reed, *Schiller*, p. 58.

13. Concerning the interdisciplinary texture of Schiller's writings, Marie-Luise Waldeck proposed that Schiller was aided in the formation of his aesthetic ideas and philosophical terminology by the concept of *Schein* (appearance) developed by J. H. Lambert in his *Neues Organon oder Gedanken über die Erforschung und Bezeichnung des Wahren und dessen Unterscheidung von Irrthum und Schein* 2 vols. (Leipzig: Wendler, 1764). Without convincing proof, however, Waldeck advances the still interesting thesis: "*Die Künstler* is a poetic formulation of the process whereby this optical concept of 'Schein' gradually acquired the aesthetic connotation which Lambert saw it potentially possessed" ("Shadows, Reflexions, Mirror-Images," *Modern Language Review* 58 [1963]: 33). She is right about the following: "This is all the more interesting because Schiller is often accused of arriving at conclusions purely by abstraction rather than by empirical observation" (p. 35). Perhaps Norbert Oellers should have taken issue with Waldeck in his contribution "Schillers 'Das Reich der Schatten' and 'Das Ideal und das Leben'—*EIN* Gedicht," in *Kulturwissenschaften. Festgabe für Wilhelm Perpeet zum 65. Geburtstag* (Bonn: Bouvier, 1980). Oeller's interpretation follows traditional scholarship when placing the poem in the Platonic tradition (versus Waldeck, who creates a modern, scientific context for the poetic writing). Waldeck's contribution is cited in *The Relations of Literature and Science: An Annotated Bibliography of Scholarship, 1880–1890*, eds. Walter Schatzberg, Ronald A. Waite and Jonathan K. Johnson (New York: Modern Language Association, 1987), p. 203; entry no. 1297. A second important study by Waldeck appeared in *Forum for Modern Language Studies* 12 (1976): 304–13.

14. David Pugh, "'Die Künstler': Schiller's philosophical programme," *Oxford German Studies* 18–19 (1989–90), p. 13.

15. Ibid., p. 15.

16. Ibid.

17. Ibid.

18. Ibid.

19. Ibid.

20. Ibid., p. 16.

21. Pugh draws a close connection here to the essay *Über Anmut und Würde*, p. 16.

22. Ibid., p. 16.

23. Ibid.

24. Ibid., p. 22.

25. Ibid.

26. It is for these reasons, as well as others, that I cannot accept the sweeping conclusion made by Arthur McCardle in his *Schiller and Swabian Pietism* that "His [Schiller's] whole life from the very beginning was a search for transcendence of earthly necessity" (p. 213).

27. For a highly informative account of the genesis of the ballad and its centrality to the friendship between Goethe and Schiller and their aspirations to realize a quality (i.e. "classical") German literature on the scale of the ancient Greeks, see Wulf Segebrecht ("Naturphänomen und Kunstidee" in *Klassik und Moderne. Die Weimarer Klassik als historisches Ereignis und Herausforderung im kulturgeschichtlichen Prozeß. Walter Müller-Seidel zum 65. Geburtstag,* eds. Karl Richter and Jörg Schönert [Stuttgart: J. B. Metzler, 1983]). Segebrecht believes that Schiller was fascinated by the theatrical-dramatic potential of the material (p. 198). On this point, Segebrecht follows the traditional conception of the writer that foregrounds the dramatist rather than the multi-talented writer. Despite Goethe's suggestion that Schiller treated the introduction of the cranes as a natural phenomenon, Segebrecht argues, Schiller concentrated on the dramatic effect. The chorus of furies, for instance, Segebrecht equates with the "moralische[n] Instanz der Bühne," as found in the essay on the stage as a moral institution, i.e., as an idea ("Idee") (p. 200). According to Segebrecht, "Die Natur [die Kraniche] ist . . . das Mittel, durch das die Kunst [der Chor] ihre Idee [die Gerechtigkeit] in das Leben hinüberträgt" (p. 202). Once again, as in traditional scholarship on Goethe and Schiller, the German scholar makes the following generalization: "Goethe und Schiller bewegen sich von polar einander entgegengesetzen [*sic*] Positionen aufeinander zu. Natur [Goethe] und Idee [Schiller], naturwissenschaftliches und idealistisches Denken, verbinden sich mit ihren zur deutschen Klassik" (p. 202). All too easily, scholarship has glided over the fact that it was Schiller who had to remind Goethe that the "Urpflanze" was merely an idea. For further elaboration of this point, see the conclusion.

28. On this general topic and the relation between dramatic art, morality and politics, see the work of Wolfgang Wittkowski.

29. Benno von Wiese, "Schillers Ballade, 'Die Kraniche des Ibykus,'" *The German Quarterly* 11 (1956): 9–23. Contrary to von Wiese, Heinz Politzer argued that the purpose of the ballad was to enchant people with the magic of terror ("Szene und Tribunal. Schillers Theater der Grausamkeit" in *Das Schweigen der Sirenen. Studien zur deutschen und österreichischen Literatur* [Stuttgart: J. B. Metzler, 1968], p. 247). Klaus Köhnke, however, emphasizes the religious effect of the poem, specifically the stage and ballad writing as a "Kanzelersatz" ("'Des Schicksals dunkler Knäul'. Zu Schillers Ballade 'Die Kraniche des Ibykus,'" *Zeitschrift für Deutsche Philologie* 108 [1989]: 481–95). Köhnke argues that the "unheard-of occurrence" of the ballad lies not in the appearance of the furies but "in der folgenreichen Verkettung der Zufälle, in 'Des Schicksals dunkle[m] Knäul'" (p. 492). From this perspective, he is able to associate the ballad with Schiller's essay on universal history (pp. 494–95), no matter how briefly.

30. *Webster's Third New International Dictionary of the English Language Unabridged,* p. 471.

31. More recent scholarship has emphasized the chain of poetry and the tension between rulership, or political dominance and literary autonomy. As noted by Wilhelm Kühlmann, "Poetische Legitimität und legitimisierte Poesie" in *Schiller und die höfische Welt,* p. 284. Kühlmann underscores the writer's dissemination of the positive traits of the Rudolf legend and the importance of conciliaton and situates the ballad in the context of late eighteenth- and early nineteenth-century reactions to the loss of Imperial rule and dynastic patriotism. Rather than emphasize the

seemingly utopian gesture of the ballad, as had Benno von Wiese ("Utopie und Geschichte," in *Geschichte im Gedicht. Texte und Interpretationen,* ed. Walter Hinck [Frankfurt a/M: Suhrkamp, 1979], pp. 87–97), Kühlmann sees in this writing "die poetische Allegorie einer aktuellen historischen Umbruchsituation, in der die Institution der Kunst zur Frage steht" (p. 294). "Der tragende Gedanke der Schillerschen Ballade, die Identität des Priesters und Sängers, besaß historischen Indiz—und Erkenntniswert" (p. 294). Problematic is Kühlmann's attempt to associate Schiller with the romantics, i.e., Friedrich Schlegel's religion of art (p. 295).

32. This aspect of Schiller's poetic writings complements the fascinating study by Peter Utz (*Das Auge und das Ohr im Text. Literarische Sinneswahrnehmung in der Goethezeit* [München: Wilhelm Fink, 1990]), who investigates the function of the eye, ear, and heart in Schiller's theory and dramatic practice. Utz suggests that Schiller not only thematized the accomplishments and deficiencies of the senses on the stage, as had Lessing, but that he turned the sensuousness of communication in drama into the "Medium einer impliziten Kritik an der zunehmenden Entfremdung, auch und gerade der Sinne" (p. 59), as he then demonstrates in the early part of his study.

33. There are quite a few differences in word choices between the original poem "Elegie") and the later "Der Spaziergang." In "Elegie," l. 12 reads: "Aber der reizende Streit löset in Wohllaut sich auf," whereas the same line in the revised version replaces the word "Wohllaut" with "Anmuth." In a letter to Wilhelm von Humboldt, Schiller noted that Voß had disallowed the use of compound nouns as trochaics in dactyls (NA 2/2A: 279). I find the substitution of "Anmuth" (from the title of the essay written near the time of the writing of "Elegie") for "Wohllaut" less convincing semantically in the light of the writer's sustained attention to musical metaphors. The earlier choice seems to fit better in this context, as well as in the light of poems such as "Das Lied von der Glocke," "Die Götter Griechenlands," and "Die Künstler," for instance, wherein Nature and history are foregrounded with the aid of various allusions to harmony and discord. From here on, I cite the later version of the "Ausgabe letzter Hand."

34. Lesley Sharpe appreciates Schiller's emphasis on "the constancy of nature, which ensures stability and the hope of renewal" (*Friedrich Schiller,* p. 202); and she observes that "This turning to the stability of nature as a source of hope sounds more like Goethe than Schiller" (p. 202). Unfortunately, she retreats when adding: "and certainly it is not an idea that occurs frequently in his poetry, for it implies a kind of identification with the external world which Schiller seems not to have felt" (p. 202). I disagree with Jochen Golz ("Individuum, Natur und Geschichte in Schillers 'Spaziergang,'" in *Friedrich Schiller. Angebot und Diskurs,* pp. 393–400), who attempts to describe the concept of Nature in this central poem. He subscribes to the traditional radical distinction between Goethe (organic Nature and development) and Schiller (idea and conflict). When taking into account Schiller's anthropology, his own study of nature, and his attention to the interrelationship between human nature and Nature, I cannot subscribe to the statement that, when compared to Goethe's understanding, Schiller's relationship to Nature is ambivalent ("stellt sich . . . als eine ambivalente Beziehung dar" [p. 398]). Among other things, the *interactionist* theory Schiller had worked out in the medical dissertations defeats Golz's pronouncement: "Für ihn [Schiller], der Natur und Geist, Leib und Seele, Sinnlichkeit und Sittlichkeit strikt voneinander abzuheben geneigt war, ist ein ganzheitlicher Naturbegriff Goethescher Prägung nicht denkbar" (p. 398). Of course not, since Goethe should not be the yardstick by which any other writer should be measured. The subject here is Schiller, not Goethe. Subscribing to the traditional (easy) dualism Goethe-Schiller and to an Hegelianized, i.e., post-Schillerian concept of the writer,

Golz follows, in part, Jürgen Stenzel ("Zum Erhabenen tauglich. Ein Spaziergang durch Schillers 'Elegie,'" *Jahrbuch der Deutschen Schillergesellschaft* 19 [1975]:167–191). Needless to say, the poem "Elegie" is not "Der Spaziergang." Günter Mieth offers a necessary corrective to Golz's remarks in the very next essay in the same volume ("Friedrich Schillers 'Spaziergang' und die lyrische Aneignung der menschlichen Gattungsgeschichte. Ein Diskussionsbeitrag," in *Friedrich Schiller. Angebot und Diskurs,* pp. 401–9). One of Mieth's most significant points is "Angeeignet wird Geschichte durch den 'Spaziergang' in der Harmonie von 'Gedankeneinheit' und 'Empfindungseinheit,'" with the caveat that it is a tension-filled harmony. Mieth also sees clearly that Schiller's poem was also an original contribution to the history of German lyric poetry. For "Inhaltiche, geschichtsphilosophische und formale, poetische Elemente fanden zu einer neuen Einheit" (p. 408). However, he too fails to account for the impact of Schiller's anthropology. The most thorough treatment thus far is Wolfgang Riedel's *"Der Spaziergang."*

35. In his fascinating examination of the poem, the historian Friedrich Meinecke discerned that the ending disclosed "die ungeheure Tragik der Geschichte" ("Schillers 'Spaziergang,'" in *Deutsche Lyrik von Weckherlin bis Benn,* ed. Jost Schillemeit [Frankfurt a.M.: Fischer, 1965], pp. 99–112), but that the writer was searching for a bridge, "um den klaffenden Hiatus zwischen Geschichte und Natur unmittelbar zu überwinden" (p. 109).

36. It is important to note the following significant change in Schiller's writing. Ll. 27–28 of the first edition read: "Und der Wohllaut der großen Natur umrauscht dich vergebens? / Dich ergreift nicht der Strom dieser harmonischen Welt?" The revised version, however, reads: "Und dir rauschen umsonst die Harmonieen des Weltalls, / Dich ergreift nicht der Strom dieses erhabnen Gesangs" (NA 2: 299). Whatever may be said about the change, it is clear that, for the writer, harmony, music and Nature are all interrelated.

37. In her insightful study "Some Word-Associations in the Writings of Hamann and Herder" in *German Studies,* Edna Purdie examined the use and etymology of terms like "Knäul" in late eighteenth-century writings. She noted that, in the writings of both Hamann and Herder, the word *Knäuel* was not used as a figure of disorder, as in the mid-twentieth century, but in the sense of unwinding in order to provide a guiding thread. However, even in the late eighteenth century, she finds, "the attempt to wind, if unsuccessful, involves entanglement; a careless unwinding of the ball creates complete confusion" (p. 155). Though the British scholar did not say so, this point provides further evidence of the Enlightenment tradition in the theories of the so-called Storm and Stress. We see that Schiller used the terms "Knoten" (and not only in the theatrical sense) and "Knäul" in a similar way. However, his writings pay attention to the problem of severing cords and strings of every kind. Hence, for Friedrich Schiller, the possibility of rupture is always immanent.

38. Traditional accounts of the poem tend to posit a dualism or antithetical structure rather than examine the implications of tension, e.g., Edgar Lohner, *Schiller und die moderne Lyrik* (Göttingen: Vandenhoeck und Ruprecht, 1964), p. 23; though Lohner did not mention the interconnection between this poem, the first medical dissertation or the later essay *Über den Gebrauch des Chors in der Tragödie* (1803). He was followed, albeit uncritically, by Ronald L. Crawford, *Images of Transience in the Poems and Ballads of Friedrich Schiller* (Berne/Frankfurt a.M./Las Vegas: Peter Lang, 1977), p. 48. Because both scholars stress Schiller's (alleged) unconditional idealism, they overlook the phenomenon of harmonious tension.

39. The discrepancy in line numbers is due to the fact that strophe 2 of the first version "Das Reich der Schatten" was deleted.

40. For this reason, I cannot subscribe to Lesley Sharpe's point that, with this

poem, "the ideal in the moral sphere as in the artistic is an effortless harmony that leaves behind all human inadequacies" (*Friedrich Schiller*, p. 208). It is likely that the idea of tranquil harmony was carried over from the Platonic tradition with its emphasis on ideal, stationary forms.

41. In Wilhelm von Humboldt's opinion, Schiller had juxtaposed the realms of the real and the ideal (NA 2/2A: 248).

42. In "Das Ideal und das Leben," the second line of this strophe reads: "Wenn dort Priams Sohn der Schlangen" (NA 2: 399). Otherwise, the strophe reads the same.

43. Schiller actually took the last four lines of the original third strophe for inclusion here and then struck the third strophe altogether. In doing so, the 1800 version intensifies the crisis of idealism.

Chapter 9. *William Tell*, or Natural Justice

1. A well-traveled avenue in the interpretation of Schiller's last completed play is the investigation of the idyll and the idyllic. E.g., Horst Rüdiger, "Schiller und das Pastorale," *Euphorion* 53 (1959): 229–51, Gert Sautermeister, *Idyllik und Dramatik im Werk Friedrich Schillers: Zum geschichtlichen Ort seiner klassischen Dramen* (Stuttgart/Berlin/Köln/mainz: Kohlhammer, 1971), and Gerhard Kaiser, "Idylle und Revolution. Schillers 'Wilhelm Tell'" in *Deutsche Literatur und Französische Revolution. Sieben Studien*, ed. Richard Brinkmann (Göttingen: Vandenhoeck und Ruprecht, 1974). Kaiser argues that, after saving the idyll, Tell returns to the same domestic circle ("das Innere des Hauses" [p. 89]). He defines idyll as forms of Nature, perceiving "daß der Mensch gut ist in dem Maße seiner Naturnähe" (p. 90), by drawing upon Ovid's *Amor*. III, Eleg. 9, l. 60 which, in German, reads: "Die Idylle ist Paradies, der Unschuld Land." "Herrschaft" is defined very loosely as "Naturform in der Gestalt patriarchalischer Beziehungen" (p. 90). But, in the final analysis, Kaiser believes (as does traditional scholarship) that Nature, for Schiller, is "eine Idee des Menschen" (p. 116), thereby robbing the concept of its substance. Indeed, too often in scholarship, the terms idyll and idyllic are made synonymous with "nature." In actuality, Schiller used the term "idyll" in a broader sense than was customary even in his own day, namely as a form of representation and a part of sentimental (and elegiac) poetry. In *Concerning Naive and Sentimental Poetry*, he made the term synonymous with unspoiled Nature or the fulfilled ideal and juxtaposed "die Natur der Kunst" to "das Ideal der Wirklichkeit" (see the footnote to NA 20: 449). The fact that Schiller never undertook a journey to Switzerland might seem to lend itself to the idea that the writer created an idealized past (Sharpe follows this school of thought here [*Friedrich Schiller*, p. 305]). But this does not preclude the possibility of the relative naturalness and beauty of the setting, as is indeed typical of Swiss landscape today. Indeed, Hermann Fähnrich has noted that Schiller's knowledge of Switzerland and the Swiss was based on a thorough study of many sources including Scheuchzer's *Naturgeschichte der Schweizer Landes* (1746) and that the writer paid special attention to "das landschaftliche Kolorit" (*Schillers Musikalität*, pp. 179–80). Concerning Schiller's theory of the idyll, Norbert Oellers comes to the sobering conclusion: "zeitig sah er ein, daß sich sein Ideal von Dichtung nicht werde realisieren lassen. Dennoch bestimmte seine Idyllen-Auffassung nachhaltig die poetische Produktion seines letzten Lebensjahrzehnts . . . er änderte seine Weltanschauung, aber weder verlor er das Ideal noch *das pädagogische Ziel seiner Kunstbemühungen* aus den Augen" ("Idylle und Politik" in *Friedrich Schiller. Kunst, Humanität und Politik*, p. 125).

2. NA 10: 131. Translations are from Sidney E. Kaplan, *Schiller: William Tell.* Hereafter: K, in the main body of the text.

3. Hermann Fähnrich, *Schillers Musikalität,* p. 180. It is important to note that in this writing external Nature and human nature are mutually cooperative. But the nature of that cooperation, while harmonious, is also one of tension.

4. Quoting Friedrich Burschell, *Schiller* (Reinbek bei Hamburg: Rowohlt, 1968): "Die Oper stimmt durch die Macht der Musik und durch eine freiere harmonische Reizung der Sinnlichkeit das Gemüt zu einer schöneren Empfängnis; hier ist wirklich auch im Pathos selbst ein freieres Spiel, weil die Musik es begleitet, und das Wunderbare, welches hier einmal geduldet wird, müßte notwendig gegen den Stoff gleichgültiger machen" (p. 494).

5. "Durch den Riß nur der Wolken / Erblickt er die Welt" (NA 10: 132).

6. "*Man hört ein dumpfes Krachen von den Bergen, Schatten von Wolken laufen über die Gegend*" (NA 10: 132).

7. Despite attempts to suppress the fact, the call for divine justice is deeply embedded in German history. It is found, for instance, at the time of the Peasant Revolt in the Anabaptist call for the institution of God's Kingdom on earth. See my book *Between Luther and Münzer,* p. 28f.

8. "Das Haus der Freiheit hat uns Gott gegründet" (NA 10: 149).

9. "Ein jeder zählt nur sicher auf sich selbst" (NA 10: 151).

10. See Hans Günther Thalheim, "Notwendigkeit und Rechtlichkeit der Selbsthilfe in Schillers *Wilhelm Tell,*" *Goethe* 73 (1956): 216–57, and Gert Ueding ("Wilhelm Tell," in *Schillers Dramen. Neue Interpretationen,* ed. Walter Hinderer [Stuttgart: Reclam, 1979], pp. 271–93) concerning the political, i.e., revolutionary ramifications of self-development.

11. Dieter Borchmeyer, in one of the finest contributions to our understanding of the play to date, draws important distinctions between the democratic principle of the sovereignty of the people, the events of the French Revolution, and the action in *Wilhelm Tell* ("*Altes Recht* und Revolution—Schillers 'Wilhelm Tell,'" in *Friedrich Schiller. Kunst, Humanität und Politik,* pp. 69–111). The basic tension stems from the claims of the Swiss to the ancient right of direct accountability to the Emperor over and against any other form of government such as princely domination (or even interference by the Church). Borchmeyer notes: "Schillers politisches Ideal ist der Vernunftstaat im Sinne des aufgeklärten Naturrechts der Revolutionsperiode, der nicht positiv an Hergebrachtes und Bestehendes anknüpft, sondern aus der Auflösung der alten Rechtsbestände hervorgeht (welche lediglich für eine Übergangszeit als notwendiges Übel toleriert werden)" (p. 88). Struck by Gerhard Kaiser's thesis concerning the idyll and revolution, Borchmeyer is led to the idea that the "idyll" of the opening scene "führt uns nicht hinter die Geschichte zurück, sondern in sie hinein" (p. 96). Gerhard Kaiser's important point ("Idylle und Revolution" cited in n. 1) that the events in the Rütli-scene usher in the eventual disintegration of the paternal order ("Vaterordnung") through a new fraternal order ("Bruderordnung") also means the complete reversal of the (political) structure of *The Robbers.* For in that early dramatic writing, the unbridgeable gap between Franz and Karl Moor precludes the possibility of a fraternal order. Indeed, Karl's desire to return home indicates the disintegration of the fraternal relationship between Karl and the robbers. However, the fact that father Moor is sickly and finally dies (as well as that of Schiller's own departure from Stuttgart and the Duke Carl Eugen) suggests that a new order might replace the old, paternal one. Drawing upon Peter Horst Neumann's fine collection of essays on Lessing and the tragic conflict of *Unmündigkeit* (*Der Preis der Mündigkeit: Über Lessings Dramen* [Stuttgart: Klett-Cotta, 1977]), Dieter Borchmeyer sees that Enlightenment ("Aufklärung") also means "die Entwicklung

eines neuen Verhältnisses zur Vater-Rolle" (p. 104). This point actually places Schiller into closer alignment with the German Enlightenment. More important, Borchmeyer draws out a connecting link between Schiller's early dramatic writings. "In diesem Konflikt zwischen zivilrechtlicher väterlicher potestas und dem naturrechtlichen Ideal des gütigen auctors werden Karl Moor, Ferdinand von Walter und Don Carlos aufgerieben" (p. 104). The loss of the father is also typical of Max Piccolomini, as Borchmeyer notes in n. 92, p. 105. From this perspective, Schiller's play does not advocate a return to an original state of nature à la Rousseau but, rather, a new order of the future based on truly democratic principles. See also Robert L. Jamison, "Politics and Nature in Schiller's *Fiesco* and *Wilhelm Tell*," in *Friedrich Schiller. Kunst, Humanität und Politik,* pp. 59–66 and the ensuing discussion (pp. 66–68). Jamison makes the insightful observation that "The reality of 'Tell' is a moral one with the moral positions implying political principles: virtue means the defense of legitimacy, and tyranny, the violation of tradition: political, moral and familial" (p. 62). Unlike Jamison, however, I do not see where, between 1783 and 1805, "politics has been displaced by nature" in Schiller's writings (p. 63). Surely, the act of Nature Tell represents has significant political ramifications. Jeffrey L. Sammons ("The Apple-Shot and the Politics of *Wilhelm Tell*," in *Friedrich von Schiller and the Drama of Human Existence,* pp. 81–88), in the spirit of Ludwig Börne, bemoans Schiller's "counterrevolutionary drama of revolution" (p. 84): "it seems to me that Schiller is an outstanding example of the unwisdom of welding a literary artist to the larger political aspirations and ideological preoccupations of society" (p. 85). The point is, however, that Schiller was not simply a literary artist. He was a writer with far wider interests than the writing of poetry. In this dramatic writing, it would seem that Nature, as embodied in Tell, carries out its own justice, one that has political ramifications.

12. "Wozu lernten wir / Die Armbrust spannen und die schwere Wucht / Der Streitaxt schwingen?" (NA 10: 160).

13. "Die Gemse reißt den Jäger in den Abgrund- / Der Pflugstier selbst, der sanfte Hausgenoß / Des Menschen, der die ungeheure Kraft / Des Halses duldsam unters Joch gebogen, / Springt auf, gereizt, wezt ein gewaltig Horn / Und schleudert seinen Feind den Wolken zu" (NA 10: 160).

14. "Du sollst ihn *hören* . . . / Zu deinem Ohr die Freudenkunde tragen" (NA 10: 164).

15. "Nichts als den Kuhreih'n und der Heerdeglocken / Einförmiges Geläut vernehm ich hier" (NA 10: 168).

16. Heinrich Mettler (*Entfremdung und Revolution: Brennpunkt des Klassischen*) sees that, unlike Kant's positive reception of the French Revolution, Schiller believed that the disruption in the world order was to be overcome through "die Revolution der 'ästhetischen Erziehung'" (p. 66), a process that necessarily involves the reader. According to Mettler, one means of advocating this type of "revolution" was through the metaphor of the clockwork. "Eine solche sowohl die Idee der Aufklärung als auch die realen politischen und sozialen Verhältnisse betreffende Revolution bringt Schiller mit der Metapher der Uhr zur Sprache" (p. 65).

17. I suggest that one of the central means to transform the reader or audience in Schiller's writings was through the creative repetition of central meaningful metaphors such as the stringed instrument.

18. Fritz Martini ("Wilhelm Tell, der ästhetische Staat und der ästhetische Mensch," *Der Deutschunterricht. Beiträge zu seiner Praxis und wissenschaftliche Grundlegung* 12 [1960]: 90–118) stressed the inner connection between the philosophical letters on aesthetic education and the poetic-dramatic work. However, rather than allow for possible differences, Martini made the drama answer to the

theory. For only by conceiving of Tell as "die eigene, in sich in ihrer autonomen Menschlichkeit bedeutungsvolle Mitte des Dramas," i.e., the autonomous province of the poetic-human, Martini argues, can the drama satisfy the aesthetic requirements that the "classical" Schiller had been used to expecting (p. 94). Martini's overeagerness to determine the (classical) form of the drama caused him to seriously undermine the social-political contours of the dramatic writing. The state, for him, is simply the aesthetic state, i.e., a work of art. "Dieser Staat der Freiheit ist der ästhetische Staat" (p. 99). As I had hoped to demonstrate in chapter 5, the aesthetic state, *following* the "Ausbildung des Empfindungsvermögens" (Letter 8) via aesthetics, the cultivated human being and the "merely" rational human being are to be fused more completely in the truly moral-rational state. For Martini, the representation of the Swiss in Schiller's drama simply projects an "Idealbild der politischen Volksgemeinschaft" (p. 99).

19. As noted also by Martini ("Wilhelm Tell") and Sharpe (*Friedrich Schiller*).

20. Marie-Luise Waldeck (*The Theme of Freedom in Schiller's Plays* [Stuttgart: Hans-Dieter Heinz Akademischer Verlag, 1986]) has observed: "Tell is a man who is truly harmonious and at one with himself, a man possessing true inner freedom" (p. 83).

21. "Die Welt gehört ihm, wollen wir allein / Die Länderkette ihm zu unterbrechen, / Die er gewaltig rings um uns gezogen?" (NA 10: 169).

22. "Von seinen Ländern wie mit einem Netz / Sind wir umgarnet rings und eingeschlossen" (NA 10: 169).

23. "Lern dieses Volk der Hirten kennen, Knabe! . . . / Sie sollen kommen, uns ein Joch aufzwingen, / Das wir entschlossen sind, *nicht* zu ertragen! /—O lerne fühlen, welches Stamms du bist!" (NA 10: 170).

24. "Die angebohrnen Bande knüpfe fest, / Ans Vaterland, ans theure, schließ dich an, / Das halte fest mit deinem ganzen Herzen" (NA 10: 170).

25. "Der fremde Zauber reißt die Jugend fort, / Gewaltsam strebend über unsre Berge. / —O unglückselge Stunde, da das Fremde, / In diese still beglückten Thäler kam, / Der Sitten frommen Unschuld zu zerstören" (NA 10: 171).

26. "Und glühend Rachgefühl hab ich gesogen, / Aus der erloschenen Sonne seines Blicks" (NA 10: 174).

27. "Doch Gott / Ist überall, wo man das Recht verwaltet, / Und unter seinem Himmel stehen wir" (NA 10: 179).

28. "Sind auch die alten Bücher nicht zur Hand, / Sie sind in unsre Herzen eingeschrieben" (NA 10: 179).

29. Hermann Fähnrich notes that the instrumental music reaches its first crescendo in this Rütli-scene (act 2, scene 1) (*Schillers Musikalität*, p. 180).

30. In his book *Tragödie und Öffentlichkeit—Schillers Dramaturgie*, Dieter Borchmeyer had determined that Tell's act is not reactionary. Referring to the function of ancient right in this play, he observes: "aber nicht in dem Sinne, daß der alte, durch die Neuerungstendenzen der Krone gestörte Zustand einfach erhalten bleibt; vielmehr erscheint die alte Freiheit am Ende des Dramas in einem neuen Zustand 'aufgehoben,' der eine höhere Stufe der politischen Entwicklung und menschlichen Entfaltung darstellt" (p. 184). The play portrays the formation of a "Gemeinwesen, das die alte (feudal-heroische) Freiheit in einer neuen (republikanischen) Freiheit aufgehen läßt und die Grundsätze moderner Staatlichkeit zu verwirklichen trachtet" (p. 185). In this earlier work, however, Borchmeyer ties Schiller's Tell much too closely to Hegel's concept of heroism (p. 180).

31. "Wir sind *ein* Volk, und einig wollen wir handeln" (NA 10: 182).

32. Fähnrich maintains that the instrumental music is not a splendid conclusion

to the scene, as it would have been in opera. Rather, it functions to introduce, or at least symbolize, the future freedom of the Swiss (*Schillers Musikalität*, p. 181).

33. Dieter Borchmeyer maintains that this is a powerful sign of "die naturhafte Bindung der politischen Ordnung" (*Tragödie und Öffentlichkeit*, p. 186).

34. As noted by Fähnrich (*Schillers Musikalität*, p. 181). "Mit dem Pfeil, dem Bogen / Durch Gebirg und Tal / Kommt der Schütz gezogen / Früh am Morgenstrahl" (NA 10: 193).

35. "Mir fehlt der Arm, wenn mir die Waffe fehlt" (NA 10: 196).

36. "Ihr seids, der mich verletzt und kränkt, ich muß / Mein Merz bezwingen, daß ich euch nicht hasse" (NA 10: 200).

37. "Euch haben sie das Netz ums Haupt geworfen" (NA 10: 200).

38. "Dort harren mein verhaßter Ehe Ketten, / Die Liebe nur—die Eure kann mich retten!" (NA 10: 202).

39. "Dann mögen dies Felsen um uns her / Die undurchdringlich feste Mauer breiten, / Und dies verschloßne sel'ge Thal allein / Zum Himmel offen und gelichtet seyn!" (NA 10: 202).

40. "Kämpfe / Fürs Vaterland, du kämpfst für deine Liebe! / Es ist *ein* Feind, vor dem wir alle zittern, / Und *eine* Freiheit macht uns alle frei!" (NA 10: 204).

41. "Unmenschlich ists, / Mit eines Vaters Angst also zu spielen" (NA 10: 214).

42. "Du kannst ja alles, Tell, an nichts verzagst du, / Das Steuerruder führst du wie den Bogen, / Dich schreckt kein Sturm, wenn es zu retten gilt, / Jetzt, Retter hilf dir selbst—du rettest alle!" (NA 10: 217).

43. "Zu weit getrieben / Verfehlt die Strenge ihres weisen Zwecks, / Und allzus-traff gespannt zerspringt der Bogen" (NA 10: 21).

44. "So bin ich hier, gerettet aus des Sturms / Gewalt und aus der schlimmeren der Menschen" (NA 10: 230).

45. "Ich seh den Knaben ewig / Gebunden stehn, den Vater auf ihn zielen, / Und ewig fliegt der Pfeil mir in das Herz" (NA 10: 234).

46. "Das Alte stürzt, es ändert sich die Zeit, / Und neues Leben blüht aus den Ruinen" (NA 10: 238).

47. "Zerrissen / Hab ich auf ewig alle fremden Bande, / Zurückgegeben bin ich meinem Volk. / Ein Schweizer bin ich und ich will es sein— / Von ganzer Seele" (NA 20: 239–40).

48. "Unter den Trümmern der Tyrannenmacht / Allein kann sie hervorgegraben werden. / Die Festen alle müssen wir bezwingen, / Ob wir vielleicht in ihren Kerker dringen" (NA 10: 242).

49. Matthijs Jolles once observed: "In 'Wilhelm Tell' gleicht die Volksstimme einer reichen orchestrierten Symphonie, voller Einzelthemen und Melodien" ("'Am Abgrund geht der Weg': Wilhelm Tell" in his *Dichtkunst und Lebenskunst: Studien zum Problem der Sprache bei Friedrich Schiller*, ed. Arthur Groos mit einem Nachwort von Elizabeth M. Wilkinson [Bonn: Bouvier, 1980], p. 294).

50. Perhaps it does not really occur to Tell "to set himself up as God's chosen instrument of vengeance," as Marie-Luise Waldeck maintains in *The Theme of Freedom in Schiller's Plays*, p. 81). But this does not preclude him from becoming that instrument to both the Swiss and the audience/reader. In this play, as the human being and Nature are intricately intermeshed, so also are Nature and God.

51. "Euch [Kinder] zu vertheidigen, eure holde Unschuld / Zu schützen vor der Rache des Tyrannen, / Will er zum Morde jetzt den Bogen spannen" (NA 10: 245).

52. "Und du / Vertraute Bogensehen, die so oft / Mir treu gedient hat in der Freude Spielen, / Verlaß mich nicht im fürchterlichen Ernst" (NA 10: 244–45). Fritz Martini had traced Tell's sense of inner freedom back to "d[em] Rein-Menschliche[n] . . . , d[er] Selbstbehauptung des Geistes" ("Wilhelm Tell," cited in n. 18, p. 112),

i.e., an intellectual or spiritual construct of freedom. Marie-Luise Waldeck also stresses Tell's "inner freedom" (*The Theme of Freedom*, p. 83), which she attributes to the harmony within himself. I have tried to show that there is a tense harmony between the human being and Nature, as represented by the crossbow, the stringed instrument of justice.

53. For Fritz Martini, Tell is an aesthetic being whose action grows "wie im 'Spiel' . . . aus der Einheit seiner eigenen, erfüllten, zur Totalität geweiteten Persönlichkeit" (p. 103), a position that is not supported by the passage just cited. Marie-Luise Waldeck, who also notes that Tell addresses his bow in this passage, seriously underestimates the representational value of the bow: "Up to this moment bow and arrow have served Tell purely in the pursuit of 'Spiel,' that is, purely as recreation and for no practical purpose of any kind" (p. 84)! We recall that S. S. Kerry had also undershot the representational value of the musical instrument in his assessment of Schiller's *Kallias* Letters (see chapter 5).

54. "Reißt ihre Kinder zu Boden und wirft sich mit ihnen ihm in den Weg" (NA 10: 252).

55. "*Man hört die vorige Musik wieder auf der Höhe des Wegs, aber gedämpft*" (NA 10: 252).

56. "Den kecken Geist der Freiheit will ich beugen. / Ein neu Gesetz will ich in diesen Landen / Verkündigen—Ich will— / *ein Pfeil durchbohrt ihn*" (NA 10: 252).

57. "*Die ganze Hochzeitgesellschaft umsteht den Sterbenden mit einem fühllosen Grausen*" (NA 10: 254).

58. "Der Tyrann / Des Landes ist gefallen. Wir erdulden / Keine Gewalt mehr. / Wir sind freie Menschen" (NA 10: 255). In the subchapter on nemesis in his book *Schillers "Wallenstein"* (München: Wilhelm Fink, 1976), Alfons Glück defined the word as "ein rächendes Schicksal, eine 'zürnende Gerechtigkeit'" (p. 133); and: "Sie stellt die durch Schuld gestörte *Ordnung* wieder her" (p. 134). Like Wolfgang Wittkowski later ("Theodizee oder Nemesistragödie?" *Jahrbuch des Freien Deutschen Hochstifts* [1980]: 177–237), Glück sees nemesis at work in history. In his study *Nature's Hidden Terror: Violent Nature Imagery in Eighteenth-Century Germany* (Columbia, South Carolina: Camden House, 1991), Robert H. Brown ascribes what he terms "The Nemesis of Violent Nature" to Schiller's *Robbers* (p. 125f.). Brown is careful not to anthropomorphize Nature "by projecting human conflicts onto nature" (p. 131). However, he overlooks Schiller's second medical dissertation. I will return to a discussion of this early writing and the topic of nemesis in Nature (or, natural justice) in the conclusion to this study. On a final note, perhaps Clemens Heselhaus's discussion of nemesis ("Die Nemesis-Tragödie. Fiesco-Wallenstein-Demetrius," *Der Deutschunterricht* [1952]: 40–59) would have been more successful had he addressed *William Tell*. See the critique by Alfons Glück, *Schillers "Wallenstein,"* p. 139.

59. "Rasch tritt der Tod den Menschen an, / Es ist ihm keine Frist gegeben, / Es stürzt ihn mitten in der Bahn, / Es reißt ihn fort vom vollen Leben, / Bereitet oder nicht, zu gehen, / Er muß vor seinen Richter stehen!" (NA 10: 255).

60. Waldeck, *The Theme of Freedom*, p. 82.

61. Fähnrich observes that the ringing of bells serves a number of functions. They announce the campaign for freedom, indicate fear and looming danger, death, and eventual freedom (*Schillers Musikalität*, p. 181).

62. There seems to be a parallel in dramatic action between Schiller's *Tell* and Lessing's *Nathan der Weise* to the extent that Recha, a Christian, is rescued from the fire by the Templar. In reality, they are supposed to be religious enemies. In Schiller's play, the supposed enemies are political.

63. "(*Eilen mit Trümmern des Gerüstes über die Scene.*) Freiheit! Freiheit! (*Das Horn von Uri wird mit Macht geblasen*)" (NA 10: 260).

64. "(*Die Landleute, Männer, Weiber und Kinder stehen und sitzen auf den Balken des zerbrochenen Gerüstes malerisch gruppiert in einem großen Halbkreis umher*)" (NA 10: 260).

65. "An heilger Stätte ist sie aufbewahrt, / Sie wird hinfort zu keiner Jagd mehr dienen" (NA 10: 270).

66. Though concerning himself primarily with the political dimension of the play, Dieter Borchmeyer observes: "Dieser Mord [Parricidas] hat nichts gemeinsam mit der Tat Tells, sondern gehört in die Reihe der Naturfrevel, deren sich die Vögte schuldig gemacht haben" ("*Altes Recht* und Revolution," cited in n. 11, p. 99).

67. "So kommt Ihr auf die *Brücke,* welche *stäubet.* / Wenn sie nicht einbricht unter eurer Schuld, / Wenn ihr sie glücklich hinter euch gelassen, / So reißt ein schwarzes *Felsentor* sich auf, / Kein Tag hats noch erhellt—da geht ihr durch, / Es führt euch in ein heitres *Thal* der Freude— / Doch schnellen Schritts müßt ihr vorüber eilen / ihr dürft nicht weilen, wo die Ruhe wohnt" (NA 10: 275).

68. Sharpe sums up one of the main points of the major secondary literature here: "These [Rudenz's] words are the fulfillment of the development of Swiss society away from the old feudal structure towards an association of free individuals" (*Friedrich Schiller,* p. 305).

69. "*Indem die Musik von neuem rasch einfällt, fällt der Vorhang*" (NA 10: 277).

70. Sharpe: "In killing Geßler he [Tell] acts for the people, not as a political man, but as a moral one in a representative act of liberation" (*Friedrich Schiller,* p. 306).

71. Borchmeyer's observation—"'Wilhelm Tell' ist das einzige 'historische' Drama Schillers, das ein politisches Ideal ungetrübt Wirklichkeit werden läßt" ("*Altes Recht* und Revolution," cited in n. 11, p. 108)—also means that the poetic-dramatic writing may serve as a culmination point rather than as an exception to his writings. The same holds for Waldeck's insight that *Wilhelm Tell* is Schiller's only play "which does not end with the necessary expiation for wrong done and the death of one or more protagonists" (*The Theme of Freedom,* p. 83).

Conclusion

1. For a judicious account of Schillers' most serious physical attacks in 1791 and 1804, see H. H. Jansen, "Schillers Krankheit und Tod aus pathologisch-anatomischer und klinischer Sicht," *Der Pathologe* 9 (1988): 187–91. Jansen's studies confirm that Schiller contracted a severe fever during a concert in Erfurt on January 3, 1791, and again on the 12th of the month while back in Jena. Following another eight days of fever, Schiller was only able to hobble around with the aid of a cane. A severe asthma attack occurred during the beginning of May in the same year. The abdominal cramps accompanying this attack remained with Schiller throughout the rest of his life. On July 24, 1804, while on a walking tour of the Dornburger Valley, the man was stricken by an almost fatal colic attack. Though he suffered some closure of the intestines, from which he never recuperated, the immediate cause of death on May 9, 1805, according to Jansen, was the pneumonia in his left [and only remaining] lung (p. 191). It is particularly interesting that the clinician should cite Thomas Mann's reference to the "zarten Instrument seines [Schiller's] Körpers" in the short story "Schwere Stunde" ["Difficult Hour"] (1905) (Jansen, p. 190).

2. Norbert Oellers, "Idylle und Politik. Französische Revolution, ästhetische Erziehung und die Freiheit der Urkantone," in *Friedrich Schiller. Kunst, Humanität und Politik,* p. 119.

3. Ibid.

4. Stephen W. Melville, *Philosophy Beside Itself: On Deconstruction and Modernism*, foreword Donald Marshall (Minneapolis: University of Minnesota Press, 1986), p. 16.

5. Ibid.

6. Sammons, "The Apple-Shot and the Politics of *Wilhelm Tell*," cited in chapter 9, n. 11, p. 83.

7. Though I am sympathetic to Robert H. Brown's view of the nemesis of Nature in this respect, I am not convinced that the violence of Nature "threatens the whole ethical order by replacing what the author calls truth with changing social realities" (*Nature's Hidden Terror*, p. 136).

8. Jeffrey L. Sammons, "The Apple-Shot and the Politics of *Wilhelm Tell*," p. 86. NA 22: 172.

9. By Hans Schavernoch, *Die Harmonie der Sphären. Die Geschichte der Idee des Welteinklangs und der Seelenstimmung* (Freiburg/Munchen: Karl Alber, 1981), pp. 32 and 31, respectively.

10. Ibid., p. 34.

11. Ibid., p. 36.

12. Ibid., p. 31.

13. Ibid., p. 36.

14. Ibid.

15. According to my notes of our lengthy discussion at the Ludwigsburg Castle on February 24, 1991. According to the Brockhaus Encyclopedia, both Plato and Johannes Kepler believed that the harmony of the spheres was discernible only by the spiritual "ear" (*Brockhaus Enzyklopädie in zwanzig Bänden* [Wiesbaden: Brockhaus, 1972], p. 720). For short overviews of the work of Pythagoras and Kepler, see *Große Naturwissenschaftler. Biographisches Lexikon. Mit einer Bibliographie zur Geschichte der Naturwissenschaften*, ed. Fritz Krafft. 2. rev. ed. (Düsseldorf: Verlag des Vereins Deutscher Ingenieure, 1986), pp. 285–87 and 198–201, respectively. In addition to Schavernoch's study, another helpful source is Hermann Köhler, "Musik bei Platon und den Pythagoreern," in *Propyläen Geschichte der Literatur*, vol. 1, *Die Welt der Antike* (Berlin: Propyläen Verlag, 1981), pp. 275–88.

16. Schavernoch, *Die Harmonie der Sphären*, p. 31.

17. Ibid., p. 39.

18. Ibid., p. 40.

19. Ibid., p. 175. Schavernoch's discussion of Schiller, however, is extremely short.

20. [Johann Friedrich Schink]. *Schillers Todtenfeyer. Gehalten auf dem hamburgischen deutschen Theater am 7tn Junii 1805* (Hamburg: Gedruckt bey Friedrich Hermann Nestler, 1805), p. 4.

21. "Wir erblicken *in ihnen* also ewig das, was uns abgeht, aber wornach wir aufgefodert sind zu ringen, und dem wir uns, wenn wir es gleich niemals erreichen, doch in einem unendlichen Fortschritte zu nähern hoffen dürfen" (NA 20: 415).

22. Klaus Berghahn, "Schiller und die Tradition," in *Friedrich Schiller zur Geschichtlichkeit seines Werkes*, p. 15.

23. Quoted by Friedrich Burschell, *Schiller*, pp. 357–58. See also *Friedrich Schiller und die Naturforschende Gesellschaft*, ed. Irmgard Kratzsch (Jena: Universitätsbibliothek der Friedrich-Schiller-Universität, 1984), and Walter Müller-Seidel, "Naturforschung und deutsche Klassik. Die Jenaer Gespräche im Juli 1794," in *Untersuchungen zur Literatur als Geschichte. Festschrift für Benno von Wiese*, eds. Vincent J. Günther, Helmut Koopmann, Peter Pütz, Hans Joachim Schrimpf (Berlin: Erich Schmidt, 1973).

24. Münchner Ausgabe 10: 919.

Appendix: Conversations with Hans-Georg Gadamer and Jürgen Habermas: A Chapter on the Reception of Friedrich Schiller in the Twentieth Century

1. Because he was still busy dictating letters, I waited for Gadamer about a quarter of an hour. After he had directed me to his office, I perused the many books on the shelves and the journals that were scattered over several end tables. Many of the books were signed copies by authors who knew the man personally and had sent him a token of their appreciation. Several volumes still had markers in them. Many unopened letters and packages lay on the desk. Gadamer entered his office at 1:45 p.m. He told me that his back was causing him problems and that his eyes prohibit him from doing much reading. Once he seated himself and began to converse, however, all conscious awareness of his physical problems dissipated instantly. Nothing seemed to hinder his ability to dialogue. He was remarkably fluent in his speech and a very good listener. Perhaps it is this, as much as his quick intellect, that makes Gadamer such a good conversationalist.

2. Ernst Cassirer, *Freiheit und Form. Studien zur deutschen Geistesgeschichte* 4 (Berlin: Bruno Cassirer, 1922). Hereafter: *FF.*

3. Ibid., p. 10f.

4. Ibid., p. 4.

5. Ibid., p. 25.

6. Ibid., p. 6.

7. Ibid., p. 9.

8. Ibid., p. 30.

9. Ibid., p. 102.

10. Ibid., p. 103.

11. Hans-Georg Gadamer, *Philosophische Lehrjahre. Eine Rückschau* (Frankfurt a.M.: Vittorio Klostermann, 1977), pp. 16–17. Hereafter: *PL.*

12. For a moving testimony, see *PL,* p. 93f.

13. This is even clearer from Cassirer's somewhat later essay "Die Methodik des Idealismus in Schillers philosophischen Schriften," in his *Idee und Gestalt. Goethe. Schiller. Hölderlin. Kleist* (Darmstadt: Wissenschaftliche Buchgesellschaft, 1975). The conception of Schiller as an idealist and the idea that German Idealism receives its "Vollendung" and "Abschluß" in Hegel has a long tradition in the twentieth century. The following number among the major contributions: A. Kewkowitz, *Hegels Ästhetik im Verhältnis zu Schiller* Diss. (Breslau, 1910); R. Kroner, *Von Kant bis Hegel* 2 vols. (Tübingen, 1921–24); Ernst Cassirer's *Freiheit und Form*; R. Haym, *Hegel und seine Zeit.* 2nd edition, ed. H. Rosenberg (Leipzig, 1927); N. Hartmann, *Die Philosophie des deutschen Idealismus,* part II: *Hegel* (Leipzig/Berlin, 1929); Helmut Kuhn, *Die Vollendung der klassischen deutschen Ästhetik* (= vol. 1 of *Die Kulturfunktion der Kunst*). See also Günter Rohrmoser, "Zum Problem der ästhetischen Versöhnung bei Schiller und Hegel," *Euphorion* 53 (1959): 351–68; and Benno von Wiese, "Das Problem der ästhetischen Versöhnung bei Schiller und Hegel," *Jahrbuch der Deutschen Schillergesellschaft* 9 (1965): 167–88. See chapter 5, n. 66.

14. *FF,* p. 422.

15. Ibid., p. 422. An example that this tradition has influenced German literary scholarship is evident from Gerhard Kaiser's description of Schiller's concept of Nature as simply "die Idee des Menschen" (chapter 9, n. 1). Klaus Berghahn continues to describe Schiller in terms of his "dualistisches Weltbild und seiner idealistischen Weltanschauung" (*Schiller. Ansichten eines Idealisten,* p. 40).

16. Ibid., p. 424.
17. Ibid., p. 423.
18. Ibid., p. 424.
19. Ibid.
20. Ibid., p. 465.
21. Ibid.
22. Ibid., p. 467.
23. Ibid., p. 468.
24. Ibid., p. 471.
25. Hans-Georg Gadamer, *Truth and Method,* p. 102. Hereafter: *TM* and *WM* (=*Wahrheit und Methode*), p. 108. Hereafter: *WM.*
26. *TM,* p. 101; *WM,* p. 107.
27. *TM,* p. 103; *WM,* p. 109.
28. *WM,* pp. 112 and 113. Joseph J. Kockelmanns notes, by contrast, that "Heidegger never states that art is play; nor does he defend the view, attributed to Schiller, that art flows from some form of 'surplus energy,' and consists in a complete and harmonious fusion of impulse and law" (*Heidegger on Art and Art Works* [Dordrecht/Boston/Lancaster: Martinus Nijhoff, 1985], p. 177).
29. *WM,* p.110; *TM,* p. 103–4.
30. *WM,* p. 87; *TM,* p. 82.
31. "Verhalte dich ästhetisch!" (*WM,* p. 87; *TM,* p. 82).
32. *WM,* p. 87; *TM,* p. 82.
33. *TM,* p. 82; *WM,* p. 88.
34. *WM,* pp. 87–88; *TM,* p. 82.
35. *WM,* p. 112; *TM,* p. 106.
36. As explored in my unpublished graduate seminar paper, "Schelling and Heidegger, and the Function of Art" (University of Washington, 1975) for Ernst Behler.
37. In Martin Heidegger, *Holzwege* 6th ed. (Frankfurt a.M: Vittorio Klostermann, 1980), p. 39. Hereafter: *Holzwege.* Translations are my own.
38. "Unverborgenheit des Seienden, das ist nie ein nur vorhandener Zustand, sondern ein Geschehnis" (*Holzwege,* p. 42).
39. Gadamer's German demonstrates how much he loves alliteration, for he wishes to determine how much "*Geschehen* in allem *Verstehen* wirksam ist" (*WM,* p. 3; *TM,* p. xxiii). Perhaps there is a subtle affinity here between Gadamer's hermeneutics and the Pythagorean theory of the harmony of the spheres, according to which, in part, the music of the celestial bodies can be discerned by the spiritual ear. See Hans Schavernoch, *Die Harmonie der Sphären* and the conclusion to the present book.
40. I retain the German here: "Literatur ist vielmehr eine Funktion geistiger Bewahrung und Überlieferung und bringt daher in jede Gegenwart ihre verborgene Geschichte ein" (*WM,* p. 166; *TM,* p. 161).
41. *TM,* p. 163.
42. Ibid.
43. Ibid.
44. Ibid.
45. Ibid., p. 164.
46. F. W. J. Schelling, *System of Transcendental Idealism,* in *Philosophies of Art and Beauty: Selected Readings in Aesthetics from Plato to Heidegger,* eds. Alfred Hofstadter and Richard Kuhns (New York: The Modern Library, 1964), p. 368.
47. *Schellings Werke,* ed. Manfred Schröter, Ergänzungsband 3: *Zur Philosophie der Kunst* (München: Beck, 1959), p. 368.
48. *Holzwege,* p. 44.

49. Ibid., p. 67.
50. Ibid., p. 44.
51. *TM*, p. 104; *WM*, p. 110.
52. *TM*, p. 105; *WM*, p. 110.
53. *TM*, p. 105; *WM*, p. 111.
54. *TM*, p. 107; *WM*, p. 113.
55. *TM*, p. 107.
56. Ibid.
57. Ibid., p. 108.
58. Ibid.
59. Ibid.
60. Ibid.
60. In Jacques Derrida, *Writing and Difference*, trans. and intro. Alan Bass (Chicago: University of Chicago Press, 1987). Hereafter: Derrida *WD*.
61. Ibid., p. 278.
62. Ibid., p. 290.
63. Ibid.
64. Ibid., p. 292.
65. *TM*, p. 63.
66. Ibid., p. 82.
67. Joel Weinsheimer, *Gadamer's Hermeneutics: A Reading of "Truth and Method"* (New Haven/London: Yale University Press, 1985), p. 92.
68. Ibid., p. 92.
69. *TM*, p. 83, n. 162.
70. Ibid., p. 82.
71. Ibid.
72. Ibid., p. 83.
73. Ibid., p. 82.
74. Weinsheimer, *Gadamer's Hermeneutics*, p. 92.
75. Ibid. In my reading, it is not Schiller's central idea of aesthetic *Bildung* that is dubious but, rather, Gadamer's notion of aesthetic differentiation. According to this notion, "The poetry of aesthetic reconciliation must seek its own self-consciousness against the prose of alienated reality" (*TM*, p. 83). This sounds very much like Herbert Marcuse's understanding though, to be sure, Gadamer's position is unresponsive to Marxist ideologies.
76. I thank Dorothea Kuhn for having reminded me of Schiller's close reading of Herder's work and to Wulf Koepke for having driven the point home.
77. Whereas Schiller does maintain that he is an idealist ("Idealist") in his correspondence to Wilhelm von Humboldt, it is, in this context, always of the formal features of the writing of literature. See chapter 4, n. 18. It should not be construed as a concession to the idealist philosophies of Schelling and Fichte, for instance, a point I made in my discussion of Schiller's disagreement with Fichte in chapter 6. Schiller wrote: "die tiefen Grundideen der Idealphilosophie bleiben ein ewiger Schatz," whereas "die poetische Produktion in Deutschland" looks "höchst kläglich" (letter of April 2, 1805, from Weimar in *Der Briefwechsel zwischen Friedrich Schiller und Wilhelm von Humboldt,* vol. 2, p. 269).
78. *TM*, p. xiv.
79. Ibid., p. xxii.
80. Ibid., p. xxiii.
81. Ibid., p. xxxv.
82. Ibid., p. xxiii.
83. Ibid.

84. Ibid., p. xxx.

85. Ibid., p. xxxvi.

86. Ibid., p. xxxviii.

87. At the time I spoke to Habermas, his attire was thoroughly middle class. He wore a darker wool jacket and slacks with a loosened tie. He was professional looking, neither over-, nor understated. Perhaps more than anything, I liked the fact that he was personable, yet anxious to engage in conversation.

88. Gadamer's decision to support Habermas is especially interesting in light of the fact that when Gadamer submitted his own dissertation at the age of 22, Nicolai Hartmann told him "daß [Paul] Natorp ein sehr schönes Gutachten geschrieben habe, er [aber] habe dann in allen Punkten das Gegenteil behauptet, und auf dieser Basis hätten sie sich auf ein Summa cum laude geeinigt" (*PL*, p. 23). Gadamer then adds that he probably would not have accepted his own dissertation, a judgment with which his wife concurs (*PL*, p. 23).

89. I am unsure of the exact title of that lecture. However, it must have been based on Habermas's dissertation *Das Absolute und die Geschichte. Von der Zwiespältigkeit in Schellings Denken* (1954).

90. Georg Lukács, *History and Class Consciousness: Studies in Marxist Dialectics*, trans. Rodney Livingstone (Cambridge, Massachusetts: MIT Press, 1971), p. 139. Hereafter: *HCC*.

91. Ibid.

92. Ibid.

93. Ibid.

94. Jürgen Habermas, *The Philosophical Discourse of Modernity: Twelve Lectures*, trans. Frederick Lawrence, 6th ed. (Cambridge, Massachusetts: MIT Press, 1992), p. 53. Hereafter: *PDM*.

95. "Gespräch mit Herbert Marcuse," in Jürgen Habermas, *Philosophisch-politische Profile*, expanded edition (Frankfurt a.M.: Suhrkamp, 1987), p. 297. Hereafter *PP*.

96. Ibid., p. 301.

97. Ibid., p. 299. The philosophy of Herbert Marcuse surfaces once again toward the end of Habermas's excursus on Schiller in the *PDM*. Here, he contends that Marcuse "specified the relationship between art and revolution in a manner similar to Schiller" (*PDM*, p. 49) and that "The late Marcuse repeats Schiller's warning against an unmediated aestheticization of life" (*PDM*, pp. 49–50).

98. Ibid., pp. 299–300.

99. Ibid., p. 301.

100. Ibid., p. 302.

101. Ibid.

102. Ibid.

103. Though Habermas believes that concepts like justice, beauty, and the like cannot be justified *theoretically*, both he and Marcuse appreciate Schelling's philosophy of art—and the idea of German idealists—that the work of art makes possible the organon of intellectual intuition ("intellektuelle Anschauung") (*PP*, p. 303).

104. See Hans-Georg Pott regarding Schiller's *Aesthetic Education of the Human Being* and Fichte's philosophy of drives (chapter 5, n. 153). In the process of determining the points of intersection and divergence between Schiller and Fichte, Pott focuses on the politics of Schiller's concepts of the beautiful.

105. In *After Philosophy: End or Transformation?* eds. Kenneth Baynes, James Bohman, and Thomas McCarthy (Cambridge, Massachusetts: MIT Press, 1987), p. 313.

106. PDM, pp. 46 and 45, respectively.

107. Ibid., p. 45.
108. Ibid.
109. Ibid.
110. Ibid., p. 63.
111. "Die Ausbildung des Empfindungsvermögens" (NA 20: 332).
112. Hoy, *The Critical Circle,* p. 126.
113. *PDM,* p. 49.
114. Ibid., p. 60.
115. Ibid., p. 48. For a thought-provoking critique of Habermas's theory of communicative action and of consensus building within a discussion of modernity, see Richard Münch, *Die Struktur der Moderne. Grundmuster und differentielle Gestaltung des institutionellen Aufbaus der modernen Gesellschaften* (Frankfurt a.M.: Suhrkamp, 1984), esp., pp. 110f. and 126. Münch charges that Habermas has not accounted for "die grundsätzliche Spannung zwischen Rationalität und Konsens auf der einen Seite und individueller Expressivität auf der anderen" (p. 110). What Habermas calls rational discourse is, for Münch, actually something greater, namely consensus building discourse. In my experience, Habermas practices consensus building but from a critically rational and socially-politically engaged manner.
116. *PDM,* p. 48.
117. Ibid.
118. Ibid.
119. Ibid.
120. Ibid., p. 50.
121. Ibid., p. 59.
122. Ibid. The German reads, in part: "besser verstehen lassen" (Jürgen Habermas, *Der philosophische Diskurs der Moderne. Zwölf Vorlesungen* [Frankfurt a.M.: Suhrkamp, 1985], p. 74).
123. Albert Divvers, "Tracing Hermeneutics," in: *Tracing Literary Theory,* ed. Joseph Notoli (Urbana: University of Illinois Press, 1987), p. 76.
124. John McGowan, *Postmodernism and Its Critics* (Ithaca, New York/London: Cornell University Press, 1991), p. 4.
125. For a good overview and critical discussion of the main differences in their orientations, see Hoy, *The Critical Circle,* pp. 117–28; and, also, Ulrich Nassen, "Hans-Georg Gadamer und Jürgen Habermas: Hermeneutik, Ideologiekritik und Diskurs," in *Klassiker der Hermeneutik,* ed. Ulrich Nassen (Paderborn/München/Wien/Zürich: Schöningh, 1982), pp. 301–21.

Bibliography

Note: The rare books that I consulted at the Deutsches Literaturarchiv in Marbach am Neckar are marked [DLA]. I thank the staff of the Deutsches Literaturarchiv in Marbach a/N for their courteous and efficient assistance in the acquisition of materials, especially for the use of Schiller's personal copy of Kant's *Kritik der Urteilskraft* from the permanent collection of the Schiller Nationalmuseum. In particular, I appreciate the assistance of Jochen Meyer, Werner Volke, Friedrich Pfäfflin, Margot Pehle, Eva Dambacher, and Frau Grüninger.

Abel, Jakob Friedrich. *Jakob Friedrich Abel. Rede über das Genie. Werden grosse Geister geboren oder erzogen und welches sind die Merkmale derselbigen? Mit einer Wiedergabe des Original-Titelblattes.* Neudruck der Rede Abels vom 14. Dezember 1776 in der Herzoglichen Militär-Akademie zu Stuttgart. Mit einem Nachwort. Edited by Walter Müller-Seidel. Marbach a.N.: Schiller Nationalmuseum, 1955.

Abusch, Alexander. *Schiller. Größe und Tragik eines deutschen Genies.* 6th ed. Berlin/Weimar: Aufbau Verlag, 1977.

Adler, Günter. "'Die Kraniche des Ibykus': die 'Szene' und das 'Tribunal'. Zu Schillers Ballade." *Der Deutschunterricht* 43 (1990): 424–28.

Albertsen, Leif Ludwig. "Ein Festspiel und kein Drama. Grösse und Grenzen der volkshaften Vaterlandsphilosophie in Schillers *Wilhelm Tell.*" In *Friedrich Schiller. Angebot und Diskurs. Zugänge/Dichtung/Zeitgenossenschaft,* edited by Helmut Brandt, 329–37. Berlin/Weimar: Aufbau Verlag, 1987.

Allison, Henry E. "The Transcendental Schematism." In his *Kant's Transcendental Idealism: An Interpretation and Defense,* 173–98. New Haven: Yale University Press, 1983.

Anonymous. *Johann Rudolf Zumsteeg.* Berlin o.J.: Hayn, n.d. [DLA]

Anonymous. *Klopstock und Schiller. Oder: Kritische Versuche über einige lyrische Gedichte des Letztern, in poetischer und moralischer Absicht.* Ellwangen/Gmünd: Ritter, 1821. [DLA]

[Arnold, Ernst.] *Johann Rudolf Zumsteeg. Seine kurze Biographie und ästhetische Darstellung seiner Werke. Bildungsbuch für junge Tonkünstler. Seitenstück zu Joseph Haydn, von demselben Verfasser.* Erfurt: Johann Karl Müller, 1810. [DLA]

Aurnhammer, Achim. "Engagiertes Erzählen: *Der Verbrecher aus verlorener Ehre.*" In *Schiller und die höfische Welt,* edited by Achim Aurnhammer, Klaus Manger, and Friedrich Strack, 254–70. Tübingen: Max Niemeyer, 1990.

———. *Schiller und die höfische Welt.* Edited by Klaus Manger and Friedrich Strack, eds. Tübingen: Max Niemeyer, 1990.

Baasner, Rainer. "'Laß es jetzt gut sein, Seni.' Zu Schillers Umarbeitung der Eröffnungsszene von 'Wallensteins Tod.'" In *Textkritik und Interpretation. Festschrift Karl Konrad Polheim zum 60. Geburtstag,* edited by Heimo Reinitzer, 177–96. Bern/Frankfurt a.M.: Peter Lang, 1987.

Bachmaier, Helmut and Thomas Rentsch, eds. *Poetische Autonomie? Zur Wechselwirkung von Dichtung und Philosophie in der Epoche Goethes und Hölderlins.* Stuttgart: Klett-Cotta, 1987.

Bahr, Ehrhard. "Geschichtsrealismus in Schillers dramatischem Werk." In *Friedrich Schiller. Angebot und Diskurs. Zugänge/Dichtung/Genossenschaft,* edited by Helmut Brandt, 282–92. Berlin/Weimar: Aufbau, 1987.

Barker, Thomas M. "Generalleutnant Octavio Piccolomini. Zur Korrektur eines ungerechten historischen Urteils." *Österreichische Osthefte* 22 (1980): 322–69.

Barner, Wilfried. "Anachronistische Klassizität. Zu Schillers Abhandlung *Über naive und sentimentalische Dichtung.*" In *Klassik im Vergleich. DFG Symposion 1990,* edited by Wilhelm VoßKamp, 62–80. Stuttgart: Metzler, 1993.

Barner, Wilfried. "Menschengeschlecht und Überlieferung. Über Schillers Traditionskonzept in Geschichte und Poesie um 1790." In *Germanistik aus interkultureller Perspektive,* 181–99. Strasbourg: Universite des Sciences Humaines, 1988.

Barner, Wilfried, Eberhard Lämmert, and Norbert Oellers, eds. *Unser Commercium. Goethes und Schillers Literaturpolitik.* Stuttgart: J. G. Cotta, 1984.

Barnes, Harry Elmer. *A History of Historical Writing.* 2nd rev. ed. New York: Dover, 1962.

Barnouw, Jeffrey. "'Freiheit zu geben durch Freiheit'. Ästhetischer Zustand—Ästhetischer Staat." In *Friedrich Schiller. Kunst, Humanität und Politik,* edited by Wolfgang Wittkowski, 138–61. Tübingen: Max Niemeyer, 1982.

———. "The Morality of the Sublime: Kant and Schiller." *Studies in Romanticism* 19 (1980): 497–514.

———. "Das 'Problem der Aktion' und *Wallenstein.* Aus dem Englischen übersetzt von Dagmar Barnouw." *Jahrbuch der Deutschen Schillergesellschaft* 16 (1972): 330–408.

Barry, Thomas F. "Love and Politics of Paternalism: Images of the Father in Schiller's *Kabale und Liebe.*" *Colloquia Germanica* 22 (1989): 21–37.

Barth, Ilse-Marie. *Literarisches Weimar.* Stuttgart: J. B. Metzler, 1971.

Baumanns, Peter. *J. G. Fichte. Kritische Gesamtdarstellung seiner Philosophie.* Freiburg/München: Karl Alber, 1990.

Baumhauer, Otto A. "Kulturwandel. Zur Entwicklung des Paradigmas von der Kultur als Kommunikationssystem. Forschungsbericht." Sonderheft *Kultur, Geschichte und Verstehen. Deutsche Vierteljahrsschrift für Literaturwissenschaft und Geistesgeschichte* 56 (1982): 1–167.

Baur, Wilfried. *Rückzug und Reflexion in kritischer und aufklärender Absicht. Schillers Ethik und Ästhetik und ihre künstlerische Gestalt im Drama.* Bern/Frankfurt a/M: Peter Lang, 1987.

Beaujean, Marion. "Zweimal Prinzenerziehung: *Don Carlos* und *Geisterseher.* Schillers Reaktion auf Illuminaten und Rosenkreuzer." *Poetica* 10 (1978): 217–35.

Beck, Adolf. "Die Krisis des Menschen im Drama des jungen Schiller." In his *Forschung und Deutung. Ausgewählte Aufsätze zur Literatur,* edited by Ulrich Fülleborn, 119–66. Frankfurt a.M./Bonn: Athenäum Verlag, 1966.

Becker-Cantarino, Bärbel. "Die 'Schwarze Legende'. Ideal und Ideologie in Schillers *Don Carlos.*" *Jahrbuch des Freien Deutschen Hochstifts 1975:* 153–73.

Behler, Ernst. "Grundlagen der Ästhetik in Friedrich Schlegels frühen Schriften." In *Früher Idealismus und Frühromantik. Der Streit um die Grundlagen der Ästhetik (1795–1805),* edited by Walter Jaeschke and Helmut Holzhey, 112–27. Hamburg: Felix Meiner, 1990.

————. "Origins of Romantic Aesthetics in Friedrich Schlegel." *Canadian Review of Comparative Literature* 7 (1980): 47–66.

————. "The Origins of the Romantic Literary Theory." *Colloquia Germanica* 2 (1968): 109–26.

————. Review of Emil Staiger, *Friedrich Schlegels Sieg über Friedrich Schiller. Vorgetragen am 13. Dezember 1980.* Heidelberg: Carl Winter, 1981, in *The German Quarterly* 57 (1984): 657–58.

————. "Die Wirkung Goethes und Schillers auf die Brüder Schlegel." In *Unser Commercium. Goethe und Schillers Literaturpolitik,* edited by Wilfried Barner, Eberhard Lämmert, and Norbert Oellers, 559–83. Stuttgart: J. G. Cotta, 1984.

Beierwaltes, Werner. *Platonismus und Idealismus.* Frankfurt a/M: Vittorio Klostermann, 1972.

Belgardt, Reinhard. "Dichtung: Zwischen Eudämonie und Ideologie. Prolegomena einer integrativen Literaturtheorie." In *Fremdsprache Deutsch,* edited by Alois Wierlacher, 410–37. München: Wilhelm Fink, 1980.

Belhalfaoui, Barbara. "*Wallensteins Tod.* Die Tragödie der Theodizee." *Recherches Germaniques* 14 (1984): 59–83.

Benn, Sheila Margaret. *Pre-Romantic Attitudes to Landscape in the Writings of Friedrich Schiller.* Berlin/New York: Walter de Gruyter, 1991.

Bennett, Benjamin. *Modern Drama and German Classicism.* Ithaca/London: Cornell University Press, 1979.

————. "Trinitarische Humanität: Dichtung und Geschichte bei Schiller." In *Friedrich Schiller. Kunst, Humanität und Politik in der späten Aufklärung. Ein Symposium,* edited by Wolfgang Wittkowski, 164–77. Tübingen: Max Niemeyer, 1982.

Berger, Kurt. "Schiller und die Mythologie. Zur Frage der Begegnung und Auseinandersetzung zwischen christlicher und antiker Tradition in der klassischen Dichtung." *Deutsche Vierteljahrsschrift für Literaturwissenschaft und Geistesgeschichte* 26 (1952): 178–224.

Berghahn, Klaus. "Ästhetik und Politik im Werk Schillers: Zur jüngsten Forschung." *Monatshefte* 66 (1974): 410–21.

————. "Das 'Pathetischerhabene'. Schillers Dramentheorie." In *Deutsche Dramentheorien. Beiträge zu einer historischen Poetik des Dramas in Deutschland,* edited by Reinhold Grimm, 214–44. Frankfurt a/M: Athenäum Verlag, 1971.

————. "Mit dem Rücken zum Publikum. Autonomie der Kunst und literarische Öffentlichkeit in der Weimarer Klassik." In *Revolution und Autonomie. Deutsche Autonomieästhetik im Zeitalter der Französischen Revolution. Ein Symposium,* edited by Wolfgang Wittkowski, 207–29. Tübingen: Max Niemeyer, 1990.

————. *Schiller. Ansichten eines Idealisten.* Frankfurt a.M.: Athenäum Verlag, 1986.

————. "Schillers mythologische Symbolik. Erläutert am Beispiel der 'Götter Griechenlands.'" In *Friedrich Schiller. Angebot und Diskurs. Zugänge/Dichtung/ Genossenschaft,* edited by Helmut Brandt, 361–81. Berlin/Weimar: Aufbau Verlag, 1987. And *Schiller. Vorträge aus Anlaß seines 225. Geburtstages,* edited by Dirk Grathoff and Erwin Leibfried, 29–48. Frankfurt a.M./Bern/New York/Paris: Peter Lang, 1991.

————. "Schiller und die Tradition." In *Friedrich Schiller zur Geschichtlichkeit seines Werkes,* edited by Klaus Berghahn, 9–24. Kronberg/Ts.: Scriptor, 1975.

————, ed. *Schiller zur Geschichtlichkeit seines Werkes.* Kronberg/Ts.: Scriptor, 1975.

———. "Volkstümlichkeit ohne Volk? Kritische Überlegungen zu einem Kulturkonzept Schillers." In *Popularität und Trivialität. Fourth Wisconsin Workshop,* edited by Reinhold Grimm and Jost Hermand, 51–75. Frankfurt a.M.: Athenäum Verlag, 1974.

———. "Zum Drama Schillers." In *Handbuch des deutschen Dramas,* edited by Walter Hinck, 157–73. Düsseldorf: Bagel, 1980.

———, ed. *Briefwechsel zwischen Friedrich Schiller und Körner.* München: Winckler, 1973.

———, ed. *Friedrich Schiller. Zur Geschichtlichkeit seines Werkes.* Kronberg/Ts.: Scriptor, 1975.

——— and Reinhold Grimm, eds. *Schiller. Zur Theorie und Praxis der Dramen.* Darmstadt: Wissenschaftliches Buchgesellschaft, 1972.

Berman, Jill. "History Can Restore Naivety to the Sentimental: Schiller's Letters on *Wallenstein.*" *Modern Language Review* 81 (1986): 369–87.

Berns, Gisela N. *Greek Antiquity in Schiller's "Wallenstein."* Chapel Hill/London: University of North Carolina Press, 1985.

Bertos, Rigas N. "Caspar David Friedrich and Friedrich Schiller." In *Nineteenth-Century Germany: A Symposium,* edited by Modris Eksteins and Hildegard Hammerschmidt, 15–27. Tübingen: Günter Narr, 1983.

Best, Alan. "Alpine Ambivalence in Schiller's *Wilhelm Tell.*" *German Life and Letters,* N.S. 37 (1984): 297–306.

Beyer, Karen. "Staatsraison und Moralität. Die Prinzipien höfischen Lebens im *Don Carlos.*" In *Schiller und die höfische Welt,* edited by Achim Aurnhammer, Klaus Manger, and Friedrich Strack, 359–76. Tübingen: Max Niemeyer, 1990.

Blum, Gerhard. *Zum Begriff des Schönen in Kants und Schillers ästhetischen Schriften.* Fulda: Verlag freier Autoren, 1988.

Blumenberg, Hans. *Die Genesis der kopernikanischen Welt.* Frankfurt a.M.: Suhrkamp, 1975.

———. *Die Lesbarkeit der Welt.* Frankfurt a.M.: Suhrkamp, 1981.

———. "Paradigmen zu einer Metaphorologie." *Archiv für Begriffsgeschichte* 6 (1960): 7–142.

Blumenthal, Lieselotte. "Schiller in Böhmen." *Jahrbuch der Deutschen Schillergesellschaft* 13 (1969): 221–50.

Blunden, Allan G. "Nature and Politics in Schiller's *Don Carlos.*" *Deutsche Vierteljahrsschrift für Literaturwissenschaft und Geistesgeschichte* 52 (1978): 241–56.

Böckmann, Paul. "Die innere Form in Schillers Jugenddramen." *Dichtung und Volkstum* 35 (1934): 439–80.

———. "Politik und Dichtung im Werk Friedrich Schillers. Festvortrag, gehalten bei der Schillerfeier der Universität Heidelberg am 9. Mai 1955." *Ruperto-Carola. Mitteilungen* 7 (1955): 25–37.

———. "Schillers *Don Karlos.* Die politische Idee unter dem Vorzeichen des Inzestmotivs." In *Friedrich Schiller. Kunst, Humanität und Politik* 33–47.

———. *Schillers Don Karlos. Edition der ursprünglichen Fassung und entstehungsgeschichtlicher Kommentar.* Stuttgart: Klett, 1974.

———. *Strukturprobleme in Schillers "Don Karlos". Vorgetragen am 24. Januar 1981.* Heidelberg: Carl Winter, 1982.

Böhler, Michael. "Die Freundschaft von Schiller und Goethe als literatursoziologisches Paradigma." *Internationales Archiv für Sozialgeschichte der deutschen Literatur* 5 (1980): 33–67.

————, Michael J. *Soziale Rolle und Ästhetische Vermittlung. Studien zur Literatur-soziologie von A.G. Baumgarten bis F. Schiller.* Bern/Frankfurt a.M.: Herbert Lang, 1975.

Bölsche, Wilhelm. "Die Metaphysik in der modernen Physiologie." *Freie Bühne* 4 (1893): 273–89.

Bogdal, Klaus-Michael. *Geschichte in der Erzählung. Heinrich von Kleists "Michael Kohlhaas". Friedrich Schiller: "Der Verbrecher aus verlorener Ehre."* Stuttgart: Klett, 1986.

Bohm, Arnd. "'Ich will den Käufer nicht betrügen': Give and Take in Schillers *Don Carlos." Seminar* 27 (1991): 203–18.

————. "Gottfried August Bürger: Texts of the Body." *Studies in Eighteenth-Century Culture* 23 (1994): 161–78.

————. "The Desublimated Body: Gottfried August Bürger." In *Subversive Sublimi-ties: Undercurrents of the German Enlightenment,* edited by Eitel Timm, 12–26. Columbia, S.C.: Camden House, 1992.

————. "Possessive Individualism in Schiller's *Die Räuber." Mosaic* 20 (1987): 31–42.

Bohn, Volker, ed. *Romantik. Literatur und Philosophie.* Frankfurt a.M.: Suhr-kamp, 1987.

Bohnen, Klaus. "Politik im Drama. Anmerkungen zu Schillers *Don Carlos." Jahr-buch der Deutschen Schillergesellschaft* 24 (1980): 15–31.

Bolten, Jürgen. *Friedrich Schiller: Poesie, Reflexion und gesellschaftliche Selbstdeu-tung.* München: Fink, 1985.

————. "Zur Genese des bürgerlichen Selbstverständnisses im ausgehenden 18. Jah-rhundert." In *Germanistik-Forschungsstand und Perspektiven. Vorträge des Deutschen Germanistentages 1984,* edited by Georg Stötzel, 492–504, 2nd part: *Ältere Deutsche Literatur. Neuere Deutsche Literatur.* Berlin/New York: Walter de Gruyter, 1985.

Bonnet, Charles. *Analytischer Versuch über die Seelenkräfte,* aus dem französischen übersetzt und mit einigen zusätzen vermehrt von Christian Gottfried Schütz. 2 vols. Bremen: J. H. Cramer, 1770–71. [DLA]

————. *Betrachtung über die Natur* . . . mit den zusätzen der italienischen Ueberset-zung des Herrn Abt Spallanzani . . . und einigen eigenen Anmerkungen hrsg. von Johann Daniel Titius. 3d ed. Leipzig: Johann Friedrich Junius, 1774. [DLA]

Borcherdt, Hans Heinrich, ed. *Schiller und die Romantiker. Briefe und Dokumente.* Stuttgart: J. G. Cotta, 1948.

Borchmeyer, Dieter. "*Altes Recht* und Revolution.—Schillers *Wilhelm Tell.*" In *Friedrich Schiller. Kunst, Humanität und Politik in der späten Aufklärung. Ein Symposium,* edited by Wolfgang Wittkowski, 69–111. Tübingen: Max Niemeyer, 1982.

————. "Ästhetische und politische Autonomie: Schillers *Ästhetische Briefe* im Geg-enlicht der Französischen Revolution." In *Revolution und Autonomie. Deutsche Autonomieästhetik im Zeitalter der Französischen Revolution. Ein Symposium,* edited by Wolfgang Wittkowski, 277–90. Tübingen: Max Niemeyer, 1990.

————. "Aufklärung und praktische Kultur. Schillers Idee der ästhetischen Erzie-hung." In *Naturplan und Verfallskritik. Zu Begriff und Geschichte der Kultur,* edited by Helmut Brackert and Fritz Wefelmeyer, 122–47. Frankfurt a.M.: Suhr-kamp, 1984.

————. "'Der ganze Mensch ist wie ein versiegelter Brief'-Schillers Kritik und

Apologie der 'Hofkunst.'" In *Schiller und die höfische Welt*, edited by Achim Aurnhammer, Klaus Manger, and Friedrich Strack, 460–75. Tübingen: Max Niemeyer, 1990.

————. *Höfische Gesellschaft und französische Revolution bei Goethe. Adliges und bürgerliches Wertsystem im Urteil der Weimarer Klassik.* Kronberg/Ts.: Athenäum Verlag, 1977.

————. "Kritik der Aufklärung im Geiste der Aufklärung: Friedrich Schiller." In *Aufklärung und Gegenaufklärung in der europäischen Literatur, Philosophie und Politik von der Antike bis zur Gegenwart*, edited by Jochen Schmidt, 361–76. Darmstadt: Wissenschaftliche Buchgesellschaft, 1989.

————. *Macht und Melancholie. Schillers "Wallenstein."* Frankfurt a.M.: Athenäum Verlag, 1988.

————. "Rhetorische und ästhetische Revolutionskritik: Edmund Burke und Schiller." In *Klassik und Moderne. Die Weimarer Klassik als historisches Ereignis und Herausforderung im kulturgeschichtlichen Prozeß. Walter Müller-Seidel zum 65. Geburtstag*, edited by Karl Richter and Jörg Schönert, 56–79. Stuttgart: J. B. Metzler, 1983.

————. "Die Tragödie vom verlorenen Vater. Der Dramatiker Schiller und die Aufklärung—Das Beispiel der *Räuber*." In *Friedrich Schiller. Angebot und Diskurs. Zugänge/Dichtung/Genossenschaft*, edited by Helmut Brandt, 160-84. Berlin/ Weimar Aufbau Verlag, 1987.

————. *Tragödie und Öffentlichkeit. Schillers Dramaturgie im Zusammenhang seiner ästhetisch-politischen Theorie und die rhetorische Tradition.* München: Wilhelm Fink, 1973.

————. *Die Weimarer Klassik. Eine Einführung.* 2 vols. Frankfurt a.M.: Athenäum Verlag, 1980.

Bowie, Andrew. *Aesthetics and Subjectivity: From Kant to Nietzsche.* Manchester/ New York: Manchester University Press, 1990.

Brackert, Helmut and Fritz Wefelmeyer, eds. *Naturplan und Verfallskritik. Zu Begriff und Geschichte der Kultur.* Frankfurt a.M.: Suhrkamp, 1984.

Braig, Friedrich. "Schillers *Philosophische Briefe* und *Don Carlos*." *Forschungen und Fortschritte* 34 (1960): 106–11.

Brandt, Helmut. "Der bleibende Schiller." In *Friedrich Schiller. Angebot und Diskurs. Zugänge/Dichtung/Zeitgenossenschaft*, edited by Helmut Brandt, 11–32. Berlin/Weimar: Aufbau Verlag, 1987.

————, ed. *Friedrich Schiller. Angebot und Diskurs. Zugänge/Dichtung/Zeitgenossenschaft.* Berlin/Weimar: Aufbau Verlag, 1987.

Bräutigam, Bernd. "Rousseaus Kritik ästhetischer Versöhnung. Eine Problemvorgabe der Bildungsästhetik Schillers." *Jahrbuch der Deutschen Schillergesellschaft* 31 (1987): 137–55.

Brastberger, Immanuel Gottlob. *Evangelische zeugnisse der wahrheit, zur aufmunterung im wahren christenthum.* Stuttgart: G. Mäntler, 1758. [DLA]

Brennecke, D. "'Schön Wie Engel, voll Walhalla's Wonne'. Altnordisches bei Schiller." *Germanisch-Romanische Monatsschrift* 35 (1985): 224–27.

Brinkmann, Richard. "Romantische Dichtungstheorie in Friedrich Schlegels Frühschriften und Schillers Begriffe des Naiven und Sentimentalischen." *Deutsche Vierteljahrsschrift für Literaturwissenschaft und Geistesgeschichte* 52 (1958): 344–71.

Brockes, Barthold Heinrich. *Herrn B. H. Brockes. Harmonische Himmels-Lust im*

*Irdischen, oder auserlesene, theils neue, theils aus dem Irdischen Vergnügen ge-
nommene, und nach den 4 Jahres-Zeiten eingerichtete Musicalische Gedichte und
Kantaten.* Mit einer Vorrede zum Druck befördert von B. H. Brockes. 2d ed.
Hamburg: Conrad König, 1744.

Brodsky, Claudia. "Freedom in Kant and Schiller: Criticism and Idealism." In
Friedrich von Schiller and the Drama of Human Existence, edited by Alexej Urgrinsky, 129–33. New York/Westport, Connecticut: Greenwood Press, 1988.

Brooks, Linda M. "Sublime Suicide: The End of Schiller's Aesthetics." In *Friedrich
von Schiller and the Drama of Human Existence,* edited by Alexej Urgrinsky,
91–101. New York/Westport, Connecticut: Greenwood Press, 1988.

————. "Sublimity and Theatricality: Romantic 'Pre-Postmodernism' in Schiller and
Coleridge." *Modern Language Notes* 105 (1990): 939–64.

Brown, Marshall. *The Shape of German Romanticism.* Ithaca/London: Cornell University Press, 1979.

Brown, Robert H. "Nature and History in Schiller's *Räuber.*" In his *Nature's Hidden
Terror. Violent Nature Imagery in Eighteenth-Century Germany.* Columbia, S.C.:
Camden House, 1991.

Bruckmann, Christoph. "'Freude! sangen wir in Thränen, Freude! in dem tiefsten
Leid.' Zur Interpretation und Rezeption des Gedichts *An die Freude* von Friedrich
Schiller." *Jahrbuch der Deutschen Schillergesellschaft* 35 (1991): 96–112.

Bruford, Walter H. *Culture and Society in Classical Weimar 1775–1806.* Cambridge:
Cambridge University Press, 1966. Translated as *Kultur und Gesellschaft im klassischen Weimar 1775–1806.* Göttingen: Vandenhoeck u. Ruprecht, 1966.

Buchwald, Reinhard. "Aus Schillers Kindheit und Jugend." *Schwäbischer Schillerverein* 41 (1936/37): 14–83.

————. "Kaspar Schiller. Major und Hofgarteninspektor des Dichters Vater. 1723–
1796." In *Schwäbische Lebensbilder,* edited by Hermann Haering and Otto Hohenstatt, vol. 1, 475–86. Stuttgart: W. Kohlhammer, 1940.

————. *Schiller.* 2 vols. Leipzig: Insel, 1937.

————. *Schiller in seiner und unserer Zeit.* Heidelberg: Pfeffer, 1946.

Buhr, Gerhard, Friedrich A. Kittler, and Horst Turk, eds. *Das Subjekt der Dichtung.
Festschrift für Gerhard Kaiser.* Würzburg: Königshausen u. Neumann, 1990.

Bürger, Peter. *Zur Kritik der idealistischen Ästhetik.* Frankfurt a.M.: Suhrkamp,
1983.

Burger, Heinz Otto. "Die bürgerliche Sitte: Schillers *Kabale und Liebe.*" In his
"Dasein heißt eine Rolle spielen": Studien zur deutschen Literaturgeschichte, 194–
210. München: C. Hanser, 1963. Burschell, Friedrich. *Schiller.* Reinbek bei Hamburg: Rowohlt, 1968.

Campbell, Keith. *Body and Mind.* 2d ed. Notre Dame: University of Notre Dame
Press, 1984.

Carlsson, Anni. *Die deutsche Buchkritik* Vol. 1: *Von den Anfängen bis 1850.* Stuttgart: Kohlhammer, 1963.

Carlyle, Thomas. *Thomas Carlyle. Leben Schillers.* Aus dem Englischen. Eingeleitet
von Goethe. Frankfurt a.M.: Heinrich Wilmans, 1830. [DLA]

————. *The Life of Friedrich Schiller: Comprehending an Examination of His Works.*
London: Taylor and Hessey, 1825. [DLA: signed Mr. Thomas Carlyle]

Casey, John. "The Noble." In *Philosophy and Literature,* edited by Phillip Griffith,
135–53. Cambridge/London: Cambridge University Press, 1984.

Cassirer, Ernst. *Freiheit und Form. Studien zur deutschen Geistesgeschichte.* Berlin: Bruno Cassirer, 1922.

———. "Die Methodik des Idealismus in Schillers philosophischen Schriften." In his *Idee und Gestalt. Goethe. Schiller. Hölderlin. Kleist,* 83–111. Darmstadt: Wissenschaftliche Buchgesellschaft, 1975.

———. *The Philosophy of the Enlightenment.* Translated by Fritz C. A. Koelln and James P. Pettegrove. Princeton: Princeton University Press, 1951.

Churchill, Frederick. "From Machine-Theory to Entelechy: Two Studies in Developmental Teleology." *Journal of the History of Biology* 2 (1969): 165–85.

Chytry, Josef. *The Aesthetic State: A Quest in Modern German Thought.* Berkeley/ Los Angeles/London: University of California Press, 1989.

Cohn, Hilde D. "Gefängnis und Gefangenschaft in Schiller's *Don Carlos.*" In *Festschrift für Bernhard Blume. Aufsätze zur deutschen und europäischen Literatur,* edited by Egon Schwarz, Hunter G. Hannum and Edgar Lohner, 81–89. Göttingen: Vandenhoeck & Ruprecht, 1967.

Collier, Peter and Helga Geyer-Ryan, eds. *Literary Theory Today.* Ithaca, New York: Cornell University Press, 1990.

Conradi-Bleibtreu, Ellen. *Die Schillers. Der Dichter und seine Familie. Leben, Lieben, Leiden in einer Epoche der Umwälzungen.* Münster: Aschendorff, 1986.

Conrady, Karl Otto, ed. *Deutsche Literatur zur Zeit der Klassik.* Stuttgart: Reclam, 1977.

Crawford, Ronald L. "Don Carlos and Marquis Posa: The Eternal Friendship." *The Germanic Review* 58 (1983): 97–105.

———. *Images of Transience in the Poems and Ballads of Friedrich Schiller.* Berne/ Frankfurt a/M./Las Vegas: Peter Lang, 1977.

Crosby, Donald H. "The Fragmented Schiller: *Welttheater* or *Regietheater?*" In *Friedrich Schiller. Kunst, Humanität und Politik in der späten Aufklärung. Ein Symposium,* edited by Wolfgang Wittkowski, 341–50. Tübingen: Max Niemeyer, 1982.

Culler, Jonathan. *On Deconstruction: Theory and Criticism after Structuralism.* Ithaca, New York: Cornell University Press, 1983.

———. *The Pursuit of Signs: Semiotics, Literature, Deconstruction.* Ithaca, New York: Cornell University Press, 1981.

Cysarz, Herbert. *Die dichterische Phantasie Friedrich Schillers.* Tübingen: Max Niemeyer, 1959.

Dahlhaus, Carl. "Formbegriff und Ausdrucksprinzip in Schillers Musikästhetik." In *Schiller und die höfische Welt,* edited by Achim Aurnhammer, Klaus Manger, and Friedrich Strack, 156–67. Tübingen: Max Niemeyer, 1990.

Dahnke, Hans-Dietrich. "Die Debatte um 'Die Götter Griechenlands.'" In *Debatten und Kontroversen. Literarische Kontroversen am Ende des 18. Jahrhunderts,* edited by Hans-Dietrich Dahnke and Bernd Leistner, 193–269. Berlin/Weimar: Aufbau, 1989.

——— and Bernd Leistner, eds. *Schiller. Das dramatische Werk in Einzelinterpretationen.* Leipzig: Reclam, 1982.

———. "Schillers *Wallenstein* und die Aktualität der Geschichte." *Impulse. Aufsätze, Quellen, Berichte zur deutschen Klassik und Romantik* 5 (1982): 63–90.

———. "Zum Verhältnis von historischer und poetischer Wahrheit in Schillers Konzeptionsbildung und Dramenpraxis." In *Friedrich Schiller. Angebot und Diskurs.*

Zugänge/Dichtung/Zeitgenossenschaft, edited by Helmut Brandt, 264–28. Berlin/ Weimar: Aufbau Verlag, 1987.

Dallmayr, Fred. "The Discourse of Modernity: Hegel and Habermas." *Journal of Philosophy* 84 (1987): 682–92.

Dau, Rud. *Geschichtsbild und klassische Lyrik. Zur Wechselbeziehung von Geschichtspublizistik und lyrischem Schaffen in Friedrich Schillers Beitrag zur "Weimarer Klassik" unter besonderer Berücksichtigung seiner klassischen Balladen.* Humboldt University (E. Berlin) Dissertation, 1973.

Dawson, Virginia P. "The Problem of Soul in the 'Little Machines' of Réaumur and Charles Bonnet." *Eighteenth-Century Studies* 18 (1984–85): 503–22.

De La Mettrie, Julien Offray. *Man a Machine: Including Frederick the Great's "Eulogy" on La Mettrie and Extracts from La Mettrie's "The Natural History of the Soul."* Philosophical and Historical Notes by Gertrude Carman Bussey. Chicago/ London: Open Court, 1927.

———. *De La Mettrie. Der Mensch eine Maschine.* Translated with a Foreword and Notes by Max Brahn. Leipzig: Dürr, 1909. [DLA]

Dembele, Soungale Remy. *Politische, ethische und ästhetische Programmatik in Schillers Jugenddramen.* University of Berlin (East) Dissertation, 1984.

Derrida, Jacques. "Structure, Sign and Play in the Discourse of the Human Sciences." In his *Writing and Difference.* Translated and introduced by Alan Bass. Chicago: University of Chicago Press, 1987: 278–93.

———. *Spurs, Nietzsche's Style/Eprons. Les Styles de Nietzsche.* Introduction by Stefano Agosti, translated by Barbara Harlow. Chicago/London: University of Chicago Press, 1979.

Deutsches Wörterbuch von Jacob und Wilhelm Grimm. Photomechanischer Nachdruck der Erstausgabe 1893. München: Deutscher Taschenbuchverlag, 1984.

Dewhurst, Kenneth and Nigel Reeves. *Friedrich Schiller: Medicine, Psychology and Literature with the first English edition of his complete medical and psychological writings.* Oxford: Sandford, 1978; Berkeley/Los Angeles: University of California Press, 1978.

Dieckmann, Friedrich. "Ein ganz neuer Schiller." *Sinn und Form* 34 (1982): 894–901.

Diecks, Thomas. "'Schuldige Unschuld': Schillers *Maria Stuart* vor dem Hintergrund barocker Dramatisierungen des Stoffes." In *Schiller und die höfische Welt,* edited by Achim Aurnhammer, Klaus Manger, and Friedrich Strack, 233–46. Tübingen: Max Niemeyer, 1990.

Dingelstedt, F. "Die erste Aufführung von Schillers *Räubern.*" *Westermans Illustrierte Deutsche Monatshefte* 5 (1858–59): 387–95.

Disselbeck, Klaus. *Geschmack und Kunst. Eine systemtheoretische Untersuchung zu Schillers Briefen "Über die ästhetische Erziehung des Menschen."* Opladen: Westdeutscher Verlag, 1987.

Divvers, Albert. "Tracing Hermeneutics." In *Tracing Literary History,* edited by Joseph Notoli. Urbana: University of Illinois Press, 1987.

Diwald, Hellmut. *Friedrich Schiller. Text von Wallensteins Tod. Dokumentation.* Frankfurt a.M./Berlin/Wien: Ullstein, 1972.

Dod, Elmar. *Die Vernünftigkeit der Imagination in Aufklärung und Romantik. Eine komparatistische Studie zu Schillers und Shelleys ästhetischen Theorien in ihrem europäischen Kontext.* Tübingen: Max Niemeyer, 1985.

Doppler, Alfred. *Der Abgrund. Studien zur Bedeutungsgeschichte eines Motivs.* Graz/Wien/Köln: Böhlau, 1968.

————. "Geschichtliche Situation und ästhetische Konzeption (Bemerkungen zu Schillers Briefen *Über die ästhetische Erziehung des Menschen*)." In *Tradition und Entwicklung. Festschrift Eugen Thurnher zum 60. Geburtstag,* edited by Werner M. Bauer, Achim Masser and Guntram A. Plangg, 283–89. Innsbruck: AMOE, 1982.

————. "Schiller und die Frühromantik." *Jahrbuch des Wiener Goethe-Vereins* 64 (1960): 71–91.

Drollinger, Carl F. *Carl Friedrich Drollinger. Gedichte.* Faksimiledruck nach der Ausgabe von 1743, kommentiert von Uwe-K. Ketelsen. Stuttgart: J. B. Metzler, 1972.

Dürrenmatt, Friedrich. *Friedrich Schiller. Eine Rede.* Zürich: Arche, 1960.

Düsing, Wolfgang. "Kosmos und Natur in Schillers Lyrik." *Jahrbuch der Deutschen Schillergesellschaft* 13 (1969): 196–220.

————. "'Das kühne Traumbild eines neuen Staates': Die Utopie in Schillers *Don Carlos.*" In *Geschichtlichkeit und Gegenwart. Festschrift für Hans-Dietrich Imscher,* edited by Hans Esselborn and Werner Keller, 194–208. Köln/Weimar/Wien: Böhlau, 1994.

Duncan, Bruce. "'An Worte läßt sich trefflich glauben'. Die Sprache der Luise Millerin." In *Friedrich Schiller. Kunst, Humanität, Politik in der späten Aufklärung. Ein Symposium,* edited by Wolfgang Wittkowski, 26–32. Tübingen: Max Niemeyer, 1982.

Dyck, Martin. *Die Gedichte Schillers. Figuren der Dynamik des Bildes.* Bern/München: Francke, 1967.

————. "Schillers Urballade—Marginalien zu einem Gestaltungsprinzip." In *Literatur als Dialog. Festschrift zum 50. Geburtstag von Karl Tober,* edited by Reingard Nethersole, 243–48. Johannesburg: Ravan Press, 1979.

Eagleton, Terry. *Literary Theory: An Introduction.* Minneapolis: University of Minnesota Press, 1983.

Eicheldinger, Martina. "Rhetorische Elemente in den Reden der Karlsschüler auf Franziska von Hohenheim (1779)." In *Schiller und die höfische Welt,* edited by Achim Aurnhammer, Klaus Manger, and Friedrich Strack, 94–110. Tübingen: Max Niemeyer, 1990.

Eichner, Hans. "The Supposed Influence of Schiller's *Über naive und sentimentalische Dichtung* on Friedrich Schlegel's *Über das Studium der griechischen Poesie.*" *The Germanic Review* 30 (1955): 260–65.

————. "Der Streit mit Schiller." in *Kritische Friedrich Schlegel Ausgabe,* edited by Ernst Behler et al., vol. 2. Paderborn/München/Wien: Ferdinand Schönigh; Zürich: Thomas Verlag, 1958f.

Elias, Norbert. "Über die Natur." *Merkur* 40 (1986): 469–81.

Ellis, John. *Narration in the German Novelle: Theory and Interpretation.* Cambridge: Cambridge University Press, 1974.

Ellis, J. M. *Schiller's Kalliasbriefe and the Study of His Aesthetic Theory.* The Hague/Paris: Mouton, 1969.

Engell, James. *The Creative Imagination: Enlightenment to Romanticism.* Cambridge, Mass./London: Harvard University Press, 1981.

Englert, Dorothea. *Literatur als Reflexionsmedium für Individualität. Systemtheoretische Studien zur Funktion des ästhetischen Sinnangebots bei Schiller und Novalis.* Frankfurt a.M./Berlin/Bern/New York/Paris/Wien: Lang, 1993.

Fähnrich, Hermann. *Schillers Musikalität und Musikanschauung*. Hildesheim: Gerstenberg, 1977.

Falk, Horst. *Der Leitgedanke von der Vollkommenheit der Natur in Schillers klassischem Werk*. Frankfurt a.M./Bern/Cirencester: Peter Lang, 1980.

Fambach, Oscar. *Schiller und sein Kreis in der Kritik ihrer Zeit. Die wesentlichen Rezensionen aus der periodischen Literatur bis zu Schillers Tod*. Berlin: Akademie, 1957.

Feldt, Michael. *Lyrik als Erlebnislyrik. Zur Geschichte eines Literatur—und Mentalitätstypus zwischen 1600 und 1900*. Heidelberg: Carl Winter, 1990.

Ferguson, Adam. *Grundsätze der Moralphilosophie*. Uebersetzt und mit einigen anmerkungen versehen von Christian Garve. Leipzig: Dyck, 1772. [DLA]

Fester, Richard. "Vorstudien zur Säkularausgabe der historischen Schriften Schillers." *Euphorion* 12 (1905): 78–142.

Fichte, Johann Gottlieb. *Fichte: Early Philosophical Writings*. Translated and edited by Daniel Breazeale. Ithaca/London: Cornell University Press, 1988.

———. *Gesamtausgabe der Bayerischen Akademie der Wissenschaften*. Edited by Reinhard Lauth and Hans Jacob. Stuttgart/Bad Canstatt: Friedrich Frommann, 1964f.

———. "Ueber Belebung und Erhöhung des reinen Interesse[s] für Wahrheit." In *Die Horen* 1 (1795): 79–93.

Finger, Ellen. "Schiller's Concept of the Sublime and Its Pertinence to *Don Carlos* and *Maria Stuart*." *Journal of English and Germanic Philology* 79 (1980): 166–78.

Fingerhut, Karlheinz. "Erstaufführung—Schillers *Kabale und Liebe*." *Der Deutschunterricht* 36 (1984): 112–17.

Fink, Gonthier-Louis. "Schillers *Wilhelm Tell*, ein antijakobinisches republikanisches Schauspiel." In *Französische Revolution und Deutsche Literatur*, edited by Karl Eibl. Hamburg: Meiner, 1986: 57–81.

Fink, Karl. *Goethe's History of Science*. Cambridge/New York: Cambridge University Press, 1991.

———. "Storm and Stress Anthropology." *History of the Human Sciences* 6 (1993): 51–71.

Finscher, Ludwig. "Was ist eine lyrische Operette? Anmerkungen zu Schillers *Semele*." In *Schiller und die höfische Welt*, edited by Achim Aurnhammer, Klaus Manger, and Friedrich Strack, 148–55. Tübingen: Max Niemeyer, 1990.

Fischer, Bernd. *"Kabale und Liebe". Skepsis und Melodrama in Schillers bürgerlichem Trauerspiel*. New York/Berne/Frankfurt a.M./Paris: Peter Lang, 1987.

Flaherty, Gloria. *Opera in the Development of German Critical Thought*. Princeton, N.J.: Princeton University Press, 1978.

Floß, Ulrich. *Kunst und Mensch in den ästhetischen Schriften Friedrich Schillers. Versuch einer kritischen Interpretation*. Köln/Wien: Böhlau, 1989.

Forster, Leonard. "A Cool, Fresh Look at Schiller's 'Das Lied von der Glocke.'" *Publications of the English Goethe-Society*. N.S. 42 (1972): 90–115.

Frank, Manfred. "Was heißt 'einen Text verstehen'?" In *Texthermeneutik, Aktualität, Geschichte, Kritik*, edited by Ulrich Nassen, 58–77. Paderborn/München/Wien/Zürich: Schöningh, 1979.

———. *Was ist Neostrukturalismus?* Frankfurt a.M.: Suhrkamp, 1984.

Frey, John R, ed. *Schiller 1759/1959: Commemorative American Studies*. Urbana: University of Illinois Press, 1959.

Fricke, Gerhard. "Die Problematik des Tragischen im Drama Schillers." *Jahrbuch des Freien Deutschen Hochstifts 1930:* 3–69.

Friedl, Gerhard. "Die Karlsschüler bei höfischen Festen." In *Schiller und die höfische Welt*, edited by Achim Aurnhammer, Klaus Manger, and Friedrich Strack, 47–76. Tübingen: Max Niemeyer, 1990.

———. *Verhüllte Wahrheit und entfesselte Phantasie. Die Mythologie in der vorklassischen und klassischen Lyrik Schillers.* Würzburg: Königshausen u. Neumann, 1987.

Frühwald, Wolfgang. "Die Auseinandersetzung um Schillers Gedicht 'Die Götter Griechenlands.'" *Jahrbuch der Deutschen Schillergesellschaft* 13 (1969): 251–71.

Frye, Lawrence O. "Schiller, Juggler of Freedoms in *Wilhelm Tell.*" *Monatshefte* 76 (1984): 73–88.

Fuhrmann, Manfred. "'Bild' und 'Gestalt' der Frau im Werk Friedrich Schillers." *Neue Sammlung* 23 (1983): 2–26.

Fukuyoshi, Masao. "Die 'Einbildungskraft' in der Umstellungszeit. Im Anschluß an J. G. Fichte." In *Zur Architektonik der Vernunft. Manfred Buhr zum sechzigsten Geburtstag*, edited by Lothar Berthold, 177–88. Berlin: Akademie-Verlag, 1987.

Fullenwider, Henry F. "Schiller and the German Tradition of Freedom of Thought." *Lessing Yearbook* 8 (1976): 117–24.

Gadamer, Hans-Georg. *Die Aktualität des Schönen.* Stuttgart: Reclam, 1977.

———. *Gesammelte Werke.* Tübingen: J. C. B. Mohr (Paul Siebeck), 1985f.

———. *Philosophical Hermeneutics.* Edited by David Linge. Berkeley/Los Angeles: University of California Press, 1977.

———. *Philosophische Lehrjahre. Eine Rückschau.* Frankfurt a.M.: Vittorio Klostermann, 1977.

———. *The Relevance of the Beautiful and Other Essays.* Translated by Nicholas Walker and edited by Robert Bernasconi. Cambridge/London/New York: Cambridge University Press, 1986.

———. "Rhetorik, Hermeneutik und Ideologiekritik. Metakritische Erörterungen zu 'Wahrheit und Methode.'" In Hans-Georg Gadamer's *Kleine Schriften I. Philosophie. Hermeneutik.* Tübingen: J. C. B. Mohr (Paul Siebeck), 1967.

———. *Truth and Method.* 2nd rev. ed. Translation revised by Joel Weinsheimer and Donald G. Marshall. New York: Crossroad, 1992.

———. "Die Universalität des hermeneutischen Problems." In his *Kleine Schriften I. Philosophie. Hermeneutik,* 101–12. Tübingen: J. C. B. Mohr (Paul Siebeck), 1967.

Garland, H. B. *Schiller. The Dramatic Writer: A Study of Style in the Plays.* Oxford: Clarendon Press, 1969.

Gerard, Alexander. *Versuch über das Genie.* Aus dem Englischen übersetzt von Christian Garve. Leipzig: Weidmanns Erben und Reich, 1776. [DLA]

Gerhard, Melitta. "'Ästhetische Erziehung' und Zukunftsausblick. Zu Goethes und Schillers Stellung gegenüber ihrer Epoche." *Jahrbuch des Freien Deutschen Hochstifts 1980:* 169–76.

Gethmann-Siefert, Annemarie. "Idylle und Utopie: Zur gesellschaftskritischen Funktion der Kunst in Schillers Ästhetik." *Jahrbuch der Deutschen Schillergesellschaft* 24 (1980): 32–67.

———. "Schiller und Lessing: Aus Geschichte(n) lernen." In *Idealismus und Aufklärung. Kontinuität und Kritik der Aufklärung in Philosophie und Poesie um 1800,* edited by Christoph Jamme and Gerhard Kurz, 259–82. Stuttgart: Klett-Cotta, 1988.

Gilde, Luise. *Friedrich von Schillers Geschichtsphilosophie. Veranschaulicht in seinen Dramen. Zum 200. Geburtstage des Dichters.* 2 vols. London: Selbstverlag, 1959.

Glassey, Roberta M. "The Concept of Freedom in Schiller's *Wallenstein.*" *Journal of European Studies* 10 (1980): 256–66.

Glück, Alfons. *Schillers "Wallenstein."* München: Wilhelm Fink, 1976.

Goethe, Johann Wolfgang. *Sämtliche Werke. Briefe, Tagebücher und Gespräche.* Edited by Hendrik Birus, et al. 40 vols. Frankfurt a.M.: Deutscher Klassiker Verlag, 1987f.

———. *Sämtliche Werke nach Epochen seines Schaffens.* Münchener Ausgabe. Edited by Karl Richter. München: Carl Hanser, 1985f.

Goetschel, Willi. *Kant als Schriftsteller.* Wien: Passagen, 1990.

Golz, Jochen. "Der Lyriker Schiller. Fragen an sein Werk." *Skamandros 1986:* 111–25.

———. "Der mäandrische Weg des Karl Moor: *Die Räuber.*" In *Schiller. Das dramatische Werk in Einzelinterpretationen,* edited by Hans-Dietrich Dahnke and Bernd Leistner, 10–41. Leipzig: Reclam, 1982.

———. "Individuum, Natur und Geschichte in Schillers 'Spaziergang.'" In *Friedrich Schiller. Angebot und Diskurs. Zugänge/Dichtung/Zeitgenossenschaft,* edited by Helmut Brandt, 393–400. Berlin/Weimar: Aufbau Verlag, 1987.

Grab, Walter. *Leben und Werke norddeutscher Jakobiner.* Stuttgart: J. B. Metzler, 1973.

Graham, Ilse. *Schiller: A Master of the Tragic Form: His Theory in His Practice.* Pittsburgh: Duquesne University Press, 1975.

———. *Schiller's Drama: Talent and Integrity.* London: Methuen, 1974.

Grassi, Ernesto. *Die Macht der Phantasie. Zur Geschichte abendländischen Denkens.* Königstein/Ts.: Athenäum, 1979.

Grathoff, Dirk and Erwin Leibfried, eds. *Schiller. Vorträge aus Anlaß seines 225. Geburtstages.* Frankfurt a.M./Bern/New York/Paris: Peter Lang, 1991.

Grimm, Jacob and Wilhelm. *Deutsches Wörterbuch.* München: Deutscher Taschenbuch, 1984.

Grimm, Reinhold and Jost Hermand, eds. *Die Klassik-Legende. Second Wisconsin Workshop.* Frankfurt a.M.: Athenäum, 1971.

Grimminger, Rolf. "Die ästhetische Versöhnung. Ideologiekritische Aspekte zum Autonomiebegriff am Beispiel Schiller[s]." In *Schillers Briefe über die ästhetische Erziehung des Menschen in einer Reihe von Briefen,* edited by Jürgen Bolten, 161–84. Frankfurt a.M.: Suhrkamp, 1984.

———. *Die Ordnung, das Chaos und die Kunst. Für eine neue Dialektik der Aufklärung.* Frankfurt a.M.: Suhrkamp, 1986.

Grossmann, Walter. "Schiller's Philosophy of History in his Jena Lectures of 1789–90." *Publications of the Modern Language Association* 69 (1954): 156–72.

Gruenter, Rainer. "Despotismus und Empfindsamkeit. Zu Schillers *Kabale und Liebe.*" *Jahrbuch des Freien Deutschen Hochstifts 1981:* 207–27.

Guthke, Karl S. "Are We Alone? The Idea of Extraterrestrial Intelligence in Literature and Philosophy from Copernicus to H. G. Wells." In *Utopian Vision. Technological Innovation and Poetic Imagination,* edited by Klaus L. Berghahn and Reinhold Grimm, 91-104. Heidelberg: Carl Winter, 1990.

———. "Haller—Glanz und Krise der Aufklärung." *Schweizer Monatshefte* 59 (1979): 134–148.

——. "Kabale und Liebe." In *Schillers Dramen. Neue Interpretationen,* edited by Walter Hinderer, 58–86. Stuttgart: Reclam, 1979.

——. *The Last Frontier: Imagining Other Worlds, from the Copernican Revolution to Modern Science Fiction.* Translated by Helen Atkins. Ithaca/London: Cornell University Press, 1990.

——. *Der Mythos der Neuzeit. Das Thema der Mehrheit der Welten in der Literatur- und Geistesgeschichte von der kopernikanischen Wende bis zur Science Fiction.* Bern/München: Francke, 1983.

——. "Der Parteien Gunst und Hass in Hamburg. Schillers Bühnenfassung des *Wallenstein.*" *Zeitschrift für Deutsche Philologie* 102 (1983): 181–200.

——. "Räuber Moors Glück und Ende." *The German Quarterly* 39 (1966): 1–11.

——. "'Richter' oder 'Leuchtöl'? Schillers letzte Worte in der Biographie." *Jahrbuch des Freien Deutschen Hochstifts 1992:* 183–204.

——. *Schillers Dramen. Idealismus und Skepsis.* Tübingen/Basel: A. Francke, 1994.

——. "Tragödie der Säkularisation. Schillers *Kabale und Liebe.*" In his *Das Abenteuer der Literatur. Studien zum literarischen Leben der deutschsprachigen Länder von der Aufklärung bis zum Exil.* Bern/München: Francke, 1981: 210–41.

——. "Wallenstein als Spiel von Spiel." *Wirkendes Wort 43* (1993): 174–96.

Habermas, Jürgen. "Erläuterungen zum Begriff des kommunikativen Handelns." In his *Vorstudien und Ergänzungen zur Theorie des kommunikativen Handelns.* Frankfurt a.M.: Suhrkamp, 1984: 571-604.

——. *Kultur und Kritik. Verstreute Aufsätze.* Frankfurt a.M.: Suhrkamp, 1973.

——. *Nachmetaphysisches Denken. Philosophische Aufsätze.* Frankfurt a.M.: Suhrkamp, 1988.

——. *The Philosophical Discourse of Modernity: Twelve Lectures.* Translated by Frederick Lawrence. 6th ed. Cambridge, Mass.: MIT Press, 1992.

——. *Der philosophische Diskurs der Moderne. Zwölf Vorlesungen.* Frankfurt a.M.: Suhrkamp, 1985.

——. *Philosophisch-politische Profile.* Expanded ed. Frankfurt a.M.: Suhrkamp, 1987.

——. "Philosophy as Stand-In and Interpreter." In *After Philosophy: End or Transformation?* edited by Kenneth Baynes, James Bohman, and Thomas McCarthy, 296–315. Cambridge, Mass.: MIT Press, 1987.

——. *Politik, Kunst, Religion. Essays über zeitgenössische Philosophen.* Stuttgart: Reclam, 1978.

——. *The Structural Transformation of the Public Sphere: An Inquiry into a Category of Bourgeois Society.* Cambridge, Mass.: MIT Press, 1989; Cambridge, England: Polity, 1989.

——. *Strukturwandel der Öffentlichkeit. Untersuchungen zu einer Kategorie der bürgerlichen Gesellschaft.* Mit einem Vorwort zur Neuauflage 1990. Frankfurt a.M.: Suhrkamp, 1990.

Hahn, Karl-Heinz. "Schillers Beitrag zur Theorie der Geschichtswissenschaft." In *Friedrich Schiller. Angebot und Diskurs. Zugänge/Dichtung/Zeitgenossenschaft,* edited by Helmut Brandt, 78–91. Berlin/Weimar: Aufbau Verlag, 1987.

——. "Schiller und die Geschichte." In *Friedrich Schiller. Zur Geschichtlichkeit seines Werkes,* edited by Klaus Berghahn, 25–54. Kronberg/Ts.: Scriptor, 1975.

Haller, Albrecht von. *Dr. Albrecht Hallers Versuch Schweizerischer Gedichte.* 3d ed. Bern: Niclaus Emanuel Haller, 1743. [DLA]

————. *First Lines of Physiology . . . A Reprint of the 1786 Edition*, with a new introduction by Lester S. King, M.D. New York/London: Johnson Reprint Corp., 1966.

Hamburger, Käte. *Philosophie der Dichter. Novalis, Schiller, Rilke.* Stuttgart: Kohlhammer, 1966.

————. "Schiller und die Lyrik." *Jahrbuch der Deutschen Schillergesellschaft* 16 (1972): 299–329.

————. "Schiller und Sartre. Ein Versuch zum Idealismus—Problem Schillers." *Jahrbuch der Deutschen Schillergesellschaft* 3 (1959): 34–70.

————. "Zum Problem des Idealismus bei Schiller." *Jahrbuch der Deutschen Schillergesellschaft* 4 (1960): 60–71.

Hammerstein, Reinhold. "'Schöne Welt, wo bist du?' Schiller, Schubert und die 'Götter Griechenlands.'" In *Musik und Dichtung: Neue Forschungsbeiträge. Viktor Pöschl zum 80. Geburtstag gewidmet,* edited by Michael von Albrecht and Werner Schubert, 305–30. Frankfurt a.M./Bern: Peter Lang, 1990.

Harrison, R. B., "The Fall and Redemption of Man in Schiller's *Kabale und Liebe.*" *German Life and Letters* 35 (1981): 5–13.

————. "'Gott ist über mir': Ruler and Reformer in the Twofold Symmetry of Schiller's *Don Carlos.*" *Modern Language Review* 76 (1981): 598–611.

Hart-Nibbrig, Christiaan L. "'Die Weltgeschichte ist das Weltgericht'. Zur Aktualität von Schillers ästhetischer Geschichtsdeutung." *Jahrbuch der Deutschen Schillergesellschaft* 20 (1976): 255–77.

Hartmann, Geoffrey H. *Criticism in the Wilderness: The Study of Literature Today.* New Haven, Connecticut/London: Yale University Press, 1980.

Hartmann, Horst. *Wallenstein. Geschichte und Deutung.* 3d. ed. Berlin: Volkseigener Verlag, 1983.

Hartmann, Nicolai. *Die Philosophie des Deutschen Idealismus.* Part 1: *Fichte, Schelling und die Romantik.* 3d ed. Berlin/New York: Walter de Gruyter, 1974.

Haupt, Johannes. "Geschichtsperspektive und Griechenverständnis im ästhetischen Programm Schillers." *Jahrbuch der Deutschen Schillergesellschaft* 18 (1974): 407–30.

Hawkes, Terence. *Metaphor.* London/New York: Methuen, 1972.

Hebel, Franz. "Menschenfreundliche Kultur. Moses Mendelssohns gegenwärtige Bedeutung." *Der Deutschunterricht* 36 (1984): 59–76.

Heftrich, Eckhard. "Das Schicksal in Schillers *Wallenstein,*" *Jahrbuch für internationale Germanistik* 27 (1990): 113–21.

Hegel, Georg Wilhelm Friedrich. "Über Wallenstein." In *Georg Wilhelm Friedrich Hegel. Werke 15: Vorlesungen über die Ästhetik III,* edited by Eva Moldenhauer and Karl Markus Michel, 618–20. Frankfurt a.M.: Suhrkamp, 1970.

Heidegger, Martin. *Holzwege.* 6th ed. Frankfurt a.M.: Vittorio Klostermann, 1980.

Heitner, Robert H. "Luise Millerin and the Shock Motif in Schiller's Early Dramas," *Germanic Review* 41 (1966): 27–44.

Hell, Victor. *Schiller. Théories esthétiques et structures dramatiques. Liberté et culture à l'épogue de la Révolution française et de l'idealisme allemand.* Paris: Aubier, 1974.

Henckmann, Wolfhart and Konrad Lotter, eds. *Lexikon der Ästhetik.* München: C. H. Beck, 1992.

Henkel, Arthur. "Wie Schiller Königinnen reden läßt. Zur Szene III,4 in der *Maria*

Stuart." In *Schiller und die höfische Welt,* edited by Achim Aurnhammer, Klaus Manger, and Friedrich Strack, 398–406. Tübingen: Max Niemeyer, 1990.

Henrich, Dieter. "Beauty and Freedom: Schiller's Struggle with Kant's Aesthetics." Translated by David R. Lachterman. In *Essays in Kant's Aesthetics,* edited by Ted Cohen and Paul Guyer, 221–57. Chicago/London: University of Chicago Press, 1982.

———. "Der Begriff der Schönheit in Schillers Ästhetik," *Zeitschrift für Philosophische Forschung* 11 (1957): 527–47.

———. "Was ist Metaphysik, was Moderne? Thesen gegen Habermas." *Merkur* 40 (1986): 495–508.

Herbst, Hildburg. "Zur Sprache des Sonnenwirts in Schillers Erzählung *Der Verbrecher aus verlorener Ehre.*" In *Friedrich Schiller. Kunst, Humanität und Politik in der späten Aufklärung. Ein Symposium,* edited by Wolfgang Wittkowski, 48–54. Tübingen: Max Niemeyer, 1982.

Herder, Johann Gottfried. *Ideen zur Philosophie der Geschichte der Menschheit.* Theil 1. Riga/Leipzig: Johann Friedrich Hartknoch, 1784. [DLA]

———. *Auch eine Philosophie der Geschichte zur Bildung der Menschheit.* Edited by Hans Dietrich Irmscher. Stuttgart: Reclam, 1990.

———. *Ideen zur Philosophie der Geschichte der Menschheit.* Edited by Martin Bollacher. Frankfurt a.M.: Deutscher Klassiker Verlag, 1989.

Hermand, Jost. "Schillers Abhandlung *Über naive und sentimentalische Dichtung* im Lichte der deutschen Popularphilosophie des 18. Jahrhunderts." *Publications of the Modern Language Association* 79 (1964): 428–41.

———. "Probleme 'interdisziplinärer' Forschung in den Kulturwissenschaften." In *Studien zur Ästhetik und Literaturgeschichte der Kunstperiode,* edited by Dirk Grathoff, 317–33. New York/Frankfurt a.M./Bern: Peter Lang, 1985.

Herrmann, Hans Peter. "Musikmeister Miller, die Emanzipation der Töchter und der dritte Ort der Liebenden. Schillers bürgerliches Trauerspiel im 18. Jh." *Jahrbuch der Deutschen Schillergesellschaft* (1984): 223–47.

——— and Martina Herrmann. *Friedrich Schiller. Kabale und Liebe.* 4th ed. Frankfurt a.M.: Moritz Diesterweg, 1988.

Herrmann, Wilhelm, ed. *200 Jahre Schillers "Räuber." Die Entstehung des Werks, Uraufführung und Inszenierungen am Nationaltheater Mannheim.* Mannheim: Städtisches Reiss-Museum, 1982.

Heselhaus, Clemens. "Wallensteinisches Welttheater." *Der Deutschunterricht* 12 (1960): 42–71.

Hess, Günter. "*Fracta Cithara* oder Die zerbrochene Laute. Zur Allegorisierung der Bekehrungsgeschichte Jacob Baldes im 18. Jahrhundert." In *Formen und Funktionen der Allegorie. Symposion Wolfenbüttel 1978,* edited by Walter Haug, 605–31. Stuttgart: J. B. Metzler, 1979.

Heubner, Kathinka "Die Kallias-Briefe von Friedrich Schiller-eine Analyse des Kunstschönen. Eine Darstellung der Kunsttheorie Friedrich Schillers mit semiotischen Mitteln." *Lili* 7 (1977): 173–87.

Heuer, Fritz. "Zu Schillers Plan einer transzendental- philosophischen Analytik des Schönen." *Philosophisches Jahrbuch* 80 (1973): 90–132.

———, and Werner Keller, eds. *Schillers Wallenstein.* Darmstadt: Wissenschaftliche Buchgesellschaft, 1977.

Heuß, Alfred. "Möglichkeiten einer Weltgeschichte heute." In his *Zur Theorie der Weltgeschichte.* Berlin: Walter de Gruyter, 1968.

Heyer, Elfriede A. "The Genesis of *Wallenstein:* From History to Drama." In *Friedrich von Schiller and the Drama of Human Existence,* edited by Alexej Urgrinsky, 71–79. New York/Westport, Connecticut: Greenwood Press, 1988.

Heyn, Gisa. *Der junge Schiller als Psychologe.* Zürich: Juris, 1966.

Hibberd, John. "Das Vorspiel zu Schillers *Wilhelm Tell* und die 'hervorzubringende Einheit.'" In *Texte, Motive und Gestalten der Goethezeit. Festschrift für Hans Reiss,* edited by John L. Hibberd and H.B. Nisbet, 151–76. Tübingen: Max Niemeyer, 1989.

Hieber, Hermann. *Der unklassische Schiller. Die Tragödie eines anständigen Menschen.* Stuttgart: Veritas, 1959.

Hilzinger, Klaus H[arro]. "Autonomie und Markt. Friedrich Schiller und sein Publikum." In *Metamorphosen des Dichters. Das Selbstverständnis deutscher Schriftsteller von der Aufklärung bis zur Gegenwart,* edited by Gunter E. Grimm. Frankfurt a.M.: Fischer Taschenbuch, 1992.

Hinck, Walter. "Schillers Zusammenarbeit mit Goethe auf dem Weimarer Hoftheater." In *Schiller und die höfische Welt,* edited by Achim Aurnhammer, Klaus Manger, and Friedrich Strack, 271–81. Tübingen: Max Niemeyer, 1990.

———, ed. *Geschichte als Schauspiel. Deutsche Geschichtsdramen. Interpretationen.* Frankfurt a.M.: Suhrkamp, 1981.

Hinderer, Walter. "Freiheit und Gesellschaft beim jungen Schiller." In his *Über deutsche Literatur und Rede. Historische Interpretationen.* München: Wilhelm Fink, 1981: 95–125.

———. "Jenseits von Eden. Zu Schillers *Wilhelm Tell.*" In *Geschichte als Schauspiel,* edited by Walter Hinck, 133–46. Frankfurt a.M.: Suhrkamp, 1981.

———. *Der Mensch in der Geschichte. Ein Versuch über Schillers "Wallenstein."* Mit einer Bibliographie von Helmut G. Hermann. Königstein: Athenäum, 1980.

———. "Die Philosophie der Ärzte und die Rhetorik der Dichter. Zu Schillers und Büchners ideologisch-ästhetischen Positionen." *Zeitschrift für Deutsche Philologie* 109 (1990). Sonderheft: 502–20.

———. "Republik oder Monarchie? Anmerkungen zu Schillers politischer Denkungsart." In *Literatur in der Demokratie. Für Walter Jens zum 60. Geburtstag,* edited by Wilfried Barner, et al., 305–14. München: Kindler, 1983.

———, ed. *Schillers Dramen. Neue Interpretationen.* Stuttgart: Reclam, 1979.

———. "Schiller und Bürger: Die ästhetische Kontroverse als Paradigma." *Jahrbuch des Freien Deutschen Hochstifts 1986:* 130–54.

———. "Der schöne Traum von der politischen Resignation: Schillers *Wallenstein*-Trilogie." In *Deutsche Dramen. Interpretationen zu Werken von der Aufklärung bis zur Gegenwart,* edited by Harro Müller-Michaels. 2 vols. Königstein: Athenäum, 1981, 1: 31–51.

———. "Utopische Elemente in Schillers ästhetischer Anthropologie." In *Literarische Utopie-Entwürfe,* edited by Hiltrud Gnüg, 173–86. Frankfurt a.M.: Suhrkamp, 1982.

———. *"Wallenstein."* In *Schillers Dramen. Neue Interpretationen,* edited by Walter Hinderer, 126–173. Stuttgart: Reclam, 1979.

Hirsch, E.D., Jr. "The Politics of Theories of Interpretation." In *The Politics of Interpretation,* edited by W. J. T. Mitchell, 321–33. Chicago/London: University of Chicago Press, 1983.

Höffe, Otfried. *Immanuel Kant.* 3d ed. München: C. H. Beck, 1992.

Hömig, Herbert and Dietrich Pfaehler, eds. *Im Bannkreis des klassischen Weimars.*

Festgabe für Hans Tümmler zum 75. Geburtstag. Bad Neustadt a.d. Saale: Pfaehler, 1982.

Hogrebe, Wolfram. "Fichte und Schiller. Eine Skizze." In *Schillers Briefe über die ästhetische Erziehung des Menschen in einer Reihe von Briefen,* edited by Jürgen Bolten, 276–89. Frankfurt a.M.: Suhrkamp, 1984.

Die Horen, eine Monatsschrift, ed. [Friedrich] Schiller. 12 vols. in 6. Tübingen: J. G. Cotta, 1795–97. [DLA]

Horkheimer, Max and Theodor Adorno. *Dialektik der Aufklärung. Philosophische Fragmente.* Frankfurt a.M.: S. Fischer, 1981.

Hoy, David Couzens. *The Critical Circle: Literature, History, and Philosophical Hermeneutics.* Berkeley/Los Angeles/London: University of California Press, 1978.

Huck, Georgina Margaret. *Schiller and the Greeks: With Special Regard to the Letters on the Aesthetic Education of Man.* Boston College Dissertation, 1972.

Hucke, Karl-Heinz. *'Jene Scheu vor allem Mercantilischen'. Schillers 'Arbeits- und Finanzplan.'* Tübingen: Max Niemeyer, 1984.

Huyssen, Andreas. *Das Drama des Sturm und Drang. Kommentar zu einer Epoche.* München: Winkler, 1980.

Ibel, Rudolf. *Schiller. Wallenstein. Wallensteins Lager. Die Piccolomini. Wallensteins Tod.* 7th ed. Frankfurt a.M./Berlin/München: Diesterweg, 1970.

Iffert, Wilhelm. *Der junge Schiller und das geistige Ringen seiner Zeit. Eine Untersuchung auf Grund der Anthologie-Gedichte.* Halle (Saale): Buchhandlung des Waisenhauses. Franckesche Stiftungen, 1926.

Immerwahr, Raymond. "Classicist Values in the Critical Thought of Friedrich Schlegel." *Journal of English and Germanic Philology* 79 (1980): 376–89.

———. "German Romanticism and the Unity of Romantic Imagination." In *On Romanticism and the Art of Translation: Studies in Honor of Edwin Hermann Zeydel,* edited by Gottfried F. Merkel, 67–81. Princeton N.J.: Princeton University Press, 1956.

Israel, Joachim. *Der Begriff Dialektik. Erkenntnistheorie, Sprache und dialektische Gesellschaftswissenschaft.* Reinbek bei Hamburg: Rowohlt, 1979.

Ives, Margaret. *The Analogue of Harmony: Some Reflections on Schiller's Philosophical Essays.* Pittsburgh: Duquesne University Press, 1970.

Jacobs, Wilhelm G. "Geschichte und Kunst in Schellings 'System des transscendentalen [sic] Idealismus.'" In *Früher Idealismus und Frühromantik. Der Streit um die Grundlagen der Ästhetik (1795–1805),* edited by Walter Jaeschke and Helmut Holzhey, 201–13. Hamburg: Felix Meiner, 1990.

Jacobson, Roswitha. "Die Entscheidung zur Sittlichkeit. Friedrich Schiller: *Der Verbrecher aus verlorener Ehre* (1786)." In *Deutsche Novellen,* edited by Winfried Freund, 15–25. München: Fink, 1993.

Jaeger, Hans-Wolf. *Politische Kategorien in Poetik und Rhetorik in der zweiten Hälfte des 18. Jahrhunderts.* Stuttgart: J. B. Metzler, 1970.

Jaeschke, Walter and Helmut Holzhey, eds. *Früher Idealismus und Frühromantik. Der Streit um die Grundlagen der Ästhetik (1795–1805).* Hamburg: Felix Meiner, 1990.

Jamison, Robert L. "Politics and Nature in Schiller's *Fiesco* and *Wilhelm Tell.*" In *Friedrich Schiller. Kunst, Humanität und Politik in der späten Aufklärung. Ein Symposium,* edited by Wolfgang Wittkowski, 59–66. Tübingen: Max Niemeyer, 1982.

Jamme, Christoph and Gerhard Kurz, eds. *Idealismus und Aufklärung. Kontinuität und Kritik der Aufklärung in Philosophie und Poesie um 1800.* Stuttgart: Klett-Cotta, 1988.

Janke, Wolfgang. *Historische Dialektik. Destruktion dialektischer Grundformen von Kant bis Marx.* Berlin/New York: Walter de Gruyter, 1977.

Jansen, H. H. "Schillers Krankheit und Tod aus pathologisch-anatomischer und klinischer Sicht." *Der Pathologe* 9 (1988): 187–91.

Janz, Rolf-Peter. "Die ästhetische Bewältigung des Schreckens. Zu Schillers Theorie des Erhabenen." In *Geschichte als Literatur: Formen und Grenzen der Repräsentation von Vergangenheit,* edited by Hartmut Eggert, Ulrich Profitlich, and Klaus R. Scherpe, 151–60. Stuttgart: Metzler, 1990.

———. *Autonomie und soziale Funktion der Kunst. Studien zur Ästhetik von Schiller und Novalis.* Stuttgart: J. B. Metzler, 1973.

———. "Schillers *Kabale und Liebe*—als bürgerliches Trauerspiel." *Jahrbuch der Deutschen Schillergesellschaft* 20 (1976): 208–28.

Jauss, Hans Robert. "Schlegels und Schillers Replik auf die 'Querelle des Anciens et des Modernes.'" In his *Literaturgeschichte als Provokation.* Frankfurt a.M.: 1970: 67–106.

Jay, Martin. "Habermas and Modernism." In *Habermas and Modernity,* edited by Richard J. Bernstein, 125–39. Cambridge, Massachusetts: MIT Press, 1985.

Jöns, Dietrich. "Das Problem der Macht in Schillers Dramen von den *Räubern* bis zum *Wallenstein.*" In *Deutsche Literatur zur Zeit der Klassik,* edited by Karl Otto Conrady, 76–92. Stuttgart: Reclam, 1977.

John, Erhard. "Zur Entwicklung von Realismusauffassung und Realismusbegriff im Gedankentausch Schillers und Goethes." In *Philosophie und Kunst. Kultur und Ästhetik im Denken der deutschen Klassik.* Weimar: Böhlau, 1987: 140–50.

Johnston, Otto W. "Mirabeau and Schiller on Education to Freedom." *Monatshefte* 76 (1984): 58–72.

———. "Schiller und das bourgeois-liberale Programm der Französischen Revolution." In *Friedrich Schiller. Kunst, Humanität und Politik in der späten Aufklärung. Ein Symposium,* edited by Wolfgang Wittkowski, 328–52. Tübingen: Max Niemeyer, 1982.

Jolles, Matthijs. "Das Bild des Weges und die Sprache des Herzens. Zur strukturellen Funktion des sprachlichen Bildes in Schillers *Wallenstein.*" *Deutsche Beiträge zur geistigen Überlieferung* 5 (1965): 109–42.

———. *Dichtkunst und Lebenskunst: Studien zum Problem der Sprache bei Friedrich Schiller.* Edited by Arthur Groos mit einem Nachwort von Elizabeth M. Wilkinson. Bonn: Bouvier, 1980.

———. "Toter Buchstabe und lebendiger Geist. Schillers Stellung zur Sprache." *Deutsche Beiträge zur geistigen Überlieferung* 4 (1964): 65–108.

Jones, Michael T. "From History to Aesthetics: Schiller's Early Jena Years." *German Studies Review* 6 (1983): 195–213.

Jonnes, Dennis. "Pattern of Power: Family and State in Schiller's Early Drama." *Colloquia Germanica* 20 (1987): 138–62.

Juhl, P. D. *Interpretation: An Essay in the Philosophy of Literary Criticism.* Princeton, N.J.: Princeton University Press, 1986.

Junker, Christoph. *Das Weltraumbild in der deutschen Lyrik von Opitz bis Klopstock.* Nachdruck der Ausgabe Berlin 1932. Nendeln/Liechtenstein: Kraus, 1967.

Kaiser, Gerhard. "Idylle und Revolution. Schillers *Wilhelm Tell.*" In *Deutsche Li-*

teratur und Französische Revolution. Sieben Studien, edited by Richard Brinkmann, 87–128. Göttingen: Vandenhoeck und Ruprecht, 1974.

———. "Krise der Familie. Eine Perspektive auf Lessings *Emilia Galotti* und Schillers *Kabale und Liebe.*" *Recherches germaniques* 14 (1984): 7–22.

———. *Vergötterung und Tod. Die thematische Einheit von Schillers Werk.* Stuttgart: J. B. Metzler, 1967.

———. *Von Arkadien nach Elysium. Schiller-Studien.* Göttingen: Vandenhoeck u. Ruprecht, 1978.

———. *Von der Aufklärung bis zum Sturm und Drang. 1730–1785.* Gütersloh: Sigbert Mohn, 1966.

———. "Wallensteins Lager. Schiller als Dichter und Theoretiker der Komödie." *Jahrbuch der Deutschen Schillergesellschaft* 14 (1970): 323–46.

Kant, Immanuel. *Immanuel Kant. Kritik der Urteilskraft.* Edited by Wilhelm Weischedel. 5th ed. Frankfurt a.M.: Suhrkamp, 1981.

———. *Immanuel Kant. Werke XI: Schriften zur Anthropologie, Geschichtsphilosophie, Politik und Pädagogik I.* Edited by Wilhelm Weischedel. Frankfurt a.M.: Suhrkamp/Insel, 1964.

Karthaus, Ulrich. "Friedrich Schiller." In *Genie und Geld. Vom Auskommen deutscher Schriftsteller,* edited by Karl Carino. Mit 34 Portraitzeichnungen von Peter Andres, 151–64. Nördlingen: Greno, 1987.

———. "Schiller und die französische Revolution." *Jahrbuch der Deutschen Schillergesellschaft* 33 (1989): 210–39 [An improved version appeared in *Schiller. Vorträge* 68–88].

Kaufman, Hans A. *Nation und Nationalismus in Schillers Entwurf "Deutsche Größe" und im Schauspiel "Wilhelm Tell." Zu ihrer kulturpolitischen Funktionalisierung im frühen 20. Jahrhurdert.* Frankfurt a.M.: Peter Lang, 1993.

Kerry, S[tanley] S. *Schiller's Writings on Aesthetics.* Manchester: Manchester University Press, 1961.

Kieffer, Bruce. "Tragedy in the Logocentric World: Schiller's *Kabale und Liebe.*" *German Studies Review* 5 (1982): 205–20.

Kiene, Hansjoachim. *Schillers Lotte. Porträt einer Frau in ihrer Welt.* Düsseldorf: Droste, 1984.

Kiesel, Helmuth. *'Bei Hof, bei Höll'. Untersuchungen zur literarischen Hofkritik von Sebastian Brant bis Friedrich Schiller.* Tübingen: Max Niemeyer, 1979.

———, and Paul Münch. *Gesellschaft und Literatur im 18. Jahrhundert. Voraussetzungen und Entstehung des literarischen Markts in Deutschland.* München: Beck, 1977.

Kittler, Friedrich. "Carlos als Carlsschüler. Ein Familiengemälde in einem fürstlichen Hause." In *Unser Commercium. Goethe und Schillers Literaturpolitik,* edited by Wilfried Barner, Eberhard Lämmert, and Norbert Oellers, 241–73. Stuttgart: J. G. Cotta, 1984.

Klein, Julie Thompson. *Interdisciplinarity: History, Theory, and Practice.* Detroit: Wayne State University Press, 1990.

Klopstock, Friedrich G. *Werke. Oden.* 2 vols. Leipzig: Georg Joachim Göschen, 1798. [DLA]

Kluge, Gerhard. "Die Kartäuserszenen in Schillers *Don Carlos.*" *Zeitschrift der Deutschen Philologie* 109 (1990). Sonderheft: 27–40.

———. "Über die Notwendigkeit der Kommentierung kleinerer Regie—und Spielanweisungen in Schillers frühen Dramen." *Editio* 3 (1989): 90–97.

————. "Zwischen Seelenmechanik und Gefühlspathos. Umrisse zum Verständnis der Gestalt Amalias. In *Die Räuber*-Analyse der Szene I,3." *Jahrbuch der Deutschen Schillergesellschaft* 20 (1976): 184–207.

Kockelmans, Joseph J. *Heidegger on Art and Art Works*. Dordrecht/Boston/Lancaster: Martinus Nijhoff, 1985.

Koc, R. "Fathers and Sons: Ambivalence Doubled in Schiller's *Räuber*." *The Germanic Review* 61 (1986): 91–104.

Köhler, Hermann. "Musik bei Platon und den Pythagoreern." In *Propyläen Geschichte der Literatur*. vol. 1: *Die Welt der Antike*. Berlin: Propyläen, 1981: 275–88.

Köhnke, Klaus. "Max Piccolomini und die Ethik des Herzens." *Acta Germanica* 11 (1979): 97–112.

————. "'Des Schicksals dunkler Knäul'. Zu Schillers Ballade 'Die Kraniche des Ibykus.'" *Zeitschrift der Deutschen Philologie* 108 (1989): 481–95.

Koepke, Wulf. "'. . . das Werk einer glücklichen Konstellation': Schillers 'Horen' und die deutsche Literaturgeschichte." In *Friedrich Schiller. Kunst, Humanität und Politik in der späten Aufklärung. Ein Symposium,* edited by Wolfgang Wittkowski, 366–82. Tübingen: Max Niemeyer, 1982.

Köpf, Gerhard. "Friedrich Schiller: 'Über Bürgers Gedichte'. Historizität als Norm einer Theorie des Lesers." In *Jahrbuch des Weiner Goethe-Vereins* 81/83 (1977–79): 263–73.

Körner, Josef. *Romantiker und Klassiker. Die Brüder Schlegel in ihren Beziehungen zu Schiller und Goethe.* Unveränderter reprografischer Nachdruck der Ausgabe Berlin 1924. Darmstadt: Wissenschaftliche Buchgesellschaft, 1971.

Kößler, Henning. *Freiheit und Ohnmacht. Die autonome Moral und Schillers Idealismus der Freiheit.* Göttingen: Vandenhoeck und Ruprecht, 1962.

Kommerell, Max. "Schiller als Psychologe." In his *Dame Dichterin und andere Essays,* edited by Arthur Henkel, 65–15. München: Deutscher Taschenbuchverlag, 1967.

Kondylis, Panajotis. *Die Aufklärung im Rahmen des neuzeitlichen Rationalismus.* Stuttgart: Klett/Cotta, 1981.

Kontje, Todd Curtis. *Constructing Reality: A Rhetorical Analysis of Friedrich Schiller's "Letters on the Aesthetic Education of Man."* New York/Berne/Frankfurt a.M./Paris: Peter Lang, 1987.

Koopmann, Helmut. "'Bestimme Dich aus Dir selbst.' Schiller, die Idee der Autonomie und Kant als problematischer Umweg." In *Friedrich Schiller. Kunst, Humanität und Politik in der späten Aufklärung. Ein Symposium,* edited by Wolfgang Wittkowski, 202–16. Tübingen: Max Niemeyer, 1982.

————. "Denken in Bildern. Zu Schillers philosophischem Stil." *Jahrbuch der Deutschen Schillergesellschaft* 30 (1986): 218–50.

————. "Der Dichter als Kunstrichter. Zu Schillers Rezensionsstragie." *Jahrbuch der Deutschen Schillergesellschaft* 20 (1976): 229–46.

————. "Dichter, Kritiker, Publikum. Schillers und Goethes Rezensionen als Indikatoren einer sich wandelnden Literaturkritik." In *Unser Commercium. Goethe und Schillers Literaturpolitik,* edited by Wilfried Barner, Eberhard Lämmert, and Norbert Oellers, 79–106. Stuttgart: J. G. Cotta, 1984.

————. "Don Karlos." In *Schillers Dramen. Neue Interpretationen,* edited by Walter Hinderer, 87–118. Stuttgart: Reclam, 1979.

————. *Drama der Aufklärung. Kommentar zu einer Epoche.* München: Winkler, 1979.

———. *Freiheitssonne und Revolutionsgewitter. Reflexe der Französischen Revolution im literarischen Deutschland zwischen 1789 und 1840.* Tübingen: Max Niemeyer, 1989.

———. *Friedrich Schiller.* 2 vols. 2d ed. Stuttgart: J. B. Metzler, 1977.

———. "*Kabale und Liebe* als Drama der Aufklärung." In *Verlorene Klassik? Ein Symposium,* edited by Wolfgang Wittkowski, 286–303. Tübingen: Max Niemeyer, 1986.

——— and Winfried Woesler, eds. *Literatur und Religion.* Freiburg/Basel/Wien: Herder, 1984.

———. *Schiller-Forschung. 1970–1980. Ein Bericht.* Marbach a.N.: Deutsche Schiller-Gesellschaft, 1982.

———. *Schiller. Eine Einführung.* München/Zürich: Artemis, 1988.

———. "Schillers *Kabale und Liebe:* das Naturrecht des Einzelnen und das Ende der bürgerlichen Sozialordnung als Ende der Aufklärung." In his *Das Drama der Aufklärung. Kommentar zu einer Epoche.* München: Winkler, 1979: 143–55.

———. "Schillers *Wallenstein*—Antiker Mythos und moderne Geschichte. Zur Begründung der klassischen Tragödie um 1800." In *Teilnahme und Spiegelung. Festschrift für Horst Rüdiger,* edited by Beda Allemann and Erwin Koppen, in cooperation with Dieter Gutzen, 263–74. Berlin/New York: Walter de Gruyter, 1975.

Koselleck, Reinhart. *Critique and Crisis. Enlightenment and the Pathogenesis of Modern Society.* Cambridge, Mass.: MIT Press, 1988.

———. "Begriffsgeschichte und Sozialgeschichte." In his *Vergangene Zukunft. Zur Semantik geschichtlicher Zeiten.* Frankfurt a.M.: Suhrkamp, 1979: 107–29.

———. *Kritik und Krise. Eine Studie zur Pathogenese der bürgerlichen Welt.* Freiburg/München: Karl Alber, 1959; 3d ed. Frankfurt a.M.: Suhrkamp, 1979.

Kowalik, Jill Anne. *The Poetics of Historical Perspectivism: Breitinger's "Critische Dichtkunst" and the Neoclassic Tradition.* Chapel Hill/London: University of North Carolina Press, 1992.

Kräupl, Günther. "Verbrechen, Justiz und Strafe bei Schiller." *Neue Justiz* 40 (1986): 409–10.

Kraft, Herbert. "Die dichterische Form der *Louise Millerin.*" *Zeitschrift der Deutschen Philologie* 85 (1966): 7–21.

———. "Über sentimentalische und idyllische Dichtung. Zweiter Teil: 'Das Ideal und das Leben.'" *Jahrbuch der Deutschen Schillergesellschaft* 20 (1976): 247–54.

———. *Um Schiller betrogen.* Pfullingen: Neske, 1978.

Kratzsch, Irmgard, ed. *Friedrich Schiller und die Naturforschende Gesellschaft zu Jena.* Mit einem Faksimile des Briefes vom 2. Februar 1794 an A. J. G. K. Batsch. Jena: Universitätsbibliothek der Friedrich-Schiller-Universität, 1984.

Krauß, Rudolf. "Das Hoftheater Herzog Karls von Württemberg," *Bühne und Welt. Zeitschrift für Theaterwesen, Litteratur und Musik* 5 (1902–03): 669–80.

———. "Die Erstaufführung von Schillers Dramen auf dem Stuttgarter Hoftheater." *Euphorion* 12 (1905): 599–627.

———. "Schiller auf der Hofbühne seines Heimatlandes." *Bühne und Welt. Zeitschrift für Theaterwesen, Litteratur und Musik* 7 (1905): 615–27.

Kühlmann, Wilhelm. "Poetische Legitimität und legitimierte Poesie: Betrachtungen zu Schillers Ballade *Der Graf von Habsburg* und ihrem literarischen Umkreis." In *Schiller und die höfische Welt,* edited by Achim Aurnhammer, Klaus Manger, and Friedrich Strack, 282–97. Tübingen: Max Niemeyer, 1990.

Kühnemann, Eugen. *Die Kantischen Studien Schillers und die Komposition des "Wallenstein."* 3 parts in 1 vol. Marburg: O. Ehrhardt's Universitätsbuchhandlung, 1889.

Kuhn, Dorothea. "Der naturwissenschaftliche Unterricht an der Hohen Karlsschule." *Medizin historisches Journal* 11 (1976): 319–34.

——. "Versuch über Modelle der Natur in der Goethezeit." In her *Typus und Metamorphose. Goethe-Studien,* edited by Renate Grumach, 159–76. Marbach am Neckar: Deutsche Schillergesellschaft, 1988.

Kuhn, Helmut. *Die Vollendung der klassischen deutschen Ästhetik durch Hegel.* Berlin: Junker u. Dünnhaupt, 1931.

Kuhn, Thomas. *The Essential Tension: Selected Studies in Scientific Tradition and Change.* Chicago: University of Chicago Press, 1977.

Kuhns, Richard. *Literature and Philosophy: Structures of Experience.* London: Routledge and Kegan Paul, 1971.

Kulenkampff, Jens. "Friedrich Schiller. Vollständiges Verzeichnis der Randbemerkungen in seinem Handexemplar der *Kritik der Urteilskraft.*" In *Materialien zu Kants "Kritik der Urteilskraft,"* edited by him, 126–44. Frankfurt a.M.: Suhrkamp, 1974.

——, ed. *Materialien zu Kants "Kritik der Urteilskraft."* Frankfurt a.M.: Suhrkamp, 1974.

Kurz, Gerhard. "Die schwierige Metapher." *Deutsche Vierteljahrsschrift für Literaturwissenschaft und Geistesgeschichte* 52 (1978): 544–57.

Kuzniar, Alice C., "Philosophic Chiliasm: Generating the Future, or Delaying the End?" *Eighteenth-Century Studies* 19 (1985): 1–20.

Kwang-Myung, Kim. *"Die vollständige anthropologische Schätzung" bei Schiller in ihrer Bedeutung für seine Ästhetik. Eine Interpretation zu Schillers philosophisch-ästhetischen Schriften.* University of Würzburg Dissertation, 1985.

Lahnstein, Peter. *Schillers Leben. Biographie.* München: List, 1982.

Lamport, F. J. "The Charismatic Hero: Goethe, Schiller, and the Tragedy of Character." *Publications of the English Goethe Society* 58 (1987–88): 62–83.

——. "Krise und Legitimitätsanspruch. *Maria Stuart* als Geschichtstragödie." *Zeitschrift der Deutschen Philologie* 109 (1990). Sonderheft: 134–45.

——. "The Silence of Wilhelm Tell." *Modern Language Review* 76 (1981): 857–68.

Lange, Victor. *The Classical Age of German Literature, 1740–1815.* New York: Holmes and Meier, 1982.

Larkin, Edward T. Review of: Klaus Berghahn, *Schiller. Ansichten eines Idealisten.* In *Goethe Yearbook* 5 (1990): 371–75.

Laufhütte, Hartmut. *Die deutsche Kunstballade. Grundlegung einer Gattungsgeschichte.* Heidelberg: Carl Winter, 1979.

Leibniz, Gottfried Wilhelm. *Monadologie.* Edited by Hermann Glockner. 2d ed. Stuttgart: Reclam, 1970.

Leidner, Alan C. "'Fremde Menschen fielen einander schluchzend in die Arme.' *Die Räuber* and the Communal Response." *Goethe Yearbook* 3 (1986): 57–71.

Leistner, Bernd. "'Ich habe deinen edlern Teil nicht retten können'. Zu Schillers Trauerspiel *Maria Stuart.*" *Zeitschrift für Germanistik* 2 (1981): 166–81.

——. "Leiden und Läuterung: *Maria Stuart.*" In *Schiller. Das dramatische Werk in Einzelinterpretationen,* edited by Hans-Dietrich Dahnke and Bernd Leistner, 167–92. Leipzig: Reclam, 1982.

―――. "Poetische Konfession und dramatisches Werk." *Impulse* 5 (1982): 9–62.

Lepenies, Wolf. *Die drei Kulturen. Soziologie zwischen Literatur und Wissenschaft.* München: Hanser, 1985.

Linden, Mareta. *Untersuchungen zum Anthropologiebegriff des 18. Jahrhunderts.* Bern/Frankfurt a.M.: Herbert und Peter Lang, 1976.

Linder, Jutta. *Schillers Dramen. Bauprinzip und Wirkungsstragie.* Bonn: Bouvier, 1989.

Linn, Rolf N. *Schillers junge Idealisten.* Berkeley/Los Angeles/London: University of California Press, 1973.

Lippuner, Heinz and Heinrich Mettler. *Friedrich Schiller: Wilhelm Tell. Das Drama der Freiheit.* Paderborn/München/Wien/Zürich: Ferdinand Schöningh, 1989.

Lloyd, Tom. "Society and Chaos: Schiller's Impact on Carlyle's Ideas about Revolution." *Clio* 17 (1987–88): 51–64.

Loewen, Harry. "The End as the Beginning: The Nature of Maria Stuart's Transformation." *Seminar* 15 (1979): 165–80.

Lohman, Knut. "Schiller: *Kabale und Liebe.*" In *Germanistik in Forschung und Lehre. Vorträge und Diskussionen des Germanistentages in Essen, 21–25. Oktober 1964,* edited by Rudolf Henß and Hugo Moser, 124–129. Berlin: E. Schmidt, 1965.

Lohner, Edgar. *Schiller und die moderne Lyrik.* Göttingen: Vandenhoeck und Ruprecht, 1964.

Lokke, Karl. "Schiller's *Maria Stuart.* The Historical Sublime and the Aesthetics of Gender." *Monatshefte* 82 (1990): 123–31.

Longyear, Rey M. *Schiller and Music.* Chapel Hill, N.C.: University of North Carolina Press, 1966.

Lovejoy, Arthur. *The Great Chain of Being: A Study of the History of an Idea.* 10th ed. Cambridge, Massachusetts: Harvard University Press, 1971.

―――. "Nature as Aesthetic Norm." In his *Essays in the History of Ideas.* Baltimore: Johns Hopkins, 1948: 42–52.

―――. "Schiller and the Genesis of Romanticism." *Modern Language Notes* 35 (1920): 1–10, and 136–46.

Lüthi, Hans Jürg. "Schillers Idee der Freiheit." *Schweizer Monatshefte für Politik, Wirtschaft, Kultur* 43 (August 1963): 449–59.

Lukács, Georg. *History and Class Consciousness: Studies in Marxist Dialectics.* Translated by Rodney Livingstone. Cambridge, Massachusetts: MIT Press, 1971.

―――. "Schillers Theorie der modernen Literatur." In his *Goethe und seine Zeit.* Bern: Francke, 1947: 108–44.

―――. "Zur Ästhetik Schillers." In *Georg Lukács Werke* 10: *Probleme der Ästhetik.* Neuwied/Berlin: Hermann Luchterhand, 1969: 17–106.

Lützeler, Paul Michael. "Literaturwissenschaft—German Studies—Interkulturelle Germanistik. Zur 'Krise' des Faches Deutsch in den USA." *Mitteilungen des Deutschen Germanistenverbandes* 37 (1990): 31–37.

Lutz, Hans. *Schillers Anschauungen von Kultur und Natur.* Berlin: E. Ebering, 1928.

Mainland, W[illiam].F[aulkner]. *Schiller and the Changing Past.* London: Heinemann, 1957.

Malsch, Wilfried. "Der Betrogene Deus iratus in Schillers Drama *Louise Millerin.*" In *Collegium philosophicum. Studien Joachim Ritter zum 60. Geburtstag.* Basel/Stuttgart: Schwabe, 1965: 157–208.

―――. "Die geistesgeschichtliche Legende der Deutschen Klassik." In *Die Klassik-*

Legende. Second Wisconsin Workshop, edited by Reinhold Grimm and Jost Hermand, 108–40. Frankfurt a.M.: Athenäum, 1971.

———. "Moral und Politik in Schillers *Don Karlos.*" In *Verantwortung und Utopie. Zur Literatur der Goethezeit. Ein Symposium,* edited by Wolfgang Wittkowski, 207–37. Tübingen: Max Niemeyer, 1988.

———. "Robespierre ad Portas? Zur Deutungsgeschichte der *Briefe über Don Carlos* von Schiller." In *The Age of Goethe Today: Critical Reexamination and Literary Reflection,* edited by Gertrud Bauer Pickar and Sabine Cramer, 69–103. München: Fink, 1990.

———. "Schillers und Friedrich Schlegels Poesiebegriffe im Licht von Herders typologischer Griechenlanddeutung." In *Perspektiven der Romantik. Beiträge des Marburger Kolloquiums zum 80. Geburtstag Erich Ruprechts,* edited by Reinhard Görisch, 9–35. Bonn: Bouvier, 1987.

Mandelbaum, Maurice. *The Anatomy of Historical Knowledge.* Baltimore: Johns Hopkins, 1977.

Manek, Anneliese Gretel. *Träger des Bösen im dramatischen Werk Schillers.* University of Freiburg/Br. Dissertation, 1964.

Mann, Golo. "Schiller als Historiker." *Jahrbuch der Deutschen Schillergesellschaft* 4 (1960): 98–109.

Mann, Michael. *Sturm-und-Drang Drama. Studien und Vorstudien zu Schillers "Räubern."* Bern/München: Francke, 1974.

———. "Zur Charakterologie in Schillers *Wallenstein.*" *Euphorion* 63 (1969): 329–339.

Mansouri, Rachid Jai. *Die Darstellung der Frau in Schillers Dramen.* New York/Berne/Frankfurt a.M./Paris: Peter Lang, 1988.

Marcuse, Herbert. "Über den affirmativen Charakter der Kultur." *Zeitschrift für Sozialforschung* 6 (1937): 5–94.

Martens, Wolfgang, ed. *Bibliographische Probleme im Zeichen eines erweiterten Literaturbegriffs. 2. Kolloquium zur bibliographischen Lage in der germanistischen Literaturwissenschaft,* Weinheim: VCH Acta humaniora, 1988.

———. "Officiana Diaboli. Das Theater im Visier des Halleschen Pietismus." *In his Literatur und Frömmigkeit in der Zeit der frühen Aufklärung.* Tübingen: Max Niemeyer, 1989: 24–29.

Martin, Uwe. "Freude, Freiheit, Götterfunken. Über Schillers Schwierigkeiten beim Schreiben von Freiheit." *Cahiers d'etudes germaniques* 18 (1990): 9–18.

Martini, Fritz. *Literarische Form und Geschichte. Aufsätze zur Gattungstheorie und Gattungsentwicklung von Sturm und Drang bis zum Erzählen heute.* Stuttgart: Metzler, 1984.

———. "Schillers Abschiedsszenen." In *Über Literatur und Geschichte. Festschrift für Gerhard Storz,* edited by Hüppauf and Dolf Sternberger, 151–184. Frankfurt a.M.: Athenäum, 1973.

———. "*Wilhelm Tell.* Der ästhetische Staat und der ästhetische Mensch." *Der Deutschunterricht* 12 (1960): 90–118.

Martinson, Steven D. *Between Luther and Münzer: The Peasant Revolt in German Drama and Thought.* Heidelberg: Carl Winter, 1988.

———. "Filling in the Gaps: 'The Problem of World-Order' in Friedrich Schiller's Essay on Universal History." *Eighteenth-Century Studies* 22 (1988): 24–46.

———. "Friedrich Schiller's *Der Verbrecher aus verlorener Ehre,* or the Triumph of the Moral Will." *Sprachkunst* 18 (1987): 1–9.

———. *On Imitation, Imagination and Beauty: A Critical Reassessment of the Concept of the Literary Artist During the Early German "Aufklärung."* Bonn: Bouvier, 1977.

———. "Reason, Revolution and Religion: Johann Benjamin Erhard's Concept of Enlightened Revolution." *History of European Ideas* 12 (1990): 221–26.

———. "Shaping the Imagination: Friedrich Schiller's Book Reviews." In *The Eighteenth-Century German Book Review,* edited by Karl J. Fink and Herbert Rowland, 137–150 Heidelberg: Carl Winter, 1995.

———. Review of: Dieter Borchmeyer, *Macht und Melancholie. Schillers "Wallenstein."* In *German Studies Review* 13 (1990): 151–53.

———. Review of: Lesley Sharpe, *Schiller and the Historical Character.* In *Monatshefte* 77 (1985): 357–58.

Marx, Werner. *Schelling: Geschichte, System, Freiheit.* Freiburg/München: Karl Alber, 1977.

Masson, Raoul. "La psycho-physiologie du jeune Schiller." *Etudes germaniques* 14 (1959): 363–73.

Maurer, Doris, ed. *Friedrich Schiller. Die Räuber. Eine Bild-Dokumentation zur Entstehungs—und Wirkungsgeschichte.* Dortmund: Harenberg Dokumentation, 1983.

Mayer, Hans. *Versuche über Schiller.* Frankfurt a.M.: Suhrkamp, 1987.

McCardle, Arthur W. *Friedrich Schiller and Swabian Pietism.* New York/Berne/Frankfurt a.M.: Peter Lang, 1986.

McCarthy, John. "The Art of Reading and the Goals of the German Enlightenment." *Lessing Yearbook* 14 (1984): 79–94.

———. *Crossing Boundaries: A Theory and History of Essay Writing in German, 1680–1815.* Philadelphia: University of Pennsylvania Press, 1989.

———. "'Morgendämmerung der Wahrheit'. Schiller and Censorship." In *"Unmoralisch an sich . . ." Zensur im 18. und 19. Jahrhundert,* edited by Herbert G. Göpfert and Erdmann Weyrauch, 231–48. Wiesbaden: Harrassowitz in Komm, 1988.

McCarthy, Thomas. *Ideals and Illusions: On Reconstruction and Deconstruction in Contemporary Critical Theory.* Cambridge, Mass.: MIT Press, 1991.

McClelland, Denny. "The Discrepancy between Kant and Schiller." In *Friedrich von Schiller and the Drama of Human Existence,* edited by Alexej Ugrinsky, 135–40. New York/Westport, Connecticut: Greenwood Press, 1988.

McGowan, John. *Postmodernism and Its Critics.* Ithaca, New York/London: Cornell University Press, 1991.

Meier, Albert. "Der Grieche, die Natur und die Geschichte. Ein Motivzusammenhang in Schillers Briefen *Über die ästhetische Erziehung* und *Über naive und sentimentalische Dichtung." Schiller-Jahrbuch* 29 (1985): 113–24.

———. "Die Schaubühne als eine moralische Arznei betrachtet. Schillers erfahrungsseelenkundliche Umdeutung der Katharsis-Theorie Lessings." *Lenz-Jahrbuch* 2 (1992): 151–162.

Meinecke, Friedrich. "Schillers 'Spaziergang.'" In *Interpretationen,* edited by Jost Schillemeit. Frankfurt a.M.: Fischer, 1965. vol. 1: *Deutsche Lyrik von Weckherlin bis Benn:* 99–112.

Meinhold, Peter. "Schillers spiritualistische Religions-philosophie und Geschichtskritik." *Zeitschrift für Religions—und Geistesgeschichte* 8 (1956): 97–128.

Melville, Stephen W. *Philosophy Beside Itself: On Deconstruction and Modernism.* Foreword Donald Marshall. Minneapolis: University of Minnesota Press, 1986.

Mendelssohn, Moses. *Moses Mendelssohn. Gesammelte Schriften. Jubiläumsausgabe,* edited by Alexander Altmann et al. Stuttgart-Bad Canstatt: Friedrich Frommann (Günther Holzboog), 1971f. vol. 1: *Moses Mendelssohn. Schriften zur Philosophie und Ästhetik,* edited by Fritz Bamberger. Faksimile-Neudruck der Ausgabe Berlin 1929 mit einem Bildnis und einem Faksimile (1971).

———. *Phädon, oder über die Unsterblichkeit der Seele in 3* Gesprächen 4th ed. Berlin: Nicolai, 1776. [DLA and the University of Arizona]

———. *Philosophische Schriften.* Erster Theil. Verbesserte Auflage. Berlin: Christian Friedrich Voss, 1777.

Menges, Karl. "Schönheit als Freiheit in der Erscheinung. Zur semiotischen Transformation des Autonomiegedankens in den ästhetischen Schriften Schillers." In *Friedrich Schiller. Kunst, Humanität und Politik in der späten Aufklärung. Ein Symposium,* edited by Wolfgang Wittkowski, 181–99. Tübingen: Max Niemeyer, 1982.

Mennemeier, Franz Norbert. "Friedrich Schlegels frühromantisches Literatur-Programm." In *Idealismus und Aufklärung. Kontinuität und Kritik der Aufklärung in Philosophie und Poesie um 1800,* edited by Christoph Jamme and Gerhard Kurz, 283–95. Stuttgart: Klett-Cotta, 1988.

Menzies, John Karl. *Schiller, Historical Truth, and the Netherlands: The Genesis of Schiller's Concept of History.* University of California at Berkeley Dissertation, 1981.

Mette, A[lexander]. "Die physiologischen Dissertationen Friedrich Schillers im Blickfeld der heutigen Medizin." *Zeitschrift für Geschichte der Naturwissenschaften, Technik und Medizin* 1 (1960): 35–49.

Mettler, Heinrich. *Entfremdung und Revolution: Brennpunkt des Klassischen. Studien zu Schillers Briefen "Über die ästhetische Erziehung des Menschen" im Hinblick auf die Begegnung mit Goethe.* Bern/München: Francke, 1977.

——— and Heinz Lippuner. *Friedrich Schiller: Wilhelm Tell. Das Drama der Freiheit.* Paderborn/München/Wien/Zürich: Schöningh, 1989.

———. *"Der Verbrecher aus verlorener Ehre* und *Wilhelm Tell.* Von Räuberhauptmann zum Erretter der Eidgenossenshaft." In *Tell und die Schweiz-die Schweiz und "Tell". Ein Schulbeispiel für die Wirkkraft von Schillers "Wilhelm Tell". Ihre Voraussetzungen und Folgen,* edited by Heinrich Mettler and Heinz Lippuner, 97–116. Thalwil/Zürich: paeda media, 1982.

Meyer, Herman. "Schillers philosophische Rhetorik." *Euphorion* 53 (1959): 313–50.

Michelfelder, Diane and Richard Palmer, eds. *The Gadamer-Derrida Encounter: Texts and Comments.* Albany, N.Y.: State University of New York Press, 1988.

Michelsen, Peter. *Der Bruch mit der Vater-Welt. Studien zu Schillers "Räubern."* Heidelberg: Carl Winter, 1979.

———. "Ordnung und Eigensinn. Über Schillers *Kabale und Liebe.*" *Jahrbuch des Freien Deutschen Hochstifts 1984:* 198–222.

Michaels, Walter Benn. "Is There a Politics of Interpretation." In *The Politics of Interpretation,* edited by W. J. T. Mitchell, 335–45. Chicago/London: University of Chicago Press, 1983.

Midell, Eike. *Friedrich Schiller. Leben und Werk.* Leipzig: Reclam, 1980.

Mielke, Andreas. "*Maria Stuart:* Hermeneutical Problems of 'One' Tragedy with 'Two' Queens." In *Friedrich von Schiller and the Drama of Human Existence,* edited by Alexej Urgrinsky, 49–61. New York/Westport, Connecticut: Greenwood Press, 1988.

Mieth, Günter. "Friedrich Schillers 'Spaziergang' und die lyrische Aneignung der menschlichen Gattungsgeschichte. Ein Diskussionsbeitrag." In *Friedrich Schiller. Angebot und Diskurs. Zugänge/Dichtung/Zeitgenossenschaft*, edited by Helmut Brandt, 401–9. Berlin/Weimar: Aufbau Verlag, 1987.

Miles, David. "Literary Sociology: Some Introductory Notes." *The German Quarterly* 48 (1975): 1–35.

Miller, J. Hillis. "Presidential Address 1986." *Publications of the Modern Language Association* 102 (1987): 281–91.

Miller, R[onald]. D[uncan]. *Interpreting Schiller: A Study of Four Plays*. Harrogate: The Duchy Press, 1986.

———. *Schiller and the Ideal of Freedom: A Study of Schiller's Philosophical Works with Chapters on Kant*. Oxford: Clarendon Press, 1970.

———. *Study of Schiller's "Letters on the Aesthetic Education of Man."* Harrogate: The Duchy Press, 1986.

Minor, J[akob]. *Schiller. Sein Leben und seine Werke*. 2 vols. Berlin: Weidmann, 1890.

Mitchell, W. J. T., ed. *The Politics of Interpretation*. Chicago/London: University of Chicago Press, 1983.

Mittelstraß, Jürgen. *Neuzeit und Aufklärung. Studien zur Entstehung der neuzeitlichen Wissenschaft und Philosophie*. Berlin/New York: Walter de Gruyter, 1970.

Möller, Horst. "Wie bürgerlich war die Aufklärung, wie aufgeklärt der Bürger?" In his *Vernunft und Kritik. Deutsche Aufklärung im 17. und 18. Jahrhundert*. Frankfurt a.M.: Suhrkamp, 1986: 289–97.

Mommsen, Katherina. "Goethes Gedicht 'Nähe des Geliebten.' Ausdruck der Liebe für Schiller, Auftakt der Freundschaft mit Zelter." *Goethe-Jahrbuch* 109 (1992): 31–44.

Moritz, Karl Philipp. *Über die bildende Nachahmung des Schönen*. Braunschweig: Schulbuchhandlung, 1788. [DLA]

Moutoux, Eugene. "The Betrayal of Friendship in Schiller's *Wallenstein* and in History. Wallenstein's Antagonists Ferdinand, Octavio, and Buttler." *Colloquia Germanica* 15 (1982): 209–24.

———. "Wallenstein: Guilty and Innocent." *The Germanic Review* 57 (1982): 23–27.

Muehleck-Müller, Cathleen. *Schönheit und Freiheit: Die Vollendung der Moderne in der Kunst. Schiller-Kant*. Würzburg: Königshausen u. Neumann, 1989.

Müller, Ernst. *Der junge Schiller*. Tübingen/Stuttgart: Rainer Wunderlich (Hermann Leins), 1947.

Müller, Hans Georg. *Friedrich Schiller. "Kabale und Liebe."* Stuttgart: Klett, 1987.

Müller, Irmgard. "'Die Wahrheit . . . von dem Krankenbett aus beweisen . . .' Zu Schillers medizinischen Studien und Bestrebungen." In *Schiller. Vorträge aus dem Anlaß seines 225. Geburtstages*, edited by Dirk Grathoff and Erwin Leibfried, 112–32. Frankfurt a.M./Bern/New York/Paris: Peter Lang, 1991.

Müller, Joachim. "Die geschichtliche Entscheidung in Schillers Dramen." In his *Wirklichkeit und Klassik. Beiträge zur deutschen Literaturgeschichte von Lessing bis Heine*. Berlin: Verlag der Nation, 1955: 149–62.

Müller, Klaus-Detlef. "Die Aufhebung des bürgerlichen Trauerspiels in Schillers *Don Karlos*." In *Friedrich Schiller. Angebot und Diskurs. Zugänge/Dichtung/Zeitgen-*

ossenschaft, edited by Helmut Brandt, 218–234. Berlin/Weimar: Aufbau Verlag, 1987.

———. "Schiller und das Mäzenat. Zu den Entstehungsbedingungen der Briefe *Über die ästhetische Erziehung des Menschen.*" In *Unser Commercium. Goethes und Schillers Literaturpolitik,* edited by Wilfried Barner, Eberhard Lämmert, and Norbert Oellers, 151–67. Stuttgart: J. G. Cotta, 1984.

Müller, Richard Matthias. "Nachstrahl der Gottheit: Karl Moor." *Deutsche Vierteljahrsschrift für Literaturwissenschaft und Geistesgeschichte* 63 (1989): 628–744.

Müller, Udo. *Friedrich Schiller: "Wallenstein."* Stuttgart: Klett, 1987.

Müller-Seidel, Walter. *Das Pathetische und Erhabene in Schillers Jugenddramen.* University of Heidelberg Dissertation, 1949.

———. "Georg Friedrich Gaus. Zur religiösen Situation des jungen Schiller." *Deutsche Vierteljahrsschrift für Literaturwissenschaft und Geistesgeschichte* 26 (1952): 76–99.

———. *Die Geschichtlichkeit der deutschen Klassik. Literatur und Denkformen um 1800.* Stuttgart: J. B. Metzler, 1983.

———. "Die Idee des neuen Lebens in Schillers *Wallenstein.*" in his *Die Geschichtlichkeit der deutschen Klassik* 127–39.

———. "Naturforschung und deutsche Klassik. Die Jenaer Gespräche im Juli 1794." In *Untersuchungen zur Literatur als Geschichte. Festschrift für Benno von Wiese,* edited by Vincent J. Günther, Helmut Koopmann, Peter Pütz, Hans Joachim Schrimpf, 61–78. Berlin: Erich Schmidt, 1973.

———. "Schillers Kontroverse mit Bürger und ihr geschichtlicher Sinn." In his *Die Geschichtlichkeit der deutschen Klassik Literatur und Denkformen um 1800,* 87–104, 307–11. Stuttgart: Metzler, 1983.

———. "Das stumme Drama der Luise Millerin." *Goethe* 17 (1955): 91–103.

———. "Verschwörungen und Rebellionen in Schillers Dramen." In *Schiller und die höfische Welt,* edited by Achim Aurnhammer, Klaus Manger, and Friedrich Strack, 422–46. Tübingen: Max Niemeyer, 1990.

Mueller-Vollmer, Kurt, ed. *The Hermeneutics Reader: Texts of the German Tradition from the Enlightenment to the Present.* New York: Continuum, 1985.

Münch, Richard. *Die Struktur der Moderne. Grundmuster und differentielle Gestaltung des institutionellen Aufbaus der modernen Gesellschaften.* Frankfurt a.M.: Suhrkamp, 1984.

Muschg, Walter. *Schiller. Die Tragödie der Freiheit. Zur zweihundertsten Wiederkehr von Schillers Geburtstag 10. November 1959.* Bern/München: Francke, 1959.

Musen-Almanach für das Jahr 1796 [also: 1797/98/99/1800]. Ed. [Friedrich] Schiller. Neustrelitz: Hofbuchhändler Michaelis, n.d. [DLA]

Namowicz, Tadeuz. "Schillers Schriften zur Geschichte in komparatistischer Sicht." In *Friedrich Schiller. Angebot und Diskurs. Zugänge/Dichtung/Zeitgenossenschaft,* edited by Helmut Brandt, 99–116. Berlin/Weimar: Aufbau Verlag, 1987.

Nassen, Ulrich. "Hans-Georg Gadamer und Jürgen Habermas: Hermeneutik, Ideologiekritik und Diskurs." In his *Klassiker der Hermeneutik,* 301–21. Paderborn/München/Wien/Zürich: Schöningh, 1982.

Natoli, Joseph, ed. *Tracing Literary Theory.* Urbana/Chicago: University of Illinois Press, 1987.

Nerjes, Guenther H. "Schiller and Carl August von Weimar." *Monatshefte* 56 (1964): 273–80.

Neubauer, John. "The Freedom of the Machine: On Mechanism, Materialism, and the Young Schiller." *Eighteenth-Century Studies* 15 (1982): 275–90.

———. "The Idea of History in Schiller's *Wallenstein*." *Neophilologus* 56 (1972): 451–63.

———. "Literature and Science." *Yearbook of Comparative and General Literature* 32 (1983): 67–75.

———. Review of Dewhurst/Reeves. In *Modern Language Notes* 95 (1980): 708–10.

Neuhouser, Frederick. *Fichte's Theory of Subjectivity*. Cambridge/New York: Cambridge University Press, 1990.

Neumann, Gerhard. "Die Anfänge deutscher Novellistik." In *Unser Commercium. Goethes und Schillers Literaturpolitik*, edited by Wilfried Barner, Eberhard Lämmert, and Norbert Oellers, 433–60. Stuttgart: J. G. Cotta, 1984.

Neuss, Raimund. *Tugend und Toleranz. Die Krise der Gattung Märtyrerdrama im 18. Jahrhundert*. Bonn: Bouvier: 1989.

Nietzsche, Friedrich. *Werke*. Edited by Karl Schlechta. München: Hanser, 1966.

Nisbet, Hugh B. *Herder and the Philosophy and History of Science*. Cambridge: Modern Humanities Research Association, 1970.

Nitschak, Horst. *Kritik der ästhetischen Wirklichkeitskonstitution. Eine Untersuchung zu den ästhetischen Schriften Kants und Schillers*. Frankfurt a.M.: Roter Stern, 1976.

Nivelle, Armand. *Kunst—und Dichtungstheorien zwischen Aufklärung und Klassik*. Berlin/New York: Walter de Gruyter, 1971.

Nollendorfs, Cora Lee. "The Role of the 'Aesthetic Subject' in the Theoretical Writings of Friedrich Schiller and Wilhelm von Humboldt: The Aesthetics of Reception in the Eighteenth Century." In *Eighteenth-Century German Authors and Their Aesthetic Theories: Literature and the Other Arts*, edited by Richard Critchfield and Wulf Koepke, 203–19; 212. Columbia, S.C.: Camden House, 1988.

Ockenden, R[aymond] C[urtis]. "*Wilhelm Tell* as Political Drama." *Oxford German Studies* 18–19 (1989–90): 23–44.

Oellers, Norbert. "Idylle und Politik. Französische Revolution, ästhetische Erziehung und die Freiheit der Urkantone." In *Friedrich Schiller. Kunst, Humanität und Politik in der späten Aufklärung. Ein Symposium,* edited by Wolfgang Wittkowski, 114–33. Tübingen: Max Niemeyer, 1982.

———. *Schiller. Geschichte seiner Wirkung bis zu Goethes Tod. 1805–1832*. 2 vols. Bonn: Bouvier, 1967.

———. *Schiller—Zeitgenosse aller Epochen. Dokumente zur Wirkungsgeschichte*. Frankfurt a.M.: Athenäum, 1970.

———. "Schillers 'Das Reich der Schatten' und 'Das Ideal und das Leben'—EIN Gedicht." In *Kulturwissenschaften. Festgabe fur Wilhelm Perpeet zum 65. Geburtstag*. Bonn: Bouvier, 1980: 292–305.

Oetinger, Friedrich Chr. *Biblisches und emblematisches Wörterbuch, dem Tellerischen Wörterbuch und andera falschen schrifterklärungen entgenen gesezt*. N.p. 1776. [DLA]

Oettinger, Klaus. "Schillers Erzählung *Der Verbrecher aus Infamie*. Ein Beitrag zur Rechtsaufklärung der Zeit." *Jahrbuch der Deutschen Schillergesellschaft* 16 (1972): 266–76.

Orton, Graham. *Schiller: Don Carlos*. London: Arnold, 1967.

Paetzold, Heinz. *Ästhetik des deutschen Idealismus. Zur Idee ästhetischer Rationali-*

tät bei Baumgarten, Kant, Schelling, Hegel und Schopenhauer. Wiesbaden: Franz Steiner, 1983.

Pannenberg, Wolfhart. "Hermeneutik und Universalgeschichte." *Zeitschrift für Theologie und Kirche* 60 (1963): 90–121.

Pape, Walter. "'Ein merkwürdiges Beispiel productiver Kritik'. Schillers *Kabale und Liebe* und das zeitgenössische Publikum." *Zeitschrift für Deutsche Philologie* 107 (1988): 190–211.

Parzeller, Marga. "Schiller und die Musik." *Goethe* 18 (1956): 282-94.

Passage, Charles. *Friedrich Schiller.* New York: Frederick Ungar, 1975.

Patterson, Michael, "Schiller at Mannheim: *The Robbers.*" In his *The First German Theatre: Schiller, Goethe, Kleist, and Büchner in Performance.* London: Routledge, 1990: 21–52.

Paulsen, Wolfgang. "Goethes Kritik am Wallenstein. Zum Problem des Geschichtsdramas in der deutschen Klassik." *Deutsche Vierteljahrsschrift für Literaturwissenschaft und Geistesgeschichte* 28 (1954): 61–83.

Pechter, Edward. "The New Historicism and Its Discontents." *Publications of the Modern Language Association* 102 (1987): 292–303.

Pehle, Margot. *Die Veröffentlichungen des Schwäbischen Schillervereins und der Deutschen Schillergesellschaft 1895–1980.* Mit einem Vorwort von Bernhard Zeller. Marbach a.N.: Deutsche Schillergesellschaft, 1980.

Peischl, Margaret T. "The Faces of Power in the Poetry of Friedrich Schiller." *Journal of English and Germanic Philology* 86 (1987): 155–64.

Perpeet, Wilhelm. "Zur Wortbedeutung von 'Kultur.'" In *Naturplan und Verfallskritik. Zu Begriff und Geschichte der Kultur,* edited by Helmut Brackert and Fritz Wefelmeyer, 21–28. Frankfurt a.M.: Suhrkamp, 1984.

Peter, Klaus. "Einleitung" to *Romantikforschung seit 1945,* edited by him, 1–39. Königstein/Ts.: Verlagsgruppe Athenäum-Hain-Scriptor-Hanstein, 1980.

———, ed. *Romantikforschung seit 1945.* Königstein/Ts.: Verlagsgruppe Athenäum, Hain, Scriptor, Hanstein [Anton Hain Meisenheim], 1980.

———. *Stadien der Aufklärung. Moral und Politik bei Lessing, Novalis und Friedrich Schlegel.* Wiesbaden: Akademische Verlagsgesellschaft Athenaion, 1980.

Peters, Günter. *Der zerrissene Engel. Genieästhetik und literarische Selbstdarstellung im achtzehnten Jahrhundert.* Stuttgart: J. B. Metzler, 1982.

Pfeiffer, Eleonora. "Die Kulturauffassung Friedrich Schillers in kulturtheoretischer Sicht." *Weimarer Beiträge* 22 (1976): 87–111.

Piedmont, Ferdinand, ed. *Schiller spielen. Stimmen der Theaterkritik. 1946–1985. Eine Dokumentation.* Darmstadt: Wissenschaftliche Buchgesellschaft, 1990.

Pillau, Helmut. *Die fortgedachte Dissonanz. Hegels Tragödientheorie und Schillers Tragödie. Deutsche Antworten auf die Französische Revolution.* München: Fink, 1981.

Pleines, Jürgen-Eckardt. *Ästhetik und Vernunftkritik. Natur-und Kunstinterpretation im Zeitalter der deutschen Klassik und Romantik.* Hildesheim/Zürich/New York: Georg Olms, 1989.

Polheim, Karl Konrad. "Studien zu Friedrich Schlegels poetischen Begriffen." *Deutsche Vierteljahrsschrift für Literaturwissenschaft und Geistesgeschichte* 35 (1961): 363–98.

———. "Von der Einheit des *Don Karlos.*" *Jahrbuch des Freien Deutschen Hochstifts 1985:* 64–100.

Polanyi, Michael. "The Creative Imagination." In *The Concept of Creativity in Science and Art,* edited by Denis Dutton and Michael Krausz, 91–108. The Hague/Boston/London: Martinus Nijhoff, 1981.

Politzer, Heinz. "Szene und Tribunal. Schillers Theater der Grausamkeit." In his *Das Schweigen der Sirenen. Studien zur deutschen und österreichischen Literatur.* Stuttgart: Metzler, 1968: 234–53.

Pott, Hans-Georg. *Die schöne Freiheit. Eine Interpretation zu Schillers Schrift "Über die ästhetische Erziehung des Menschen in einer Reihe von Briefen."* München: Wilhelm Fink, 1980.

Prändl, Julie D. *Spirited Women Heroes: Major Female Characters in the Dramas of Goethe, Schiller and Kleist.* New York/Frankfurt a.m./Bern: Peter Lang, 1983.

Price, Cora Lee. "Wilhelm von Humboldt und Schillers Briefe über die ästhetische Erziehung des Menschen." *Jahrbuch der Deutschen Schillergesellschaft* 11 (1967): 358–73.

Propyläen Geschichte der Literatur IV: Aufklärung und Romantik. 1700–1830. Berlin: Propyläen, 1983.

Pütz, Peter. *Die deutsche Aufklärung.* Darmstadt: Wissenschaftliche Buchgesellschaft, 1978.

Puffett, Derrick, "Some Reflections on 'Literaturoper.'" *German Life and Letters* 35 (1981–82): 238–40.

Pugh, David. "Aesthetic and Moral Autonomy in Schiller's 'Gedankenlyrik.'" In *Revolution und Autonomie. Deutsche Autonomieästhetik im Zeitalter der Französischen Revolution. Ein Symposium,* edited by Wolfgang Wittkowski, 314–23. Tübingen: Max Niemeyer, 1990.

——— Vaughn. *Conflict and Harmony: A Study of Schiller's Philosophical Writings.* University of Toronto Dissertation 1986.

———. "'Die Künstler': Schiller's philosophical programme." *Oxford German Studies* 18–19 (1989–90).

———. "Schiller as Platonist." *Colloquia Germanica* 24 (1991): 273–95.

Puntel, Kai. *Die Struktur künstlerischer Darstellung. Schillers Theorie der Vesinnlichung in Kunst und Literatur.* München: 1986.

Purdie, Edan. "Some Word-Associations in the Writings of Hamann and Herder." In *German Studies. Presented to Leonard Ahsley Willoughby by Pupils, Colleagues and Friends on his Retirement.* Oxford: Basil Blackwell, 1952: 144–58.

Raabe, August. *Idealistischer Realismus. Eine genetische Analyse der Gedankenwelt Friedrich Schillers.* Bonn: Emil Semmel, 1962.

Rainer, Ulrike. *Schillers Prosa. Poetologie und Praxis.* Berlin: Erich Schmidt, 1988.

Ranke, Wolf. *Dichtung unter den Bedingungen der Reflexion. Interpretationen zu Schillers philosophischer Poetik und ihren Auswirkungen im "Wallenstein."* Würzburg: Königshausen u. Neumann, 1990.

Rasch, Wolfdietrich. "Schillers Aufsatz über die Anfänge der Menschheitsgeschichte." In *Friedrich Schiller. Kunst, Humanität und Politik in der späten Aufklärung. Ein Symposium,* edited by Wolfgang Wittkowski, 220–27. Tübingen: Max Niemeyer, 1982.

———. "Zum Verhältnis der Romantik zur Aufklärung." In *Romantik. Ein literaturwissenschaftliches Studienbuch,* edited by Ernst Ribbat, 7–22. Königstein/Ts.: Athenäum, 1979.

Reed, T[erence] J. "Coming of Age in Prussia and Swabia: Kant, Schiller, and the Duke." *Modern Language Review* 86 (1991): 613–26.

Reichardt, Johann Friedrich. *Deutschland*. 4 vols. Berlin: Johann Friedrich Unger, 1976. [DLA: "Außerordentlich seltene Zeitschrift aus der Zeit der Klassik . . . "; E. A. Arnold's signature of 1833 is on the first page.]

Reichmann, Eberhard. *Die Herrschaft der Zahl. Quantitatives Denken in der deutschen Aufklärung*. Stuttgart: J. B. Metzler, 1968.

————. *Schiller*. Oxford/New York: Oxford University Press, 1991.

Regin, Derec. *Freedom and Dignity: The Historical and Philosophical Thought of Schiller*. The Hague: M. Nijhoff, 1965.

Reinhardt, Hartmut. "Das 'Schicksal' als Schicksalsfrage. Schillers Dramatik in romantischer Sicht: Kritik und Nachfolge." *Aurora* 50 (1990): 63–86.

————. "Schillers *Wallenstein* und Aristoteles." *Jahrbuch der Deutschen Schillergesellschaft* 20 (1976): 278–337.

————. "Die Wege der Freiheit. Schillers 'Wallenstein'-Trilogie und die Idee des Erhabenen." In *Friedrich Schiller. Kunst, Humanität und Politik in der späten Aufklärung. Ein Symposium*, edited by Wolfgang Wittkowski, 252–69. Tübingen: Max Niemeyer, 1982.

Ribbat, Ernst, ed. *Romantik. Ein Literaturwissenschaftliches Studienbuch*. Königstein/Ts.: Athenäum, 1979.

Richards, David B. "The Problem of Knowledge in *Wallenstein*." In *Goethezeit. Studien zur Erkenntnis und Rezeption Goethes und seiner Zeitgenossen. Festschrift für Stuart Atkins*, edited by Gerhart Hoffmeister, 231–42. Bern/München: Francke, 1981.

Richter, Karl. "Die kopernikanische Wende in der Lyrik von Brockes bis Klopstock." *Jahrbuch der Deutschen Schillergesellschaft* 12 (1968): 132–69.

————. *Literatur und Naturwissenschaft. Eine Studie zur Lyrik der Aufklärung*. München: Wilhelm Fink, 1972.

Ricoeur, Paul. "History and Hermeneutics." In *Philosophy of History and Action: Papers Presented at the First Jerusalem Philosophical Encounter, December 1974*, edited by Yirmiahu Yovel, 3–20. Dordrecht: D. Reidel, 1978.

Riecke-Niklewski, Rose. *Die Metaphorik des Schönen. Eine kritische Lektüre der Versöhnung in Schillers 'Über die ästhetische Erziehung des Menschen in einer Reihe von Briefen.'* Tübingen: Max Niemeyer, 1986.

Riedel, Wolfgang. *Die Anthropologie des jungen Schiller*. Würzburg: Königshausen u. Neumann, 1985.

————. "Die Aufklärung und das Unbewußte: Die Inversionen des Franz Moor." *Jahrbuch der Deutschen Schillergesellschaft* 37 (1993): 198–220.

————. *"Der Spaziergang." Ästhetik der Landschaft und Geschichtsphilosophie der Natur bei Schiller*. Würzburg: Königshausen und Neumann, 1989.

Rieder, Heinz. *Schiller. Religion und Menschenbild*. Stuttgart: Wilhelm Braumüller (Wien), 1966.

Rippere, Vicky. *Schiller and "Alienation."* Bern/Frankfurt a.M.: Peter Lang, 1981.

Roberts, David. "After Adorno: Modernism and Postmodernism." In his *Art and Enlightenment. Aesthetic Theory after Adorno*, 117–151. Lincoln/London: University of Nebraska Press, 1991.

Roe, Shirley A. *Matter, Life and Generation: Eighteenth-Century Embryology and the Haller-Wolff Debate*. Cambridge/New York: Cambridge University Press, 1981.

Rohrmoser, Günter. "Zum Problem der ästhetischen Versöhnung. Schiller und Hegel." *Euphorion* 53 (1959): 351–68.

———. *Das Elend der Kritischen Theorie. Theodor Adorno, Herbert Marcuse, Jürgen Habermas.* 2d ed. Freiburg: Rombach, 1970.

Rohs, Peter. *Johann Gottlieb Fichte.* München: C. H. Beck, 1991.

Rolleston, James. "The Legacy of Idealism. Schiller Mörike and Biedermeier Culture." *Modern Language Quarterly* 51 (1990): 491–512.

Rorty, Richard. "Posties." Review of: Jürgen Habermas, *Der Philosophische Diskurs der Moderne: Zwölf Vorlesungen.* In *The London Review of Books* (March 9, 1987): 41–44.

Rosalewski, Willy. *Schillers Ästhetik im Verhältnis zur Kantischen.* Heidelberg: Carl Winter, 1912.

Rothschuh, K[arl]. E[d]. *Geschichte der Physiologie. English.* Huntington, N.Y.: R. E. Krieger, 1973.

Rousseau, G[eorge] S. *Pre-and Post-Modern Discourses: A Three-Volume Set.* vol. 2: *Enlightenment Crossings.* Manchester: Manchester University Press; New York: St. Martin's Press, 1991.

———. "Medicine and the Muses: an approach to literature and medicine." In *Literature and Medicine During the Eighteenth Century,* edited by Roy Porter and M. Roberts, 23–57. London: Routledge, 1993.

Rudloff-Hille, Gertrud. *Schiller auf der deutschen Bühne seiner Zeit.* Berlin/Weimar: Aufbau, 1969.

Rudolf, Ludwig. *Schiller-Lexikon. Erläuterndes Wörterbuch zu Schiller's Dichterwerken.* Unter Mitwirkung von Karl Goldbeck. 2 vols. 2d ed. New York: Burt Franklin, 1971.

Rüdiger, Horst. "Schiller und das Pastorale." *Euphorion* 53 (1959): 229–51.

Rüsen, Jörn. "Bürgerliche Identität zwischen Geschichtsbewusstsein und Utopie: Friedrich Schiller." In *Schiller. Vorträge aus Anlaß seines 225. Geburtstages,* edited by Dirk Grathoff and Erwin Leibfried, 178–93. Frankfurt a.M./Bern/New York/Paris: Peter Lang, 1991.

Ruppelt, Georg. *Schiller im nationalsozialistischen Deutschland. Der Versuch einer Gleichschaltung.* Stuttgart: J. B. Metzler, 1979.

Ryder, Frank. G. "Schiller's *Tell* and the Cause of Freedom." *The German Quarterly* 48 (1975): 487–504.

Saeculum Weltgeschichte. 7 vols. Freiburg/Basel/Wien: Herder, 1965–75.

Sallman, Klaus. "Schillers Pathos und die poetische Funktion des Pathetischen." *Jahrbuch der Deutschen Schillergesellschaft* 27 (1983): 202–21.

Sammons, Jeffrey. "The Apple-Shot and the Politics of *Wilhelm Tell.*" In *Friedrich von Schiller and the Drama of Human Existence,* edited by Alexej Urgrinsky, 81–88. New York/Westport, Connecticut: Greenwood Press, 1988.

Sattes, H., "Der junge Schiller und das Leib-Seele Problem." *Der Nervenarzt* 27 (1956): 128–32.

Sauerland, Karol. "Goethes, Schillers, Fr. Schlegels und Novalis' Reaktionen auf die neuen politischen, konstitutionellen und sozialphilosophischen Fragen, die die Französische Revolution aufwarf." In *Daß eine Nation die ander verstehen möge. Festschrift Marian Syrocki zu seinem 60. Geburtstag,* edited by Norbert Honsza and Hans-Gert Roloff, 615–37. Amsterdam: Rodopi, 1988.

———. "Schiller und die Französische Revolution." *Skamandros 1986:* 79–89.

Sautermeister, Gert. "Aufklärung und Körpersprache. Schillers Drama auf dem Theater heute." In *Klassik und Moderne. Die Weimarer Klassik als historisches Ereignis und Herausforderung im kulturgeschichtlichen Prozeß. Walter Müller-*

Seidel zum 65. Geburtstag, edited by Karl Richter and Jörg Schönert, 618–40. Stuttgart: J. B. Metzler, 1983.

―――. *Idyllik und Dramatik im Werk Friedrich Schillers: Zum geschichtlichen Ort seiner klassischen Dramen.* Stuttgart/Berlin/Köln/Mainz: Kohlhammer, 1971.

―――. *"Maria Stuart.* Ästhetik, Seelenkunde, historisch-gesellschaftlicher Ort." In *Schillers Dramen. Neue Interpretationen,* edited by Walter Hinderer, 174–216. Stuttgart: Reclam, 1979.

―――. "Unverjährte Aufklärung. Schillers *Der Verbrecher aus verlorener Ehre.*" *Die Horen* 30 (1985): 273–79.

―――. "Vom Nutzen des Theaters für die Philologie. Schillers Räuber—unverjährt." In *Schiller. Vorträge aus Anlaß seines 225. Geburtstages,* edited by Dirk Grathoff and Erwin Leibfried, 49–67. Frankfurt a.M./Bern/New York/Paris: Peter Lang, 1991.

Saville, Anthony. *Aesthetic Reconstructions: The Seminal Writings of Lessing, Kant and Schiller.* Oxford: Basil Blackwell, 1987.

Sayce, Olive. "Das Problem der Vieldeutigkeit in Schillers ästhetischer Terminologie." *Jahrbuch der Deutschen Schillergesellschaft* 6 (1962): 149–77.

Schanze, Helmut. *Romantik und Aufklärung. Untersuchungen zu Friedrich Schlegel und Novalis.* Nürnberg: Hans Carl, 1966.

Schavernoch, Hans. *Die Harmonie der Sphären. Die Geschichte der Idee des Welteinklangs und der Seelenstimmung.* Freiburg/München: Karl Alber, 1981.

Scheier, Claus-Artur. "Die Frühromantik als Kultur der Reflexion." In *Früher Idealismus und Frühromantik. Der Streit um die Grundlagen der Ästhetik (1795–1805),* edited by Walter Jaeschke and Helmut Holzhey, 69–79. Hamburg: Felix Meiner, 1990.

Schelling, Friedrich Wilhelm Joseph. *Erster Entwurf eines Systems der Naturphilosophie. Zum Behuf seiner Vorlesungen.* Jena/Leipzig: Christian Ernst Gabler, 1799. [DLA]

―――. *System des transcendentalen Idealismus.* Tübingen: J. G. Cotta, 1800. [DLA]

―――. *Vom Ich als Princip der Philosophie oder über das Unbedingte im menschlichen Wesen.* Tübingen: Jakob Friedrich Heerbrandt, 1795. [DLA]

―――. *Texte zur Philosophie der Kunst.* Edited by Werner Beierwaltes. Stuttgart: Reclam, 1982.

―――. *Werke, nach der Originalausgabe in neuer Anordnung.* Edited by Manfred Schröter. Ergänzungsband 3: *Zur Philosophie der Kunst.* München: Beck, 1959.

Scherpe, Klaus. "Die Räuber." In *Schillers Dramen. Neue Interpretationen,* edited by Walter Hinderer, 9–36. Stuttgart: Reclam, 1979.

―――. "Friedrich Schiller. *Die Räuber.*" In *Dramen des Sturm und Drang. Interpretationen.* Stuttgart: Reclam, 1987: 161–211.

―――. "Schillers *Räuber*—theatralisch." *Der Deutschunterricht* 35 (1983): 61–77.

Schieder, Theodor. "Schiller als Historiker." *Historische Zeitschrift* 190 (1960): 31–54.

Schiller, Friedrich. *Friedrich Schillers medizinisch-philosophische Jugendarbeiten.* Edited by Alexander Mette. Berlin: Volk und Gesundheit, 1959.

―――. *Mary Stuart: A Tragedy.* Translated by Sophie Wilkins. Woodbury, N.Y./London/Toronto/Sydney: Barron's, 1959.

―――. *Medizinische Schriften. Eine Buchgabe der Deutschen Hoffmann-La Roche AG aus Anlaß des 200. Geburtstages des Dichters 10. November 1959.* Miesbach/Obb.: Wilhelm Friedrich Mayr, 1959.

————. *On the Aesthetic Education of Man in a Series of Letters.* Edited and translated with an introduction, commentary and glossary of terms by Elizabeth M. Wilkinson and Leonard A. Willoughby. Oxford: Clarendon Press, 1967.

————. *Plays.* Edited by Walter Hinderer. 2 vols. New York: Continuum, 1983.

————. *The Robbers. Wallenstein.* Translation with an introduction by F. J. Lamport. London: Penguin, 1979.

————. *Über die ästhetische Erziehung des Menschen in einer Reihe von Briefen. Text, Materialien, Kommentar.* Edited by Wolfgang Düsing. München: Hanser, 1981.

————. *Über Kunst und Wirklichkeit. Schriften und Briefe zur Ästhetik.* Edited by Claus Träger. Leipzig: Reclam, 1984.

————, ed. *Neue Thalia.* 1792–93. [DLA]

————, ed. *Rheinische Thalia.* Mannheim: Schwan, 1785. [DLA]

————. *Schillers Briefe über die ästhetische Erziehung des Menschen in einer Reihe von Briefen.* Edited by Jürgen Bolten. Frankfurt a.M.: Suhrkamp, 1984.

————. *Schillers Leben dokumentarisch in Briefen, zeitgenössichen Berichten und Bildern.* Edited by Walter Hoyer. Köln: Kiepenhauer un. Witsch, 1967.

————. *Werke. Nationalausgabe. Historisch-Kritische Ausgabe.* Edited by Julius Petersen and Friedrich Beißner/Lieselote Blumenthal and Benno von Wiese/Norbert Oellers. Weimar: Böhlau, 1943f.

————. *Werke und Briefe in zwölf Bänden.* Edited by Klaus Harro Hilzinger et al. Frankfurt a.M.: Deutscher Klassiker, 1988f.

Schiller: Aspekte neuerer Forschung. Sonderheft zur Zeitschrift für deutsche Philologie 109 (1990).

Schiller, Johann Caspar. *Betrachtungen über landwirtschaftliche Dinge in dem Herzogthum Württemberg, ausgesetzt von einem Herzoglichen Offizier.* Stuttgart: Cotta, 1767–69. [DLA]

————. *Von der Baumzucht im Großen.* Neustrelitz: Michaelis, 1793. [DLA]

Schings, Hans-Jürgen. "Freiheit in der Geschichte: Egmont und Marquis Posa im Vergleich." In *Geschichtlichkeit und Gegenwart. Festschrift für Hans-Dietrich Irmscher,* edited by Hans Esselborn and Werner Keller, 174–93. Köln/Weimar/Wien: Böhlau, 1994.

————. "Das Haupt der Gorgone. Tragische Analysis und Politik in Schillers *Wallenstein.*" In *Das Subjekt der Dichtung. Festschrift für Gerhard Kaiser,* edited by Gerhard Buhr, Friedrich A. Kittler, and Horst Turk, 283–307. Würzburg: Königshausen u. Neumann, 1990.

————. "Die Illuminaten in Stuttgart. Auch ein Beitrag zur Geschichte des jungen Schiller." *Deutsche Vierteljahrsschrift für Literaturwissenschaft und Geistesgeschichte* 66 (1992): 48–87.

————. *Melancholie und Aufklärung. Melancholiker und ihre Kritiker in Erfahrungsseelenkunde und Literatur des 18. Jahrhunderts.* Stuttgart: J. B. Metzler, 1977.

————. "Philosophie der Liebe und Tragödie des Universalhasses. *Die Räuber* im Kontext von Schillers Jugendphilosophie (I)." *Jahrbuch des Wiener Goethe-Vereins* 84–85 (1980–81): 71–95.

————. "Schillers *Räuber:* Ein Experiment des Universalhasses." In *Friedrich Schiller. Kunst, Humanitat und Politik in der späten Aufklärung. Ein Symposium,* edited by Wolfgang Wittkowski, 1–21. Tübingen: Max Niemeyer, 1982.

————. "Triumph des Erhabenen, Untergang des Mitleids: Theorie der hohen Tragödie von Schiller bis Hegel." In his *Der mitleidigste Mensch ist der beste Mensch. Poetik des Mitleids von Lessing bis Büchner,* 46–53. München: Fink, 1980.

Schink, Johann Friedrich. *Schillers Todtenfeyer. Gehalten auf dem hamburgischen deutschen Theater am 7ten Junii 1805.* Hamburg: Friedrich Hermann Nestler, 1805. [DLA]

Schipperges, Heinrich. *Kosmos Anthropos. Entwürfe zu einer Philosophie des Leibes.* Stuttgart: Klett-Cotta, 1981.

———. "Der Medicus Schiller und das Konzept seiner Heilkunde." In *Schiller und die höfische Welt,* edited by Achim Aurnhammer, Klaus Manger, and Friedrich Strack, 134–47. Tübingen: Max Niemeyer, 1990.

Schlaffer, Hannelore. "Die Ausweisung des Lyrischen aus der Lyrik: Schillers Gedichte." In *Das Subjekt der Dichtung. Festschrift für Gerhard Kaiser,* edited by Gerhard Buhr, Friedrich A. Kittler, and Horst Turk, 519–32. Würzburg: Königshausen u. Neumann, 1990.

Schlegel, Friedrich. *Die Griechen und Römer. Historische und kritische Versuche über das Klassische Alterthum.* Erster Band. Neustrelitz: Hofbuchhändler Michaelis, 1797. [DLA]

Schlunk, Jürgen. "Vertrauen als Ursache und Überwindung tragischer Verstrickung in Schillers *Räubern.* Zum Verständnis Karl Moors." *Jahrbuch der Deutschen Schillergesellschaft* 27 (1983): 185–201.

Schmidt, Jochen. *Die Geschichte des Genie-Gedankens. 1750–1945.* vol. 1: *Von der Aufklärung bis zum Idealismus.* Darmstadt: Wissenschaftliche Buchgesellschaft, 1985.

Schmidt, Meinolf. *Die ästhetischen Kategorien Schillers als Weg zum Verständnis und zur Vermittlung des "Wallenstein."* Frankfurt: Lang, 1988.

Schmidt, Michael R. *Schillers "Verbrecher."* University of Munich Dissertation, 1987.

Schmidt-Neubacher, Joachim. *Tyrannei und der Mythos vom Glück. Drei Essays zu Lessing, Schiller und Goethe.* Frankfurt a.M.: Rita Fischer, 1981.

Schminank, Hans. "Stand und Entwicklung der Naturwissenschaften im Zeitalter der Aufklärung." In *Lessing und die Zeit der Aufklärung.* Göttingen: Vandenhoeck u. Ruprecht, 1968: 30–76.

Schmitt, F. "Krankheit und Schaffen bei Friedrich Schiller." *Allgemeine Zeitschrift für Psychiatrie* 105 (1937): 1–34.

Schmitz, Heinz-Gerd. *Die Glücklichen und die Unglücklichen. Politische Eudämonologie, ästhetischer Staat und erhabene Kunst im Werk Friedrich Schillers.* Würzburg: Königshausen und Neumann, 1992.

Schueller, H. M. "Schelling's Theory of the Metaphysics of Music." *Journal of Aesthetics and Art Criticism* 15 (1956–57): 461–76.

Schulin, Ernst. "Einleitung" to his *Universalgeschichte.* Köln: Kiepenheuer und Witsch, 1974.

Schulte, Hans H. *Werke der Begeisterung: Friedrich Schiller. Idee und Eigenart seines Schaffens.* Bonn: Bouvier, 1980.

Schulz, Gerhard. "Schillers *Wallenstein* zwischen den Zeiten." In *Geschichte als Schauspiel. Deutsche Geschichtsdramen. Interpretationen,* edited by Walter Hinck, 116–32. Frankfurt a.M.: Suhrkamp, 1981.

Schulz, Günter. "Die erste Fassung von Fichtes Abhandlung *Über Geist und Buchstab in der Philosophie In einer Reihe von Briefen* 1795. Ein Beitrag zum Verhältnis Fichte-Schiller." *Goethe* 17 (1955): 114–41.

Schulz, Walter. *Metaphysik des Schwebens. Untersuchungen zur Geschichte der Ästhetik.* Pfullingen: Günther Neske, 1985.

Schulze, Wilhelm. "Schillers Kritik an Kant." *Blätter für württembergische Kirchengeschichte* 89 (1989): 202–45.

Schwäbisches Magazin von gelehrten Sachen auf das Jahr 1775 [–1780]. Edited by Balthasar Haug. Stuttgart: Erhardische Schriften. [DLA]

Schwäbischer Musenalmanach. Auf das Jahr 1782. Edited by Gotthold Friedrich Stäudlin. Tübingen: Johann Georg Cotta, 1782.

Schwäbische[r] Schillerverein, ed. *Marbacher Schillerbuch. Zur hundersten Wiederkehr von Schillers Todestag.* Stuttgart/Berlin: J. G. Cotta, 1905. [University of Arizona copy; signed Leonard Forster ex libris Karl Breul.]

Schwerte, Hans. "Simultaneität und Differenz des Wortes in Schillers *Wallenstein.*" *Germanisch-Romanische Monatsschrift* 15 (1965): 15–25.

Science and Metaphor: The Historical Role of Scientific Theories in Forming Western Culture. Edited by Richard Olson. Belmont, Calif.: Wadsworth, 1971.

Seeba, Hinrich. "Historiographischer Idealismus? Fragen zu Schillers Geschichtsbild." In *Friedrich Schiller. Kunst, Humanität und Politik in der späten Aufklärung. Ein Symposium,* edited by Wolfgang Wittkowski, 229–49. Tübingen: Max Niemeyer, 1982.

———. "Literatur und Geschichte. Hermeneutische Ansätze zu einer Poetik der Geschichtsschreibung." In *Akten des VI. Internationalen Germanisten-Kongresses.* Bern/Frankfurt a.M./Las Vegas: Lang, 1980: 201–8.

———. "Das wirkende Wort in Schillers Balladen." *Jahrbuch der Deutschen Schillergesellschaft* 14 (1970): 275–322.

Segebrecht, Wulf. "Naturphänomen und Kunstidee. Goethe und Schiller in ihrer Zusammenarbeit als Balladendichter, dargestellt am Beispiel der 'Kraniche des Ibykus.'" In *Klassik und Moderne. Die Weimarer Klassik als historisches Ereignis und Herausforderung im kulturgeschichtlichen Prozeß. Walter Müller-Seidel zum 65. Geburtstag,* edited by Karl Richter and Jörg Schönert, 194–206. Stuttgart: J. B. Metzler, 1983.

Seidel, Siegfried. "Friedrich Schiller. Die Überwindung des subjektiven Idealismus." *Weimarer Beiträge* 5 (1959). Sonderheft: 149–68.

———, ed. *Der Briefwechsel zwischen Friedrich Schiller und Wilhelm von Humboldt.* 2 vols. Berlin: Aufbau Verlag, 1962.

Seidlin, Oskar. "Schillers *Don Carlos* nach 200 Jahren." *Jahrbuch der Deutschen Schillergesellschaft* 27 (1983): 477–92.

———. "Schiller's 'Treacherous Signs': The Function of the Letters in his Early Plays." In *Schiller 1759/1959. Commemorative American Studies,* edited by John R. Frey, 129–46. Urbana, Ill.: University of Illinois Press, 1959.

———. "Das Vorspiel zu Wilhelm Tell." In *Untersuchungen zur Literatur als Geschichte: Festschrift für Benno von Wiese,* edited by Vincent J. Günther, Helmut Koopmann, Peter Pütz, Hans Joachim Schrimpf, 112–28. Berlin: Schmidt, 1973.

———. "*Wallenstein:* Sein und Zeit." *Der Monat* 15 (1963): 28–42.

Seifert, Siegfried. "Autor und Publikum. Fragen des literarischen Marktes in der Sicht des Herausgebers Schiller." *Skamandros 1986:* 68–78.

Sengle, Friedrich. "Die Klassische Kultur von Weimar, sozialgeschichtlich gesehen." *Internationales Archiv für Sozialgeschichte der deutschen Literatur* 3 (1978): 68–86.

428   HARMONIOUS TENSIONS

Sharpe, Lesley. *Friedrich Schiller: Drama, Thought and Politics.* Cambridge/New York: Cambridge University Press, 1991.

———. "National Socialism and Schiller." *German Life and Letters* 36 (1982–83): 156–65.

———. "Die Reisen des verlorenen Sohns. Eine These zu Schillers *Räubern.*" *Zeitschrift für Deutsche Philologie* 109 (1990): Sonderheft: 3–15.

———. *Schiller and the Historical Character: Presentation and Interpretation in the Historiographical Works and in the Historical Dramas.* Oxford: Oxford University Press, 1982.

———. *"Der Verbrecher aus verlorener Ehre:* An Early Exercise in Schillerian Psychology." *German Life and Letters* 33 (1980): 102–10.

Sheehan, James J. *German History, 1770–1866.* Oxford: Clarendon, 1989.

Shelley, Percy Bysshe. *A Defence of Poetry;* Thomas Love Peacock, *The Four Ages of Poetry.* Edited by John E. Jordan. Indianapolis/New York: Bobbs-Merrill, 1965.

Siekmann, Andreas. "Friedrich Schillers Differenzierung von historischer und poetischer Wahrheit." *Wirkendes Wort* 36 (1986): 9–15.

Simons, John. *Friedrich Schiller.* Boston: Hall, 1981.

Simpson, David, ed. *German Aesthetic and Literary Criticism: Kant, Fichte, Schelling, Schopenhauer, Hegel.* Cambridge/London/New York: Cambridge University Press, 1984.

———, ed. *German Aesthetic and Literary Criticism from Lessing to Hegel.* Cambridge/London/New York: Cambridge University Press, 1984.

Sin Oh, Han. *Studien zu Schillers ästhetischen Schriften und ihren verwandtschaftlichen Beziehungen zu ostasiatischem Gedankengut.* University of Bonn Dissertation, 1966.

Sokel, Walter. "Die politische Funktion botschaftsloser Kunst. Zum Verhältnis von Politik und Ästhetik in Schillers Briefen 'Über die ästhetische Erziehung des Menschen.'" In *Revolution und Autonomie. Deutsche Autonomieästhetik im Zeitalter der Französischen Revolution. Ein Symposium,* edited by Wolfgang Wittkowski, 264–72. Tübingen: Max Niemeyer, 1990.

Sommerhage, Claus. "Schillers Lyrik. Eine Apologie." *Weimarer Beiträge* 38 (1992): 19–30.

Sørensen, Bengt Algot. *Herrschaft und Zärtlichkeit: Der Patriarchalismus und das Drama im 18. Jahrhundert.* Münich: C. H. Beck, 1984.

———. *Schillers Jugenddramen und das familiale Wertsystem seiner Zeit.* Odense: University of Odense, Germanistik-Institut, 1985.

South, Marie-Luise. *Der Doppelsinn des Lebens. Dialektische Rhetorik als Strukturprinzip in Schillers "Wallenstein."* University of California at Berkeley Dissertation, 1970.

Spranger, Eduard. *Schillers Geistesart gespiegelt in seinen philosophischen Schriften und Gedichten.* Berlin: Akademie der Wissenschaften, 1941.

Stafford, Barbara Maria. *Body Criticism: Imaging the Unseen in Enlightenment Art and Medicine.* Cambridge: MIT Press, 1991.

Stahl, E[rnest] L. *Friedrich Schiller's Drama: Theory and Practice.* Oxford: Clarendon Press, 1954; reprinted 1961.

Stahl, Jürgen. "Dialektisches Denken in der Geschichtsphilosophie Friedrich Schillers unter besonderer Beachtung der theoretischen Schriften." *Wissenschaftliche Zeitschrift* (Jena) 33 (1984): 65–73.

Staiger, Emil. *Friedrich Schiller.* Zürich: Atlantis, 1967.

————. *Friedrich Schillers Sieg über Schiller. Vorgetragen am 13. Dezember 1980.* Heidelberg: Carl Winter, 1981.

Steinbach, D. "Das Interesse an Franz Moor oder: Leseprozesse als Erkenntnisprozesse. Anmerkungen zur literarischen Hermeneutik." *Der Deutschunterricht* 33 (2/1981): 91–103.

Steinberg, Heinz. "Sekundär-Literatur der letzten Jahre. Zum Beispiel Schiller." *Buch und Bibliothek* 37 (1985): 248–51.

Steinhagen, Harald. "Der junge Schiller zwischen Marquis de Sade und Kant: Aufklärung und Idealismus." *Deutsche Vierteljahrsschrift für Literaturwissenschaft und Geistesgeschichte* 56 (1982): 135–57.

Steinhagen, Harald. "Schillers *Wallenstein* und die Französische Revolution." *Zeitschrift für Deutsche Philologie* 109 (1990). Sonderheft: 77–98.

Stenzel, Jürgen. "Über die ästhetische Erziehung eines Tyrannen. Zu Schillers Ballade 'Die Burgschaft.'" In *Gedichte und Interpretationen* 3: *Klassik und Romantik,* edited by Wulf Segebrecht, 169–80. Stuttgart: Reclam, 1984.

————. "Zum Erhabenen tauglich. Spaziergang durch Schillers 'Elegie.'" *Jahrbuch der Deutschen Schillergesellschaft* 19 (1975): 167–91.

Sternberger, Dolf. "Beim Lesen von Moses Mendelssohns *Phaedon.*" In *Digressionen. Wege zur Aufklärung. Festgabe für Peter Michelsen,* edited by Gotthardt Frühsorge, Klaus Manger, and Friedrich Strack, 93–106. Heidelberg: Carl Winter, 1984.

————. "Politische Helden Schillers." In *Schiller und die höfische Welt,* edited by Achim Aurnhammer, Klaus Manger, and Friedrich Strack, 307–17. Tübingen: Max Niemeyer, 1990.

Storz, Gerhard. "Gesichtspunkte für die Betrachtung von Schillers Lyrik." *Jahrbuch der Deutschen Schillergesellschaft* 12 (1968): 259–74.

————. *Der Dichter Friedrich Schiller.* Stuttgart: Ernst Klett, 1959.

————. *Klassik und Romantik. Eine stilgeschichtliche Darstellung.* Mannheim/Wien/ Zürich: Bibliographisches Institut, 1972.

Strack, Friedrich. "Ein Herold höfischer Musen: Schiller in der Karlsschule." In *'O Fürsten der Heimath! Glückliches Stutgard': Politik, Kultur und Gesellschaft im deutschen Südwesten um 1800,* edited by Christoph Jamme and Otto Pöggeler, 187–203. Stuttgart: Klett-Cotta, 1988.

————. "Schillers Festreden." In *Schiller und die höfische Welt,* edited by Achim Aurnhammer, Klaus Manger, and Friedrich Strack, 111–26. Tübingen: Max Niemeyer, 1990.

Streicher, Andreas. *Schillers Flucht von Stuttgart und Aufenthalt in Mannheim von 1782 bis 1785.* Edited by Paul Raabe. Stuttgart: Reclam, 1968.

Strube, Werner. "Schillers Kallias-Briefe oder über die Objektivität der Schönheit." *Literaturwissenschaftliches Jahrbuch* N.F. 18 (1977): 115–31.

Süvern, Wilhelm. *Über Schillers Wallenstein in Hinsicht auf griechische Tragödie.* Berlin: Reimer, 1800.

Sulzer, Johann George. *Allgemeine Theorie der Schönen Künste.* Theile 1–4. Neue und vermehrte Auflage. Leipzig: Weidmann, 1792. [DLA]

Sulzer, Johann Heinrich. *Dr. Sulzers Abgekürzte Geschichte der INSECTEN. Nach dem Linaeischen System.* 2 parts. Winterthur: H. Steiner u. Comp., 1776. [DLA]

Sutermeister, H. M. *Schiller als Arzt. Ein Beitrag zur Geschichte der psychosomatischen Forschung.* Bern: Francke, 1955.

Swales, Erika. *Maria Stuart*. London: Grant and Cutler, 1988.

Sychrava, Juliet. *Schiller to Derrida: Idealism in Aesthetics*. Cambridge/New York: Cambridge University Press, 1989.

Szondi, Peter. "Das Naive ist das Sentimentalische. Zur Begriffsdialektik in Schillers Abhandlung." In his *Schriften II*, edited by Jean Bollack et al., 59–105. Frankfurt a.M.: Suhrkamp, 1978.

Taubeneck, Steven A. "From Schiller to Derrida: Genealogy and Deconstruction of the Individual." In *Friedrich von Schiller and the Drama of Human Existence*, edited by Alexej Urgrinsky, 103–8. New York/Westport, Connecticut: Greenwood Press, 1988.

Taylor, Charles. *Hegel*. Cambridge/London/New York/Melbourne: Cambridge University Press, 1975.

Thalheim, Hans-Günther. "Notwendigkeit und Rechtlichkeit der Selbsthilfe in Schillers *Wilhelm Tell*." *Goethe* 73 (1956): 216–57.

———. "Zeitalterkritik und Zukunftserwartung. Zur Grundkonzeption in Schillers früher Dramatik." In *Friedrich Schiller. Angebot und Diskurs. Zugänge/Dichtung/ Zeitgenossenschaft*, edited by Helmut Brandt, 141–59. Berlin/Weimar: Aufbau Verlag, 1987.

———. "Zum Problem des geschichtlich handelnden Menschen bei Schiller." *Weimarer Beiträge* 25 (1979): 5–21.

Theopold, Wilhelm. *Der Herzog und die Heilkunst. Die Medizin an der Hohen Carlsschule zu Stuttgart*. With the cooperation of Robert Uhland. Köln/Berlin: Deutscher Ärtze Verlag, 1967.

———. *Der Regimentsmedikus Friedrich Schiller und die Medizin seiner Zeit*. Stuttgart: Gentner, 1968.

———. *Schiller. Sein Leben und die Medizin im 18. Jahrhundert*. Stuttgart: Gustav Fischer, 1964.

Tieftrunk, J.H. "Über den Einfluß der Aufklärung und Revolutionen." In *Aufklärung und Gedankenfreiheit. Adam Bergk, Jon. Ludw. Ewald, J. G. Fichte u.a. Fünfzehn Anregungen, aus der Geschichte zu lernen*, edited by Zwi Batscha, 195–205. Frankfurt a.M.: Suhrkamp, 1977.

Tschierske, Ulrich, *Vernunftkritik und ästhetische Subjektivität. Studien zur Anthropologie Friedrich Schillers*. Tübingen: Max Niemeyer, 1988.

Toellner, Richard. *Albrecht von Haller. Über die Einheit im Denken des letzten Universalgelehrten*. Wiesbaden: Steiner, 1971.

Tomberg, Friedrich. *Politische Ästhetik. Vorträge und Aufsätze*. Darmstadt: Luchterhand, 1973.

———. "Schiller auf dem Weg von Kant zur Moderne." In *Friedrich Schiller. Angebot und Diskurs. Zugänge/Dichtung/Zeitgenossenschaft*, edited by Helmut Brandt, 49–61. Berlin/Weimar: Aufbau Verlag, 1987.

Tschierske, Ulrich. *Vernunftkritik und ästhetische Subjektivität. Studien zur Anthropologie Friedrich Schillers*. Tübingen: Max Niemeyer, 1988.

Turk, Horst. "Die Kunst des Augenblicks. Zu Schillers *Wallenstein*." In *Augenblick und Zeitpunkt. Studien zur Zeitstruktur und Zeitmetaphorik in Kunst und Wissenschaften*, edited by Christian W. Thomsen and Hans Holländer, 306–24. Darmstadt: Wissenschaftliche Buchgesellschaft, 1984.

Ueberweg, Friedrich. *Schiller als Historiker und Philosoph. Mit einer biographischen Skizze Ueberwegs von Fr. A. Lange*. Edited by Moritz Brasch. Leipzig: Carl Reißner, 1884.

Ueding, Gert. *Friedrich Schiller.* München: C. H. Beck, 1990.

———. "Rhetorik und Ästhetik in Schillers theoretischen Abhandlungen." In *Friedrich Schiller. Zur Geschichtlichkeit seines Werkes,* edited by Klaus Berghahn, 159–95. Kronberg/Ts.: Scriptor, 1975.

———. *Schillers Rhetorik. Idealistische Wirkungsästhetik und rhetorische Tradition.* Tübingen: Max Niemeyer, 1971.

———. "Wilhelm Tell." In *Schillers Dramen. Neue Interpretationen,* edited by Walter Hinderer, 271–93. Stuttgart: Reclam, 1979.

Urgrinsky, Alexej, ed. *Friedrich von Schiller and the Drama of Human Existence.* New York/Westport, Connecticut: Greenwood Press, 1988.

Utz, Peter. *Das Auge und das Ohr im Text. Literarische Sinneswahrnehmung in der Goethezeit.* München: Wilhelm Fink, 1990.

———. *Die ausgehöhlte Gasse: Stationen der Wirkungsgeschichte von Schillers "Wilhelm Tell."* Königstein: Athenäum, 1984.

———. "Schiller's Dramaturgy of the Senses: The Eye, the Ear, and the Heart." In *Friedrich von Schiller and the Drama of Human Existence,* edited by Alexej Urgrinsky, 13–19. New York/Westport, Conn.: Greenwood Press, 1988.

Vaerst-Pfarr, Christa. "Semele—Die Huldigung der Künste." In *Schillers Dramen. Neue Interpretationen,* edited by Walter Hinderer, 294–315. Stuttgart: Reclam, 1979.

van Ingen, Ferdinand. "Macht und Gewissen: Schillers *Maria Stuart.*" In *Verantwortung und Utopie. Zur Literatur der Goethezeit. Ein Symposium,* edited by Wolfgang Wittkowski, 283–309. Tübingen: Max Niemeyer, 1988.

Vander Meulen, Ross. "The Theological Texture of Schiller's *Wilhelm Tell.*" *Germanic Review* 53 (1978): 56–62.

Vazsonyi, Nicholas. "Schillers *Don Carlos:* Historical Drama or Dramatized History." *New German Review* 7 (1991): 26–41.

Veeser, Aram, ed. *The New Historicism.* New York/London: Routledge, 1989.

Vierhaus, Rudolf, ed. *Aufklärung als Prozeß.* Hamburg: Meiner, 1988.

Vieweg, Klaus. "Anthropologie und Weltgeschichte—Kant und Schiller." In *Friedrich Schiller. Angebot und Diskurs. Zugänge/Dichtung/Zeitgenossenschaft,* edited by Helmut Brandt, 92–98. Berlin/Weimar: Aufbau Verlag, 1987.

Völker, Ludwig. "Schiller and the Problem of Lyrical Subjectivity: *Expression* and *Concept.*" In *Friedrich von Schiller and the Drama of Human Existence,* edited by Alexej Urgrinsky, 141–48. New York/Westport, Connecticut: Greenwood Press, 1988.

Volkmann-Schluck, Karl Heinz. *Die Kunst und der Mensch: Schillers Briefe über die ästhetische Erziehung des Menschen.* Frankfurt a.M.: Klostermann, 1964.

von Dalberg, Karl Theodor. "Von der Natur der äusserlichen Sinne und Empfindungen." *Der Arzt* 2 (1769): 98–112.

von Humboldt, Wilhelm. *Über Schiller und den Gang seiner Geistesentwicklung. Mit Bildnissen Humboldts und Schillers.* Nachwort von Theodor Heuss. Marbach a.N.: Schiller Nationalmuseum, 1952.

von Matthisson, Friedrich. *Friedrich v. Matthisson's Litterarischer Nachlaß nebst einer Auswahl von Briefen seiner Freunde. Ein Supplement zu allen Ausgaben seiner Schriften.* 4 vols. Berlin: August Mylius, 1832.

von Weizsäcker, Richard. "Das Theater." In his *Die politische Kraft der Kultur,* 81–95. Reinbek bei Hamburg: Rowohlt, 1987.

von Wiese, Benno. *Friedrich Schiller.* Stuttgart: J. B. Metzler, 1959; 4th ed., 1978.

———. "Friedrich Schiller. Erbe und Aufgabe." In *Germanistik in Forschung und Lehre. Vorträge und Diskussionen des Germanistentages in Essen 21.-25. Oktober 1964,* edited by Rudolf Henss and Hugo Moser, 65–87. Berlin: Erich Schmidt, 1965.

———. "Geschichte und Drama." *Deutsche Vierteljahrsschrift für Literaturwissenschaft und Geistesgeschichte* 16 (1942): 412–34.

———. *Die deutsche Tragödie von Lessing bis Hebbel.* 6th ed. Hamburg: Hoffmann u. Campe, 1964.

———. *Die Dramen Schillers. Politik und Tragödie.* Leipzig: Bibliographisches Institut, 1938.

———. "Schiller als Geschichtsphilosoph und Geschichtsschreiber." In his *Von Lessing bis Grabbe. Studien zur deutschen Klassik und Romantik,* 41–57. Düsseldorf: August Bagel, 1968.

———. "'Der Tod kann kein Übel sein . . .' Zu Schillers 175. Todestag am 9. Mai 1980." In *Jahrbuch der Deutschen Schillergesellschaft* 24 (1980): 68–86.

———. "Die Utopie des Ästhetischen bei Schiller." In his *Zwischen Utopie und Wirklichkeit,* 81–101. Düsseldorf: Bagel, 1963.

———. "Utopie und Geschichte." In *Geschichte im Gedicht. Texte und Interpretationen,* edited by Walter Hinck, 87–97. Frankfurt a.M.: Suhrkamp, 1979.

von Wolzogen, Caroline. *Schillers Leben, verfaßt aus Erinnerungen der Familie, seinen eignen Briefen und den nachrichten seines Freundes Körner.* 2 parts in 1 volume. Stuttgart/Tübingen: J. G. Cotta, 1830. [signed Emilie von Gleichen] [DLA]

Vorländer, Karl. *Immanuel Kant. Der Mann und das Werk.* 3d ed. Hamburg: Felix Meiner, 1992.

Wagner, Fritz. *Zur Apotheose Newtons. Künstlerische Utopie und naturwissenschaftliches Weltbild im 18. Jahrhundert.* München: Verlag der Bayerischen Akademie der Wissenschaften, 1974.

Wagner, Gerhard and Heinz Zipprian, "Intersubjectivity and Critical Consciousness: Remarks on Habermas's Theory of Communicative Action." *Inquiry* 34 (1991): 49–62.

Wagner, Hans. *Ästhetik der Tragödie von Aristoteles bis Schiller.* Würzburg: Königshausen u. Neumann, 1987.

Wagner, Heinrich. *Geschichte der Hohen Carls-Schule. Mit Illustrationen von Carl Alexander von Heideloff.* 2 vols. Würzburg: C. Etlinger, 1856–57.

Waldeck, Marie-Luise. "Further Thoughts on the Genesis of a Key Concept in Schiller's Aesthetic Thinking." *Forum for Modern Language Studies* 12 (1976): 304–13.

———. "Shadows, Reflexions, Mirror-Images and Virtual 'Objects' in 'Die Künstler' and Their Relation to Schiller's Concept of 'Schein.'" *Modern Language Review* 58 (1963): 33–37.

———. *The Theme of Freedom in Schiller's Plays.* Stuttgart: Hans-Dieter Heinz Akademischer Verlag, 1986.

Waldmann, Walter. "Zu Veränderungen der Aneignung des klassischen Erbes auf den Bühnen der DDR, insbesondere der Dramen Friedrich Schillers." *Wissenschaftliche Zeitschrift* (Rostock) 34 (1985): 72–82.

Weber, Peter. "Schillers *Horen*-ein zeitgerechtes Journal? Aspekte publizistischer Strategien im ausgehenden 18. Jahrhundert." In *Friedrich Schiller. Angebot und Diskurs. Zugänge/Dichtung/Zeitgenossenschaft,* edited by Helmut Brandt, 451–63. Berlin/Weimar: Aufbau Verlag, 1987.

Weber, Samuel. "Capitalizing History: *The Political Unconscious.*" In his *Institution and Interpretation,* afterword by Wlad Godzich, 40–58. Minneapolis: University of Minnesota Press, 1987.

Weigand, Paul. "Schiller's Dramas as Opera Texts." *Monatshefte* 46 (1954): 249–59.

Weimar, Klaus. "Die Begründung der Normalität. Zu Schillers *Wallenstein.*" *Zeitschrift für Deutsche Philologie* 109 (1990). Sonderheft: 99–116.

Weinsheimer, Joel. *Gadamer's Hermeneutics: A Reading of "Truth and Method."* New Haven/London: Yale University Press, 1985.

———. *Philosophical Hermeneutics and Literary Theory.* New Haven/London: Yale University Press, 1991.

Weiss, Wisso. "Schiller als Papierliebhaber." *Marginalien. Zeitschrift für Buchkunst und Bibliophilie* 40 (1970): 70–74.

Weisstein, Ulrich. "Romanticism: Transcendentalist Games or 'wechselseitige Erhellung der Künste?'" *Colloquia Germanica* 2 (1968): 47–69.

Wellek, Rene. "The Attack on Literature." In his *The Attack on Literature and Other Essays.* Chapel Hill: University of North Carolina Press, 1982: 3–18.

———. "The Concept of Romanticism in Literary History." In his *Concepts of Criticism,* edited with an intro. by Stephen G. Nichols, Jr., 128–98. New Haven Conn.: Yale University Press, 1963.

Wells, G. A. "Interpretation and Misinterpretation of Schiller's *Kabale und Liebe.*" *German Life and Letters* 38 (1984–85): 448–61.

———. "Schiller's *Wilhelm Tell* and the Methodology of Literary Criticism." *Oxford German Studies* 16 (1985): 36–46.

———. "Villainy and Guilt in Schiller's *Wallenstein* and *Maria Stuart.*" In *Deutung und Bedeutung: Studies in German and Comparative Literature Presented to Karl-Werner Maurer,* edited by Brigitte Schludermann et al., 100–17. The Hague: Mouton, 1973.

Wentzlaff-Eggebert, Friedrich Wilhelm. *Schillers Weg zu Goethe.* 2d expanded ed. Berlin: Walter de Gruyter, 1963.

———. "Zur Kommentierung von Schillers philosophischen Schriften." *Zeitschrift für Deutsche Philologie* 84 (1965): 170–82.

Wenzel, Manfred. "Die Anthropologie Johann Gottfried Herders und das klassische Humanitätsideal." In *Die Natur des Menschen. Probleme der Physischen Anthropologie und Rassenkunde (1750–1850),* edited by Gunter Mann and Franz Dumont, 137–67. Stuttgart/New York: Gustav Fischer, 1990.

Werner, Hans-Georg. "Ein Beitrag zur Deutung der Wallenstein-Trilogie Friedrich Schillers. Das Verhältnis des Dichters zur Geschichte." *Wissenschaftliche Zeitschrift* (Halle) 10 (1961): 1043–57.

———. "Vergegenwärtigung von Geschichte in Schillers *Dom Karlos.*" In *Friedrich Schiller. Angebot und Diskurs. Zugänge/Dichtung/Zeitgenossenschaft,* edited by Helmut Brandt, 235–49. Berlin/Weimar: Aufbau Verlag, 1987.

Wernly, Julia. *Prolegomena zu einem Lexikon der ästhetisch-ethischen Terminologie Friedrich Schillers.* Leipzig: Haessel, 1909.

Wertheim, Ursula. "Einige Aspekte der Revolutionserfahrungen in Schillers dramatischen Werken und theoretischen Schriften nach 1789." In *Philosophie und Geschichte. Beiträge zur Geschichtsphilosophie der deutschen Klassik,* edited by Erhard Lange, 238–50. Weimar: Hermann Böhlaus Nachfolger, 1983.

Wessell, Leonard P., Jr. *The Philosophical Background to Friedrich Schiller's Aesthetics of Living Form.* Frankfurt a.M.: Bern, 1982.

————. "Schiller and the Genesis of German Romanticism." *Studies in Romanticism* 10 (1971): 176–98.

White, Hayden. *Metahistory: The Historical Imagination in Nineteenth-Century Europe.* Baltimore/London: Johns Hopkins, 1973.

————. "The Politics of Historical Interpretation: Discipline and De-Sublimation." In *The Politics of Interpretation,* edited by W. J. T. Mitchell, 119–43. Chicago/London: University of Chicago Press, 1983.

————. "The Problem of Change in Literary History." *New Literary History* 7 (1975): 97–111.

Widmann, Joachim. *Johann Gottlieb Fichte. Einführung in seine Philosophie.* Berlin/New York: Walter de Gruyter, 1982.

Widmaier, Fritz Theodor. *Die Weltanschauung und Ästhetik der Popularphilosophie und ihr Einfluß auf Friedrich Schiller.* University of Southern California Dissertation, 1968.

Wieland, Christoph Martin, ed. *Der Neue Teutsche Merkur vom Jahre 1795.* Weimar: Hoffmann; Leipzig: Göschen, 1795. [DLA]

Wiener, Jon. "Deconstructing de Man." *The Nation.* January 9, 1988: 22–24.

Wilcox, Kenneth. "On Sublimation and Suppression in the Works of Schiller." In *The Germanic Review* 55 (1980): 146–51.

Wilkie, Brian and James Hurt, eds. *Literature of the Western World.* vol. 1: *The Ancient World Through the Renaissance.* 3d ed. New York: Macmillan, 1992.

Wilkinson, Elizabeth M. *Schiller: Poet or Philosopher?* Oxford: Clarendon Press, 1961.

————. "Schiller und die Idee der Aufklärung. Betrachtungen anläßlich der Briefe über die ästhetische Erziehung." *Jahrbuch der Deutschen Schillergesellschaft* 4 (1960): 42–59.

———— and Leonard A. Willoughby. "Nachlese zu Schillers Ästhetik." *Jahrbuch der Deutschen Schillergesellschaft* 11 (1967): 374–403.

————. "'The Whole Man' in Schiller's Theory of Culture and Society: On the Virtue of a Plurality of Models." In *Essays in German Language, Culture and Society,* edited by Siegbert Salomon Prawer, Thomas R. Hinton, and Leonard Forster, 177–210. London: University of London, 1969.

Winckelmann. Writings on Art. Edited by David Irwin. London: Phaidon, 1972.

Windfuhr, Manfred. "Evolution oder Revolution? Goethes und Schillers Stellung zur französischen Revolution." In *Wer wird nicht einen Dichter loben? Literatur: Verständnis und Vermittlung. Eine Anthologie für Wilhelm Gössmann zum 65. Geburtstag,* edited by Joseph A. Kruse, Monika Salmen, and Klaus-Hinrich Roth, 97–110.

Wirtembergisches Repertorium der Literatur. Eds. Friedrich Schiller and J.W. Petersen. Stücke 1–3. [Selbstverlag], 1782–83. Düsseldorf: Cornelsen, 1991. [DLA]

Wirth, Andreas. *Das schwierige Schöne. Zu Schillers Ästhetik. Auch eine Interpretation der Abhandlung 'Über Matthissons Gedichte'(1794).* Bonn: Bouvier, 1975.

Witte, William. "Schiller: Der Denker und die Gabe des Lieds." *Monatshefte* 68 (1976): 41–50.

Wittkowski, Wolfgang. "Einleitung. Zur Konzeption ästhetischer Autonomie in Deutschland." In *Revolution und Autonomie. Deutsche Autonomieästhetik im Zeitalter der Französischen Revolution. Ein Symposium,* edited by him, 1–29. Tübingen: Max Niemeyer, 1990.

————. "Ethik und Politik in Schillers Dramen. Germanistik im Banne der materialistischen Geschichtsphilosophie oder worum es bei Schiller geht." *Zeitschrift für Germanistik* N.F. 2 (1992): 31–50.

———. "Höfische Intrige für die gute Sache. Marquis Posa und Octavio Piccolomini." In *Schiller und die höfische Welt,* edited by Achim Aurnhammer, Klaus Manger, and Friedrich Strack, 378–97. Tübingen: Max Niemeyer, 1990.

———. "Introduction: Schiller's Idealism—How 'Idealistic' Is It?" In *Friedrich von Schiller: The Drama of Human Existence,* edited by Alexej Urgrinsky, 1–9. New York/Westport, Connecticut: Greenwood Press, 1988.

———. "Octavio Piccolomini. Zur Schaffensweise des *Wallenstein*-Dichters." *Jahrbuch der Deutschen Schillergesellschaft* 5 (1961): 10–57.

———, ed. *Revolution und Autonomie. Deutsche Autonomieästhetik im Zeitalter der Französischen Revolution. Ein Symposium.* Tübingen: Max Niemeyer, 1990.

———. "Theodizee oder Nemesistragödie? Schillers *Wallenstein* zwischen Hegel und politischer Ethik." *Jahrbuch des Freien Deutschen Hochstifts 1980:* 177–237.

———. "'Der Übel größtes aber ist die Schuld'. Nemesis und politische Ethik in Schillers Dramen." In his *Friedrich Schiller. Kunst, Humanität und Politik in der späten Aufklärung. Ein Symposium,* 295–304. Tübingen: Max Niemeyer, 1982.

———, ed. *Friedrich Schiller. Kunst, Humanität und Politik in der späten Aufklärung. Ein Symposium.* Tübingen: Max Niemeyer, 1982.

———, ed. *Verantwortung und Utopie. Zur Literatur der Goethezeit. Ein Symposium.* Tübingen: Max Niemeyer, 1988.

———, ed. *Verlorene Klassik? Ein Symposium.* Tübingen: Max Niemeyer, 1986.

Wolf, Maria. "Der politische Himmel. Zum astrologischen Motiv in Schillers *Wallenstein.*" In *Schiller und die höfische Welt,* edited by Achim Aurnhammer, Klaus Manger, and Friedrich Strack, 223–32. Tübingen: Max Niemeyer, 1990.

Wolgast, Eike, "Schiller und die Fürsten." In *Schiller und die höfische Welt,* edited by Achim Aurnhammer, Klaus Manger, and Friedrich Strack, 6–30. Tübingen: Max Niemeyer, 1990.

Württembergischer Geschichts-und Altertums-Verein, ed. *Herzog Karl Eugen von Württemberg und seine Zeit.* 2 vols. Eßlingen a.N.: Paul Neff (Max Schreiber), 1907.

Zedler, Johann Heinrich. *Großes vollständiges Universal-Lexikon Aller Wissenschaften und Künste.* Leipzig/Halle: Johann Heinrich Zedler, 1741f. [DLA]

Zeller, Bernhard and Walter Scheffler, eds. *Friedrich Schiller. Eine Dokumentation in Bildern.* Marbach a.N.: Schiller-Nationalmuseum; Frankfurt a.M.: Insel, 1977.

———, eds. "Jakob Friedrich Abel. 1751–1829 (Vortrag im Heimatverein Schorndorff am 9. November 1962)." *Heimatbuch für Schorndorf und Umgebung. Festschrift zum 75. Geburtstag von Dr. Reinhold Maier,* edited by I. C. Roster, 87–99. Schondorff: Herman Schmid, 1964.

Zeller, Bernhard, ed. *Klassiker in finsteren Zeiten. 1933–1945.* 2 vols. Marbach a.N.: Deutsche Schillergesellschaft, 1983.

———, ed. *Schau-bühne. Schillers Dramen 1945–84. Eine Ausstellung des Deutschen Literaturarchivs und des Theatermuseums der Universität zu Köln.* Marbach a.N.: Schiller-Nationalmuseum, 1984.

———, ed. *Schillers Leben und Werk in Daten und Bildern.* Frankfurt a.M.: Insel, 1966.

———, ed. *Schiller. Reden im Gedenkjahr 1955. Im Auftrag der Deutschen Schillergesellschaft.* Stuttgart: Klett, 1955.

——, ed. *Schiller. Reden im Gedenkjahr 1959. Im Auftrag der Deutschen Schiller-gesellschaft.* Stuttgart: Klett, 1961.

——, ed. *Schillers Schwabenreise. 1793–1794. Bilder, Briefe, Berichte.* Stuttgart: Höhere Fachschule f.d. Graph Gewerbe, 1959.

Zima, Peter V. *Literarische Ästhetik. Methoden und Modelle der Literaturwissenschaft.* Tübingen: Francke, 1991.

Zimmermann, Johann Georg. *Von der Erfahrung in der Arzneykunst.* 2 vols. Neue Auflage. Zürich: Orell, Geßner, Füßli and Compag., 1787. [DLA]

Zimmermann, Rolf Christian. *Das Weltbild des jungen Goethe. Studien zur hermetischen Tradition des deutschen 18. Jahrhunderts.* 2 vols. München: Fink, 1969/1979.

Index

Page numbers in italics refer to illustrations.